Hong Kong
Macau & Guangzhou
a Lonely Planet travel survival kit

Robert Storey

Hong Kong, Macau & Guangzhou

8th edition

Published by
Lonely Planet Publications
Head Office: PO Box 617, Hawthorn, Vic 3122, Australia
Branches: 155 Filbert St, Suite 251, Oakland, CA 94607, USA
10 Barley Mow Passage, Chiswick, London W4 4PH, UK
71 bis rue du Cardinal Lemoine, 75005 Paris, France

Printed by
SNP Printing Pte Ltd, Singapore

Photographs by

Glenn Beanland	Rob Flynn	Nicko Goncharoff
Richard I'Anson	Paul Steel	Robert Storey
Tony Wheeler		

Front cover: Incense (known as *xiang* – literally, fragrance) is ubiquitous in temples, but is also used at the small shrines which many Hong Kongers dedicate to household deities. (Richard I'Anson)

First Published
1978

This Edition
March 1997

Although the author and publisher have tried to make the information as accurate as possible, they accept no responsibility for any loss, injury or inconvenience sustained by any person using this book.

National Library of Australia Cataloguing-in-Publication Data

Storey, Robert
Hong Kong, Macau & Guangzhou

8th ed.
Includes index.
ISBN 0 86442 410 8.

1. Hong Kong – Guidebooks. 2. Macao – Guidebooks. 3. Guangzhou (China) – Guidebooks.
I. Storey, Robert. Hong Kong, Macau & Canton. 7th ed. II. Title. III. Title: Hong Kong, Macau & Canton. 7th ed. (Series : Lonely Planet travel survival kit).

915.12504

text & maps © Lonely Planet 1997
photos © photographers as indicated 1997

Robert Storey

Devoted mountain climber and computer hacker, Robert has had a number of distinguished careers, including monkeykeeper at a zoo and slot machine repairman in a Las Vegas casino. After running out of money while travelling, Robert finally got a decent job as an English teacher in Taiwan. Robert then diligently learnt Chinese, wrote Lonely Planet's *Taiwan* guide and became a respectable citizen and a pillar of the community. With Las Vegas still in his blood, Robert was lured into a Macau casino one crazed weekend, and was thus inspired to write this book so he could pay his way back to Taiwan. Now safely home, Robert has devoted the rest of his life to serious pursuits such as studying Chinese calligraphy and writing a computer program that will allow him to win at the roulette tables.

From the Author

I'm deeply grateful to a number of residents in Hong Kong, Macau and Guangzhou who generously donated their time, energy and enthusiasm to provide helpful information as well as a bit of companionship to a weary travel writer on the road. In Hong Kong, special thanks go to Lynne Medhurst, Ron Gluckman and Peter Danford of Lamma Island, Andre De Smet in Kowloon, and Larry Feign and Aine Fligg on Lantau Island. In Macau I am particularly grateful to Peggy Wong for her valuable assistance. Friendly expats in Guangzhou who came to my aid include Stephanie Salmon, Bobbie Boudreau, Jane Hulka, and Grant & Barbara Pearse. Also thanks to others who provided valuable input, including Martin Grumet in the USA and Chiu Miaoling from Taiwan.

This Book

The 1st edition of this book was researched and written by Carol Clewlow, and since then it has gone through several incarnations under the influence of a number of people. The 2nd edition was updated by Jim Hart, with a Guangzhou section added by an Australian student who had lived and studied in China for some time. The 3rd and 4th editions were updated by Alan Samalgalski. The 5th, 6th, and 7th editions were major rewrites done by Robert Storey.

From the Publisher

This edition was knocked into shape at Lonely Planet's headquarters in Melbourne, Australia. Wielding the editorial hammer and chisel were Mic Looby and Greg Alford, with David Andrew providing the high-polish proofing. Sally Jacka, Verity Campbell, Valerie Tellini and Chris Love drove the mapping, design and layout machinery. Thanks to Trudi Canavan for her illustrations and to David Kemp and Adam McCrow for the front and back covers, respectively. Once again, special thanks to computer guru Dan Levin for creating the pinyin script.

Thanks

We've had a number of letters carrying useful information from people 'out there', even the odd letter from People's Republic Chinese. With thanks to everyone, and apologies to anyone who's been left out, we'd like to mention:

Sharon Adams, Scott Anderson, Stephen Anderson, Marshall Berdan, J Bergmann, C Betts, LA Bodker, Ulrike Bohm, R Brooks, K deBruijn, David Burgess,

Jay Davidson, Kelsey Dorogi, Angela Jill Durose, Gaby Eidenberg, Robert Eidschun, Caroline & Martin Evans, John Fender, Michael Fysh, Melanie Gafield, Dolores Graham, PG Griffin, A Hagquist, David Hall, Jennifer Henderson, Jennifer Holland, D Huddleston, Arved Jacast, Tony Jensen, Michael & Elizabeth Johnson, Gwen Jones, Graham Knight, R Lever, Torng Lih, Annette McGloin, Robert Meyer, David Miller, RF Monch, John Morgan, Judith O'Hare, James Parsons, E Philipson, B Pieters, Johanna Polensberg, Robert Salter, Sara Scates, PC Shum, JA Searle, Elaine Slade, Jon Taffs, Judith Tan, Hideaki Ueda, Nicholas Uloth, Mike Unrau, J Walker, Robert Williams, John Wilson, Neal Wright

Warning and Request

No place in the world changes more rapidly than Hong Kong. Every time you turn around, the local street market becomes a shopping mall, a cheap youth hostel changes into a 60-storey skyscraper, and even the beach is transformed into reclaimed land. In Hong Kong they build like there's no tomorrow – and perhaps there won't be after 1997. So if you find things better or worse, recently opened or long since closed, please write and tell us and help make the next edition better.

Your letters will be used to help update future editions and where possible, important changes will also be included in a Stop Press section in reprints.

We greatly appreciate all information that is sent to us by travellers. Back at Lonely Planet we employ a hard-working readers' letters team to sort through the many letters we receive. The best ones will be rewarded with a free copy of the next edition or another Lonely Planet guide, if you prefer. We give away lots of books, but, unfortunately, not every letter/postcard receives one.

Contents

AROUND GUANGZHOU 406

HEALTH 446

GLOSSARY 454

INDEX 455

Map Legend

BOUNDARIES

.... International Boundary
.... Regional Boundary

ROUTES

.... Freeway
.... Highway
.... Major Road
.... Unsealed Road or Track
.... City Road
.... City Street
.... Railway
.... Underground Railway
.... Tram
.... Walking Track
.... Walking Tour
.... Ferry Route
.... Cable Car or Chairlift

AREA FEATURES

.... Parks
.... Built-Up Area
.... Pedestrian Mall
.... Market
.... Christian Cemetery
.... Non-Christian Cemetery
.... Beach or Desert
.... Rocks

HYDROGRAPHIC FEATURES

.... Coastline
.... River, Creek
.... Intermittent River or Creek
.... Rapids, Waterfalls
.... Lake, Intermittent Lake
.... Canal
.... Swamp

SYMBOLS

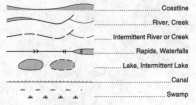

✪ CAPITAL		National Capital
◉ Capital		Regional Capital
⬬ CITY		Major City
● City		City
● Town		Town
● Village		Village
▪ ▼		Place to Stay, Place to Eat
⚱ ⛉		Cafe, Pub or Bar
✉ ☎		Post Office, Telephone
❶ ❸		Tourist Information, Bank
◒ ℗		Transport, Parking
🏛 ⛫		Museum, Youth Hostel
⛺ ⚑		Caravan Park, Camping Ground
✚ ✚		Church, Cathedral
◪ ✡		Mosque, Synagogue
⊞ ▮		Buddhist Monastery, Temple
✛ ★		Hospital, Police Station

◔ ⓟ		Embassy, Petrol Station
✈ ✝		Airport, Airfield
⊞ ✿		Swimming Pool, Gardens
❖ 🐘		Shopping Centre, Zoo
⚘ 🌲		Winery or Vineyard, Picnic Site
⬅ A25		One Way Street, Route Number
🏛 ⚱		Stately Home, Monument
Ⓜ ▣		Metro Station, Tomb
⌒ ⚑		Cave, Golf Course
▲ ※		Mountain or Hill, Lookout
⚲ ⚟		Lighthouse, Shipwreck
)(◎		Pass, Spring
⚑ ⚘		Beach, Surf Beach
∴		Archaeological Site or Ruins
		Ancient or City Wall
		Tunnel
		Railway Station

Introduction

Hong Kong is the final chapter of a colonial saga that began almost 150 years ago, and 1997 marks both a beginning and an end for this famed corner of mainland China.

Most people think of Hong Kong as an island; it is, but not just one. There are 236 islands plus a chunk of mainland bordering the Chinese province of Guangdong – a mere dot on the map compared to the rest of China. Much of it is uninhabited while other parts, especially Hong Kong Island itself, are among the most densely populated areas in the world.

Hong Kong Island is the heart of it all, and the oldest part in terms of British history (the British acquired it in 1841). The centre of Hong Kong Island is the business district of Central where the greater part of the territory's business life goes on. New office blocks, and the rents, shoot up almost daily to accommodate the ever-growing financial elite who want to be part of the Asian Wall St.

From Central it's a seven-minute ferry ride across one of the world's great harbours to the Kowloon Peninsula on the mainland. The tip of Kowloon is the shopping and tourist ghetto of Tsim Sha Tsui, and beyond that are the high-rise commercial and industrial estates.

Beyond Kowloon lie the New Territories, which includes not only the mainland area bordering China but also the lesser-known islands which make up Hong Kong. The New Territories form the bulk of Hong Kong territory.

So why go to Hong Kong? Contrary to popular belief, it's more than just a place to buy a duty-free musical watch. Hong Kong is one of the world's great trading ports and provides an eye-opener on how to make the most from every sq km, since space is Hong Kong's most precious commodity.

Hong Kong supports an almost-intact traditional Chinese culture, in contrast to the rest of the mainland where the old culture was attacked and weakened by the Cultural Revolution of the 1960s. There are empty

hills where you can walk for an afternoon and barely see another person, and there are remote rural villages where lives have changed little over many generations.

Most travel agents and package tours allow a week at the most for visiting Hong Kong – enough time for a whistle-stop tour of a half-dozen attractions plus the obligatory shopping jaunt. But if you give yourself longer and make the effort to get out of Central and Tsim Sha Tsui, you will find a lot more. Hong Kong is only the start.

An hour's hydrofoil ride away is the 500-year-old Portuguese colony of Macau. To the north of Hong Kong and adjoining the New Territories is the special economic zone of Shenzhen, where the People's Republic has been packing foreign money into development schemes designed to help modernise the entire country. Another special economic zone, Zhuhai, is adjacent to Macau and has turned into a pricey resort playground for Hong Kong Chinese.

Northwards up the Pearl River is Guangzhou (formerly Canton), the chief city of Guangdong Province, the ancestral home of the Cantonese people and the most accessible part of China.

HONG KONG

Facts about Hong Kong

HISTORY

'Albert is so amused at my having got the island of Hong Kong,' wrote Queen Victoria to King Leopold of Belgium in 1841. But while her husband could see the funny side of this apparently useless little island off the south coast of China, considerably less amused was the then British foreign secretary, Lord Palmerston. He considered the acquisition of Hong Kong a massive bungle. 'A barren island with hardly a house upon it!' he raged in a letter to the man responsible for the deal, Captain Charles Elliot.

Western Traders

Hong Kong must stand as one of the more successful results of dope running. The story really begins upriver, in the city of Guangzhou, where the British began trading with China on a regular basis in the late 17th century.

The British were not the first Westerners on the scene: regular Chinese contact with the modern European nations began in 1557, when the Portuguese were given permission to set up a base in nearby Macau. Jesuit priests also arrived and in 1582 were allowed to establish themselves at Zhaoqing, a town west of Guangzhou. Their scientific and technical knowledge aroused the interest of the imperial court and a few priests were permitted to live in Beijing.

The first trade overtures from the British were rebuffed by the Chinese, but Guangzhou was finally opened to trade with Europeans in 1685. From then on British ships began to arrive regularly from the East India Company bases on the Indian coast, and traders were allowed to establish 'factories' (offices and residences) near Guangzhou to export tea and silk.

From the end of the 17th century the British and French started trading regularly at Guangzhou, followed by the Dutch, Danes, Swedes and Americans.

Even so, the opening of Guangzhou was an indication of how little importance was placed on trade with the Western barbarians. Guangzhou was considered to exist on the edge of a wilderness far from Nanjing (Nanking) and Beijing, which were the centres of power under the isolationist Ming (1368-1644) and Qing (1644-1911) dynasties. As far as the Chinese were concerned, only the Chinese empire was civilised and the people beyond its frontiers were barbarians. The Qing could not have foreseen the dramatic impact the Europeans were about to have on their country.

In 1757 the fuse to the Opium Wars was lit when, by imperial edict, a Guangzhou merchants' guild called the Co Hong gained exclusive rights to China's foreign trade, paid for with royalties, fees, kickbacks and bribes.

Numerous restrictions were forced on the Western traders: they could reside in Guangzhou from about September to March only; they were restricted to Shamian Island on Guangzhou's Pearl River, where they had their factories; and they had to leave their wives and families downriver in Macau (though not all found this a hardship). Also, it was illegal for foreigners to learn Chinese or to deal with anyone except the Co Hong. The traders complained about the restrictions and the trading regulations, which changed daily. Nevertheless trade flourished, though mainly in China's favour because tea and silk had to be paid for in cash (usually silver).

Trade in favour of China was not what the Western merchants had in mind and in 1773 the British unloaded a thousand chests at Guangzhou, each containing almost 70 kg of Bengal opium. The intention was to balance, and eventually more than balance, their purchases of Chinese goods. The Chinese taste for opium grew exponentially.

Emperor Dao Guang, alarmed at the drain of silver from the country and the increasing number of opium addicts, issued an edict in

1796 totally banning the drug trade. But the foreigners had different ideas, and with the help of the Co Hong and corrupt Chinese officials the trade flourished.

In 1839 the emperor appointed Lin Zexu commissioner of Guangzhou, with orders to stamp out the opium trade. Meanwhile, the British superintendent of trade, Captain Charles Elliot, was under instructions from Lord Palmerston to solve the trade problems with China.

It took Lin just a week to surround the British in Guangzhou, cut off their food supplies and demand they surrender all opium in their possession. The British stuck it out for six weeks until they were ordered by their own Captain Elliot to surrender 20,000 chests of opium – an act which earned him their undying hatred. Lin then had the 'foreign mud' destroyed in public at the small city of Humen by the Pearl River.

Having surrendered the opium, Elliot tried unsuccessfully to negotiate with Lin's representative. The British then sent an expeditionary force to China, under Rear Admiral George Elliot (a cousin of Charles Elliot), to extract reprisals, secure favourable trade arrangements and obtain the use of some islands as a British base.

The force arrived in June 1840, blockaded Guangzhou and sailed north, occupying or blockading a number of ports and cities on the coast and the Yangzi River, and ultimately threatening Beijing itself. The emperor, alarmed, lost confidence in Lin and authorised Qi Shan to negotiate with the two Elliots, whom he persuaded to withdraw from northern China. In January 1841, after further military actions and threats, Qi agreed to the Convention of Chuan Bi. Among other concessions, this unofficially ceded Hong Kong Island to the British.

The convention was repudiated by both sides. Qi, it is said, was hauled back to Beijing in chains for selling out the emperor. And despite his country's repudiation of the treaty, British Commodore Gordon Bremmer led a contingent of naval men ashore and claimed Hong Kong Island for Britain on 26 January 1841.

In late February, Captain Charles successfully attacked the Bogue forts at Humen (where the opium had earlier been destroyed), took control of the Pearl River and laid siege to Guangzhou, withdrawing in May after extracting $6 million and other concessions from the Guangzhou merchants.

In August 1841, a powerful British force sailed north and seized Xiamen, Ningbo, Shanghai and other ports. With Nanjing (Nanking) under immediate threat, the Chinese were forced to accept the Treaty of Nanking which, among other things, officially ceded the island of Hong Kong to the British 'in perpetuity'.

That wasn't the end of the fighting. In 1856 war broke out again over the interpretation of earlier treaties and over the boarding of the British-owned merchant ship *Arrow*, by Chinese soldiers searching for pirates. French troops joined the British in this war, while Russia and the United States lent naval support. The war was brought to an end by the Treaty of Tientsin (Tianjin), which permitted the British to establish diplomatic representation in China.

In 1859 a flotilla carrying the first 'British envoy and minister plenipotentiary' to Beijing attempted to force its way up the Pei Ho River, despite Chinese warnings. It was fired upon by the Chinese forts on both shores and sustained heavy losses. With this excuse, a combined British and French force invaded China and marched on Beijing. Another treaty, the Convention of Peking (Beijing), was forced on the Chinese. Along with other concessions, this ceded the Kowloon Peninsula and nearby Stonecutters Island to the British.

Hong Kong made its last land grab in a moment of panic 40 years later when China was on the verge of being parcelled up into 'spheres of influence' by the Western powers and Japan, all of which had sunk their claws into the country. The British army felt it needed more land to protect the colony, and in June 1898 the Second Convention of Peking presented Britain with the New Territories on a 99-year lease, beginning 1 July 1898 and ending 1 July 1997.

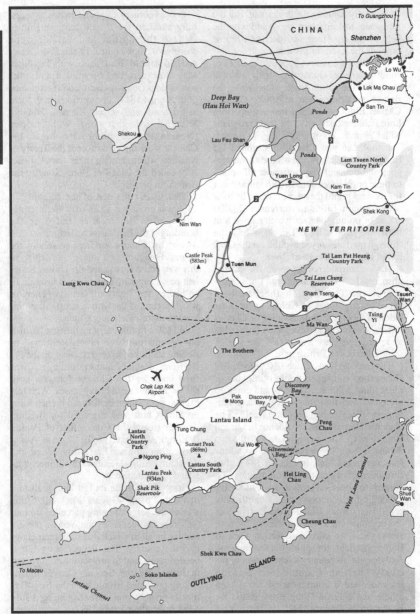

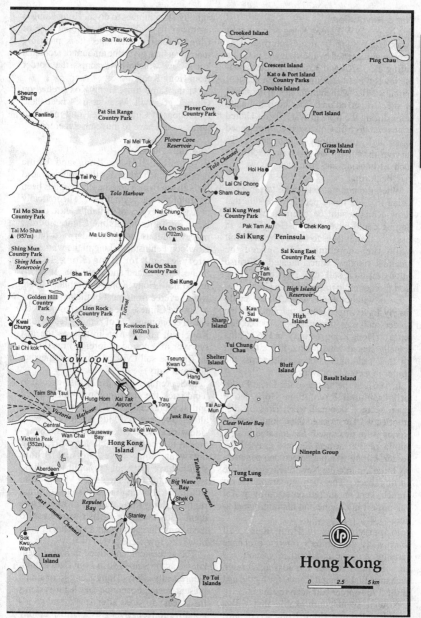

HONG KONG

Hong Kong

0   2.5   5 km

War & Revolution

Just before WWII Hong Kong began a shift away from trade to manufacturing. This move was hastened by the civil war in China during the 1920s and 30s, and by the Japanese invasion of the country – when Chinese capitalists fled with their money to the safety of the British colony. The crunch finally came during the Korean War, when a United States embargo on Chinese goods threatened to strangle the colony economically. To survive, the colony had to develop industries such as banking and insurance, as well as manufacturing.

When the communists came to power in China in 1949 many people were sure that Hong Kong would be overrun. Militarily, Beijing could have overrun Hong Kong in less time than it takes to make fried rice. But while the communists denounced the 'unequal treaties' which created a British colony on their soil, they recognised Hong Kong's economic importance to China.

Even without force, the Chinese could simply have ripped down the fence on the border and sent the masses to peacefully settle on Hong Kong territory. In 1962 China actually staged what looked like a trial run for this, sending 70,000 people across the border in a couple of weeks.

In 1967, at the height of the Great Proletarian Cultural Revolution, Hong Kong again seemed doomed when riots by disgruntled workers rocked the colony. Several bombs were detonated. In the same year, a militia of 300 armed Chinese crossed the border, killing five policemen and penetrating three km into the New Territories before pulling back. The then governor, David Trench, kept an aircraft on stand-by at Kai Tak airport in case he and his family had to flee.

Property values in Hong Kong fell sharply, as did China's foreign exchange earnings as trade and tourism ground to a halt. Perhaps it was the loss of foreign exchange that sobered China, for by the end of the 1960s order had been restored.

Now it seems unthinkable that China would undermine Hong Kong's economy, although it continues to do so. Hong Kong is estimated to be the source of about 30% of China's foreign exchange. It is probably more than that, given the amount of technical know-how which flows across the border from Hong Kong.

At the same time, Hong Kong relies on China's goodwill. Without the cheap land and labour of China, Hong Kong manufacturers would have to move elsewhere.

The 1997 Blues

Economically, Hong Kong and China depend on each other. Yet the problem faced by both the British and the Chinese has been the colony's fate beyond 1997. Theoretically at least, the expiry of Britain's lease on the New Territories means the Chinese border moves south as far as Boundary Rd on the Kowloon Peninsula, taking in the whole territory except for Hong Kong Island, Stonecutters Island and Kowloon. It's hard to see how Hong Kong can remain viable when severed from most of the population.

For the Chinese, the problem has not been one of economics, but of keeping face. Hong Kong will go down in history as the last survivor of a period of foreign imperialism on Chinese soil (Macau being a somewhat different story).

In September 1984 the British agreed to hand back the entire colony – lock, stock and skyscrapers – to China in 1997. An alternative was to divide it – leaving each side with a useless piece, and Britain hanging on to a colony which, arguably, it did not want. Some have said that Britain should have just shut up about the whole issue, forcing China to seek a Macau-style solution – allowing the British to continue running Hong Kong with no formal agreement. However, the British were keen to have something on paper. Once they got it, however, few were proud of it.

The agreement, enshrined in a document known as the Sino-British Joint Declaration, theoretically allows Hong Kong to retain its present social, economic and legal systems for at least 50 years after 1997. And so it's goodbye to Hong Kong as a British colony and hello to Hong Kong as a Special Administrative Region (SAR) of China. The Chinese catch phrase for this is 'one country, two systems', meaning Hong Kong is permitted to retain its capitalist system after 1997 while across the border the Chinese continue with a system which they label socialist.

In 1988, as a follow-up to the Joint Declaration, Beijing published *The Basic Law for Hong Kong*, a hefty document resembling a constitution. The Basic Law permits the preservation of Hong Kong's legal system and guarantees the right of property and ownership. It allows Hong Kong residents to retain the right to travel in and out of the colony; permits Hong Kong to remain a free port and to continue independent membership of international organisations; and guarantees employment after 1997 for the colony's civil servants (both Chinese and foreigners). The rights of assembly, free speech, association, travel and movement, correspondence, choice of occupation, academic research, religious belief and the right to strike are all included.

But few Hong Kongers have much faith in the agreement. China's own constitution also makes lofty guarantees of individual freedoms and respect for human rights. Such guarantees have proven to be empty promises. Beijing has made it abundantly clear that it will not allow Hong Kong to establish its own democratically elected government. Although some low-level officials will be chosen by election, Hong Kong's new leaders are to be appointed. Not that Hong Kong has ever been a true democracy. The British, after all, have installed a succession of governors who were neither elected nor native-born.

The Basic Law provides Beijing with options to interfere in Hong Kong's internal affairs to preserve public order, public morals and national security. Beijing also demanded that Britain remove its Ghurkha battalion, to be replaced by the People's Liberation Army (PLA). This has generated both fear and scepticism. China says it's a matter of 'national sovereignty', but sceptics say it's an attempt to suppress democracy and

dissent. It may also be a matter of pure greed – the British military and Ghurkha battalion were sitting on some extremely valuable chunks of real estate, such as the HMS Tamar Naval Centre in Central. Attempts to transfer these bases to civilian use before the handover were adamantly rejected by Beijing – the PLA could stand to gain literally billions of US dollars out of its new home.

Hong Kong's fledgling pro-democracy movement has denounced the Joint Declaration as the new 'unequal treaty' and the Basic Law as a 'basic flaw'. Britain stands accused of selling out the best interests of Hong Kong's people in order to keep good economic relations with China. It's also been pointed out that Hong Kong residents never had any opportunity to vote for or against these agreements – the negotiations were held entirely behind closed doors.

China's pro-democracy movement reached its zenith in the latter half of May 1989, when about one million people took part in protests in and around Beijing's Tiananmen Square. Hong Kong responded with its own demonstrations, and 500,000 people marched through the streets of Hong Kong in support of democracy. On 4 June, the People's Liberation Army gave its response: tanks were sent into Tiananmen Square, protesters were gunned down and a wave of arrests followed.

In Hong Kong, more than one million people attended rallies to protest against the Beijing massacre. Confidence plummeted – the Hong Kong stock market fell 22% in one day, and a great deal of capital headed to safer havens overseas.

The final five years of British rule were characterised by increasing Chinese hostility towards Britain. The Basic Law is unclear on the issue of democracy, but the British have belatedly recognised that it would be wise to clarify just how Hong Kong's future leaders will be chosen. Chris Patten, Hong Kong's last British governor, has been adamant that Hong Kong should have at least limited democracy. China has reacted by issuing hysterical threats – that public debts could be repudiated after 1997, that China might decide to 'take back' Hong Kong before 1997, etc. But the real bombshell was when China announced in 1996 that it would disband Hong Kong's democratically-elected legislature and replace it with one appointed by Beijing (see the Government & Politics section in this chapter). And for good measure, Hong Kong's new Bill of Rights would also be repealed by Beijing.

Of course, not all Hong Kongers have had to become citizens of the People's Republic because of the handover. About 60,000 people flee Hong Kong every year, and in opinion polls, about 40% of Hong Kongers say that they want to emigrate. Those with money and good technological skills have little difficulty emigrating, and about one million Hong Kongers hold foreign passports.

Ironically, the outward migration of money and talent is creating a vacuum which is being filled by foreigners. But Beijing has said it wants Hong Kong to be run by 'Hong Kong people'.

In its brief 160 years Hong Kong has been transformed. What was originally a 'barren island with hardly a house upon it' is now a highly developed city-state. Yet, a cloud of pessimism hangs over the city. Ultimately, Hong Kong's fate will be determined by the political dramas that unfold in Beijing.

And what of the opium trade that started it all? It folded by mutual consent in 1907, by which time the trading companies had diversified sufficiently to put their sordid pasts behind them without fear of financial ruin. In a twist of poetic justice, Hong Kong now has a serious dope problem and about 38,000 addicts – a constant reminder of the territory's less than creditable beginnings.

GEOGRAPHY

Hong Kong's 1070 sq km is divided into four main areas – Kowloon, Hong Kong Island, the New Territories and the Outlying Islands.

Kowloon is a peninsula on the north side of the harbour. The southern tip of this peninsula (Tsim Sha Tsui) is the biggest tourist area and is where most of the hotels are. Kowloon proper only includes the land south of Boundary Rd, a mere 12 sq km. North of Boundary Rd is New Kowloon, which is part of the New Territories.

Hong Kong Island covers 78 sq km, or roughly 7% of Hong Kong's land area. The island is on the south side of the harbour and

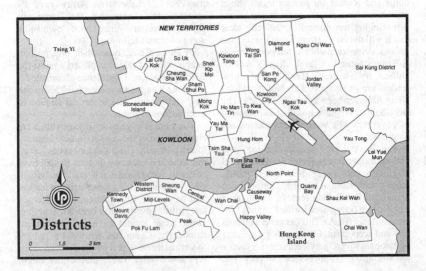

Districts

is the main business area, with numerous tourist hotels and sightseeing spots. Towering above the skyscrapers is the Peak, Hong Kong's premier scenic viewpoint.

The New Territories occupy 980 sq km, or 91% of Hong Kong's land area, and are sandwiched between Kowloon and the Chinese border. Foreign visitors rarely make the effort to visit the New Territories even though there is much to offer. About one third of Hong Kong's population lives here.

The Outlying Islands refers to any island apart from Hong Kong Island. Officially, they are part of the New Territories and make up about 20% of Hong Kong's total land area. There are actually 234 islands and while many are tiny rocks, the largest (Lantau) is nearly twice the size of Hong Kong Island (there were 235 islands until Stonecutters Island was absorbed by the Kowloon peninsula by land reclamation). Most tourists never make it to any of these islands, which is a shame since they offer a

taste of tranquil village life and in some ways are the best part of Hong Kong.

Within these four main areas are numerous neighbourhoods. Hong Kong Island is divided into Central, Wan Chai, Causeway Bay, Quarry Bay and so on, while Kowloon districts include Tsim Sha Tsui, Yau Ma Tei, Mong Kok, Hung Hom, etc.

CLIMATE

Hong Kong is perched on the south-east coast of China just a little to the south of the Tropic of Cancer. This puts the colony on much the same latitude as Hawaii or Calcutta, but the climate is not tropical. This is because the huge land mass of Asia generates powerful blasts of Arctic wind that blow during winter. In summer, the seasonal wind (monsoon) reverses and blows from the south, bringing humid tropical air.

Winter is chilly. It never snows or freezes, but it's cold enough to wear a warm sweater or coat. Many travellers arrive at the airport

---

Winds of Change

'Typhoon' is the Chinese word for big wind. Hong Kong's deadliest typhoon struck on 2 September 1937, when more than 1000 boats sank and about 2500 people drowned. Since then, many other severe typhoons have lashed Hong Kong, but in this age of weather satellites they no longer arrive without warning.

Typhoons can hit as early as May, but the peak season is from mid-July to mid-October. They vary in size from tropical storms to severe super-typhoons. If one just brushes past Hong Kong, it will bring a little rain and that might only last for half a day. If it scores a direct hit, the winds can be deadly and it may rain for days on end.

Typhoons are really not much fun even if you are safely entrenched in a hotel room. You can't go outside during a bad typhoon and most businesses shut down. Sitting around a hotel with nothing to do might not be the worst fate, but if the electric power is cut it can be rather unpleasant. In the worst-case scenario, the water pumps will fail too because there's no electricity to run them. Given these possibilities, it would be prudent to stock up on food, water, candles, matches and a torch if a big typhoon is heading your way. A battery-operated radio or tape player helps to pass the time. Keep extra batteries on hand.

When a typhoon becomes a possibility, warnings are broadcast continuously on TV and radio. Signal one goes out when there is a tropical storm centred within 800 km of Hong Kong. This is followed by signals three and eight, by which time offices are closed and everyone goes home while there is still public transport. There used to be other in-between signals with consecutive numbers, but this got too confusing so a simplified system was introduced - hence the odd jumps in the numbering.

Signals nine and 10 are rare. Nine means the storm is expected to increase significantly in strength. Ten means that hurricane-force winds are expected. This signal usually indicates a direct hit on Hong Kong.

Warning bulletins are broadcast at two minutes to every hour and half-past every hour whenever a signal of eight or more is hoisted. If you are without a radio, or miss a bulletin, there is a number you can call (☎ 2835-1473).

Signals are hoisted at various vantage points throughout Hong Kong, on both sides of the harbour. There's also a system of white, green and red lights. See the *Yellow Pages* for details. ■

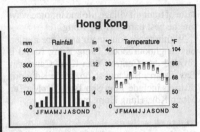

Hong Kong

in shorts and T-shirt, totally unprepared. Winter also tends to be windy and frequently cloudy. Not much rain falls, but when it does, it's usually a chilly, depressing drizzle that lasts for days on end. Because of a low cloud ceiling, the mountains are often shrouded in mist, which means it isn't too good for visiting the Peak and other scenic outlooks. Winter weather usually continues into March, often ending when the Arctic wind abruptly stops blowing. But even during winter, there are windless days when the weather gets amazingly balmy.

Autumn, from October until early December, is the best time to visit. The weather is generally sunny and dry. Typhoons sometimes occur in October, but not often, and November usually has ideal weather.

Spring is a short season in Hong Kong, but it's also a good time to visit. It's generally warm by the end of March and stays pleasant until the end of May. In March or April, an occasional wind will swoop out of the north and send temperatures plummeting for a few days. Big thunder showers become more frequent as June approaches. June tends to be the wettest month and the beginning of the summer monsoon. The Chinese call this the 'plum rain'.

Summer is hot and humid. The weather is sunny, but big thunder showers can occur suddenly.

ECOLOGY & ENVIRONMENT

Hong Kong is an urbanised, consumer-oriented, throw-away society. For years people have been throwing their rubbish into Victoria Harbour and now the harbour is starting to throw it back. Water pollution has become one of Hong Kong's most serious ecological problems. After watching fishing boats plucking fish out of the chemical-laden harbour, many foreigners have given up eating fresh seafood in Hong Kong (the locals seem indifferent).

In the past, little or no attention was paid to environmental protection, but the concept is slowly beginning to take root. Private industry has taken a few fledgling initiatives – for example, some stores (Giordano's, Wellcome supermarkets, etc) give a discount to people who don't require a bag. And other businesses have periodically donated funds to environmental causes.

The Hong Kong government has established an Environmental Protection Department (EPD) with a staff of nearly 1000. The bulk of funding goes on programmes to improve waste disposal and curb water pollution.

In spite of some mild waste-disposal regulations and environmental awareness publicity campaigns, Hong Kong's increasing population will probably only lead to more ecological degradation. Many feel that China's takeover means even weaker environmental regulations.

Green Power (☎ 2314-2662), at Jordan Rd, Yau Ma Tei, is Hong Kong's home grown environmental group. It appears that members of this organisation have their work cut out for them.

FLORA & FAUNA
Flora
Back in 1841, the British foreign secretary Lord Palmerston disparaged Hong Kong as a 'barren island with hardly a house upon it'. While the lack of houses was nothing unusual, the barrenness certainly was. With abundant rainfall and a warm climate, the British might well have expected to find a dense jungle on the shores of south China. Instead, they found Hong Kong to be decidedly leafless, a situation that persists today.

The simple reason for this is that Hong Kong's earlier inhabitants cut down all the trees. Massive tree cutting by settlers started as long ago as the Sung dynasty (960 -

1279 AD) and continued until the hills were stripped bare. Green politics were not fashionable in those days, and no effort was made to replant. With the forests removed, heavy summer thunder showers quickly eroded Hong Kong's steep slopes, and the lack of topsoil has prevented the forests from regenerating.

These days, most uninhabited regions of Hong Kong are grasslands. Somewhat ironically, the only areas of Hong Kong that have seen any reafforestation are those inhabited by humans. The British were never happy about the lack of shade during the scorching summers, and planted quick-growing species around their colonial residences. As for the Chinese, some have planted groves in an attempt to please the spirits of the deceased. Trees and other plants with commercial value, like bamboo, have been planted in small groves in agricultural regions, but other than in the New Territories and the more remote islands, there is precious little forest in Hong Kong today.

Fauna

The loss of forest has also meant loss of habitat for large animals. Although some small creatures survive in the Outlying Islands, there are very few large animals remaining – unless you count businessmen.

Weighing in at over 100 kg are wild boars, found in some rural spots and regarded as pests because they dig up crops. Much more delicate are barking deer (also called muntjacs), which are found even on the high slopes of Hong Kong Island. Early British settlers encountered leopards and tigers, but the last tiger seen in the New Territories was shot in 1915. The Chinese leopard cat (weighing only two to five kg) is still found in remote parts of the territory and other small mammals still around include ferret badgers, otters, masked palm civets, porcupines, shrews and bats. Wild monkeys survive, but are thought to be the descendants of escaped pets. The rat population of Hong Kong has apparently benefited from the arrival of humans.

An interesting creature is the Chinese pan-

golin, a scaly mammal that resembles an armadillo. When attacked, it rolls itself up into an unappetising ball. Unfortunately, its existence is threatened because the Chinese regard its flesh as a tonic and aphrodisiac.

Country Parks & Reserves

It surprises many visitors to learn that 40% of Hong Kong's total land area is protected by 21 country parks. Watershed protection was the major reason for putting these areas off-limits to development and private motor vehicles – all of Hong Kong's 17 reservoirs lie within park boundaries. Nevertheless, hikers, campers, birdwatchers and other nature-lovers all benefit. Most of the country parks are in the New Territories and the Outlying Islands, but the higher mountainous slopes of Hong Kong Island are also protected.

GOVERNMENT & POLITICS

Unfortunately, Hong Kong has had more politics than government in recent years.

Hong Kong is not a democracy, and Beijing is determined to make sure it doesn't become one. Now that China's ruling elite has sent the British-appointed governor packing, a 'provisional legislature' is set to evolve under the auspices of a Chinese-appointed chief executive. The Legislative Council (Legco) remains in theory, but it may well lose something in the translation.

Legco's role has been to frame legislation, enact laws and control government expenditure. The means by which its members are chosen has stirred up a storm of controversy which now hangs like a black cloud over Hong Kong. Until recently, the issue was simple – Britain appointed Legco members and that was it. But Chris Patten, Hong Kong's last governor, began to introduce a more democratic process after his appointment in 1992. Three years later, Legco members were chosen by direct election, which outraged Beijing. Hong Kong's Democratic Party, led by the charismatic Martin Lee, came out on top in the election while pro-Beijing candidates were trounced. China's solution to this problem is as simple as it is inevitable – remodel Legco Chinese-style.

Below the legislative level, the contentious issue of who runs Hong Kong is a little more mundane. The Urban Council is in charge of the day-to-day running of services on Hong Kong Island and Kowloon, including street cleaning, garbage collection, food hygiene, hawkers' licences and the like. In the New Territories, the Regional Council has much the same function.

On the next rung down are the District Boards, set up in 1982 to give Hong Kong residents a degree of control over their local area. The boards consist of government officials and elected representatives from the local area. The problem is that these boards have little (if any) real power because the seats are sought by a small number of candidates who are voted in by the small proportion of the electorate who bother to vote.

Staff in government departments and other areas of administration are under the umbrella of the Hong Kong Civil Service, which employs about 173,000 people. Until recently, several thousand of these employees were expats, many of whom held top policy-making positions. However, the number of expats in such positions of power has dwindled dramatically. The officer corps in the 27,000-strong police force has seen a similar shift in its expat power base. British professionals are no longer recruited for top administrative posts in the territory's police force. The Joint Declaration decrees that expats cannot head major government departments, nor can they hold deputy positions in some departments. But below these levels, they may still be employed.

The colonial government of the 1990s has been seen as generally efficient and free of corruption. It hasn't always been so. Hong Kong's police and civil service were a disgrace until 1974, when the British established the Independent Commission Against Corruption (ICAC). The ICAC was given far-reaching powers, and within three years it had nearly crushed corruption in Hong Kong. To prosecute, the ICAC only needs to show that a civil servant has wealth disproportionate to his or her income – it's not necessary to prove that the unexplained wealth was obtained illegally. Not only can the defendant be imprisoned, but they must also turn over the ill-gotten gains to the government.

Unfortunately, China has no independent judiciary and corrupt senior officials openly thumb their nose at the law. Many observers predict the same fate for Hong Kong, convinced that the ICAC will be intimidated by Communist Party officials and that corruption will once again flourish. Already, the ICAC has seen a sharp increase in the number of cases it prosecutes as quality civil servants emigrate abroad and their replacements succumb to graft.

The Chinese Communist Party (CCP) has a long history in Hong Kong, going back at least to 1949 when the party came to power in China. The CCP's Hong Kong arm is the Hong Kong Macau Work Committee, headed by the director of the New China (Xinhua) News Agency's Hong Kong branch, which is Beijing's official mouthpiece in the territory.

Another connection between Hong Kong and China is the 50 or so Hong Kong delegates to the NPC (China's rubber-stamp parliament). Add to that the other peculiar body, the Chinese People's Political Consultative Conference, which seems to be in charge of providing an image of a united front between China, Macau, Hong Kong and Taiwan. The NPC has 16 Hong Kong delegates, all top people from banking, business, commerce, education, trade unions, the media and so on – and all reliably pro-Beijing.

ECONOMY

Regarded by many as a paragon of capitalism, Hong Kong is a hard-working, competitive, money-oriented society. Its *laissez faire* economic policies have been a capitalist's dream: free enterprise and free trade, low taxes, a hard-working labour force, a modern and efficient port, excellent worldwide communications, and a government famous

The slippery dip. To many observers Hong Kong's existence has never seemed so precarious as it does with the imminent handover to China. Illustration by Mic Looby.

for a hands-off approach. When it comes to regulating business, the slogan of the Hong Kong government has always been 'positive non-intervention'.

Generally, Hong Kong has been moving towards capital-intensive rather than labour-intensive industries. Most of the manual labour is now being performed across the border in China. Within Hong Kong itself, industries like telecommunications, banking, insurance, tourism and retail sales have pushed manufacturing to the background. The shift from manufacturing to services has been accompanied by a dramatic increase in wages. Hong Kong actually enjoys the best of both worlds: a high standard of living with a well-educated workforce and sophisticated service industries – and a nearby pool of sweatshop labour to do the dirty work.

The basic philosophy of Hong Kong's manufacturers has been 'export or die'. While the domestic market certainly isn't overlooked, around 90% of manufactured goods head to other lands. The largest proportion goes to the USA (45%); other large markets are China, Britain, West Germany, Japan, Canada, Australia and Singapore. With an official unemployment rate of less than 2%, Hong Kong actually suffers from a labour shortage, something of a rarity in the

Asian region. Much of the lower-level work (domestic servants, construction workers, etc) is performed by imported labour, chiefly from the Philippines. But with the influx of Chinese labour from now on, many of these foreigners may be kicked out of their jobs, and out of Hong Kong.

One should not forget tourism, Hong Kong's second-largest earner of foreign exchange after textiles. And it's no longer just Westerners who make tourism such a lucrative business – despite high costs, Hong Kong is a favourite destination of visitors from China.

Hong Kong has a very small agricultural base – only 9% of the total land area is suitable for crop farming, and even that is shrinking fast. Less than 2% of the population is engaged in agriculture or fishing and, again, these numbers continue to decline.

Most food is imported, although Hong Kong's farming and fishing industries are efficient. A sizeable ocean fishing industry employs about 29,000 people working 5000 fishing vessels. But most of Hong Kong's food is brought in from the mainland – even McDonald's gets its potatoes and vegies from China.

Because of its limited natural resources, Hong Kong depends on imports for virtually

HONG KONG

all its requirements, including water – more than 50% is pumped from China. To pay for all these imports Hong Kong has to generate enough foreign exchange through exports, tourism and overseas investments. So far, the city has had no problem paying its bills, and one of the government's 'problems' has been what to do with the surplus revenue!

Only about 350,000 people of the 2.5 million-strong workforce are unionised, which appears to suit Hong Kong capitalists as much as the Chinese government. It's argued that the People's Republic believes a strong independent union movement could become the focus of mass political discontent, which cannot be allowed because it will upset Hong Kong's 'stability and prosperity'.

The living standards and wages of most people in Hong Kong are much higher than those in China and most other Asian countries – only Japan ranks higher in the statistics. Hong Kong is one of Asia's 'four little tigers' (also called 'four little dragons'). The other economic powerhouses in this weight division are Korea, Singapore and Taiwan. While China's per-capita Gross National Product is around US$500, in Hong Kong it's about US$23,000.

Maximum personal income tax is no more than 15%, company profits tax is 16.5% and there are no capital gains or transfer taxes. But the money is far from being evenly spread and the government supports only meagre spending on social welfare.

Hong Kong's importance to China is manifold. For the first three decades after the communist takeover in China in 1949, China was largely content to sell Hong Kong foodstuffs, raw materials and fuel. Hong Kong bought the produce and in return provided China with a large proportion of its foreign-exchange earnings, as it continues to do. Chinese investment has been steadily increasing and now amounts to more than a third of all direct foreign investment in Hong Kong.

But all this capital does not necessarily cheer Hong Kong's business community. On the Chinese mainland, the government's policy has frequently been to invite foreign companies to invest, learn their technology secrets and then strangle them with red tape. Foreign companies which have survived in China have often been forced into highly unfavourable joint-venture operations that leave the lion's share of profits to the Chinese. And now history seems to be repeating itself. In 1996, China Inc flexed its muscles and pressured Swire Pacific to sell (at bargain-basement prices) 25% of Cathay Pacific Airlines to Chinese state-run enterprises. And the Chinese government, citing 'national security' concerns, seems to have set its sights on Hongkong Telecom (currently controlled by Britain's Cable & Wireless). In the early 1990s, China scuttled a deal by a British-backed consortium to build a new container terminal, but in the end decided it could be built if China's state-run companies owned a lucrative part of it. Hong Kong's pessimists insist that China's real intention is to monopolise the lucrative business in the city. The Chinese government, of course, denies the charge.

Hong Kong's economy, for the moment, is booming, yet many companies are making contingency plans should things ever turn sour. Will Hong Kong be the boomtown of the East, or will the government kill the goose that lays the golden eggs? Get a good seat, the drama could be about to unfold.

POPULATION & PEOPLE

Hong Kong's official population is about 6.4 million, with an annual growth rate of 2.1%. The overall density of the population works out to be about 5800 people per sq km, but this figure is rather deceiving since there is an extremely wide variation in density from area to area. Some urban areas have tens of thousands of people per sq km, stacked into multi-block, high-rise housing estates, while many areas are genuinely rural. And many of the Outlying Islands are uninhabited.

The colony's phenomenally dense population is largely a product of the events in China in the first half of this century: in 1851, the colony's population was a mere 33,000.

The Qing dynasty collapsed in 1911/12 and during the 1920s and 30s the wars between the Kuomintang (now the ruling party of Taiwan), Chinese warlords, the communists and the Japanese made Chinese flee to the safer shores of Hong Kong. By 1931 there were 880,000 people living there. When war between China and Japan erupted in 1937 (the Japanese having occupied Manchuria several years before) and Guangzhou fell a year later, another 700,000 people fled to Hong Kong.

The Japanese attacked the colony on 8 December 1941, the same time as the attack on Pearl Harbour, and occupied it for the next three and a half years. Mass deportations of Chinese civilians, aimed at relieving the colony's food shortage, reduced the population to 600,000 by 1945, but the displaced people began returning after the war. When Chiang Kai-shek's Kuomintang forces were defeated by the communists in 1949, another 750,000 followed, bringing the total population to about 2.5 million.

From the 1950s to the 70s there was a varying flow of immigrants (they're no longer called refugees) across the border from China. In two years alone at the end of the 70s, the population rose by a quarter of a million as a result of Chinese immigration – some legal, but most of it not.

About 98% of Hong Kong's population is ethnic Chinese, most of whom have their origins in China's Guangdong Province. About 60% were born in the colony. About 35% of the population lives in Kowloon, 21% on Hong Kong Island, 42% in the New Territories and 2% in the Outlying Islands.

If any groups can truly claim to belong to Hong Kong, they are the Tankas, the nomadic boat people who have fished the local waters for centuries, and the Hakka, who farmed the New Territories long before the British thought about running the Union Jack up a flagpole. The Hakka are a distinct group which emigrated from north to south China centuries ago to flee persecution. Hakka means 'guest'. Hakka women can be recognised in the New Territories by their distinctive spliced-bamboo hats with wide brims and black cloth fringes.

About 400,000 expats permanently reside (legally) in Hong Kong, plus an unknown number of illegals who usually don't stay for long. In descending order, the top 10 foreign nationalities living in Hong Kong (both legally and illegally) are: Filipinos, Americans, British, Thais, Canadians, Indians, Australians, Japanese, Malaysians and Nigerians.

A very touchy issue in 1997 has been what will happen to 'foreigners' who were born in Hong Kong and hold Hong Kong passports. Some are half-Chinese or quarter-Chinese, but Beijing has indicated that citizenship can only be endowed on those Hong Kongers of 'pure Chinese descent'. In other words, racial purity, not place of birth, is the deciding factor and this threatens to render many people stateless. The 15,000 or so Hong Kong-born Indians have protested loudly, demanding either full Chinese citizenship or British passports. The Filipinos and Nigerians are a likely target for mass expulsion – after all, they have no legitimate citizenship claim and China would rather replace them with cheap Chinese workers. For that matter, many British nationals may suddenly become unwelcome.

EDUCATION

Hong Kong's education system closely follows the British model. Primary education is free and compulsory. At secondary level students begin to specialise: some go into a university or college preparatory programme while others select vocational education combined with apprenticeships.

At tertiary level, education is fiercely competitive. Only about 5% of students who sit university entrance exams actually gain admission. This is less of a problem for wealthy families, who simply send their children abroad to study.

Campuses

Hong Kong has four universities. Hong Kong University, established in 1911, is the oldest. The campus is on the west side of Hong Kong Island in the Mid-Levels area. The Chinese University of Hong Kong is at Ma Liu Shui in the New Territories. It was officially established in 1963 on a beautiful campus. The Hong Kong University of Science & Technology, which admitted its first students in 1991, is in Tai Po Tsai in the south-east of the New Territories.

The newest institute is the City University of Hong Kong. The campus is on Tat Chee Ave, very close to Kowloon Tong MTR station. This school was formerly known as City Polytechnic of Hong Kong. This is not to be confused with the Hong Kong Polytechnic, in the Hung Hom area, which was established in 1972.

ARTS
Dance
Lion Dances Chinese festivals are never sombre occasions – when the religious rites are over at any festival there is generally a lion dance, some opera or a show by a visiting puppeteer.

Celebrations in Chinatowns throughout the world have made the lion dance synonymous with Chinese culture. There is no reason why it should be. The lion is not indigenous to China and the Chinese lion is a strictly mythical animal.

The lion dance is universally associated with Chinese festivals and can be seen in Chinatowns all over the world.

Music
Hong Kong's home grown variety of music consists of soft-rock love melodies. The songs are usually sung in Cantonese and are collectively known as 'Canto-pop'. Pop songs sung in Mandarin are also imported from Taiwan and sometimes even mainland China. Most Chinese find Western-style hard rock too harsh and grating. Conversely, most Westerners have little regard for Canto-pop, though it would no doubt be more appealing if you learn to speak Cantonese.

If you have a strong interest in music (and especially if you're a musician yourself), you might want to drop in at the Music Union (☎ 2312-2688), flat F, 1st floor, Comfort Building, 88 Nathan Rd, Tsim Sha Tsui. Despite its spot in a grimy commercial block, this place is a lively music venue for local performers. Gigs are held regularly in a little lounge that resembles a low-key jazz bar. The musicians are usually Cantonese, but *gwailos* ('ghost people' or 'foreign devils') are also welcome to perform. Though it's not a bar, juice and beer are served during live performances. You can also buy CDs put out by local artists here. There is a 10,000-CD lending library, but it's open only to members. There's also a local musicians' noticeboard.

Film
Hong Kong has one of the most robust film industries in Asia. The good news for foreigners is that most Hong Kong-made films have English subtitles even though the sound track is in Cantonese or Mandarin.

Hong Kong is especially famous for kungfu epics, such as the Bruce Lee series. Unfortunately, a lot of what is produced now doesn't come up to the high standards set by Lee.

Jackie Chan is one movie hero who has picked up where Lee left off, becoming the closest thing Hong Kong has to a living god. Now Chan's outrageous slapstick style is leading the Asian assault on Hollywood. His blockbuster *Rumble in the Bronx* leapt to the top of the US cinema charts in its first weekend of release.

You can find plenty of Hong Kong martial arts movies on video. The lead characters are more often than not super killers with supernatural abilities. They fly through the air, jump over buildings and heal dying people with 10 seconds of *qigong* (kungfu meditation).

But not every Hong Kong film maker is a kungfu fightin'. Other genres include dramas from Chinese history, comedies and heartbreaking love stories. At the 1996 Hong Kong film festival, *Hu-du-men* by Shu Kei was judged by many amateurs to be the most interesting film of the year.

Hong Kong's leading movie companies are Shaw Brothers, with its huge Movietown studios on Clearwater Bay Rd in the New Territories, and Golden Harvest, which started the Bruce Lee series. Hong Kong films are exported to Chinese communities all over the world, and many are shown in Taiwan and China. In the West, many Chinese grocery stores display Hong Kong videos for hire among the sacks of rice and bean curd.

Unfortunately, Hong Kong's criminal gangs have been trying to take over the industry and could well destroy it; producers and stars are fleeing to avoid both the gangsters and the changes wrought by the Chinese handover.

Theatre
Chinese Opera Few Chinese festivals are complete without an opera performance. There are probably more than 500 opera performers in Hong Kong and opera troupes from China make regular appearances.

Chinese opera is a world away from the Western variety. It is a mixture of singing, speaking, mime, acrobatics and dancing that can go on for five or six hours.

Three types of Chinese opera are performed in Hong Kong. Top of the line among Chinese culture buffs is reckoned to be the so-called 'Beijing opera' – a highly refined style which uses almost no scenery but a variety of traditional props. More 'music hall' is the Cantonese variety, which usually has a 'boy meets girl' theme, and often incorporates modern and foreign references. The most traditional, Chaozhou, is now the least performed of the three. It is staged almost as it was in the Ming dynasty, with stories from Chaozhou legends and folklore, and always contains a moral.

There are at least two venues worth checking for opera performances. One is the City Hall Theatre near the Star Ferry terminal in Central. The other is the Lai Chi Kok Amusement Park in Kowloon. Probably the best time to see Chinese opera is during the annual Hong Kong Arts Festival (around February or March) and the Festival of Asian Arts (held every two years around October or November). The Hong Kong Tourist Association has the latest information.

Puppets Puppets are the oldest of the Chinese theatre arts. Styles include rod, glove, string and shadow. The rod puppets, visible only from waist up, are fixed to a long pole with short sticks for hand movements. The puppets are made from camphor wood and the main characters have larger heads than the rest of the cast. The shadow variety are made from leather and cast shadows on to a silk screen. Most performances relate tales of past dynasties. The most likely place to see performances is on TV – live shows are somewhat rare these days.

Although puppets are the oldest of Chinese theatre arts, the most likely place to see a performance these days is on TV.

SOCIETY & CONDUCT
Traditional Culture

Face Having 'big face' is synonymous with prestige, and prestige is important in the Orient. All families, even poor ones, are expected to have big wedding parties and throw around money like water, in order to 'gain face'.

Much of the Chinese obsession with materialism is really to do with gaining face. Owning nice clothes, a big car (even if you can't drive), a piano (even if you can't play it), imported cigarettes and liquor (even if you don't smoke or drink), will all help gain face. Therefore, when taking a gift to a Chinese friend, try to give something with snob appeal, such as a bottle of imported liquor, perfume, cigarettes or chocolate. This will please your host and help win you points in the face game.

The whole concept of face seems very childish to Westerners and most never learn to understand it, but it is important in the East.

Chinese Zodiac Astrology has a long history in China and is integrated with religious beliefs. As in the Western system of astrology, there are 12 zodiac signs. However, unlike the Western system, your sign is based on the year, rather than the day, you were born. Still, this is a simplification. The exact day and time of birth is also carefully considered in charting an astrological path.

If you want to know your sign in the Chinese zodiac, look up your year of birth in the chart. However, it's a little more complicated than this because Chinese astrology goes by the lunar calendar. The Chinese Lunar New Year falls in late January or early February, so the first month will be included in the year before.

It is said that the animal year chart originated when Buddha commanded all the beasts of the earth to assemble before him. Only 12 animals came and they were rewarded by having their names given to a specific year. Buddha also decided to name each year in the order in which the animals arrived – the first was the rat, then the ox, tiger, rabbit and so on.

Many festivals are held throughout the year in accordance with the lunar calendar. Some festivals only occur at the end of the 12-year cycle, and some occur only once in 60 years. This is because each of the 12 animals is influenced at different times by five elements: metal, wood, earth, water and fire. The full cycle takes 60 years (5 x 12) and at the end of this time there is a 'super festival'.

Being born or married in a particular year is believed to determine one's fortune. In this era of modern birth-control techniques and abortion, Chinese parents will often carefully manipulate the birth times of their children. The year of the dragon sees the biggest jump in the birth rate, closely followed by the year of the tiger. A girl born in the year of the pig could have trouble getting married!

Fortune-Tellers Having your fortune told can be fun. It can also be dangerous. The

Chinese Zodiac

Rat	1924	1936	1948	1960	1972	1984	1996
Ox/Cow	1925	1937	1949	1961	1973	1985	1997
Tiger	1926	1938	1950	1962	1974	1986	1998
Rabbit	1927	1939	1951	1963	1975	1987	1999
Dragon	1928	1940	1952	1964	1976	1988	2000
Snake	1929	1941	1953	1965	1977	1989	2001
Horse	1930	1942	1954	1966	1978	1990	2002
Goat	1931	1943	1955	1967	1979	1991	2003
Monkey	1932	1944	1956	1968	1980	1992	2004
Rooster	1933	1945	1957	1969	1981	1993	2005
Dog	1934	1946	1958	1970	1982	1994	2006
Pig	1935	1947	1959	1971	1983	1995	2007

danger is the psychological problems that can occur when someone's fortune is bleak. One friend was told that she would die by the age of 23. Three fortune-tellers made the same prediction. She became very depressed and nearly gave up trying to live. It almost became a self-fulfilling prophecy, but the last time I saw her she was 26 and still very much alive. She swears that she will never see another fortune teller again.

So how did three fortune-tellers manage to make the same alarming prediction? Quite simply, they used the same methods. For example, one line on your palm is your life line – a short one indicates a short life. Other lines indicate health, wealth, happiness and the number of children or spouses you might have. Also, astrologers use the same reference when charting an astrological path. Some people do their own fortune-telling at home using the Chinese *Almanac*, a sort of annual horoscope.

The business of fortune-telling is lucrative, and it's how many Hong Kong temples pay their bills. The most popular venue for fortune-telling is Sik Sik Yuen (Wong Tai Sin Temple) next to Wong Tai Sin MTR station. Other possibilities include the Tin Hau temple in Yau Ma Tei and several smaller temples in Wan Chai. Palmists (who also read faces) set up at the Temple St night market in Yau Ma Tei. If you decide, as many tourists do, to find out what fate has in store for you, keep the preceding warning in mind.

Your Age Are you sure you know how old you are? You might be less than certain after seeing how the Chinese work it out. Since the Chinese calculate age from the moment of conception, a baby is already going on one when it leaves the womb. The seventh day on the Chinese lunar calender is also 'everyone's birthday'. Some more modern Chinese follow the solar calendar, so they have yet another birthday. Then, of course, there is the date·of birth itself to add to the list.

Fungshui (Geomancy) The Chinese word *fungshui* literally means 'wind-water'. West-

erners call it geomancy, the art (or science if you prefer) of manipulating or judging the environment to produce good fortune. If you want to build a house or find a suitable site for a grave then you call in a geomancer. The Chinese warn that violating the principles of good fungshui can have serious consequences. Therefore, fungshui masters are consulted before an apartment block is built, a highway laid down, telephone poles erected or trees lopped.

Trees may have a spirit living inside, and for this reason some villages and temples in the New Territories still have fungshui groves to provide a place for the good spirits to live. Attempts to cut down fungshui groves to construct new buildings have sometimes led to massive protests and even violent confrontations – the solution may be a large cash payment to the village to 'placate the spirits'.

Businesses that are failing may call in a fungshui expert. Sometimes the solution is to move a door or window. If this doesn't do the trick, it might be necessary to move an ancestor's grave. The location of an ancestor's grave is an especially serious matter. If the grave is in the wrong spot, or facing the wrong way, then there is no telling what trouble the spirits might cause. If a fungshui master is not consulted, and the family of the deceased suddenly runs into an episode of bad luck, then it's time to see a Taoist priest who knows how to deal with the ghosts who are causing all the trouble.

Hong Kong produces some architectural wonders – the Lippo Centre in Central, for example, is all lumps and bumps and mirrored glass. But no matter how attractive or innovative, any office tower built without the blessings of a fungshui expert could be a financial disaster – no one but foreigners would rent offices in it. One prominent building had to be completely renovated and worked over by Taoist priests after it was 'discovered' that the faces of wolves could be seen in the marble decor. Evidently, the spirits of wolves had been trapped in the marble and the tenants quickly moved out of this haunted place. Fortunately, the priests were able to save the building and prevent the landlord from going bankrupt, but it was a close call indeed.

Construction of Hong Kong's underground Mass Transit Railway (MTR) began with an invocation by a group of Taoist priests who paid respects to the spirits of the earth whose domain was about to be violated

Dos & Don'ts

Clothing Hong Kong is a very fashion-conscious city. The Chinese generally judge a person by their clothing far more than a Westerner would. Still, Hong Kong is cosmopolitan – they've seen it all, so you can get away with wearing almost anything. Revealing clothing is OK – shorts, miniskirts and bikinis (at the beach only) are common. However, nude bathing is a definite no-no.

Although Hong Kongers are usually tolerant when it comes to dress, there is one exception – thongs (flip flops). Thongs are OK to wear in hotel rooms or maybe the corridor of your hotel, but not in its lobby and most definitely not outdoors (except around a swimming pool or beach). Many restaurants and hotels will not let you in the door wearing thongs. Many Westerners ignore this unwritten rule, and although the police won't arrest you for wearing thongs in public, you will be looked upon with contempt.

Ironically, sandals are perfectly acceptable. The difference between sandals and thongs is the strap across the back of the ankle. As long as the strap is there, it's OK. No strap, and you're dressed indecently.

Handy Hints Always hand a piece of paper to somebody using both hands. This shows respect. This is especially true if that person is somebody important, like a public official, your landlord or a business associate. If you only use one hand, you will be considered rude.

Colour Codes Every colour symbolises something to the Chinese, and red is normally a happy colour. However, a grand exception is made for red ink. The reason for this is subject to speculation – perhaps red ink looks too much like blood. Regardless of the long-forgotten reason, do not write a note in red. If you want to give someone your address or telephone, write in any colour but red. Messages written in red convey anger, hostility or unfriendliness.

White is the colour of death, and it's only appropriate to give white flowers at funerals. And a man should never wear a green hat because this indicates that his wife is having an affair!

Killer Chopsticks Leaving chopsticks sticking vertically into the bowl is a bad omen. This resembles incense sticks in a bowl of ashes, a sure death sign.

Gift Giving This is a complicated issue with the Chinese. It's good manners when visiting people at their homes to bring some sort of gift, especially if you've been invited for a meal. Flowers are OK, or a box of chocolates. Money is not generally appropriate (and indeed would be an insult), but there are times when you are supposed to give money – weddings, funerals and (for children) the Chinese Lunar New Year. The money should be given in a red envelope (sold in stationery shops all over Hong Kong).

To complicate matters still further, a Chinese with good manners is supposed to refuse (at least once, maybe twice) any gift you want to offer. You are supposed to insist. They will then 'reluctantly' accept it. To accept a gift too readily is considered greedy and will cause the recipient to lose face. But this really makes it hard to know if that person is really trying to refuse the gift because they don't want it, or if they really want it but must make a token refusal to save face.

If you receive a present that is gift-wrapped, it is customary not to open it in front of the giver. If you open it immediately, it makes you look greedy.

RELIGION

In Chinese religion, Taoism, Confucianism and Buddhism have become inextricably entwined. Ancestor worship and ancient animist beliefs have also been incorporated into the religious milieu.

Top: Take a peek. Every visitor to Hong Kong should treat themselves to the view from Victoria Peak at night.

Bottom: Traditional vessels known as junks have plied the China coast for centuries. Today they are most commonly seen in Aberdeen Harbour.

RICHARD I'ANSON

GLENN BEANLAND

RICHARD I'ANSON

Top: The glass and steel of Kowloon's skyscrapers have their own beauty.
Bottom Left: The Bank of China building is one of Central's most distinctive landmarks.
Bottom Right: The only way is up in the scramble for living space on Hong Kong Island,
yet the New Territories feature open spaces and peaceful country parks.

In Hong Kong there are approximately 600 temples, monasteries and shrines. Most are tiny but some are enormous, such as the Po Lin Monastery on Lantau Island; the Ten Thousand Buddhas Monastery at Sha Tin; and the Sik Sik Yuen (Wong Tai Sin Temple) in Kowloon.

Buddhism

Buddhism was founded in India in the 6th century BC by Siddhartha Gautama of the Sakya clan. Siddhartha was a prince brought up in luxury, but he became discontented with the physical world when he was confronted with the sights of old age, sickness and death. He despaired of finding fulfilment on the physical level, since the body was inescapably subject to these weaknesses.

Around the age of 30 Siddhartha broke from the material world and sought 'enlightenment' by following various yogic disciplines. After several failed attempts he devoted the final phase of his search to intensive contemplation. One evening as he sat beneath a banyan tree, he slipped into a deep meditation and emerged after achieving enlightenment. His title 'Buddha' means 'the awakened' or 'the enlightened one'.

. Buddha founded an order of monks and preached his ideas for the next four decades until his death around 480 BC. To his followers he was known as Sakyamuni, the 'silent sage of the Sakya clan'. It is said that Gautama Buddha was not the only Buddha – the fourth, in fact – and is not expected to be the last.

The cornerstone of Buddhist philosophy is the view that all life is suffering. Everyone is subject to the traumas of birth, sickness, decrepitude, fear and death. The cause of suffering is desire – the desires of the body and the desire for personal fulfilment. Happiness can only be achieved if these desires are overcome.

Buddhism developed in China during the 3rd to 6th centuries AD. In the middle of the 1st century AD the religion had gained the interest of the Han emperor Ming, who sent a mission to the west; the mission returned in 67 AD with Buddhist scriptures, two Indian monks and images of the Buddha. Centuries later other Chinese monks, like Xuan Zang, journeyed to India and returned with Buddhist scriptures, which were then translated from the original Sanskrit to Chinese.

Buddha wrote nothing; the writings that have come down to us date from about 150 years after his death. By the time these texts came out, divisions had already appeared within Buddhism. At some stage Buddhism split into two major schools: Theravada and Mahayana.

The Theravada, or 'doctrine of elders', holds that the path to nirvana is an individual pursuit. It centres on monks and nuns who make the search for nirvana a full-time profession. This school maintains that people are alone in the world and must tread the path to nirvana on their own; Buddhas can only show the way. The Theravada school is the Buddhism of Sri Lanka, Myanmar (Burma), Thailand, Laos and Cambodia.

The Mahayana (or 'big school') holds that since all existence is one, the fate of the individual is linked to the fate of others. The Buddha did not just point the way and float off into his own nirvana, but continues to offer spiritual help to others seeking nirvana. The Mahayana is the Buddhism of Vietnam, Japan, Tibet, Korea, Mongolia and China.

Taoism

Originally a philosophy, Taoism evolved into a religion. Unlike Buddhism, which was imported from India, Taoism is truly a Chinese home-grown religion. While Buddhism is found throughout East Asia, Taoism is seldom practised by non-Chinese.

The philosophy of Taoism originated with Laozi (Laotse), who lived in the 6th century BC. Very little is known about Laozi and some have questioned whether or not he existed. His name simply means the old one. Laozi is believed to have been the custodian of the imperial archives for the Chinese government and Confucius is supposed to have consulted him.

Laozi (or someone else) left behind a record of his beliefs, a slim volume entitled the *Dao De Qing* or *The Way and its Power*. It is doubtful that Laozi ever intended his philosophy to become a religion. Chang Ling is more

Chinese Gods

Chinese religion is polytheistic, ie having many divinities. Every Chinese house has its kitchen or house god, and trades have their gods too. Students worship Wan Chung, the deified scholar. Shopkeepers pray to Tsai Shin, god of riches. Every profession has its own god, and numerous temples in Hong Kong and Macau are dedicated to certain gods or goddesses. The following are some of the important local divinities.

Tin Hau Queen of heaven and protector of seafarers, she is one of the most popular goddesses in Hong Kong. In Macau she is known as Ah Ma or 'Mother' and in Taiwan she is known as Matsu. In Singapore she is Ma Chu Po or 'Respected Great Aunt'.

In Hong Kong Tin Hau has about 250,000 fishing people as followers and there are about two dozen temples dedicated to her dotted around the territory. The most famous is Tai Miu ('Great Temple') at Joss House Bay in the New Territories east of Hong Kong Island. Others are on Cheung Chau Island, at Sok Kwu Wan on Lamma Island, on Market St in Kowloon's Yau Ma Tei district, on Tin Hau Temple Rd in Causeway Bay, and at Stanley on Hong Kong Island.

Tin Hau is a case of the deification of a real person. She was born on an island in Fujian Province between 900 AD and 1000 AD. After her death the cult of Tin Hau spread along the coast of China.

Kwun Yum The Buddhist equivalent of Tin Hau is Kuanyin (Kwun Yum in Hong Kong), the goddess of mercy, who stands for tenderness and compassion for the unhappy lot of mortals. Kwun Yum temples are at Repulse Bay and Stanley on Hong Kong Island, and at Cheung Chau in the Outlying Islands. There are some temples in Macau also, where the goddess is called Kuan Iam.

Kuanti Soldiers pray to Kuanti, the red-faced god of war. Kuanti was a great warrior who lived at the end of the Han dynasty (206 BC to 220 AD) and is worshipped not only for his might in battle but because he is the embodiment of right action, integrity and loyalty. The life of Kuanti is told in an old Chinese legend called *The Story of the Three Kingdoms*.

Kuanti is not a cruel tyrant delighting in battle and the slaying of enemies. Rather, he can avert war and protect people from its horrors. He is also the patron god of restaurants, pawn shops and literature, as well as the Hong Kong police force and secret societies such as the Triad organisations.

Kuanti temples are at Tai O on Lantau Island and the Man Mo (literally 'civil and military') Temple on Hollywood Rd, Hong Kong Island.

---

or less credited with formally establishing the Taoist religion in 143 BC.

Understanding Taoism is not simple. The word *tao* (pronounced 'dao'), means 'the way'. It is considered indescribable, but might be interpreted as the guiding path, the truth or the principle of the universe.

One of the main principles of Taoism is the concept of *wuwei* or 'doing nothing'. A quote, attributed to Laozi: 'Do nothing, and nothing will not be done,' emphasises this principle. The idea is to remain humble, passive, non-assertive and non-interventionist. Qian Sima, a Chinese historian who lived from 145 BC to 90 BC, put it another way: 'Do not take the lead in planning affairs or you may be held responsible.'

Non-intervention or 'live and let live' ideals are the keystones of Tao. Harmony and patience are needed, and action is obtained through inaction. Taoists like to note that water, the softest substance, will wear away stone, the hardest substance.

Just as there have been different interpretations of Tao, there have been different interpretations of *De* – 'the power', which has led to three distinct kinds of Taoism in China.

Unlike philosophical Taoism, which has many Western followers, Chinese Taoism is a religion. It has been associated with alchemy and the search for immortality, which attracted the patronage of Chinese rulers before Confucianism gained the upper hand.

As time passed, Taoism increasingly became wrapped up in the supernatural, self-mutilation, hot-coal dances, witchcraft, fortune-telling and magic. All this is evident if you visit a Taoist temple during the ghost month or certain other festivals.

Pak Tai Like all gods for special localities, Pak Tai keeps an eye out for his area, Cheung Chau Island.

Like Kuanti, Pak Tai is a military protector of the state and there are various stories about his origins. Chinese ancestors are the spiritual guardians of their descendants, and Pak Tai is the guardian of society. When chaos reigns and there is destruction he is believed to descend from heaven to restore peace and order.

On the island of Cheung Chau, Pak Tai is revered as a life-giver, having intervened to end a plague which hit the island at the end of the last century. A large temple on Cheung Chau, the Temple of Jade Vacuity, is dedicated to him.

This wooden carving from the 12 or 13th century depicts Kuanyin, the Goddess of Mercy.

Tam Kung This god is worshipped only along a small stretch of the southern Chinese coast which includes Macau and Hong Kong. One theory is that he was actually the last emperor of the Southern Song dynasty (1127 AD to 1279 AD) which was overrun by Kublai Khan's Mongol armies. The emperor was a boy of eight or nine years and is now worshipped under the pseudonym of Tam Kung. A temple for Tam Kung can be seen in Shau Kei Wan on Hong Kong Island and Coloane Village in Macau.

Wong Tai Sin This god watches over the housing settlement of the same name in Kowloon. Wong Tai Sin's popularity had a meteoric rise in Hong Kong after a man and his son brought a painting of him from Guangdong Province in 1915. They installed the painting and an altar in a small temple in Wan Chai. A temple was built in Kowloon in 1921 and his popularity grew further.

For all that, Wong Tai Sin had a humble beginning as a shepherd boy in Zhejiang Province. At 15 he was taught by an immortal how to make a herb that could cure all illnesses – thus, he is worshipped by the ill. Wong Tai Sin also spent 40 years in seclusion doing various miraculous things like turning white boulders into sheep (which perhaps explains why he is worshipped by business people, who want to turn white elephants into profitable companies). ■

Confucianism

Confucius is regarded as China's greatest philosopher and teacher. The philosophy of Confucius has been borrowed by Japan, Korea, Vietnam and other neighbours of China. Confucius never claimed to be a religious leader, prophet or god, but his influence has been so great in China that Confucianism is regarded as a religion by many.

Confucius (551 to 479 BC) lived through a time of great chaos known as the Warring States Period. He emphasised devotion to parents and family, loyalty to friends, justice, peace, education and humanitarianism. A great reformer, Confucius preached the virtues of good government. His philosophy led to China's renowned bureaucracy and the system of civil service and university entrance examinations, where a person gained position through ability and merit rather than through noble birth and connections.

Confucius preached against such evils as corruption, war, torture and excessive taxation. He was the first teacher to open his school to all students on the basis of their eagerness to learn. The philosophy of Confucius is most easily found in the *Lunyu* or *The Analects*. Many quotes have been taken from this work, the most famous perhaps being the Golden Rule. The Western version of this rule is 'Do unto others as you would have them do unto you'. The Confucian version is written in the negative, 'Do not do unto others what you would not have them do unto you'.

The glorification of Confucius began only after his death, but eventually his ideas permeated every level of Chinese society – government offices presupposed a knowledge of the Confucian classics and spoken proverbs trickled down to the illiterate masses.

During the Han dynasty (206 BC to 220 AD), Confucianism effectively became the state religion. In 130 BC it was made the basic discipline for training government officials, and remained so almost until the end of the Qing dynasty, in 1911.

In 59 AD, sacrifices were ordered to Confucius in all urban schools. In the 7th and 8th centuries, during the Tang dynasty, temples and shrines were built to him and his original disciples. During the Song dynasty *The Analects* became the basis of all education.

Although Confucius died almost 2500 years ago, his influence remains strong in China. The Chinese remain solidly loyal to friends, family and teachers. The bureaucracy and examination system still thrives and a son is generally favoured over a daughter. It can be said that much of Confucian thought has become Chinese culture as we know it.

Chinese Religion Now

On a daily level, the Chinese are much less concerned with the high-minded philosophies and asceticism of Buddha, Confucius or Laozi than they are with the pursuit of worldly success, the appeasement of the dead and the spirits, and the seeking of hidden knowledge about the future.

The most important word in the Chinese popular religious vocabulary is *joss*, meaning luck. The Chinese are too astute to leave something as important as luck to chance. Gods have to be appeased, bad spirits blown away and sleeping dragons soothed to keep joss on your side. No house, wall or shrine is built until an auspicious date for the start of construction is chosen and the most propitious location is selected. Incense has to be burnt, gifts presented and prayers said to appease the spirits who might inhabit the construction site.

Integral parts of Chinese religion are death, the after-life and ancestor worship. Chinese funerals are usually lavish drawn-out events since the body can only be buried on an auspicious day. When the day finally comes, it's signalled first by the clash of cymbals and the moan of oboes. Next comes the clover-shaped coffin and grief-stricken mourners, some paid to weep and many wearing ghost-like outfits with white hoods. A fine spread of roast pigs and other foods, not to be eaten but offered to the gods for the one gone beyond, accompanies the funeral.

A grave site is chosen on the side of a hill with a good view for the loved one who must lie there. At the grave the mourners burn paper models of material treasures like cars and boats, as well as bundles of paper money, to ensure that the dead person is getting the good things of the first life in the great beyond. Just as during the Shang dynasty, when the dead were said to look after the welfare of the living, the living continue to take care of the dead.

Other Religions

Hong Kong has a cosmopolitan population, and many religious denominations are represented. There are about 500,000 Christians (about 55% Catholic, 45% Protestant), Sikhs from India, around 50,000 Muslims and over 1000 Jews.

If you want to pursue the matter of Hong Kong's non-Buddhist and non-Taoist religions, you can contact one of the following places of worship:

Anglican
   St John's Cathedral, 4-8 Garden Rd, Central (☎ 2523-4157)
Bahai
   flat C-6, 11th floor, Hankow Centre, Middle Rd, Tsim Sha Tsui (☎ 2367-6407)
Christian Scientist
   31 MacDonnell Rd, Central (☎ 2524-2701)
Hindu
   Happy Valley (☎ 2572-5284)
Jewish
   Ohel Leah Synagogue, 70 Robinson Rd, Mid-Levels (☎ 2801-5440)
Methodist
   271 English Methodist Church, Queen's Rd East, Wan Chai (☎ 2575-7817)
Mormon
   Church of the Latter Day Saints, 7 Castle Rd, Mid-Levels, Central (☎ 2559-3325)
Muslim
   Islamic Union, 40 Oi Kwan Rd, Wan Chai (☎ 2575-2218)

Quaker
Society of Friends, 3rd floor, conference room, Mariners Club, Middle Rd, Tsim Sha Tsui (☎ 2697-7283)

Roman Catholic
St Joseph's, 37 Garden Rd, Central (☎ 2552-3992)

Sikh
371 Queen's Rd East, Wan Chai (☎ 2574-9837)

LANGUAGE

While the Chinese have about eight main dialects, about 70% of the population of China speaks the Beijing dialect (commonly known as Mandarin) which is the official language of the People's Republic. For details see the Facts about Guangzhou chapter. Hong Kong's two official languages are English and Cantonese. Cantonese is a southern Chinese dialect, spoken in Guangzhou and the surrounding Guangdong Province, Hong Kong and Macau.

While Cantonese is used in Hong Kong in everyday life, English is the primary language of commerce, banking and international trade, and is also used in the law courts. However, many have noticed a sharp decline in the level of English-speaking proficiency. Those Hong Kong Chinese who speak excellent English are usually also the wealthiest, and they are the people who can emigrate most easily. Those left behind are the working classes, who speak primarily Cantonese.

On the other hand, the ability to speak Mandarin is on the increase. There has been a large percentage of Mandarin speakers in Hong Kong since the 1950s because so many refugees fled from China. Until recently, the younger generation has generally not bothered studying Mandarin, preferring English as a second language. The new political realities are now changing attitudes. Despite China's promises that virtually nothing will change after 1997, most Hong Kongers believe that Mandarin will soon be the official language. Furthermore, Mandarin is far easier to learn for a Cantonese native speaker than English.

Short-term visitors can get along fine in Hong Kong without a word of Cantonese, especially in the tourist zones. All street signs and public transport information is bilingual, so there is no problem getting around.

Most expatriates in Hong Kong never learn the local language. This is mainly because they spend their time in the company of other expats. Of course, the few foreigners willing to expend the considerable effort required to learn Cantonese are rewarded with a level of understanding and camaraderie not achievable otherwise.

The Spoken Language

Cantonese differs from Mandarin as much as

The Word on the Street

While Hong Kong's expatriate community tries to speak the Queen's English, some Chinese words have been incorporated into the local English vernacular. *Taipan* means a big boss, usually in a large company, which is referred to as a *hong*. A *godown* is a warehouse. An *amah* is a servant, usually a woman who babysits and takes care of the house.

A *cheongsam* (*qipao* in Mandarin) is a tight-fitting Chinese dress with a slit up the side. You may well see receptionists at upmarket restaurants wearing one, and it's also the gown favoured by honeymoon brides. The dress originated in Shanghai and was banned in China during the Cultural Revolution.

A foreigner is often referred to as a *gwailo* – a Cantonese word which literally means 'ghost person', but which is more accurately translated as 'foreign devil'. It used to have a negative connotation, but these days many foreigners call themselves gwailos without giving it a second thought. More polite terms would be *sai yan* (Westerner) or *ngoi gwok yan* (foreigner), but gwailo is what you'll hear most often.

The word *shroff*, frequently used in Hong Kong, is not derived from Chinese – it's an Anglo-Indian word meaning cashier.

And finally there is the word *junk*. It might be rubbish in English, but to the Chinese it's a mid-sized fishing boat. The traditional models had sails, but these days diesel engines do the job. ∎

French differs from Spanish. Speakers of both dialects can read Chinese characters, but a Cantonese speaker will pronounce many of the characters differently from a Mandarin speaker. For example, when Mr Ng from Hong Kong goes to Beijing the Mandarin-speakers will call him Mr Wu. If Mr Wong goes from Hong Kong to Fujian Province the character for his name will be read as Mr Wee, and in Beijing he is Mr Huang.

Tones

A linguist once described the Chinese language as being notable for its 'phonetic poverty'. This should not be taken to mean that Chinese lacks a rich or expressive vocabulary – indeed, it's just the contrary. What the linguist meant is that the number of possible sounds which can be uttered in Chinese is very limited. In Mandarin Chinese there are just 410 possible sounds that can make up a syllable, and in Cantonese only slightly more. Compared to most other languages, this is phonetic poverty indeed. This results in many homonyms (sound-alike words). Thus, the Cantonese word for 'four' sounds just like the words for 'death', 'silk', 'lion', 'private', 'master', and 'affair'. While the abundant homonyms are great for making puns and word plays, the sound-alike words are terribly confusing to the foreign student of Cantonese.

The Chinese language compensates for the lack of phonetic variety with tones. Mandarin has four tones but Cantonese has at least six (linguists argue about the seventh). Adding tone to a syllable has the effect of multiplying the number of phonetic possibilities several times over. This is sufficient to make Chinese just as linguistically rich as any modern language.

While intonation is not always crucial, in most cases the difference in tone will be a deciding factor in the meaning of a word. If you get the tones mixed, you can say something entirely different from what was intended. The seven tones of Cantonese are illustrated by the following example, using the vowel *a* and the syllable *wan*:

Tone	Name	Vowel	Syllable	Meaning
1	high-falling	à	wàn	to review
2	high-rising	á	wán	look for
3	middle-level	a	wan	to hold
4	high-level	ã	wãn	to review
5	low-falling	àh	wàhn	cloud
6	low-rising	á	wán	to license
7	low-level	ah	wahn	to transport

In the preceding example it's worth noting that Nos 1 and 4 have the same meaning. This is the source of dispute between linguists. These two tones do not seem to differentiate anything, and in Hong Kong most people cannot distinguish the two. However, in parts of Guangdong Province there does seem to be a difference. Unless your Cantonese becomes extremely fluent, you shouldn't concern yourself with this.

You may run into a few old language textbooks which claim that Cantonese actually has 10 tones, the additional three being called 'clipped tones'. Linguists have generally rubbished this argument, and the 'clipped tones' are now referred to as 'clipped sounds'. What happens is that the final consonants *m, n* and *ng* are 'clipped' under certain circumstances. That is, they change pronunciation to become *p, t* and *k*, respectively. Thus, the Cantonese word *sam* can be transformed into *sap* in certain contexts. To use an example from English, the word 'burnt' is often pronounced 'burned'.

The Written Language

Officially, written Chinese has about 50,000 pictographs or characters which symbolise objects or actions. However, most of these are archaic and only about 5000 remain in common use. There are at least 2000 essential characters which you would need to know to read a newspaper.

It is often said that Chinese is a monosyllabic language. That is, each word is only one syllable long. However, the point is hotly debated by linguists and I don't accept it myself. It is true that each character is only one syllable long and each character has meaning, but the dispute is over what constitutes a word. For example, the spoken

Cantonese word for 'coral' is *shaan-woo*, which is clearly two syllables. In written form, both syllables are represented by individual characters. While a literate Chinese speaker would understand either of these two characters to mean coral, as a practical matter the syllables are always used together in conversation. It might be more accurate to say that Chinese uses a monosyllabic writing system.

All Chinese use mostly the same characters, though the Cantonese have invented over 400 which are not understood by Mandarin speakers. And even though Cantonese and Mandarin speakers can read the same newspaper, they pronounce all the characters differently. All Chinese can read the same newspaper, but with some difficulty. One problem is that a Cantonese word might be two syllables which would require two characters to write, whereas the equivalent in Mandarin might require three characters. This really becomes a problem when foreign words are borrowed – the Cantonese borrowed the English word for 'taxi' *(diksi)* which is two characters, whereas Mandarin speakers have kept the three-character traditional form *(chuzuche)*.

There is another complication. In the 1950s, the Chinese government introduced a system of simplified characters in an effort to make the written script easier to learn and increase literacy in the country. Unfortunately, apart from China, only Singapore has adopted these simplified forms. The result is that many of the characters you'll see in Hong Kong are written quite differently from the same ones in China. The simplified characters have actually made it more difficult for students, since they end up having to study both systems.

In Hong Kong, Chinese characters can be read from left to right, right to left, or top to bottom. In China itself the government has been trying to get everyone to read and write from left to right.

Romanisation

The People's Republic uses a Romanisation system known as *pinyin* which, while very accurate once you learn its peculiarities, only works for the Mandarin dialect. You cannot use it to Romanise Cantonese. An explanation of the pinyin system is in the Guangzhou section.

For Cantonese the situation is far messier. Unfortunately, several competing systems of Romanisation exist and no single one has emerged as an official standard. Hong Kongers are not forced to learn Romanisation in school, so asking a Cantonese native speaker to Romanise a Chinese character produces mixed results. The lack of an established standard creates a good deal of confusion for foreigners trying to master the vagaries of Cantonese pronunciation.

A number of Romanisation schemes have come and gone, but at least three have survived and are currently used in Hong Kong: Meyer-Wempe, Sidney Lau and Yale. You are likely to encounter all of them if you make any serious study of the language.

The Meyer-Wempe system is the oldest in current use. Until Sidney Lau came along, it was the one most likely to appear on maps, street signs and in books about Hong Kong. The reason for its popularity is simply its age – the first past the post usually has the best chance of becoming the standard because people resist change. Unfortunately, Meyer-Wempe is also highly confusing. One of its oddities is the use of apostrophes in words to distinguish aspirated sounds (pronounced with a puff of air) from unaspirated sounds. Map and book publishers tend to drop the apostrophes, thus leaving readers unable to distinguish *p* from *b* and *t* from *d*.

The Sidney Lau system fixed this defect and several others. Lau was the principal of the Government Language School for civil servants, and he also broadcast the popular Cantonese by Radio teaching series which started in 1961. The Sidney Lau system has been widely adopted by publishers.

The Yale system is the most phonetically accurate and the one generally preferred by foreign students. It's the system adopted by the Chinese University of Hong Kong for the New Asia Yale in China Language Institute.

There are a number of textbooks and dictionaries based on this system. Unfortunately, it's the least used of the Romanisation schemes.

There is in fact a fourth Romanisation system, called the International Phonetic Alphabet (IPA). However, this is a purely academic system and adds some special symbols which are not part of the Roman alphabet. Linguists are fond of the system, but you are not likely to encounter it outside academic circles.

The following table illustrates the notable differences between the three major Romanisation systems:

Meyer-Wempe	Sydney Lau	Yale
p'	p	p
p	b	b
t'	t	t
t	d	d
k'	k	k
k	g	g
ch'	ch	ch
ts	j	j
k'w	kw	kw
kw	gw	gw
s,sh	s	s
i,y	y	y
oo,w	w	w
oeh	euh	eu
ui	ui	eui
un	un	eun
ut	ut	eut
o	o	ou
oo	oo	u
ue	ue	yu

Some have wondered about the placement of spaces and hyphens in Chinese words. 'Hong Kong' is sometimes written 'Hongkong', though you will probably not see 'Shanghai' as 'Shang Hai' or 'Beijing' as 'Bei Jing'. Chinese often hyphenate their given names, so you may find Sun Yatsen written as Sun Yat-sen. The confusion comes from the fact that every syllable in Chinese is written with a separate character, but when transcribed into Romanised form a name is usually written as a multisyllabic

word. In Mandarin there is a standard rule – names are kept as one word (thus 'Shanghai' and 'Beijing'). However, Cantonese has not adopted any such standard, so in this book we use what is most commonly accepted (thus 'Hong Kong'). The hyphenation of names is falling into disuse and is therefore best avoided.

Phrase List

Even if you never gain fluency, knowing a few simple Cantonese phrases can be useful. Hong Kong is not known as a very friendly place, yet even a small attempt to speak the local vernacular will bring smiles to the faces of Chinese people you meet. Here are a few phrases to get you started:

Pronouns
I
   ngo 我
you
   nei 你
he, she, it
   keui 他
we, us
   ngodei 我們
you (plural)
   neidei 你們
they, them
   keuidei 他們

Greetings & Civilities
hello, how are you?
   nei hou 你好
good morning
   jou san 早晨
goodbye
   joi gin 再見
thank you
   m goido zei 唔該/多謝
you're welcome
   m saihaakhei 不客氣
I'm sorry/excuse me
   deuimjyu 對不起

Useful Expressions
I want...
   ngo yiu... 我要

I want to buy...
ngo yiu maai... 我要買...
yes, have
yau 有
no, don't have
m yau 沒有
How much does it cost?
gei siu chin 多少錢
too expensive
taai gwaige 太貴
Waiter, the bill
fogei, maai daan 伙記埋單
I don't understand
ngo m meng ba 我聽不懂
Wait a moment
deng chan 等一下

Necessities
toilet paper
chi ji 廁紙
tissue paper
ji gan 紙巾
tampons
wai sang ming tiu 衛生棉條
sanitary pads (Kotex)
wai seng gan 衛生巾
sunscreen (UV) lotion
tai you yau 太陽油
laundry service
sai yee chung sum 洗衣中心

Getting Around
I want to go to the...
ngo you hoi 我要去...
airport
fei gei chang 飛機場
MTR station
dei tip zam 地鐵站
KCR station
fo chei zam 火車站
LRT station
heng bin ti lou 輕便鐵路
Star Ferry
ting seng ma tau 天星碼頭
I'm lost
ngo dong sat lou 我蕩失路
Where is the...?
...hai bin dou 在那裡
telephone
din wah 電話

post office
yau go 郵局
toilet
ji sou 廁所
Turn right
yau jwin 右轉
Turn left
jwo jwin 左轉
Go straight
yet zet zau 一直走
Turn around
jwin gou wan 轉個彎
I want to hire a bicycle
ngo yu jo daan chei 我要租單車

Emergencies
I'm sick
ngo beng la 我生病
I'm injured
ngo sau cheung 我受傷
hospital
yi yun 醫院
police
geng cha 警察
Fire!
fo jok 火燭
Help!
gau meng ah 救命啊
Thief!
siu tau 小偷
pickpocket
pa sau 扒手
rapist
keng gan ze 強姦者

Numbers

0	*leng*	零
1	*yet*	一
2	*yi, leung*	二, 兩
3	*sam*	三
4	*sei*	四
5	*m*	五
6	*lok*	六
7	*chat*	七
8	*ba*	八
9	*gau*	九
10	*sap*	十
11	*sap yet*	十一
12	*sap yi*	十二
20	*yi sap*	二十

21	*yi sam yet*	二十一
100	*yet ba*	一百
200	*leung ba*	兩百
1000	*yet chin*	一千
2000	*leung chin*	兩千
10,000	*yet man*	一萬
20,000	*leung man*	兩萬
100,000	*sap man*	十萬
200,000	*yi sap man*	二十萬

Time

What is the time?

  gei dim 幾點

hour

  dim 點

minute

  fan 分

Facts for the Visitor

PLANNING

When to Go

Hong Kong is worth visiting at any time of year, although you may save a little on airfares and hotels by visiting during winter. Take care to avoid major holiday times – particularly the Chinese Lunar New Year (late January or early February), when prices double, businesses shut down and every tourist site is packed to the armpits with locals trying to get away from it all. Easter and the summer school holidays are also busy times.

There are special events at various times of the year which may interest you. See the Public Holidays & Special Events section in this chapter for details.

What Kind of Trip?

You can tackle Hong Kong solo, with friends and family, with a tour, do a mad dash, or stay in one spot and pursue special interests. Hong Kong's variety lends itself to just about any type of journey.

Maps

There are a couple of good maps of Hong Kong worth picking up. Some of the best city maps are the *Kowloon Street Plan* and its companion the *Hong Kong Street Plan*, which you can buy in bookshops.

Even more detailed and highly recommended is a small atlas called the *Hong Kong Guide – Streets & Places*, which has complete maps and an index of all the buildings and streets in Hong Kong. It's available at the Government Publications Centre in the Government Offices Building, 66 Queensway, Admiralty. This is also the place to pick up the excellent *Countryside* series of maps, a boon for hikers. These maps cover all major hiking areas, including Hong Kong Island, the New Territories and the Outlying Islands.

The map most people use is the freebie put out by the Hong Kong Tourist Association (HKTA). Also look for the *AOA Street Map*, a freebie sponsored by the Hong Kong Association of Travel Agents and the Hong Kong Hotels Association. It's covered with advertisements, but is very good for finding your way around the lower Kowloon and Hong Kong urban areas.

Hong Kong is full of free maps, but ChequePoint moneychangers charge for theirs (HK$30) without saying so! Among your given paperwork will be hidden a receipt for the map, but most travellers don't realise they've been charged until too late (sorry, no refunds).

Rudy Samson

What to Bring

As little as possible. Many travellers try to bring everything and the kitchen sink. Keep in mind that you can and will buy things in Hong Kong and elsewhere, so don't burden yourself with a lot of unnecessary junk.

That advice having been given, there are some things you will want to bring from home. But the first thing to consider is what kind of bag you will use to carry all your goods.

Backpacks are the easiest type of bag to carry and a frameless or internal-frame pack is the easiest to manage on buses and trains. Packs that close with a zipper can usually be secured with a padlock. Of course, any pack can be slit open with a razor blade, but a padlock will usually prevent pilfering.

A daypack can be handy. Leave your main luggage at the hotel or in lockers. A beltpack is OK for maps, extra film and other miscellanea, but don't use it for valuables such as your travellers' cheques and passport, as it's an easy target for pickpockets.

If you don't want to use a backpack, a shoulder bag is much easier to carry than a suitcase. Some cleverly designed shoulder bags can double as backpacks by re-arranging a few straps. If you must have a suitcase, get one with wheels. Cases with wheels and a pull-out handle are even better.

'Lightweight' and 'compact' are two words that should be etched in your mind when you're deciding what to bring. Saw the handle off your toothbrush if you have to – anything to keep the weight down! You only need two sets of clothes – one to wear and one to wash. You will, no doubt, be buying clothes along the way – you can find some real bargains in Hong Kong, Macau and China. However, don't believe the labels – 'large' in Asia is often equivalent to 'medium' in the West. Asian clothing manufacturers would be wise to visit a Western tourist hotel to see what 'large' really means.

Nylon running or sports shoes are best – comfortable, washable and lightweight. If you're going to be in cold weather, buy them oversized and wear with heavy wool socks – it's better than carrying a pair of boots. A pair of thongs (flip flops) is useful footwear for indoors and shower rooms.

A Swiss army knife (even if not made in Switzerland) comes in handy, but you don't need one with 27 separate functions. Basically, you need one small sharp blade, a can opener and bottle opener – a built-in magnifying glass or backscratcher isn't necessary.

The secret of successful packing is plastic bags or nylon 'stuff bags' – they not only keep things separate, they keep them clean and dry.

The following is a checklist of things you might consider packing, but don't feel obligated to take everything – you can buy all of them in Hong Kong.

Passport, money, money belt, air ticket, address book, business cards, visa photos, Swiss army knife, electric immersion coil (for heating water), cup, camera & accessories, sunglasses, alarm clock, leak-proof water bottle, torch (flashlight) with batteries, comb, compass, daypack, long pants, short pants, long shirt, T-shirt, nylon jacket, overcoat, sweater, rain cover for backpack, rainsuit or poncho, razor, razor blades, shaving cream, sewing kit, spoon, sun hat, sunscreen (UV lotion), toilet paper, tampons, toothbrush, toothpaste, dental floss, deodorant, shampoo, underwear, socks, thongs (flip flops), nail clippers, tweezers, mosquito repellent, vitamins, headache tablets, laxative, Lomotil, birth control and any special medications you use.

A final thought: airlines do lose bags from time to time – there's a much better chance of it not being yours if it is tagged with your name and address *inside* the bag as well as outside. Other tags can always fall off or be removed.

HIGHLIGHTS
Top Ten

The trip on the Peak Tram to Victoria Peak has been practically mandatory for visitors since it opened in 1888. It's fascinating to take a 30-minute ride on a sampan through one of Hong Kong's fishing harbours (Cheung Chau's is best). Equally interesting is a ride on Hong Kong Island's trams. Exploring the Outlying Islands by ferry is one of Hong Kong's best-kept secrets. Hong Kong's got some amazingly good beaches – and the best way to reach them is by boat or as part of a hiking trip. Similarly, no hiker could resist the MacLehose, Lantau or Hong Kong trails – all which offer some of the world's most breathtaking views. Amusement park enthusiasts will find Ocean Park hard to beat. Party animals can eat, drink and dance the night away at Lan Kwai Fong and Wan Chai. Lunch at a good dim sum restaurant is one of the great pleasures of the Orient, and of course, shopping is what Hong Kong is famous for.

Lastly, there are some who insist that the highlight of their visit to Hong Kong was Macau. See the Macau chapters of this book for details.

Bottom Ten

The lifts at Chungking Mansions. Kai Tak Airport (soon to be closed, thank goodness). Nathan Rd camera shops. The Chinese New Year, unless you get invited to a family feast. China's puppet 'Hong Kong and Macau Affairs Office' which issues one puke-inspiring policy statement after another. Public toilets – if you can find one. The 'copy watch' spruikers. Hong Kong's Chinese-language newspapers (if you can't read Chinese, be grateful). Statue Square on Sunday. The high prices for everything (except Big Macs and clothing).

TOURIST OFFICES
Local Tourist Offices
The enterprising Hong Kong Tourist Association (HKTA) is definitely worth a visit. Staff are efficient and helpful and they have reams of information, most of it free. The HKTA also sells (at reasonable cost) a few publications, plus postcards, T-shirts and other souvenirs.

You can call the HKTA hotline (☎ 2807-6177) from 8 am to 6 pm from Monday to Friday, and from 9 am to 5 pm on weekends and holidays.

The HKTA operates a hotel booking service in the arrival hall of the airport. They don't deal with the real cheapies, but can usually find you a room starting from the two-star level on up to five stars. As an added benefit, booking through the HKTA (or most other travel agencies) nets you a discount of 20% to 30% off the walk-in rate. You'll find HKTA offices at:

Star Ferry Terminal, Tsim Sha Tsui, Kowloon. Open 8 am to 6 pm Monday through Friday, and from 9 am to 5 pm weekends and holidays.
Shop 8, basement, Jardine House, 1 Connaught Place, Central. Open 9 am to 6 pm weekdays, and 9 am to 1 pm on Saturdays. Closed on Sundays and holidays.
Buffer Hall, Kai Tak airport, Kowloon City. Open 8 am to 10.30 pm daily. Information is provided for arriving passengers only.
Head Office (☎ 2807-6543), 11th floor, Citicorp Centre, 18 Whitfield Rd, North Point. This is a business office – not for normal tourist enquires.

If you have access to a fax, you can take advantage of the HKTA's Infofax service. The data available includes HKTA member hotels, restaurants, places to shop and so on. If dialling from within Hong Kong, the fax number is 11 digits (fax 9006-077-1128), but from abroad it's only 10 digits including the country code (fax (852) 177-1128). To use this service, if the fax machine has a handset, pick it up first and then dial; if the machine has no handset, set it to polling mode before dialling. After you connect you'll receive a list of topics and the appropriate fax numbers to call to receive the data. You can call this service from abroad and there is no charge beyond what you pay for an international phone connection. If calling from within Hong Kong, the local phone company tacks on a charge of HK$2 per minute between 8 am and 9 pm, reduced to HK$1 from 9 pm to 8 am.

HKTA Offices Abroad
Australia
    Level 4, 80 Druitt St, Sydney, NSW 2000 (☎ (02) 9283 3083)
Canada
    3rd floor, Hong Kong Trade Centre, 9 Temperance St, Toronto, Ontario M5H 1Y6 (☎ (416) 366-2389)
France
    Escalier C, 8ème étage, 53 Rue François 1er, 75008, Paris (☎ 01 47 20 39 54)
Germany
    Humboldt Strasse 94, D-60318 Frankfurt am Main (☎ (069) 959-1290)
Japan
    4th floor, Toho Twin Tower Building, 1-5-2 Yurakucho, Chiyoda-ku, Tokyo 100 (☎ (03) 3503-0735)
    8th floor, Osaka Saitama Building, 3-5-13 Awaji-machi, Chuo-ku, Osaka 541 (☎ (06) 229-9240)
Korea (South)
    c/o Glocom Korea, Suite 1105, Paiknam Building, 188-3 Ulchiro 1-ga, Chung-gu, Seoul (☎ (02) 778-4403)
New Zealand
    PO Box 2120, Auckland (☎ (09) 575-2707)
Singapore
    9 Temasek Blvd, 34-03 Suntec Tower Two (☎ 532-3668)
South Africa
    c/o Development Promotions, PO Box 9874, Johannesburg 2000 (☎ (011) 339-4865)
Taiwan
    9th floor, 18 Chang'an E Rd, Section 1, Taipei (☎ (02) 581-2967)
    Hong Kong Information Service (☎ (02) 581-6061)
Spain
    c/o Sergat España SL, Pau Casals 4, 08021 Barcelona (☎ (03) 414-1794)
UK
    5th floor, 125 Pall Mall, London, SW1Y 5EA (☎ (0171) 930-4775)
USA
    Suite 200, 610 Enterprise Drive, Oak Brook, IL 60521 (☎ (630) 575-2828)

5th floor, 590 Fifth Ave, New York, NY 10036-
4706 (☎ (212) 869-5008)
Suite 1220, 10940 Wilshire Blvd, Los Angeles,
CA 90024-3915 (☎ (310) 208-4582)

VISAS & DOCUMENTS
Passport
A passport is essential for visiting Hong
Kong, and if yours is within a few months of
expiration get a new one now. Losing your
passport is very bad news – getting a new one
means a trip to your embassy or consulate
and usually a long wait while they send faxes
or telexes (at your expense) to confirm that
you exist. If you'll be staying a long time in
Hong Kong, it's wise to register your passport with your consulate or embassy – this
makes the replacement process much
simpler.

Visas
For most visitors to Hong Kong a passport is
all that's required.

UK citizens (or Commonwealth citizens
born in Britain or Hong Kong) can normally
stay for up to 12 months without a visa, and
it is possible to stay longer. Australians,
Canadians and New Zealanders get a three-
month, visa-free stay. Citizens of most
Western European countries are also permitted to stay for three months without a visa,
depending on which country they're from.
Americans can stay for one month without a
visa.

Officially, visitors have to show they have
adequate funds for their stay and that they
have an onward ticket, or a return ticket to
their own country. In practice this rule is
seldom enforced, except when a visa is
required. Visitors from the following countries *must* have a visa:

Afghanistan, Albania, Bulgaria, Cambodia, China,
CIS (former USSR), Cuba, Czech & Slovak Repub-
lics, Hungary, Iran, Iraq, Laos, Lebanon, Libya, Mon-
golia, Myanmar (Burma), North Korea, Oman,
Romania, Somalia, Sudan, Syria, Taiwan, Tonga,
Vietnam, Yemen, Yugoslavia and all stateless persons.

Visitors are not permitted to take up employment, establish any business or enrol as

students. If you want to enter for employment, education or residence you should
have a work visa and be able to show means
of support in Hong Kong. Beware: some
visitors have been refused entry simply for
carrying a CV!

Visa Extensions In Hong Kong, enquire at
the Immigration Department (☎ 2824-6111),
2nd floor, Immigration Tower, 7 Gloucester
Rd, Wan Chai.

In general, visa extensions are not readily
granted unless there are special circumstances
– cancelled flights, illness, registration in a
legitimate course of study, legal employment,
marriage to a local, etc.

Photocopies
It's wise to keep photocopies of vital documents in a separate place. They should
include a copy of your passport's data pages,
birth certificate, credit cards, airline tickets
and a list of your travellers' cheque serial
numbers. To this you might as well add an
emergency stash of about US$50 or more.
Also leave a copy of all these things with
someone at home.

If you're travelling with your spouse, a
photocopy of your marriage licence just
might come in handy should you become
involved with the law, hospitals or other
bureaucratic authorities.

If you're planning on working or studying
in Hong Kong, it could be helpful to have
copies of transcripts, diplomas, letters of reference and other professional qualifications.
But again, be warned: customs officials can
be tough on job-seekers arriving without
work visas.

Travel Insurance
Whatever insurance you have at home is
probably not valid in Hong Kong. There are
various types of travel insurance policies.
Some will cover losses due to theft, accident,
illness and death (at least your relatives
benefit). The best policies might reimburse
you for an air ticket if you're forced to fly
home in an emergency.

Travel insurance is something you should

arrange before you venture abroad. You can, of course, purchase an insurance policy after arrival in Hong Kong. Rates vary, so shop around. Some of the banks are in the business of selling medical and travellers' insurance – HongkongBank is one such place. If interested, drop by the banks and pick up their brochures in English describing what sort of policies are available.

See the Health chapter in this book for information about health insurance policies.

Driving Licence & Permits

Driving Licence Any foreigner over the age of 18 with a valid international driving permit can drive in Hong Kong for up to 12 months. If you're staying longer, you'll need a Hong Kong licence. Apply to the Transport Department Licensing Division (☎ 2804-2600, 24-hour hotline), 41st floor, Immigration Tower, 7 Gloucester Rd, Wan Chai. There is another centre for vehicle registrations on the 3rd floor, United Centre, 95 Queensway, Wan Chai. If you have a licence from your home country bring it along, as it may save you having to get a learner's permit, taking a driving course or doing the driving test. The learner's-permit-driving course routine is a drag – it takes lots of time and costs lots of money – so avoid it if you can.

International Driving Permit If you plan to be driving abroad, get an international driving permit from your local car association or motor vehicle department *before* you leave home. Although a scant few countries will issue an international driving permit if you just show a licence from your home country, Hong Kong is definitely *not* one of those places.

In many countries international driving permits are valid for one year only so there's no sense getting one far in advance of departure. However, some countries issue permits valid for three years.

Hostel Card

An International Youth Hostel Federation (IYHF) card can be of some limited use in Hong Kong and nearby Macau. However,

the vast majority of travellers will not need one because private hostels or guesthouses are where most backpackers stay. For information on Hong Kong's hostels, see the Accommodation section in this chapter.

Student & Youth Cards

If you're a student or you're under 27, you can get an STA Youth Card. If you're aged 13 to 26, you qualify for an International Student Identity Card (ISIC), which entitles you to a number of discounts on airfares, trains, museums, etc. To get this card, enquire at your campus; they can also be issued by the Hong Kong Student Travel Bureau.

International Health Certificate

Useful (though not essential) is an International Health Certificate to record any vaccinations you've had. This can also be issued in Hong Kong.

Other Documents

Visitors and residents are advised to carry identification at all times in Hong Kong. It needn't be a passport – anything with a photo on it will do. This is because the immigration authorities do frequent spot checks to catch illegal workers and those who overstay their visas. If you have no ID, you could find yourself being 'rounded up'.

The Chinese are very impressed by business cards, so bring some along. Alternatively, make use of the 'Express Card' machines, which can whip out customised cards in less than 10 minutes. The machines are found mostly in MTR and KCR train stations – Central MTR station has several. For HK$25 you get 40 cards.

CONSULATES
Foreign Consulates in Hong Kong

Below are some of the diplomatic missions in Hong Kong. There's a complete list in the *Yellow Pages* under Consulates. Some of the smaller countries are represented by honorary consuls who are normally businesspeople employed in commercial firms – so it's advisable to phone beforehand to find out if they're available. Beijing – keen to keep consulate powers limited to the 'Special Administration Region' of Hong Kong – is slowly phasing out diplomats who hold dual accreditation in mainland China.

Australia
23rd & 24th floor, Harbour Centre, 25 Harbour Rd, Wan Chai (☎ 2827-8881)

Britain
c/o Overseas Visa Section, Hong Kong Immigration Department, 24th & 25th floors, Immigration Tower, 7 Gloucester Rd, Wan Chai (☎ 2802-3300)

Canada
11th-14th floor, Tower One, Exchange Square, 8 Connaught Place, Central (☎ 2810-4321)

China
Visa Office of the Ministry of Foreign Affairs, 5th floor, lower block, 26 Harbour Rd, Wan Chai (☎ 2827-1881)

France
26th floor, Admiralty Centre, Tower Two, 18 Harcourt Rd, Admiralty (☎ 2529-4316)

Germany
21st floor, United Centre, 95 Queensway, Admiralty (☎ 2529-8855)

Indonesia
6-8 Keswick St & 127 Leighton Rd, Causeway Bay (☎ 2890-4421)

Japan
Exchange Square, 8 Connaught Place, Central (☎ 2526-0796)

Korea (South)
5th floor, Far East Finance Centre, 16 Harcourt Rd, Central (☎ 2529-4141)

Macau
British Trade Commission, Bank of America Tower, Lambeth Walk, Admiralty (☎ 2523-0176)

Malaysia
24th floor, Malaysia Building, 50 Gloucester Rd, Wan Chai (☎ 2527-0921)

Myanmar (Burma)
Room 2421-2425, Sung Hung Kai Centre, 30 Harbour Rd, Wan Chai (☎ 2827-7929)

New Zealand
Room 3414, Jardine House, Connaught Rd, Central (☎ 2526-7898)

Philippines
Room 603, United Centre, 95 Queensway, Admiralty (☎ 2866-8738)

Singapore
Room 901, 9th floor, Tower One, Admiralty Centre, 18 Harcourt Rd, Admiralty (☎ 2527-2212)

South Africa
27th floor, Sunning Plaza, 10 Hysan Ave, Causeway Bay (☎ 2577-3279)

Taiwan
Chung Hwa Travel Service, 4th floor, Lippo Tower, 89 Queensway, Admiralty (☎ 2525-8315)

Thailand
8th floor, Fairmont House, 8 Cotton Tree Drive, Central (☎ 2521-6481)

USA
26 Garden Rd, Central (☎ 2523-9011)

Vietnam
Visa office, 15th floor, Great Smart Tower, 230 Wan Chai Rd, Wan Chai (☎ 2591-4517)

CUSTOMS

Even though Hong Kong is a duty-free port, there are still items on which duty is charged. In particular, there are high import taxes on cigarettes and alcohol. The duty-free allowance for visitors is 200 cigarettes (or 50 cigars or 250g tobacco) and one litre of alcohol. Apart from these limits there are no other import tax worries, so you can bring in reasonable quantities of almost anything without paying taxes or obtaining permits. An exception is ivory, which requires a bureaucratic tangle of permits.

Of course, you can't bring anything deemed illegal into Hong Kong. This includes fireworks. Hong Kongers returning from Macau and China are often vigorously searched for this reason. Not surprisingly, firearms are strictly controlled and special permits are needed to import them. Non-lethal weapons like chemical mace and stun guns are also prohibited – a few female travellers have run afoul of this rule.

Customs officers are on the alert for drug smugglers. If you're arriving from Thailand or Vietnam, expect a rigorous examination of luggage.

Have some sympathy for the enormous job that customs officials must perform. Aside from air passengers, more than 700 ships a day pass through Hong Kong's harbour. Obviously, not all ships can be inspected. One customs official told me that the biggest problems are with ships from South-East Asia (carrying heroin) and from the USA (smuggling guns and ammunition).

This is in addition to small speedboats from China, which bring in guns, drugs and illegal immigrants.

BAGGAGE STORAGE

If you're going to be visiting Macau, Guangzhou or points beyond but will be returning to Hong Kong, consider the virtues of leaving your heavy junk behind. Most hotels and even some budget hostels have left-luggage rooms. There is usually a charge for this service, which can be anything from very cheap to totally outrageous – be sure to enquire first to avoid any unpleasant surprises when you come back to pick up the bag.

There is a left-luggage room at Kai Tak airport. Each bag you want to store will cost you HK$100 per day, though it's only HK$40 if you collect it the same day. There are no discounts for long-term storage, nor are there any discounts for storing a large number of bags.

The last option is lockers, but you'll have to search hard. There are a few around the major railway stations of the KCR system and at the ferry piers for Macau and China. Hong Kong's lockers are high-tech – there are no keys. Instead, when you close the locker door, the machine spits out a numbered ticket. You have to punch in this number if you ever want to see your bag again, so keep the ticket where you won't lose it or write the number down elsewhere. Some lockers have a three-day maximum storage time – read the instructions carefully.

MONEY
Costs

A recent survey found that Hong Kong is the second most expensive city in the world – only Tokyo is dearer. And if the inflationary trend of the past few years continues, Hong Kong may have the dubious distinction of being even pricier than Tokyo by the turn of the century.

If money is no object, then Hong Kong can accommodate you – there are plenty of hotels costing over US$300 a day. And there are plenty of restaurants that are willing to present you with a bill that could bankrupt a third-world country.

For those of more humble means, it's possible to survive in Hong Kong for under HK$200, but it will require a good deal of self-discipline. Accommodation is the biggest expense, but you can get it down to HK$50 a night by staying in grotty dormitories. Food is actually quite reasonable if you choose your restaurants carefully – you can keep the eating bill down to HK$60 a day if you patronise bottom-end fast food barns or buy your own from supermarkets. Transport is cheap only because distances are short – on a per-km basis, Hong Kong's prices are world class.

The main way to cut costs is to control yourself – shopping in Hong Kong can be addictive. Many people find all those cameras and electronic goodies on sale to be irresistible and suddenly decide they need to buy all sorts of things they don't need at all! Nightlife is also a temptation – discos, pubs and pricey restaurants have been the downfall of many budget travellers.

Carrying Money

Hong Kong has its share of pickpockets. Rather than lose your precious cash and travellers' cheques (not to mention passport), large amounts of money and other valuables should be kept far from sticky fingers. Various devices which can usually thwart pickpockets include pockets sewn on the inside of your trousers, Velcro tabs to seal pocket openings, or a money belt or pouch under your shirt.

Cash

While US dollars are preferred, all major and many minor foreign currencies can be readily exchanged. However, it may be difficult to get rid of foreign coins – many banks and money changers will not accept them.

Travellers' Cheques

US-dollar travellers' cheques are easiest to exchange, but you shouldn't have any significant problem changing other commonly traded currencies such as pounds sterling, Japanese yen or Australian dollars.

If your travellers' cheques are lost or stolen, some places to call for replacements include: American Express (☎ 2885-9331); Citicorp (☎ 2821-7215); Thomas Cook (☎ 2854-0575, 2854-1388); and Visa (☎ 2523-8152).

ATMs

Automatic Teller Machine cards from a number of foreign banks will work in Hong Kong auto-teller machines. Look for machines advertising international bank settlement systems such as GlobalAccess, Cirrus, Interlink, Plus, Star, Accel, The Exchange and Explore. Visa, MasterCard and American Express will work in many machines as well. HongkongBank, Standard Chartered Bank and Citibank seem to have very compatible machines. The rear side of your ATM card should tell you which systems will work with your card.

Midland Bank customers can use their cash cards in the ATMs of the HongkongBank (which owns Midland). Hong Kong's ATMs pay in Hong Kong dollars only.

Credit Cards

Credit cards accepted by most places are American Express, Visa, Carte Blanche, Diners Club, JCB and MasterCard. Major charge and credit cards are accepted by many restaurants and shops in Hong Kong.

Some shops may try to add a surcharge to the cost of the item if you charge your purchase against your card. In theory this is prohibited by the credit-card companies, but in this case I have some sympathy for the shops. Credit-card companies normally charge the shops a commission on each purchase – up to 5% – but they insist that this charge not be passed on to the customer for the obvious reason that it would hurt the credit-card business. To get around this many shops say that there is no commission charged if you use a credit card, but there is a 5% discount if you pay cash.

The following companies are the major issuers of plastic money:

American Express
24-hour hotline (☎ 2885-9366), Kowloon office, 1st floor, 25 Kimberley Rd, Tsim Sha Tsui (☎ 2732-7327)
Citibank
24-hour hotline (☎ 2823-2323), Hopewell Centre, Queen's Rd East, Wan Chai
Diners Club
24-hour hotline (☎ 2529-9223), 11th floor, Dorset House, Taikoo Place, 979 King's Rd, Quarry Bay
JCB
28 Hankow Rd, Tsim Sha Tsui; room 507, Hong Kong Pacific Centre, Connaught Rd, Central (☎ 2366-7203)
MasterCard
Dah Sing Financial Centre, Gloucester & Fleming Rds, Wan Chai (☎ 2598-8038, 2598-4108)
Visa
Lippo Tower, Tamar St, Admiralty (☎ 2523-8152)

International Transfers

International telegraphic transfers are fast and efficient. All major banks in Hong Kong can do it, the two most popular being HongkongBank and Hang Seng Bank.

A specialist in telegraphic transfers is Western Union (☎ 2528-5631), shop 2038, 2nd floor, United Centre, 95 Queensway, Admiralty.

If having money wired to you, it's useful if the sender includes your passport number along with your name. You can also have the money wired directly into a bank account. Anyone can open a bank account in Hong Kong – there is no need to have a residence visa. Accounts can be opened in Hong Kong dollars or almost any other major currency (even in gold!).

Currency

When making a large purchase such as a camera, many shops will accept payment in US dollars (and sometimes other currencies) but may give you slightly less than the official rate. However, for most of your everyday needs, you'll have to pay in Hong Kong dollars.

The Hong Kong dollar is divided into 100 cents. There are different banknote designs in circulation, although the notes are inter-changeable.

Bills are issued in denominations of $10 (green), $20 (grey), $50 (blue), $100 (red), $500 (brown) and $1000 (yellow). Coins are issued in denominations of $10, $5, $2, $1, 50 cent, 20 cent and 10 cent. China has recently insisted that the 'colonial' image of Queen Elizabeth II be removed from all newly minted Hong Kong coins. This was done and the new coins look pretty drab now – just whose face will appear on them in years to come is anybody's guess.

Currency Exchange

Since 1983, the Hong Kong dollar has been rigidly tied to the US dollar at a rate of US$1 = HK$7.8. However, the Hong Kong dollar is permitted to float within a very narrow range of this level and has now risen to its maximum permitted value. Pessimists are expecting a run on the Hong Kong dollar as China takes over.

The following exchange rates are current at the time of publication:

Australia	A$1	=	HK$5.98
Britain	UK£1	=	HK$11.96
Canada	C$1	=	HK$5.63
China	Y$1	=	HK$0.93
France	Ffr1	=	HK$1.55
Germany	DM1	=	HK$5.25
Indonesia	100 rp	=	HK$0.33
Japan	¥100	=	HK$7.25
Korea (South)	W100	=	HK$0.95
Malaysia	RM1	=	HK$3.10
Netherlands	G1	=	HK$4.51
New Zealand	NZ$1	=	HK$5.28
Philippines	P1	=	HK$0.30
Singapore	S$1	=	HK$5.46
South Africa	R1	=	HK$1.72
Switzerland	Sfr1	=	HK$6.47
Taiwan	NT$1	=	HK$0.28
Thailand	1B	=	HK$0.31
USA	US$1	=	HK$7.74
Vietnam	d1	=	HK$0.71

Changing Money

Hong Kong has no exchange controls – locals and foreigners can send large quantities of money in or out as they please, and even play the local stock market while they're at it. Hong Kong is, in fact, the financial centre of Asia simply because it is unregulated. How much China interferes with this financial freedom after 1997 is the big question that keeps bankers awake at night.

Banks theoretically give the best exchange rates, but they tack on a HK$50 service charge for each transaction. You'd have to change over US$200 at a time to make this worthwhile. Streetside money changers in tourist areas (ChequePoint is the best known) give relatively poor rates, though you can often bargain over a large transaction (you'd still do better at a bank). The money changers inside Chungking Mansions, on Nathan Rd, give the best rates, but not the money changers nearest the main entrance. Unison Foreign Exchange at the back of nearby Mirador Mansions is also good.

Exchange rates are always posted, and the best way to know if you're getting a good deal is to look at the spread (the difference between the buy and sell rates): a large spread means you're getting a bad deal. Some comparative exchange rates at the time of writing are (for US$1): ChequePoint, HK$7.05; ChequePoint after bargaining, HK$7.40; airport money changers, HK$7.30; hotel desks, HK$7.40; Hang Seng Bank if you change US$200, HK$7.45; Hang Seng Bank if you change US$1000, HK$7.65; Chungking Mansions money changers, HK$7.70.

Bank hours are from 9 am to 4 pm Monday to Friday, and from 9 am to noon or 1 pm on Saturday. ChequePoint operates 24 hours a day. Chungking Mansions money changers are open daily from approximately 9 am to 9 pm.

Black Market

No foreign currency black market exists in Hong Kong. If anyone on the street does approach you to change money, then you're being set up to be ripped off.

Tipping & Bargaining

The good news is that historically the

Chinese never had the habit of tipping. The bad news is that Westerners have introduced this vulgar custom to Hong Kong. Feel no obligation to tip taxi drivers (they make plenty as it is), but it's almost mandatory to tip hotel porters (bellhops) at least HK$10. If you make use of the porters at the airport, HK$2 per suitcase is normally expected.

Fancy hotels and restaurants stick you with a mandatory 10% service charge which is supposedly your tip. Nevertheless, many staff expect more, especially from free-spending tourists. It is said that Japanese tourists are the best tippers, Westerners the worst. Let your conscience be your guide. If you think the service was great, you might want to leave them something. Otherwise don't bother – there's no need to reward rotten service.

Bargaining is expected in Hong Kong's tourist districts, but less so elsewhere. Sadly, some people (both Chinese and foreigners) turn it into a ruthless contest of 'in your face' East-West rivalry. Some tourists operate on the theory that you can always get the goods for half the price originally quoted. My philosophy is that if you can bargain something down to half price, then you shouldn't buy in that shop anyway because they were trying to rip you off in the first place. If they're that crooked (and many are, particularly in the Tsim Sha Tsui tourist ghetto), they will probably find other ways to cheat you, like selling electronics with missing components, or a secondhand camera instead of a new one. In an honest shop, you shouldn't be able to bargain more than a 10% discount, if they'll bargain at all.

Price tags should be displayed on all goods. If they aren't, you've undoubtedly entered one of those business establishments with 'flexible' (read rip-off) prices. For more details, see the Things to Buy section in this chapter, and the Things to Buy sections for Kowloon and Hong Kong Island.

POST & COMMUNICATIONS

For some weird reason, the cheapest places to buy postcards of Hong Kong are the very places you'd think would be tourist rip-offs– Kai Tak airport (at the DFS Kai Tak market, six for HK$6) and the Peak Galleria (HK$1 each, when the same cards go for HK$2 to HK$4 almost everywhere else).

Postal Rates

Local Mail Rates for Hong Kong mail in HK$ are as follows:

Weight Not Over	Letters & Postcards	Printed Matter
30g	1.20	1.10
50g	1.90	1.60
100g	2.60	2.20
250g	3.80	3.20
500g	7.50	6.50
1 kg	15.40	10.50
2 kg	26.00	

International Airmail The Hong Kong postal service divides the world into two distinct zones. Zone 1 is China, Japan, Taiwan, South Korea, South-East Asia, Indonesia and India. International airmail rates in HK$ are as follows:

	Zone 1	Zone 2
Letters & Postcards		
first 10g	2.10	2.60
each additional 10g	1.10	1.20
Aerogrammes	2.10	2.10
Printed Matter		
first 10g	1.60	2.10
each additional 10g	0.70	0.90

International Surface Mail The postal service also divides the world in two parts, but not the same zones as for airmail. Area 1 is China, Macau and Taiwan. Area 2 is all other countries. The rates for Area 2 in HK$ are as follows:

Weight Not Over	Letters & Postcards	Printed Matter	Small Packet
20g	2.30	2.10	4.60
50g	4.00	3.60	4.60
100g	5.30	4.60	4.60
250g	10.50	9.40	9.40
500g	20.00	17.50	17.50
1 kg	35.00	31.00	31.00
2 kg	56.00	45.00	45.00

Speedpost What Hong Kong calls 'Speedpost' is often called EMS (express mail service) elsewhere. Letters and small parcels sent by Speedpost should reach almost any destination in the world in four days or less. Furthermore, anything sent by Speedpost is automatically registered.

The rates for Speedpost vary enormously according to destination but bear little relation to actual distance. For example, a 250g Speedpost letter to Australia costs HK$90 but to China it's HK$95 and to Singapore HK$70! The main factors seem to be the availability of air transport and efficiency of mail handling at the destination country. Every post office has a schedule of fees and a Speedpost timetable available on request.

Sending Mail

On Hong Kong Island, the General Post Office is on your right as you alight the Star Ferry. On the Kowloon side, one of the most convenient post offices is at 10 Middle Rd, east of the Ambassador Hotel and Nathan Rd, Tsim Sha Tsui (this one has a stamp vending machine outside – a big convenience after hours). Another good post office (which is less crowded) is in the basement of the Albion Plaza, 2-6 Granville Rd, just off Nathan Rd, Tsim Sha Tsui. All major post offices are open Monday to Friday from 8 am to 6 pm, Saturday from 8 am to 2 pm and are closed on Sunday and public holidays.

Allow five days for delivery of letters, postcards and aerogrammes to the UK and the USA. Speedpost reduces delivery time by about half. Sea mail is slow, so allow from six to 10 weeks for delivery to the UK and the USA.

Receiving Mail

There are poste restante services at the GPO and other large post offices. Mail will be held for two months. Simply address an envelope c/o Poste Restante, GPO Hong Kong, and it will go to the Hong Kong Island side. If you want letters to go to the Kowloon side, they should be addressed to Poste Restante, 10 Middle Rd, Tsim Sha Tsui, Kowloon.

If you decide to take up residence or do business, realise that there is a very long waiting list for post office boxes.

Courier Service

Hong Kong's post office offers Speedpost (EMS). Express document and small parcel service (32 kg limit) is also offered by privately-owned courier companies. Some of these companies will also ship larger items, though not as express deliveries. All of these companies have numerous pick-up points, so call for the one nearest you. Well-known competitors in this market include:

DHL
> (☎ 2765-8111, 24 hours), express service centres found in all major MTR stations; sales office (☎ 2572-7631) at East Point Centre, Yee Wo and Great George Sts, Causeway Bay

Federal Express
> (☎ 2730-3333); also in Admiralty MTR station (☎ 2865-3302); and China Hong Kong City (☎ 2736-7780), Canton Rd, Kowloon

TNT Express
> (☎ 2331-2663), Pacific Trade Centre, 2 Kai Hing Rd, Kwun Tong (near Kai Tak airport)

United Parcel Service, or UPS
> (☎ 2735-3535), rooms 602-610, North Tower, Harbour City, World Finance Centre, Tsim Sha Tsui

Telephone

Hongkong Telecom, a joint-venture more than 58% owned by Britain's Cable & Wireless, has until recently enjoyed a monopoly on phone services (but not pagers). In 1994 three other companies (New T&T, Hutchison and New World) were permitted into the market, but the lucrative long-distance monopoly will continue until the year 2006. Monopolies usually charge high rates for poor service, but Hongkong Telecom is something of an exception – service is good and long-distance rates are the lowest in Asia.

All calls made within Hong Kong are local calls and therefore free, except for public pay phones which cost HK$1 per local call with no extra charges for chatting a long time. The pay phones normally accept HK$2 coins but do *not* give change, though you can make a second call by pressing the 'FC' (Follow-on Call) button before hanging up.

Hong Kong should hang its head in shame over the lack of public phones. Some say the problem is due to virtually everyone having a cellular phone. It seems to be a classic chicken and egg problem – there are no public phones because everyone has a cellular phone, or else everyone has a cellular phone because there are no public phones. For peons like me who don't own a cellular phone, finding a place to make a call can be frustrating. There aren't many phone booths on the street, you're best bet is indoors – check the hotel lobbies, convenience stores, ferry terminals, MTR stations and post offices. There are free courtesy phones in the reception area of the airport (useful for contacting hotels).

If you want to phone overseas, it's cheapest to use an IDD (International Direct Dialling) telephone. You can place an IDD call from most phone boxes, but you'll need a stack of HK$5 coins handy if your call is going to be anything but very brief. An alternative is to buy a 'phonecard', which comes in denominations of HK$50, HK$100 or HK$250. You can find phones that take these cards in shops, on the street or at Hongkong Telecom offices. 'Duet' phones accept coins and phonecards.

The aforementioned phonecard should not be mistaken for the 'Hello Phonecard', also available from Hongkong Telecom. It charges the same rates as regular phonecards but can be used to call from *any* phone (coin phone, private phone, etc). The disadvantage is that you have to dial a special code first. Hello phonecards are available in denominations of HK$100, HK$200 and HK$300.

To make an IDD call from Hong Kong, first dial 001, then the country code, area code and number. If the area code begins with a zero, you must omit that zero when dialling from abroad. So to call Melbourne (area code 03) in Australia (country code 61), you would dial 001-61-3-XXXX XXXX. If you're using someone else's phone and you want to know how much the call cost, dial

003 instead of 001 and the operator will call back to report the cost.

If you go to Hongkong Telecom, there are three options for overseas phone calls: operator-connected calls – paid in advance with a minimum of three minutes; international direct dialling (IDD) which you dial yourself after paying a deposit – the unused portion of your deposit is refunded; and reverse charges (collect), which requires a small deposit refundable if the charge is accepted or the call doesn't get through. The cost of long-distance calls is listed in the *Business Telephone Directory*. You can place international calls at the following Hongkong Telecom offices:

Hermes House
    10 Middle Rd, Tsim Sha Tsui, Kowloon. Open 24
    hours a day, including public holidays.
Shop B
    basement, Century Square, 1-13 D'Aguilar St,
    Central, open 24 hours including holidays.
Unit D-37
    Passenger Terminal Building, Kai Tak airport,
    Kowloon City. Open 8 am to 11 pm daily, includ-
    ing public holidays.
Unit D-915
    (restricted to departing passengers), Departure
    Hall, Kai Tak airport, Kowloon City.

You can apply for a phone account at Hongkong Telecom offices, or at Telecom CSL offices (of which there are 23 in Hong Kong).

If you're staying in Hong Kong for more than a few months and make frequent calls to the USA, it's worthwhile to sign up for call-back services with a US-based company such as PrimeCall (☎ (800) 698-1232; email primecal@compumedia.com) or NewWorld (☎ (201) 996-1670; Website http://www.new-worldtele.com), 1402 Teaneck Rd, Suite 114, Teaneck, NJ 07666, USA.

Some useful phone numbers and prefixes include the following:

Ambulance, Fire, Police, Emergency	☎ 999
Calls to China	☎ 012
Credit-Card Billing	☎ 011
Crime Report, Police Business	☎ 2527-7177
Directory Assistance	☎ 1081
Fire Hazard Complaints	☎ 2723-8787
Hong Kong's Country Code	☎ 852

IDD Prefix	☎ 001
International Directory Assistance	☎ 013
International Operator	☎ 010
Taxi Complaints	☎ 2527-7177
Time & Weather	☎ 18501

If you don't have the cash on hand, an easy way to make reverse-charge (collect) calls or bill to a credit card is to use a service called Home Direct. This service is not offered to every country. One way to make a Home Direct call is to use a special telephone on which you simply push a button and you are immediately connected to an operator in that country – these special phones are found in airports and a few major hotels. You can also make a Home Direct call on an ordinary telephone by dialling one of the following numbers:

Australia	
Optus	☎ 800-0161
Telstra	☎ 800-0061
Canada	☎ 800-1100
China	☎ 800-0186
France	☎ 800-0033
Germany	☎ 800-0049
Indonesia	☎ 800-0062
Japan	
IDC	☎ 800-0181
KDD	☎ 800-0081
Korea (South)	
Dacom	☎ 800-0083
KT	☎ 800-0082
Macau	☎ 800-0853
Malaysia	☎ 800-0060
New Zealand	
TNZI	☎ 800-0064
CLEAR	☎ 800-0164
Portugal	☎ 800-0351
Singapore	☎ 800-0065
South Africa	☎ 800-0027
Taiwan	☎ 800-0886
Thailand	☎ 800-0066
UK	
MCL	☎ 800-1144
BT	☎ 800-0044
USA	
AT&T	☎ 800-1111
MCI	☎ 800-1121
Sprint	☎ 800-1877
Hawaii	☎ 800-1188

Phone Directories There are more phone directories than you would expect! Currently, the line-up includes the *Yellow Pages*

for Consumers (three volumes, all English & Chinese); the *Yellow Pages for Businesses* (one volume, English only); the *Business White Pages Telephone Directory* (one volume, English & Chinese); the *Residential Directories* (three volumes, all English & Chinese); and the *Hong Kong Fax Directory* (one volume, English & Chinese). These guides are available from Telecom CSL shops.

Cellular Phones & Pagers Hong Kong boasts the world's highest per-capita usage of cellular telephones and pagers. Even if you don't take up permanent residence, it might be worth knowing that you can rent this equipment too. And to answer an often-asked question: yes, cellular phones and pagers *do* work inside the MTR.

Cellular phones can be rented from Rentel (☎ 2828-6600), 5th floor, Allied Kajima Building, 138 Gloucester Rd, Wan Chai. Hongkong Telecom does not rent cellular phones, but will happily sell you one.

Pagers can be rented from a wide variety of sources. Hongkong Telecom charges a HK$10 per month rental fee plus a usage fee of HK$230 for the service. The bad part is that there is a HK$500 deposit which is *not* refundable unless you use the pager for more than six months.

Some other companies rent and sell pagers at slightly lower prices. Look in the *Yellow Pages* under Pagers to find an extensive list. Cheapest of the lot is said to be ABC Communications (☎ 2710-0333), 40 Waterloo Rd, Kowloon Tong, but there are more convenient branches in the MTR stations at Central and Tsim Sha Tsui. In Mong Kok you can contact Star Paging (☎ 2771-1111), 602 Nathan Rd, or New World Paging (☎ 2781-6688), 558 Nathan Rd. Hutchison Paging is the largest in the Hong Kong paging market and has service centres in the following locations:

51 Des Voeux Rd, Central; 10 Harcourt Rd, Central; 133 Thomson Rd, Wan Chai; 294 Hennessy Rd, Wan Chai; 480 Hennessy Rd, Wan Chai; 7 Paterson St, Causeway Bay; Peninsula Centre, Tsim Sha Tsui East; 16 Carnarvon Rd, Tsim Sha Tsui

Telecom CSL Shops This is where you go to apply for service, pay bills, rent pagers, purchase equipment and phone directories. The list of these shops is too extensive to reproduce here, but some of the major ones are as follows:

Shop 60, lower ground floor, Silvercord Shopping Centre, 30 Canton Rd, Tsim Sha Tsui; 221 Nathan Rd, Yau Ma Tei; 501 Nathan Rd, Yau Ma Tei; shop 116, Prince's Building, Chater Rd & Ice House St, Central; Shop B, ground floor, International Building, 141 Des Voeux Rd, Central; 46 Hennessy Rd, Wan Chai; 66 Percival St, Causeway Bay

Fax, Telegraph, Email & Telex

You can send a fax from any office of Hong-kong Telecom. To send a one-page fax (A4 size) they charge HK$15 within Hong Kong; HK$30 for South-East Asia; HK$35 to Australia, New Zealand, Canada, USA and UK; and HK$45 to all other countries. For HK$15 per page, you can also receive a fax here. Be sure the sending party puts your name and your Hong Kong telephone number on the top of the page.

Most hotels and even many youth hostels allow their guests to send and receive faxes. The surcharge for sending is usually 10% above cost, and receiving is normally HK$10 per page.

Hongkong Telecom's fully digital fibre-optic lines ensure good quality transmission within Hong Kong. However, if dialling your own fax for an overseas transmission, you should use the international prefix 002 (for a data line) rather than 001 (for a voice line).

CallFax 1783 Determined to stay at the fore-front of fax technology, Hong Kong Telecom has introduced CallFax 1783, a hi-tech version of the *Yellow Pages*. By dialling a certain code, you can have *Yellow Pages* listings sent to you by fax. Besides catering to those who are too lazy to look things up in the phone book, the system has the one advantage of always having the most current listings. This service is free. There are three basic steps to using the system:

1. Using a touchtone phone or fax machine with handset (or if no handset, set to polling mode), dial the CallFax gateway number, which is 1783. You will then hear instructions on how to receive your fax.
2. Enter the five-digit CallFax code for the *Yellow Pages* classification you need. You must look up this number in the printed CallFax index available from the phone company, or in the printed *Yellow Pages* Fast Find index. If you don't have either of these, the index is also available by fax – dial 1783 followed by CallFax code 20000.
3. If you're using a fax machine, press the 'start' button. If you're using a touchtone telephone, enter your fax number and hang up. Either way, the information you've requested should be sent to your fax machine within minutes.

Telegraph Hongkong Telecom (☎ 2888-2888) is the place to go for sending international or local telegrams. They also have a hotline (☎ 1000) which operates 24 hours a day.

Email Hong Kong is one of the most wired cities in cyberspace and competition keeps the cost for email services low. If you have an account with CompuServe, you can connect by dialling the CIS node (☎ 3002-8332). For members of America Online, there is an Aol-Globalnet access number for Hong Kong (☎ 2519-9040).

Infonauts residing in Hong Kong who want to surf the Internet will find a wide selection of companies ready, willing and able to make the connection. There are 33 companies providing on-ramps to the Net at the time of writing, and more will no doubt be setting up shop unless China subverts their efforts. The following list, by no means complete, comprises Internet service providers with more than 100 dial-up data lines in Hong Kong:

Asia On-Line
    ☎ 2837-8888; data 3004-5115; fax 2882-2358
    email info@asiaonline.net
    http://www.asiaonline.net
Chevalier Internet
    ☎ 2953-3300; data 3002-6838; fax 2750-7687
    email info@chevalier.net
    http://www.chavalier.net
CompuServe
    ☎ 2833-1500; data 3002-8332; fax 2506-3445
    email 74777.1372@compuserve.com
    http://www.compuserve.com

HKNet
 ☎ 2110-3388; data 3006-0088; fax 2110-0088
 email info@hknet.com
 http://www.hknet.com
Hong Kong Star Internet
 ☎ 2781-6552; data 3002-0000; fax 2770-3157
 email info@hkstar.com
 http://www.hkstar.com
Hong Kong Supernet
 ☎ 2358-7924; data 3002-9000; fax 2770-3157
 email info@hk.super.net
 http://hk.super.net
IBM Global Network
 ☎ 2515-4511; data 3004-9009; fax 2556-3156
 email hkibm281@ibmmail.com
 http://www.ibm.net
InterServe
 ☎ 2314-5906; data 3002-9388; fax 2317-5622
 email info@interserve.com.hk
 http://www.interserve.com.hk

Cyber-surfers may also want to visit Kublai's Cyber Diner (☎ 2529-9117), 3rd floor, One Capital Place, 18 Luard Rd, Wan Chai.

Telex Telex is old technology, having been rendered obsolete by fax and email. However, there are still a few ancient telex machines around. The main branches of Hong Kong Telecom can send and receive telexes for you.

BOOKS
Lonely Planet
Lonely Planet publishes other guides to the region, including *North-East Asia on a shoe-string*, *South-East Asia on a shoestring*, *China – travel survival kit*, the *Cantonese phrasebook* and the *Mandarin phrasebook*.

Guidebooks
There are some special-interest guidebooks which you might want to look into if you stay in Hong Kong a while.

Leisure Guide to Hong Kong is a recent guide which has proven popular.

Setting Up in Hong Kong and *Living in Hong Kong* are useful for those planning a long stay.

Associations and Societies in Hong Kong has a self-explanatory title. It's published by the Hong Kong Tourist Association (HKTA).

The Hong Kong Guide, 1893 is available as a reprint and makes fascinating reading. The travel information is somewhat out of date.

Hong Kong, part of the series of Insight Guides by Apa Productions, has outstanding photographs and a very readable text.

The *Journal of the Royal Asiatic Society* is published annually by the RAS (☎ 2551-0300), GPO Box 3864, Hong Kong. Each volume delves into different topics, everything from history to flora and fauna.

A guide of a more general nature is *Keeping Your Life, Family and Career Intact While Living Abroad* by Cathy Tsang-Feign.

Nature Guides
The Government Publications Centre sells the definitive nature guides to Hong Kong's flora, fauna, geography and geology. A good book to start with is *Hong Kong Animals* by Dennis Hill and Karen Phillipps. There are also quite a few other *Hong Kong Fill-in-the-blank* guides, including *Hong Kong Insects*, *Hong Kong Trees*, *Hong Kong Shrubs* and *Hong Kong Poisonous Plants*. The Urban Council also chips in with the *Illustrated Guide to the Venomous Snakes of Hong Kong*.

Audubon Society types should be enthralled with the *New Colour Guide to Hong Kong Birds* by C Viney and K Phillipps. *Hong Kong Country Parks* by Stella Thrower is an excellent introduction if you want to walk in the countryside. Ditto for *The Hong Kong Countryside* by CAC Herklots.

Magic Walks by Kaarlo Schepel is an excellent guide to walking the New Territories and the Outlying Islands. This one is not a government publication and can be picked up from commercial bookshops.

Travel
The Taipan Traders by Anthony Lawrence is one of the Formasia series of books. A large sketchbook, it depicts many portraits by Asia's finest painters. *Great Cities of the World – Old Hong Kong* is another interesting Formasia book.

Hong Kong by Ian Lloyd and Russell

Spurr is a good pictorial and part of the series of Times Editions.

History & Politics

A History of Hong Kong by GB Endacott, published in 1958, is a classic which has everything you'd ever want to know about Hong Kong's past. It's not to be confused with *A History of Hong Kong* by Frank Welsh – same title but different author and publisher. This 624-page tome was published in 1993.

The government's annual report is entitled *Hong Kong 1990, Hong Kong 1991*, etc. In addition to the excellent photographs, the text is a gold mine of information about the government, politics, economy, history, arts and just about any other topic relevant to Hong Kong.

Maurice Collis' *Foreign Mud* tells the sordid story of the opium wars. Another version of the same story is *The Opium War* by the Foreign Language Press in Peking.

Hong Kong Illustrated, Views & News 1840-1890, compiled by John Warner, is a large sketchbook and history of the colony.

The Taipans – Hong Kong's Merchant Princes tells the story of the Western managers (taipans) who profiteered during the opium wars.

A prolific writer and respected magistrate, Austin Coates wrote *Whampoa – Ships on the Shore*, a history of the Hong Kong & Whampoa Dock Company, formed in 1863 and one of the first big companies to be founded in Hong Kong. He also wrote *Myself a Mandarin*.

The Other Hong Kong Report is a fascinating and somewhat cynical rebuttal to the government's optimistic annual report.

Some of the gloom surrounding the British retreat is captured in *Hong Kong, Epilogue to an Empire*, by Jan Morris, in a lively mix of past and present, fact and myth.

Fragrant Harbour by John Warner has many early photographs of Hong Kong.

Humour

Larry Feign doesn't pull any punches with his hilarious political cartoons which graced the pages of the *South China Morning Post* before China took office and Feign was given the boot. His best works have been released in a series of books. Some titles to look for include *The World of Lily Wong* and *The Adventures of Super Lily*. Feign's latest book, *Banned in Hong Kong*, includes cartoons which were censored by the *Post* before Feign's employment was abruptly terminated. You can find these books in shops all over Hong Kong, including (ironically) the South China Morning Post Family Bookshop.

Nuri Vittachi, a writer for the *Far Eastern Economic Review* has published numerous humorous tracts including *The Hong Kong Joke Book*, *Only in Hong Kong* and *Travellers' Tales*.

Author George Adams writes books with a humorous bent, including *True Hong Kong Confessions*, *Games Hong Kong People Play*, *Wicked Hong Kong Stories*, *The Great Hong Kong Sex Novel* and *Hong Kong Watching*.

General

Certainly the most famous fiction set in Hong Kong is *The World of Suzie Wong* by Richard Mason. It was written in 1957 and the movie was filmed in Hong Kong in 1960, but it still makes an excellent read.

Spy-thriller author John Le Carré wrote a fascinating tale, *The Honourable Schoolboy*. It's a story of espionage in Hong Kong and Indochina in the early 1970s.

The marathon-length *Tai-Pan* by James Clavell will certainly help pass idle hours, although it's not a very realistic version of Hong Kong's early days of ships and traders. The sequel to *Tai-Pan* is another epic-length book, *Noble House*.

Also set in Hong Kong and China are Robert Elegant's *Dynasty* and *Mandarin*.

Triad by Derek Lambert is a violent fictional account of the Chinese underworld.

The Occult World of Hong Kong by Frena Bloomfield may fascinate you or give you nightmares.

The private lives of Hong Kong families are captured in *Chinese Walls* by Sussy

Chako and *The Monkey King* by Timothy Mo. *An Insular Possession*, also by Timothy Mo, is a novel set in pre-colonial Hong Kong.

Bookshops

Kowloon One of the biggest and best bookshops is Swindon Books (☎ 2366-8001), 13 Lock Rd, Tsim Sha Tsui. There are also smaller branches: shop 346, 3rd floor, Ocean Terminal, Tsim Sha Tsui; and at the Star Ferry Pier, Tsim Sha Tsui.

Times Books (☎ 2367-4340) is hidden in the basement of Golden Crown Court at 66-70 Nathan Rd, Tsim Sha Tsui. There is a branch (☎ 2722-6583) in Tsim Sha Tsui East in Houston Centre, lower ground floor, shop LG-23.

The South China Morning Post Family Bookshop is on the 3rd floor, Ocean Terminal in Tsim Sha Tsui, and on the ground floor of the Tung Ying Building, Granville Rd (at Nathan Rd).

Chung Hwa Book Company (☎ 2782-5054), 450 Nathan Rd, Yau Ma Tei, stocks many books in Chinese as well as in other languages.

Hong Kong Island Times Books (☎ 2525-8797) is in the Hong Kong Club Building, 3 Jackson Rd, Central (just west of the Ritz-Carlton Hotel). The second Times Books (☎ 2525-0043) is in the basement of the Haleson Building, 1 Jubilee St, Central (west side of Central Market). There is another Times Books (☎ 2504-2383) on the 3rd floor of the World Trade Centre, 280 Gloucester Rd, Causeway Bay.

Arguably the best bookshop on Hong Kong Island is Cosmos Books (☎ 2866-1677; fax 2861-1541), 30 Johnston Rd, in Wan Chai. The basement houses Chinese books while English books are found on the mezzanine floor.

There is a South China Morning Post Family Bookshop (☎ 2522-1012) at the Star Ferry terminal on Hong Kong Island. There is another in Times Square, Matheson St, Causeway Bay.

There is a very wide selection of books at the Hong Kong Book Centre (☎ 2522-7064) in the basement at 25 Des Voeux Rd, Central.

The Bookazine Company has a fine little bookshop directly opposite the HKTA office in the basement of Jardine House (☎ 2523-1747) in Central. Bookazine has a larger store in Alexandra House (☎ 2524-9914), 7 Des Voeux Rd, Central. And there is a third Bookazine (☎ 2501-5926) in shop G31, Hutchison House, 10 Harcourt Rd, Central.

The Commercial Press (☎ 2890-8028), 9 Yee Wo St, Causeway Bay, is more notable for its selection of Chinese books though it does have a decent stock of English titles too.

Asahiya Japanese Bookstore is only of interest if you're studying Japanese. It's in Daimaru Household Square (Kingston & Gloucester Rd), Causeway Bay (don't confuse it with the Daimaru Department Store on Paterson St).

Joint Publishing Company (☎ 2525-0102), 9 Queen Victoria St (opposite the Central Market) is an outstanding store to find books about China or books and tapes for studying the Chinese language.

Not to be overlooked is the Government Publications Centre on the ground floor of the Government Offices Building, 66 Queensway, Admiralty.

Libraries

The main library is at City Hall, high block, Central, just one street to the east of the Star Ferry terminal. However, they will not let you make photocopies of anything which is copyrighted (which means just about everything). As a result, most of their reference books have had pages ripped out of them by frustrated students.

The American Library (☎ 2501-0088), 51 Garden Rd, Central, has good research facilities and *does* allow you to make photocopies.

CD ROM

Hong Kong produces a number of interactive CD ROMs for the local market. These have a mostly Cantonese dialogue, though English subtitles are not uncommon. Their content is not exactly inspiring, though perhaps they reveal one side of Hong Kong's culture. A quick browse of the CD racks at a computer arcade in Kowloon produced this list of locally made titles: *Karaoke Canto-Pop, God of Gambling, Triad Women, Daughter of Darkness, Blood Lust, I Ching – Book of Erotic Changes, Woman with Four Husbands, Sex School* and *Kung Fu Devil*.

ONLINE SERVICES

There are heaps of online services dealing with Hong Kong issues, and a simple Net search on the words 'Hong Kong' will turn up all sorts of intriguing possibilities. Lonely Planet contributes to this medium – check out http://www.lonelyplanet.com on the World Wide Web.

Larry Feign, the artist whose political cartoons got him blacklisted from the Hong Kong newspapers, has fought back by going online. His Web site includes some hilarious cartoons, a glossary of Hong Kong terminology and a who's who list. For a good laugh, browse Lily Wong's home page (http://www.asiaonline.net/lilywong).

BC Magazine has the inside scoop on Hong Kong's entertainment and nightlife scene. Check out its home page (http://ourworld.compuserve.com/homepages/puregoodness/bconline.htm).

Information changes on the Internet so quickly that it's impossible to say what the hottest sites will be at the time you read this. At the moment, some good possibilities include:

Asian Sources Online
   the centre of Asian trade on the World Wide Web,
   http://www.asiansources.com
Hong Kong government information
   http://www.info.gov.hk
Hong Kong information page
   http://www-geog.hkbu.edu.hk/hkwww.html
Hong Kong jobs
   http://www-geog.hkbu.edu.hk/career.html£hk
Hong Kong Tourist Association
   http://www.hkta.org

FILMS

A few foreign films with a Hong Kong theme include *Hardboiled, Farewell My Concubine* and *Rumble in the Bronx*. If you're interested in learning a bit more about made-in-Hong Kong films, see the Arts section in the Facts about Hong Kong chapter.

If you live in a Western country and want to pick up some videos about Hong Kong, your best bet would be to visit some of the video rental shops located in a 'Chinatown' (such as in San Francisco, Melbourne, etc). Most of the videos you can expect to find will have Chinese dialogue with English subtitles, though you may find some Western-made movies as well. Watching these videos can give you at least a little insight into Hong Kong society.

NEWSPAPERS & MAGAZINES

Hong Kong is the leading information and news centre in Asia. It became that way largely because the government kept its hands off the media, although the British colonial government occasionally used its powers of censorship to avoid upsetting China. In 1989, a documentary entitled *Mainland China 1989* was censored because it was likely 'to seriously damage good relations with other territories'. Other documentaries critical of China (such as *The Dying Rooms* released in 1996) are simply never shown in Hong Kong. What will happen after 1997 is the big question on every publisher's mind. Lu Ping, China's director of the Hong Kong and Macau Affairs Office, has said that Hong Kong's currently free press will face 'some restrictions' after 1997.

Many Hong Kong reporters, nervous about their future, already practice self-censorship to avoid upsetting China. They have good reason to be nervous. In September, 1993, reporter Xi Yang – working for the Hong Kong-based *Ming Pao Daily News* – published some mundane financial statistics about interest rates and gold policies which were to be announced in a Chinese politician's speech. In Hong Kong this would have been regarded as nothing more than a financial reporter's scoop and would have gone largely unnoticed. However, the Chinese government decided it was 'espionage' and had Xi arrested for stealing state banking secrets. His incredibly harsh 12-year sentence triggered massive protests in Hong Kong, but Beijing remained unmoved. There seems to be little doubt that China was sending a message to Hong Kong reporters – toe the line, or else.

The Chinese government is, of course, most concerned about newspapers published in Chinese. Newspapers published in English are currently far more daring than their Chinese counterparts. There are nearly 50 Chinese language newspapers in Hong Kong, though admittedly most are just advertising sheets. There are less than 10 serious newspapers in Hong Kong, and two of them (*Wen Wei Po* and *Ta Kung Pao*) read as if they were printed in Beijing already.

With the demise of the *Eastern Express*, the only local English-language newspapers are the *South China Morning Post* and *Hong Kong Standard*. The *Post* has the largest circulation (and is rumoured to be the most profitable newspaper in the world). However, the newspaper often practises self-censorship so as not to offend China, a practice which has become more noticeable recently. The *Hong Kong Standard* is rather thin on news, though it's notable for its weekly computer section.

Three international newspapers produce Asian editions which are printed in Hong Kong. These are the *Asian Wall Street Journal, USA Today* and the *International Herald Tribune*. The IHT is put together by the *New York Times* and *Washington Post*, but is only available outside the USA.

Many magazines are published in Hong Kong, but the most outstanding is the *Far Eastern Economic Review*, which focuses on news throughout Asia. *Asiaweek* is also published in Hong Kong, as well as the Asian editions of *Time* and *Newsweek*.

HK Magazine has the scoop on nightlife and entertainment in this city. The magazine is published weekly and is free. The best place to find it is at pubs or cafes frequented by gwailos ('foreign devils'), or at some trendy bookshops. For subscription

information, ring the office (☎ 2850-5065; fax 2543-4964; email asiacity@hk.super.net).

BC Magazine is a monthly freebie covering wining and dining in Hong Kong. For subscription info or to place an ad, ring the office (☎ 2976-0876; fax 2976-0973).

RADIO & TV
RTHK (Radio Television Hong Kong) is a government-funded but editorially independent (for now) broadcasting system which dominates the airwaves. In 1996, the Chinese government once again upset everyone by demanding access to RTHK to broadcast Beijing's point of view. The British authorities refused to cooperate, but how much longer RTHK can maintain its independent editorial content is a big question.

The most popular English-language radio stations are RTHK Radio 3 (567 kHz AM, 1584 kHz AM, 97.9 mHz FM, 106.8 mHz FM); RTHK Radio 4 (classical music, 97.6 to 98.9 mHz FM); RTHK Radio 6 (BBC World Service, 675 kHz AM, 24 hours a day); Commercial Radio (864 kHz AM); Metro News (1044 kHz AM); Hit Radio (99.7 mHz FM); FM Select (104 mHz FM); Quote AM (alternative & dance music, 864 kHz AM). The English-language newspapers publish a daily guide to radio programmes.

Hong Kong's terrestrial TV stations are run by two companies, Television Broadcasts (TVB) and Asia Television (ATV). Each company operates one English-language and one Cantonese-language channel, making a total of four stations in Hong Kong. The two English stations are TVB Pearl (channel 3) and ATV World (channel 4). The two Cantonese stations are called TVB Jade (channel 1) and ATV Home (channel 2). The programme schedule is listed daily in the English-language newspapers.

Since people in Macau also read Hong Kong newspapers, programmes from the Macau station (TdM) are listed, but the signal is too weak to be received in Hong Kong. TdM has wanted to broadcast to Hong Kong for years, but the Hong Kong government has strenuously objected, claiming that this would cause interference. Many suspect the real reason is that Hong Kong's two stations would prefer not to have any competition.

If your hotel is connected to a satellite dish, you'll be able to receive Hong Kong's STAR TV along with CNN, BBC and a host of other stations.

Cable TV is available in Hong Kong, although foreign newscasts are censored when politically sensitive topics are involved.

VIDEO SYSTEMS
In a nutshell, the problem is that no universal TV broadcasting standard exists. Due to the influence of Britain, Hong Kong subscribes to the PAL broadcasting standard. The three most common standards are PAL (used in Australia, Hong Kong, New Zealand, UK, most of Europe), SECAM (France, Germany, Luxembourg) and NTSC (Canada, Japan, Korea, Latin America, USA). See under Video in the Things to Buy section later in this chapter.

PHOTOGRAPHY & VIDEO
Film & Equipment
Almost everything you could possibly need in the way of film, camera and photographic accessories is available in Hong Kong. Stanley St on Hong Kong Island is the place to look for reputable camera stores.

If you're a professional photographer, you are no doubt prepared for every contingency with an assortment of film, at least three lenses, filters, a tripod and perhaps an extra camera body.

However, the average traveller doesn't want to be weighed down by 10 kg of heavy metal. In this case, the best option may be to invest in a pocket-sized electronic point-and-shoot camera. Connoisseurs of photography will no doubt moan and groan at this advice, but it should be pointed out that some of the more expensive models come with an amazing variety of features. A high-end point-and-shoot camera should have a zoom lens (preferably 28 mm to 120 mm), fill flash, self-timer, remote control and special modes for night photos and exposure com-

pensation. The latter feature allows you to manually brighten or darken the exposure. This is particularly important if you use slide film – slides tend to come out too dark when used in automatic cameras.

Real enthusiasts may want to buy two or three cameras – one for colour slide film, one for colour prints and one for black & white. While it is possible to get prints made from slides (or even slides made from prints) and black & white made from colour, the best results are achieved when you use the proper film to begin with.

If you'll be doing a lot of shooting indoors, consider the virtues of high-speed films like ASA 400 and above.

Photography
Hong Kong offers some visually striking scenery, but getting good pictures can often be challenging. The first problem is the fickle weather – it can be cloudy for months on end, though at other times the sun beats down without mercy. In mountainous areas such as Victoria Peak, you may encounter fog as thick as pea soup. Photography is further complicated by the fact that there are numerous opportunities to take pictures indoors, where lighting is generally poor and you'll need a wide-angle lens to manoeuvre in close quarters. Hong Kong's bright lights can be very photogenic at night, assuming you understand the intricacies of night-time photography.

Video
Making a good travel video is a complex subject that would require a book in itself (indeed, such books are available in Hong Kong and elsewhere). For the budding amateur, general considerations include equipment, light, sound and avoiding camera shudder.

A more detailed discussion of video equipment is found in the Things to Buy section of this chapter.

Restrictions
You can't photograph customs and immigration procedures at the airport, ferry terminals

and overland border crossings. There are signs advising you of this fact. Nor can you photograph security measures, such as x-ray machines, metal detectors, machine gun-toting airport police, etc. I have personally been prevented from taking photos of the runways and parked aircraft.

Ironically, there is a local aviation club-house within Kai Tak airport where, after paying a small entrance fee, you can take photos of planes landing and taking off. The clubhouse is open to everyone, foreigners and locals alike.

China has traditionally been hyper-para-noid about foreigners 'stealing state secrets'. It's possible that there will be more restrictions placed on what you can and cannot film as time marches on. The best advice is to keep your eyes open for an increasing number of 'No Photography' signs.

Photographing People

There are three basic approaches to photographing people. One is the polite 'ask for permission and pose it' shot, which is sometimes rejected. Another is the 'no-holds barred and upset everyone' approach. The third is surreptitious, standing half a km away with a metre-long telephoto lens.

Not being a particularly friendly place, asking permission to photograph people in Hong Kong seldom produces any cooperation. Fortunately, the locals are pretty much used to camera-clicking foreign tourists, and won't normally throw a fit if you take a photo of them. Young students seem to enjoy having their photo taken and may even ham it up for the camera.

When it comes to being photographed by family and friends, Hong Kongers are generally big on people shots. Most have a collection of several thousand photos of themselves. Usually, they prefer to be photographed standing in front of something (a temple, a boat, a karaoke lounge, etc). Hong Kongers tend to be not much impressed by photos which lack people, no matter how beautiful the scenery. Some foreigners have been taken aback when showing their prize (but people-less) pictures to Hong Kong

friends, who take a quick look and pronounce the photos 'boring'.

Airport Security

The dreaded x-ray machines are officially marked 'film-safe', and most travellers will not need to worry about their film being fogged by x-rays. However, professional photographers using ultra-sensitive film (such as ASA 1000) do need to worry about this, especially if the film is repeatedly exposed to even mild x-rays. One way to combat the problem is to use lead-lined bags, but it's probably safer and easier to simply get the film physically inspected.

TIME

Hong Kong Standard Time is eight hours ahead of GMT/UTC. Hong Kong does not have daylight-saving time. When it's noon in Hong Kong it's also noon in Singapore, Manila and Perth; 8 pm the previous day in Los Angeles; 11 pm the previous day in New York; 4 am in London; and 2 pm in Melbourne and Sydney.

ELECTRICITY
Voltage & Cycle

The standard is 220V, 50 Hz (cycles per second) AC. Electrical shops in Hong Kong and elsewhere sell handy pocket-sized transformers which will step down the electricity to 110V, but most mini-transformers are only rated for 50W. This is sufficient for an electric razor or laptop computer but *not* for those electric heater coils that some travellers carry to make tea and coffee. If in doubt, most appliances have a wattage rating printed somewhere on the bottom. Overloading a transformer can cause it to melt. Luxury tourist hotels often have razor outlets with multi-fittings to suit different plugs and voltages.

Apart from needing the right voltage, a few electric motors need the right frequency of current to work properly. For example, your 60 Hz clock will run slow on 50 Hz current, although it shouldn't harm the motor.

Plugs & Sockets

In Hong Kong, the electricity outlets are designed to accommodate three round prongs, though some newer buildings are wired with three square pins of the British design. Inexpensive plug adaptors are widely available in Hong Kong supermarkets. Remember that adaptors are *not* transformers. If you ignore this warning and plug a 110V appliance into a 220V outlet, it will be sparks and fireworks.

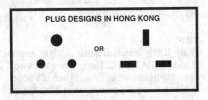

PLUG DESIGNS IN HONG KONG

OR

WEIGHTS & MEASURES

The international metric system is in official use in Hong Kong. In practice, traditional Chinese weights and measures are still common.

If you want to shop in the local markets, become familiar with Chinese units of weight. Things are sold by the *leung*, which is equivalent to 37.5g, or the *catty* – about 600g. There are 16 leung to the catty.

Gold is sold by the *tael*, which is exactly the same as a leung, and you will find many banks selling gold in Hong Kong. The Chinese have a long history of putting their wealth into gold as they generally have little faith in paper money. The rapid inflation that China has experienced in the past makes it easy to understand why.

Hong Kong currently uses the British system of counting floors in a building. The street level is the ground floor and the next one up is the 1st floor. The Chinese system is different – street level is the 1st floor. It's entirely possible that the Chinese system will be put into place after 1997.

LAUNDRY

There is no need to hide your dirty laundry as there are plenty of places in Hong Kong which will clean it cheaply. Many hotels, even the cheap youth hostels, have a laundry service. If they don't, just ask where one is. Prices are normally HK$25 for three kg. If it's less than three kg you still pay the same, so you might want to throw your clothes together with a friend's.

Three convenient laundry services in Tsim Sha Tsui include:

Purity Laundry, 25 Chungking Arcade, Chungking Mansions, 30 Nathan Rd; Posh Wash (☎ 2739-8424), 13th floor, Mirador Arcade, 58 Nathan Rd; and Carlye Steam Laundry, Golden Crown Court, 66-70 Nathan Rd.

For dry-cleaning, you can try the chain store with the unforgettable name of Clean Living. There are branches all around, but convenient ones are in the MTR stations.

HEALTH

See the separate Health chapter at the end of this book.

TOILETS

You need a strong bladder to visit Hong Kong – the city suffers from a real scarcity of public toilets. There are a few, but you have to know where to look for them – perhaps my next project will be to write a guidebook entitled *Public Toilets in Hong Kong – a travel survival kit*. So far, the HKTA has not produced a brochure on the matter. Parks generally have public toilets; there is one in the Central Market on Hong Kong Island, and another hidden in a basement off Lan Kwai Fong. Past the turnstiles of the Star Ferry are public toilets, though there are none on the boat itself.

Most irritating is the fact that all the major touristy shopping malls have toilets, but keep the doors locked so only employees with keys can use them. Ocean Centre, arguably the busiest tourist mall, is a notorious example and even goes so far as to put a sign on the rest room doors saying 'staff only'. Perhaps what's needed is a massive protest – if all the tourists

Left: Trams make slow but dignified progress along Central's crowded thoroughfares. A tram trip is an ideal way to sightsee.

Top Right: Budget accommodation, Nathan Road, Kowloon.

Bottom Right: Kowloon's distinctive clock tower is all that remains of the old KCR station.

RICHARD I'ANSON

GLENN BEANLAND

GLENN BEANLAND

RICHARD I'ANSON

RICHARD I'ANSON

NICKO GONCHAROFF

Top: Signage clamours for attention along busy Nathan Road, Kowloon.
Middle: Signs in both English and Chinese clutter the streets of Sheung Wan.
Bottom: Wheels of fortune. Luxury cars reflect only wealth and status – not
practicality – in this crowded city.

would just urinate on the floor, the shop-owners might get the message. Barring that, the only recourse is to seek out the toilets in fast-food outlets (though not all have them) and in some of the large department stores.

If you find a public toilet you probably won't find toilet paper, so bring your own. You'd be wise to keep a stash with you at all times.

WOMEN TRAVELLERS
Safety Precautions
While Hong Kong poses no special dangers for women, unpleasant incidents can occur. It might be worth noting that some of the agencies advertising for Western women to work as models, escorts and extras in films are in fact fronts for prostitution. One woman who responded to such an offer had this to say:

OK, I should have known better. I left as soon as possible amid threats, and quite frankly I was really frightened. My friend who was interested in model-ling stayed, but soon found out that the entire business was just to find European girls to have sex with Chinese men.

I was old enough and had money enough in Hong Kong to refuse these people who were obviously hoping to intimidate or force us into working for them, but I think some people would be too scared to say no, as they were extremely persistent!

I had gone to see this man, Mr Chan, out of idle curiosity and ended up very frightened! I'd like other women to be warned, as they tried very hard to conceal the true nature of their business and Mr Chan is extremely charming and pleasant to start with.

What to Wear
In fashion-conscious Hong Kong almost anything goes, including miniskirts, hot pants, torn pants, blue jeans, halter tops, see-through blouses, see-through under-wear, etc. The last word that would describe Hong Kong is 'conservative'. Of course, being too blatant can attract more attention than you really want, but that's true any-where in the world. What you wear depends mainly on what image you want to project. Just remember that when you step across the border into China a different set of rules applies.

Organisations
Hong Kong has heaps of organisations cater-ing to the various interests of women. These are just a few:

HK Association of Business & Professional Women
GPO Box 1526, Hong Kong
(☎ 2869-6536; fax 2869-6556)
HK Association of University Women
GPO Box 11708, Hong Kong
HK Council of Women
GPO Box 819, Hong Kong
HK Federation of Women
flat B, 10th floor, Jonsim Place, 228 Queen's Rd East, Wan Chai (☎ 2833-6131; fax 2833-6909)
HK Federation of Women's Centres
S8-9, 2nd floor, Lai Kwai House, Kai Kwok Estate, Kowloon (☎ 2386-6256; fax 2728-0617)
HK Women's Welfare Club – Eastern District
4th floor, 210 Java Rd, North Point
(☎ 2561-2709; fax 2811-5982)
HK Women's Welfare Club – Western District
60 Bridger St, Sheung Wan
(☎ 2548-1536; fax 2540-5003)
International Women's League
2nd floor, 136A Nathan Rd, Tsim Sha Tsui
(☎ 2723-4393; fax 2367-8511)
Lady Executive Club
GPO Box 6830
(fax 2877-9531, 2362-3726)
League of Women Voters
GPO Box 1683 (fax 2849-5114, 2987-1522)
Women Business Owners Club
room 2700, Vicwood Plaza, 199 Des Voeux Rd, Central (☎ 2540-0446; fax 2543-5555)
Women in Publishing Society
room 409, Yu Yuet Lai Building, 43-55 Wyndham St, Central
(fax 2591-9853, 2526-0378)

GAY & LESBIAN TRAVELLERS
In general, the Chinese regard gays and les-bians as being afflicted with some sort of (Western) mental illness. As elsewhere, gays in Hong Kong receive more overt hostility than lesbians. In the not-too-distant past, anyone openly gay was liable to be arrested. These days, discrimination is more subtle, but being gay or lesbian in Hong Kong is enough to get you fired from a job. What the future holds for the Hong Kong gay commu-nity is yet another topic for debate.

SENIOR TRAVELLERS
Hong Kong is just about as user-friendly to

senior travellers as any Western city. With decent medical care, well-stocked pharmacies, air-conditioning and good public transport, Hong Kong offers most of the modern conveniences that make travel safe and comfortable. However, some seniors may have difficulty negotiating the steep hills or the steps on pedestrian overpasses and in the MTR stations.

There are half-price discounts for seniors (age 65 and over) on buses and ferries, and on MTR and KCR trains. There are also discounts for seniors (age 60 and over) in museums and on organised tours. Some upmarket hotels also have discounts for seniors, though these are somewhat bogus because anyone can get good discounts at a hotel by booking through a travel agent – you aren't likely to get it twice.

DISABLED TRAVELLERS

As mentioned in the foregoing section for senior travellers, disabled persons have to cope with some substantial obstacles, such as the stairs at the MTR stations, narrow crowded footpaths and steep hills. Persons whose sight, hearing or walking ability is impaired must be extremely cautious of Hong Kong's crazy drivers, who almost *never* yield to pedestrians.

On the other hand, taxis are not hard to find and most buildings have lifts. Wheelchairs can negotiate most of the ferries (lower deck only), but don't attempt to move around on hoverferries.

In some (but not all) upmarket hotels there are specially designed rooms for disabled persons. Those which provide such rooms are indicated under Places to Stay in the Kowloon and Hong Kong Island chapters.

TRAVEL WITH CHILDREN

Except for the dangers posed by traffic, Hong Kong is a pretty good travel destination if you want to bring the kids along. Food and sanitation are of a high enough standard that you needn't fear for their health, and there is plenty to keep them amused (Ocean Park, video games, STAR TV, etc).

A number of upmarket hotels give special concessions for families with children (reduced rates or free extra bed, etc). Most public transport offers half-price fares for children under the age of 12.

If your children are in fact teenagers, useful summer camp programmes are offered through the Outward Bound School (☎ 2792-4333, 2792-0055).

Lonely Planet publishes a guide entitled *Travel with Children* which has some useful tips about this particular aspect of journeying abroad.

USEFUL ORGANISATIONS

The Community Advice Bureau (☎ 2524-5444, 2815-5444) is where volunteer expats answer questions for new Hong Kong foreign residents. Since it's a volunteer organisation, don't bother them with a lot of trivia. If you've been living in Hong Kong a while, perhaps you'd like to volunteer some time too.

The Hong Kong Information Services Department (☎ 2842-8777) is on the ground, 1st, 4th, 5th and 6th floors of Beaconsfield House, 4 Queen's Rd, Central. They can answer specific questions or direct you to other government agencies that can handle your enquiry. It's best to try the HKTA before resorting to the Information Services Department.

Since the likelihood of getting ripped off by shopkeepers is high, it's good to know about the Hong Kong Consumer Council (☎ 2856-3113). There is a useful branch office (☎ 2926-1088) in the Tsim Sha Tsui tourist rip-off zone at the corner of Granville and Nathan Rds. It has a complaints and advice hot line (☎ 2929-2222) and an Advice Centre (☎ 2921-6228) at 38 Pier Rd, Central.

If you get robbed, you can obtain a loss report for insurance purposes at the Central Police Station, 10 Hollywood Rd (at the top end of Pottinger St) in Central. There is also a crime hotline (☎ 2527-7177), but this is *not* for emergencies.

If you've been ripped off by your employer, take your complaint to the Labour Department (☎ 2717-1771, 24 hours), or drop by their office in the Harbour Building,

38 Pier Rd, Central. Of course, that's assuming you're working legally to begin with.

A lot of Westerners go to work in Hong Kong and it's pretty easy to get a job in the pubs and nightclubs. However, quite a few of these places are not adverse to treating their staff pretty badly as they know they'll be moving on and are usually desperate for the money. Some pubs are notorious for making deductions from wages for any reason. However, Hong Kong does have quite strong employment protection legislation. The Labour Department has a 24-hour hotline for answering questions. One pub tried to deduct HK$600 from my wages, but a quick phone call told me my rights and I eventually got my money.

Clive Searle

If you're in the publishing, music or software business and your goods are being pirated, you can try complaining to the Intellectual Property Department (☎ 2961-6800), 24th & 25th floors, Wu Chung House, 213 Queen's Rd East, Wan Chai. This is also the place for registering copyrights, trademarks and patents.

The Royal Asiatic Society (☎ 2551-0300), GPO Box 3864, is dedicated to helping its members or visitors learn more about the history and culture of Hong Kong. The RAS organises lectures and field trips, operates a lending library and puts out publications of its own. The RAS was founded in London in 1823 and has branches in several Asian countries.

St John's Cathedral Counselling Service (☎ 2525-7202) provides help to all those in need.

If you're interested in doing business in Hong Kong, you might want to consult the Hong Kong Chamber of Commerce (☎ 2523-7177), 902 Swire House, 9-25 Chater Rd, Central. Perhaps even more to the point is the Hong Kong Trade Development Council (☎ 2584-4333; fax 2824-4333), 38th floor, Office Tower Convention Plaza, 1 Harbour Rd, Wan Chai, which also has a Web address (http://www.tdc.org.hk).

Know any government officials you want to get rid of? Call the Report Centre of the Independent Commission Against Corruption (ICAC) (☎ 2526-6366).

Other organisations which could do you some good include: the American Chamber of Commerce, 1030 Swire House, Central (☎ 2526-0165); the British Chamber of Commerce, Shui On Centre, Harbour Rd, Wan Chai (☎ 2824-2211); and the British Council, ground floor, Easey Commercial Building, 255 Hennessy Rd, Wan Chai (☎ 2879-5100).

DANGERS & ANNOYANCES
Rudeness

'Give us your money and get the hell out!' is the motto of many Hong Kong shopkeepers and hotel owners. The biggest complaint of travellers is that Hong Kong people are often appallingly rude, pushy and impatient. This impression partly results from the fact that most foreigners deal mainly with people in the tourist trade rather than the typical Hong Kong resident. However, this is a thin excuse. Sales clerks in Taiwan, Korea, Japan or the Philippines are generally cheerful and friendly, but this is seldom the case in Hong Kong.

You may encounter sales clerks who pretend you don't even exist – go into a supermarket and ask a clerk 'where can I find coffee' and they just pretend to have a hearing problem. In bookshops you may find clerks chatting away happily on the telephone to their friends, ignoring your query about a certain book. At other times, you get half way through your question when the clerk cuts you off abruptly with the reply 'out of stock'. The excuse that they don't speak English is also a thin one – even in countries where English is nonexistent, clerks who don't understand what you're saying just smile, laugh or shrug their shoulders. In Hong Kong, the reaction is more likely to be irritation and hostility. When they do smile, it usually means that they're Thais or Filipinos. The Hong Kong Tourist Association is aware of the problem, and has attempted to educate people to smile, say 'hello' and 'thank you'. Unfortunately, their efforts have been less than stunningly successful.

It's not just tourists who complain. Many native Hong Kongers also feel that their home town is far less friendly than it should be. Furthermore, Chinese from other parts of China feel that not only Hong Kong, but the

Cantonese in general are the least hospitable people in the entire country. This doesn't mean that you will never encounter an amiable person in Hong Kong. Within this sea of frowning faces, there are smiles. You might even meet someone who will be polite, helpful, friendly and generous, and not expect anything in return. Sadly, such experiences are all too rare, especially if you're a only a short-term visitor.

Crime

Despite Hong Kong's obvious prosperity and low unemployment rate, there are plenty of people who live on the margin of society and will resort to crime to earn a living. This includes Western travellers, some of whom arrive in Hong Kong totally broke with no prospects for employment. There have been disturbing reports of foreigners having had their backpacks burgled by their room mates in youth hostels. One fellow I know had his wallet, passport and travellers' cheques lifted during the two minutes he spent taking a shower at a hostel, and the only other people in the place were other travellers. So if something of yours is stolen, don't automatically assume that the guilty party is a local Chinese.

If you set a bag down and don't keep an eye on it, the whole thing may disappear in seconds. A number of people have had all their luggage nicked this way in the airport when they wandered off for a minute to use the toilets or change money. You probably wouldn't leave your bags unattended in a third-world country, but tourists just assume that it's OK in wealthy Hong Kong – unfortunately, it's not OK. The same principle applies in restaurants and pubs – if your bag doesn't accompany you to the toilet, don't expect to find it when you return. Again, if your bag is pinched this way the thief could well be a foreigner.

In a form of poetic justice, the colony's opium-based founding has rebounded and Hong Kong now has a serious dope problem. There are an estimated 38,000 drug addicts in Hong Kong, 90% of whom are male. While female addicts mostly finance their habit through prostitution, the men resort to more aggressive crimes such as pickpocketing, burglary and robbery. The effect on travellers is that you have to be careful with your valuables. However, it is generally safe to walk around at night, though it's best to stick to well-lit areas. Tourist districts like Tsim Sha Tsui are heavily patrolled by the police and there is little danger of violent crime, though pickpocketing can occur anywhere.

Scams

Hong Kong is a pretty prosperous place, so not surprisingly it attracts an increasing number of poverty-stricken workers in search of employment. Not all these people find the proverbial pot of gold at the end of the rainbow, and some turn to crime in order to survive.

Increasingly, we're getting letters from young, gullible travellers who have become the victims of these schemes. Typically, a young traveller is approached by a 'trustworthy' man or woman who offers 'friendship'. Under a pretext, the tourist is lured to the new friend's place and introduced to some more friends. Next, the traveller is offered a part in a 'get-rich-quick scheme'. At first they claim that the tourist need not provide any money. But later, more money is needed for the operation than was originally thought and they ask the tourist to hand over a hefty amount. Alone against a band of complete strangers, the tourist is likely to give money in a despairing attempt to stay alive.

LEGAL MATTERS

Most foreigners who get into legal trouble in Hong Kong are usually involved with drugs, either as a consumer or a seller. All forms of dope are highly illegal in Hong Kong. It makes no difference whether it's heroin, opium or marijuana – the law makes no distinction. If police or customs officials find dope or the equipment for smoking it in your possession, you can expect to be arrested immediately. Selling drugs can land you in serious hot water indeed, and being a foreigner doesn't get you off the hook.

Card Tricks

Watch out for the card scam, a common trick in Bangkok but now (in my experience) being perpetrated by Filipinos in Hong Kong. An extremely innocent looking Filipino struck up a casual conversation with me as I was awaiting a ferry at the Tsim Sha Tsui terminal. He asked where I was from, and when I said Vancouver, Canada he remarked on what a coincidence it was that his sister was going to study there. As she had never gone so far away before and just happened to be with him in Hong Kong, he asked if it might be possible for me to come back to his hotel and speak with her. Being a good sport, I agreed.

When we arrived at his guesthouse in the lovely Chungking Mansions, his 'sister' wasn't there but his 'brother', who just happened to be a croupier in Macau, was. Since we had some time to kill before the sister returned, the croupier was quite eager to show me some card tricks. We started with a basic tutorial on blackjack and then got onto the topic of how easy it was to cheat, with him using card-shark techniques and me playing along. He emphasised how these techniques were secret and how he might 'lose his job' if it were revealed that he had shown these methods to me.

The conversation, naturally, turned to the scam. Essentially he proposed that he could loan me some money and we would perpetrate the scheme at the casino in Macau then split the profits 50:50 afterwards. First, of course, we had to practise. He was quite eager for me to stick around to 7 pm, when an informal card game with his friends would be taking place. Unfortunately for him, it just so happened that I had to return to the hostel that night to meet a friend for dinner. I was, 'of course', still interested in the idea so I promised to meet him at the ferry terminal at 9 am the next day. This never did quite materialise as I 'slept in', missed the appointment and caught my evening flight out of Hong Kong.

Robert Meyer

Depending on the quantity found, the sentence for possession or smuggling of narcotics can be several years' jail in addition to large fines. China is likely to introduce the death penalty after 1997.

Under the British, Hong Kong had a legal system that included an independent judiciary and a Bill of Rights. China long ago announced that it would suspend the Bill of Rights, and the independent judiciary is unlikely to last under Chinese rule. Politics, expediency and outright bribery are likely to play a stronger rule in Hong Kong's future courts – this could work either for or against you if you find yourself accused of a crime.

At least for the moment, Hong Kong does have a Legal Aid Department (☎ 2537-7677), 24th to 27th floors, Queensway Government Offices, 66 Queensway, Admiralty.

BUSINESS HOURS

Office hours are Monday through Friday from 9 am to 5 pm, and on Saturday from 9 am to noon. Lunch hour is from 1 to 2 pm and many offices simply shut down and lock the door at this time. Banks are open Monday through Friday from 9 am to 4.30 pm and do not close for lunch – on Saturday they are open from 9 am to 12.30 pm.

Stores and restaurants that cater to the tourist trade keep longer hours, but almost nothing opens before 9 am. Even tourist related businesses shut down by 9 or 10 pm, and many will close for major holidays, especially Chinese Lunar New Year.

PUBLIC HOLIDAYS & SPECIAL EVENTS

Western and Chinese culture combine to create an interesting mix of holidays. Trying to determine the exact date of each is a bit tricky since there are two calendars in use in Hong Kong – the Gregorian solar calendar and the Chinese lunar calendar. The two calendars do not correspond exactly because a lunar month is only 28 days. To keep the two calendars in relative harmony, an extra month is added to the lunar calendar once every 30 months. The result is that the Lunar New Year, the most important Chinese holiday, can fall anywhere between 21 January and 28 February on the Gregorian calendar.

Many of the Chinese festivals go back hundreds, perhaps thousands, of years – their true origins are often lost in the mists of time. The reasons for each festival vary and you will generally find there are a couple of tales to choose from. The Hong Kong Tourist Association's free leaflet, *Chinese Festivals & Special Events*, will tell you the exact dates that festivals are celebrated in the current year.

It's likely that China will sooner or later abolish all Western-inspired holidays, and that some socialist holidays (like International Labour Day) will be added. The following list of holidays and festivals reflects the dispensation at the time we go to press.

New Year

The first week day in January is a public holiday.

Chinese Lunar New Year

The first day of the first moon is the Chinese Lunar New Year, also known as the Spring Festival. The first, second and third day of the first moon are public holidays. Almost everything closes but you won't starve in the tourist areas.

This is a festival for the family, with little for the visitor to see except a fireworks display on New Year's Eve. Starting the New Year well is said to ensure good fortune for the entire year. Therefore, houses are cleaned, debts paid off and feuds, no matter how bitter, are ended – even if it's only for the day. Pictures of gods are pasted around the front doors of houses to scare off bad spirits, along with messages of welcome on red paper to encourage the good ones.

By tradition, everyone asks for double wages. The garbage collector, the milkman and so on get *lai see* (lucky money) in red envelopes as tips – good reasons for the traditional Chinese Lunar New Year greeting *kung hey fat choi* which literally means 'good wishes, good fortune'.

It costs double to get your hair cut in the week leading up to the Chinese Lunar New Year. Even cinemas put their prices up. It's not the time to go to China, as hordes of Hong Kong people cram the trains and every other form of transport to get there.

It is worth seeing the huge flower fairs where, on Chinese New Year's Eve, the Chinese buy lucky peach blossoms, kumquat trees and narcissi from the hundreds of flower sellers. Victoria Park in Causeway Bay, Hong Kong Island, is the place to go for this, although it's jam-packed. Other than that, there isn't

much else to see at Chinese Lunar New Year. You might catch a lion dance in a street, but if not, you will certainly see one specially laid on in the top tourist hotels.

The first day of the first moon usually falls at the end of January or the beginning of February. For the remainder of this century, the schedule is: 7 February 1997, 28 January 1998, 16 February 1999 and 5 February 2000.

Lantern Festival

Also known by its Chinese name *Yuen Siu*, this is not a public holiday but is more interesting than the Chinese Lunar New Year. At the end of the Chinese New Year celebrations, customarily the 15th day of the first moon (middle or end of February), lanterns in traditional designs are lit in homes, restaurants and temples. Out in the residential areas, you'll see people carrying lanterns through the streets. The Lantern Festival is also a holiday for lovers.

Easter

In Hong Kong, Easter is a three-day public holiday starting from Good Friday and running through Easter Sunday. Although many Westerners don't realise it, the date of Easter is fixed by the lunar calendar, falling somewhere in March or April. It seems unlikely that Easter will survive much longer as a public holiday in Hong Kong.

Ching Ming

Ching Ming is very much a family affair. It is a time for visiting graves, traditionally to call up ancestors to ask if they are satisfied with their descendants. Graves are cleaned and food and wine left for the spirits, while incense and paper money are burned for the dead. Some people follow the custom of pasting long strips of red and white paper to the graves to indicate that the rituals have been performed. The festival is thought to have its origins during the Han period, about 2000 years ago, when ancestors' tombs were swept, washed and repaired.

Ching Ming is a public holiday and is not a particularly good time to visit Hong Kong, though not nearly so bad as the Chinese

Lunar New Year. Many people take a three-or four-day holiday. Banks and many other businesses close for Ching Ming, public transport is extremely crowded and the border crossing into China turns host to a near riot.

Ching Ming is traditionally celebrated at the beginning of the third moon, but the calendar has been slightly adjusted so that it always falls during the first week of April.

Tin Hau Festival

Although it's not a public holiday, this is one of Hong Kong's most colourful occasions. Tin Hau, patroness of fishing people, is one of the colony's most popular goddesses.

Junks are decorated with flags and sail in long rows to Tin Hau temples around the colony to pray for clear skies and good catches. Often her image is taken from the temple and paraded through the streets. Shrines from the junks are carried to the shore to be blessed by Taoist priests.

The best place to see the festival and the fortune telling, lion dances and Chinese opera that follow is at the site of Tin Hau's best-known temple, the Tai Miu Temple in Joss House Bay. It's not accessible by road and is not on the normal ferry route, but at festival time the ferry company puts on excursion trips which are usually packed.

Another main Tin Hau temple is at Sok Kwu Wan on Lamma Island. The Tin Hau temple at Stanley on the south coast of Hong Kong Island was built in 1767 and is said to be the oldest building in Hong Kong.

The Tin Hau Festival is traditionally held on the 23rd day of the third moon, and will fall on the following dates: 29 April 1997, 19 April 1998, 8 May 1999 and 27 April 2000.

Cheung Chau Bun Festival

The Bun Festival of Tai Chiu is held in May on Cheung Chau Island, traditionally on the sixth day of the fourth moon. Precise dates are decided by village elders on the island about three weeks before it starts. A Taoist festival, it is one of the festival calendar highlights, and there are three or four days of religious observances.

While not a public holiday, it is definitely worth getting to Cheung Chau for. Festival information is in the Outlying Islands chapter.

Birthday of Lord Buddha

Also referred to as the Bathing of Lord Buddha, this is not a public holiday but can still be quite interesting. The festival is celebrated on the eighth day of the fourth moon. For the remainder of this century it will fall on the following dates: 14 May 1997, 3 May 1998, 22 May 1999 and 11 May 2000.

Like most Buddhist festivals, it's rather more sedate than Taoist celebrations. The Buddha's statue is taken from monasteries and temples and ceremoniously bathed in water scented with sandalwood, ambergris (a waxy substance secreted from the intestine of a sperm whale and often found floating in the sea), garu wood, turmeric and aloes (a drug used for clearing the bowels, made from the fleshy, spiny-toothed leaves of the aloe tree). The mixture is drunk by the faithful, who believe it has great curative powers.

While Lantau Island is the best place to observe this event because of its many Buddhist monasteries, most people visit only Po Lin, the largest and best known of them. Extra ferries operate for the crowds.

The New Territories has several Buddhist temples worth visiting at this time, such as the Ten Thousand Buddhas Monastery in Sha Tin, or the Miu Fat Monastery at Lam Tei.

Dragon Boat Festival

A main public holiday, *Tuen Ng* – Double Fifth (fifth day, fifth moon) or the Dragon Boat Festival – is normally held in June. It's a lot of fun despite the fact that it commemorates the sad tale of Chu Yuan, a 3rd-century BC poet-statesman who hurled himself into the Mi Lo River in Hunan Province to protest against the corrupt government. The people who lived on the banks of the river raced to the scene in their boats in an attempt to save him but were too late. Not unmindful of his sacrifice, the people later threw dumplings into the water to keep the hungry fish away from his body.

Traditional rice dumplings are still eaten in memory of the event and dragon-boat races are held in Hong Kong, Kowloon and the Outlying Islands. See the races at Shau Kei Wan, Aberdeen, Yau Ma Tei, Tai Po and Stanley, and on Lantau and Cheung Chau Islands. The boats are rowed by teams from Hong Kong's sports and social clubs. International dragon-boat races are held at Yau Ma Tei.

This lunar holiday will fall on the following dates: 9 June 1997, 28 June 1998, 18 June 1999 and 6 June 2000.

Queen's Birthday
This public holiday is normally held on a Saturday in June. The Monday after is also a public holiday. Expect this holiday to be axed after 1997.

Birthday of Lu Pan, Master Builder
Legends say that Lu Pan was a real person, born around 507 BC and later deified. A master architect, magician, engineer, inventor and designer, Lu Pan is worshipped by anyone connected with the building trade. Ceremonies sponsored by the builders' guilds are held at Lu Pan Temple in Kennedy Town, Hong Kong Island. The celebration occurs around mid- to late-July. It's a minor holiday.

Maidens' Festival
This is a minor holiday and you might not even notice anything special taking place. Also known as the Seven Sisters Festival, this celebration for girls and young lovers is held on the seventh day of the seventh moon (about mid-August).

It has its origins in an ancient Chinese story about two celestial lovers, Chien Niu the cowherd and Chih Nu the spinner and weaver. One version says that they became so engrossed in each other that they forgot their work. As a punishment for this, the Queen of Heaven decided that they should be separated by being placed on either side of a river which she cut through the heavens

with her hairpin. The King of Heaven took pity on the lovers and said they could meet once a year – but provided no bridge across the river. So magpies (regarded as birds of good omen) flocked together, spread their wings and formed a bridge so the lovers could be reunited.

At midnight on the day of this festival prayers are offered by unmarried girls and young men to Chien Niu and Chih Nu. Prayers are also directed to Chih Nu's six sisters, who appear in another version of the story. The main offerings made to the seven sisters are cosmetics and flowers.

Ghost Month
On the first day of the seventh moon (late August or early September), the gates of hell are opened and 'hungry ghosts' are freed for two weeks to walk the earth. Hungry ghosts are the spirits of those who were unloved, abandoned or forgotten by the family, or suffered a violent death. On the 14th day, called the Yue Lan Festival, hungry ghosts receive offerings of food from the living before returning down below.

Paper cars, paper houses and paper money are burnt, and then become the property of the ghosts.

People whose relatives suffered a violent death are particularly concerned to placate the spirits. Many people will not swim, travel, get married, move house or indulge in other risky activities during this time.

The ghost month is an excellent time to visit Taoist temples in Hong Kong, as they are usually packed with worshippers burning incense and making offerings. There are also lots of Cantonese opera performances – presumably to give the ghosts one good night out before they go back down below for another year. This is not a public holiday, so there aren't any problems with crowded buses, trains and hotels.

Liberation Day
Celebrated on the last Monday in August, this public holiday commemorates the liberation of Hong Kong from Japan after World

War II. The preceding Saturday is also a public holiday.

Mid-Autumn Moon Festival

This festival is held in September, on the 15th night of the eighth moon. Because it begins at night, the day after is a public holiday.

Although the observance of the moon is thought to date back to much earlier times, today the festival recalls an uprising against the Mongols in the 14th century when plans for the revolution were passed around in cakes.

Moon cakes are still eaten and there are many varieties – all delicious. The various fillings include coconut, dates, nuts, lotus, sesame seeds and sometimes an egg.

Everyone heads for the hilltops, where they light special lanterns with candles inside and watch the moon rise. The Peak Tram is crammed, as is all transport to the New Territories, where hillsides abound. For young couples, it's a romantic holiday – a time to be together and watch the moon.

The Mid-Autumn festival will be celebrated on the following dates: 16 September 1997, 5 October 1998, 24 September 1999 and 12 September 2000.

Birthday of Confucius

Confucius' birthday is in early October and religious observances are held by the Confucian Society in the Confucius Temple at Causeway Bay. It's a minor holiday that usually passes unnoticed by most Hong Kongers.

Cheung Yeung Festival

While not an especially interesting occasion, the Cheung Yeung Festival is a public holiday.

The story goes that back in the Eastern Han dynasty (in the first two centuries AD), an old soothsayer advised a man to take his family away to a high place for 24 hours to avoid disaster. When the man returned to his village he found every living thing had been destroyed and only he and his family had survived. Many people head for the high

spots again to remember the old man's advice. The Cheung Yeung Festival is held in mid- to late October.

Christmas & Boxing Day

Christmas (25 December) and the day after (Boxing Day) are, of course, public holidays. Again, both could possibly be axed by China after 1997.

OTHER EVENTS

There are literally hundreds of cultural and special-interest events throughout the year. The HKTA publishes a complete schedule every month. Exact dates vary from year to year, so if you want to time your visit to coincide with a particular event, it would be wise to contact the HKTA beforehand. A brief rundown of important annual events includes:

HK Arts Festival – An assortment of exhibitions and shows, usually held in January.

Orienteering Competition – Sponsored by the Urban Council, this event is usually staged in January in Tai Tam Country Park.

HK Festival Fringe – The Fringe Club supports budding artists and performers from Hong Kong and elsewhere. This three-week festival occurs from late January to February.

HK Golf Open – This is held at the Royal Hong Kong Golf Club, usually in February.

HK International Marathon – Organised by the Hong Kong Amateur Athletic Association, this major event is held in Sha Tin, usually in March.

HK Food Festival – Sponsored by the HKTA and usually held in March.

HK International Film Festival – Organised by the Urban Council, this event usually occurs in March or April.

HK International Handball Invitation Tournament – Organised by the Hong Kong Amateur Handball Association, this event is in March or April.

Sotheby's Auction – This usually occurs in April.

HK Computer Expo – This takes place in May.

International Dragon Boat Festival – Usually falling in June, this international festival is usually held the week after the Chinese dragon-boat races.

Davis Cup – This tennis tournament is usually held in July.

International Arts Carnival – This unusual summer festival promotes performances by children's groups. The carnival usually falls in July or August.

Asian Regatta – Organised by the Hong Kong Yachting Association, this event usually occurs in October.

Festival of Asian Arts – This is one of Asia's major international events, attracting performers from Australia as well as nearby countries. This festival usually occurs in October or November.

ACTIVITIES

Hong Kong may not have downhill skiing, but the city offers plenty of ways to keep fit and have fun at the same time.

Anyone who is serious about sports should contact the South China Athletic Association (☎ 2577-6932; fax 2890-9304), 88 Caroline Hill Rd, Causeway Bay, Hong Kong Island. The SCAA has numerous indoor facilities for bowling, tennis, squash, ping pong, gymnastics, fencing, yoga, judo, karate, billiards and dancing. Outdoor activities include golf and there is also a women's activities section. Membership is cheap and a discounted short-term membership is available for visitors.

Another excellent place is the Hong Kong Amateur Athletic Association (☎ 2574-6845; fax 2838-4959), room 913, Queen Elizabeth Stadium, 18 Oi Kwan Rd, Wan Chai. All sorts of sports clubs have activities here or hold members' meetings.

Hong Kong's largest sporting facility is the Jubilee Sports Centre (☎ 2605-1212), also known as the Hong Kong Sports Institute. It's near Fo Tan KCR station, Sha Tin, New Territories. This one is mainly Chinese and gwailos are in the minority, but it's a good place to meet locals who might have the same interests as you.

Bowling

Some of the best facilities are at the South China Athletic Association (☎ 2577-6932), 88 Caroline Hill Rd, Causeway Bay. Also on Hong Kong Island is Fourseas Bowling Centre (☎ 2567-0703), Cityplaza Shopping Centre, Tai Koo Shing MTR station.

In Kowloon, bowling alleys tend to be located in the backwaters. One of the most accessible is Top Bowling (☎ 2334-5022), Basement, Site II, Whampoa Gardens, Hung Hom. You can also try the Telford Bowling

Centre (☎ 2755-0200), Telford Gardens, near Kowloon Bay MTR station. Another obscure place is the Mei Foo Sun Chuen Bowling Centre (☎ 2742-5911), 1st floor, 95C Broadway St, Lai Chi Kok.

Billiards & Snooker

The Chinese are crazy about these games, but most facilities are rather makeshift and in places where gwailos rarely go. Probably the most accessible venues are in Tsim Sha Tsui East, and include the Peninsula Billiards Club (☎ 2739-0638), 3rd floor, Peninsula Centre, and the Castle Billiards Club (☎ 2367-9071), Houston Centre.

In Central you can check out the Olympic Billiard Association (☎ 2815-0456), Hollywood Commercial Centre, Hollywood Rd & Old Bailey St. In Wan Chai, there are two good places, Jim Mei White Snooker (☎ 2833-6628), 339 Jaffe Rd, and Winsor Billiard Company (☎ 2575-5505), 10 Canal Rd West. In Causeway Bay there is Kent Billiard & Snooker Association (☎ 2833-5665), Elizabeth House, Jaffe Rd and Percival St. In Quarry Bay you can find Far East Billiards & Snooker City (☎ 2565-9727), 969 King's Rd.

If you make it to the Outlying Islands, you can play at the Cheung Chau Billiards Association (☎ 2981-3576), 95 Hoi Pong Rd, Cheung Chau.

Canoeing

To find enthusiasts of this sport, contact the Canoe Union (☎ 2572-7008; fax 2838-9037), room 1010, Queen Elizabeth Stadium, 18 Oi Kwan Rd, Wan Chai. Canoeing facilities are available through the Tai Mei Tuk Water Sports Centre (☎ 2665-3591), Regional Council, Tai Mei Tuk, Tai Po, New Territories. You can also enquire at the Wong Shek Water Sports Centre (☎ 2328-2370), Wong Shek Pier, Sai Kung, New Territories. Alternatively, there is the Chong Hing Water Sports Centre (☎ 2792-6810), West Sea Coffer Dam, High Island Reservoir, Sai Kung, New Territories.

Computer Clubs & BBSs

Hong Kong's economic prosperity, low-priced computer equipment and the large

English-speaking expatriate community all make this an ideal place for computer hobbyists. You can seek the company of fellow computer freaks by joining a computer club, or plug in a modem and dial up an electronic bulletin board system (BBS).

Probably the first thing you should do is visit a bookshop and purchase a copy of *The Datafile*, Hong Kong's only locally produced computer magazine (at least in English). In the back is a listing of all the English-language Hong Kong BBS phone numbers. There are also Chinese BBSs around, but you need Chinese software and the ability to read it if this option is to be any use at all. Subscriptions to *The Datafile* cost HK$100 annually, but that could change so ring them up (☎ 2791-2446) or write (PO Box 127, Sai Kung). The magazine also operates the Houston BBS (☎ 2735-0613).

Like BBSs, computer clubs come and go, but the HKTA publication *Associations & Societies in Hong Kong* also lists a few. One of the biggest is the Computer Club of Hong Kong (☎ 2308-1021; fax 2308-1023), room 1408, Join-In Commercial Centre, 33 Lai Chi Kok Rd, Mong Kok, Kowloon. Another is the Hong Kong Computer Society (☎ 2834-2228; fax 2834-3003), unit D, 1st floor, Luckifast Building, 1 Stone Nullah Lane, Wan Chai, and with a modem you can contact BISSIG, their BBS (☎ 2572-3145).

The *South China Morning Post* has a small computer section every Tuesday and this can be another source of information about activities for computer buffs.

Cricket

Just north of Deepwater Bay is the Hong Kong Cricket Club (☎ 2574-6266), 137 Wong Nai Chung Gap Rd, Hong Kong Island. The scenery from the playing fields is stunning.

On the other side of Victoria Harbour is the Kowloon Cricket Club (☎ 2367-4141), 10 Cox's Rd, Yau Ma Tei.

Additional information may be obtained by contacting the Hong Kong Cricket Association (☎ 2859-2414; fax 2559-7528), c/o School of Professional & Continuing Educa-

tion, University of Hong Kong, Pok Fu Lam Rd, Hong Kong Island.

Cycling

There are bicycle paths in the New Territories, mostly around Tolo Harbour. The paths run from Sha Tin to Tai Po and continue up to Tai Mei Tuk. You can rent cycles in these three places, but it's very crowded on weekends. On a week day you may have the paths to yourself.

Bicycle rentals are also available at Shek O on Hong Kong Island, and Mui Wo on Lantau Island.

The *Hong Kong Cycling Association* (☎ 2573-3861; fax 2834-3715) can be contacted at room 1013, Queen Elizabeth Stadium, 18 Oi Kwan Rd, Wan Chai. Or try the *Hong Kong Cyclist Club* (☎ 2788-3898; fax 2788-0093), shop 17, Fu Chak House, Chak On Estate, Sham Shui Po, Kowloon.

Fishing

Sports fishing from small-sized yachts is a popular activity for resident gwailos. To organise a trip, contact the Hong Kong Amateur Fishing Society (☎ 2730-0442), Lucky House, 15th floor, flat D, 18-24 Jordan Rd, Yau Ma Tei, Kowloon.

While there are virtually no restrictions on sea fishing, it's a different story with fishing at freshwater reservoirs. There are restrictions on the quantity and size of fish taken from reservoirs, and the fishing season is from September through March. A licence is required, and can be obtained from the Water Authority (☎ 2824-5000) in Causeway Bay. Those applying for a licence must be at least 14 years old.

Fitness Centres

If pumping iron, sauna, aerobics and other such activities are what you need, you can try The Gym (☎ 2877-8337), 18th floor, Melbourne Plaza, 33 Queen's Rd, Central.

Golf

There are four golf courses in Hong Kong. On weekends they are crowded and you pay more. The Royal Hong Kong Golf Club

(RHKGC) permits visitors, but you must pay green fees and hire equipment. The RHKGC has two venues: the less expensive one is the 9-hole course at Deepwater Bay (☎ 2812-7070) on the south side of Hong Kong Island. For visitors playing 18 holes, the fee is HK$350, or HK$450 for the whole day. Visitors accompanied by a member are charged HK$130 on weekdays, rising to HK$225 on weekends. Operating hours are 9.30 am to 2.30 pm from May to August, and 9.30 am to 1.30 pm from September to April.

The RHKGC operates a more expensive course at Fanling (☎ 2670-1211) in the New Territories. For 18 holes, green fees are HK$850 for Hong Kong residents (non-members), or HK$1100 for overseas visitors. However, overseas visitors accompanied by a member can play for HK$250 on weekdays, or HK$650 on weekends. The course is open from 7.30 am to 6 pm.

The Discovery Bay Golf Club (☎ 2987-7271) on Lantau Island offers impressive mountain and coastal scenery. The charge for 18 holes is HK$700 on week days (8 am until dusk) or HK$1500 on weekends (7.30 am until dusk). Visitors accompanied by a member are charged HK$280 on weekdays, HK$850 on weekends.

The Clearwater Bay Golf & Country Club (☎ 2719-5936) is on the Sai Kung Peninsula in the New Territories. Overseas visitors are charged HK$1100, but those with a Hong Kong ID card pay HK$850. Guests accompanied by a member are charged HK$300 on weekdays, or HK$600 on weekends.

Handball
You can play at the Indoor Handball Court in Kowloon Park in Tsim Sha Tsui, or at Victoria Park in Causeway Bay. Otherwise, contact the Handball Association (☎ 2574-6934; fax 2834-6937), room 911, Queen Elizabeth Stadium, 18 Oi Kwan Rd, Wan Chai.

Hiking
Although trekking in Hong Kong is less challenging than the Nepal Himalaya, some basic equipment is necessary. Most important is a full water bottle. Other useful items include food, a rainsuit, sun hat, toilet paper, maps and compass. Boots are not really necessary – indeed, some people suffer lower back pain after hiking in heavy boots. The best footwear is generally a good pair of running shoes. If you're prone to getting blisters, take some plaster. Of course, just how much equipment you decide to drag along depends on how far you plan to walk.

Good maps will save you a lot of time and trouble. Check out the *Countryside* series of maps, available from the Government Publications Centre in the Government Offices Building, 66 Queensway, Admiralty.

Track conditions vary widely – not all are concreted paths. *Countryside* maps may describe a track as 'unmaintained/impassable'. This term may mean as little as the path is not concreted, to as much as the path is genuinely difficult or impossible to locate.

Serious walkers should remember that the high humidity during spring and summer is tiring. November through March are the best months for strenuous treks. At high elevations, like at the youth hostel at Ngong Ping on Lantau, it can get very cold so it's essential to bring warm clothes and even a down sleeping bag if you're staying the night.

The sun can be merciless, so a hat and/or UV lotion are essential. There is little shade here because there are few trees on the slopes of Hong Kong's mountains. One effect of this is that landslides still occur during heavy rainstorms, posing another hazard to hikers.

Very few hiking areas in Hong Kong are dangerous, but there have been several injuries and some deaths. The victims are mostly inexperienced walkers taking foolish risks. It is wise to stick to the established trails and heed the signs saying 'Steep and Seasonally Overgrown' or 'Firing Range'.

Snakes are rarely encountered, and your best way of avoiding them is to stick to trails and avoid walking through dense undergrowth. If you see a snake, the best thing to do is to walk away from it. Most snakes are shy of creatures larger than themselves, including humans, and will try to avoid you. However, most snakes will attack when cornered. Hikers get bitten when they accidentally step on a snake or attempt to beat the creature with a stick.

Mosquitoes are a nuisance, so a good mosquito repellent is essential. Autan and Off! are popular brands of repellent available from Hong Kong drugstores. Mosquito coils (incense) are also effective when you're resting, but should not be used inside a tent or any other enclosed area as they are a fire hazard and the smoke contains a poison that isn't particularly good for your lungs.

Hiking in Hong Kong has become so popular that many trails are crowded on weekends, so try to schedule your walks during weekdays. The four longest trails are (in descending order): the MacLehose Trail (New Territories), Wilson Trail (Hong Kong Island & New Territories), Lantau Trail (Lantau Island) and the Hong Kong Trail (Hong Kong Island). See the relevant chapters in this book for details.

To contact hiking clubs, call the Federation of Hong Kong Hiking & Outdoor Activities Groups (☎ 2720-4042), PO Box 79435, Mong Kok Post Office, Mong Kok, Kowloon. More serious climbers should perhaps try the Mountaineering Association (☎ 2391-6892), room 1308, Argyle Centre, Phase I, 688 Nathan Rd, Mong Kok, Kowloon; or the Mountaineering Union (☎ 2747-7003; fax 2770-7115), PO Box 70837, Kowloon Central Post Office, Kowloon.

Horseback Riding

Hong Kong's size limits opportunities for horseback riding. The Hong Kong Riding Union (☎ 2762-0810), 76 Waterloo Rd, Kowloon Tong, organises rides in the New Territories. You can also call the Hong Kong Equestrian Centre (☎ 2607-3131), 7½ Miles Tai Po Rd, New Territories. Limited riding is possible at the Lantau Tea Gardens (☎ 2985-5718) at Ngong Ping on Lantau Island. On Hong Kong Island, riding lessons are available at the Pok Fu Lam Riding School (☎ 2550-1059, 2550-1359), 75 Pok Fu Lam Reservoir Rd.

The clubs and riding schools organise competitions, and if you want to participate

then apply one or two months in advance. Some major events include the Mini-Hunter Trials, Lo Wu Spring Show and Lo Wu Autumn Show.

Karting

The big event of the year for karting enthusiasts is the Hong Kong Kart Grand Prix, held in late November or early December. For more details you can contact the Hong Kong Kart Club (☎ 2574-7466), 18th floor, Caltex House, 258 Hennessy Rd, Wan Chai.

Lawn Bowling

Victoria Park in Causeway Bay has facilities for lawn bowling. These are open on week days in the afternoon only, but all day on weekends. There is a Lawn Bowls Association (☎ 2891-5156; fax 2838-2416), GPO Box 1823, Central. The same phone and fax numbers are shared by the Ladies Lawn Bowls Association, but there is a different mailing address (GPO Box 7387, Central).

Martial Arts

Kungfu Many forms of martial arts *(wushu)* were developed in East Asia, but most are based on Chinese kungfu (also spelt *gongfu*). For more information try the following associations:

Judo Association
    room 902, Queen Elizabeth Stadium,
    18 Oi Kwan Rd, Wan Chai
    (☎ 2891-3879; fax 2834-8935)
Karatedo Association
    room 1006, Queen Elizabeth Stadium,
    18 Oi Kwan Rd, Wan Chai
    (☎ 2891-9705; fax 2834-6264)
Taekwondo Association
    room 1004, Queen Elizabeth Stadium,
    18 Oi Kwan Rd, Wan Chai
    (☎ 2891-2036, 2891-2104)
South China Athletic Association
    88 Caroline Hill Rd, Causeway Bay
    (☎ 2577-6932; fax 2890-9304)
YMCA
    Salisbury Rd, Tsim Sha Tsui (☎ 2369-2211)

Outward Bound

The Outward Bound School (☎ 2792-4333, 2792-0055) teaches wilderness survival, but also organises orienteering courses, camping and barbecues. It's geared towards helping young adults build character and self-esteem, but the organisation is not limited to teenagers. The address is Tai Mong Tsai, New Territories.

Parachuting

It's not a very economical sport, but you can't beat it for thrills. If you get your jollies by diving out of aircraft, contact the Hong Kong Parachute Club (☎ 2891-5447; fax 2891-5481), flat 4, block A, 18th floor, Grandview Towers, 126 Kennedy Rd, Hong Kong Island.

Paragliding

If floating on air appeals to you, the place to contact is the Hong Kong Paragliding Association (☎ 2803-2779). The club has three sites for regular meets: Big Wave Bay on Hong Kong Island, nearby Dragon's Back at Shek O and Sunset Peak on Lantau Island. A four-day training course is required for beginners, which costs HK$1500. This course can be spread out over a long period – up to a whole year – and once it is completed you're qualified to use the three sites. The training spot for beginners is none of the foregoing, but rather at Pai Mai Tuk, Tai Po, in the New Territories.

Running

If you'd like a morning jog with spectacular views, nothing beats the path around Victoria Peak on Harlech and Lugard Rds. Part of this is a 'fitness trail' with various exercise machines (parallel bars and the like). Almost as spectacular is the jog along Bowen Rd, which is closed to traffic and runs in an east-west direction in the hills above Wan Chai. As long as there are no horse races at the time, the racecourse at Happy Valley is an excellent place to run. There is also a running track in Victoria Park in Causeway Bay.

On the Kowloon side, a popular place to run is the Promenade which runs along the waterfront in Tsim Sha Tsui East. It's not a

very long run, but the views are good and it's close to many of the hotels.

The Hong Kong International Marathon is held on the second day of the Chinese Lunar New Year. This has become a cross-border event and part of the course passes through China. The Coast of China Marathon is held in March. Contact the HKTA for more information on upcoming marathons.

If you like easy runs followed by beer and good company, consider joining Hash House Harriers (☎ 2376-2299; fax 2813-6517), 3rd floor, 74 Chung Hom Kok Rd, Stanley, Hong Kong Island. You do not need to be in particularly good shape to participate. The Hash is an international organisation geared towards young people and the young at heart.

If you're looking for folks to run with, contact the Distance Runners Club (☎ 2829-6254; fax 2824-1220), GPO Box 10368. There is a Ladies Road Runners Club (☎ 2317-5933; fax 2317-5920), PO Box 20613, Hennessy Rd Post Office, Wan Chai.

There is a running clinic every Thursday morning from 7 to 8.30 am. For information, call the Adventist Hospital (☎ 2574-6211 ext 777).

If you take running seriously, contact the Triathlon Association (☎ 2609-2972; fax 2609-2958), room 4B, 18th floor, block E, Wah Lok Industrial Centre, 37-41 Shan Mei St, Fo Tan, Sha Tin, New Territories.

Sauna & Massage

The art of massage has a long history in China. Sauna baths are popular in Hong Kong and many bathhouses offer a good massage service. During the chilly winter season there is probably no better way to relax. The *legitimate* places are suitable for both men and women. The saunas tend to be crowded in the evenings. Prices typically range from around HK$100 to HK$170 per hour, but ask first. The high-priced places are mainly found in Tsim Sha Tsui East, but you can do better than this.

Many less respectable establishments are for men only and offer 'additional services'. The legitimate saunas are listed in the *Yellow Pages* under Baths; questionable ones are listed under Massage or Escort. The advertisements make interesting reading even if you never make use of their services.

The most incredible sauna is Sunny Paradise (☎ 2831-0123), 339-347 Lockhart Rd, Wan Chai. Services include saunas, jacuzzis and massage for both males and females. Another very good one in the same area is Hong Kong Sauna (☎ 2834-7230), 389 Jaffe Rd, Wan Chai. Also consider New Paradise Health Club (☎ 2574-8807), 416 Lockhart Rd, Wan Chai. Over in Kowloon, another reputable establishment is Crystal Spa (☎ 2722-6600), Basement 2, Harbour Crystal Centre, 100 Granville Rd, Tsim Sha Tsui. In pricey Tsim Sha Tsui East there's VIP Sauna (☎ 2311-2288), 13th floor, Autoplaza, 65 Mody Rd.

Scuba Diving

Diving enthusiasts should contact the Underwater Association (☎ 2572-3792; fax 2849-6499), room 910, Queen Elizabeth Stadium, 18 Oi Kwan Rd, Wan Chai. An alternative is the Sea Dragons Skindiving Club (☎ 2891-2113), GPO Box 10014, Hong Kong.

Bunn's Diving Equipment (☎ 2572-1629), ground floor, shop E & G, Kwong Sang Hong Building, 188 Wan Chai Rd, Wan Chai, organises dives every Sunday from 9 am to 4.30 pm at a cost of HK$280. Bunn's (☎ 2380-5344) also has another branch on the ground floor, 217 Sai Yee St, Mong Kok.

Skating

One of the best ice skating rinks in Hong Kong is on the first floor of Cityplaza-Two (☎ 2885-4697), Cityplaza Shopping Centre, 18 Tai Koo Shing Rd, Quarry Bay. The easiest way to get there is to take the MTR to Tai Koo station.

On the Kowloon side, the best rink is Whampoa Super Ice (☎ 2774-4899) in basement two of the Whampoa Gardens Shopping Complex in Hung Hom. Further afield is Riviera Ice Chalet (☎ 2407-1100), 3rd floor, Riviera Plaza, 28 Wing Shun St, Tsuen Wan, New Territories.

If you are interested in ice dancing or ice hockey, contact the Hong Kong Ice Activities Association (☎ 2827-5033; fax 2827-2698), room B8, 9th floor, Causeway Centre, 28 Harbour Rd, Wan Chai. This is also the location of the Ice Dance Union and Ice Hockey Association.

If you prefer wheels to blades, Rollerworld at Cityplaza Shopping Centre at Quarry Bay can accommodate you. There's also a roller rink in Telford Gardens shopping mall, next to Kowloon Bay MTR station.

The Hong Kong Amateur Roller Skating Association (☎ 2887-0296; fax 2887-9646) is at Braemar Hill Mansions, Sports Centre, 29 Braemar Hill Rd, North Point.

Soccer

Soccer has caught the imagination of the Chinese, so competition for playing fields is keen. There isn't much trouble getting a soccer pitch during working hours, but forget it on weekends, holidays or during the evening.

If you want to get serious about competing in matches, contact the Football Association (☎ 2712-9122; fax 2760-4303), 55 Fat Kwong St, Ho Man Tin, Kowloon. The association has a women's division.

There are over 130 soccer pitches in Hong Kong, and you can call the Urban Services Department to locate the ones nearest to you. The Urban Services Department is itself segmented into neighbourhood divisions, so look in the Business Telephone Directory to find the branch relevant to your area. Some notable soccer pitches include:

Hong Kong Island:
    Blake Garden, Po Hing Fong, Sai Ying Pun
    King George V Park, Hospital Rd, Sai Ying Pun
Kowloon:
    Kowloon Park, Tsim Sha Tsui
    Kowloon Tsai Park, La Salle Rd, Shek Kip Mei
    MacPherson Playground, Sai Yee St, Mong Kok
    Morse Park, Fung Mo St, Wong Tai Sin
Wan Chai:
    Southern Playground, Hennessy Rd
Causeway Bay:
    Victoria Park

Squash

There are about 600 public squash courts in Hong Kong, but they become totally packed-out in the evening or on holidays. The most modern facilities are to be found at the Hong Kong Squash Centre (☎ 2869-0611), 23 Cotton Tree Drive, Central, next to Hong Kong Park. Book in advance. This is also the home of the Hong Kong Squash Rackets Association, which has done much to promote the sport. There are also squash courts in the Queen Elizabeth Stadium, Wan Chai. In the New Territories, you can play squash at the Jubilee Sports Centre (☎ 2605-1212), near Fo Tan KCR station, Sha Tin.

Swimming

Except for Kowloon and the north side of Hong Kong Island, there are good beaches throughout the area. The most accessible are on the south side of Hong Kong Island but some of these are becoming increasingly polluted. The best beaches can be found on the Outlying Islands and in the New Territories. See those chapters for details. The longest beach in Hong Kong is Cheung Sha on Lantau Island.

There is an official swimming season from 1 April to 31 October. At this time, the 42 gazetted public beaches in Hong Kong are staffed with lifeguards. When the swimming season is officially declared finished, the beaches become deserted no matter how hot the weather.

Conversely, from the first day of the official swimming season until the last, expect the beaches to be chock-a-block on weekends and holidays. On weekdays, it's not bad at all. During the official season, all beaches controlled by the Urban Council or the Urban Services Department are patrolled by lifeguards. A red flag means the water is too rough for swimming and a blue flag means it's unsafe for children and weak swimmers. At most of the beaches you will find toilets, showers, changing rooms, refreshment stalls and sometimes restaurants. The usual life-saving hours are from 9 am to 6 pm on week days, but are extended to 7 pm on weekends during July and August.

Hong Kong's Urban Council operates 13 public swimming pools. During school-term week days the pools are nearly deserted. There's an excellent pool in Kowloon Park, Tsim Sha Tsui, and Victoria Park, Causeway Bay.

There's a fine indoor pool at Morrison Hill School in Wan Chai, which is five minutes by foot from the British Council (see Wan Chai map). There's a great outdoor pool at the Sai Kung Sports Centre, Sai Kung town, New Territories.

Waterworld, next to Ocean Park in Aberdeen, offers outdoor pools and water slides.

You can contact the Amateur Swimming Association (☎ 2572-8594) at room 1003, Queen Elizabeth Stadium, 18 Oi Kwan Rd, Wan Chai. Or try the Winter Swimming Association, 10th floor, Success Commercial Building, 245 Hennessy Rd, Wan Chai (☎ 2511-8363).

Table Tennis & Badminton

It's widely acknowledged that the Chinese are the best table tennis players in the world. It's not so widely known that they are also badminton enthusiasts. Contact the Badminton Association (☎ 2838-4066), Queen Elizabeth Stadium, 18 Oi Kwan Rd, Wan Chai. There are similar facilities at the South China Athletic Association (☎ 2577-6932), 88 Caroline Hill Rd, Causeway Bay. You can also find facilities at the Aberdeen Indoor Games Hall (☎ 2553-6663), 168 Wong Chuk Hang Rd, Aberdeen.

T'ai Chi

This form of slow-motion shadow boxing has been popular in China for centuries. It is basically a type of exercise, but it's also an art form.

T'ai chi (also known as *taijiquan*) differs from kungfu in that the latter is performed at much higher speed and with the intention of doing bodily harm. Kungfu also often employs weapons. T'ai chi is not a form of self-defence but the movements are similar to kungfu.

T'ai chi is very popular among old people and also with young women who believe it will help keep their bodies beautiful. The movements are supposed to develop the breathing muscles, promote digestion and improve muscle tone. A modern innovation is to perform t'ai chi movements to the thump of disco music supplied by a portable cassette tape player.

Although there are books written about t'ai chi, the only way to learn properly is to find a good teacher. You'll have to get up early since the Chinese traditionally do this exercise in the park at the crack of dawn. The most popular park for t'ai chi is Victoria Park in Causeway Bay, Hong Kong Island. Other popular venues include the Zoological and Botanic Gardens in Central, and Kowloon Park in Tsim Sha Tsui.

To study t'ai chi, contact the Hong Kong Taichi Association (☎ 2395-4884), 11th floor, 60 Argyle St, Mong Kok, Kowloon.

Tennis

The Hong Kong Tennis Centre (☎ 2574-9122) is at Wong Nai Chung Gap, a spectacular pass in the hills between Happy Valley and Deep Water Bay on Hong Kong Island. It's open from 7 am until 11 pm, but it's only easy to get a court during working hours.

There are 13 courts in Victoria Park (☎ 2570-6186) which can be booked and are open from 6 am until 11 pm. There are four courts open from 6 am until 7 pm at Bowen Road Sports Ground (☎ 2528-2983), Bowen Rd, Mid-Levels.

The South China Athletic Association (☎ 2577-6932), 88 Caroline Hill Rd, Causeway Bay, also operates the tennis courts at King's Park, Yau Ma Tei, Kowloon. Other facilities in Kowloon are at Tin Kwong Rd Playground, Tin Kwong Rd, Kowloon City and at Kowloon Tsai Park, Inverness Rd, Shek Kip Mei.

In the New Territories, you can play tennis at the Jubilee Sports Centre (☎ 2605-1212), near Fo Tan KCR station, Sha Tin, and at the Sai Kung Sports Centre, Sai Kung town.

The Hong Kong Tennis Association (☎ 2890-1132) is in Victoria Park. This is the place to ask questions about available facilities and upcoming events. Spectators may be interested in the Hong Kong Open Tennis Championship, held every September. In October, there's the Hong Kong Tennis Classic in Victoria Park.

Toastmasters Club

The purpose of this organisation is to give you practice in public speaking, to practice English (if it's not your native language) and to meet people. For some, it's a sort of dating service.

Actually, Toastmasters is not one organisation – there are many informal clubs that use the same name or some variation of it. The sponsors of the clubs are often companies who want to teach speaking skills to their employees and thus build self-confidence. One is Victoria Toastmasters (☎ 2867-7938; fax 2810-0218), c/o Asia Insurance Company, 16th floor, World Wide House, 19 Des Voeux Rd, Central. Another is Hong Kong Toastmasters, GPO Box 9243, Central (☎ 2525-6060; fax 2521-7990).

Waterskiing

The main venues for waterskiing are on the south side of Hong Kong Island at Deep Water Bay, Repulse Bay, Stanley and Tai Tam. The south side of Lamma Island also attracts waterskiers. The price of participating is something like HK$250 per hour unless you have your own boat and equipment.

Places to contact include the Deep Water Bay Speedboat Company (☎ 2812-0391), Lot 702, Island Rd and Hong Kong Waterski Association, 35 Tsing Yi Rd, Tsing Yi Island (☎ 2431-2290).

Windsurfing

The best months for windsurfing are September through December, when a steady north-east monsoon blows. Windsurfing during a typhoon is not recommended! Equipment rentals are available in the New Territories at the Windsurfing Centre (☎ 2792-5605), Sha Ha (just past Sai Kung). Also check out Tai Po Sailboard Centre, Chan Uk Chuen, 77 Ting Kok Rd, Tai Po, New Territories. Ditto for the Tai Mei Tuk Water Sports Centre

(☎ 2665-3591), Regional Council, Tai Mei Tuk, Tai Po, New Territories.

Perhaps the best spot is on Cheung Chau Island at the Outdoor Cafe (☎ 2981-8316), Tung Wan Beach. Rentals are HK$70 for two hours, or HK$200 for a full day. Tuition (if you need it) costs HK$450 for five hours.

At Stanley Main Beach on Hong Kong Island you can try the Pro Shop (pager 2112-8238-287) and Wind Surf Pro Motion (☎ 2813-2372). Shek O is another good place on Hong Kong Island for windsurfing.

Rental fees are typically from HK$50 to HK$80 per hour. Around December, Stanley Beach becomes the venue of the Hong Kong Open Windsurfing Championship.

The place to check for more information is the Windsurfing Association of Hong Kong (☎ 2866-3232; fax 2865-6849), room 801, Fortune Building, 13-15 Thomson Rd, Wan Chai.

Yachting & Sailing

Major yacht harbours are at Aberdeen and Causeway Bay on Hong Kong Island, at Hebe Haven in the New Territories and at Discovery Bay on Lantau Island.

This is not exactly an inexpensive activity. The Royal Hong Kong Yacht Club is the largest gwailo yachting organisation in Hong Kong, but you can contact any of the following:

Aberdeen Boat Club
    20 Shum Wan Rd, Aberdeen (☎ 2552-8182)
Aberdeen Marina Club
    8 Shum Wan Rd, Aberdeen (☎ 2555-8321)
Discovery Bay Marina Club
    Discovery Bay, Lantau Island (☎ 2987-9591)
Hebe Haven Yacht Club
    10½ Miles, Hirams Highway, Pak Sha Wan,
    Sai Kung, New Territories
    (☎ 2719-9682; fax 2358-1017)
Royal Hong Kong Yacht Club
    Kellett Island, Causeway Bay
    (☎ 2832-2817; fax 2572-5399)
Yachting Association
    room 906, Queen Elizabeth Stadium,
    18 Oi Kwan Rd, Wan Chai
    (☎ 2574-2639; fax 2572-0701)

The Corum China Sea Race is held every other year during Easter. The yachts race from Hong Kong to Manila.

One way to make a boat trip very affordable is to get together a group and rent a junk for the day. A 16m junk can accommodate around 28 persons and costs HK$2500 to HK$2800 per day (eight hours), so you needn't be independently wealthy to participate. Costs tend to be higher on weekends and holidays. This is a popular form of recreation for gwailo office parties or birthday celebrations and is best accomplished in the Outlying Islands, at fishing harbours like Aberdeen, or from piers in the New Territories. Check the *Yellow Pages* – there are heaps of listings under Boats – Charter & Rental. A place to try is Charterboats (☎ 2555-73497; fax 2555-7340), ground floor, Aberdeen Marina Tower, 8 Shum Wan Rd, Aberdeen. Or in the city you can try Jubilee (☎ 2530-0530; fax 2845-2469), room 604, Far East Consortium Building, 121 Des Voeux Rd, Central.

Traditional Chinese junks can still be seen in waterways around Hong Kong, especially near Aberdeen.

Other

The following is a list of some other associations and clubs which have activities that could be of interest:

Archery Association
room 911, Queen Elizabeth Stadium, 18 Oi Kwan Rd, Wan Chai (☎ 2574-0635)
Artists' Society
PO Box 74029, Kowloon Central Post Office, Kowloon (☎ 2778-2557)
Artists' Guild
1st floor, 5 Mui Hing St, Happy Valley (☎ 2833-0096; fax 2572-9155)
Arts Festival Society
13th floor, Hong Kong Arts Centre, 2 Harbour Rd, Wan Chai (☎ 2824-3555; fax 2824-3798)
Astronomical Society
GPO Box 2872, Central (☎ 2547-4543; fax 2715-2345)
Backgammon Club
room 526, Hollywood Plaza, 610 Nathan Rd, Mong Kok (☎ 2782-2721)
Balloon & Airship Club
12B Bella Vista, 15 Silver Terrace Rd, Clearwater Bay, Kowloon (☎ 2719-2046; fax 2719-6597)
Basketball Association
room 1101, Queen Elizabeth Stadium, 18 Oi Kwan Rd, Wan Chai (☎ 2546-1823)
Birdwatching Society
GPO Box 12460, Central
Boxing Association
room 1004, Queen Elizabeth Stadium, Wan Chai (☎ 2572-2932)
Buddhist Association
1st floor, 338 Lockhart Rd, Wan Chai (☎ 2574-9371; fax 2834-0789)
Green Power (environmental group)
room 705, Nathan Centre, 580 Nathan Rd, Mong Kok, Kowloon (☎ 2770-9368; fax 2782-3160)
Fencing Association
room 1004, Queen Elizabeth Stadium, 18 Oi Kwan Rd, Wan Chai (☎ 2891-4448; fax 2833-6715)
Fringe Festival
2 Lower Albert Rd, south block, Central (☎ 2521-7251; fax 2868-4415)
Gymnastic Association
room 905, Queen Elizabeth Stadium, 18 Oi Kwan Rd, Wan Chai (☎ 2573-4159; fax 2838-9075)
Human Rights Commission
3rd floor, 52 Princess Margaret Rd, Ho Man Tin, Kowloon (☎ 2713-9165; fax 2761-3326)
International Kite Association
ground floor, 8 Kau Yuk Rd, Yuen Long, New Territories (☎ 2477-9867; fax 2473-3934)

Mensa (for persons whose IQ is in the top 2%)
GPO Box 9858, Central (☎ 2310-3111; fax 2849-7018)
Orienteering Club
PO Box 20142, Hennessy Rd Post Office, Wan Chai (☎ 2555-2105)
Orienteering Association
room 910, Queen Elizabeth Stadium, 18 Oi Kwan Rd, Wan Chai (☎ 2891-2691; fax 2893-5654)
Photographic Society
21st floor, Wayson Commercial House, 68-70 Lockhart Rd, Wan Chai
Raja Yoga Centre
room 16B, Hung On Building, 3 Tin Hau Temple Rd, North Point (☎ 2806-3008; fax 2887-0104)
Rugby Football Union
A1401, Seaview Estate, 2 Watson Rd, North Point (☎ 2566-0719; fax 2807-3840)
Scout Association of Hong Kong
Morse House, 9 Cox's Rd, Yau Ma Tei, Kowloon (☎ 2367-3096; fax 2311-4701)
Weightlifting Association
room 1005, Queen Elizabeth Stadium, 18 Oi Kwan Rd, Wan Chai (☎ 2893-9725)

COURSES
Language

If you want to study Chinese seriously, the Chinese University in Hong Kong offers regular courses in Cantonese and Mandarin. Classes can be arranged through the New Asia Yale in China Language Institute, associated with the university. There are three terms a year – one 10-week summer term and two regular 15-week terms. The university does not provide dormitories, so you must make your own living arrangements.

Somewhat less popular but still OK is the course at Hong Kong University, School of Professional & Continuing Education (☎ 2859-2787, 2859-2791), Pok Fu Lam, Hong Kong Island. There is a branch (☎ 2547-2225) on the 9th floor, West Tower, Shun Tak Centre, Sheung Wan.

There are a number of private language schools which cater to individuals or companies. These informal schools offer more flexibility and will even dispatch a teacher to a company to teach the whole staff if need be. Some to consider include:

British Institute
also known as Chinese Language Institute of

Hong Kong, room 1701, Yue Shing Commercial Building, 15 Queen Victoria St, Central (☎ 2523-8455)

Personal Education
3rd floor, One Hysan Ave, Causeway Bay (☎ 2577-8002)

Staff Service Hong Kong
room 3702 B Peregrine Tower, Lippo Centre, 89 Queensway, Admiralty (☎ 2810-9822)

WORK

Stretching the cash? Legally speaking, under the British system, there were only three groups of foreigners who did not need employment visas for Hong Kong: UK citizens, British passport holders or registered British subjects. Such people were granted a 12-month stay on arrival, after which extensions were merely a formality.

As for foreign nationals, including Australians, Americans and Canadians, to work in Hong Kong you are meant to get an employment visa from the Hong Kong Immigration Department before you arrive. This is no longer very easy to arrange – you need a job skill which cannot easily be performed by a local, and your employer must be willing to sponsor you.

Under-the-table employment certainly exists, but there are stiff penalties for employers who hire foreigners illegally. Despite the rules and risks plenty of Westerners find temporary illegal work in Hong Kong. Discretion is strongly advised!

If you arrive as a visitor and get a job, you will probably have to leave at some point, apply for a visa, and return when it is obtained – and the easy-fix quick run to Macau and back is not as foolproof as it used to be. Westerners are normally granted a six-month work visa. Extensions should be applied for a month before the visa expires.

Many travellers drop into Hong Kong looking for short-term work to top up cash reserves before heading off to other destinations in Asia. Some wind up staying much longer than originally planned – the place is full of people who stopped for a few months to replenish the coffers and are still there 15 years later (swearing that they hate the place and plan to leave any day now!).

Success in finding work depends largely on what skills you have. Professional people such as engineers, computer programmers and accountants will have no problem landing a job, especially now that Hong Kong's well-educated class is emigrating in droves to Canada, Australia and elsewhere. However, those who do not possess rare high-technology skills are at a distinct disadvantage.

Of course, the 1997 takeover has affected Hong Kong's job market: many skilled and talented Chinese people are fleeing. Furthermore, as Mandarin Chinese gains in popularity the level of spoken English is declining rapidly. Those who could speak good English have already emigrated or soon will. All this is creating job opportunities for foreigners – businesses needing English-speaking staff are often unable to find local Chinese with the necessary linguistic or technical skills. The big irony is that China's attempt to rid itself of colonialism is instead making China more dependent than ever on the foreign devils.

Some suggest registering with Hong Kong personnel agencies, and others suggest checking the classified sections of the local newspapers. Indeed, there is a free newspaper called *Recruit* (look for it in MTR stations) which has nothing but help-wanted ads. Although looking through the newspaper is not a total waste of time, the reality is that most foreigners who have found work in Hong Kong have done so by going door to door and asking. As in most other places, who you know can count for more than what you know. Also, pay attention to how you look – whether you're beautiful or not, the way you dress will make a difference in fashion-conscious Hong Kong.

The legal minimum wage in Hong Kong is a meagre HK$3500 per month, which works out to approximately HK$20 per hour for full time. These are starvation wages, so you must reach an agreement on salary before you begin any job. In general, unskilled foreign labourers (bartenders, English teachers, etc) can negotiate salaries from HK$40 to HK$70 per hour. Your nationality makes a difference – unfair as it might seem, Filipinos and Thais earn considerably less than Westerners for doing the same work.

Teaching

It's fairly easy to pick up work teaching conversational English, though you may find yourself doing a lot of commuting between part-time jobs. Teaching English is not always as easy as it sounds. If your students are good, it can be a pleasure, but if their English is very poor, teaching them can be both boring and frustrating. However, it provides an opportunity to meet local people.

Qualified teachers with British passports, or a British spouse, could try applying to the British Council (☎ 2879-5138), ground floor, Easey Commercial Building, 255 Hennessy Rd, Wan Chai, for full- or part-time teaching posts.

Translating

If you're fluent in one or more foreign languages then you might get work as a translator. You can find dozens of such companies listed in the Yellow Pages for Consumers under Translators & Interpreters. Some of the well-known ones include: Abraham, Wong, Hoffman & Associates (☎ 2522-8836; fax 2519-7604); Alpha Interlingua (☎ 2543-0188; fax 2541-2468; email 100314.1412@compuserve.com); Polyglot (☎ 2851-7232; fax 2545-9537).

Bars & Restaurants

Good places to start looking are bars and Western restaurants in Lan Kwai Fong, Wan Chai and Tsim Sha Tsui. Besides finding bartending or waitressing work, you may meet people in gwailo bars and restaurants with tips on English-teaching opportunities, modelling jobs, secretarial work and so on.

Movies & Modelling

Occasionally Westerners can find work standing around as extras in Hong Kong movies (long hours and little pay). Some people even try busking, but this does not seem to be highly lucrative.

Modelling is another possibility for both men and women. Modelling agencies are listed in the Yellow Pages for Businesses, but again, contacts are vital and the agencies are only of limited help.

Babysitting

For females, paid babysitting is an option. Contact Rent-a-Mum (☎ 2817-9799), 88B Pok Fu Lam Rd, Hong Kong Island.

Smuggling

One form of employment which requires no work visa is smuggling. It's also far more risky than you might be led to believe by prospective 'employers'. Supposedly, the idea is that you cart a bagful of perfectly legal goodies – such as one watch, one cassette player, one camera, one diamond ring or some other valuable item to a place such as Vietnam or India, where imports of such foreign-made goods are heavily taxed or prohibited. Westerners are employed by professional smugglers who are usually Hong Kong Chinese. The theory is that the customs people are less likely to stamp the goodies on a Western passport, thus requiring you to exit with them. Once you pass customs, you hand the goods to an accompanying Hong Kong Chinese, who then zips off to sell them. You either get a fee for this service and go back to Hong Kong to do it again, or else you've gained a free air ticket to South Korea or Nepal and saved some money. These small-time smuggling expeditions are commonly known as 'milk runs'.

It all sounds very benign, but the risks are not something that your Chinese boss will reveal to you. When I was in Hong Kong, a traveller living in Chungking Mansions was solicited to smuggle seven kg of gold into Nepal and was offered US$2000 for his trouble. He got caught and was given four years in prison. Another traveller I met got caught at Seoul airport wearing three mink coats under his jacket – he was fined and given two months in jail before being booted out of the country. Even worse is the possibility that your employer will use you as a 'mule' to smuggle drugs hidden inside your electronic goodies. There is even a lucrative market in stolen microchips and blasting caps, and while you might not recognise these goods for what they are, trained customs agents will.

MOVING TO HONG KONG
Moving Companies

If you're moving a household, you'll need the services of a moving company. The following companies do both international and local moves: Asian Express (☎ 2893-1000); Columbia International (☎ 2547-6228); Prudential Moving (☎ 2648-9282); Jardine International (☎ 2563-6653); Santa Fe Transport (☎ 2574-6204); Universal Removal (☎ 2866-0151; fax 2520-2857).

Storage

A number of moving companies offer both short-term and long-term storage of household and commercial items. For a fee, they'll be happy to move the items in question and place them in a warehouse. Many of the warehouses (or *godowns* as they are known in Hong Kong) are in the To Kwa Wan district of Kowloon, near Kai Tak airport. Some companies milking this market include:

Fortune International
    8 Lok Yip Rd, Fanling, New Territories
    (☎ 2770-2077, 2676-5981)
Lap Sing Transportation
    1st floor, 27 Shim Luen St, To Kwa Wan, Kowloon (☎ 2571-8177; fax 2887-8147)
Superior Removal
    4th floor, block A, 126 Wing Lok St, Sheung Wan
    (☎ 2545-7883; fax 2854-2746)
Tung Shun Transportation
    1st floor, 12 Tsun Fat St, To Kwa Wan, Kowloon
    (☎ 2363-3086; fax 2362-0019)
Yan Yan Transportation
    3rd floor, flat B, 366 Hennessy Rd, Wan Chai
    (☎ 2891-4388; fax 2783-0715)

ACCOMMODATION

If you're looking for dirt-cheap accommodation, Hong Kong is no paradise. High land prices mean high prices for tiny, cramped rooms. Even though new hotels are constantly being built, demand always seems to exceed supply. Still, you can usually find a room without too much hassle, although this can be difficult during peak holidays times like Chinese Lunar New Year and Easter.

Reservations

Hong Kong does not suffer from a shortage of hotel rooms, so reservations are not essential except during peak holiday times and during special events.

As elsewhere in the world, Hong Kong hotels want deposits for advance reservations. The better-organised hotels can arrange this through a credit card.

The HKTA runs a hotel-booking counter at the airport, and while it won't find you a rock-bottom hovel, it will do its best to get you something. This can be especially useful if you arrive at night – it's no joy carting your luggage around the streets looking for elusive beds at midnight.

You can get as much as a 30% discount at mid-range and luxury hotels if you book through certain travel agents. One agent offering this service is Traveller Services (☎ 2375-2222; fax 2375-2233), room 1012, Silvercord Tower 1, 30 Canton Rd, Tsim Sha Tsui. The hotel booking desk at Kai Tak airport also gets you better rates than the walk-in prices.

Camping

Camping is permitted next to most IYHA youth hostels (it's prohibited at the Ma Wui Hall and Bradbury Lodge hostels). You have to pay a camping fee of HK$25 which permits you to use the hostels' toilet and washroom facilities.

Camping is generally prohibited on the 42 public beaches patrolled by lifeguards, but should be OK at remote beaches.

Also, several government and independent campsites exist on Lantau Island and in the New Territories (see the New Territories chapter for details). Some campsites are listed in the HKTA camping leaflet.

Because of limited fuel availability, the most useful kind of camping stove is the type which uses throw-away gas canisters. They are a litter problem but there aren't many alternatives. A few high-tech camp stoves can use diesel fuel, which is readily available. Kerosene is very difficult to find and ditto for 'white gas'. Hong Kong locals bring bags of charcoal for cooking in picnic and camping areas.

Rental Accommodation

For definition purposes, a long stay means a month or more. Many hotels offer big discounts for monthly rentals.

Not to be overlooked are the hotels and holiday flats on Lamma, Cheung Chau and Lantau Islands – many of these are reasonably cheap if rented by the month, though very expensive for short-term stays. Lamma is particularly popular, with rents typically around HK$5000 for a two-bedroom flat. Equivalent accommodation in Kowloon or Hong Kong Island would cost around HK$7000 or more for a smaller place. Of course, you have to tolerate a long commute if you work in the city.

The trendy gwailo housing estates all boast excellent surroundings, fine sea views, security guards and prices to match. Rents start at around the HK$9000 level for a studio flat and move up to around HK$20,000, or even HK$30,000 for three bedrooms. Many Westerners who can afford such accommodation don't pay for it – their company does. On Hong Kong Island, you can find these estates on the Peak, the Mid-Levels, Pok Fu Lam (especially Baguio Villa), Happy Valley (Stubbs Rd), Deep Water Bay, Repulse Bay, Stanley and Shek O. In the New Territories, check out Tai Po (Hon Lok Yuen), Yuen Long (Fairview Park), Clearwater Bay and Sai Kung. In the Outlying Islands, only Discovery Bay on Lantau falls into this category.

The cheapest flats are in the ugly public housing estates and tend to be concentrated in Kowloon. Fully half of all Hong Kongers live in these places. Pets, particularly dogs, are prohibited though people raise them surreptitiously.

Some Westerners have moved out to the New Territories towards Tuen Mun, Sha Tin and Tsuen Wan, while others have chosen to live on the outlying islands. It's easier to find accommodation in the New Territories and islands and rents are cheaper than in the centre, but the problem is commuting. Rush-hour traffic in Hong Kong grinds to a halt, though it's tolerable if you take the MTR, KCR or a ferry. Nevertheless, expect all forms of public transport to be packed during rush hour.

An important factor in determining the cost of rent is the age of a building. Usually the younger the apartment block the higher the rents. Since even moderate Hong Kong rents are still high by international standards, most single people share flats.

Flats are generally rented with little or no furniture, but used furnishings can sometimes be bought from departing foreigners. Check the noticeboards at expat pubs or around expat housing areas (Lamma Island, for example, has a noticeboard by the ferry pier).

One little trick that many gwailos have discovered is that practically all Chinese have a strong fear of anything associated with death. Consequently, apartments with views overlooking cemeteries are always cheaper and almost always rented by foreigners. If you understand the principles of *fungshui* (geomancy), then finding a flat with bad fungshui gives you bargaining power over the landlord when deciding what your rent should be.

If you are stuck for accommodation, 'leave' flats are worth investigating. Employees on contract are rewarded every couple of years with long holidays and usually rent their flats out while they are away. The usual duration is three months, during which time you are responsible for the rent and the wages of the *amah* (servant). Occasionally people even offer the flat rent-free with just the amah's wages to pay, in order to have someone keep an eye on the place. Nice work if you can get it. Leave flats are listed under a separate heading in the classified advertisements of the *South China Morning Post*.

The best place to look for flats is in the classified sections of the English-language newspapers. Having a Chinese person to check the Chinese-language newspapers can be a tremendous help too.

Then of course there are the real estate agents. Look in the *Yellow Pages* under Estate Agents.

Short-termers may be interested in 'serviced apartments', which are high-priced flats rented out for a short term (maybe one to three months). Look in the *Yellow Pages* under Serviced Apartments. Occasionally the property sections of the English-language newspapers also carry advertisements.

If you're lucky enough to be moving to Hong Kong on contract you'll probably have your hotel room paid for you while you hunt for a flat. That's the custom in Hong Kong and if that isn't in your contract then you haven't negotiated very well.

Residential burglaries are a problem in Hong Kong, so keep security in mind. A steel door helps and many places have bars on the windows. Change the locks when you move in. A building with security guards is best, but this is a luxury you have to pay for.

If you're going to be doing business in Hong Kong, a number of companies can rent you an instant office. You can simply rent an office with phone and fax, or you can rent secretaries and translators as well. Prices depend on how many staff you want, size, location, the length of the lease, etc. Most places require a three-month minimum. The HKTA can supply you with a list of companies that rent business offices.

As for buying property: Hong Kong's property prices are among the highest in the world. Another problem is just whether or not China will continue to respect the property rights of foreigners. Currently, a flat in a public housing estate goes for about HK$1 million, if you can find one. Flats elsewhere usually sell for a mere HK$5 million.

Hostels
The Hong Kong Youth Hostels Association (☎ 2788-1638; fax 2788-3105), room 225, block 19, Shek Kip Mei Estate, Kowloon, sells International Youth Hostel Federation (IYHF) cards for HK$90 to Hong Kong resi-

dents (HK$120 for non-residents). They can also give you a members' handbook which shows the locations of the hostels. You can purchase various hostel paraphernalia here (guide books, patches, etc). The office is inconveniently located in a hideous housing estate near Shek Kip Mei MTR station. It is possible to buy membership cards at the hostels – be sure to bring a visa-sized photo along and some ID.

Prices for a dormitory bed range from HK$25 to HK$50 a night, and a few hostels have family rooms for four persons at HK$200 per room. If you're not a member of the IYHF, you can still stay at the hostels, but you'll be charged considerably more – it pays to get the card if you're staying more than a few days.

Air-conditioning is available at some hostels during summer. Except for Ma Wui Hall (which is open all day), on week days they close between 10 am and 4 pm (they *may* stay open all day on weekends). All hostels are shut between 11 pm and 7 am – forget about late-night partying. Normally, travellers are not permitted to stay more than three days, but this can be extended if the hostel has sufficient empty beds.

As at youth hostels in other countries, you are required to own a special IYHF sleeping sheet (you can buy or rent these at the hostels) and you must do a few simple cleaning chores. Advance booking is required for some hostels and this can be done by either writing, telephoning or going to the head office.

Some of the more remote hostels shut down during mid-week, especially in winter. On the other hand, many are full to overflowing during the school holidays. For these reasons, you'd best ring up in advance to make sure a bed is available. If making a booking more than three days in advance, ring the HKYHA head office and secure a booking reference number. You can take this number to the hostel head office or any branch of the HongkongBank and pay in to account number 002-645414-004 – be sure to keep the receipts to give to the hostel manager. International computerised book-

Tout and About

One thing to be cautious about are touts who hang around the airport to solicit backpackers with offers of cheap rooms. Sometimes they really do have good, cheap rooms, but you can't be sure until you actually see what you're getting. The problem is that if you go with them, see the room and decide that you don't like it, you might be faced with demands to pay HK$100 or more 'service charge' for the trouble they took to guide you from the airport. Some of them will even present the namecards of hostels and guesthouses which have been highly recommended in the Lonely Planet book, and then take you to some dump.

I was approached at the airport by one man claiming to represent Man Hing Lung Guesthouse, and he showed me the namecard 'to prove it'. I asked if I could keep the namecard and go find the place by myself, but he said no, he wanted to guide me. As it turned out, I was already familiar with Man Hing Lung because I had stayed there before, so I went there by myself and was astonished when the owner said he was all full and had not sent any touts to the airport to solicit business. I later heard the same story from other hostels. The moral of the story is that if they won't give you the namecard and allow you to find the place by yourself, it's probably a fraud.

The same applies when you get off the airport bus. A tout meets the A1 bus from the airport and asks travellers where they are staying. Whatever guesthouse they name, The tout says he works for it, then takes him to his shoddy, illegal dump of a hostel. No wonder his hostel has no sign on the door.

Jason Gau

ings are also possible. If you want to reserve a bed less than three days before your anticipated stay, call directly to the hostel and make the booking with the manager. The phone numbers of the individual hostels are listed in the Places to Stay sections of the relevant chapters in this book.

Warning Theft is a constant worry at any dormitory-style accommodation. The problem here is your fellow travellers, not the management of the hostel. Most hostels have lockers available – be sure to use them. Remember, it only takes a minute for your camera or Walkman to walk away.

Guesthouses

This is where most budget travellers wind up staying. The guesthouses are most numerous in dilapidated buildings in the Tsim Sha Tsui neighbourhood and in Causeway Bay on Hong Kong Island. A few places still have dormitory beds, but these are not numerous. Expect to pay around HK$50 to HK$80 for a dormitory bed. For private rooms, prices start in the HK$150 range for doubles and can reach HK$500 for deluxe class. It definitely pays for two people to share a room as it costs little or no extra.

Hotels

Except in the Outlying Islands, there are no hotels that could be called 'budget accommodation'. Low-end places in the city are all guesthouses. Furthermore, there seem to be fewer and fewer hotels in the mid-range category – as time goes by, everything is moving upmarket. Luxury hotels are abundant in Hong Kong – apparently somebody can afford them.

Hong Kong does not suffer from a shortage of hotel rooms, so reservations shouldn't be necessary during off-peak times. However, during major holidays and special events you may not get your first choice of rooms unless you've reserved something. There is a hotel reservations hotline (☎ 2383-8380) which saves phoning around.

The star ratings mentioned in this book are assigned by the China National Travel Association, but it is not necessarily true that you will find a five-star place to be significantly superior to a four-star or even three-star hotel. Star ratings are fairly controversial – take them as a general guide only.

You can be reasonably sure that any luxury hotel has whatever you need; a more pressing consideration than facilities will probably be whether or not you like the location. For Kowloon, Tsim Sha Tsui East is the newest and most modern area and fairly close to the airport (at least until the airport moves sometime in 1998). Nearby Tsim Sha Tsui is older, more crowded and a bit more tattered, but tourist shopping and dining facilities are ubiquitous. On the Hong Kong Island side, there are several big hotels in the heart of Central and a lot more further east in Wan Chai and Causeway Bay.

If you stay in any proper hotels you will find a 10% service charge and a 5% government tax added to your bill, but you won't be troubled with either in the cheap places.

FOOD

The Chinese don't ask 'Have you eaten yet?'. Instead they say 'Have you eaten rice yet?'. Rice is an inseparable part of Chinese culture – the key to survival in their long history. Among older, more conservative Chinese, wasting rice is practically a sin. If they see you've left half your rice uneaten, they may regard you with disdain. The attitude is more decadent among the wealthy younger generation.

Another thing which has changed is the variety of food. There are few places on earth with a more cosmopolitan cuisine than Hong Kong, and the locals like to boast that their city has the best food in the world.

Unfortunately, eating well in Hong Kong is no longer cheap, although with effort you can still get a good meal for a few dollars. A lot depends on the surroundings. If you're willing to eat from pushcarts and styrofoam boxes while standing or sitting on plastic stools, then you can save a bundle. Plush, spacious surroundings are dear mainly because a high proportion of the price of a restaurant meal goes to pay for the space occupied by the customer's bottom.

Even though Hong Kong is justly famous for its Chinese food, you may find yourself engaged in a frustrating search for a place to actually sample the stuff. Travellers find themselves eating a lot more Big Macs than they originally intended. Cost is one reason, as fast food is significantly cheaper than a meal at many Chinese restaurants. Another reason is that after a few months in Asia

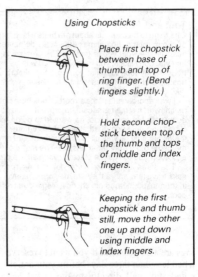

Using Chopsticks

Place first chopstick between base of thumb and top of ring finger. (Bend fingers slightly.)

Hold second chopstick between top of the thumb and tops of middle and index fingers.

Keeping the first chopstick and thumb still, move the other one up and down using middle and index fingers.

many travellers find that they can't stand the sight of one more noodle.

However, the bizarre truth is that many Westerners are driven to eat fast food because of the peculiar attitude of Hong Kong restaurateurs. Most Chinese restaurants only list Western food in the English menu and list Chinese food in Chinese characters only – they actually seem to not want Western customers eating 'their' food. Unable to decipher the Chinese menu, frustrated travellers turn to the English menu and end up eating hot dogs and spaghetti, while the Chinese at adjacent tables feast on Peking duck, egg rolls and steamed dumplings.

Finding top-notch Chinese restaurants is easy, but finding one that's cheap can take perseverance. And it's especially hard to find a cheap but good restaurant with an English menu. One possible solution to all this is to explore the street stalls, known as *dai pai dong* in Cantonese. There are no menus to struggle with, so just point to what you want. However, even finding street stalls is becoming more and more difficult, especially in the tourist zones like Tsim Sha Tsui and Causeway Bay. The night markets like Temple St in Yau Ma Tei and Apliu St in Sham Shui Po are the best bet.

Several good books on eating out in Hong Kong are available at any of the English-language bookshops. The trouble with such books is that they go out of date quickly. Listed places go bust or are under new management (with a consequent deterioration in service, or raised prices) and new places open all the time.

The HKTA's *Dining and Entertainment Guide*, which is updated annually, is aimed at the well-heeled tourist rather than the budget backpacker. Nevertheless it's free, so ask at any HKTA office for a copy.

Chinese restaurants often try to gouge customers. Once you enter, they feel it's a licence to charge you whatever they want. I am referring to medium- and high-priced restaurants, not the cheap ones. Besides a 10% service charge, they try to charge you for tea you didn't order or drink. One place charged me for tea because the beer I ordered was served in the same glass that is used for tea. Of course, they charged me for the beer too. Another place tried to force me to accept a whole pitcher of beer just for myself, when I just ordered a glass. When Chinese restaurants make a mistake, they argue with the customer to try to force them to take or pay for the item.

If a bar or a restaurant brings an appetiser such as peanuts, they will charge you for it even though you did not ask for it or eat any. It's a good idea to check the bill before paying because they often make mistakes in favour of the restaurant. Unless I was getting together with friends, I would only eat at the low-priced Chinese joints, where there's usually not a service charge and they don't try to cheat you.

John Harkness

Snacks

There are plenty of Western-style snacks, as indicated by all those Dairy Farm Creameries (ice-cream shops).

The more traditional Chinese snacks are various seafood-type dishes, often served on a bamboo skewer. Squid on a stick is one such example. Fish ball soup served in a styrofoam cup is a modern variation of a traditional snack. You mostly buy these Cantonese munchies from pushcarts. These tend to gather late at night in strategic locations,

like in front of the off-track betting parlours or the ferry piers.

Thousand-year-old eggs (also known as hundred-year-old eggs) are a Cantonese speciality – these are duck eggs soaked in a chemical solution for several days. This turns the white of the egg green and the yolk a greenish-black. In the old days, the eggs were soaked in horse urine. Most Westerners say these eggs smell and taste like ammonia.

Main Dishes

Over many centuries the Chinese have perfected a unique style of cooking which they regard as a fine art. Being a large country, China can be divided into many geographical areas, each with its own style of cooking, and the ingredients used tend to reflect what is available in that region.

For example, northern China is suitable for raising wheat, so noodles, dumplings and other wheat-based dishes are most common. In the south, where the climate is warm and wet, rice dominates as the basic staple. Coastal areas are where seafood is best. The Sichuan area, where spices grow well, is famous for fiery hot dishes.

However, it is not only geography that determines which ingredients are used. Tradition and culture play a part. The Cantonese, the least squeamish among Chinese, are known for their ability to eat virtually anything. Hong Kong is a dog-eat-dog society, and the only reason you don't find canines on the menu is because the British have prohibited it. That may well change, because just across the border in Guangzhou you'll find dogs, cats and rats on the menu. Most won't admit it publicly, but many Westerners who live in Hong Kong have joined the cross-border weekend dog-eating expeditions to Guangzhou.

The Chinese take the notion of 'you are what you eat' quite literally. Consequently, animals with physical and possible sexual prowess are widely sought. Snake meat, for example, is considered good for your health. The more venomous the snake, the greater its reputation as a revitaliser and cure-all. Cobras are a favourite. Little old ladies drink the blood because they believe it cures arthritis. Some men are convinced the blood is an aphrodisiac. Everyone knows that tigers are strong, so tiger meat is much in demand. Being a rare animal, the meat is very expensive – especially the sexual organs.

Of course, not all Hong Kongers are interested in eating the testicles of endangered species. Less bizarre meat dishes include pork, duck, beef and fish.

The Government Publications Centre in the Government Offices Building, 66 Queensway, Admiralty, sells books with colour photos and recipes for various dishes with both English names and Chinese characters. If you want to take it further, the YWCA offers Chinese cooking classes.

It's not unusual for a meal to be served with small dishes filled with various sauces. The most popular with Cantonese food is hot

---

Table Manners

Chinese meals are social events. The idea is to order many dishes (at least one per person) and then share. The Chinese think nothing of sticking their chopsticks into a communal dish, which is one reason why hepatitis is still a problem in Hong Kong (and even worse in China). You may prefer to use a serving spoon.

Apart from the communal dishes, everyone gets an individual bowl of rice or small soup bowl. Proper etiquette demands that you hold the bowl near your lips and shovel the contents into your mouth with chopsticks (or a spoon for soup).

As an alternative to holding the bowl up to your mouth, place a spoon in your left hand and the chopsticks in the right, then push the food on to the spoon. Then use the spoon as you normally would. Chinese food is never eaten with a knife or fork.

If the food contains bones, just put them out on the tablecloth or, if you want to be extra polite, into a separate bowl (most people use the tablecloth). You needn't use a napkin to hide the spitting out of bones. As you'll discover, Chinese people generally leave a big mess when they finish eating. Restaurants know this and are prepared – they change the tablecloth after each customer leaves.

Soup is usually eaten at the end of a meal, rather than at the beginning. ∎

---

mustard sauce. If they don't put it on the table, you can ask for it.

I've never seen salt shakers in a Chinese restaurant unless they also served Western food, but they sometimes have pepper. Often you will find several small bottles on the table containing soy sauce, vinegar and sesame oil. Most Westerners like soy sauce, but the vinegar and sesame oil are definitely an acquired taste. The Chinese often mix all three together. The vinegar is usually a very dark colour and is easily confused with the soy sauce, so taste some first before dumping it on your food. The Chinese don't dump sauces on their food – they prefer to pour some into a separate dish and dip the food into it.

China's regional variations are well represented in Hong Kong as a result of immigration from the mainland. There are four major styles of Chinese cuisine; Beijing-Shandong, Sichuan-Hunan, Shanghainese and Cantonese-Chaozhou. Somewhere in between comes vegetarian food, and the innovation commonly known as 'fast food'.

Except for the last two categories, you probably won't know or care which style you're eating. For the benefit of culinary connoisseurs, a brief rundown follows.

Cantonese & Chaozhou This is southern Chinese cooking and the one for which Hong Kong is famous. Cooking methods include lots of steaming, boiling and stir-frying.

Specialities are abalone, shark's fin soup (very expensive), roast pig and a dish known as Dragon's Duel Tiger, which is a combination of wild cat and snake meat. The Chinese do interesting things with edible fungi (more politely called 'truffles') of which there are numerous species with different tastes.

Pigeon is a Cantonese speciality served in various ways, including with lemon or oyster sauce, but the gourmet's delight is as a plain roast.

Dim sum is a snack-like variation consisting of all sorts of little delicacies. It's justifiably famous and highly addictive stuff. Dim sum is a uniquely Cantonese dish for breakfast or lunch. The term dim sum means 'a snack'. If the characters are translated literally, dim sum means 'to touch the heart'. The act of eating dim sum is usually referred to as *yum cha*, which literally means 'to drink tea', since it is always served with dim sum meals.

Eating dim sum is a social occasion and something you should do in a group. If you're by yourself, try to round up three or four other travellers for a dim sum lunch. Of course, you can eat dim sum alone, but the problem is that it consists of many separate dishes which are meant to be shared. You can't simply order a plate of dim sum. Having several people to share with you means you can try many different dishes.

Dim sum delicacies are normally steamed in a small bamboo basket. Typically, each basket contains four identical pieces, so four people would be an ideal number for a dim sum meal. You pay by the number of baskets you order. The baskets are stacked up on pushcarts and rolled around the dining room.

You don't need a menu, just stop the waiter or waitress and choose something from the cart, and it will be marked down on your bill. Don't try to order everything at once. Each pushcart has a different selection, so take your time and order many different dishes from different carts. It's estimated that there are about 1000 dim sum dishes. Usually dim sum is not expensive – HK$25 per person is about average for breakfast, or perhaps HK$40 for a decent lunch.

Dim sum restaurants are normally brightly lit and very large – it's rather like eating in an aircraft hangar. Nevertheless, it can get very crowded, especially at lunch time.

The restaurants normally open about 7.30 am and close about 2.30 pm, and many are also shut between 10 and 11.30 am. Arriving after lunch is probably not a good idea as the best food will be gone. Some dim sum connoisseurs say late morning, at 10.30 or 11 am, is the ideal time to arrive, though not all places are open at those hours. The operating hours are often extended on weekends or public holidays, starting earlier and ending later. It can also be very crowded on weekends and sometimes you have to wait for a seat or join the stampede. In the evening, when dim sum is no longer served, many restaurants become dinner nightclubs and charge high prices.

Beijing & Shandong Beijing and Shandong cuisine comes from the cold north of China. Since this is China's wheat belt, steamed bread, dumplings and noodles figure more prominently than rice.

The better Beijing restaurants put on quite a show of noodle making for tourists. This is done by hand – the chef adroitly twirls the dough, stretches it, divides it into two strands, stretches, divides into four, and so on until the noodles are thin as threads.

The most famous speciality is Peking duck, served with pancakes and plum sauce. Another northern speciality is Mongolian hotpot, composed of assorted meats and vegetables cooked in a burner on the dining table – it's so good in Hong Kong that it's hard to believe it can be so bad in Mongolia. Hotpot is usually eaten during winter. Bird's-nest soup is a speciality of Shandong cooking.

Another popular dish, beggar's chicken, was supposedly created by a beggar who stole the Emperor's chicken and then had to bury it in the ground to cook it. The chicken is stuffed with mushrooms, pickled Chinese cabbage, herbs and onions, then wrapped in lotus leaves, sealed in clay and baked all day in hot ashes.

Shanghainese Of all Chinese cuisines, this one is my least favourite. Shanghainese cooking is noted for its use of seafood, but it's heavy and oily. Many Westerners say it's greasy, tasteless and disgusting, although the liberal use of spices can make it almost palatable. Eels are popular, as is drunken chicken, cooked in wine. Other things to try are some of the cold-meat-and-sauce dishes; ham-and-melon soup; bean curd (tofu) and brown sauce; braised meat balls; deep-fried chicken; and pork ribs with salt and pepper.

Sichuan & Hunan Sichuan food is the hottest of the four major categories – it's great stuff if you like spicy food, but keep the drinking water handy! Specialities include frogs' legs and smoked duck. Other dishes to try are shrimps with salt and garlic; dried chilli beef; bean curd with chilli; bear paws braised in brown sauce; fish in spicy bean sauce; and aubergines in garlic.

Hunan food is a variation, and often hot and spicy like Sichuan cuisine. Ducks, chickens and seafood are usually on the menu.

Vegetarian Strict Buddhists (a distinct minority in Hong Kong) are traditionally vegetarians, and the Chinese are masters at adding variety to vegetarian cooking. Large monasteries often have vegetarian restaurants, though you can also find a scattering of such restaurants in Kowloon and on Hong Kong Island.

Vegetarian food is based on soybean curd (tofu) – but the Chinese do some miraculous things with it. 'Fish' can be made by layering pieces of dried bean curd, or fashioned from mashed taro root. Not only do they make it taste like any food you could think of, they make it look like it as well. *Lo lun chai* is a delicious mixed vegetable dish, a meal in itself. Try also the noodle and bean curd dishes, *congee* (rice porridge), fried spring rolls, sweet-and-sour and sweet corn soup.

An option you shouldn't overlook is Hong Kong's Indian restaurants. Indian vegetarian cuisine is considerably spicier than its Chinese counterpart. Some Indian restaurants are exclusively vegetarian, but most offer a combined menu. Even if you're not vegetarian, it's worth trying some of the tasty meatless dishes, such as *biryani*.

Other Asian Food Many Asian people apart from Chinese live in Hong Kong have found it profitable to go into the restaurant business. Indian restaurants are particularly abundant, but you won't have trouble finding just about any other Asian cuisine, from Korean *bulgogi* (barbecue) and *kimchi* to an Indonesian *satay* or *gado gado*.

Japanese food is never cheap. A Japanese meal will cost at least double what you'd spend for a similar level of service in a Chinese restaurant. It's interesting to speculate why. A lot of Japanese come to Hong

Kong, and since they're used to paying exorbitant prices anyway, perhaps local restaurateurs want to make them feel at home. Bring a credit card or a suitcase full of cash.

Fast Food
No matter what negative feelings you might have about fast food, after two months or more in China, the sight of rice and noodles becomes intolerable for many travellers, who find themselves dreaming of milk shakes and French fries.

Seven out of 10 of the busiest McDonald's branches in the whole world are in Hong Kong. If you were expecting to find them chock full of Westerners, then you're in for a surprise – most of the customers are Chinese. The Chinese attach no stigma to eating fast food, and in fact it actually has some snob appeal. Hanging out with an Egg McMuffin is considered chic.

The Chinese have their own versions of fast food, some which isn't bad at all. In my opinion, the king of Chinese fast-food

---

Power Eating

The Chinese love banquets and look for any excuse to have one. Not all banquets are free – especially at weddings, you are expected to bring a cash gift placed in a red envelope. Find out in advance if you are supposed to do this and how much you should give.

When the banquet begins, you may at first be disappointed – it will seem as if there isn't enough food on the table. Nevertheless, eat slowly to avoid feeling satisfied because one course will follow another. You will often be urged to eat more and more, no matter how full you are. About 10 to 12 courses is considered normal at a banquet.

At banquets, eat little or no rice. Rice at banquets is considered a filler and if you're eating a 12-course meal you'll soon become full - with seven courses yet to come.

There is plenty of toasting between courses. The host raises a glass and says *gam bei* (literally 'dry glass') which basically means bottoms up! You do not have to empty your glass, just take small sips, especially since Chinese liquor is powerful. Some people who can't handle strong alcohol fill their glass with tea instead. However, you definitely must go along with the toast. ■

outlets is *Fairwood*. The plastic red clown face over the door puts off many foreigners, but the meals can compete with those served in mid-range Western restaurants. Some dishes disappoint though – the 'salad' is basically a bowl of mayonnaise.

Another homegrown fast-food chain is *Café de Coral*. It gets mixed reviews, but has gradually improved over the years. Some of the dishes are good and the Chinese are absolutely crazy about the place.

Ka Ka Lok Fast Food Shop does quick meals of rice, meat and vegies that you take away in a styrofoam box. It is fast, filling and cheap, and does a good job catering to the budget end of the fast food market.

Maxim's is a well-known Hong Kong chain of fast-food restaurants and cake shops. Known for plastic enamel decor and staff who speak no English, it's not a big hit with Westerners. The Chinese food is passable and the cakes are OK, but the Western egg & sausage breakfasts look as if they've been spray-painted onto the plate. I rate this one near the bottom.

Desserts

The Cantonese have always been the best bakers among the Chinese by a wide margin. Part of this may be Western influence, since the Cantonese had the earliest contact with the West. Nevertheless, there are certain specialities which seem to be distinctly homegrown. Things to look for include custard tarts (best when served hot), steamed buns with sweet bean-paste inside, coconut snowballs (sweet rice-flour balls dressed with coconut slices) and various other sweets dressed with coconut and sesame seeds.

Incidentally, you do not find fortune cookies in Cantonese or any other real Chinese cuisine. They are a foreign invention.

Fruit

Besides mundane peaches, pears and apples, Hong Kong imports a wide variety of fruit from Australia and South-East Asia. Many of these are excellent, though some tropical varieties spoil rapidly after being picked and are definitely the worse for wear. You'll also find that prices are several times higher than in the Philippines, Thailand or Vietnam. Treats to look for include:

carambola – This is also known as star fruit, because that's what it looks like from one angle.

durian – This large fruit has tough spiky skin which looks impenetrable. After breaking it open with a big knife and peeling off the skin (not difficult), you'll encounter the next obstacle, a powerful odour that many can't stand. The creamy fruit is actually delicious and even used to make ice cream in South-East Asia. The season is approximately April through June. Durians spoil fairly easily and cost a bundle.

jackfruit – This large segmented fruit is fine stuff when ripe, but positively awful if it's not.

longan – The name means 'dragon eyes' in Chinese. The skin is brown, but otherwise the taste is similar to lychees. The season is from around June through early August.

lychee – This red pulpy fruit with white flesh and a single large (inedible) seed is one of the main agricultural exports of China. It grows well in Guangdong Province, just across the border from Hong Kong. There is even a lychee carbonated soft drink, which is fine stuff. China's lychee season is from April through June.

mangosteen – Cut these in two and scoop out the delicious pulp with a spoon.

mango – These are sweet, pulpy and very messy to eat. Although the season is late spring and summer, you can easily buy dried mango at any time of year. The Chinese also eat green (unripe) mangos out of season, but pickled and sweetened – the taste is sour but not bad.

papaya – This delicious fruit is available all year round in Hong Kong. The abundant black seeds from the centre of the fruit can be dried and used as herbal medicine. The seeds have been successfully used to treat amoebic dysentery, but the taste is awful. By contrast, the fruit is delicious stuff and is even used to make milk shakes.

pomelo – It's similar to a large grapefruit but tougher.

rambutan – This fruit is very similar to the lychee except for the 'hairy' skin.

Dim Sum 點心

barbecued pork buns
  cha siu bau 叉燒飽
bean curd chicken roll
  gai chuk 雞紮
bean curd pork roll
  seen chuk guen 鮮竹卷

fried spring rolls
tsun guen 春卷
fried green pepper
yeung chen chiu 叉燒飽
fried rice flour triangle
ham shui kok 咸水餃
fried taro puff
woo kok 竽角
fried chicken feet
fung jau 鳳爪
fried flour triangle
jar fun gwor 炸粉果
minced pork dumpling
guon tong gau 灌湯餃
pork & shrimp dumplings
siu mai 燒賣
rice flour triangle
fun gwor 粉果
rice wrapped in lotus leaf
ho yip fan 荷葉飯
rice dumpling in bamboo leaf
gwor ching chung 裹蒸粽
rice flour & shrimp roll
har cheung fun 蝦腸粉
shark's fin dumpling
yee chi gau 魚翅餃
spicy spare ribs
pai gwat 排骨
steamed shrimp dumplings
har gau 蝦餃
steamed tripe
ngau pak yip 牛柏葉
steamed meat buns
siu lung bau 小龍飽
steamed minced beef balls
san juk ngau yuk 山竹牛肉

Dim Sum Desserts
coconut pudding cubes
yeh jap go 椰汁糕
coconut snowball
nor mai chi 糯米茲
custard tart
daan tart 蛋撻
steamed egg pudding
dun gai daan 炖雞蛋
steamed lotus paste bun
lin yung bau 蓮蓉飽

sticky cake & nuts
ma chai 馬仔
sweet red bean porridge
hung dow sa 紅豆沙
wrapped coconut, peanut & sesame
pun yip kok 蘋葉角

Fruits 水果
carambola
yong tou 楊桃
durian
laulin 榴蓮
jackfruit
taishui boluo 大樹菠蘿
longan
long an 龍眼
lychee
lai chi 荔枝
mangosteen
san juk 山竹
mango
mong gow 芒果
papaya
mok gwa 木瓜
pomelo
sa tin yau 沙田柚
rambutan
fan gwai lo lai chi 番鬼佬荔枝

DRINKS
Non–alcoholic Drinks
Tea In Chinese restaurants tea is often served free of charge, or at most you'll pay HK$1 for a big pot which can be refilled indefinitely. On the other hand, coffee is seldom available except in Western restaurants or coffee shops, and is never free.

When your teapot is empty and you would like a refill, signal this by taking the lid off the pot. To thank the waiter or waitress for pouring your tea, tap your fingers on the table. You needn't say thank you. The finger-tapping is only done for tea, not for when food is brought.

There are three main types of tea: green or

unfermented; *bolai* fermented, also known as black tea; and oolong, which is semi-fermented. There are many varieties of tea. Jasmine tea *(heung ping)* is a blend of tea and flowers which is always drunk straight, without milk or sugar. Most of the tea is imported from China, but some comes from India and Sri Lanka. Hong Kong has only one tea plantation (at Ngong Ping on Lantau Island) and it's basically a tourist attraction.

Fleecy No, 'fleecy' is not just what shop-owners on Nathan Rd do to tourists – it's also the name of a sweet cold drink. The distinguishing feature of a fleecy is that it contains some sort of lumpy mixture, usually red or green mung beans, but sometimes pineapple or other fruit. An interesting ingredient sometimes used is black grass jelly. Milk or ice cream is usually part of the mixture, but not always. You can sample these drinks almost anywhere, even in Chinese fast-food restaurants.

Soft Drinks Of course, there isn't a single street in Hong Kong where you can't buy Coke, Pepsi, Fanta, Sprite and Hi-C Lemon Tea.

Alcoholic Drinks

In free-market Hong Kong, you can easily find most major brands of imported alcohol. Excellent beer is available everywhere, and San Miguel even has a brewery in Hong Kong.

In more expensive restaurants, drinks are extortionately priced, particularly wine. This doesn't necessarily mean that the wine will be good, though: what the Chinese generally call 'wine' is what Westerners call hard liquor, similar to whisky or rum. Many of these 'wines' are brewed from grains like rice, sorghum and millet. To the Western palate, they more closely resemble petrol. *Siu hing* is a rice-based wine, the fiery *go leung* is distilled from sorghum and *mao tai* is made from millet. Some of this stuff makes a reasonable substitute for paint thinner. More closely resembling wine is *ng ka pay*, which has a sweet taste and is made with herbs. The Chinese seldom dilute their alcohol – they drink it just as it comes from the bottle.

You may have an opportunity to see the finger game, a type of drinking game in which the loser is obliged to empty his glass ('his' is appropriate as women seldom play).

In Hong Kong, the drinking age in bars is 18 years, but even little children can buy booze in supermarkets.

Happy Hour The cheapest way to get drunk is to buy a bottle of Chinese rice wine (used for cooking), preferably in a brown paper sack, and sit in Kowloon Park to finish it off. However, if you would prefer a more cheerful atmosphere, you can save considerably by taking advantage of the happy hours. During certain hours of the day, several bars, discos and nightclubs give substantial discounts on drinks. Some places give you drinks for half-price during happy hour, while others let you buy one drink and give you the second one free. Usually, happy hour is in the late afternoon or early evening, but the times vary too much for there to be any hard rule. If you enter a bar during happy hour, take note of the time when it ends. Otherwise, you may linger too long and wind up paying more than you expected.

Drinks Vocabulary
ice cold
  dong 凍
ice cubes
  bingfai 冰塊
hot
  yit 熱

Cold Drinks
water
  soi 水
mineral water
  kong chwin soi 礦泉水
fizzy drink (soda)
  hesoi 汽水
Coca-Cola
  hohau holok 可口可樂
Diet Coke
  gamfei holok 減肥可樂

Fanta Orange
fantat changchap 芬達橙汁
Sprite
shwe bae 雪碧
lemon tea (cold)
dong lengmeng cha 凍檸檬茶
carrot juice
hong lobak chap 紅蘿蔔汁
orange juice
chang chap 橙汁
starfruit juice
yong tou chap 楊桃汁
sugarcane juice
gam chei chap 甘蔗汁
papaya milkshake
mougwa aulai 木瓜牛奶
pineapple milkshake
boluo laisek 菠蘿奶昔
watermelon milkshake
saigwa laisek 西瓜奶昔

Fleecy
Red Bean
hongdau bing 紅豆冰
Green Bean
lokdau bing 綠豆冰
Black Grass Jelly
leungfan 涼粉
Fruit Punch
zap gou bing 雜果冰
Pineapple
boluo bing 菠蘿冰

Tea & Coffee
tea
cha 茶
black tea
zai cha 齋茶
tea with milk
lai cha 奶茶
lemon tea
lengmeng cha 檸檬茶
green tea
luk cha 綠茶
chrysanthemum tea
gukfa cha 菊花茶
jasmine tea
heung pin cha 茉莉花茶
oolong tea
oolong cha 烏龍茶

hot chocolate
ye jugulek 熱朱古力
Ovaltine
ye ouwahtin 熱阿華田
Horlicks
ye holahak 熱好立克
coffee with milk
gafei 熱咖啡
black coffee
zai fei 齋啡

Alcohol
beer
beijau 啤酒
Carlsberg Beer
gasiba 加士百
Lowenbrau Beer
lowenbo 盧雲堡
San Miguel Beer
sangle bei 生力啤
Tsingtao Beer
chingdo beijau 青島啤酒
whiskey
waisigei 威士忌
vodka
fukte ga 伏特加
red grape wine
hung jau 紅酒
white grape wine
ba jau 白酒
rice wine
mai jau 米酒
Mao Tai
mao toi 茅台

ENTERTAINMENT
In Hong Kong, you get what you pay for. This applies as much to entertainment as it does to shopping. Outside of sitting around Chungking Mansions and smashing cockroaches with a rolled up newspaper, most forms of amusement require money.

Fortunately, if your needs are simple, it doesn't have to cost a lot. You can get at least a few hours of free or almost free nightlife by exploring the street markets, the *dai pai dongs*, which are usually bustling with activity from about 8 pm to 11 pm. There are plenty of cheap snacks from pushcarts for about HK$3, and occasionally you will be entertained by a Cantonese opera performing on a makeshift stage in the street.

Harbour cruises can be taken day or night, but these are not cheap. See the Tours section in the Getting Around chapter.

The Saturday and Sunday English-language newspapers have weekend entertainment inserts which list nightspots. Also have a look at the *Dining and Nightlife* pamphlet published by the Hong Kong Tourist Association. The pamphlet only gives you a vague idea of what a place is like, but it lists many with a telephone number, address and operating hours.

For cinemas, concerts and various cultural performances, you can book tickets over the phone from Ticket Master (☎ 2317-6666) in the World Commerce Centre, 30 Canton Rd, Tsim Sha Tsui. The way it works is you book your ticket over the phone using a credit card and then collect the ticket at the theatre from a vending machine. Other competitors in this business are TeleTIX (☎ 2850-5500).

URBTIX (☎ 2734-9009) is run by the Urban Council and mainly books tickets for shows in municipal theatres. URBTIX has outlets at City Hall in Central, the Hong Kong Arts Centre in Wan Chai and the Hong Kong Cultural Centre in Tsim Sha Tsui. You don't need a credit card, but must pick up your tickets within three days of making your reservation.

Cinemas

While most major Western films play in Hong Kong cinemas, there is considerable anxiety that China's takeover will result in more and more films being deemed 'unacceptable' by the authorities. At the moment, almost all Western films play in Hong Kong. However, the cinemas have a tendency to cut movies, in part because Hong Kong has a mild form of film censorship, but also because cinema owners find it more profitable to shorten the films to get one or two extra showings a day (plus a few advertisements).

Young people in Hong Kong are crazy about the movies. Most popular are American and locally-made violent films featuring psychopathic killers. Theatres tend to be jam-packed and it is often necessary to buy your ticket a day in advance if you want a seat. Most theatres start selling tickets three days before the actual showing.

Your ticket will have an assigned seat number and you are expected to sit only there. Choose where you want to sit when you buy your ticket and remember that all the best seats sell out early. You may well be approached by ticket scalpers when you arrive at the cinema, but given Hong Kong's reputation as a counterfeit centre who knows if these scalped tickets are real or fake?

To find out what's on at the cinemas look in the *South China Morning Post* or the *Hong Kong Standard*, which list the English-language movies, show times and telephone numbers.

Concerts & Cultural Events

To find out more about the avant-garde cultural scene, check *BC Magazine* and *HK Magazine*. Both are free and available from expat pubs, cafes and some bookshops. Keep your eyes and ears open for information on the annual Hong Kong Festival Fringe – a four-week event which includes everything from drama and dance to mime and street shows.

The *South China Morning Post* and *Hong Kong Standard* have cultural sections which should give you the latest scoop on art exhibitions, film festivals, opera, meetings, concerts, beauty pageants, lion dances, and so on.

The Hong Kong Tourist Association, the Urban Council and the Arts Centre also have programmes, information about which can be obtained from the Arts Centre or HKTA offices. Their weekly cultural calendar should be enough to keep you informed of events such as performances by Cantonese opera troupes, piano recitals, Fujianese puppet shows, Chinese folk singers and exhibits of Chinese watercolours.

Some of the yearly main events include a Western arts festival in February or March, the Hong Kong International Film Festival at about Easter, the Hong Kong Food Festival in August or September, the Hong Kong Asian Arts Festival in October, a major tennis tournament, a rugby tournament and a Lawn Bowling Classic. The various Hong Kong Tourist Association offices around the world can be contacted for information on precise dates.

Cultural Centres

You can ring up Hong Kong's cultural centres to ask about upcoming performances. However, it would seem that this doesn't always work too well:

I rang up the Coliseum to find out who would be playing at the evening concert and was told 'a bunch of gwailos'. I said 'well yes, but what's the name of the band?' They said 'just some gwailos from England, with long hair and guitars'.

Jenny Chan

The following are the main entertainment venues on Kowloon side:

Hong Kong Cultural Centre – (☎ 2734-2010) 10 Salisbury Rd, Tsim Sha Tsui, is home to the Philharmonic Orchestra and Chinese Orchestra .

Hong Kong Coliseum – (☎ 2355-7234), 9 Cheong Wan Rd, Hung Hom, a huge 12,500-seat indoor facility next to the Kowloon-Canton Railway station. The lousy acoustics make this a rather poor place to hold concerts, but this is where most big-name acts perform.

Ko Shan Theatre – (☎ 2334-2331), Ko Shan Rd, Hung Hom (near the KCR station) holds some small performances.

Cultural centres on Hong Kong Island include the following:

Hong Kong Stadium – (☎ 2839-7300), So Kan Po, about 300m due east of the horse race track at Happy Valley. This is Hong Kong's largest venue for cultural and sporting events and can seat 40,000. This is where Hong Kong's Rugby Sevens are staged. Unfortunately, complaints about noise from local wealthy residents has made this venue a non-starter for rock concerts.

Academy for the Performing Arts – 1 Gloucester Rd, Wan Chai (☎ 2584-8514)

Arts Centre – 2 Harbour Rd, Wan Chai (☎ 2877-1000)

City Hall Theatre – Edinburgh Place, right next to the Star Ferry terminal in Central (☎ 2921-2840)

Queen Elizabeth Stadium – 18 Oi Kwan Rd, Wan Chai, is the site for both sporting events and large rock concerts (☎ 2575-6793)

Institute for Promotion of Chinese Culture – room 1001-5, 5 Shun Tak Centre, 200 Connaught Rd, Sheung Wan (☎ 2559-4904)

Sheung Wan Civic Centre – 5th floor, 345 Queen's Rd, Sheung Wan (☎ 2853-2678)

Sai Wan Ho Civic Centre – 111 Shau Kei Wan Rd, adjacent to Sai Wan Ho MTR station (☎ 2568-3721)

The New Territories chips in with three cultural centres of its own:

Sha Tin Town Hall – 1 Yuen Ho Rd, Sha Tin (☎ 2694-2536)

Tuen Mun Town Hall – 3 Tuen Hi Rd, Tuen Mun (☎ 2452-7300)

Tsuen Wan Town Hall – Yuen Tun Circuit, Tsuen Wan (☎ 2414-0144)

Discos

Hong Kong has some outstanding discos, mostly in the Wan Chai district of Hong Kong Island. The disco scene remains popular with foreigners, but surprisingly the fad has come and gone for the Chinese. Karaoke has proved to be a formidable competitor and has drawn away much of the Chinese clientele.

Hostess Clubs

How does it feel to be legally mugged in Hong Kong? To find out, just visit one of the many sleazy-looking topless bars along Peking Rd (and adjacent streets) in Tsim Sha Tsui.

Be wary of places where an aggressive tout, sometimes female, stands at the front door, and tries to persuade you to go inside. In the past they would grab travellers by the arm and try to pull them inside, but the government finally banned this practice after numerous complaints. However, the rules are suspended during the Chinese Lunar New Year, when you practically have to beat them off with a stick. By the way, they often solicit couples, not just males.

Very likely there will be signs on the front door promising 'Drinks Only HK$40' and naughty pictures to stimulate interest.

Inside, a cocktail waitress, usually topless and often wearing nothing but her knickers, will serve you a drink. She will probably be friendly and chat for a few minutes. It will be one of the most expensive conversations of your life, because after a pleasant five-minute chat you will be presented with a bill for about HK$500.

When you protest, they will undoubtedly point to the tiny sign prominently posted on the wall behind a vase which informs you of the HK$400 service charge for talking to the waitress. If you baulk at paying this fee, don't be surprised if two muscular thugs suddenly happen to be standing by your elbows. Congratulations, you've now met Hong Kong's notorious Triads. They accept travellers' cheques. If you really don't have enough money to pay, try bargaining – it works anywhere else in Hong Kong. Or be as gwailo as possible, and ask to call your embassy – they might let you off easy if they think you're loony.

This introduction to Hong Kong's hostess clubs wasn't meant to frighten you off. If you really want to be waited on by almost-naked women, that's fine, but do realise that it will cost big bucks. In Hong Kong, you get what you pay for. Don't think that you can quietly sit in the back of the room and sip your beer and get out for HK$40. That doesn't happen unless you're a card-carrying Triad member.

Hostess clubs come in two varieties – the sleaze-pits which are mostly found in Tsim Sha Tsui, and 'respectable establishments' which are mostly in Tsim Sha Tsui East. The difference is that the sleaze-pits blatantly try to cheat customers, while the respectable pits don't need to cheat – they are very up-front about their high prices. The line-up of Mercedes' and Rolls-Royces outside the door should suggest just what sort of clientele these places cater to. The respectable hostess clubs offer live music, featuring Filipino bands, and topless dance shows (that is, the dancers are topless, not the Filipino bands). An evening out in any of these places could easily cost a cool HK$1000 or more. This is beyond the means of most middle-class Hong Kongers, which explains why nearby Macau is so popular.

Karaoke

Not many foreigners get into this, but the Chinese love it. The word *karaoke* (empty music) was borrowed from Japanese. Basically, it's sing-along video tapes. Most of the songs are in Chinese, but they have English too.

Mahjong

If you walk down the side streets of Hong Kong, sooner or later you are bound to hear the rattle of mahjong pieces. Mahjong is so popular in Hong Kong that there are licensed mahjong centres where one can meet other players and gamble all day. Hong Kong is a good place to play mahjong, but there is a lot of local talent and you'll be up against the pros. If you want to visit a mahjong centre, get a Chinese person to take you.

There are various forms of illegal gambling: private poker matches are popular, and hard-core gambling addicts attend dog fights and (I kid you not) cricket fights. To participate in such illegal forms of gambling you will need the help of local Chinese.

Mahjong is played with coloured tiles engraved with patterns and Chinese characters. Mahjong games are often played far into the night.

Pubs

Since the British influence has been substantial in Hong Kong, it's not surprising that British-style pubs are plentiful – especially in the tourist areas. Often the owners are British or Australian, and you can expect authentic decor, meat pies, darts and sometimes Aussie bush bands. Depending on where you go, beers typically cost HK$35 a pint, which is likely more expensive than the shirt you'll be wearing if you've bought any clothes in Hong Kong. Overall, Lan Kwai Fong on Hong Kong Island is best for pubs, but there are plenty on the Kowloon side as well.

Video Game Arcades

If you have an urge to test your skills at Sega Rally or Street Fighter, check out one of the ubiquitous video arcades.

SPECTATOR SPORT

Sporting events are well covered in the sports section of Hong Kong's English-language newspapers. There are a number of special tournaments for which competition for tickets is keen. Since these sporting events don't fall on the same day every year, contact the HKTA for the current info.

Rugby

The Chinese aren't really big on rugby, but many expats are. The biggest match of the year – the Cathay Pacific-HongkongBank Seven-a-Side Rugby Tournament (just call it the 'Rugby Sevens') – is held in late April or early March. Teams come from all over the world to participate in the three-day event. Tickets are hard to come by and often require connections to get. Some big companies allocate them to their employees – otherwise, join the queues the night before tickets go on sale.

Soccer

Both Chinese and expats are soccer enthusiasts. Regular matches are played at Hong Kong Stadium at So Kon Po, about 300m due east of the Happy Valley horse race track on Hong Kong Island.

Tennis

Several international tennis tournaments are held annually in Hong Kong. The largest is the Salem Open (held in April) and the Marlboro Championship (usually in October). The tournaments are held in Victoria Park in Causeway Bay.

Horse Racing

Gambling is deeply ingrained in Chinese culture, though, to be fair, it was the British who introduced horse racing to Hong Kong. And, without a doubt, horse races are now Hong Kong's biggest spectator sport.

Apart from mahjong games and the twice-weekly Mark Six Lottery, which raises money for the government, racing is the only form of legal gambling in Hong Kong – which is why Macau is so popular with the gambling-addicted Chinese. The first horse races were held in 1846 at Happy Valley racecourse on Hong Kong Island, and became an annual event. Now there are about 65 meetings per year at Hong Kong's two racecourses, and about 450 races in all. The newer and larger track is at Sha Tin in the New Territories, and has seats in an air-conditioned enclosure which can accommodate 70,000 people (See New Territories chapter).

While you don't need your passport to attend a race, you do need one if you want to get a tourist ticket. And these special tickets are worthwhile, especially when the race track is crowded (as it frequently is). There have been times when up to 50,000 race fans have been turned away because of insufficient seating! But if you quality for a tourist ticket, you can get in anyway, and the tourist ticket allows you to walk around next to the finish area where you can get wonderful views of the races. In order to qualify, your passport must show that you've been in Hong Kong for less than 21 days.

The HKTA has Come Horse Racing tours to Happy Valley and Sha Tin. See the Organised Tours section in the Getting Around chapter for details.

The racing season is from late September to June. Normally, races at Sha Tin are held on Saturdays from 1 to 6 pm. At Happy

Valley, races are normally on Wednesday evenings from about 7 to 11 pm. However, this schedule isn't followed religiously. Sometimes extra races are held on Sundays or holidays. Check with the HKTA in late September or early October to get the schedule for the coming season.

Betting is organised by the Royal Hong Kong Jockey Club (RHKJC). Many types of betting combinations are available, such as the quinella (picking the first and second place getters) or double quinella (picking the first and second from two races); there is also the treble (picking the winner from three specific races); and the six-up (picking the first or second from all six of the day's races).

Off-track betting is also permitted. The RHKJC maintains off-track betting centres at 39-41 Hankow Rd in Tsim Sha Tsui, at 64 Connaught Rd in Central and elsewhere.

If you want to attend the races, a seat in the public stands at Happy Valley cost just HK$10. A visitor's badge to sit in the members' box costs HK$50. These badges can be purchased at the gate on the day of the race, or up to two days in advance at any branch of the RHKJC.

You are not allowed to bring portable phones into the track – special small lockers are available to store them in!

THINGS TO BUY

'Shop till you drop' is the motto of many visitors to Hong Kong. And while it's true that the city resembles one gigantic shopping mall, a quick look at price tags should convince you that Hong Kong is not quite the bargain it's cracked up to be. Imported goods like Japanese-made cameras and electronic gadgets can be bought for roughly the same price in many Western countries. However, what makes Hong Kong shine is the variety – if you can't find it in Hong Kong, it probably doesn't exist.

That having been said, there are bargains to be had on locally manufactured products. Goods which require low technology but much manual labour to produce are the best bargains, including clothing, footwear and luggage. The reason for this is the cheap labour just next door in the People's Republic.

The HKTA can give you some information to get you started, but don't accept it as gospel. They publish a handy little booklet, called *Shopping*, which recommends shops that are HKTA members – though I have found some of these members to be less than charitable. The HKTA publishes an *Official Shopping Guide*, which is worth reading.

Duty Free

'Duty free' is just a slogan here. Hong Kong is a duty free port, and the only imported goods on which duty is paid are alcohol, tobacco, perfumes, cosmetics, cars and some petroleum products. Although many shops in Hong Kong display a big sign proclaiming 'Duty-Free Goods' there is little reason to bother with them as they cater mostly to a Japanese clientele who are already accustomed to being ripped off.

The only true duty-free shops in Hong Kong are the liquor and tobacco stores in the airport which you find in the departure area *after* you pass through immigration and the security check. The other so-called duty-free shops in the check-in area of the airport are just expensive shops. In general, almost anything – cameras, electronics, jewellery, and so on – will be cheaper when you buy it outside duty-free shops.

If you want to buy duty-free cigarettes and liquor, you might do better just buying these on the aircraft itself. The other option is to buy from the duty-free shops in Macau (at the ferry pier) or at the border crossing at Shenzhen where you enter Hong Kong from China. Or just wait until you get to another country – most other airports in Asia offer better deals on duty-free items than what you find in Hong Kong's airport.

Guarantees

There are too many cases of visitors being sold defective equipment, and retailers then refusing to honour warranties. Every guarantee should carry a complete description of the item (including model and serial numbers) as well as the date of purchase, the name and address of the shop it was purchased from and the shop's official stamp.

Many imported items come with a warranty registration with the word 'Guarantee only valid in Hong Kong'. If it's a well-known brand name, you can often return this card to the importer in Hong Kong to get a warranty card for your home country. It's best to do this while you're still in Hong Kong, as doing it by post from abroad is chancy.

A common practice is to sell grey-market equipment (ie imported by somebody other than the official local agent). Such equipment may have no guarantee at all, or the guarantee might only be valid in the country of manufacture (which will probably be either China or Japan).

If you buy goods such as cameras and computers at discount prices, then make sure – if you really need the latest model – that the model hasn't been superseded. The agent or importer can tell you this. Contacting an agent is one way of obtaining a detailed explanation of what each model actually does, though many agents aren't interested in talking to you. The HKTA *Shopping* guide has a list of sole agents and their phone numbers in the back of the pamphlet.

Always check prices in a few shops, take your time and return to a shop several times if necessary. Don't buy anything expensive in a hurry and always get a manufacturer's guarantee that is valid worldwide. When comparing prices, on cameras for example, make sure you're comparing not only the same camera body but also the same lenses and any other accessories.

Refunds & Exchanges

Many shops will exchange goods if they are defective, or in the case of clothing, if the garment simply doesn't fit. Be sure to keep receipts and go back to the store as soon as possible.

Forget about refunds. They are almost never given in Hong Kong. This applies to deposits as well as final payment. If you put a deposit on something, don't ever expect to see that money again.

Rip-offs

Caveat emptor, or 'buyer beware', are two words which should be embedded in your mind while shopping in Hong Kong, especially during that crucial moment when you hand over the cash.

Rip-offs do happen. While most shops are honest, there are plenty which are not. The longer you shop in Hong Kong, the more likely it is that you'll run into a shopkeeper who is nothing but a crook. It would be wise to learn how to recognise the techniques of rip-off artists in order to avoid them.

The HKTA recommends that you only shop in stores which display the HKTA membership sign. This sounds like great advice except that many of the best stores are not HKTA members. Furthermore, many of the thieving camera and video shops in Tsim Sha Tsui *are* HKTA members. Indeed, the *worst* shop I've ever done business with in Hong Kong was an HKTA member (no longer though, I'm happy to report). In other words, you should take the HKTA's seal of approval with a grain of salt.

The most common way to cheat tourists is simply to overcharge. In the tourist shopping district of Tsim Sha Tsui, you'll rarely find price tags on anything. Checking prices in several stores therefore becomes essential. However, shopkeepers know that tourists compare prices in several locations before buying, so they will often quote a reasonable or ridiculously low price on a big-ticket item, only to get the money back by overcharging on small items or accessories. You may be quoted a reasonable price on a camera, only to be gouged on the lens cap, neck strap, case, batteries and flash. If you realise that you are being ripped off and casually ask why you're being charged 10 times the going rate for a set of batteries, you'll probably be told in no uncertain terms to 'get the hell out'.

Overcharging is easy to spot, so many dishonest shopowners are more sneaky. They sometimes remove vital components that should have been included free (like the connecting cords for the speakers on a stereo system) and demand more money when you return to the shop to get them.

You should be especially wary if they want to take the goods into the back room to 'box it up'. This provides ample opportunity to remove essential items that you have already paid for. The camera case, included free with most cameras, will often be sold as an accessory. Another tactic is to replace some of the good components with cheap or defective ones. Only later will you discover that the 'Nikon' lens turns out to be a cheap copy. When it's time to put your equipment in the box, it's best if you do it yourself.

Another sneaky ploy is to knowingly sell defective merchandise. Your only safeguard is to inspect the equipment carefully before handing over the cash.

Also be alert for signs of wear and tear – the equipment could be secondhand. Whatever you do, insist on getting an itemised receipt. You should avoid handing over the cash until you have the goods in hand and they've written a receipt.

There is really no reason to put a deposit on anything unless it is being custom-made for you, like a fitted suit or a pair of glasses. Some shops might ask for a deposit if you're ordering a very unusual item that they wouldn't normally stock, but this isn't a common practice.

Here are a few experiences of dissatisfied customers:

They took a deposit and demanded an extra $800 for the camera when I came for delivery...used abusive language and started fights.

I signed a receipt for a US$200 disc player. They had another receipt underneath the first one and produced a $30 record player when they went to put the disc player in a box. So I ended up with a $30 record player which cost $200 – and a receipt for a record player (switched!).

Couldn't be worse. They try to provoke you to start a fight!

Getting Help

There isn't much you can do if a shop simply overcharges. However, if you discover that the goods are defective or something is missing, return to the shop immediately with the goods and receipt. Sometimes it really is an honest mistake and they will clear the problem up at once. Honest shopkeepers will exchange defective goods or replace missing components. On the other hand, if the shop intentionally cheated you, expect a bitter argument.

If you feel you were defrauded, don't expect any help from the police. There is an unfortunate lack of consumer protection in Hong Kong. However, there are a few agencies that might be able to help you.

The first place to try is the HKTA (☎ 2807-6543), 11th floor, Citicorp Centre, 18 Whitfield Rd, North Point. If the shop is one of their members they can lean on them, but don't expect miracles. If you file a written complaint, the only penalty the HKTA can impose is to revoke the shop's membership (which incidentally, costs HK$15,000 in annual dues).

If you can't get satisfaction at the HKTA, another place to try is the Consumer Council (☎ 2304-1234), which has 16 advice centres. The Small Claims Tribunal (☎ 2825-4667) is the place to contact for claims less than HK$15,000. The Community Advice Bureau (☎ 2524-5444) can help you find a lawyer.

As a last desperate measure, you can take matters into your own hands. By this I don't mean you should punch the shopkeeper, which might be fun but isn't legal (unless, of course, they punch first). However, it is entirely legal to stand outside the shop and tell others about your experience. Some pickets have successfully gotten back their money after driving away other customers. However, this can be an exhausting way to spend your time in Hong Kong and results are by no means guaranteed.

Fake Goods

Watch out for counterfeit-brand goods. Fake labels on clothes are the most obvious example, but there are fake Rolex watches, fake Gucci leather bags, fake jade, fake jewellery, fake herbal medicines, and even some fake electronics. Obviously there's more risk buying electronic goods than buying clothes, shoes or luggage, though I was nearly crippled by some fake Reebok shoes because they hurt so much. The pirated music tapes and CDs are often of poor quality and have a tendency to rapidly deteriorate.

Hong Kong's customs agents have been cracking down particularly hard on the fake electronics and cameras, and this problem seems all but solved. However, counterfeit name-brand watches seem to be very common. If you discover that you've been sold a fake brand-name watch when you thought you were buying the genuine article, it would be worth your while to contact the police or customs because this is definitely illegal. Also beware of factory rejects.

Shopping Hours

There are no hard and fast shopping hours in Hong Kong, but shops in the four main shopping areas are generally open as follows:

Central and Western districts 10 am to 6 pm; Causeway Bay and Wan Chai 10 am to 10 pm; Tsim Sha Tsui, Yau Ma Tei and Mong Kok 10 am to 9 pm; and Tsim Sha Tsui East 10 am to 7.30 pm. Causeway Bay is the best part of town for late-night shopping.

Most shops are open seven days a week, but on Sundays or holidays many only open from 1 to 5 pm. Street markets are open every day and well into the night (with the exception of the Jade Market in Kowloon, which is open from 10 am to 3.30 pm). Almost everything closes for two or three days during the Chinese New Year holiday period. However, just before the Chinese New Year is the best time to make expensive purchases – everything goes on sale at that time because the stores want to clear out old stock.

Cheapest Places to Shop

Hong Kong merchants can be divided into two general categories; those who cater to tourists only and those who sell to the general populace. Those who live entirely off the tourist trade base their marketing philosophy on a simple mathematical equation: Tourist = Sucker. The best way to counter this is to get away from tourist land, which basically means get away from Tsim Sha Tsui.

The Kowloon and Hong Kong Island chapters both give a good rundown of places to shop outside the tourist combat zone. Also, don't overlook the New Territories: one of the most impressive shopping malls in Hong Kong is the Sha Tin New Town Plaza. With a little more effort, you can visit the Tuen Mun Town Plaza in the north-west part of the New Territories; it can be reached by hoverferry.

Street Markets The reason why Hong Kong teenagers look so chic, despite having no income beyond their lunch money, is that it is possible to buy just about anything in the street markets and clothing alleys. Prices are typically less than half of what you would pay in the boutiques.

They can be found at Temple St (open from about 8 to 11 pm) in Yau Ma Tei, Tung Choi St (noon to 10 pm) in Mong Kok, and Apliu St (noon to 9 pm) in Sham Shui Po. These sell clothes, cassettes, watches, ballpoint pens with built-in digital clocks, radios, knives, cheap jewellery, naughty postcards, potions, lotions, false teeth and hundreds of other items.

Street markets and alleys are truly a bargain for clothing, but because of the largely Chinese clientele clothes sizes are mainly small. To complicate matters, you can't try on garments such as trousers before you buy. You're also taking a chance on quality. Most of the time you can ignore monograms – Hong Kong is monogram-mad and makes excellent reproductions of fashion luggage, handbags and clothes as well as copies of labels.

Factory Outlets In my opinion, it's barely worth chasing these places down. You *can* get bargains here on overruns, but the selection is decidedly limited and there are a fair few factory rejects among the occasional gems. Also, the best factory outlets tend to be in far-off neighbourhoods among the warehouses rather than in five-star hotel districts. But since tourists will often go to great lengths to search out these places, most charge only slightly less for their stylish clothing than you could buy it for in retail shops. Overall, the street markets are a better bargain. Still, if you've got the time to search, you might get a great deal on those leather trousers you've always wanted (even if the zipper is missing), or that silk shirt with one sleeve longer than the other.

Always check purchases carefully for defects as factory outlets rarely give refunds or exchanges. Many outlets post a sign saying 'All Sales Are Final' – and they mean it. Some places will accept credit cards, but most won't. If they do accept credit cards they'll often offer a discount if you pay cash, so be sure to ask.

If you're going to spend some time hunting down factory outlets, it's essential that you get *Hong Kong Factory Bargains* by Dana Goetz, widely available from bookshops throughout Hong Kong. The book gives a thorough rundown on what's available and where to find it.

A wide range of goods is available from factory outlets, such as jewellery, carpets, camphor chests, leatherwork, silks, shoes, handbags, ceramics and imitation antiques.

What to Buy
Antiques & Curios How do you tell a real Ming vase from a fake when the cracks and chips and age discolouration have been cleverly added? Hong Kong factories quite legitimately turn out antique replicas. Many dealers state when a piece is a reproduction and some even restrict their sales to these items. Unfortunately, others don't feel the necessity to tell customers/suckers.

The Tang dynasty ran from 618 AD to 906; the Song from 960 to 1279; the Ming from 1368 to 1644 and the Qing from 1566 to 1911. So a Qing vase might be less than 100 years old, which in Western terms would hardly qualify as an antique. Basically, if you don't know what to look for or who to buy, then don't – the serious purchase of antiques is not for the tourist on a stopover!

There are still many beautiful items to buy

in Hong Kong, including fine examples of Chinese art and craft – not necessarily antique, which doesn't matter as long as you don't pay antique prices.

For what it's worth, the annual International Asian Antiques Fair is held in Hong Kong.

Appliances & Electronics Remember that most electrical appliances in Hong Kong are designed to work with 220V. Some thoughtful manufacturers now equip their computers, stereos and video machines with international power supplies that automatically sense the voltage and adapt to it – others include a little switch for 110/220V operation. Hong Kong's standard plug design, which uses three round prongs, is not used by many other countries, but plugs are easily changed or you can buy an adaptor in Hong Kong. If the shop can't supply you with the correct adaptor, ask the store to change the plug for you, which they should do free of charge.

Cameras Much could be said about buying cameras, and in fact much was already said in the Photography & Video section of this chapter. Other pointers to keep in mind when shopping for a camera is to never buy one that doesn't have a price tag, which basically precludes 99% of the shops in Tsim Sha Tsui. Stanley St in Central is the place to look for cameras (see the Things to Buy section in the Hong Kong Island chapter). Tsim Sha Tsui has a couple of shops on Kimberley Rd dealing in used cameras (see Things to Buy in the Kowloon chapter).

The new digital cameras are interesting in that the photographs can be transferred directly to a computer and stored on a CD ROM, or outputted to a colour laser printer. This might be of interest to people who write software or make CD ROMs, but will probably not interest the average user.

If you're thinking about buying a digital camera simply to save money on photoprocessing, you might as well forget it – you'd have to take many thousands of pictures to offset the cost of the equipment. Furthermore, digital photos are not nearly as high in resolution as those taken with photographic film. Of course, all this may change – digital cameras, colour laser printers and CDR (CD writable) drives have been rapidly improving in quality and prices have been coming down. Nevertheless, it will be some years before the state of the art advances enough to interest the average user who wants some snapshots to show the loved ones at home.

Carpets When you talk about buying a fine Oriental carpet, you're talking serious money. Not surprisingly, the cost depends on the size, type of material and intricacy of the design. There are hand-knotted or machine-knotted carpets, and hand-woven wall hangings. Fancy decorative carpets can be made of wool or silk – these are obviously not for wiping your feet on.

It's difficult to give advice about what constitutes a fine carpet, because everyone has their own tastes. You need to do a lot of looking and cost comparison. The HKTA's *Shopping* booklet gives a long list of places selling carpets. What their pamphlet doesn't say is that the further away you get from tourist land, the cheaper prices become.

Clothes China has a raging export-oriented textile industry, and Hong Kong is the export gateway. While you can often find this stuff more cheaply in China, the quality is vastly superior in Hong Kong – China tends to dump all its cheap junk on the domestic market.

An interesting phenomenon in recent years has been the proliferation of Hong Kong clothing manufacturers which have adopted Italian names. Chief among these are Giordano and Bossini. While the clothes are about as Italian as chopsticks, the quality is not bad at all and prices are low to moderate. There are numerous, easily found, outlets around Hong Kong – prices are fixed, there's no bargaining and you can often pick up items on sale.

Hong Kong has long been famous for custom-made clothes and tailors exist in profusion. Most are ethnic Indians – the Chinese

seem to be slowly abandoning this particular market niche. To find a tailor, all you need to do is walk around the shopping arcades in the tourist zones and show a passing interest – you'll practically be kidnapped. There are often pamphleteers hanging around Nathan Rd, ever eager to inform you about their custom-tailor services. There are also plenty of listings in the *Yellow Pages for Consumers* and the HKTA can produce a list longer than a Chinese scroll painting. Some tailors require you to buy their material, while others will let you bring your own. The more time you give the tailor, the more fittings you will have and the better the outcome is likely to be.

Computers Hong Kong is a popular place to buy personal computers. While prices are competitive, it is also important to pay careful attention to where and what you buy. Computers are prone to breakdowns, so finding a shop with a good reputation for honesty is vital. Before leaving Hong Kong it's important to run the computer continuously for several days to make sure it is free of defects.

You may have your own ideas about what kind of computer you want to buy, but if you're leaving Hong Kong you would be wise to choose a name-brand portable computer with an international warranty, such as Hewlett-Packard, Compac or Acer. A portable computer is a whole lot easier to transport than a desktop machine, and if it's a name-brand computer it should have an international warranty. If it does break down, parts and service will be easier to find.

Many shops will be happy to sell you a generic (no-name) desktop computer custom-designed to whatever configuration you desire. Buying a generic desktop machine might make sense if you will be living in Hong Kong for at least a year (the typical warranty period). Assuming that the shop stays in business for a year, the warranty will probably be honoured. However, if the dealer proves to be inept or dishonest, then you may have to go elsewhere for repairs and pay for the service. In general, buying a brand name is safer.

You may be hit with a steep import tax when you return to your home country Save your receipt, because the older the machine is the less you're likely to pay in import duty. The rules in many countries say that the machine is tax-exempt if over one year old, and some shops in Hong Kong will even write you a back-dated receipt on request for just this purpose!

Some Hong Kong computer shops still sell pirated computer software, although the authorities have cracked down on this. Bear in mind that besides being illegal, pirated programs often contain computer viruses – there is even one called 'AIDS' and wearing a condom offers no protection whatsoever.

Ivory For years, ivory jewellery, chopsticks and ornaments were big sellers in Hong Kong, fuelling the demand for tusks and contributing to the slaughter of Africa's already depleted elephant population. In 1989, the Hong Kong government signed the CITES (Convention on International Trade in Endangered Species) treaty which effectively bans the import of raw ivory. The USA, Japan and western European nations have all signed the CITES, as have many other countries.

Since the agreement was reached, the elephants have been making a roaring comeback. Unfortunately, this hasn't been entirely welcomed in some African and Asian countries, where they compete with humans for food and living space. Every now and then there is talk of lifting the ban and commercially herding the elephants, but so far it hasn't happened.

In the meantime, the only carved ivory products being sold in Hong Kong are those which were supposedly manufactured before the ban went into effect. Those who want to sell such ivory need to have all sorts of documentation proving where and when the goods were made. The importing and exporting of ivory is still technically possible with a licence from Hong Kong and from the other country involved, but it's a legal minefield and hardly worth the trouble.

Jade The Chinese attribute various magical qualities to jade, including the power to prevent aging and keep evil spirits away.

It's a pity then that jade doesn't have the magical ability to prevent lying. Fake jade exists – the deep green colour associated with some jade pieces can be achieved with a dye pot, as can the white, green, red, lavender and brown of other pieces. Green soapstone and plastic can be passed off as jade too.

Most so-called Chinese jade sold in Hong Kong comes from South Africa, New Zealand, Australia and the USA. One trick of jade merchants is to sell a supposedly solid piece of jade jewellery which is actually a thin slice of jade backed by green glue and quartz.

It is said that the test for jade is to try scratching it with a steel blade – real jade will not scratch. Another story is that water dropped on real jade will form droplets if the stone is genuine.

There are two different minerals which can be called jade: jadeite from Myanmar (Burma) and nephrite (commonly from Canada, China, New Zealand and Taiwan). Unfortunately, you would have to know your Burmese jade pretty well to avoid being fooled. While the colour green is usually associated with jade, a milk-white shade is also highly prized. Shades of pink, red, yellow, brown, mauve and turquoise come in between.

The circular disc with a central hole worn around many necks in Hong Kong represents heaven in Chinese mythology. In the old days, amulets and talismans of jade were worn by Chinese court officials to denote rank, power and wealth. One emperor was reputed to have worn jade sandals, and another gave his favourite concubine a bed of jade.

Jewellery If you have ever tried to sell a secondhand diamond ring to a jewellery shop, you no doubt already know that the price of used jewellery is a fraction of what it costs new. Yet shops which buy secondhand jewellery turn around and sell it for close to what it costs new.

The moral of the story is that buying jewellery as an investment is a non-starter. Don't buy jewellery in Hong Kong (or anywhere else) with the idea that you can sell it for more in your home country. The only way to make money from jewellery is to be well connected with a supplier and to have your own retail outlet.

One of the great myths of the jewellery business is that the high prices in the stores reflect the rarity of the materials. While it's true that uncut diamonds sold in bulk cost far more than zircons, the high prices charged reflect the fact that people are willing to pay a lot for shiny rocks and metals. Prestige is something you pay for. A ring with US$5 worth of raw materials can sell for US$100 in the stores. If the materials are worth US$100, the retail price can be US$1000. And so on.

Part of what you pay for is the labour involved in making the rocks look good. The jewellery export business is big in Hong Kong. This is because gemstones are imported, cut, polished, set and re-exported using cheap Chinese labour. In theory, this should make Hong Kong a cheap place to purchase jewellery. In practice, retail prices are only marginally lower than elsewhere.

Your only real weapon in getting a decent price is the intense competition in Hong Kong. Jewellery has a large mark-up and there is considerable latitude for bargaining. However, the jewellers have a weapon of their own, namely the inability of the common tourist to judge good quality jewellery from bad. Can you distinguish a pure diamond from a zircon? A flawed diamond from a perfect one? Most people cannot. To become an expert on jewellery requires considerable training. The law requires jewellers to stamp the content on gold and platinum products, but that isn't much help when it comes to judging gems.

If you don't know what to look for in jewellery, you should at least be careful about where you buy. If the items you want to buy do not have price tags attached, that's

a serious danger sign and you should go elsewhere. Shops in the trendy shopping arcades of the Tsim Sha Tsui tourist combat zone are going to be most expensive.

Opals are said to be the best value in Hong Kong because this is where they are cut. Diamonds are generally not a good deal, because the world trade is mostly controlled by a cartel. Hong Kong does not have a diamond-cutting industry and must import from Belgium, India, Israel and the USA.

A couple of reputable jewellers will issue a certificate that not only states exactly what you are buying, but guarantees that the shop will buy it back at a fair market price. It's worthwhile buying from one of these places – if you later become dissatisfied with your purchase, you can at least get most of your money back on a trade-in. Two chain stores which give this guarantee are King Fook and Tse Sui Luen. Exact addresses of their branches are given in the Things to Buy sections for Kowloon and Hong Kong Island.

Finally, after you've bought something and want to find out how badly you got ripped off, you can have it appraised. This is a service you get charged for, and some stones (such as diamonds) may have to be unset for testing. You can contact the Gemmological Association of Hong Kong (☎ 2366-6066) for the current list of approved appraisers. Two places which do appraisals are De Silva (☎ 2522-0639), Two Pacific Place, Central; and Valuation Services (☎ 2810-6640), 11 MacDonnell Rd, Central.

Leathers & Luggage As with clothing, the manufacture of luggage and leather goods is low-tech and labour intensive, which means that China is the perfect place to open a factory. Lots of what gets produced in mainland China is pure junk – zippers and straps that break instantly, and 'leather' that often proves to be vinyl.

Fortunately, most of what gets sent to the Hong Kong market is export quality, but check carefully because there is still a lot of rubbish on sale. All the big brand names like

Gucci and Louis Vuitton are on display in Hong Kong department stores, and you'll find some local vendors in the leather business with odd names like Mandarina Duck and Companion Reptile. To be sure, you'll find a wide selection and a big spread in prices.

The best advice for buying this kind of stuff is to take your time to carefully inspect zippers, straps and stitching. Look on the inside of the luggage, as the outside may be tough leather or nylon but the inside could be cheap vinyl. Decide early on if you need an expensive label or just durability at the lowest possible price.

Watches Watch stores are ubiquitous in Hong Kong and you can find everything from a Russian army timepiece to Rolex and scuba-diving watches. As always, you should avoid the shops which do not put price tags on their merchandise, which pretty much precludes buying anything along Nathan Rd in Tsim Sha Tsui. The big department stores are quite all right, but compare prices.

It's worth knowing that watch cases do not have to be expensive to ensure a quality watch: the internal workings (simply known as the 'movement') are 90% of the battle. There is a thriving industry in Hong Kong taking top-quality Swiss movements and putting them into cheap made-in-China cases. While you do want to find a case that isn't going to rust, you can easily solve the green-wrist syndrome if you buy a leather rather than a metal watchband. A waterproof watch is another ball game – if it's made in China, let the seller dunk it into a glass of water to prove that it is indeed waterproof. If you really want a fancy gold case sporting a famous label that's fine, but it's something you will pay dearly for.

About every third person you encounter on Nathan Rd in Tsim Sha Tsui seems to be yelling 'copy watch!' in your ear. This is not some sort of traditional Chinese greeting, but

---

The Triads

At one time the Triads, or secret societies, may have been a positive influence in China. It is said they opposed the corrupt and brutal Manchu (Qing) dynasty and aided the revolution that brought down the Manchus in 1911. The fact that Kuanti, the God of War, has been adopted by the Triads has probably lent some respectability to these organisations.

Unfortunately, the Triads that exist now are the Chinese equivalent of the Mafia. Sporting such catchy names as Bamboo Union and 14K, the Triads have been increasingly successful at recruiting disaffected teenagers in Hong Kong's high-rise housing estates. Initially offering young people a bit of companionship and adventure, the 'fun' soon turns to illegal gambling, extortion, protection rackets, the smuggling of drugs and weapons, prostitution, loan sharking and sometimes robberies of banks and jewellery shops. Like most such organisations, once you join a Triad you cannot quit. Gwailos are not welcome – even the Triad-controlled prostitution business centred in Mong Kok and Sham Shui Po shuns foreign clientele.

Membership in a Triad is illegal in Hong Kong – it's even illegal to claim to be a member. Yet the Triads seem to be growing and have been trying to use their vast wealth to muscle into legitimate businesses: a recent target has been Hong Kong's movie industry. Many fear that the growing influence of the Triads will drive out legitimate businesses and hurt Hong Kong's economy in the long term.

It was the communists who smashed the Triad-controlled opium selling business in Shanghai after the 1949 revolution. The Triads have not forgotten, and 1997 has seen many Hong Kong-based criminals moving their operations to ethnic Chinese communities in places like Australia, Canada and the USA. Even the poverty-stricken Philippines has received some of this 'overseas investment' – Triad-arranged kidnappings of wealthy Chinese families living in the Philippines has become a growth industry. Ironically, some Triads are expanding into mainland China, establishing links with corrupt government officials and high-ranking soldiers in the People's Liberation Army (PLA).

Foreigners visiting Hong Kong seldom encounter Triad members directly except possibly in two places – the 'copy-watch' spruikers along Nathan Rd and the bouncers in sleazy hostess clubs. Fortunately, it's easy enough to avoid doing business with these unpleasant characters – buy a Swatch instead, and do your drinking in Lan Kwai Fong or Wan Chai. ■

HONG KONG

an attempt to sell you a fake Rolex or Seiko. Just why this is tolerated by the Hong Kong authorities has always mystified me – after all, it is illegal and the government is always claiming to be 'cracking down' on counterfeiters. The police have even found fake watches in shops displaying the HKTA logo. Perhaps official willingness to look the other way has something to do with the fact that this business is controlled by Hong Kong's notorious Triad criminal gangs.

Perhaps you don't mind doing business with the Triads and don't care about the morality of buying counterfeit merchandise, but consider this: these fake Rolexes have a nasty habit of losing 10 to 15 minutes of time per day, and then stop working at all after a month. If by some miracle it lasts longer than that, the 'gold' watchband starts to turn your wrist green. But at least you got a 'bargain', didn't you?

Video This catch-all term 'video' refers to a number of commercial products you might wish to buy: a TV set, video tape player (also known as video cassette recorder or VCR), the video tapes themselves, and a video camera (camcorder) to make your own movies.

In the Tsim Sha Tsui rip-off zone, practically every video shop has a demonstration TV set up in the rear of the store. You can expect a demonstration in which only the most expensive 'digital' video camera produces a crisp image. What you won't be told is that the TV is rigged so that it will only work properly with the overpriced digital model. You also won't be told that the 'digital' model is not digital at all, but an ordinary camera for which you get to pay double.

The problem of rip-offs can best be avoided by not shopping in Tsim Sha Tsui. However, life isn't so simple – it is also important to understand a few basics of TV broadcasting if you want to purchase a VCR, video tapes or camcorder.

Hong Kong's standard for video and TV broadcasting is PAL. Unfortunately, there are additional complications to consider –

a PAL-standard TV bought in Hong Kong may not work for you, even if your home country uses PAL, because the stations might be adjusted to different frequencies. A few manufacturers have started offering multi-standard TVs that can be adjusted to PAL, NTSC or SECAM with the flick of a switch, but these models cost more. Some multi-standard systems show colour in one mode only, so read the manuals carefully before purchasing.

If you're interested in purchasing a VCR, you'll have the same problem – a VCR must be compatible with your TV. You can't connect a PAL video player to an NTSC TV or vice versa. Also, the video player won't work if it uses a frequency different from that used by your TV set, though this problem can be adjusted by a technician (for a fee). The same is true of camcorders – they must be compatible with the VCR and TV with which they will be used. Again, there is such a thing as a multi-standard VCR which can work with PAL, NTSC and SECAM, but you pay extra for this feature.

Again, you've got the same problem when purchasing video tapes. If you buy a prerecorded video tape off the shelf in Hong Kong, it will almost certainly be PAL standard. If your home country uses NTSC or SECAM, you won't be able to view this tape unless you have one of those new multi-standard VCRs.

If multi-standard TVs and multi-standard VCRs exist, is there also such a thing as a multi-standard camcorder? The answer is no. If you want to buy a camcorder, you must decide which standard you want, PAL, NTSC or SECAM. A wrong choice would be a costly mistake, so pay careful attention to the labels.

Video tapes come in two sizes: VHS and 8 mm. Virtually all pre-recorded tapes and all VCRs are VHS size. The 8 mm tapes are very small, making them ideal for use in small hand-held camcorders. If you produce a movie on 8 mm tape, many companies offer a service to transfer it to a VHS tape for home viewing. A more important complication is the new improved 'super-video'

(S-video) variation. This is a high-resolution variation of the VHS and 8 mm standard, called Super-VHS (S-VHS) and Hi-Band 8 mm (Hi-8), respectively. You cannot play an S-video tape on a standard VCR. However, an S-VCR can play standard video tapes.

Having told you that, I now have to admit that I was lying. Somebody recently introduced a more compact version of VHS, known as VHS-Compact (VHS-C). It's smaller than standard VHS but larger than 8 mm. And yes, there is a high-resolution variation, Super-VHS-Compact (S-VHS-C). Technology marches on.

If you've managed to digest all this, you still have one more hurdle to clear – audio standards. Video tapes come with the ability to reproduce sound, and the latest rage is to have stereo sound quality. In the VHS format, there is VHS Hi-Fi, while 8 mm chips in with the new PCM audio format. If you want to enjoy this improved sound quality, you have to buy equipment that can record it and play it back.

There is such a thing as a laser disk, more accurately called a video disk. These offer a few advantages over tapes: longevity, the ability to jump from one point in a movie to any other, and they can freeze a frame without the annoying flutter of tapes. The drawback is that you can't make your own recordings on laser disks unless you invest in big-money equipment. The real reason to buy laser disks and a laser disk player is to watch quality pre-recorded movies. For most people, this is not a wise option because the number of movies available for rental on laser disks is relatively small.

Confused? You ought to be. The problem is that what is standard today is likely to be obsolete tomorrow. There has been much talk about introducing super high-resolution 'double-scan' TVs and digital TVs with pictures so clear they practically leap off the screen. Wouldn't it be nice if the various countries in the world could agree on a single standard? Don't hold your breath.

Getting There & Away

AIR

Airports & Airlines

Hong Kong is the major gateway to China and much of East Asia. Consequently, international air service is excellent and competition keeps fares relatively low compared to neighbouring countries. The only problem is flying during the holiday crunch – the Chinese Lunar New Year. Christmas and Easter can also be difficult times to get reservations.

Hong Kong's Kai Tak airport is named after a Mr Kai and a Mr Tak who once owned the land. As airports go, it has an unusual set of problems. To begin with, it's the fourth busiest in the world and the single runway has to accommodate one landing every two minutes (the maximum permitted by international regulations). Furthermore, it was designed in the 1930s before the skyscrapers were built and when aircraft had propeller engines. The result is that nowadays high-rise residents get to look *down* on approaching jumbo jets! The gridlocked air traffic and heart-in-teeth landings among the skyscrapers may have you wishing you'd purchased extra life insurance, but Kai Tak in fact has a good safety record. Unfortunately, elbow-to-armpit crowds, impossibly long queues at immigration and massive delays at the baggage claim area are all too common.

Kai Tak's shortcomings were long ago noted and a new airport is under construction at Chek Lap Kok, on the north side of Lantau Island. However, everyone concedes that Chek Lap Kok's single runway will be instantly inundated from the moment it opens. A proposal to build a second runway has been approved, and airport officials admit that even with a third runway the airport will probably be saturated by around the year 2005.

On all flights, carry-on hand baggage must be able to fit in a space no larger than 22.5 cm x 35 cm x 55 cm. At least in Hong Kong, the security guards at the airport attempt to enforce this regulation (most other airports are more slack). Putting all non-breakable items into your checked luggage makes sense, but the price for overweight baggage can be high – usually 1% of the first-class airfare for each kg.

The current slogan of the HKTA is 'Stay Another Day', but if you don't reconfirm your onward ticket you may have to stay another week or longer. The easiest place to reconfirm is right in the airport on arrival, but you can do it by telephone or by dropping in to the airlines' branch offices.

Aeroflot
New Henry House, 10 Ice House St, Central (☎ 2537-2611)

Aerolineas Argentinas
Takshing House, Theatre Lane & Des Voeux Rd, Central (☎ 2521-2307)

Air Canada
Room 1002, Wheelock House, 20 Pedder St, Central (☎ 2522-1001)

Air France
Room 2104, Alexandra House, 7 Des Voeux Rd, Central (☎ 2524-8145)

Air India
42nd floor, Gloucester Tower, 11 Pedder St, Central (☎ 2522-1176)

Air Lanka
27th floor, Lippo Tower, Lippo Centre, 89 Queensway, Central (☎ 2521-0708)

Air Mauritius
c/o Mercury Travel, St George's Building, Ice House St & Connaught Rd, Central (☎ 2523-1114)

Air New Zealand
Room 1601, 8 Cotton Tree Drive, Central (☎ 2524-9041)

Air Niugini
Room 705, Century Square, 1-13 D'Aguilar St, Central (☎ 2524-2151)

Air Panama
Century House, Hart Ave, Tsim Sha Tsui (☎ 2369-9883)

Air Seychelles, Heng Shan Centre, Queen's Rd East, Wan Chai (☎ 2866-8826; 22821-3881)

Alitalia
Vicwood Plaza, 199 Des Voeux Rd, Central (☎ 2543-6998)

All Nippon
Room 2512, Pacific Place Two, 88 Queensway, Admiralty (☎ 2810-7100)

American Airlines
Room 1738, Swire House, 9 Connaught Rd, Central (☎ 2826-9269)

Ansett Australia
Unit A, 26th floor, United Centre, 95 Queensway, Admiralty (☎ 2527-7883)

Asiana
Gloucester Tower, 11 Pedder St (☎ 2523-8585)

Biman Bangladesh
Kai Tak airport, Kowloon City (☎ 2329-8036)

British Airways
30th floor, Alexandra House, 7 Des Voeux Rd Central (☎ 2868-0303)

CAAC (Civil Aviation Administration of China)
Ground floor, 10 Queen's Rd, Central
Ground floor, Mirador Mansion, 54-64B Nathan Rd, Tsim Sha Tsui (☎ 2861-0322)

Canadian Airlines International
Ground floor, Swire House, 9-25 Chater Rd, Central (☎ 2868-3123)

Cathay Pacific
Ground floor, Swire House, 9-25 Chater Rd, Central Sheraton Hotel, 20 Nathan Rd, Tsim Sha Tsui (☎ 2747-1888)

China Airlines (Taiwan)
3rd floor, St George's Building, Ice House St and Connaught Rd, Central

Continental Micronesia
New Henry House, 10 Ice House St, Central (☎ 2525-7759)

Delta
Two Pacific Place, Admiralty (☎ 2526-5875)

Dragonair
World Wide House, 19 Des Voeux Rd, Central (☎ 2590-1188)

Emirates
Gloucester Tower, 11 Pedder St, Central (☎ 2526-7171)

EVA Air
Gloucester Tower, 11 Pedder St, Central (☎ 2810-9251)

Finnair
Caroline Centre, 28 Yun Ping Rd, Causeway Bay (☎ 2926-2048)

Garuda Indonesia
2nd floor, Sing Pao Centre, 8 Queen's Rd, Central (☎ 2840-0000)

Gulf Air
Room 2508, Caroline Centre, 28 Yun Ping Rd, Causeway Bay (☎ 2881-8993)

Iberia
19th floor, Chung Hing Commercial Building, 62-63 Connaught Rd, Central (☎ 2542-3228)

Japan Air Lines
20th floor, Gloucester Tower, 11 Pedder St, Central (☎ 2523-0081)

Japan Asia
20th floor, Gloucester Tower, 11 Pedder St, Central (☎ 2521-8102)

Jardine Airways
30th floor, Alexandra House, 7 Des Voeux Rd, Central (☎ 2868-0768)

Kenya
Liu Chong Hing Bank Building, Des Voeux Rd & Theatre Lane, Central (☎ 2523-6054)

KLM Royal Dutch
Room 2201, World Trade Centre, 280 Gloucester Rd, Causeway Bay (☎ 2808-2118)

Korean Air
11th floor, South Seas Centre, Tower II, 75 Mody Rd, Tsim Sha Tsui East (☎ 2733-7111)

Ladeco Chilean
Chung Hing Commercial Building, 62-63 Connaught Rd, Central (☎ 2542-3228)

LanChile
Windsor House, 311 Gloucester Rd (at Great George St), Causeway Bay (☎ 2882-1327)

Lauda Air (Austria)
Pacific House, Zetland St, Central (☎ 2525-5222)

Lufthansa
The Landmark, 11 Pedder St, Central (☎ 2868-2313)

Malaysia Airlines
Room 1306, Prince's Building, 9-25 Chater Rd, Central (☎ 2521-8181)

Myanmar Airways
Asia Standard Tower, Queen's Rd & Pottinger St, Central (☎ 2526-0100)

New Zealand International
Jardine House, 1 Connaught Place, Central (☎ 2845-8458)

Northwest Airlines
29th floor, Alexandra House, 7 Des Voeux Rd, Central (☎ 2810-4288)

Pakistan International
Room 401A, Empire Centre, Mody Rd, Tsim Sha Tsui East (☎ 2366-4770)

Philippine Airlines
Room 6, ground floor, East Ocean Centre, 98 Granville Rd, Tsim Sha Tsui East (☎ 2369-4521)

Qantas
Room 1433, Swire House, 9-25 Chater Rd, Central (☎ 2842-1438)

Royal Brunei Airlines
Room 1406, Central Building, 3 Pedder St, Central (☎ 2869-8608)

Royal Nepal Airlines
Room 704, Lippo Sun Plaza, 28 Canton Rd, Tsim Sha Tsui (☎ 2375-9151)

Sabena Belgian
Heng Shan Centre, Queen's Rd East, Wan Chai (☎ 2528-2738)

Air Travel Glossary

Baggage Allowance This will be written on your ticket: usually one 20 kg item to go in the hold, plus one item of hand luggage.

Bucket Shop An unbonded travel agency specialising in discounted airline tickets.

Bumped Just because you have a confirmed seat doesn't mean you're going to get on the plane – see Overbooking.

Cancellation Penalties If you have to cancel or change an Apex ticket there are often heavy penalties involved. Insurance can sometimes be taken out against these penalties. Some airlines impose penalties on regular tickets as well, particularly against 'no show' passengers.

Check-In Airlines ask you to check in a certain time ahead of the flight departure (usually 2 hours on international flights). If you fail to check in on time and the flight is overbooked the airline can cancel your booking and give your seat to somebody else.

Confirmation Having a ticket written out with the flight and date you want doesn't mean you have a seat until the agent has checked with the airline that your status is 'OK' or confirmed. Meanwhile you could just be 'on request'.

Full Fares Airlines traditionally offer first class (coded F), business class (coded J) and economy class (coded Y) tickets. These days there are so many promotional and discounted fares available from the regular economy class that few passengers pay full economy fare.

No-Shows No-shows are passengers who fail to show up for their flight; sometimes because of

---

Sempati Air (Indonesia)
Tung Ying Building, Granville Rd at Nathan Rd, Tsim Sha Tsui (☎ 2368-5151)

Singapore Airlines
United Centre, 95 Queensway, Admiralty (☎ 2520-2233)

South African Airways
30th floor, Alexandra House, Central (☎ 2877-3277)

Swissair
8th floor, Tower II, Admiralty Centre, 18 Harcourt Rd, Central (☎ 2529-3670)

THAI Airways
United Centre, 95 Queensway, Admiralty
Shop 124, 1st floor, World Wide Plaza, Des Voeux Rd and Pedder St, Central
Omni, The Hongkong Hotel, 3 Canton Rd, Tsim Sha Tsui (☎ 2529-5681)

Trans World Airlines
Mezzanine floor, Sun House, 90 Connaught Rd, Central (☎ 2851-1411)

United Airlines
29th floor, The Landmark, Gloucester Tower, 11 Pedder St, Central Star House, 3 Salisbury Rd, Tsim Sha Tsui (☎ 2810-4888)

Varig Brazilian
Central Plaza, Gloucester & Fleming Rds, Wan Chai (☎ 2511-1234)

Viasa Venezuelan
Chung Hing Commercial Building, 62-63 Connaught Rd, Central(☎ 2542-3228)

Vietnam Airlines
Peregrine Tower, Lippo Centre, 89 Queensway, Admiralty (☎ 2810-6880)

Virgin Atlantic
Suite 4104, 41st floor, Lippo Tower, Lippo Centre, 89 Queensway, Admiralty (☎ 2532-6060)

Buying Tickets

You will have to choose between buying a ticket to Hong Kong then making other arrangements when you arrive, and buying a ticket allowing various stopovers around Asia. For example, such a ticket could fly you from Sydney to London with stopovers in Denpasar, Jakarta, Hong Kong, Bangkok, Calcutta, Delhi and Istanbul.

There are a host of other deals which travel agents will offer in order to sell you a cheaper ticket. Fares will vary according to your point of departure, the time of year, how direct the flight is and how flexible you can be. Whatever you do, buy air tickets from a travel agent. The airlines don't deal directly in discount tickets, only the travel agents do. However, not every travel agent offers discount tickets, and those that do can vary widely. It's a good idea to call the airline first and see what their cheapest ticket costs – use that as your starting point when talking to travel agents. Thanks to intense competition, most tickets sold these days are discounted.

Many travel agents hesitate to sell you the

unexpected delays or disasters; sometimes they simply forget, sometimes because they made more than one booking and didn't bother to cancel the one they didn't want. Full-fare passengers who fail to turn up are sometimes entitled to travel on a later flight. The rest of us are penalised (see Cancellation Penalties).

On Request An unconfirmed booking for a flight, see Confirmation.

Overbooking Airlines hate to fly empty seats and since every flight has some passengers who fail to show up (see No-Shows) airlines often book more passengers than they have seats. Usually the excess passengers balance those who fail to show up but occasionally somebody gets bumped. If this happens guess who it is most likely to be? The passengers who check in late.

Reconfirmation At least 72 hours before departure time of an onward or return flight you must contact the airline and 'reconfirm' that you intend to be on the flight. If you don't do this the airline can delete your name from the passenger list and you could lose your seat. You don't have to reconfirm the first flight on your itinerary or if your stopover is less than 72 hours. It doesn't hurt to reconfirm more than once.

Transferred Tickets Airline tickets cannot be transferred from one person to another. Travellers sometimes try to sell the return half of their ticket, but officials can ask you to prove that you are the person named on the ticket. This is unlikely to happen on domestic flights, but on an international flight tickets may be compared with passports. ■

cheapest ticket available. This is not always because they want to squeeze more money out of you. Airlines have cheap special deals, but the number of such seats may be limited, and there are often severe restrictions. With the cheapest tickets, you often have to pay the travel agent first and then pick up the ticket at the airport. Nevertheless, these cheap tickets may be worth the extra trouble. If you want the cheapest flight, tell the agent, and then make sure you understand what restrictions, if any, apply.

It's important to realise that when you buy a discounted air ticket from a travel agent, you must also go back to that agent if you want to obtain a refund – the airlines will not refund your money directly unless you paid full fare. This can be quite a hassle if you decide to change your route half way through. In that case, you'd have to return to the place where you purchased the ticket to recoup the unused portion. Of course, you could mail the ticket to a reliable friend and they could try getting a refund for you, but don't count on it. It's also true that some travel agents (and airlines) are extremely slow to issue refunds – delays of up to a year are not uncommon!

Most airlines divide the year into 'peak' (expensive), 'shoulder' (less expensive) and 'off' (cheapest) seasons. In the northern hemisphere, peak season is June through September and off season is November through February. However, holidays (Christmas and Chinese Lunar New Year) will be treated as peak season even though they come during off season. In the southern hemisphere, the seasons are reversed.

Despite the name, 'normal economy-class tickets' are *not* the most economical way to go. Essentially, they are full-fare tickets. On the other hand, they give you maximum flexibility and are valid for 12 months. Also, if you don't use them they are fully refundable by the airlines, as are unused sectors of a multiple ticket.

'Group tickets' are well worth considering. You usually do *not* need to travel with a group. However, once the departure date is booked it may be impossible to change – you can only depart when the 'group' departs, even if you never meet another group member. The good news is that the return date can usually be left open, but there could be other restrictions – you might have to complete the trip in 60 days, or perhaps only fly off-season or during weekdays. It's important to ask the travel agent what conditions and restrictions apply to any tickets you intend to buy.

APEX (Advance Purchase Excursion)

tickets are sold at a discount but will lock you into a rigid schedule. Such tickets must be purchased two or three weeks ahead of departure, do not permit stopovers and may have minimum and maximum stays as well as fixed departure and return dates. Unless you must return at a certain time, it's best to purchase APEX tickets on a one-way basis only. There are stiff cancellation fees if you decide not to use your APEX ticket.

'Round-the-world' tickets are usually offered by an airline or combination of airlines, and let you take your time (six months to a year) moving from point to point on their routes for the price of one ticket. The main restriction is that you have to keep moving in the same direction; another drawback is that because you are usually booking individual flights as you go, and can't switch carriers, you can get caught out by flight availabilities, and have to spend more or less time in a place than you want.

One thing to avoid is a 'back-to-front' ticket. These are best explained by example – if you want to fly from Japan (where tickets are relatively expensive) to Hong Kong (where tickets are much cheaper), you can pay by check or credit card and have a friend or travel agent in Hong Kong mail the ticket to you. The problem is that the airlines have computers and will know that the ticket was issued in Hong Kong rather than Japan, and they will refuse to honour it. Consumer groups have filed lawsuits over this practice with mixed results, but in most countries the law protects the airlines, not consumers. In short, the ticket is only valid starting from the country where it was issued. The only exception to this rule is if you purchase a full-fare (non-discounted) ticket, but of course that robs you of the advantage you gain by purchasing a back-to-front ticket.

If the ticket is issued in a third location (such as the USA), the same rule applies. You cannot fly from Japan to Hong Kong with a ticket mailed to you from the USA – if you buy a ticket in the USA, you can fly from there to Japan and then to Hong Kong and thus enjoy a discounted price, but you can't start the journey from Japan. Again, an exception is made if you pay full fare and thus negate your savings.

'Frequent-flyer' plans have proliferated in recent years and are now offered by most airlines, even some budget ones. Basically, these allow you a free ticket if you chalk up so many km with the same airline. The plans aren't always as good as they sound – some airlines require you to use all your frequent-flier credits within one year or you lose the lot. Sometimes you find yourself flying on a particular airline just to get frequent flier credits, and the ticket may well be considerably more expensive than what you might have got elsewhere. Since frequent-flier programmes first got off the ground in the USA, some airlines require that you have a US or Canadian mailing address, though you don't have to be a citizen or resident of either country. Many airlines have 'blackout' periods – peak times when you cannot use the free tickets you obtained under a frequent-flier programme. When you purchase the ticket be sure to give the ticket agent your frequent-flier membership number, and again when you check in for your flight. A common complaint seems to be that airlines forget to record your frequent-flier credits when you fly with them – save all your boarding passes and ticket receipts and be prepared to push if no bonus is forthcoming. In this regard I've personally had much trouble with United Airlines, and for this reason I no longer fly with them. Taiwan's China Airlines also has a frequent flier programme, but it isn't too good – to qualify for a free ticket you must fly 160,000 km, which is equivalent to eight round-trip flights from Los Angeles to Taipei. North-West Airlines has the most generous frequent-flier programme, offering a free ticket after you've flown 32,000 km.

Some airlines offer student card holders discounts of up to 25% on their tickets. In some countries, an official-looking letter from the school is also needed. You also must be aged 26 or less. These discounts are generally only available on ordinary economy-class fares.

You wouldn't get one, for instance, on an APEX or a round-the-world ticket since these are already discounted.

Courier flights can be a bargain if you're fortunate enough to find one. The way it works is that an air freight company takes over your entire checked baggage allowance. You are permitted to bring along a carry-on bag, but that's all. In return, you get a steeply discounted ticket. These arrangements usually have to be made a month or more in advance and are only available on certain routes. Such flights are occasionally advertised in the newspapers, or contact air freight companies listed in the phone book.

Buying Tickets in Hong Kong Be careful about Hong Kong travel agencies – rip-offs do occur. It happens less now than it used to, but Hong Kong has long been plagued with bogus travel agents and fly-by-night operations that appear shortly before peak holiday seasons and dupe customers into buying non-existent airline seats and holiday packages. One way to tell is to see if they are listed in the telephone book, since fly-by-night operations don't stay around long enough to get listed.

The most common trick is a request for a non-refundable deposit on an air ticket. You pay a deposit for the booking, but when you go to pick up the tickets they say the flight is no longer available. However, there will be another flight available at a higher price – sometimes 50% more! This sales tactic is commonly referred to as 'bait and switch' – it's illegal in many countries, but apparently perfectly legal in Hong Kong.

It is best not to pay a deposit, but rather to pay for the ticket in full and get a receipt clearly showing that there is no balance due, and that the full amount is refundable if no ticket is issued. Tickets are normally issued the next day after booking, but you must pick up the really cheap tickets (ie, group tickets) yourself at the airport from the 'tour leader' (who you will never see again once you've got the ticket). One caution: when you get the ticket from the tour leader, check it carefully because occasional errors occur. For example, you may be issued a ticket with the return portion valid for only 60 days when you paid for a ticket valid for one year, etc.

If you think you have been ripped off, and the agent is a member of the HKTA, the organisation can apply some pressure (and apparently has a fund to handle cases of outright fraud). Even if an agent is a member of the HKTA they do not have to comply with any set of guidelines.

Since mid-1985 all travel agencies offering outward-bound services must be licensed. A fund was also set up to compensate cheated customers. It could be worth enquiring about it if you get ripped-off.

The travel agent that I often use in Hong Kong is *Traveller Services* (☎ 2375-2222; fax 2375-2233), Room 1012, Silvercord Tower 1, 30 Canton Rd, Tsim Sha Tsui.

Phoenix Services (☎ 2722-7378; fax 2369-8884) Room B, 6th floor, Milton Mansion, 96 Nathan Rd, Tsim Sha Tsui, is scrupulously honest and gets good reviews from travellers.

You can also try *Shoestring Travel* (☎ 2723-2306; fax 2721-2085) Flat A, 4th floor, Alpha House, 27-33 Nathan Rd, Tsim Sha Tsui. The service is not friendly, but the prices are in the same range as the others.

Hong Kong Student Travel Bureau is really no cheaper than the other agencies, though this place can offer a discount for ISIC card holders. They have several branch offices, the most useful being at Star House (☎ 2730-3269), Room 1021, 10th Floor, Tsim Sha Tsui; and Wing On Central Building (☎ 2810-7272), Room 901, 26 Des Voeux Rd, Central.

If you're staying on the Hong Kong Island side, an agent who gets good recommendations is Natori Travel (☎ 2881-8482; fax 2576-0311), Room 2102A, Goldmark, 502 Hennessy Rd, Causeway Bay.

Travellers with Special Needs
Most international airlines can cater to special needs – travellers with disabilities, people with young children and even children travelling alone. Check with the airline to be sure.

HONG KONG

Special dietary needs (vegetarian, kosher, etc) can also be catered to with advance notice. However, the 'special meals' usually aren't very special – they often consist of salad, fruit, bread and dessert. They're edible, but nothing to write home about.

Airlines usually carry babies up to two years of age at 10% of the relevant adult fare; a few may carry them free of charge. Reputable international airlines usually provide nappies (diapers), tissues, talcum and all the other paraphernalia needed to keep babies clean, dry and half happy. For children between the ages of four and 12, the fare on international flights is usually 50% of the regular fare or 67% of a discounted fare.

Australia

As an alternative to flying direct between Australia and Hong Kong, you can often get free stopovers in either Singapore or Bangkok, especially if you fly with Singapore Airlines or THAI Airways, respectively.

Australia is not a cheap place to fly from, and airfares to Asia are absurdly expensive considering the distances flown. However, there are a few ways of cutting the costs.

Among the cheapest regular tickets available in Australia are APEX tickets. The cost depends on your departure date from Australia.

It's possible to get reductions on the cost of APEX and other fares by going to the student travel offices and/or some of the travel agents in Australia that specialise in discounting.

The weekend travel sections of newspapers like *The Age* (Melbourne) or the *Sydney Morning Herald* are good sources of travel information.

In Melbourne, Flight Centre is well worth trying. They have offices throughout the inner city (☎ 13 1600). The main office is at 353 Little Collins St, Melbourne. They also have branches in central Sydney (☎ (02) 9235-3522), Brisbane (☎ (07) 3221-9211) and Darwin (☎ (08) 8941-8 002.

A one-way/return Melbourne-Hong Kong ticket starts from about A$915/1150. Darwin-Hong Kong begins at about A$535/985.

Canada

With half of Hong Kong emigrating to Vancouver, you would expect to find year-round super-cheap airfares on this competitive route. In fact, fares are not terribly low, and there is a considerable variation by season. The following airfares are offered on Cathay Pacific and Canadian Airlines:

	Low Season	Shoulder Season	High Season
One Way	US$501	US$566	US$644
Return	US$916	US$1046	US$1202

Fares are slightly cheaper if you fly Northwest Airlines, though you are obliged to make a transit stop in Seattle.

Getting discount tickets in Canada is much the same as in the USA – go to the travel agents and shop around until you find a good deal. There are a number of good agents in Vancouver for discounted tickets. You may want to try CUTS, Canada's national student bureau, which has offices in most Canadian cities (you don't have to be a student).

Europe

Most West European cities are good places for buying discount air tickets. In Antwerp, WATS has been recommended. In Zurich, try SOF Travel and Sindbad. In Geneva, try Stohl Travel. In the Netherlands, NBBS is a reputable agency. Frankfurt is Germany's gateway to Hong Kong, with direct flights on Lufthansa.

In Germany there are some quarterly magazines available which specialise in price information for flights all over the world (*Reise & Preise*, *Reisefieber*, etc).

From most cities in Western Europe, rock bottom one-way/return fares to Hong Kong begin at US$410/640.

Guam

Guam has emerged as a popular honeymoon spot and a favoured location for Chinese and Japanese film crews making karaoke movies. Although Guam is just four hours' flying from Hong Kong, air fares cost as much as a flight to the US west coast (a 13-hour flight)!

Continental Micronesia has a monopoly on direct Hong Kong-Guam flights, but other airlines offer lower fares if you make a stopover. For example, one-way/return on Continental is US$589/810, but Asiana Airlines charges only US$444/625 with a stopover in Seoul.

Indonesia

Garuda Airlines has direct flights from Jakarta to Hong Kong, and from Denpasar to Hong Kong via Jakarta. Cheap discount air tickets out of Indonesia can be bought from travel agents in Kuta Beach in Bali and in Jakarta. There are numerous airline ticket discounters around Kuta Beach – several are on the main strip, Jalan Legian. You can also buy discount tickets in Kuta for departure from Jakarta. In Jakarta, there are a few discounters on Jalan Jaksa. Bottom-end one-way/return prices for Hong Kong-Jakarta are currently 552,240 rp/1,020,240 rp.

Japan

Japan is not a good place to buy cheap air tickets. In fact, I can't think of anything you can buy cheaply in Japan, not even rice. The cheapest way to get out of Japan is by ferry to either Taiwan or Korea. However, if you need an air ticket, some well-established Tokyo travel agents where English is spoken include STA (☎ 5269-0751) and Ikebukuro (☎ 5391-2922).

For tickets purchased in Hong Kong, a Hong Kong-Tokyo one-way/return flight costs around HK$1989/3869.

Korea (South)

Some of the best deals are available from Joy Travel Service (☎ (02) 776-9871; fax 756-5342), 10th floor, 24-2 Mukyo-dong, Chung-gu (directly behind City Hall). The Korean International Student Exchange Society (KISES) (☎ (02) 733-9494), room 505, YMCA building, Chongno 2-ga, Seoul, is also very good. The lowest one-way/return prices on the Hong Kong-Seoul route are W160,555/266,505.

New Zealand

Air New Zealand and Cathay Pacific fly directly from Auckland to Hong Kong. APEX fares are the cheapest way to go, but you have to pay for your ticket at least 21 days in advance and spend a minimum of six days overseas. The lowest-priced one-way/return tickets available on the Hong Kong-Auckland run are NZ$835/1222.

Singapore

A good place for buying cheap air tickets in Singapore is Airmaster Travel, 46 Bencoolen St. Other agents advertise in the *Straits Times* classified columns. One-way/return Hong Kong-Singapore tickets start at S$280/409.

Taiwan

The cheapest one-way/return fares on the Hong Kong-Taipei or Hong Kong-Kaohsiung routes are NT$4124/5223.

With an ISIC or STA youth card, discounts are available from Youth Travel International (☎ (02) 721-1978), suite 502, 142 Chunghsiao E Rd, Section 4, Taipei. This place also issues these cards to qualified individuals.

Otherwise, look for discount travel agencies which advertise in the local English-language newspapers, the *China Post* or *China News*. An agent I've dealt with and found to be very reliable is Jenny Su Travel (☎ (02) 594-7733; fax 592-0068), 10th floor, 27 Chungshan N Rd, Section 3, Taipei.

Thailand

In Bangkok, Student Travel in the Thai Hotel is helpful and efficient. Travel agents on Khao San Rd are also heavily into discounting. Discounted one way/return fares start at 3485B/5454B.

Other Asian Countries

For one-way return tickets purchased in Hong Kong, some sample fares include: Beijing HK$2293/4353; Guangzhou HK$600/1000; Hanoi HK$2184/4173; Ho Chi Minh City (Saigon) HK$2410/4594; Kuala Lumpur HK$3005/3565; Kathmandu HK$2348/3970; Manila US$1000/

1485; Pnomh Penh US$2075/ 3237; Yangon (Rangoon) US$3005/5775.

The USA

There are some very good open tickets which remain valid for six months or one year (opt for the latter) and allow multiple stopovers, but don't lock you into any fixed dates of departure. For example, there are cheap tickets between the US west coast and Hong Kong with stopovers in Japan and Korea for very little extra money – the departure dates can be changed and you have one year to complete the journey. However, remember that it's easy to get locked out during the Chinese Lunar New Year and other peak times.

Usually, and not surprisingly, the cheapest fare to whatever country is offered by a bucket shop owned by someone of that particular ethnic origin. San Francisco is the bucket-shop capital of America, though some good deals can be found in Los Angeles, New York and other cities. Discounters can be found through the *Yellow Pages* or the major daily newspapers. Those listed in both Roman and Oriental scripts are invariably discounters. A more direct way is to wander around San Francisco's Chinatown where most of the shops are – especially in the Clay St and Waverly Place area. Many of these are staffed by recent arrivals from Hong Kong and Taiwan who speak little English. Enquiries are best made in person. One place popular with budget travellers is Wahlock Travel in the Bank of America Building on Stockton St.

It's not advisable to send money (even cheques) through the post unless the agent is very well established – some travellers have reported being ripped off by fly-by-night mail-order ticket agents. Nor is it wise to hand over the full amount to Shady Deal Travel Services unless they can give you the ticket straight away – most US travel agencies have computers that can spit out the ticket on the spot.

Council Travel, with an office on Bush St, is the largest student travel organisation and, though you don't have to be a student to use them, they do have specially discounted student tickets.

One of the cheapest and most reliable travel agents on the west coast is Overseas Tours (π (800) 222-5292), 475 El Camino Real, room 206, Millbrae, CA 94030. Another good agent is Gateway Travel (π (214) 960-2000, (800) 441-1183), 4201 Spring Valley Rd, Suite 104, Dallas, TX 75244. Both of these places seem to be trustworthy for mail-order tickets.

The price of flights is obviously affected by which US city you start out from. The lowest one-way/return fares to Hong Kong are as follows: Honolulu US$350/600; Los Angeles US$355/640; New York US$380/ 740.

The UK

Airfare discounting is a long-running business in the UK and it's wide open. The various agents advertise their fares and there is nothing under-the-counter about it at all. To find out what's going, there are a number of magazines in Britain which have good information about flights and agents. The listings magazine *Time Out*, the Sunday papers and the *Evening Standard* carry ads for cheap airfares. Also look out for *TNT Magazine* and *Southern Cross*.

Discount tickets are mostly available in London – you won't find your friendly travel agent out in the country offering cheap deals. The danger with discounted tickets in Britain is that some of the 'bucket shops' (as British ticket-discounters are known) are unsound. Sometimes the backstairs over-the-shop travel agents fold up and disappear after you've handed over the money and before you've received the tickets. Get the tickets before you hand over the cash.

Two reliable London bucket shops are Trailfinders, in Earls Court, and STA, which has several offices. In Bristol, look up Regent Holidays.

Flights from London and Manchester to East Asian destinations are cheapest on THAI, Singapore Airlines, Malaysia Airlines and Cathay Pacific. These airlines do not charge extra if passengers want to stop over en route, and in fact offer stopover packages which encourage it. There are also direct flights on Lufthansa and Air France – both are significantly more expensive than the aforementioned Asian-based carriers.

From London, the cheapest current one-way/return fares are approximately £273/390.

LAND
Europe

From Europe, you can reach Hong Kong by rail, though most travellers following this route also tour China along the way. Don't take this rail journey just to save money – a direct flight from Europe to Hong Kong works out to be about the same price and sometimes less. The idea is to get a glimpse of Russia, Mongolia and China along the way.

It's a long haul. The most commonly taken routes are from western Europe to Moscow, then on to Beijing via the Trans-Manchurian or Trans-Mongolian Railway. From Beijing there are trains to Guangzhou, and from there express trains to Hong Kong. The minimum time needed for this rail journey (one way) is 10 days, though most travellers will spend at least a month in China before finally arriving in Hong Kong.

More details are provided in Lonely Planet's *China – travel survival kit*, *Mongolia – travel survival kit* and *North-East Asia on a shoestring*. For still more depth, there's the *Trans-Siberian Handbook* by Bryn Thomas.

Travel Service Asia (☎ 07371-4963; fax 07371-4769), Kirchberg 15, 7948 Dürmentingen, Germany, is highly recommended for low prices and good service. In the UK, one of the experts in budget rail travel is Regent Holidays (UK (☎ (0117) 9211711; fax 9254866), 15 John St, Bristol BS1 2HR. Another agency geared towards budget travellers is Progressive Tours (☎ (071) 262-1676), 12 Porchester Place, Connaught Square, London W2 2BS. Several travellers have recommended Scandinavian Student Travel Service (SSTS), 117 Hauchsvej, 1825 Copenhagen V, Denmark. One agent in Germany catering to the Trans-Siberian market with tours of Mongolia thrown

in is Mongolia Tourist Information Service (☎ (030) 784-8057), Postfach 62 05 29, D-1000 Berlin 62.

If you want to go from Beijing to Moscow, you can book the ticket in Hong Kong at Moonsky Star (☎ 2723-1376; fax 2723-6653; email 100267.2570@compuserve.com; http://www.hk.super.net/shrine/monkey.htm), 4th floor, block E, flat 6E, Chungking Mansions, 36 Nathan Rd, Tsim Sha Tsui, Kowloon. In the same building you can also book at Time Travel (☎ 2366-6222; fax 2739-5413), 16th floor, block A, Chungking Mansions, 36 Nathan Rd, Tsim Sha Tsui, Kowloon.

It can be hard to book this trip during the summer peak season. Off-season shouldn't be a problem, but plan as far ahead as possible.

South-East Asia

The Vietnam-China border has finally opened up to rail travellers, and overland travel by bus between Cambodia and Vietnam (at Moc Bai) is now reasonably safe. Things are still dicey on the Thai-Cambodian border, but if that gets sorted out then rail and road journeys from Singapore and Bangkok to Hong Kong would be entirely feasible.

SEA

Considering the renowned beauty of Hong Kong Harbour, it's a pity so few people can arrive by ship. The days of cheap passage on a cargo ship are mostly over, though it's not impossible to get on as a paying or even working passenger on either a yacht or freighter. If you want to exit Hong Kong this way, try posting a notice on the board in the *Mariners' Club* (☎ 2368-8261), 11 Middle Rd, Tsim Sha Tsui, Kowloon.

Of course, there are luxurious passenger ships making cruises of the Far East, but these are anything but cheap. About the only cheap ships are those coming from China, such as the popular Haikou-Hong Kong cruise. If luxury cruises appeal to you, see a travel agent.

DEPARTURE TAX

Airport departure tax is HK$100. It's free if

you can persuade the airport personnel that you're under the age of 12.

If leaving by sea, there is a departure tax of HK$26, but it's an 'invisible' tax since it's included in the price of the ticket.

ORGANISED TOURS

It's so easy to organise a tour yourself after you've arrived in Hong Kong that it hardly pays to do so beforehand. See the following Getting Around chapter for details.

WARNING

Remember that all prices published in this book are subject to change. Inflation is the scourge of travel writers – today's quoted prices start to look very quaint six months after publication. Furthermore, travel agents we've recommended in this book can go bad or bankrupt, or get swallowed up in corporate raids. In other words, you may have to do a bit of research yourself to find out who's offering the best deals on tickets this year.

Getting Around

Hong Kong is small and crowded, which makes public transport the only practical way to move people. Consequently public transport is cheap, fast, widely used and generally efficient. It is mostly privately owned and operates at a profit.

If you want to master all the intricacies of Hong Kong's complex system of buses, minibuses, trams and ferries, pick up the book *Public Transport in Hong Kong – A Guide to Services* published by the Transport Department. This guide describes the routes in excruciating detail. Indeed, the worst thing about it is that it inundates you with information, some of it confusing, and it doesn't contain maps. The guide can be purchased from the Government Publications Centre in the Government Offices Building, 66 Queensway, Admiralty.

AIRPORT

Hong Kong's Kai Tak airport is due to close when the all-new Chek Lap Kok airport opens. This momentous event is scheduled to occur in April 1998, though further postponements are possible of this already much-delayed project. Except where noted, the following information applies only to Kai Tak airport.

Airport buses, simply known as 'Airbuses', depart from just outside the arrival hall and go past most major hotels. One goes to Kowloon and the other two to Hong Kong Island. The buses have plenty of room for luggage and charge half fares for children under 12. No change is given on any of the buses, but there is an airport bus service centre right outside the airport exit that will give change for HK$10 notes. Departures are every 15 to 20 minutes throughout the day. Except for Airbus A5, buses to the airport begin at 7.40 am and stop at midnight. From the airport into the city, buses start running at 7 am and final departures are also at midnight.

Touts at the bus stop often try to persuade backpackers to come with them to guesthouses. If you want, you can ask them for their business card, but it's unwise to go with them because they will often insist you stay at their place since they guided you into town. Furthermore, many of these touts do not work for the places they claim, but will take you to a much inferior guesthouse.

The Airbus services are very convenient. There are six services – A1 to Tsim Sha Tsui (HK$12.30); A2 to Wan Chai, Central and the Macau Ferry Terminal (HK$19); A3 to Causeway Bay (HK$19); A5 to Tai Koo Shing (HK$19); A7 to Kowloon Tong MTR station (HK$6.70); A20 to Causeway Bay, Wan Chai and Central (the fare varies by destination but is generally HK$19).

The A1 service to Tsim Sha Tsui in Kowloon is the most heavily used by budget travellers. It goes down Nathan Rd past Chungking Mansions, then turns around at the Star Ferry terminal and heads back, making numerous stops en route.

There is an Airbus brochure at the departure area with a map showing the bus routes. The Hong Kong Tourist Association (HKTA) also has this brochure.

Of course, taxis are an option. There are often unbelievably long queues at the airport taxi stands, but the lines move quickly. In the city, taxis can be hard to get at peak times and it will sometimes be faster just to take the Airbus. But if you've got plenty of luggage or you're staying somewhere off the main bus routes, a taxi can be the best option. A taxi from the airport to Tsim Sha Tsui costs around HK$35; to Central figure on around HK$90 (including the tunnel fare).

Traffic jams are common during rush hour so start out early to avoid missing your flight. The Cross-Harbour Tunnel is a serious bottleneck, so many taxi drivers will try to persuade you to let them take the East-Harbour Tunnel (this will cost you more but can save considerable time). Alternatively, if you're coming from Hong Kong Island during peak hour and your luggage isn't excessive, you might

125

Hong Kong Island

Bus	From	To	Via	Frequency
1	Central-Rumsey St	Happy Valley	Wanchai Rd	12-20 min
2	Macau Ferry Pier	Shau Kei Wan	Hennessy Rd	12 min
3	Central-Rumsey St	Kennedy Town	Bonham Rd	7-20 min
6	Exchange Square	Stanley Prison	Repulse Bay	10-20 min
6A	Exchange Square	Stanley Fort	Repulse Bay	30 min
7	Central-pier 7	Aberdeen	Pok Fu Lam	12-15 min
9	Shau Kei Wan	Shek O	Chai Wan Rd	15-36 min
11	Central-pier 7	Tiger Balm Gardens	Queensway	10-12 min
14	Sai Wan Ho pier	Stanley Fort	Shau Kei Wan Rd	20-30 min
15	Exchange Square	Victoria Peak	Queen's Rd East	15-30 min
15B*	Tin Hau MTR	Victoria Peak	Yee Wo St	20 min
18*	West Point	North Point	Connaught Rd	10-15 min
26	Tiger Balm Gardens	Hollywood Rd	Hennessy Rd	12 min
61	Exchange Square	Repulse Bay	Queen's Rd East	20-30 min
63!	North Point Ferry	Stanley Prison	King's Rd	30 min
64*	Exchange Square	Chung Hom Kok	Repulse Bay	20-30 min
65*	North Point Ferry	Stanley	Yee Wo St	20-30 min
70	Exchange Square	Aberdeen	Aberdeen Tunnel	5-10 min
72	Causeway Bay	Wah Fu	Aberdeen Tunnel	10-20 min
73	Wah Fu	Stanley Prison	Aberdeen	15-30 min
90	Exchange Square	Ap Lei Chau	Aberdeen Tunnel	6-10 min
170	Sha Tin KCR	Wah Fu	Causeway Bay	12-20 min
260	Exchange Square	Stanley Prison	Aberdeen Tunnel	12-20 min
262	Exchange Square	Chung Hom Kok	Repulse Bay	20-30 min
543	Exchange Square	Wah Fu	Aberdeen Tunnel	15-20 min

* Sunday & holidays only
! No service on Sunday & holidays

Kowloon

Bus	From	To	Via	Frequency
1	Star Ferry	Wong Tai Sin	Nathan Rd	5-10 min
1A	Star Ferry	Kwun Tong	Nathan Rd	4-10 min
2	Star Ferry	Lei Cheung Uk	Lai Chi Kok Rd	5-10 min
2C	Star Ferry	Shek Kip Mei	City University	20-30 min
5	Star Ferry	Choi Hung	Kai Tak Airport	4-9 min
5C	Star Ferry	Diamond Hill	Kai Tak Airport	6-12 min
6	Star Ferry	Mei Foo	Nathan Rd	7-15 min
6A	Star Ferry	Lai Chi Kok	Nathan Rd	8-15 min
7	Star Ferry	Lok Fu MTR	Waterloo Rd	7-15 min
8	Star Ferry	Jordan Rd Ferry	Kowloon KCR	10-15 min
8A	Jordan Rd	Whampoa Gardens	Whampoa Plaza	9-18 min
9	Star Ferry	Choi Hung	Kai Tak Airport	8-18 min
11	Jordan Rd Ferry	Wong Tai Sin	Kai Tak Airport	5-10 min
14	China Ferry	Kwun Tong	Jordan Rd	9-15 min
14C	Kwun Tong MTR	Lei Yue Mun	Kwun Tong Rd	18-35 min
100	Tsim Sha Tsui	Causeway Bay	Nathan Rd	5-6 min

even want to cross the harbour by subway or ferry, then take the A1 or A7 bus.

My wife arrived alone at Kai Tak airport and didn't really have any idea how and where to get a taxi, or how much it would be. She was looking a little lost and unsure of herself when she was accosted by a man claiming that no taxis were available because of a storm and he would transport her to her hotel for HK$250. Despite the fact that she is an intelligent professional she accepted, although she first talked him down to HK$170. It turned out that there was no shortage of taxis and a cab fare would have been about HK$35. My wife was lucky that she only was cheated of money and arrived safely. She easily could have been assaulted, robbed, etc. Apparently the man had some sort of official-looking badge hanging around his neck. Please warn your readers of this.

Mike Charles

HONG KONG

New Territories

Bus	From	To	Via	Frequency
48X	Tsuen Wan	Fo Tan	Sha Tin	8-20 min
51	Tsuen Wan Ferry	Kam Tin	Route Twisk	7-20 min
52X	Sham Shui Po	Tuen Mun	Tsuen Wan	13-20 min
54	Yuen Long	Shek Kong	Kam Tin	15-25 min
60M	Tsuen Wan	Tuen Mun	Ma Wan Pier	5-10 min
60X	Jordan Rd Ferry	Tuen Mun	Tsuen Wan	5-15 min
64K	Yuen Long	Tai Po KCR	Kam Tin	5-15 min
68M	Tsuen Wan	Yuen Long	Tuen Mun	4-12 min
68X	Jordan Rd Ferry	Yuen Long	Tuen Mun	5-15 min
70	Jordan Rd Ferry	Sheung Shui	Sha Tin-Tai Po	10-25 min
75K	Tai Po KCR	Plover Cove	Tai Mei Tuk	13-25 min
77K	Yuen Long	Fanling	Kam Tin	14-25 min
78K	Sheung Shui	Sha Tau Kok	Fanling KCR	20-35 min
81	Jordan Rd Ferry	Fo Tan	Nathan Rd	6-12 min
81C	Kowloon KCR	Ma On Shan	Sha Tin	6-15 min
91	Choi Hung	Clearwater Bay	University Rd	12-16 min
92	Choi Hung	Sai Kung	Hebe Haven	6-15 min
94	Sai Kung	Wong Shek Pier	Pak Tam Chung	30-60 min
96R*	Choi Hung	Wong Shek Pier	Sai Kung	10-25 min
299	Sai Kung	Sha Tin	Ma On Shan Rd	12-20 min

* Sunday & holidays only

When Chek Lap Kok airport finally opens, it will be connected to the city by a high-speed train. This will be able to cruise at 135 km/h, and it will take 23 minutes to travel between Central and the new airport. The air terminal itself will be so huge that it will require a transport system of its own, including a 750m-long driverless train system and 2.5 km of moving walkways. The passenger terminal will be 1.2 km in length.

BUS

The extensive bus system offers a bewildering number of routes that will take you just about anywhere in Hong Kong. Most visitors use the buses to explore the south side of Hong Kong Island and the New Territories. The north side of Hong Kong Island and most of Kowloon are well-served by the Mass Transit Railway (MTR).

In Central, the most important bus terminal is on the ground floor right under Exchange Square (just west of the GPO). In Kowloon, the Star Ferry bus terminal is the most crucial.

Finding the bus terminals is the easy part – figuring out which bus you want may take some effort. One useful fact to memorise is

that any bus number ending with the letter K (78K, 69K, etc) means the route connects to the Kowloon-Canton Railway. Similarly, bus numbers ending with M (51M, 68M, etc) go to the MTR stations. Those ending with R are recreational buses and normally run on Sunday, public holidays or for special events like the races at Happy Valley. Buses with an X are express. Air-conditioning is used without mercy even in winter – bring gloves so you don't get frostbite. Whether you want it or not, air-conditioning costs extra. Children under the age of four can ride for free if accompanied by an adult, children aged five to 11 pay half fare.

Three companies run the vast majority of Hong Kong's buses. China Motor Bus (CMB) Company operates the blue and white buses on Hong Kong Island, and the Kowloon Motor Bus (KMB) Company runs the red and cream buses in Kowloon. Citybus is a relatively new contender which offers excellent service all over Hong Kong (and even to Guangzhou). Citybus has a relatively small piece of the transport pie, but expect this company to expand its routes rapidly.

The HKTA has some useful free handouts

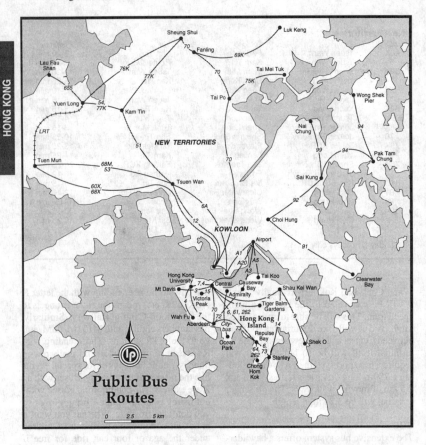

Public Bus Routes

0   2.5   5 km

on bus routes in Kowloon, Hong Kong Island and the New Territories.

Most buses run from about 6 am until midnight, but the 121 and 122 are all-night buses which operate through the Cross-Harbour Tunnel every 15 minutes from 12.45 to 5 am. Bus No 121 runs from Macau Ferry Pier on Hong Kong Island, then through the tunnel to Chatham Rd in Tsim Sha Tsui East before continuing to Choi Hung on the east side of the airport. Bus No 122 runs from North Point on Hong Kong Island, through the Cross-Harbour Tunnel, Chatham Rd South in Tsim Sha Tsui East, the

northern part of Nathan Rd and on to Lai Chi Kok in the north-west part of Kowloon. You can catch them right near the tunnel entrances on either side of the harbour.

Bus fares range from HK$2.50 for the shortest routes without air-conditioning, up to HK$30 for air-conditioned deluxe buses on the longest route in the New Territories. A typical trip will cost around HK$5. Drop the exact fare into the box next to the driver as you board the bus. No change is given so keep a collection of coins with you all the time.

When you want to get off just yell out

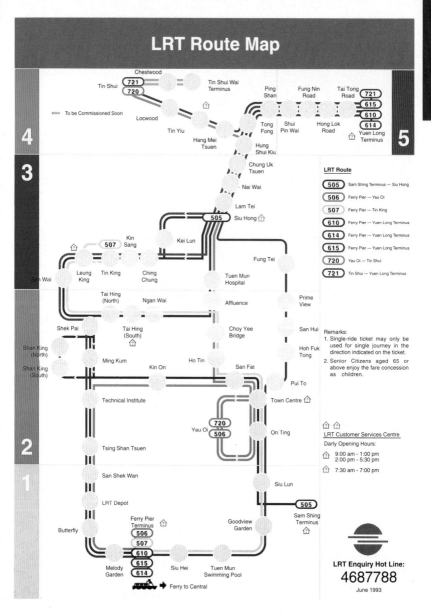

LRT Route Map

LRT Route

505	Sam Shing Terminus — Siu Hong
506	Ferry Pier — Yau Oi
507	Ferry Pier — Tin King
610	Ferry Pier — Yuen Long Terminus
614	Ferry Pier — Yuen Long Terminus
615	Ferry Pier — Yuen Long Terminus
720	Yau Oi — Tin Shui
721	Tin Shui — Yuen Long Terminus

Remarks:
1. Single-ride ticket may only be used for single journey in the direction indicated on the ticket.
2. Senior Citizens aged 65 or above enjoy the fare concession as children.

LRT Customer Services Centre

Daily Opening Hours:

9:00 am - 1:00 pm
2:00 pm - 5:30 pm

7:30 am - 7:00 pm

LRT Enquiry Hot Line:
4687788

June 1993

Light Rail Transit
(Reproduced courtesy of Kowloon-Canton Railway Corporation)

RICHARD I'ANSON

RICHARD I'ANSON

Top: Wong Tai Sin Temple nestles among the towers of Kowloon. Wong Tai Sin is a popular Taoist god who, among other things, gives tips on horse races.
Bottom: Sung Dynasty Village, Kowloon, features wax figures in authentic dress and re-enactments of life in a Chinese village 10 centuries ago.

anything – the drivers usually don't speak much English. If you want to feel like a local, the Cantonese yell *yau lok*.

Minibus

This is a cream-coloured bus with a red stripe down the side. It usually seats 16 people. Its final destination is written in Chinese and English on the sign at the front, but you'll have to squint to see the English squeezed in above the Chinese.

You can hail a minibus just as you do an ordinary taxi. It will stop almost anywhere, but not at the stops for the large KMB and CMB buses or in the restricted zones where it's unsafe to stop. The fares are not much higher than on the large buses. There's no standing room on a minibus so they won't pick up more passengers than they have seats.

Fares range from HK$2 to HK$6, you pay when you get off, and drivers usually can give change. Minibuses to the New Territories can be picked up at the Jordan Rd ferry pier in Kowloon or at Choi Hong MTR station.

Maxicab

Maxicabs are like minibuses, but have a green stripe and operate on fixed routes and stop at designated places. Fares vary according to distance, running between HK$1 and HK$8. You pay when you get on and no change is given.

TRAM

One of the world's great travel bargains, Hong Kong's trams are tall, narrow, double-decker streetcars that trundle along the northern side of Hong Kong Island.

The tram line was built in 1904 on what was then the shoreline of Hong Kong Island, which should help you appreciate just how much land Hong Kong has reclaimed from the sea. Although the tram has been in operation since then, the vehicles you see were built in the 1950s and 1960s.

The trams are not fast but they are cheap and fun. For a flat fare of HK$1.20 (dropped

in a box beside the driver when you leave – no change) you can go as far as you like, whether it's one block or the end of the line. Children pay half price. If you want to go in style, ordinary trams can be chartered for a mere HK$475 per hour, or you can rent an antique model for HK$750 per hour. Ring up (☎ 2311-3509) to make a booking. Trams operate between 6 am and 1 am. On each route they run with a frequency of between two and seven minutes.

Try to get a seat at the front window upstairs to enjoy a first-class view of life in Hong Kong while rattling through the crowded streets. If you don't get a seat, like during the rush hours, the ride isn't so entertaining.

The routes overlap. Some start from Kennedy Town and run to Shau Kei Wan, but others run only part of the way and one turns south to Happy Valley. The eight routes are as follows:

From (west)	To (east)
Kennedy Town	Causeway Bay
Kennedy Town	Happy Valley
Kennedy Town	North Point
Kennedy Town	Shau Kei Wan
Shau Kei Wan	Happy Valley
Western Market	Causeway Bay
Western Market	Shau Kei Wan
Whitty Street	North Point

TRAIN
Mass Transit Railway (MTR)

One of the world's most modern metro systems, the MTR is clean, fast and safe. Trains run every two to four minutes from 6 am to 1 am daily on three lines (see map).

The cheapest fare is HK$4, while the most expensive is HK$12.50. For short hauls, the MTR is more expensive than other public transport. If you want to cross the harbour from Central to Tsim Sha Tsui, the MTR is about five times the price of the Star Ferry and without the view, and only marginally faster. But if you go further, like to Tsuen Wan in the New Territories, the MTR is considerably faster than a ferry and a bus, and almost the same price. Also, it's air-conditioned, which you may find worth paying for in summer.

Riding the MTR is dead easy – just follow the signs. Everything is automated, from the ticket-vending machines to the turnstiles. Ticket machines take HK$5, HK$2, HK$1 and 50c pieces, but do not give change. If you put in a HK$5 coin for a HK$4 ticket the next person gets a HK$1 discount! There are change machines that accept coins only – notes must be changed at the information desks or minibanks. Once you pass through the turnstiles, you have 90 minutes to complete the journey or the ticket becomes void.

The MTR uses 'smart tickets' with a magnetic coding strip on the back. When you pass through the turnstile, the card is encoded with the station identification and time. At the other end, the exit turnstile sucks in the ticket, reads where you came from, the time and how much you paid, and lets you through if you pass the test.

You can't buy return tickets, but there are 'common stored-value' tickets for making multiple journeys. These are available in denominations of HK$70, HK$100 and HK$200, and are definitely worthwhile if you use the MTR frequently. They can also be used on the Kowloon-Canton Railway except for Lo Wu station (the Chinese border station). You gain some benefit from buying the larger denominations – the encoded value of the HK$100 ticket is HK$103, and the HK$200 ticket is worth HK$212. Another benefit is the 'last ride bonus' – even if there's just 10c remaining on the ticket, you can have one last ride anywhere. The single-journey MTR tickets must be used the same day, so it's no good buying one to use tomorrow. You can buy these tickets at the minibanks in the MTR stations.

There's also a 'tourist ticket' – better known as the 'sucker ticket' – which is valid for HK$20 worth of travel but costs HK$25! As compensation, you get to keep the ticket as a souvenir.

Children aged two or under can travel free and there are special child/student tickets which are much cheaper than adult prices.

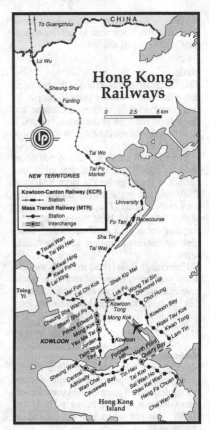

These can only be used by children aged 3 to 11.

Passengers aged 12 or over can only use the child/student tickets if they are students carrying a Hong Kong Student Travel Card – an International Student Identity Card (ISIC) is not acceptable. You might be tempted to buy a child/student ticket to save money, after all, how can the machine know you aren't a student? However, the MTR is well-patrolled by plain-clothes police and closed-circuit TV. If you're spotted buying a child/student ticket, you may have some explaining to do.

MTR & KCR Timetable

Station Name	First Train	Lo Wu	Kowloon	Last Train to: Tsuen Wan	Sheung Wan	Chai Wan
Admiralty	6.05am	–	–	12.56am	12.55am	1.00am
Causeway Bay	6.01am	–	–	12.51am	12.51am	1.03am
Central	6.07am	–	–	12.54am	12.57am	12.58am
Chai Wan	5.55am	–	–	12.35am	12.35am	–
Cheung Sha Wan	6.13am	–	–	1.11am	1.43am	1.43am
Choi Hung	5.57am	–	–	12.36am	12.36am	12.48am
Diamond Hill	5.59am	–	–	12.38am	12.38am	12.46am
Fanling KCR	6.08am	12.58am	12.14am	–	–	–
Fortress Hill	6.08am	–	–	12.48am	12.48am	1.07am
Fo Tan KCR	5.50am	12.40am	12.32am	–	–	–
Heng Fa Chuen	5.57am	–	–	12.37am	12.37am	1.17am
Jordan	6.03am	–	–	1.02am	12.52am	12.52am
Kowloon KCR	5.35am	12.25am	–	–	–	–
Kowloon Bay	6.03am	–	–	12.33am	12.33am	12.50am
Kowloon Tong	6.04am	–	–	12.43am	12.43am	12.43am
Kowloon Tong KCR	5.41am	12.31am	12.41am	–	–	–
Kwai Hing	6.04am	–	–	1.21am	12.34am	12.34am
Kwun Tong	6.07am	–	–	12.30am	12.30am	12.53am
Lai Chi Kok	6.11am	–	–	1.13am	12.41am	12.41am
Lai King	6.07am	–	–	1.17am	12.37am	12.37am
Lam Tin	6.09am	–	–	12.29am	12.29am	12.55am
Lok Fu	6.02am	–	–	12.41am	12.41am	12.43am
Lo Wu KCR	6.01am	–	12.08am	–	–	–
Mei Foo	6.09am	–	–	1.15am	12.39am	12.39am
Mong Kok	6.09am	–	–	1.06am	12.48am	12.48am
Mong Kok KCR	5.38am	12.28am	12.44am	–	–	–
Ngau Tau Kok	6.05am	–	–	12.31am	12.31am	12.52am
North Point	6.06am	–	–	12.46am	12.46am	1.08am
Prince Edward	6.08am	–	–	1.07am	12.46am	12.46am
Quarry Bay	6.04am	–	–	12.44am	12.44am	1.10am
Sai Wan Ho	6.01am	–	–	12.41am	12.41am	1.13am
Sham Shui Po	6.14am	–	–	1.09am	12.44am	12.44am
Sha Tin KCR	5.48am	12.38am	12.34am	–	–	–
Shau Kei Wan	5.59am	–	–	12.39am	12.39am	1.15am
Shek Kip Mei	6.06am	–	–	12.45am	12.45am	12.45am
Sheung Shui KCR	6.44am	11.56pm	12.12am	–	–	–
Sheung Wan	6.05am	–	–	12.46am	12.56am	
Tai Koo	6.02am	–	–	12.42am	12.42am	1.12am
Tai Po KCR	6.00am	12.50am	12.22am	–	–	–
Tai Wai KCR	5.45am	12.35am	12.37am	–	–	–
Tai Wo KCR	6.03am	12.53am	12.19am	–	–	–
Tai Wo Hau	6.01am	–	–	1.23am	12.31am	12.31am
Tsim Sha Tsui	6.05am	–	–	1.00am	12.54am	12.54am
Tsuen Wan	6.00am	–	–	12.30am	12.30am	
University KCR	5.54am	12.44am	12.28am	–	–	–
Wan Chai	6.03am	–	–	12.53am	12.53am	1.01am
Wong Tai Sin	6.00am	–	–	12.39am	12.39am	12.44am
Yau Ma Tei	6.01am	–	–	1.04am	12.50am	12.50am

Smoking, eating and drinking are not permitted in the MTR stations or on the trains (makes me wonder about all those Maxim's Cake Shops in the stations). The fine for eating or drinking is HK$1000, while smoking will set you back HK$2000. Busking, selling and soliciting are also prohibited activities. You are not supposed to carry large pieces of luggage, but 'large' is subject to interpretation. Apparently, backpacks and suitcases are OK, but don't try moving furniture.

There are no toilets in either the trains or the stations. If you leave something on the train and nobody steals it, you might be able to reclaim your goods at the lost property office at Admiralty station between 11 am and 6.45 pm, Monday to Saturday. There is also a passenger information hotline (☎ 2750-0170).

Kowloon-Canton Railway (KCR)

This line runs from Kowloon to the border crossing at Lo Wu. Most trains terminate at the border, but special express trains run all the way through to Guangzhou. You can change from the MTR to the KCR at Kowloon Tong station. The southernmost station on the line, at Hung Hom, is easily reached from Tsim Sha Tsui by taking the green minibus No 6 from Hankow Rd (south of Peking Rd). 'Common stored-value' tickets and tourist tickets for the MTR can be used on the KCR for every station but Lo Wu. You are not supposed to ride up to Lo Wu station unless you plan to cross the border into Shenzhen.

Fares are from HK$3 to HK$8, except for the train to the border at Lo Wu, which costs HK$29. Another oddity is the train service to the horse race track near Sha Tin – trains run only on race days and are priced up to HK$14.50. The KCR is a good way to get to various parts of the New Territories – see the New Territories chapter for more details.

The lost property office for the KCR is in Sha Tin KCR station.

Light Rail Transit (LRT)

The latest addition to the alphabet soup of Hong Kong trains is the LRT. This is rather like a modern, air-conditioned version of the tram, but it follows the road and stops at designated stations. It's much faster than the tram, at times reaching a maximum speed of 70 km/h.

The LRT only runs in the New Territories, connecting the city of Tuen Mun with Yuen Long, but may be extended to connect with the MTR and KCR.

There are five LRT lines connecting the various small districts in the area. The system operates from 5.30 am to 12.30 am Monday to Saturday, and from 6 am to midnight on Sundays and holidays. The LRT terminus in Tuen Mun is at the hoverferry pier, where you can reach Central on Hong Kong Island

in 30 minutes. Fares vary by distance and tickets are purchased from vending machines. Children and seniors are entitled to a half-fare discount. The system of fare collection is unique for Hong Kong – there are no gates or turnstiles and customers are 'trusted' to pay. However, that 'trust' is enforced by occasional police spot checks.

TAXI

When a taxi is available, there should be a red 'For Hire' sign displayed in the windscreen and the 'Taxi' sign on the roof should be lit up at night. Taxis cannot stop at bus stops or where a yellow line is painted next to the kerb. A driver who ignores these rules risks a HK$300 fine, so be sure to position yourself correctly.

In Kowloon and Hong Kong Island, taxis are red. In the New Territories they are green. On Lantau Island, the colour code is blue.

The New Territories taxis are cheapest but they are not permitted to pick up or put down passengers in Kowloon or Hong Kong Island. It's often hard to get taxis during rush hour, when it rains or during shift changes (around 4 pm). Taxis are also in great demand after midnight, when public transport dwindles. Officially, there are no late-night or extra-passenger charges. Unofficially, during heavy rains and after midnight many drivers try to charge double (supposedly illegal) – just pretend you 'don't understand' and pay the metered fare.

In Hong Kong and Kowloon, the flagfall is HK$14 for the first two km and HK$1.20 for every additional 200m. In the New Territories, flagfall is HK$12 for the first two km, thereafter HK$1 for every 200m. There is a luggage fee of HK$5 per bag but not all drivers insist on this. Most drivers carry very little change (to deter robbers), so keep a supply of coins and HK$10 bills.

If you go through either the Cross-Harbour Tunnel or Eastern Harbour Crossing, you'll be charged an extra HK$20. The toll is only HK$10, but the driver is allowed to assume that he won't get a fare back so you have to pay. You're charged extra for other tunnels as follows: Aberdeen HK$5; Lion Rock HK$6;

Shing Mun HK$5; Tate's Cairn HK$4; and Tseung Kwan O HK$3. There is no charge for the tunnel under Kai Tak airport.

All taxis should have a card listing the top 50 destinations in Cantonese, English and Japanese – very useful since a lot of drivers don't speak English. Even if the card doesn't name your specific destination, it will certainly list somewhere nearby. The card is usually kept above the driver's sun visor.

If you feel a taxi driver has ripped you off, get the licence number and call the police hotline (☎ 2527-7177) with the details about when, where and how much. Drivers have some reason to fear the police – getting a taxi licence is extremely difficult and it can be revoked if the driver breaks the rules. The number of licences ('medallions' in taxi driver lingo) is limited and they are obtained through competitive bidding. The going rate is now something like HK$2 million – you can buy a house in Hong Kong for less than that!

Also contact the police if you leave something of value in a taxi – the majority of drivers are reasonably honest and will turn in lost property.

CAR & MOTORCYCLE
Road Rules
Driving is on the left side of the road – the same as Australia and Britain but the opposite to China. Seat belts must be worn by the driver and all front-seat passengers. The police are strict and there are Draconian fines for traffic violations.

Driving in crowded Hong Kong has been made deliberately expensive in order to discourage it. The motor vehicle import tax is 100% and the petrol tax is more than 100%. Vehicle registration (based on engine size) averages about HK$8000 annually and liability insurance is compulsory.

For details about driving licences, see the Facts for the Visitor chapter, Visas & Documents (Driving Licence & Permits).

Rental
The best advice I can give about renting a car is don't! Except for touring some of the backwaters in the New Territories, a car

saves no time at all. The MTR doesn't have to stop for traffic lights, and taking the bus will often be faster and cheaper than driving. The reason is that parking in the city is a nightmare, and it's likely that you'll have to park so far away from your destination that the travel time saved will be used up walking to and from the car park. Most Hong Kongers own cars to gain 'face', not because they have any need for a motor vehicle. Expats with fragile egos buy cars for the same reason.

Several companies offer a variety of cars for self-drive or chauffeur-driven rental; even Rolls-Royces are available. You'll find car rental agencies listed in the *Yellow Pages* under Motorcar Renting & Leasing. The following agencies are HKTA members:

Ace
mezzanine floor, 16 Min Fat St, Happy Valley (☎ 2893-0541)
Avis
ground floor, Bonaventure House, 85 Leighton Rd, Causeway Bay (☎ 2890-6988)
Intercontinental
21st floor, Lane Crawford House, 70 Queen's Rd, Central (☎ 2532-1388)
Windsor
basement 1, Bayview Mansion, 21 Moreton Terrace, Causeway Bay (☎ 2577-9031)

You normally get unlimited km at no extra cost and discounts if you rent for a week or more. Many car-rental outlets and the big hotels offer chauffeur-driven cars, but using this service for one day could easily cost more than your hotel room. Motorcycles seem impossible to rent, but can be bought if you're staying long enough.

BICYCLE
Cycling in Kowloon or Central would be suicidal, but in quiet areas of the islands or the New Territories a bike can be quite a nice way of getting around. The bike-rental places tend to run out early on weekends.

Some places where you can rent bikes and ride in safety include; Shek O on Hong Kong Island; Sai Kung, Sha Tin and Tai Mei Tuk (near Tai Po) in the New Territories; Mui Wo

(Silvermine Bay) on Lantau Island; and on the island of Cheung Chau.

WALKING

Despite the concrete, glass and steel, Hong Kong presents plenty of good opportunities for walking. There are many interesting walks around Hong Kong and Kowloon, as well as more rural walks on the Outlying Islands and in the New Territories, some of which are described in the relevant chapters.

Also useful is the HKTA free leaflet *Six Walks*. One 50-km walk winds across Hong Kong Island from Shek O to Victoria Peak, with the 3.5-km Peak circuit walk as the starting or finishing stretch.

Selected Walks in Hong Kong, by Ronald Forrest and George Hobbins, describes walks of varying lengths in all regions.

TRAVELATOR

Hong Kong's latest transport scheme is attracting widespread attention. Officially dubbed the 'Hillside Escalator Link' but commonly known as the 'travelator', this novel system looks like something out of a science-fiction movie. Basically, the system consists of elevated escalators and moving walkways. It's presently 800m long, making it the longest such system in the world.

One of Hong Kong's long-standing problems is that many well-to-do residents live in the Mid-Levels, the lower portion of the Peak, but work in the skyscraper forest below. The roads are narrow and the distance is more vertical than horizontal, making the walk home a strenuous climb. The result is a rush-hour nightmare of bumper-to-bumper taxis, minibuses and private cars. The travelator is aimed at solving this problem by getting people out of their vehicles entirely. To judge from the rush-hour crowds, the project has been a smashing success.

Although construction ran 500% over budget, no one is complaining and there's talk of expanding the system. Other cities are watching with interest. Score another first for Hong Kong.

RICKSHAW

This was once the main means of public transport in Hong Kong. Rickshaws were invented by an American Baptist missionary in Japan in 1871 and quickly caught on in Hong Kong.

That was then and this is now – rickshaws are just for photograph-taking. Licences to operate a rickshaw have not been issued for decades and the remaining drivers are so old and frail you might have to put them in the rickshaw and do the hauling yourself. You have to bargain the fare with them. For only a photograph they'll ask at least HK$30 but you can often get them down to HK$15. The fare escalates dramatically if you ask them to take you any distance, even around the block. Agree on the fare first and ignore demands for more. If the rickshaw drivers try to cheat you, threaten to call the police.

BOAT

Hong Kong's ferries are almost always faster than the buses, and cheaper too. There are discounts for children under 12. As long as you are not prone to seasickness, the boats are fun and the harbour views are stunning when the weather cooperates. Though you'll find that many people break the rules, smoking is prohibited on all ferries and the fine for violating this is HK$4000.

Sad to say, all of the cross-harbour ferries now prohibit bicycles. This means that the only way to get a bicycle across the harbour is in the boot (trunk) of a taxi. However, bicycles are permitted on the Outlying Island ferries (but *not* the hoverferries).

Cross-Harbour Ferries

Practically every visitor takes a ride on the Star Ferry, which is also an essential mode of transport for commuters. The ferries have names like Morning Star, Evening Star, Celestial Star, Shining Star, Twinkling Star, etc. You should definitely take the trip on a clear night if you can.

There are actually three Star Ferries, but by far the most popular is the one running between Tsim Sha Tsui (the lower tip of Kowloon) and Central (Edinburgh Place).

The trip takes seven minutes, enough time to knock off some great photos. For adults, lower and upper deck costs HK$1.70 and HK$2, respectively. Children under 12 receive a discount. The coin-operated turnstiles do not give change. You can get change from the ticket window if you take the upper deck, but the lower deck does not have a ticket window.

I find the lower deck more interesting for photography purposes, but it's worth the extra 30c to go top deck at least once. The top deck is less crowded and gives a different perspective of the harbour.

The Star Ferry is not the only show in town. The Hong Kong Ferry (HKF) Company operates a number of useful ferries and hoverferries.

Hoverferries are about twice as fast as conventional boats. They are also far more modern, with aircraft-type seats (no one stands) and air-conditioning. They are exciting to ride but not particularly smooth. When the water is rough, they bounce along like a stone skipping across a pond. If you're prone to seasickness, don't get on a hovercraft after eating a big plate of greasy pork chops and lasagne. You won't have the option of getting rid of this unpleasant mess over the side as the windows on hoverferries don't open.

The following schedules are for ferries connecting Hong Kong Island to Kowloon and the New Territories.

Star Ferry

Tsim Sha Tsui
> Central (Edinburgh Place), every five to 10 minutes from 6.30 am until 11.30 pm

Tsim Sha Tsui
> Wan Chai, every 10 to 20 minutes from 7.30 to 10.50 pm

Hung Hom
> Central (Edinburgh Place), every 12 to 20 minutes (every 20 minutes on Sunday & public holidays) from 7 am to 7.20 pm

Hong Kong Ferry (HKF)

Central
> Yau Ma Tei (Jordan Rd), every 15 to 20 minutes from 6.15 am to midnight

Hung Hom
> North Point, every 20 minutes from 6.03 am to 10.40 pm

Hung Hom
> Wan Chai, Monday to Friday every 15 to 20 minutes from 6.30 am to 9.50 pm, reduced schedule on Saturday and no service on Sunday & public holidays

Kowloon City
> North Point, every 20 minutes from 6.05 am to 10.25 pm

Kwun Tong
> North Point, every 15 minutes from 7 am to 8 pm

HKF Hoverferry

Tsim Sha Tsui East
> Central (Queen's Pier), every 20 minutes from 8 am to 8 pm

Tsuen Wan
> Central (Pier 6), every 15 to 20 minutes from 7 am to 5.30 pm

Tuen Mun (Butterfly Beach)
> Central (Pier 5), every five to 15 minutes from 6.45 am to 7.40 pm

Tuen Mun (Gold Coast)
> Central (Edinburgh Place), Monday to Saturday from Central at 8.05, 8.45 and 9.35 am, 12.30, 1.30, 2.30, 4.30, 5.30, 6.55, 8.30 and 10 pm; Monday to Saturday from Gold Coast at 7.20, 7.40, 8, 8.50, 9.30 and 10.30 am, 1.30, 2.30, 3.30, 5.30, 6.10, 4.45 and 9.15 pm; Sunday & public holidays from Central at 9.30 and 10.30 am, 12.30, 1.30, 2.30, 3.30, 4.30, 5.35, 7, 8.30 and 10 pm; Sunday & public holidays from Gold Coast at 9.30 and 10.30 am, 12.30, 1.20, 2.20, 3.20, 4.20, 5.20, 6.20, 7.45 and 9.15 pm

All visitors to Hong Kong should treat themselves to a night-time cruise on the Star Ferry to see one of the world's great harbours at its best.

Kaidos

A *kaido* is a small- to medium-sized ferry which can make short runs on the open sea. Few kaido routes operate on regular schedules, preferring to adjust supply to demand. There is a sort of schedule on popular runs like the trip between Aberdeen and Lamma Island. Kaidos run most frequently on weekends and holidays when everyone tries to 'get away from it all'.

A *sampan* is a motorised launch which can only accommodate a few people. A sampan is too small to be considered seaworthy, but can safely zip you around typhoon shelters like Aberdeen Harbour.

Bigger than a sampan, but smaller than a kaido, is a *walla walla*. These operate as water taxis on Victoria Harbour. Most of the customers are sailors living on ships anchored in the harbour.

Even if you're not a sailor, walla wallas are useful to late-night carousers who need to get across the harbour after the MTR and regular ferries stop running. Your other late-night options are taxis or bus Nos 121 and 122 (see Buses section for details). On Hong Kong Island you catch walla wallas from Queen's Pier (east side of the Star Ferry Pier). On the Kowloon side, walla wallas can be found at the Kowloon Public Pier (just east of Star Ferry Pier).

Other Ferries

If you want to visit islands more remote than Hong Kong Island, see the chapters on the New Territories and Outlying Islands.

HELICOPTER

This is not exactly for the typical commuter or tourist, but if you've got cash to burn (HK$4000 for 30 minutes), you can charter a helicopter for an aerial tour. The place to contact is Heliservices (☎ 2523-6407, 2802-0200), 22nd floor, St George's Building, Ice House St & Connaught Rd, Central. The helipad is at Fenwick Pier St in Wan Chai, and there is another at Shek Kong airfield in the New Territories.

ORGANISED TOURS

There are so many tours available it's impossible to list them all. You can get one to just about anywhere in Hong Kong. Some popular destinations include the Sung

Dynasty Village, Ocean Park, Stanley, the Outlying Islands, or the duck farms in the New Territories.

Tours can be booked through the HKTA, travel agents, large tourist hotels or the tour companies themselves. There are discounts for children under 16 and seniors 60 and over. Children six years and under are admitted free.

Watertours
 There are currently 20 of these popular tours, covering such diverse places as Victoria Harbour and Cheung Chau Island. Book these trips through a travel agent or call Watertours (☎ 2724-2856, 2739-3302). Costs vary enormously according to which tour you choose – the current price range is from HK$40 to HK$600.

Harbour Cruises
 These are offered by the Star Ferry Company, and you book at the Star Ferry Pier. There are both day and evening cruises. Cost: HK$150 for adults, HK$110 for children. Options include the 'noonday gun' cruise, 'seafarers' cruise, 'afternoon Chinese tea' cruise, a 'sundown' cruise and 'harbour lights' cruise. The daytime cruises last a little over one hour while night cruises are just one hour in duration.

Open Top Tram Tours
 For about 70 minutes, you ride a special tram with its roof missing. Cost: HK$150 for adults, HK$110 for children. Book at the Star Ferry Pier (☎ 2366-7024, 2845-2324).

Come Horseracing Tour
 You get to sit in the Visitors' Box of the Members' Enclosure of the Royal Hong Kong Jockey Club. A Western lunch or dinner is thrown in. The tour follows the racing season, and to be eligible you must be 18 or older, hold a foreign passport and have been in Hong Kong less than 21 days. There is a dress code of sorts (consult the tour pamphlet for details). Cost: HK$490. Tour conducted by the HKTA.

Heritage Tour
 This covers historical sights, including Lei Cheng Uk, a 2000-year-old burial chamber. Trips are run on Monday, Wednesday, Friday and Saturday. Cost: HK$300 for a five-hour tour (HK$260 for seniors aged 60 and over). Tour conducted by the HKTA.

Family Insight Tour
 You visit public-housing estates and see how the people live. You get to visit a family's apartment, a rest home and a large Taoist temple. The tour runs on Thursday only and lasts four hours. Cost: HK$260 for adults, HK$220 for children (under

16) and seniors (60 or over), special offers for families. Tour conducted by the HKTA.

Land Between Tour

This popular six-hour tour covers the New Territories. Cost: HK$365 for adults, HK$315 for children (under 16) and seniors (age 60 or over), special offers for families. The tour is offered daily except Sunday and public holidays. Tour conducted by the HKTA.

Sports & Recreation Tour

You get to use the facilities at the Clearwater Bay Golf & Country Club. This includes the golf course, jacuzzi, swimming pool, tennis courts and a meal. The meal is free, most of the facilities are not. Cost: HK$400 (HK$350 for seniors aged 60 and over) for the tour. Other charges include: HK$850 for green fees; HK$60 per hour (per court) for tennis courts; HK$35 (per person) for the swimming pool; and HK$250 for two hours (per room) for table tennis. Use of the sauna is free. The tour runs on Tuesday and Friday only. Tour conducted by the HKTA.

Kowloon

The name Kowloon is thought to have originated when the last emperor of the Sung dynasty passed through the area during his flight from the Mongols. He is said to have counted eight peaks on the peninsula and commented that there must therefore be eight dragons here – but was reminded that since he himself was present there must be nine.

Kowloon is thus derived from the Cantonese words *kau,* meaning nine, and *loong,* for dragon. It covers a mere 12 sq km of highrise buildings extending from the Tsim Sha Tsui waterfront to Boundary St.

TSIM SHA TSUI

The tourist ghetto of Tsim Sha Tsui lies at the very tip of the Kowloon Peninsula. About one sq km of shops, restaurants, topless bars charging rip-off prices, fast-food places and camera and electronics stores are clustered on either side of Nathan Rd.

Clock Tower

Adjacent to the Star Ferry and the new Cultural Centre, the 45m-tall clock tower is all that remains of a train station that once existed at the tip of the Kowloon Peninsula. The station – the southern terminus of the Kowloon-Canton Railway (KCR) – was built in 1916 and torn down in 1978. The clock tower was built in 1922. A colonial-style building with columns, the station was too small to handle the large volume of passenger traffic. The new Kowloon KCR station, where many travellers begin their journey to China, is a huge, modern building in Hung Hom to the north-east of Tsim Sha Tsui.

Hong Kong Cultural Centre

Adjacent to the Star Ferry pier, the Cultural Centre (☎ 2734-2009) is one of Hong Kong's landmarks. The complex includes a concert hall, able to seat 2100 people, and a cinema that accommodates 1800, a smaller theatre with 300 seats, an arts library, two restaurants and a garden. On the south side of the building is a viewing area where you can admire Victoria Harbour, also known as Hong Kong Harbour. The Cultural Centre is open week days except Thursday from 10 am to 6 pm (including Saturday), and from 1 to 6 pm on Sunday and public holidays.

Hong Kong Museum of Art

The Cultural Centre complex incorporates the Museum of Art (☎ 2734-2167). Included in the collection are paintings, calligraphy, rubbings, ceramics, bronze pieces, lacquerware, jade, cloisonné and embroidery.

It's closed on Thursday, otherwise operating hours are week days (including Saturday) from 10 am to 6 pm, and Sunday and public holidays from 1 to 6 pm. Full-price admission is HK$10, while children and seniors (aged 60 and over) pay half.

Hong Kong Space Museum

This is the peculiar building shaped like half a golf ball at 10 Salisbury Rd, adjoining the Cultural Centre. It's divided into three parts: the Space Theatre (planetarium), the Hall of Space Science and the Hall of Astronomy.

Exhibits include a lump of moon rock, models of rocket ships, telescopes, time lines and videos of moon walks – all very educational and worth a look. The Mercury space capsule piloted by astronaut Scott Carpenter in 1962 is displayed.

Opening times for the exhibition halls are week days (except Tuesday) from 1 to 9 pm, and from 10 am to 9 pm on weekends and public holidays. Admission for adults is HK$10, children and seniors are charged half price.

The Space Theatre has about seven shows each day (except Tuesday), some in English and some in Cantonese, but headphone translations are available for all shows. Check times with the museum. Admission to the Space Theatre is HK$28, or HK$14 for students and seniors (over 60). Children under the age of three are not admitted to the theatre (☎ 2734-2722).

Star House

This building occupies a prime piece of turf right next to the Star Ferry. Astronomical rents are charged for ground-floor shops, but they are recouped from the constant flow of tourists. There is a Watson's chemist – the cheapest place around here to buy film, which you might need for photographing the harbour. Most of the stores inside the arcade are overpriced, but check out Chinese Arts & Crafts (owned by the People's Republic). The McDonald's here is believed to be the busiest in the world.

Ocean Terminal

Next door to Star House, the long building jutting into the harbour is the Ocean Terminal. There always seems to be an ocean liner moored here full of elderly millionaires. To meet their needs, the terminal and adjoining Ocean Centre are crammed with ritzy shops in endless arcades. It's not the place for cheap souvenir hunting but interesting for a stroll. On the waterfront is a small park, built on a pier, which has benches and good views of the harbour.

Peninsula Hotel

One of Hong Kong's most prestigious landmarks, the Peninsula used to be *the* place to stay in Hong Kong. It's on Salisbury Rd and was once right on the waterfront, but land reclamation has extended the shoreline south another block.

Before WWII it was one of several prestigious hotels across Asia where everybody who was anybody stayed. The list included the Raffles in Singapore, the Taj in Bombay, the Cathay (now called the Peace) in Shanghai and the Strand in Yangon (Rangoon).

The hotel's lobby offers high-ceiling splendour. It is worth paying the extra dollars for a cup of coffee or a beer here to enjoy the rarefied atmosphere and to spot people spotting other people. The rich and famous

definitely stay here, but don't expect to see them hanging around the lobby.

Nathan Rd

The main drag of Kowloon was named after the governor, Sir Matthew Nathan, around the turn of the century. It was promptly dubbed 'Nathan's Folly' since Kowloon at the time was sparsely populated and such a wide road was thought unnecessary. The trees that once lined the street are gone and some would say the folly has remained.

Now the lower end of the road is known as the Golden Mile, after both its real estate prices and its ability to suck money out of tourists' pockets.

Kowloon Park

'Shrinking Park' might be a better name for this place. This was once the site of the Whitfield Barracks for British and Indian troops, but I remember a time when the park bordered Nathan Rd and was filled with trees, flowers, joggers and strolling couples. Both the troops and the natural environment are gone. Now the park is hidden behind the Yue Hwa Chinese Products store on Nathan Rd and concrete blocks on Austin Rd. Most tourists staying in nearby hotels are not aware that the park exists.

Just as well, because the park is so artificial that it might as well be indoors. Some recent creations include the Sculpture Walk, a grotesque outdoor 'art gallery' made up of metal tubes. Other 'highlights' include an aviary, a space-age indoor sports hall, fountains, concrete plazas, a museum and numerous other intrusions. The multiple swimming pools are perhaps the park's finest feature – they're even equipped with waterfalls. Of course, it's packed on summer weekends. There are still a few magnificent old trees left in the park, but just wait – they'll get those too. All that's missing are plastic talking animals, but those may be installed by the time you read this. Admission is free. The park is open from 6.30 am to 11.30 pm.

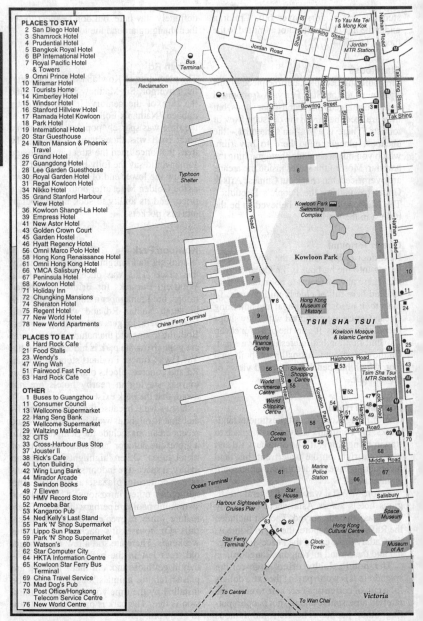

PLACES TO STAY
2 San Diego Hotel
3 Shamrock Hotel
4 Prudential Hotel
5 Bangkok Royal Hotel
6 BP International Hotel
7 Royal Pacific Hotel
   & Towers
9 Omni Prince Hotel
10 Miramar Hotel
12 Tourists Home
14 Kimberley Hotel
15 Windsor Hotel
16 Stanford Hillview Hotel
17 Ramada Hotel Kowloon
18 Park Hotel
19 International Hotel
20 Star Guesthouse
24 Milton Mansion & Phoenix
    Travel
26 Grand Hotel
27 Guangdong Hotel
28 Lee Garden Guesthouse
30 Royal Garden Hotel
31 Regal Kowloon Hotel
34 Nikko Hotel
35 Grand Stanford Harbour
    View Hotel
36 Kowloon Shangri-La Hotel
39 Empress Hotel
41 New Astor Hotel
43 Golden Crown Court
45 Garden Hostel
46 Hyatt Regency Hotel
56 Omni Marco Polo Hotel
58 Hong Kong Renaissance Hotel
61 Omni Hong Kong Hotel
66 YMCA Salisbury Hotel
67 Peninsula Hotel
68 Kowloon Hotel
71 Holiday Inn
72 Chungking Mansions
74 Sheraton Hotel
75 Regent Hotel
77 New World Hotel
78 New World Apartments

PLACES TO EAT
8 Hard Rock Cafe
21 Food Stalls
23 Wendy's
47 Wing Wah
51 Fairwood Fast Food
63 Hard Rock Cafe

OTHER
1 Buses to Guangzhou
11 Consumer Council
13 Wellcome Supermarket
22 Hang Seng Bank
25 Wellcome Supermarket
29 Waltzing Matilda Pub
32 CITS
33 Cross-Harbour Bus Stop
37 Jouster II
38 Rick's Cafe
40 Lyton Building
42 Wing Lung Bank
48 Mirador Arcade
48 Swindon Books
49 7 Eleven
50 HMV Record Store
52 Amoeba Bar
53 Kangaroo Pub
54 Ned Kelly's Last Stand
55 Park 'N' Shop Supermarket
57 Lippo Sun Plaza
59 Park 'N' Shop Supermarket
60 Watson's
62 Star Computer City
64 HKTA Information Centre
65 Kowloon Star Ferry Bus
    Terminal
69 China Travel Service
70 Mad Dog's Pub
73 Post Office/Hongkong
    Telecom Service Centre
76 New World Centre

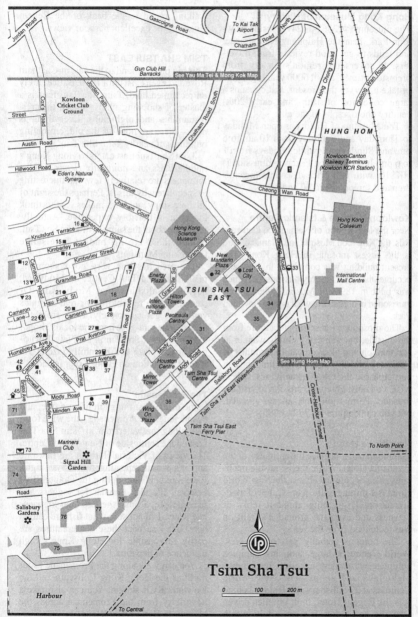

Tsim Sha Tsui

0   100   200 m

Hong Kong Museum of History

The museum (☎ 2367-1124) is inside Kowloon Park, near the Haiphong Rd entrance, and tends to get good reviews from travellers. It covers the region's history from prehistoric times (about 6000 years ago, give or take a few) to the present, and contains a large collection of 19th- and early 20th-century photographs of the city.

The Museum of History is open Monday to Thursday and Saturday from 10 am to 6 pm, and Sunday and public holidays from 1 to 6 pm. It is closed on Friday. Admission is HK$10, with half-price discounts for children and seniors (aged 60 and over).

Kowloon Mosque & Islamic Centre

Near the intersection of Nathan and Cameron Rds, the Kowloon Mosque and Islamic Centre is the largest mosque in Hong Kong. The present building was completed in 1984 and occupies the site of the previous mosque, which was built in 1896 for Muslim Indian troops garrisoned in barracks at what is now Kowloon Park.

The mosque is interesting to admire from the outside, but you can't simply wander in and take photos like you can in Buddhist or Taoist temples. If you are a Muslim, you can participate in the religious activities. Otherwise, you must obtain permission to visit the mosque. Permission isn't always granted, but you can enquire (☎ 2724-0095).

New World Hotel

You might call this place the antithesis of the Peninsula Hotel. While the Peninsula maintains an air of colonial charm, the New World Hotel is a shining, glittering symbol of modernisation. Everything about it reeks of newness and even the ground it's built on was reclaimed from the sea.

The hotel is actually part of the New World Centre, a large shopping complex complete with many excellent restaurants, nightclubs and shops. The New World Centre is at 22 Salisbury Rd. Hidden behind it is the Regent Hotel, built on piles driven into the sea floor. It's definitely worth walking round to the back of the Regent Hotel for the excellent harbour views.

TSIM SHA TSUI EAST

This big piece of land to the east of Chatham Rd didn't even exist until 1980. Built entirely on reclaimed land, Tsim Sha Tsui East is a cluster of shopping malls, hotels, theatres, restaurants and nightclubs. Everything is new – there are none of the old, crumbling buildings of nearby Tsim Sha Tsui.

Tsim Sha Tsui East caters to Hong Kong's middle class and *nouveaux riches*. Oddly, foreigners are relatively few. It's interesting to speculate why this is. Perhaps the sight of all those shiny buildings makes visitors think the area is horribly expensive. Actually, prices are about the same as in Tsim Sha Tsui, though there are no budget hotels like Chungking Mansions.

The area has one very good shopping mall, Tsim Sha Tsui Centre, 66 Mody Rd, between Salisbury and Mody Rds. Of course, if you're looking for real bargains you must get completely away from the tourist zone and go where the locals shop – try the malls at Sha Tin in the New Territories, or Cityplaza and Kornhill Plaza at Tai Koo MTR station on Hong Kong Island.

The Promenade

Some of the best things in life are free, and this includes the Promenade – the wide footpath along the waterfront in Tsim Sha Tsui East on the south side of New World Centre. The views of Victoria Harbour are first-rate and it's worth repeating the trip at night. Races are held here during the Dragon Boat Festival. It's also popular for joggers and fisherpeople, despite the less than immaculate water. I'm not sure what fish are caught here, but I suspect these sea creatures are partly responsible for Hong Kong's high incidence of hepatitis.

You can walk along the Promenade as far north as the Hong Kong Coliseum and the Kowloon KCR station. You can also take a hoverferry from the Promenade across the harbour to Hong Kong Island.

Hong Kong Science Museum

The Science Museum (☎ 2732-3232) is at 2 Science Museum Rd (near the corner of Chatham Rd South and Granville Rd). This multi-level complex houses over 500 exhibits. Admission is HK$25 for adults, HK$12.50 for students and seniors (aged 60 and over). Operating hours are 1 to 9 pm Tuesday through Friday, and 10 am to 9 pm on weekends and public holidays. The museum is closed on Monday. From the Star Ferry terminal, you can get there on green minibus No 1 – get off at the last stop.

HUNG HOM
Whampoa Gardens

In the middle of a high-rise housing estate is the Whampoa, a full-sized concrete model of a luxury cruiser. While not very seaworthy, the 'ship' is impressive – 100m long and four decks tall. The whole thing is actually a fancy shopping mall with stores, restaurants, a cinema and a playground (top deck). The basement harbours more shops and a car park. It was built by one of Hong Kong's largest companies, Hutchison Whampoa.

The good ship Whampoa is a little off the

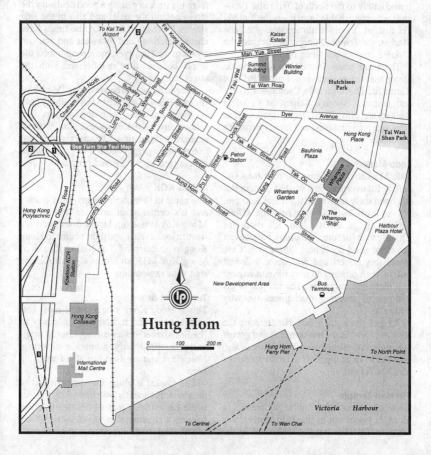

Hung Hom

beaten tourist track, but not difficult to reach. It's at the corner of Shung King and Tak Fung Sts. You can get there from Tsim Sha Tsui by taking green minibus No 6 from Hankow Rd (south of Peking Rd). There is also a Star Ferry to Hung Hom that lands at the waterfront a couple of blocks away from the Whampoa.

Other features of Hung Hom include Hong Kong Polytechnic and the 12,500-seat Hong Kong Coliseum, which hosts concerts and sporting events.

YAU MA TEI

Immediately to the north of Tsim Sha Tsui – and indistinguishable from it – is the Yau Ma Tei district. Its chief attraction is the Jade Market, the Temple St night market and the Chinese emporiums along Nathan Rd.

There are many interesting walks to do along the streets between Jordan Rd and Kansu St. These include Canton Rd (ivory and mahjong shops), Saigon St (a street market) and Ning Po St (paper items such as kites and paper houses, and luxury items for the dead).

Jade Market

Jade Market is on Kansu St, near the Gascoigne Rd overpass, just west of Nathan Rd. It's open daily between 10 am and 3.30 pm, but go early as you may find the sellers packing up at about 1 pm. It's more for Chinese than for foreign tourists, but you can get some good deals here. Some sellers are reasonably honest and will quote a decent price – with others you may have to engage in a marathon bargaining session just to get it down to shopping-mall prices (so why bother?).

To get there take bus No 9 from the Kowloon Star Ferry bus terminal and get off at Kowloon Central Post Office. You can also take the MTR and get off at either Jordan or Yau Ma Tei stations.

Tin Hau Temple

Between Market and Public Square Sts, a block or two north of the Jade Market, is a sizeable Tin Hau temple, dedicated to the goddess of seafarers. To the right, as you face the main temple, is a row of fortune-tellers. The temple complex also houses an altar dedicated to Shing Wong (god of the city) and To Tei (god of the earth). The temple is open daily from 8 am to 6 pm.

Temple St

The liveliest night market in the city, Temple St (and Shanghai St which runs parallel to it) *used to be* the place to go for cheap clothes, cheap food, watches, footwear, cookware and everyday items. The problem here is that tourists have driven prices up. However, there is a trick to getting a good deal – try the stores behind the stalls and also in the side streets. More often than not, the stores have cheaper clothing and footwear and you can try them on. However, most people miss the stores because they're obsessed with the street stalls.

Temple St used to be known as 'Men's St' because this was a place to buy clothing only for men, but these days the vendors will relieve any tourist of excess cash without sexual discrimination. The street is at its best in the evening from about 8 to 11 pm, when it's clogged with stalls and people.

MONG KOK

The name in Cantonese means 'busy point', and it's certainly an accurate description. Mong Kok is one big buy-and-sell, and it's worth a look even if you didn't come to Hong Kong to go shopping. The Nathan Rd exit of Mong Kok MTR station is a good place to start your exploration.

Tung Choi St

This is Hong Kong's largest and most colourful street market. It is known locally as 'Ladies Market' because Tung Choi St originally featured only women's clothing. Nowadays you can find just about anything here.

The market is along the southern end of the street. Frequently overlooked by tourists is the far northern part of the street, which features a large number of pet shops selling ornamental fish. It's interesting to walk through the area – every store displays large and colourful aquariums. Tung Choi St is two blocks east of Nathan Rd, off Argyle St.

Bird Market

The most exotic sight in Mong Kok is the Bird Market. It's on Hong Lok St, an obscure alley on the south side of Argyle St, two blocks west of Nathan Rd. In crowded Hong Kong, few people keep dogs and cats, but birds are highly prized as pets – especially if they can sing. Aside from the hundreds of birds on display, large bags of live grasshoppers are for sale. The birds seem to live pretty well: the Chinese use chopsticks to feed the grasshoppers to their feathered friends, the cages are elaborately carved from teak and bamboo, and the water and food dishes are ceramic.

There has been talk for years about moving the Bird Market, but for now it's where it's always been. If you find it has taken flight, contact the HKTA to track down it's new location.

NEW KOWLOON

Surrounding Kowloon proper is an area of about 30 sq km known as New Kowloon. It includes places such as Sham Shui Po and Lai Chi Kok in the west, and Kwun Tong in the east. Strictly speaking, these places are part of the New Territories, but they tend to be included in Kowloon in everyday usage of the name. Boundary St marks the border between Kowloon and the New Territories, and this would have become the new border had Britain and China failed to reach an agreement on Hong Kong's future.

New Kowloon West

Wong Tai Sin Temple (Sik Sik Yuen) This large and active Taoist temple was built in 1973 and is adjacent to the Wong Tai Sin housing estate. It is dedicated to the god of the same name. The image of the god in the main temple was brought to Hong Kong from China in 1915 and installed in a temple in Wan Chai until being moved to the present site in 1921. For information on Wong Tai

Sin see the Religion section in Facts about Hong Kong.

On Sunday afternoon the temple is crowded with worshippers burning joss sticks and making offerings of food. Some bring their own carefully prepared dishes, others buy oranges from the fruit stalls that engulf the entrance. The incense is burnt, the offerings are made (but not left behind, the gods can't be all that hungry and no one wants good food to go to waste) and the fortune sticks are cast.

Near the temple is an arcade with about 150 booths operated by fortune-tellers. Some of them speak good English, so if you really want to know what fate has in store for you, this is your chance to find out. Just off to one side of the arcade is a small open area where you can get a magnificent view of Lion Rock, one of Hong Kong's landmarks.

In the rear of the complex is the Good Wish Garden, a small replica of Beijing's Summer Palace. It's open every day except Monday from 9 am to 4 pm, and admission is HK$2.

Also towards the rear of the compound is the Nine Dragon Wall Garden, modelled after a mural in Beijing's Beihai Park. Admission is free but a small donation is expected.

Getting to the temple is easy. Take the MTR to Wong Tai Sin station then follow the signs in the station to come out in front of the temple.

The temple is open daily from 7 am to 5 pm. The busiest times are around the Chinese Lunar New Year, on Wong Tai Sin's birthday (the 23rd day of the 8th lunar month), during the 7th lunar month (the ghost month) and most Sundays. There is no admission fee for this or any other temple in Hong Kong, but they've become used to tourists dropping a few coins (HK$1 will do) into the donation box by the entrance.

Sung Dynasty Village The village was part of the Lai Chi Kok Amusement Park before it was hyped up as an authentic re-creation of a Chinese village from 10 centuries ago.

It's a type of Chinese Disneyland/super-

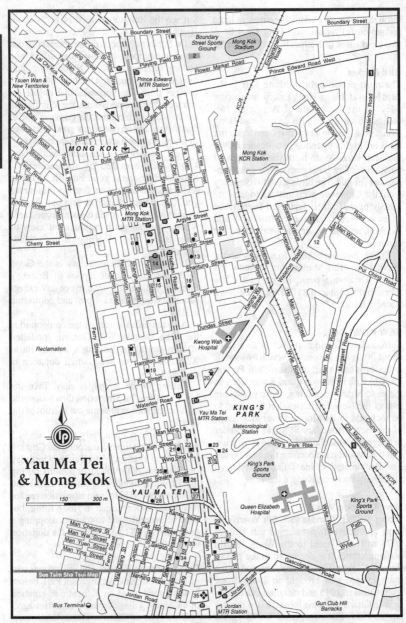

Yau Ma Tei & Mong Kok

0   150   300 m

market where craftspeople and villagers walk around in period costume, engaging in Sung dynasty (960-1279 AD) pursuits, such as fortune-telling, blacksmithing, woodcarving and getting married.

Sweets and pastries can be bought with coupons made to look like Sung money, but if you want a gown, paperweight or other souvenirs from the village shop you'll need 20th century cash.

Beneath the Restaurant of Plentiful Joy lies a wax museum which houses figures of people from Chinese history.

There are four cultural shows daily, each lasting 40 minutes. The schedule could change, but currently it's 11 am, 2.15, 4 and 7 pm.

The Sung Dynasty Village is open from 10 am to 8.30 pm daily. Admission is HK$120. It drops to HK$80 on weekends and public holidays between 12.30 and 5 pm.

The HKTA can book you on a tour if you're so inclined. These cost HK$150, but for a higher tariff (HK$209 to HK$242) a snack or meal can be thrown in. The tour includes transport from Tsim Sha Tsui or Central plus the services of a guide.

You can, of course, get there without a tour bus or guide. You have a choice of travelling by MTR or bus. From the Kowloon Star Ferry bus terminal take bus No 6A, which terminates near the Sung Dynasty Village.

From Hong Kong Island, take the vehicular ferry to the Jordan Rd ferry terminal – then catch bus No 12 to the park.

Taking the MTR will involve a 15-minute walk. Catch the train to Mei Foo station and from there head north along Lai Wan Rd. Turn left at the junction with Mei Lai Rd, at the end of which is the Sung Dynasty Village.

Lai Chi Kok Amusement Park Adjacent to the Sung Dynasty Village is the Lai Chi Kok Amusement Park. It's got the standard dodgem cars, shooting galleries and balloons for the kiddies, but the ice-skating rink may be of interest for the sports-minded. There is also a theatre that has Chinese opera performances. Operating hours for the park are Monday to Friday from noon to 9.30 pm, and from 10 am to 9.30 pm on weekends and public holidays. Admission is HK$15.

Lei Cheng Uk Museum (Han Tomb) The Lei Cheng Uk Museum (☎ 2386-2863) at 41 Tonkin St, Lei Cheng Uk Estate, is a branch of the Museum of History. The site is a late Han dynasty (25 to 220 AD) burial vault.

Hong Kong's earliest surviving historical monument, it was discovered in 1955 when workers were levelling the hillside for a

HONG KONG

housing estate. The tomb consists of four barrel-vaulted brick chambers, in the form of a cross, around a domed central chamber. The tomb is estimated to be more than 1600 years old and is behind the museum, encased in a concrete shell for protection.

The museum is open daily (except Thursday) from 10 am to 1 pm, and from 2 to 6 pm. On Sunday and public holidays it's open from 1 to 6 pm. Admission is free.

To get there, take bus No 2 from the Kowloon Star Ferry bus terminal and get off at Tonkin St. The nearest MTR station is Cheung Sha Wan, a five-minute walk from the museum.

Sham Shui Po Follow the signs at Sham Shui Po MTR station to Apliu St and you can't miss the enormous street market, which features everything from clothing to CDs at rock-bottom prices.

Descend back into the MTR and come up on the north-east side of the tracks to find the Golden Shopping Centre, 146-152 Fuk Wa St, the place to see the latest in computers and other high-tech wizardry. Two blocks further north-east at 85-95 Un Chau St (between Kweilin and Yen Chow Sts) is the New Capital Computer Plaza.

There is a chic, multi-storey shopping mall called the Dragon Centre above the bus depot on the west corner of Yen Chow St and Cheung Sha Wan Rd – it's sign-posted in the MTR. It's doesn't look like a shopping centre at first glance – an external escalator takes you up from the street level beside the bus depot to the first shopping level.

The building towers above the surrounding apartment blocks and from the top level you can see tall buildings in Central! The lifts and escalators are all glass-sided (you can see the return steps going underneath the escalators) and each floor has a choice of escalator – you can go up one floor or skip the next and go up two: this is useful if you're aiming for the top floor, where there's a great food hall. Food here is cheap and plentiful (HK$20 to HK$30 buys a huge meal of soup, egg, pork and rice). It's packed on

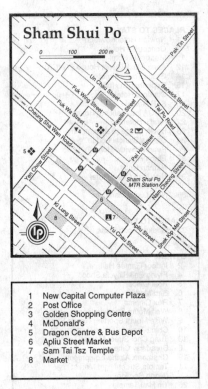

Sham Shui Po

1	New Capital Computer Plaza
2	Post Office
3	Golden Shopping Centre
4	McDonald's
5	Dragon Centre & Bus Depot
6	Apliu Street Market
7	Sam Tai Tsz Temple
8	Market

weekends with family groups and it can be hard to find a seat during lunchtime. There's also a skating rink on the floor below the food centre, and a roller coaster suspended above the shopping floors (though it's not always operating).

New Kowloon East

Lei Yue Mun To the east of the airport is a residential neighbourhood called Kwun Tong, and a bit further south-east is a rapidly modernising fishing village called Lei Yue Mun. *Lei yue* means 'carp' and *mun* is 'gate', and 'carp gate' refers to the channel separating eastern Kowloon from neighbouring Hong Kong Island.

While you aren't likely to find the 'village' reminiscent of ancient China, it's one of

---

Unmansionables

For a real-life vision of hell, take a look down the light wells of Chungking Mansions' D block. It's dark, dirty, festooned with pipes and wires and covered in what looks like the debris of half a century. Why bother to put rubbish in the bin when it's so much easier to throw it out the window? Discarded plastic bags fall only halfway before lodging on a ledge or drainpipe. Soon they're joined by old newspapers, used toilet paper, underwear, half-eaten food, an expired rat (was it too dirty for him too?).

In 1993, the building's electric transformer blew up, blacking out the Mansions for a whole week – the place probably looked a lot better that way.

As for the lifts, they're a little slice of hell all their own. A buzzer sounds when one too many people have clambered aboard them and a sign inside one helpfully announces: 'The Irresponsible for Accident due to Overloading'. ∎

Hong Kong's prime seafood venues. Locals dive into plates full of prawns and crabs, oblivious to the screech of jets from soon-to-be-closed Kai Tak airport. I'd rather eat seafood at the quiet restaurants in the Outlying Islands, but Hong Kongers with a passion for seafood and little love of boats prefer Lei Yue Mun.

The neighbourhood is colourful and lively at night when the diners arrive en masse. You can get there on bus No 14C from Kwun Tong MTR station – take it to the end of the line (Sam Ka Tsuen terminal).

PLACES TO STAY – BOTTOM END

For definition purposes, 'bottom end' in Hong Kong is any place where you can get a double room for under HK$500.

Chungking Mansions

There is probably no other place in the world like *Chungking Mansions*, the bottom-end accommodation ghetto of Hong Kong. This huge high-rise dump at 36-44 Nathan Rd, in the heart of Tsim Sha Tsui, is almost like a city in itself. Virtually all needs in life can be catered for here – everything from finding a room to eating, shopping and getting your hair cut.

For years there has been much talk about tearing down Chungking Mansions because it's an eyesore and a fire trap, but the cost would be huge, and the Hong Kong government tends to take a 'hands-off' approach to private enterprise.

A crackdown on fire-safety violations finally came at the end of 1993, and many

tinderbox guesthouses were shut down. Others survived by upgrading their standards – the new building codes require smoke alarms, sprinklers and walls made of fireproof material. However, the recent emigration of many competent civil servants has seen fire safety codes slacken once again. There has been an increase in hostels featuring walls made of plywood, and sprinkler systems consisting of a bucket of water. If you're going to stay, at least tap on the wall of your room to be sure it isn't made of cardboard.

The character of Chungking has changed in other ways in recent years – the place now serves as a long-term boarding house for workers from developing countries. This has actually driven prices and standards down, and matchbox rooms are often occupied by two, three or even four persons. Backpackers have started migrating to guesthouses in other buildings, but Chungking is still the cheapest place to stay in Hong Kong.

Adding some spice to your stay here are the occasional midnight raids by the police. Mostly they are looking for illegal immigrants – if your passport is at some embassy awaiting visa stamps, this could create a problem. At least try to have a receipt for your passport from the travel agency, a photocopy of your passport and some other picture ID card. Another purpose of the police raids is supposedly to round up foreign prostitutes, though the police do little more than hassle them if they haven't overstayed their visas. The one thing travellers really have to watch out for is drugs – a few grams of hashish in your backpack could leave you with a lot of explaining to do.

HONG KONG

The entrance to Chungking Mansions is via Chungking Arcade facing Nathan Rd. Wander around and you will find lifts labelled A to E. There are only two tiny overworked lifts for each 17-storey block. Long lines form in front of the lifts in A and B blocks. It's often faster to take the stairs if you think you can cope with up to 17 storeys.

Despite the dilapidated appearance of the building, most of the little hotels are OK – generally clean and often quite comfortable, though rooms are the size of closets. Chungking is a good place to eat cheaply too: there are several low-priced restaurants, mostly run by Indians and Pakistanis. The ground floor is filled with shops selling everything imaginable, though the mezzanine floor has better deals.

Bargaining for a bed is certainly possible when business is slack. You can often negotiate a cheaper price if you stay a long time, but never do that the first night. Stay one night and find out how you like it before handing over two weeks' rent. Once you pay, there are no refunds. Be certain to get a receipt. Paying for a room in advance so that you can have it on a certain day is *not* advised. If that cheap room suddenly becomes 'not available', threaten to call the police.

If you're too tired to go from door to door looking for a room, just hang out in the lobby with your luggage. There are plenty of touts who will approach you with offers of cheap rooms.

Prices listed here are only a guide and vary with the season, peaking in summer and during certain holidays such as Easter. No one is quite certain how Chungking will change after 1997 – will the Chinese take-over increase business (causing prices to rise), or will it drive the backpackers away permanently? Or will Beijing just decide to tear down the place (or billet PLA troops here?). Only time will tell.

As a general guide, a single room in Chungking starts in the HK$150 to HK$180 range, reaching about HK$250 or higher for larger rooms with attached bath. A double (two people in one bed) costs about HK$20 more, but it can be HK$50 more if you require twin beds.

Dormitories There are now only a few places in Chungking Mansions offering dormitories, though there are dormitories elsewhere in Tsim Sha Tsui (see the following Other Cheapies section). All Chungking dorms cost HK$50 per bed.

United Guesthouse, A block, 17th floor, is the penthouse of Chungking's hostels (in terms of location, not in terms of facilities). Go up on the roof for incredible views.

The ever-popular *Travellers' Hostel* (☎ 2368-7710), A block, 16th floor, is a Chungking Mansions landmark. Aside from dorms, there are double rooms with/without attached bath for HK$160/180.

The 12th floor of A block is where you'll find the friendly *Super Guesthouse*.

On the 6th floor of A block is *New World Hostel* (☎ 2723-6352). This place also has double rooms for HK$180.

Friendship Travellers Hostel (☎ 2311-0797, 2311-2523), B block, 6th floor, has mixed dormitory accommodation. Double rooms cost HK$120 to HK$150.

Also in B block on the 6th floor is *Kamal Dormitory*.

The only other dormitories are offered by *Splendid Asia Guesthouse* in B block, 4th floor.

Guesthouses – A block This block has the densest concentration of guesthouses. The main drawback is the frequent long queues to get into the lifts. You may find yourself using the stairs more than you expected, which wouldn't be so terrible except that the stairwells are incredibly filthy and the cockroaches show no fear. Still, A block is popular.

16th floor
  Travellers' Hostel (☎ 2368-7710), doubles HK$170
15th floor
  Happy Guesthouse singles are HK$180 with shared bath, HK$200 with private bath; *Park Guesthouse* – (☎ 2368-1689), clean, air-conditioned and friendly, rooms with shared bath HK$120, with private bath HK$160 *Ocean Guesthouse*
14th floor
  New Grand Guesthouse; *Hawaii Guesthouse* (☎ 2366-6127), a good deal at HK$160 for rooms with attached bath

13th floor
> *Capital Guesthouse* (☎ 2366-3455), friendly place, has rooms with attached bath for HK$170; *Rhine Guesthouse*, doubles with attached bath HK$160

12th floor
> *Peking Guesthouse* (☎ 2723-8320), has very friendly management and is very clean, recommended, all rooms have air-conditioning and start at HK$180

11th floor
> *New International Guesthouse* (☎ 2369-2613), has doubles with attached bath for HK$200 to HK$400, best rooms have air-conditioning, TV and a personal refrigerator

8th floor
> *New Asia Guesthouse*, clean and well-kept; *New Mandarin Guesthouse* (☎ 2366-1070), is clean and has singles from HK$150 with a shared bath to HK$180 with an attached private bath; *Tom's Guesthouse* (☎ 2722-4956), small rooms with attached bath start at HK$180

7th floor
> *Double Seven Guesthouse*; *First Guesthouse*; *Pay Less Guesthouse*

6th floor
> *London Guesthouse* (☎ 2724-5000) looks very fancy. It has singles from HK$180 with TV, telephone and air-conditioning; *New World Hostel* (☎ 2723-6352), doubles HK$180

4th & 5th floors
> *Chungking House* (☎ 2366-5362; fax 2721-3570), the most upmarket place in Chungking Mansions with singles/twins at HK$345/440, all rooms with attached bath

Guesthouses – B block This block has almost as many guesthouses as A block, so you may still have to queue for the lifts. The stairwells support a rather large amount of wildlife, including a rare species of aggressive cockroach indigenous to this region of Chungking Mansions. Be grateful for the stray cats as they keep the rats in check.

17th floor
> *Amar Guesthouse* (☎ 2368-4869)

16th floor
> *Tom's Guesthouse*, very friendly, doubles HK$200

15th floor
> *Carlton Guesthouse* (☎ 2721-0720), is a very clean, very tidy place with friendly people, doubles HK$130 to HK$150

14th floor
> *Dashing Guesthouse*, doubles HK$150

13th floor
> *New Washington Guesthouse* (☎ 2366-5798), is friendly, clean and popular, doubles start from HK$190

12th floor
> *Hong Kong Guesthouse* (☎ 2723-7842), has singles for HK$170 and doubles for HK$220 with TV and air-conditioning

10th floor
> *Kowloon Guesthouse* (☎ 2369-9802), singles HK$115, one of the larger places in this block and seems to be popular with Nigerians

9th floor
> *Happy Guesthouse*, doubles HK$180 to HK$220

7th floor
> *New York Guesthouse* (☎ 2339-5986), doubles with shared bath HK$160

4th floor
> *Harbour Guesthouse*

3rd floor
> *Dragon Inn* single rooms with shared bath HK$160

Guesthouses – C block The one great advantage of staying in C block is that there are seldom queues for the lifts. Also, the stairwells and hallways are much cleaner than elsewhere in Chungking Mansions. Just why is uncertain – perhaps C block has its own indigenous culture.

16th floor
> *Tom's Guesthouse* (☎ 2367-9258) is clean, friendly and popular, good singles for HK$180; *Garden Guesthouse* (☎ 2368-0981), is also an excellent place

15th floor
> *Carlton Guesthouse*, typically clean and quiet, as you'd expect in C block

13th floor
> *Osaka Guesthouse* and *New Grand Guesthouse* (☎ 2311-1702), same owner, all rooms have private bath and TV, with a price range from HK$150 to HK$250

11th floor
> *Marria Guesthouse*, Indian-run and looks very clean, rooms start at HK$180

10th floor
> *Kowloon Guesthouse*, a room with shared/ private bath costs HK$170/200

9th floor
> *Harbour Guesthouse*

7th floor
> *New Chungking Guesthouse* (☎ 2368-0981), very clean and pleasant

6th floor
New Brother's Guesthouse (☎ 2724-0135), is good but all rooms have shared bath only, prices start at HK$160
4th floor
Maharaja Guesthouse; *Ranjeet Guesthouse*

Guesthouses – D block
This part of Chungking is almost as tattered and dirty as A and B blocks. It rates fourth in terms of the number of guesthouses, but there seems to be a lot of traffic here and you sometimes have to queue for the lifts.

16th floor
New Shanghai Guesthouse
13th floor
New Guangzhou Guesthouse (☎ 2724-1555), is not particularly friendly but has OK singles from HK$190
8th floor
Fortuna Guesthouse (☎ 2366-4524), looks newish and nice
6th floor
Regent Inn Guesthouse
5th floor
Royal Inn and *Royal Plaza Inn* (☎ 2367-1424), sign says 'deluxe rooms' but they aren't, singles with shared bath HK$150, with attached bath HK$250
4th floor
Head Sun Guesthouse, rather so-so; *Lai Wei Guesthouse*, a well-kept place; *Mt Everest Guesthouse*, recently renovated, newish-looking
3rd floor
Princess Guesthouse

Guesthouses – E block
Like C block, this area is a backwater which is relatively clean and quiet. There are very few guesthouses here, especially after the fire safety crackdown. There are light to moderate queues for the lifts, a breeze from the south-east if your room has windows and a chance of showers if the plumbing is working.

14th floor
Far East Guesthouse (☎ 2368-1724), has doubles from HK$220, rooms are clean and have a telephone, TV and air-conditioning
13th floor
Mandarin Guesthouse
12th floor
International Guesthouse

8th floor
Yan Yan Guesthouse
6th floor
Regent Inn Guesthouse (☎ 2722-0833), seems nice enough, with a phone, TV and air-conditioner in each room. However, singles with shared bath are pricey at HK$220

Mirador Arcade
Mirador Arcade at 58 Nathan Rd is like a scaled-down version of Chungking Mansions, but considerably cleaner and roomier. It's on Nathan Rd between Mody and Carnarvon Rds, one block north of Chungking Mansions. The place caught fire in 1988, but that actually did it some good – the building has since had a pretty thorough renovation. Much of the back-packer clientele has moved here in recent years, with the result that there can be heavy queues for the lifts during peak hours (daytime). Ask about discounts if you want to rent long-term.

Dormitories Hostels in Mirador typically charge HK$50 to HK$60 for a dorm bed. The current line-up of places with dorms is as follows:

Ajit Guesthouse – (☎ 2369-1201), 12th floor, flat F3
Blue Lagoon Guesthouse – (☎ 2721-0346), 3rd floor, flat F2
City Guesthouse – (☎ 2724-2612), 9th floor
Garden Hostel – (☎ 2721-8567), 3rd floor, flat F4
London Guesthouse (☎ 2369-0919), 13th floor, flat F2, not recommended
Mini Hotel – (☎ 2367-2551), 7th floor, flat F2
New Garden – (☎ 2311-2523), 13th floor, flat F4, dorms most expensive at HK$70
Star Guesthouse – (☎ 2311-9095), 4th floor, flat F2B

Guesthouses Starting from the top floor, there's the clean and friendly *First-Class Guesthouse* (☎ 2724-0595; fax 2724-0843). Rooms all have attached bath and cost HK$200 to HK$350. It's on the 16th floor, flat D1.

My favourite in Mirador is *Man Hing Lung* (☎ 2722-0678; fax 2311-8807) on the 14th floor in flat F2. Spotlessly clean rooms all come equipped with private bath, air-conditioning and TV. Singles cost HK$200 to HK$280 and doubles are HK$320 to HK$360. If you arrive by yourself and want a room mate, the very friendly management can put you in with another traveller.

The 14th floor also chips in with the *Wide Sky Hotel* (☎ 2312-1880; fax 2723-3463) in flat F3. Rooms cost HK$300 to HK$380.

On the 13th floor is the *New Garden Hotel* (☎ 2311-2523; fax 2368-5241). Singles with shared bath are HK$120, rising to HK$200 for rooms with private bath. Salubrious doubles with private bath and telephone cost HK$200 to HK$320. This is one of the largest guesthouses in the building.

Ajit Guesthouse (☎ 2369-1201), 12th floor, flat F3, is deservedly popular with travellers. Clean rooms with shared bath cost HK$150, with private bath it's HK$250.

Also on the 12th floor is *Cosmic Guesthouse* (☎ 2721-3077; fax 2311-5260), flat A2. Often there's no one around watching over the place, but if you find someone rooms start at HK$200.

Kowloon Hotel (☎ 2311-2523; fax 2368-5241) on the 10th floor has shared bathrooms at HK$120 to HK$300.

On the 9th floor in flat B5 is the *Mini Garden Guesthouse* (☎ 2367-8261; fax 2780-1709). The rooms look rather depressing, but are cheap at HK$160.

On the 6th floor, flat A3, is the *Oriental Pearl Hostel* (☎ 2723-3439; fax 2723-1344). Doubles with attached bath cost HK$250, but the place could be cleaner.

Loi Loi Guesthouse (☎ 2367-2909; fax 2723-6168), 5th floor, flat A2, is new, clean and very nice. Doubles/triples cost HK$220/360.

Star Guesthouse (☎ 2311-9095; fax 2312-0085), 4th floor, flat F2B, is a friendly place dishing up rooms with attached bath for HK$190.

Garden Hostel, 3rd floor, flat F4 (☎ 2721-8567), is popular for no apparent reason – it's almost always full. Rooms with shared bath cost HK$200.

Lily Garden Guesthouse (☎ 2366-2575), 3rd floor, flat A9, is new and nice. Rooms are small but clean. With outside bath a room costs HK$200 – with the bath inside it's HK$300 to HK$350.

Other Cheapies

YMCA Salisbury (☎ 2369-2211), 41 Salisbury

Rd, Tsim Sha Tsui, is certainly *not* a budget hotel. However, it's intriguing to backpackers because on the fifth floor there are dorm beds for HK$180 each (four beds per room). That's more than three times what you'd pay in the Mirador Arcade, but 'the Y' is plush. There are restrictions however – check-in 2 pm and check-out 11 am, no one can stay more than seven consecutive nights and they don't accept walk-in guests when their passports show that they have been staying in HK for more than 10 days.

Golden Crown Guesthouse (☎ 2369-1782) Golden Crown Court, 5th floor, 66-70 Nathan Rd, Tsim Sha Tsui, was once popular, but went downhill and is now being taken over by new management. No word yet on how this will affect prices or standards. Previously it was rather overpriced at HK$80 for a dormitory, HK$300 for a single with no bath!

Also on the 5th floor of Golden Crown Court (but hidden in the back), is the spotlessly clean and highly recommended *Wah Tat Guesthouse* (☎ 2366-6121; fax 2311-7195). Singles/doubles cost HK$250/300 and more luxurious rooms go for HK$350.

The *STB Hostel* (☎ 2710-9199; fax 2385-0153), operated by the Hong Kong Student Travel Bureau, costs HK$200 in the dormitory, HK$500 for doubles (twin beds), and HK$600 for a triple room. Many travellers don't think this place is worth the price. The hostel is on the 2nd floor at Great Eastern Mansion, 255-261 Reclamation St, Mong Kok, on the corner of Reclamation and Dundas Sts, a few blocks north-west of Yau Ma Tei MTR station.

Star Guesthouse (☎ 2723-8951), 6th floor at 21 Cameron Rd, is immaculately clean. *Lee Garden Guesthouse* (☎ 2367-2284) is on the 8th floor, D block, 36 Cameron Rd, close to Chatham Rd South. Both guesthouses are run by the same owner, the charismatic Charlie Chan. Rooms with shared bath are HK$280 to HK$350; or HK$370 to HK$440 with private bath.

Tourists Home (☎ 2311-2622; fax 2368-8580) is on the 6th floor, G block, Champagne Court, 16 Kimberley Rd. Singles/doubles are HK$320 to HK$380. All rooms have an attached private bath.

The Lyton Building, 32-40 Mody Rd, has two decent guesthouses but neither is cheap. *Lyton House Inn* (☎ 2367-3791) is on the 6th floor of block 2, and costs HK$400 for a double. *Frank's Mody House* (☎ 2724-4113) on the 7th floor of block 4 has doubles for HK$350 to HK$550.

The *New Lucky Mansions*, 300 Nathan Rd (entrance on Jordan Rd), near Jordan MTR station in Yau Ma Tei, is in a slightly better neighbourhood than most of the other guesthouses. There are eight places here to choose from in various price ranges. The rundown from top floor to bottom is as follows:

Great Wall Hotel – (☎ 2388-7675; fax 2388-0084), also known as *Sky Guesthouse*, 14th floor, singles/doubles cost HK$350/400
Ocean Guesthouse – (☎ 2385-0125; fax 2782-6441), 11th floor, singles/doubles HK$300/350
Nathan House – (☎ 2780-1302), 10th floor, doubles HK$400, usually full
Overseas Guesthouse – 9th floor, singles/doubles with shared bath HK$180/190, clean and friendly
Tung Wo Guesthouse – 9th floor, singles HK$180, cheap but not so nice
Hilton Inn – (☎ 2770-4880), 3rd floor, singles/doubles HK$250/300, a bit dreary
Hakkas Guesthouse – (☎ 2770-1470), 3rd floor, singles/doubles HK$280/350, *not* recommended

Also in Yau Ma Tei is Cumberland House, at 227 Nathan Rd. Here on the 5th floor you'll find *International House* (☎ 2730-9276), with rooms in the HK$400 to HK$500 range. On the 6th floor is the friendly *City Guesthouse* (☎ 2730-0212) where singles/doubles are HK$300/350.

PLACES TO STAY – MIDDLE

The following places fall into the two- to three-star category, and have doubles in the HK$500 to HK$1000 range:

Bangkok Royal – (☎ 2735-9181; fax 2730-2209), 2-12 Pilkem St, Yau Ma Tei, 70 rooms, singles HK$440 to HK$620, doubles HK$520 to HK$700. Facilities: bar, coffee shop, restaurants (American, Cantonese & Thai). Near Jordan MTR station.
Booth Lodge – (☎ 2771-9266; fax 2385-1140), 11 Wing Sing Lane, Yau Ma Tei, 54 rooms, doubles HK$580 to HK$950. This place is run by the Salvation Army. Near Yau Ma Tei MTR station.

Caritas Bianchi Lodge – (☎ 2388-1111; fax 2770-6669), 4 Cliff Rd, Yau Ma Tei, singles HK$650, doubles HK$750, triples HK$950. Near Yau Ma Tei MTR station.
Caritas Lodge – (☎ 2339-3777; fax 2338-2864), 134 Boundary St, Mong Kok, 40 rooms, singles HK$490, doubles HK$560, triples HK$790. Near Prince Edward MTR station.
Evergreen Hotel – (☎ 2780-4222; fax 2385-8584), 42-52 Woosung St, Yau Ma Tei, 68 rooms. Doubles HK$650 to HK$700, triples HK$980. Facilities: business centre, in-house video and Cantonese restaurant. Near Jordan MTR station.
Holy Carpenter Guesthouse – (☎ 2362-0301; fax 2362-2193), 1 Dyer Ave, Hung Hom, 14 rooms, doubles HK$570, triples HK$680. This church-affiliated guesthouse is in a rather remote spot, but apparently a few people do stay here.
Imperial – (☎ 2366-2201; fax 2311-2360), 30-34 Nathan Rd, Tsim Sha Tsui, 215 rooms, singles HK$750 to HK$1400, doubles HK$850 to HK$1500, suites HK$2100 to HK$2600. Facilities: bar, business centre, conference room, hotel doctor, in-house video and restaurants (Cantonese & Italian). Three stars. Near Tsim Sha Tsui MTR station.
International – (☎ 2366-3381; fax 2369-5381), 33 Cameron Rd, Tsim Sha Tsui, 89 rooms, singles HK$480 to HK$780, doubles HK$640 to HK$950, suites HK$1250 to HK$1450. Facilities include a bar, hotel doctor, Chaozhou and French restaurants. Near Tsim Sha Tsui MTR station.
King's Hotel – (☎ 2780-1281; fax 2782-1833), 473 Nathan Rd, Yau Ma Tei, 72 rooms, singles HK$430 to HK$450, doubles HK$540 to HK$570. Near Yau Ma Tei MTR station.
Mariners' Club – (☎ 2368-8261), 11 Middle Rd, Tsim Sha Tsui, is a church-affiliated hostel for sailors and members only, singles/doubles are HK$462/590. Near Tsim Sha Tsui MTR station.
Nathan – (☎ 2388-5141), 378 Nathan Rd, Yau Ma Tei, 186 rooms, doubles HK$980 to HK$1050, suites HK$1250 to HK$1380. Facilities: business centre, coffee shop and Cantonese restaurant. Near Jordan MTR station.
San Diego – (☎ 2735-3855), 181 Woosung St, Yau Ma Tei, doubles HK$980. Near Jordan MTR station.
New San Diego – (☎ 2710-4888), 125 Chi Wo St, Yau Ma Tei, doubles HK$850 to HK$920. Near Jordan MTR station.
Newton – (☎ 2787-2338; fax 2789-0688), 58-66 Boundary St, Mong Kok, 175 rooms, doubles HK$890 to HK$1460, suites HK$3000. Facilities: bar, business centre, coffee shop, conference room, disabled rooms, hotel doctor, in-house video and international restaurant. Three stars. Near Prince Edward MTR station. (There's also

a Newtown Hotel of a similar standard in North Point on Hong Kong Island).

Shamrock – (☎ 2735-2271; fax 2736-7354), 223 Nathan Rd, Yau Ma Tei, 147 rooms, singles HK$750 to HK$970, doubles HK$850 to HK$1070, suites HK$1100 to HK$1170. Facilities: bar, coffee shop and restaurants (American & Malaysian). Near Jordan MTR station.

YMCA International House – (☎ 2771-9111; fax 2771-5238), 23 Waterloo Rd, Yau Ma Tei, 419 rooms, doubles HK$800 to HK$1000, suites HK$1130 to HK$1500. Three stars. Near Yau Ma Tei MTR station.

YWCA – Anne Black Guesthouse – (☎ 2713-9211; fax 2761-1269), badly located near Pui Ching and Waterloo Rds in Mong Kok – official address is 5 Man Fuk Rd, up a hill behind a Caltex petrol station. There are 169 rooms for women only, singles HK$350 to HK$550, doubles HK$470 to HK$720. Facilities include a coffee shop, Chinese and Western restaurants and a conference room. Three stars. (Sort of) near Yau Ma Tei MTR station.

PLACES TO STAY – TOP END

You can get as much as 30% off at many hotels (three-star and above) by booking your room through a local travel agency. A rundown of Kowloon's top-end hotels follows:

BP International – (☎ 2376-1111; fax 2376-1333), 8 Austin Rd, Tsim Sha Tsui, 535 rooms, doubles HK$980 to HK$1700, suites HK$2800. Facilities: bar, coffee shop, conference room, disabled rooms, exercise centre, Cantonese restaurant. Near Jordan MTR station.

Concourse – (☎ 2397-6683; fax 2381-3768), 20 Lai Chi Kok Rd, Mong Kok, 430 rooms, doubles HK$1050 to HK$1850, suites HK$2450. Facilities: bar, business centre, coffee shop, conference room, night club, hotel doctor, in-house video, restaurants (Korean & Chinese). Three stars. Near Prince Edward MTR station.

Eaton – (☎ 2782-1818; fax 2782-5563), 380 Nathan Rd, Yau Ma Tei, 392 rooms, doubles HK$770 to HK$1950, suites HK$2200. Facilities: bar, hairdresser-barber shop, business centre, coffee shop, conference room, disabled rooms, in-house video, restaurants (Asian, Cantonese & Western). Four stars. Near Jordan MTR station.

Grand Stanford Harbour View – (☎ 2721-5161; fax 2369-5672), 70 Mody Rd, Tsim Sha Tsui East, 579 rooms, singles HK$2000 to HK$3000, doubles HK$2150 to HK$3450, suites HK$4400 to HK$10,650. Facilities: bar, barber shop, business centre, coffee shop, conference room, disabled rooms, exercise centre, in-house video, outdoor swimming pool, restaurants (Cantonese,

French, Italian & international). Near Tsim Sha Tsui MTR station.

Grand Tower – (☎ 2789-0011; fax 2789-0945), 627-641 Nathan Rd, Mong Kok, 536 rooms, doubles HK$1100 to HK$1750, suites HK$3000 to HK$4200. Facilities: bar, coffee shop, conference room, hotel doctor, international restaurant. Three stars. Near Mong Kok MTR station.

Guangdong – (☎ 2739-3311; fax 2721-1137), 18 Prat Ave, Tsim Sha Tsui, 234 rooms, doubles HK$1200 to HK$1600, suites HK$2200 to HK$3200. Facilities: coffee shop, hotel doctor, in-house video, restaurants (Western & Cantonese). Three stars. Near Tsim Sha Tsui MTR station.

Harbour Plaza – (☎ 2621-3188; fax 2621-3311), 20 Tak Fung St, Hung Hom, 415 rooms. Doubles HK$1900 to HK$3000, suites HK$3800 to HK$16,500. Facilities: bar, barber shop, business centre, coffee shop, conference room, disabled rooms, exercise centre, hotel doctor, in-house video, outdoor swimming pool and restaurants (Chinese, Western & Japanese).

Holiday Inn Golden Mile – (☎ 2369-3111; fax 2369-8016), 46-52 Nathan Rd, Tsim Sha Tsui, 600 rooms, singles HK$1550, doubles HK$1900 to HK$2510, suites HK$4800 to HK$8000. Facilities: bar, hairdresser-barber shop, business centre, coffee shop, conference room, exercise centre, hotel doctor, in-house video, outdoor swimming pool, restaurants (Western & Cantonese). Four stars. Near Tsim Sha Tsui MTR station.

Hyatt Regency – (☎ 2311-1234; fax 2739-8701), 67 Nathan Rd, Tsim Sha Tsui, 723 rooms, doubles HK$2150 to HK$2850, suites HK$5500 to HK$16,000. Facilities: bar, hairdresser-barber shop, business centre, coffee shop, conference room, disabled rooms, hotel doctor, in-house video and restaurants (Western, Japanese & Cantonese). Near Tsim Sha Tsui MTR station.

Kimberley – (☎ 2723-3888; fax 2723-1318), 28 Kimberley Rd, Tsim Sha Tsui, 532 rooms, doubles HK$1300 to HK$1800, suites HK$2100 to HK$4000. Facilities: bar, hairdresser-barber shop, business centre, coffee shop, conference room, disabled rooms, exercise centre, hotel doctor, in-house video and restaurants (Cantonese & Japanese). Near Tsim Sha Tsui MTR station.

Kowloon – (☎ 2369-8698; fax 2739-9811), 19-21 Nathan Rd, Tsim Sha Tsui, 736 rooms, doubles HK$1320 to HK$2300, suites HK$2900 to HK$4100. Facilities: bar, hairdresser-barber shop, business centre, coffee shop, hotel doctor and restaurants (Cantonese & Italian). Four stars. Near Tsim Sha Tsui MTR station.

Kowloon Shangri-La – (☎ 2721-2111; fax 2723-8686), 64 Mody Rd, Tsim Sha Tsui East, 717 rooms, doubles HK$2100 to HK$3800, suites

HK$3200 to HK$16,000. Facilities: bar, hairdresser-barber shop, business centre, coffee shop, disabled rooms, exercise centre, hotel doctor, indoor swimming pool, in-house video and restaurants (Cantonese, Western, French & Japanese). Near Tsim Sha Tsui MTR station.

Majestic – (☎ 2781-1333; fax 2781-1773), 348 Nathan Rd, Yau Ma Tei, 387 rooms, doubles HK$1200 to HK$1600, suites HK$2800. Facilities: bar, business centre, coffee shop, hotel doctor, in-house video and restaurant. Four stars. Near Jordan MTR station.

Metropole – (☎ 2761-1711; fax 2761-0769), 75 Waterloo Rd, Yau Ma Tei, 487 rooms, doubles HK$1180 to HK$1780, suites HK$3000 to HK$5800. Facilities: bar, business centre, coffee shop, conference room, hotel doctor, in-house video, outdoor swimming pool and restaurants (Cantonese & Western). Four stars. Near Yau Ma Tei MTR station.

Miramar – (☎ 2368-1111; fax 2369-1788), 130 Nathan Rd, Tsim Sha Tsui, 550 rooms, doubles HK$1700 to HK$2800, suites HK$4200 to HK$16,000. Facilities: bar, hairdresser-barber shop, business centre, coffee shop, conference room, exercise club, hotel doctor, indoor swimming pool, in-house video and restaurants (Cantonese & Western). Four stars. Near Tsim Sha Tsui MTR station.

New Astor – (☎ 2366-7261; fax 2722-7122), 11 Carnarvon Rd, Tsim Sha Tsui, 148 rooms, doubles HK$1100 to HK$1600, suites HK$3000. Facilities: business centre, coffee shop, conference room, hotel doctor, in-house video and restaurants (Cantonese & Western). Three stars. Near Tsim Sha Tsui MTR station.

New World – (☎ 2369-4111; fax 2369-9387), 22 Salisbury Rd, Tsim Sha Tsui, 543 rooms, singles HK$1750 to HK$2600, doubles HK$1950 to HK$2600, suites HK$2800 to HK$6400. Facilities: bar, hairdresser-barber shop, business centre, coffee shop, conference room, exercise centre, hotel doctor, in-house video, outdoor swimming pool and restaurants (Cantonese & Western). Five stars. Near Tsim Sha Tsui MTR station.

Nikko – (☎ 2739-1111; fax 2311-3122), 72 Mody Rd, Tsim Sha Tsui East, 461 rooms, doubles HK$1980 to HK$3180, suites HK$5000 to HK$13,000. Facilities: bar, hairdresser-barber shop, business centre, coffee shop, conference room, exercise centre, disabled rooms, hotel doctor, in-house video, outdoor swimming pool and restaurants (Cantonese, French & Japanese). Four stars. Near Tsim Sha Tsui MTR station.

Omni Marco Polo – (☎ 2736-0888; fax 2736-0022), Harbour City, Canton Rd, Tsim Sha Tsui, 440 rooms, doubles HK$1700 to HK$2100, suites HK$2800 to HK$6700. Facilities: bar, hairdresser-barber shop, business centre, coffee shop, conference room, hotel doctor and restaurants (Western & French). Four stars. Near Tsim Sha Tsui MTR station.

Omni Prince – (☎ 2736-1888; fax 2736-0066), Harbour City, Canton Rd, Tsim Sha Tsui, 396 rooms, doubles HK$1700 to HK$2250, suites HK$2800 to HK$3200. Facilities: bar, business centre, coffee shop, conference room, hotel doctor, outdoor swimming pool and restaurants (International & South-East Asian). Near Tsim Sha Tsui MTR station.

Omni Hongkong – (☎ 2736-0888; fax 2736-0011), Harbour City, Canton Rd, Tsim Sha Tsui, 665 rooms, doubles HK$2050 to HK$3670, suites HK$3300 to HK$11,500. Facilities: bar, hairdresser-barber shop, business centre, coffee shop, conference room, hotel doctor, outdoor swimming pool and restaurants (Cantonese, Chaozhou, Western, French & Japanese). Near Tsim Sha Tsui MTR station.

Park – (☎ 2366-1371; fax 2739-7259), 61-65 Chatham Rd South, Tsim Sha Tsui, 430 rooms, singles HK$1400 to HK$1600, doubles HK$1500 to HK$1700, suites HK$2200 to HK$4200. Facilities: bar, hairdresser-barber shop, business centre, coffee shop, conference room, disabled rooms, hotel doctor, in-house video and restaurants (Cantonese & Western). Near Tsim Sha Tsui MTR station.

Pearl Seaview – (☎ 2782-0882; fax 2388-1803), 262-276 Shanghai St, Yau Ma Tei, 253 rooms, singles HK$780 to HK$1180, doubles HK$1180 to HK$1480, suites HK$2200 to HK$2500. Facilities: bar, doctor, in-house video and international restaurant. Three stars. Near Yau Ma Tei MTR station.

Peninsula – (☎ 2366-6251; fax 2722-4170), Salisbury Rd, Tsim Sha Tsui, 300 rooms, doubles HK$2600 to HK$3800, suites HK$4900 to HK$38,000. Facilities: bar, hairdresser-barber shop, business centre, coffee shop, conference room, exercise centre, hotel doctor, in-house video and restaurants (Cantonese, Western, French & Swiss). The hotel is known for its stunning traditional architecture. Near Tsim Sha Tsui MTR station.

Prudential – (☎ 2311-8222; fax 2311-4760), 222 Nathan Rd, Yau Ma Tei, 434 rooms, singles HK$1150 to HK$1700, doubles HK$1230 to HK$1780, suites HK$2100 to HK$3980. Facilities: bar, business centre, coffee shop, disabled rooms, doctor, in-house video and outdoor swimming pool. Near Jordan MTR station.

Ramada – (☎ 2311-1100; fax 2311-6000), 73-75 Chatham Rd South, Tsim Sha Tsui, 205 rooms, doubles HK$1080 to HK$1780, suites HK$2480 to HK$3680. Facilities: bar, business centre, coffee shop, conference room, hotel doctor, in-house video and restaurants (American & Japanese). Four stars. Near Tsim Sha Tsui MTR station.

Regal Airport – (☎ 2718-0333; fax 2718-4111), 30 Sa Po Rd, Kowloon City (next to airport), 389 rooms, singles HK$1500 to HK$2250, doubles HK$1650 to HK$2500, suites HK$3850 to HK$10,000. Facilities: bar, hairdresser-barber shop, business centre, coffee shop, conference room, night club, hotel doctor, in-house video and restaurants (Western, French, Cantonese & Chaozhou). Three stars.

Regal Kowloon – (☎ 2722-1818; fax 2369-6950), 71 Mody Rd, Tsim Sha Tsui East, 592 rooms, singles HK$1850 to HK$2550, doubles HK$2000 to HK$2700, suites HK$4000 to HK$10,000. Facilities: bar, hairdresser-barber shop, business centre, coffee shop, conference room, night club, exercise centre, doctor, in-house video and restaurants (Cantonese, international, French & Japanese). Four stars. Near Tsim Sha Tsui MTR station.

Regent – (☎ 2721-1211; fax 2739-4546), 18 Salisbury Rd, Tsim Sha Tsui, 602 rooms, doubles HK$2200 to HK$3500, suites HK$3800 to HK$22,000. Facilities: bar, hairdresser-barber shop, business centre, coffee shop, conference room, exercise centre, doctor, in-house video, outdoor swimming pool and restaurants (Cantonese & Western). Near Tsim Sha Tsui MTR station.

Renaissance – (☎ 2375-1133; fax 2375-6611), 8 Peking Rd, Tsim Sha Tsui, 500 rooms, doubles HK$2050 to HK$2900, suites HK$3200 to HK$13,500. Facilities: bar, hairdresser-barber shop, business centre, coffee shop, disabled rooms, exercise centre, doctor, in-house video, outdoor swimming pool, squash court, restaurants (American, Italian & Cantonese). Near Tsim Sha Tsui MTR station.

Royal Garden – (☎ 2721-5215; fax 2369-9976), 69 Mody Rd, Tsim Sha Tsui East, 422 rooms, singles HK$1900 to HK$2400, doubles HK$2000 to HK$2500, suites HK$3500 to HK$8200. Facilities: bar, hairdresser-barber shop, business centre, coffee shop, conference room, exercise centre, doctor, indoor swimming pool, outdoor swimming pool, in-house video, tennis court and restaurants (Cantonese, Western, Italian & Japanese). Near Tsim Sha Tsui MTR station.

Royal Pacific – (☎ 2736-1188; fax 2736-1212; email rphotel@hk.linkage.net), China Hong Kong City complex, 33 Canton Rd, Tsim Sha Tsui, 675 rooms, doubles HK$1250 to HK$2750, suites HK$2200 to HK$8600. Facilities: bar, hairdresser-barber shop, business centre, coffee shop, conference room, exercise club, doctor, in-house video, squash courts and Swiss restaurant. Near Tsim Sha Tsui MTR station.

Salisbury YMCA – (☎ 2369-2211; fax 2739-9315), 41 Salisbury Rd, Tsim Sha Tsui, 366 rooms, singles HK$800, doubles HK$945 to HK$1155, suites

HK$1595 to HK$1895. Some rooms with harbour views. Facilities: bar, hairdresser-barber shop, business centre, coffee shop, conference room, disabled rooms, exercise centre, indoor swimming pool, squash courts, tennis courts and restaurants (Asian & Western). Four stars. Near Tsim Sha Tsui MTR station.

Sheraton – (☎ 2369-1111; fax 2739-8707), 20 Nathan Rd, Tsim Sha Tsui, 798 rooms, singles HK$2200 to HK$3280, doubles HK$2400 to HK$3480, suites HK$3300 to HK$7800. Facilities: bar, hairdresser-barber shop, business centre, coffee shop, conference room, disabled rooms, exercise centre, doctor, in-house video, outdoor swimming pool and restaurants (American, Cantonese, Western, Indian & Japanese). Five stars. Near Tsim Sha Tsui MTR station.

Stanford Hillview – (☎ 2722-7822; fax 2723-3718), 13-17 Observatory Rd, Tsim Sha Tsui, 163 rooms, doubles HK$1200 to HK$1700, suites HK$2400. Facilities: bar, business centre, coffee shop, conference room, doctor, in-house video and restaurants (American, Cantonese, French, German & Italian). Three stars. Near Tsim Sha Tsui MTR station.

Stanford – (☎ 2781-1881; fax 2388-3733), 118 Soy St, Mong Kok, 194 rooms, doubles HK$1100 to HK$1600. Facilities: bar, business centre, coffee shop, conference room, hotel doctor, in-house video and restaurants (American, Asian, Chinese, French & German). Three stars. Near Mong Kok MTR station.

Windsor – (☎ 2739-5665; fax 2311-5101), 39-43A Kimberley Rd, Tsim Sha Tsui, 166 rooms, doubles HK$1100 to HK$1450, suites HK$2450. Facilities: bar, business centre, coffee shop, conference room, doctor, in-house video and Cantonese restaurant. Near Tsim Sha Tsui MTR station.

PLACES TO EAT
Breakfast

The window of the *Wing Wah Restaurant* (☎ 2721-2947) is always filled with great-looking cakes and pastries. It's at 21A Lock Rd near Swindon bookshop and the Hyatt Regency. Either take it away or sit down with some coffee. Prices are very reasonable and this place has kept me alive for years. Inexpensive Chinese food is also served and – a rare treat for a Hong Kong budget Chinese cafe – there is an English menu.

Just down the street is *Big John* (☎ 2739-6035) at 17 Lock Rd, where you can get superb breakfasts for about HK$20.

HONG KONG

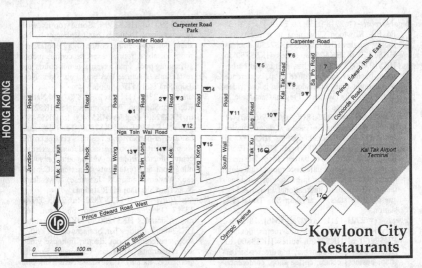

1	Indoor Market
2	Ruaen Pae Thai Restaurant
3	Golden Wheat Thai Restaurant
4	Post Office
5	Phuket Thai Restaurant
6	Heng (Sau) Thai Restaurant
7	Regal Airport Hotel
8	Thai Wah Restaurant
9	Indian Curry Hut
10	Golden Harvest Thai Restaurant
11	Taste of India Restaurant
12	Wong Chun Chun Cantonese-Thai Restaurant
13	Cambo Thai Restaurant
14	Thai Farm Restaurant
15	Golden Orchid Thai Restaurant
16	No 5 Bus Stop
17	Airbus Bus Stop

Deep in the bowels of *every* MTR station you can find *Maxim's Cake Shops*. The cakes and pastries look irresistible, but don't sink your teeth into the creamy delights until you're back on the street as it is prohibited to eat or drink anything in the MTR stations or on the trains – HK$1000 fine if you do.

There is a chain of bakeries around Hong Kong with the name *St Honore Cake Shop*; there's no English sign on their stores although you'll soon recognise their ideogram. You can find one at 221 Nathan Rd, Yau Ma Tei, and a smaller one at 12 Cameron Rd, Tsim Sha Tsui.

Uncle Russ is a takeaway muffin and coffee vendor on the north side of Peking Rd where it intersects with Canton Rd (official address is 2 Canton Rd). The muffins are possibly the best in Hong Kong and the coffee is top-flight. This is one of the few places where you can get decaffeinated coffee, and you can also buy coffee beans for home brewing.

Delifrance is a coffee shop notable for its pastries, muffins, submarine sandwiches, quiche and bouillabaisse, not to mention coffee. You'll find one branch in the Hyatt Arcade at 67 Nathan Rd and another in Carnarvon Plaza, 20 Carnarvon Rd, Tsim Sha Tsui.

Asian

An unusual place that gets rave reviews is *The Spice Market* (☎ 2777-6046), 3rd floor, Omni Prince Hotel, Harbour City, Canton Rd, Tsim Sha Tsui. This restaurant features spicy cuisine from various Asian countries, such as India,

Indonesia, Japan, Malaysia and Singapore. The all-you-can-eat buffets are moderately priced, but be careful when ordering à la carte as some items cost more than the silverware. Operating hours are from 6 to 12.30 am.

American

Dan Ryan's Chicago Grill (☎ 2735-6111), shop 200, Ocean Terminal, Harbour City, Canton Rd, Tsim Sha Tsui. The theme here is 'Chicago', including a model elevated rail system (the MTR is faster though).

If this isn't your style, west coast cuisine can be had at the *San Francisco Steak House* (☎ 2735-7576), 7 Ashley Rd, Tsim Sha Tsui. If you've got a thick wallet or sturdy credit cards, you can fill up on steak and lobster, baked potatoes, jumbo onion rings and toasted garlic bread.

Chinese

Tsim Sha Tsui's Chinese restaurant alley is *Hau Fook St*. A few blocks east of Nathan Rd, it doesn't appear on many tourist maps. Walking north from the intersection of Carnarvon and Cameron Rds, it's the first lane on your right. Unfortunately, most of the places here don't have English menus.

Street Stalls A traditional place for cheap eats is the *Temple St Night Market* in Yau Ma Tei. The street market starts at about 8 pm and begins to fade at 11 pm. Pushcart cuisine includes fish balls or squid on a skewer, as well as a few unidentifiable creatures (maybe you're better off not asking). There are also plenty of mainstream indoor restaurants with variable prices. Although many locals are drawn here by the seafood restaurants, any Hong Kong resident will tell you that much fresher marine cuisine is served up in the Outlying Islands and New Territories (see relevant sections for more information).

Dim Sum This is normally served from around 11 am to 3 pm, but a few places have it available for breakfast. The following places were chosen for their reasonable prices, but you can certainly get more atmosphere by spending more:

Canton Court – (☎ 2739-3311), Guangdong Hotel, 18 Prat Ave, Tsim Sha Tsui, dim sum served from 7 am to 3 pm

Eastern Palace – (☎ 2730-6011), 3rd floor, Omni Hongkong Hotel, Shopping Arcade, Harbour City, Canton Rd, Tsim Sha Tsui, dim sum served from 11.30 am to 3 pm

Harbour View Seafood – (☎ 2722-5888), 3rd floor, West Wing, Tsim Sha Tsui Centre, 66 Mody Rd, Tsim Sha Tsui East, dim sum served from 11 am to 5 pm, restaurant closes at midnight, stunning harbour views

New Home – (☎ 2366-5876), 19-20 Hanoi Rd, Tsim Sha Tsui, dim sum served from 7 am to 4.30 pm

North China Peking Seafood – (☎ 2311-6689), 2nd floor, Polly Commercial Building, 21-23 Prat Ave, Tsim Sha Tsui, dim sum served from 11 am to 3 pm

Orchard Court – (☎ 2317-5111), 1st & 2nd floors, Ma's Mansion, 37 Hankow Rd, Tsim Sha Tsui, dim sum served from 11 am to 5 pm

Oriental Harbour Restaurant – (☎ 2723-3885), 2nd floor, Tsim Sha Tsui Centre, 66 Mody Rd, Tsim Sha Tsui East, good harbour views (try to get a table by the window), dim sum hours are 11 am to 3 pm

Tai Woo – (☎ 2369-9773), 14-16 Hillwood Rd, Yau Ma Tei (near Jordan MTR station), dim sum served from 11 am to 4 pm

Wu Kong Shanghai – (☎ 2366-7244), basement, Alpha House, 27 Nathan Rd, Tsim Sha Tsui, dim sum hours 11.30 am to midnight (most unusual!). The crispy fried eels are very nice.

Sichuan If spicy Sichuan cuisine is on your mind, try the *Fung Lum Restaurant* (☎ 2367-8686), 1st floor, Polly Commercial Building, 21-23 Prat Ave, Tsim Sha Tsui.

Snake All major Cantonese restaurants serve snake, especially in the evening. Even upmarket hotel restaurants are getting into the act. The restaurant at the *Nikko Hotel*, 72 Mody Rd, Tsim Sha Tsui East, is one such place. Prices are not cheap.

Fast Food

Oliver's has a branch on the ground floor at the Ocean Centre on Canton Rd, Tsim Sha Tsui. It's a great place for breakfast – inexpensive bacon, eggs and toast. The sandwiches are equally excellent – the bread is so good you'll probably take home a loaf from their adjacent delicatessen. The restaurant packs out during lunch hour, but is blissfully uncrowded at other times.

McDonald's occupies key strategic locations in Tsim Sha Tsui. Late night restaurants are amazingly scarce in Hong Kong, so it's useful to know that two McDonald's in Tsim Sha Tsui operate 24 hours a day: at 21A-B Granville Rd, and 12 Peking Rd. There is also a McDonald's at 2 Cameron Rd, and another at Star House opposite the Star Ferry pier.

Domino's Pizza (☎ 2765-0683), Yue Sun Mansion, Hung Hom, does not have a restaurant where you can sit down to eat. Rather, pizzas are delivered to your door within 30 minutes of phoning in your order. If the pizza arrives even a few minutes late, you get a HK$10 discount. If it's 45 minutes late, the pizza is free.

Other fast-food outlets in Kowloon include:

Café de Coral – mezzanine floor, Albion Plaza, 2-6 Granville Rd, Tsim Sha Tsui; 54A Canton Rd

Fairwood Fast Food – 6 Ashley Rd, Tsim Sha Tsui; basement two, Silvercord Shopping Centre, corner Haiphong and Canton Rds

Hardee's – Regent Hotel arcade, south of Salisbury Rd at the southern tip of Tsim Sha Tsui

Jack in the Box – ground floor, Tsim Sha Tsui Centre, 66 Mody Rd, Tsim Sha Tsui East, has some Mexican food

Ka Ka Lok Fast Food Shop – 55A Carnarvon Rd, Tsim Sha Tsui; 16A Ashley Rd (enter from Ichang St), Tsim Sha Tsui; 79A Austin Rd, Yau Ma Tei; Peninsula Centre, Mody Square, Tsim Sha Tsui East. Mostly takeaway Chinese food.

KFC 2 – Cameron Rd, Tsim Sha Tsui; 241 Nathan Rd, Yau Ma Tei

Pizza Hut – lower basement, Silvercord Shopping Centre, corner Haiphong and Canton Rds, Tsim Sha Tsui; shop 008, Ocean Terminal, Harbour City, Canton Rd, Tsim Sha Tsui; 1st floor, Hanford House, 221C-D Nathan Rd, Yau Ma Tei; port A, basement 1, Autoplaza, 65 Mody Rd, Tsim Sha Tsui East

Spaghetti House – 3B Cameron Rd; 1st floor, 57 Peking Rd; basement, 6-6A Hart Ave; 1st floor, 38 Haiphong Rd, Tsim Sha Tsui. The pizzas are ordinary but this place seems to be popular.

Wendy's – basement, Albion Plaza, 2-6 Granville Rd, just off Nathan Rd, Tsim Sha Tsui

Filipino

The *Mabuhay* (☎ 2367-3762), 11 Minden Ave serves good Filipino and Spanish food. Many Filipino expats eat here.

Indian

You won't have trouble finding restaurants dishing up Indian and similar Pakistani and Sri Lankan cuisine in Kowloon, but some places have an inexplicable 'members only' rule. To eat in these places, you must be a member, though absolutely anyone can become a member by paying about HK$20 for a membership card, which is valid for one year. The card is usually sent to you by post rather than issued on the spot, and from my experience this can take weeks. I suppose that this enhances the restaurants' prestige, but it seems to me like a good way to drive away business. Fortunately, not all Indian restaurants have this requirement.

Gurkha Club (☎ 2724-2014), 2nd floor, Haiphong Mansion, 53-55 Haiphong Rd (enter from Lock Rd), does Indian & Nepali food. There is also a good selection of vegetarian dishes here.

Koh-i-Nor (☎ 2368-3065), 3-4 Peninsula Mansion, 16C Mody Rd, is just around the corner from Chungking Mansions and offers a much more salubrious environment. There are meat dishes and vegetarian meals on the menu.

Surya Restaurant (☎ 2366-9902), is buried among the shops inside the Lyton Building at 34-48 Mody Rd. It's as good a place as any to get your biryani mutton, lamb keema sali and chicken tikka. The restaurant is open from noon until midnight.

In the flashy Tsim Sha Tsui East neighbourhood is *Woodlands* (☎ 2369-3718), shops 5 & 6, ground floor, Mirror Tower, 61 Mody Rd. This place specialises in spicy vegetarian food.

Gaylord (☎ 2376-1001), 1st floor, 11 Ashley Centre, 23-25 Ashley Rd, is an upmarket establishment which serves highly rated tandoori delights.

The top-end in terms of flashy surroundings is *Bukhara* (☎ 2369-1111 ext 3921), 2nd floor, Sheraton Hotel, 20 Nathan Rd. Probably the best value here is the tandoori luncheon buffet, which is priced at a very reasonable HK$88.

GLENN BEANLAND

GLENN BEANLAND

RICHARD I'ANSON

Top: Antique shops in Cat St, Sheung Wan, overflow with bric-a-brac.
Bottom Left: Antique shop near Man Mo Temple, Sheung Wan.
Bottom Right: The wares at the Bird Market, Mong Kok, are bought for the pleasure of their song.

RICHARD I'ANSON

ROBERT STOREY

GLENN BEANLAND

Top Left: Fruit and vegetable stalls in Gresson St Market, Wan Chai.
Top Right: Indoor fish market, Hong Kong Island.
   Bottom: Market forces. A fruit and vegetable vendor keeps in touch with the world
   outside his stall in Central.

Chungking Mansions The greatest concentration of cheap Indian and Pakistani restaurants is in Chungking Mansions, at 36-44 Nathan Rd. Despite the grotty appearance of the entrance to the Mansions, many of the restaurants are surprisingly plush inside. A meal of curried chicken and rice, or curry with chapattis and dhal, will cost around HK$30 per person.

Start your search for Indian food on the ground floor of the arcade. The bottom of the market belongs to *Kashmir Fast Food*, *Pita Palace* and *Lahore Fast Food*. These open early, so you can have curry, chapattis and heartburn for breakfast. Other perks include free drinking water and a roll of toilet paper on each table for tidying up. But neither of these two restaurants offer any kind of cheery atmosphere and the stools are uncomfortable – it's no place to linger.

The mezzanine floor of Chungking Mansions has a better selection of Indian-style fast-food eateries, with more comfortable seating. Here you can sample the wares at *Nepal Fast Food* (☎ 2739-5979) which offers free delivery to any place in the Mansions. Also on this floor is *Sher-E-Punjab* and *Bismillah Fast Food*.

Further upstairs in Chungking Mansions there are many places with better food and ambience. Prices are still low, with set meals from HK$35 or so. The following are presented in alphabetical order rather than in order of price or quality:

Delhi Club – (☎ 2368-1682), 3rd floor, C block, one of the best and it offers free delivery
Islamabad Club – (☎ 2721-5362), 4th floor, C block, Indian and Pakistani halal food, looks decent
Khyber Pass Club Mess – (☎ 2721-2786), 7th floor, E block, has good food served in more-or-less acceptable surroundings
Mumtaj Mahal Club – (☎ 2721-5591), 12th floor, C block, good if you're staying in this block
Nanak Mess – (☎ 2368-8063), 11th floor, A block, flat A4, decent but not one of the top spots
New Madras Mess – (☎ 2368-5021), 16th floor, D block, Muslim and vegetarian halal food, grotty atmosphere
Pakistan Mess – 4th floor, C block, Pakistani halal food

Royal Club Mess – (☎ 2369-7680), 5th floor, D block, Indian and vegetarian, with free delivery
Sher-I-Punjab Club Mess – (☎ 2368-0859), 3rd floor, B block, Nepali and Indian food
Swagat – (☎ 2722-5350), 1st floor, the top-rated Indian restaurant in the Mansions but also the most expensive
Taj Mahal Club Mess – (☎ 2722-5454), 3rd floor, B block, excellent food, excellent value – a personal favourite
Taj Mahal Takeaway – ground floor arcade, not to be confused with the above-mentioned Taj Mahal, this is probably the best place to get quick, inexpensive samosas and pakoras

Indonesian

The *Java Rijsttafel* (☎ 2367-1230), Han Hing Mansion, 38 Hankow Rd, Tsim Sha Tsui, serves 'rijsttafel' – literally meaning a rice table. This place packs out with Dutch expats, most of whom complain that the same thing is a lot cheaper in Amsterdam. Two delicious rijsttafels will set you back about HK$300.

There is also the *Indonesia Restaurant* (☎ 2367-3287) at 66 Granville Rd, Tsim Sha Tsui, which is good for a *gado gado* and a side order of prawn crackers.

Italian

A great Italian restaurant is *Valentino* (☎ 2721-6449) at 16 Hanoi Rd. Also highly rated is *La Taverna* (☎ 2376-0674), Astoria Building, 36-38 Ashley Rd, Tsim Sha Tsui.

Pizza World (☎ 2367-1983) ground floor, New World Centre, 22 Salisbury Rd, is extremely popular and has the best salad bar in Hong Kong – the large salad for HK$35 is a meal in itself.

French

Elegant French cuisine is available at *Au Trou Normand* (☎ 2366-8754), 6 Carnarvon Rd, Tsim Sha Tsui.

Japanese

If you want cheap Japanese food, make it yourself. Japanese restaurants charge Japanese prices. You can economise by looking for informal ones without the fish ponds and young Filipinas in geisha costumes playing ukuleles. Some places to consider include:

Ah-So – (☎ 2730-3392), 159 Craigie Court, World Finance Centre, Harbour City, Canton Rd, Tsim Sha Tsui

Hanamizuki – (☎ 2369-3988), mezzanine floor, Kimberley Hotel, 28 Kimberley Rd, Tsim Sha Tsui

Kyozasa – (☎ 2739-1336), Wing On Plaza, 62 Mody Rd, Tsim Sha Tsui East

Matsuzaka – (☎ 2724-3057), UG23-28 South Seas Centre, 75 Mody Rd, Tsim Sha Tsui East

Nagoya – (☎ 2739-5566), 1st floor, 21A Lock Rd, Tsim Sha Tsui

Sui Sha Ya – (☎ 2722-5001), ground floor, 9 Chatham Rd, Tsim Sha Tsui

Unkai – (☎ 2369-1111 ext 2), 3rd floor, Sheraton Hotel

Korean

There are several excellent and easily accessible Korean restaurants. A good one is *Seoul House* (☎ 2314-3174), 35 Hillwood Rd, Yau Ma Tei.

Another place is *Manna*, a chain restaurant with outlets in Tsim Sha Tsui at 83B Nathan Rd (☎ 2721-2159); Lyton Building, 32B Mody Rd (☎ 2367-4278); and 6A Humphrey's Rd (☎ 2368-2485).

Korea House (☎ 2367-5674), Empire Centre, 68 Mody Rd, Tsim Sha Tsui East.

Malaysian

Banana Leaf Curry House (☎ 2721-4821), 3rd floor, Golden Crown Court, 68 Nathan Rd, dishes up Malaysian food served on a banana leaf. Outstanding fruit juices go down well with spicy Singapore noodles.

Thai

Thai food can be devastatingly hot but delicious. An excellent Thai restaurant is *Royal Pattaya* (☎ 2366-9919), 9 Minden Ave, Tsim Sha Tsui. This place has a vegetarian menu if you prefer.

Also good is *Wong Chun Chun* (☎ 2721-0099), 21-23 Prat Ave, Tsim Sha Tsui. Visiting Thais seem to enjoy the food at *Bangkok Royal Hotel* (☎ 2735-9181), 2-12 Pilkem St, Yau Ma Tei.

The neighbourhood just opposite the passenger terminal building at Kai Tak Airport is Kowloon City. While it wouldn't be called one of Hong Kong's notable scenic spots, it has an unusually high concentration of Thai residents and therefore Thai restaurants. There are also a few Indian restaurants in the neighbourhood. The selection of places to eat is so good and prices so reasonable (by Hong Kong standards) that it's almost worth a trip out here just for a meal. Alternatively, if you've got a few hours to kill while waiting for a flight, this could be your last chance to pig out in Hong Kong.

You can get here by catching any of the Airbuses (A1, A2 or A3) and crossing Prince Edward Road (follow the pedestrian overpass into the Regal Airport Hotel). However, it makes more sense to take bus No 5 from the Kowloon Star Ferry terminal because it is cheaper and lands you closer to the restaurants. The nearest MTR station is Lok Fu, but that's still a rather long walk. Places to eat in this neighbourhood include:

Cambo Thai – (☎ 2716-7318), 15 Nga Tsin Long Rd
Golden Harvest Thai – (☎ 2383-6131), 19-21 Kai Tak Rd
Golden Orchid Thai – (☎ 2383-3076), Nos 6 & 12, Lung Kong Rd
Golden Wheat Thai – (☎ 2718-1801), 34 Nam Kok Rd
Heng (Sau) Thai – (☎ 2383-9159), 68 Kai Tak Rd
Indian Curry Hut – (☎ 2716-6182), 37 Sa Po Rd
Phuket Thai – (☎ 2716-6616), 74 Tak Ku Ling Rd
Ruaen Pae – (☎ 2382-2320), 27 Nam Kok Rd
Taste of India – (☎ 2716-5128), 24 South Wall Rd
Thai Farm – (☎ 2382-0992), 21-23 Nam Kok Rd
Thai Wah – (☎ 2716-7877, 2382-7117), Nos 24 & 38 Kai Tak Rd
Wong Chun Chun Cantonese-Thai – (☎ 2383-4680), 70-72 Nga Tsin Wai Rd, and at 29-33 Lung Kong Rd

Vegetarian

Bodhi (☎ 2739-2222), 1st floor, 32-34 Lock Rd, Tsim Sha Tsui (you can also enter at 81 Nathan Rd), is one of Hong Kong's biggest vegetarian restaurants. Dim sum is dished up from 11 am to 5 pm.

Also excellent is *Pak Bo Vegetarian Kitchen* (☎ 2366-2732), 106 Austin Rd, Tsim Sha Tsui; there's another branch (☎ 2380-2681) at 787 Nathan Rd, Mong Kok.

Though Westerners may be put off by a restaurant whose name begins with 'fat', *Fat Siu Lam*

(☎ 2388-1308) is a pretty good place for vegie cuisine. It's at 2-3 Cheong Lok St, Yau Ma Tei.

Vietnamese

One excellent place is *Café de La Paix Vietnamese Cuisine* (☎ 2721-4665) at 25 Hillwood Rd, Yau Ma Tei. There is another branch (☎ 2721-2747) just down the street in Hermes Commercial Centre, corner of Hillwood and Nathan Rds.

Another good place is *Golden Bull* (☎ 2369-4617), Level 1, Unit 17, New World Centre, 18 Salisbury Rd, Tsim Sha Tsui. There is another branch (☎ 2730-4866) at unit 101, Ocean Centre, Harbour City, Canton Rd, Tsim Sha Tsui.

Western

Hugo's (☎ 2311-1234 ext 877) on the 2nd floor of the Hyatt Regency Hotel offers some of the best and most expensive Western food in Kowloon. The more-than-you-can-eat brunch costs a cool HK$430, but for children it's a mere HK$310. Open 7 am to 11 pm. The Hyatt is at 67 Nathan Rd.

If you're watching the budget, the *Café* (in the same hotel) has buffet luncheons for HK$150 (HK$100 for children).

The Bostonian (☎ 2375-1133) inside the Ramada Renaissance Hotel, 8 Peking Rd, Tsim Sha Tsui, is ostensibly a seafood restaurant. However, it has the most knock-out buffet in Kowloon.

Budget or expensive? It's up to you! The Bostonian specialises in fresh seafood and good steaks. 'Not for the budget traveller' you say, but wait. They offer a steak dinner that can be cut three ways – the 'girly' portion, the 'manly' portion and the 'animal' portion. The animal portion is a ridiculous size and only for the traveller who hasn't eaten properly while on the road in the past six months. Order this, *eat it all* and you don't have to pay for it! Tips: pass on the free bread, don't drink too much water and don't have soup for a starter. Actually, don't have a starter at all, because if you don't eat all that steak you'll have to pay about HK$500 for it!

Martin Lai

It's perhaps not too extravagant to have a fixed-price lunch on the first floor veranda of the exceedingly posh *Peninsula Hotel*. The 'curry tiffin' on Saturday is particularly good for

HK$175, this includes the main course, dessert and coffee, but *not* drinks – stick to water or the bill can easily get wildly out of control. A glass of wine is HK$110 and orange juice is HK$50; this must be how the hotel pays for its fleet of Rolls-Royces – painted what else but 'peninsula green'. The lunches are popular – book a table (☎ 2366-6251).

Planet Hollywood (☎ 2377-7888), 3 Canton Rd, Tsim Sha Tsui, is very pricey but that hasn't dented its popularity. Examples of what's on the menu include: burgers HK$80, beers HK$32 to HK$40, desserts HK$45 to HK$55, pastas HK$80 to HK$95, wine by the glass HK$40, dinner for four HK$855.

Planet Hollywood, the restaurant of Willis, Stallone and Schwarzenegger, has what must be the very best brownie in the whole world, though it's quite expensive.
Tatjena Steinecke

Self Catering

If you're looking for the best in cheese, bread and other imported delicacies, check out the delicatessen at *Oliver's* on the ground floor of Ocean Centre on Canton Rd. Here you'll find such exotica as blue cheese, Melba toast, imported Belgian chocolate cookies and German black bread.

A health food store with everything from wholemeal bread to Tiger's Milk health bars is *Eden's Natural Synergy* (☎ 2368-0725), ground floor, 28 Hillwood Rd, Tsim Sha Tsui.

See's Candies (☎ 2735-6488), 119B Ocean Terminal, Harbour City, Canton Rd, Tsim Sha Tsui, is of special interest to chocolate junkies.

For true backpackers' cuisine like muesli, yoghurt and peanut butter, you've got to hit the supermarkets – and Hong Kong's are exceedingly well stocked. The biggest surprise is that prices are very reasonable. A few good supermarkets in Tsim Sha Tsui and Yau Ma Tei include:

Park 'N' Shop – south-west corner, Peking Rd & Kowloon Park Drive; second basement, Silvercord Shopping Centre, 30 Canton Rd
Wellcome – inside the Dairy Farm Creamery (ice-cream parlour), 74-78 Nathan Rd, open until 10 pm; north-west corner of Granville and Car-

narvon; basement, Star House (next to Star Ferry pier)

Yue Hwa Chinese Products – basement, 301 Nathan Rd, Yau Ma Tei (near Jordan MTR station), both Western products and Chinese exotica (tea bricks, flattened chickens, etc)

Ice Cream

Haagen-Dazs at 67 Nathan Rd is the premier spot for ice-cream delights. There is another branch at Kai Tak airport in case you need an emergency rum & raisin cone or zesty lemon sorbet before you board your flight.

Dairy Farm is a good place to pick up a fast takeaway fix – you'll find a closet-sized branch at 74 Nathan Rd.

ENTERTAINMENT

All things considered, Hong Kong Island is more interesting for nightlife, particularly the Lan Kwai Fong area in Central. See the Hong Kong Island chapter for details. That said, you can certainly find ways of keeping yourself entertained on the Kowloon side, but keep in mind that this is not a cheap city for late-night carousing.

Cinemas

The more popular English-language cinemas in Kowloon include:

Astor – (☎ 2781-1833), Eaton Hotel, Astor Plaza, 380 Nathan Rd, Yau Ma Tei

Broadway – (☎ 2332-5731), 6 Sai Yeung Choi St, Mong Kok

Chinachem – (☎ 2311-3000), Chinachem Golden Plaza, 77 Mody Rd, Tsim Sha Tsui East

Dynasty – (☎ 2399-0363), 4 Mong Kok Rd, Mong Kok

Empire – (☎ 2771-8933), 60 Soy St, Yau Ma Tei

Harbour City – (☎ 2735-6916), World Shipping Centre, Canton Rd, Tsim Sha Tsui

Liberty – (☎ 2730-6148), 26A Jordan Rd, Yau Ma Tei

London – (☎ 2736-8282), 219 Nathan Rd, Yau Ma Tei

Mandarin – (☎ 2396-3110), Hung Hom Commercial Centre, Hung Hom

Majestic – (☎ 2782-0272), 348 Nathan Rd, Yau Ma Tei

Miramar – (☎ 2736-0108), Park Lane Square, Kimberley & Nathan Rds, Tsim Sha Tsui

Newport – (☎ 2385-7151), 23 Jordan Rd, Yau Ma Tei

Ocean – (☎ 2377-2100), Omni Hongkong Hotel, 3 Canton Rd, Tsim Sha Tsui

Silvercord – (☎ 2317-1083), 30 Canton Rd

South China – (☎ 2388-1755), 180 Portland St, Mong Kok

Space Museum – (☎ 2721-2361), near the Star Ferry in Tsim Sha Tsui also shows excellent films in the planetarium.

UA Whampoa – (☎ 2303-1040), Whampoa Garden, Hung Hom

Night Markets

The biggest night market and the one most popular with tourists is the Temple St market in Tsim Sha Tsui (near Jordan MTR station). The market gets going about 8 pm and closes around midnight.

Another big market is at Tung Choi St in Mong Kok. It is geared more towards selling clothing and operates mostly in the daytime.

Pubs & Clubs

Rick's Cafe (☎ 2367-2939), basement, 4 Hart Ave, is popular with the Tsim Sha Tsui backpacker set. However, it gets expensive for men on Friday and Saturday night after 10 pm, when there's a HK$100 cover charge (free for women though).

Jouster II (☎ 2723-0022), shops A & B, Hart Ave Court, 19-23 Hart Ave, Tsim Sha Tsui, is a fun multi-storey place with medi-aeval decor – check out the knight in shining armour and miniature drawbridge. Normal hours are noon to 3 am, except on Sundays when it's from 6 pm to 2 am. Happy hour is anytime before 9 pm.

It seems that half the Western travellers who visit Hong Kong leave the city with a T-shirt emblazoned with the 'Hard Rock Cafe' moniker. If all these people actually eat at the *Hard Rock Cafe* (☎ 2377-8118), then business must be booming. Check it out yourself. There are two locations – the big one is at 100 Canton Rd and a smaller branch is inside the Star Ferry terminal. Open from 11.30 am to 3 am.

Ned Kelly's Last Stand (☎ 2376-0562), 11A Ashley Rd, open 11 am to 2 am, became famous as a real Australian pub, complete with meat pies. Now it's known mainly for its Dixieland jazz and Aussie folk music. It has a good party atmosphere (at least if you can tolerate Dixieland), but the volume is set on high so it's no place for quiet conversation.

Amoeba Bar (☎ 2376-0389), 22 Ashley Rd, Tsim Sha Tsui, has local live music from around 9 pm, and the place doesn't close until about 6 am.

The *Red Lion Inn* (☎ 2317-6289), 15 Ashley Rd, is just down the street from the Amoeba. A feature of this pub is that customers are invited to sing along with the band.

The *Kangaroo Pub* (☎ 2376-0083), 1st & 2nd floors, 35 Haiphong Rd, Tsim Sha Tsui, is an Aussie pub in the true tradition. This place does a good Sunday brunch.

Mad Dogs Pub (☎ 2301-2222), basement, 32 Nathan Rd, is a popular Aussie-style pub. From Monday through Thursday it's open from 7 am until 2 am, but from Friday through Sunday it's 24-hour service.

Presumably, the preceding inspired *Mad Cats* (☎ 2723-1651) at 11 Hanoi Rd. Thankfully, no one has yet opened a pub in Hong Kong called *Mad Cows*.

Delaneys (☎ 2301-3980), 3-7A Prat Ave, Tsim Sha Tsui, serves good Irish food and has performances of fine Irish folk music. Happy hour is from 3 to 8 pm and the place closes up around 1 am.

Watering Hole (☎ 2312-2288), basement, 1A Mody Rd, Tsim Sha Tsui, is very popular with travellers and close to Chungking Mansions.

Schnurrbart (☎ 2366-2986), 9-11 Prat Ave, is the place to get your German dark beer on tap.

Knutsford Terrace, if you can find it, is a narrow alley that has suddenly becoming trendy with diners and late-night revellers – some say it's Kowloon's answer to Lan Kwai Fong (see the Hong Kong Island chapter). The alley is one block north of Kimberley Rd (not Kimberley St) and runs parallel to it – enter from Observatory Rd. At 4-5 Knutsford Terrace is *Bahama Mama's* (☎ 2368-2121), notable for its tropical decor, and the *Big Tree Pub* (☎ 2721-1686). At 14 Knutsford Terrace is a fine Spanish bar/restaurant called *El Cid* (☎ 2312-1898). Nearby is *Tutto Bene* (☎ 2316-2116), a charming Italian restaurant whose name means 'everything's fine'.

If you'd like to see what the Cantonese jet-set does for entertainment, visit *Catwalk*

(☎ 2369-4111 ext 6380) in the New World Hotel at 22 Salisbury Rd. Music is Latin salsa style, but there's a karaoke lounge and a video wall. When dancing, be careful not to get poked in the eye by a cellular telephone. On Friday and Saturday evenings, the cover charge is a cool HK$200, though this lands you two drinks. It's open from 9 pm to at least 2.30 am.

Lost City (☎ 2311-1111) is aptly named – you could indeed get lost in this enormous place. The 'city' is divided into 12 theme areas with a bar about the size of the Star Ferry in the middle. This place is devoted mostly to Cantonese tastes, and as such has a large disco and karaoke section. The high prices scare off most foreigners, but if you'd like to have a look it's in the Chinachem Golden Plaza, 77 Mody Rd, Tsim Sha Tsui East.

If you're looking for a quiet romantic place with harbour views, you could try the *Sky Lounge* (☎ 2739-1111) in the Hotel Nikko, 72 Mody Rd, Tsim Sha Tsui East. It's open from 4 pm to 1.30 am.

Hostess Clubs

Many of these places are real sleaze pits and make a habit of cheating foreigners through hidden 'service charges'. The ones in Tsim Sha Tsui are particularly bad, but it's more above-board in Tsim Sha Tsui East. See the Entertainment section in the Facts for the Visitor chapter for details of hostess bar scams.

Bottoms Up (☎ 2721-4509), 14 Hankow Rd, is probably the most famous girlie club in Hong Kong. This is only because one brief scene in the 007 movie *The Man with the Golden Gun* was filmed here in the 1970s. The 'famous scene' consisted of a near-naked Chinese cocktail waitress squatting on the bar pouring a drink for James Bond. Bottoms Up has been milking this public relations coup ever since. Unfortunately, there is nothing particularly elegant about this place, though the bar was probably a more fitting setting for Mr Bond than Chungking Mansions.

All of the following places are considered 'respectable establishments', though they are expensive.

A popular place with Chinese tycoons is

China City Night Club (☎ 2723-3278), 4th floor, Peninsula Centre, 67 Mody Rd, Tsim Sha Tsui East. Open daily from noon to 4 am.

Club Bboss (☎ 2369-2883), New Mandarin Plaza, 14 Science Museum Rd, Tsim Sha Tsui East, bills itself as a 'Japanese-style nightclub'. Certainly the prices are Japanese-style. With more than 1000 hostesses of 'various nationalities', it's a good place to practise your Tagalog or Thai (if you don't mind paying HK$1000 an hour for lessons).

Club Deluxe (☎ 2721-0277), L-301, New World Centre, Salisbury Rd, Tsim Sha Tsui, is a good place to burn up money, especially in the VIP karaoke suites. Opening hours are from 8 pm to 3 am. The club features, among other things, an indoor waterfall.

Video Game Parlours

Blow away bad guys and zap evil extraterrestrials at any of the following video game centres:

328 Game Centre – (☎ 2366-6657), 26 Cameron Rd, Tsim Sha Tsui
First Rate Game Centre – (☎ 2388-5267), 17 Waterloo Rd, Yau Ma Tei
Houston Game Centre – (☎ 2722-4295), Houston Centre, Tsim Sha Tsui East
Ka Lok TV Games Centre – (☎ 2384-4069), 51B Jordan Rd, Yau Ma Tei
Million Ways Game Centre – (☎ 2713-1760), 77 Waterloo Rd, Yau Ma Tei
Shun Hoi Games Centre – (☎ 2332-7933), 3D Waterloo Rd, Yau Ma Tei
Shun Sheung Games Centre – (☎ 2710-8933), 13 Temple St, Yau Ma Tei

THINGS TO BUY

Oh yeah, shopping. I guess some people come to Hong Kong for that. In Tsim Sha Tsui, you don't have to look for a place to shop, the shopping comes to you – people are constantly trying to stuff advertisements into your hands. Finding a place to buy a loaf of bread is almost impossible along the streets crammed with shops peddling clothes, watches, cameras, jewellery, eyeglasses and electronics. It's capitalism run amok, and more than a few travellers who came to Hong Kong just to pick up a China visa suddenly catch the buying fever. Try to exercise some restraint, or attend a local meeting of Shopperholics Anonymous.

If you've decided that you need to do some serious shopping, then Hong Kong is as good a place as any to go on a buying binge. However, if you're looking to make some expensive purchases like cameras, video and stereo equipment, please memorise the following sentence: Tsim Sha Tsui is a rip-off. While it's quite all right to purchase clothing here, you should look elsewhere when buying pricey hi-tech items.

Appliances & Electronics Sham Shui Po is a good neighbourhood to search for electrical and electronic goodies. You can even buy (and sell) secondhand appliances here. If you take any of the west exits from the MTR at Sham Shui Po station, you'll find yourself on Apliu St. There are numerous good shops here – one I've had success with is Success Electronics at No 220. Apliu St is one of the best areas in Hong Kong to go searching for the numerous permutations of plug adaptors you'll need if you're heading for China.

Mong Kok is another good neighbourhood for electronic gadgetry. Starting from Argyle St and heading south, explore all the side streets running parallel to Nathan Rd, such as Tung Choi, Sai Yeung Choi, Portland, Shanghai, and Reclamation Sts. In this area you can buy just about everything imaginable.

Backpacks Hong Kong is a good place to pick up gear for hiking, camping and travelling. Mong Kok is by far the best neighbourhood to look for this stuff, though there are a couple of places in nearby Yau Ma Tei. Some places worth checking out include:

Chamonix Alpine Equipment
   (☎ 2388-3626), On Yip Building, Shanghai St
Grade VI Alpine
   (☎ 2782-0202), 115 Woosung St, Yau Ma Tei
Mountaineer Supermarket
   (☎ 2397-0585), 395 Portland St, Mong Kok
Perfect Corporation
   (☎ 2366-1273), basement, 132 Austin Rd, Yau Ma Tei
Tang Fai Kee Military
   (☎ 2385-5169), 248 Reclamation St, Mong Kok

Three Military Equipment Company
(☎ 2395-5234), 83 Sai Yee St, Mong Kok

Cameras Tsim Sha Tsui is perhaps the most expensive place in Asia, if not the world, to buy photographic equipment. It's amazing there aren't more murders here when you consider the way the camera shops blatantly cheat tourists. This particularly applies to Nathan Rd. No shops here put price tags on the equipment and charging double or more is standard. In this neighbourhood, camera equipment is only 'reasonably-priced' when it's broken, second-hand or components are missing. Stanley St in Central is probably the best neighbourhood for camera equipment (see Hong Kong Island chapter), or go up to Mong Kok or the shopping malls in Sha Tin (see the New Territories chapter).

From my own experience, the two best camera shops in Tsim Sha Tsui are in Champagne Court at 16 Kimberley Rd. One is Kimberley Camera Company (☎ 2721-2308), and the other is David Chan (☎ 2723-3886). There are actually price tags on the equipment here, a rare find in Tsim Sha Tsui. These places also sell used equipment – there is some latitude for bargaining.

Chinese Emporiums One branch of Yue Hwa Chinese Products is at the Park Lane Boulevard on Nathan Rd, just north of the Kowloon Mosque. Look for the two-storey block that looks like the world's longest garage.

The People's Republic owns Chinese Arts & Crafts, which has two branches in Tsim Sha Tsui: at Silvercord Shopping Centre, 30 Canton Rd, near the corner of Haiphong Rd; and at Star House, at the corner of Salisbury and Canton Rds. There is another branch in Yau Ma Tei at 239 Nathan Rd (near Jordan MTR station). Everything has price tags and no bargaining is necessary.

Chung Kiu Chinese Products is also worth investigating. Branches are at 17 Hankow Rd, Tsim Sha Tsui; 528-532 Nathan Rd, Yau Ma Tei; and 47-51 Shantung St, Mong Kok.

Clothing You'll find the best buys at the street markets at Tong Choi St in Mong Kok and Apliu St in Sham Shui Po. If you want to search around Tsim Sha Tsui, the best deals are generally found on the eastern end of Granville Rd. Giordano's has an outlet at Golden Crown Mansion, 66-70 Nathan Rd. Bossini has one of its many stores at Granville House, 53 Granville Rd, Tsim Sha Tsui. Another good place is the mezzanine floor of Chungking Mansions (not the ground floor).

Britain's well-known Marks & Spencer chain has a branch in Tsim Sha Tsui at shops 102 & 254, Ocean Centre, Harbour City, Canton Rd.

There are many amazingly fancy and expensive boutiques in Tsim Sha Tsui and the prices don't seem to faze the hordes of free-spending Hong Kongers. A good example of the genre is *Green Peace* (☎ 2302-2062) at 1 Peking Rd. It's worth visiting just to check out the posh decor.

There are many factory outlets in Hung Hom, especially in Kaiser Estates. If you want to track them down, consult Dana Goetz's book *Hong Kong Factory Bargains*. A few notable ones in the neighbourhood include High Fashion Corner (☎ 2334-6411), Winner Building, 32-D Man Yue St; Vica Moda Dresses (☎ 2334-8363, 2765-7333), ground floor, Summit Building, 30 Man Yue St and Kaiser Estate Phase Two, 51 Man Yue St.

Computers Star Computer City, on the second floor in Star House at 3 Salisbury Rd, is the largest complex of computer shops in Tsim Sha Tsui. While it's not the cheapest place in Hong Kong to find computers, it's not the worst (that honour goes to nearby Nathan Rd). Bargaining is advised – honesty is in short supply in this neighbourhood. The highest mark-ups (blatant overcharging) are on small items like floppy disks and printer cartridges – you can often get a 50% discount just by asking for it. From the outside of the building it's not immediately obvious how to get inside this complex; as you face Star House from the harbour side, there are two main entrances with escalators leading up to the mezzanine level. The computer shops are all cleverly concealed in there.

Mong Kok Computer Centre has three floors of computer stores. It's geared more towards

Herbal Medicine

Western visitors often become so engrossed buying cameras and electronic goods that they forget Hong Kong is famous for something else – herbal medicine.

Nearby Guangzhou is less expensive for buying Chinese medicines, but in Hong Kong there are more chemists who can speak English and prices really aren't much higher. Also, in Hong Kong it's easier to find everything you want in one place and there's less problem with counterfeit medicines.

Chinese herbalists have all sorts of treatments for stomach aches, headaches, colds, flu and sore throat. They also have herbs to treat long-term problems like asthma. Many of these herbs seem to work. Whether or not Chinese medicine can cure more serious illnesses like cancer and heart disease is debatable.

In general, Chinese medicine works best for the relief of unpleasant symptoms (pain, sore throat, etc) and for some serious long-term conditions which resist Western medicines, such as migraine headaches, asthma and chronic backache. A well-known Chinese cure-all, the ganoderma mushroom, seems to work well on certain chronic intestinal diseases. And in the case of migraine headaches, herbs may well prove more effective than Western painkillers. But for acute life-threatening conditions, such as heart problems or appendicitis, it's still wise to see a Western doctor.

When reading about the theory behind Chinese medicine, the word 'holistic' appears often. Basically, this means that Chinese medicine seeks to treat the whole body rather than focusing on a particular organ or disease.

Another point to be wary of when taking herbal medicine is the tendency of some manufacturers to falsely claim that their product contains potent and expensive ingredients. For example, some herbal formulas may list the horn of the endangered rhinoceros. Widely acclaimed as a cure for fever, sweating and hot flushes, rhino horn is so rare it's practically impossible to buy. Any formula listing rhinoceros horn may, at best, contain water buffalo horn. By contrast, the Chinese demand for antlers now supports a whole industry of deer ranchers in New Zealand, Germany and the UK.

One benefit of Chinese medicine is that there are generally few side-effects. Compared to a drug like penicillin which can produce allergic reactions and other serious side-effects, herbal medicines are fairly safe. Nevertheless, herbs are still medicines, and not candy. There is no need to gobble herbs if you're feeling fine to begin with.

In Chinese medicine, a broad-spectrum remedy such as snake gall bladder may be good for treating colds, but there are many different types of colds. The best way to treat a cold with herbal medicine is to see a Chinese doctor and get a specific prescription. The pills on sale in herbal medicine shops are generally broad-spectrum, while a prescription remedy will usually require that you take home a bunch of specific herbs and cook them into a thick broth.

If you visit a Chinese doctor, you might be surprised by what he or she discovers about your body. For example, the doctor will almost certainly take your pulse and may tell you that you have a 'slippery' or 'thready' pulse. Chinese doctors have identified more than 30 different kinds of pulses. A pulse can be 'empty', 'leisurely', 'bowstring', or even 'regularly irregular'. The doctor may then examine your tongue, and pronounce that you have 'wet heat', as evidenced by a slippery pulse and a red greasy tongue.

Many Chinese medicines are powders that come in vials. Typically, you take one or two vials a day. Some of these powders taste OK, but others are very bitter and difficult to swallow. If you can't tolerate the taste, you may want to buy some empty gelatin capsules and fill them yourself with the powder.

A good place to purchase herbal medicines is Yue Hwa Chinese Products Emporium at the north-west corner of Nathan Rd and Jordan Rd, just above Jordan MTR station. Before buying anything, explain your condition to a Chinese chemist and ask for a recommendation. They consider this part of their job.

There are plenty of books available to learn more about Chinese medicine. One of the easiest to understand is *The Web That Has No Weaver: Understanding Chinese Medicine*, by Ted Kaptchuk.

If you want a more advanced text, *The Theoretical Foundations of Chinese Medicine*, by Manfred Porkert is good. However, the author has been criticised for introducing many Latin terms which make the book more difficult to read. ∎

the local Cantonese-speaking market than foreigners, but you can generally get better deals here than in Tsim Sha Tsui. The computer centre is at the intersection of Nelson and Fa Yuen Sts in Mong Kok.

The Golden Shopping Centre, basement and

1st floor, 146-152 Fuk Wah St, Sham Shui Po, has a good selection of computers, accessories and components. The nearby New Capital Computer Plaza, 85-95 Un Chau St, is also excellent. Both places are signposted in Sham Shui Po MTR station.

Department Stores My favourite store in Hong Kong is the main branch of Yue Hwa Chinese Products at 301 Nathan Rd, Yau Ma Tei (corner of Nathan and Jordan Rds). Unlike the touristy branch in Tsim Sha Tsui, this store has a wide assortment of practical, everyday, locally produced and imported items (not just from China). There is also some Chinese exotica like herbal medicine. However, it's not a high-fashion store – if it's famous labels you crave, look elsewhere.

Wing On is an upmarket department store where you can find Gucci handbags, Calvin Klein underwear, Chanel No 19 perfume and Rolex watches (real ones). There are three branches in Kowloon: 361 Nathan Rd, Yau Ma Tei; 620 Nathan Rd, Mong Kok; and Wing On Plaza, Mody Rd, Tsim Sha Tsui East. Another Hong Kong department store is Sincere, 83 Argyle St, Mong Kok. Lane Crawford has a store in Manson House, 74 Nathan Rd, Tsim Sha Tsui.

Dragon Seed operates a three-storey store at Albion Plaza, 2-6 Granville Rd, Tsim Sha Tsui.

The major Japanese department store in Tsim Sha Tsui is Mitsukoshi, 28 Canton Rd. If you're really interested in Japanese wares, it's better to visit the stores in Causeway Bay on Hong Kong Island.

Eyeglasses Nathan Rd in Tsim Sha Tsui is lined with opticians charging high prices for low quality, but the rude service is free. I always get my spectacles made on the 3rd floor of Yue Hwa Chinese Products, 301 Nathan Rd, Yau Ma Tei.

Gems If it's coloured rocks you're after, the following are HKTA members – for what that's worth:

Chaumont
    (☎ 2368-7331), 10th floor, Metropole Building, 57 Peking Rd, Tsim Sha Tsui
Opal Mine
    (☎ 2721-9933), Burlington House Arcade, 92 Nathan Rd, Tsim Sha Tsui

Jewellery King Fook and Tse Sui Luen are two chain stores which guarantee to buy back any jewellery they sell at its wholesale price. Of course, be sure you get the certificate and realise that you need to be in Hong Kong to take advantage of the buy-back plan. There isn't supposed to be any difference in price from one branch to another, but you might do better to avoid Tsim Sha Tsui. Branches are located as follows:

King Fook
    Hotel Miramar Princess Shopping Plaza, 118-130 Nathan Rd, Tsim Sha Tsui (☎ 2313-2768); ground floor, 644 Nathan Rd, Mong Kok (☎ 2789-2008); shop A-C, ground floor, 26 Jordan Rd, Yau Ma Tei (☎ 2735-1017); 611-615 Nathan Rd, Mong Kok (☎ 2388-8108)

Tse Sui Luen
    ground floor, 315 Nathan Rd, Yau Ma Tei (☎ 2332-4618); ground floor, TSL Building, 335 Nathan Rd, Yau Ma Tei (☎ 2782-0110); ground floor, 343 Nathan Rd, Yau Ma Tei (☎ 2332-1468); G1 & G2, ground floor, Nathan Centre, 580 Nathan Rd, Mong Kok (☎ 2770-2322); shop AR1005, ground floor, Park Lane Square, 132-134 Nathan Rd, Tsim Sha Tsui (☎ 2739-6673); ground floor, 125-127 Ma Tau Wai Rd, Hung Hom (☎ 2766-2613); block B, ground floor, Summit Building, 30 Man Yue St, Hung Hom (☎ 2333-4221 ext 633)

Pharmaceuticals Hong Kong is a good place to stock up on everyday practical items, especially if you're headed into the backwaters of China, where shaving cream and deodorant are unimaginable luxuries. Watson's is Hong Kong's biggest chain store in the pharmaceutical arena, and there is no need to give their addresses here because there seems to be one on every street corner. However, I have found prices to be somewhat better at Mannings, a much smaller chain. There is one in Tsim Sha Tsui on the lower ground floor, shop 37-47, Silvercord Shopping Centre, 30 Canton Rd.

Toys These can be found everywhere, but perhaps the biggest in Hong Kong is Toys R Us (☎ 2730-9462), shop 003, basement, Ocean Terminal, Harbour City, Tsim Sha Tsui.

Music & Software HMV is a chain store, and the largest branch is at the north-west corner of Hankow and Peking Rds. This place has five floors of music, making it one of the largest CD selections in the world.

Check out the upper floors for classical music. Prices are about average for Hong Kong. The store is open from 10 am until midnight.

A chain store named KPS is another good place to buy CDs and music tapes. Computer software (legal copies, that is) are also sold at substantial discounts. There are several branches, but the easiest one to find is in the basement of Silvercord Shopping Centre (☎ 2730-3055) at 30 Canton Rd and is open from 10 am to 10 pm. There is another KPS (☎ 2388-1380) on the 3rd floor of Chong Hing Square, 601 Nathan Rd, Mong Kok.

You can also pick up cheap CDs at the Temple St night market and from shops in Mong Kok, but the selection is limited.

Sporting Goods Some stores catering to sports enthusiasts include:

Bunn's Diving Equipment
  (☎ 2380-5344), ground floor, 217 Sai Yee St, Mong Kok
Bunn's Sportoo
  (☎ 2302-1379) (water sports), shop 015, Marine Deck, Ocean Terminal, Harbour City, Canton Rd, Tsim Sha Tsui
Flying Ball Bicycle Shop
  (☎ 2381-5919), 201 Tung Choi St (near Prince Edward MTR station), Mong Kok
Golf 18
  (☎ 2367-1188), Shop 7, Hong Kong Pacific Centre, 28 Hankow Rd, Tsim Sha Tsui
International Elite Divers Training Centre
  (☎ 2381-2789), ground floor, Fulland Court, 256 Fa Yuen St, Mong Kok

Pro-Shop
  (☎ 2723-6816) (windsurfing equipment), 1st floor, front unit, Ocean View Court, 31 Mody Rd, Tsim Sha Tsui
Wah Shing Diving Equipment
  (☎ 2391-4084), ground floor, 2B-2C Larch St, Mong Kok
Windsurf Boutique
  (☎ 2366-9911; fax 2369-8403), shop 19-23, Rise Commercial Building, 5-11 Granville Circuit, Tsim Sha Tsui
Wind 'N' Surf
  (☎ 2366-9293), Flat 3, Block A, 1st floor, Carnarvon Mansion, 10 Carnarvon Rd, Tsim Sha Tsui

Tourist Shopping Malls Exploring the malls in tourist land is not a total waste of time. True, you can probably find what you need elsewhere for less money, but sometimes the extra you pay in Tsim Sha Tsui is worth it to avoid having to track down the same goods elsewhere. Also, the malls are interesting tourist attractions in themselves.

In the tourist zone of Tsim Sha Tsui, there are three big complexes in a row on Canton Rd: Ocean Terminal, nearest the Star Ferry; Ocean Centre; and Harbour City. Across the street at 30 Canton Rd is Silvercord. The New World Centre is on Salisbury Rd, adjacent to the New World Hotel.

In Tsim Sha Tsui East, the biggest mall is the Tsim Sha Tsui Centre at 66 Mody Rd (between Salisbury and Mody Rds). There are other malls here and you could probably spend days exploring them.

Hong Kong Island

The commercial heart of Hong Kong pumps away on the north side of Hong Kong Island, where banks and businesses, high-rise apartment blocks and hotels cover a good part of its 78 sq km.

From the Star Ferry the island looks unbelievably crowded, and on the lower levels it certainly is, but from 40m up on the Peak you realise how much space is left.

As well as moving up the hill for more building space, Hong Kong keeps on moving out. Reclamation along the harbour edge continues to add the odd quarter km every so often, and buildings once on the waterfront are now several hundred metres back. At the rate things are going, some cynics have suggested that the harbour will completely disappear in another decade.

The south side of Hong Kong Island has a completely different character to the north. For one thing, there are some fine beaches here and the water is actually clean enough to swim in. The best beaches are at Big Wave Bay, Deep Water Bay, Shek O, Stanley and Repulse Bay. Expensive villas are perched on the hillsides, and the impression is more like the French Riviera than crowded Hong Kong. Unfortunately, huge, multi-storey apartment blocks have been going up in recent years, though there's still a long way to go before it overtakes Kowloon.

It's easy to circumnavigate the island by public transport, starting from Central and taking a bus over the hills to Stanley, then heading clockwise along the coast back to the Star Ferry terminal.

CENTRAL

Central is most people's first impression of Hong Kong Island since it's where the Star Ferry lands. As you leave the ferry terminal, immediately on your right is the General Post Office, in front of which is towering Jardine House with its distinctive port hole windows. The HKTA operates a tourist information centre in the basement arcade.

Cenotaph

To reach the main part of Central you have to cross Connaught Rd. Straight ahead as you leave the Star Ferry is the pedestrian underpass which surfaces at the side of the Cenotaph. This forlorn looking monument is a memorial to Hong Kongers who died in the two world wars.

Just to the east of the Cenotaph is the Hong Kong Club, the last bastion of the British empire.

Statue Square

The Cenotaph occupies a tiny sliver of Statue Square, but the main part of the square is across the street on the south side of Chater Rd. Statue Square is notable for its collection of fountains and places to sit, and every Sunday is transformed into the unofficial gathering place for expat Filipinos (ethnic Thais gather nearby, just west of the Star Ferry pier). A bronze statue of the former chief manager of the Hong Kong & Shanghai Bank (HongkongBank), Sir Thomas Jackson, graces the square. The ornate colonial building on the east side of the square is the former Supreme Court, now elevated to the lofty title of Legislative Council (Legco) Chamber. In the front is a statue of the blindfolded Greek goddess Themis, representing justice.

Hong Kong & Shanghai Bank Building

At the south side of Statue Square (at Des Voeux Rd, along which the trams run) you come face to face with the bizarre-looking headquarters of the Hong Kong & Shanghai Banking Corporation (HongkongBank). Designed by architect Norman Foster, it cost over US$1 billion and was the most expensive building in the world at the time of its completion in 1985. Opinions differ on whether this place is an architectural masterpiece or a

HONG KONG

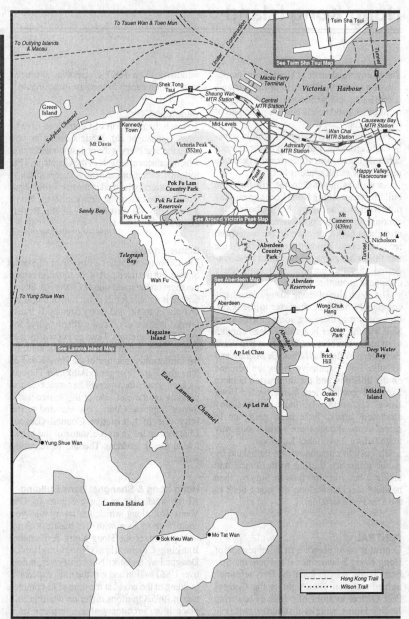

Legend:
- – – – Hong Kong Trail
- ·········· Wilson Trail

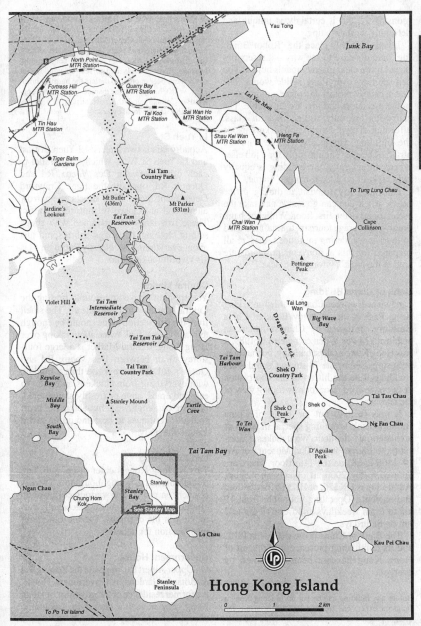

Hong Kong Island

monstrosity, but it certainly is unique and definitely worth visiting.

Locals call this place the 'Robot Building', and it's easy to see why – it resembles one of those clear plastic models built so you can see how everything inside works. The gears, chains, motors and other moving parts of the escalators and lifts are all visible. The stairwells are only walled in with glass, affording dizzying views to workers inside the building. Obviously, people who are afraid of heights should apply for a job elsewhere. Structurally, the building is equally radical, built on a 'coat-hanger' frame.

Definitely try to visit it during office hours, when you can go inside and take the escalator up to the first floor. While the bank doesn't encourage tourism, the staff are used to tourists wandering in. Indeed, they're all prepared for this as souvenir postcards are sold at the bank's information desk.

Bank of China Building

Sandwiched between Chater Garden and Hong Kong Park is the 74-storey Bank of China Building, designed by Chinese-American architect I M Pei. When completed in 1989, it was Hong Kong's tallest building, but has now been surpassed by the 78-storey Central Plaza Building. Ride the lift up to the observation deck on the 73rd floor for a sweeping view of the harbour.

It may be tall, but the Bank of China Building itself is nothing special in terms of architectural splendour. What makes it interesting to tourists is the Tsui Museum of Art (☎ 2868-2688) on the 11th floor. There are approximately 2000 art objects on display. Admission is HK$20, or HK$10 for children and students. Operating hours are from 10 am to 6 pm weekdays and from 10 am to 2 pm on Saturdays.

The Bank of China is owned by the PRC, and its dominating presence in the heart of Hong Kong has not been welcomed by everyone.

Before any building can be put up in Hong Kong a fungshui expert has to be called in to ensure the design, position and alignment don't bring bad luck, or even worse. Well, the Bank of China's fungshui is bad news – not for the Bank of China but for the buildings around it. Reportedly, the Bank of China positively radiates bad vibes (all those sharp corners, the spikes on the roof, etc) and some neighbouring buildings have actually had to seal up windows or cover them over in order to deflect the harmful influence. With China, 1997, the dispute over Legco [Legislative Council] and the new airport, it's hardly surprising, say the local cynics.

Li Yuen St

Actually this is two streets: Li Yuen St East and Li Yuen St West, which run parallel to each other between Des Voeux Rd and Queen's Rd, opposite the Lane Crawford Department Store. Both streets are narrow alleys and are closed to motorised traffic. These two lanes are crammed with shops selling clothing, handbags, fabrics and just about everything else. Nearby Pottinger St is also worth looking into.

Central Market

You shouldn't have any trouble finding the Central Market – just sniff the air. The smell from the fish section alone should be enough to make China think twice about taking over Hong Kong. Central Market is a large four-storey affair between Des Voeux Rd and Queen's Rd. It's more a zoo than a market, with everything from chickens and quail to eels and crabs, alive or freshly slaughtered. Fish are cut lengthwise, but above the heart so that it continues to beat and pump blood around the body.

Lan Kwai Fong

This is Hong Kong's chief disco, pub, bar, restaurant and party neighbourhood. There is a luncheon crowd and various coffee shop afternoon hang-outs, but the place really gets rocking in the evenings. See the Entertainment section for details.

Government House

On Upper Albert Rd, opposite the Zoological & Botanic Gardens, is Government House, the former residence of the governor of Hong Kong. For now, it's closed to the public except for one day in March (always a

Though its days as an administrative seat are numbered, the stately lines of Government House recall Hong Kong's colonial beginnings.

Sunday) when the azaleas are in bloom. At this time the place is swamped with locals and tourists.

The original sections of the building date back to 1858. Other features were actually built to Japanese designs during the war, when Japan occupied the colony and the Japanese governor wanted to establish a residence and administrative centre worthy of his role.

Zoological & Botanic Gardens

First established in 1864, the gardens are home to statues, hundreds of species of birds, exotic trees, plants and shrubs. Captive breeding of endangered species is carried out here.

Among the statues is one of the innovative Sir Arthur Kennedy, the first governor to invite Chinese to government functions. If you go to the gardens at about 8 am the place will be packed with Chinese toning up with a bit of t'ai chi before work. The gardens are divided by Albany Rd, with the botanics and the aviaries in the first section, off Garden Rd, and the zoologicals in the other. Admission is free.

The gardens are at the top end of Garden Rd, which runs past the US consulate – an easy walk, but you can also take bus No 3 or No 12 to the stop in front of Jardine House on Connaught Rd. The bus takes you along Upper Albert Rd and Caine Rd on the northern boundary of the gardens. Get off in front of the Caritas Centre (at the junction of Upper Albert and Caine Rds) and follow the path uphill to the gardens.

Hong Kong Park

This is one of the most unusual parks in the world – it was deliberately designed to look anything but natural. Rather, the park emphasises synthetic creations such as its fountain plaza, conservatory (greenhouse), aviary, artificial waterfall, indoor games hall, visual arts centre, playground, viewing tower, museum and t'ai chi garden. For all that, the park is beautiful in its own weird way, and makes for dramatic photography with a wall of skyscrapers on one side and mountains on the other.

Within the park is the **Flagstaff House Museum** (☎ 2869-0690), the oldest Western-style building still standing in Hong Kong, dating from the mid-19th century. Enter from Cotton Tree Drive. The museum houses a Chinese tea-ware collection, including pieces

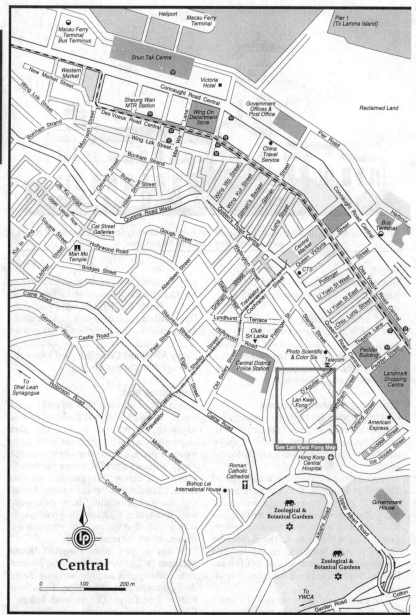

Central

0   100   200 m

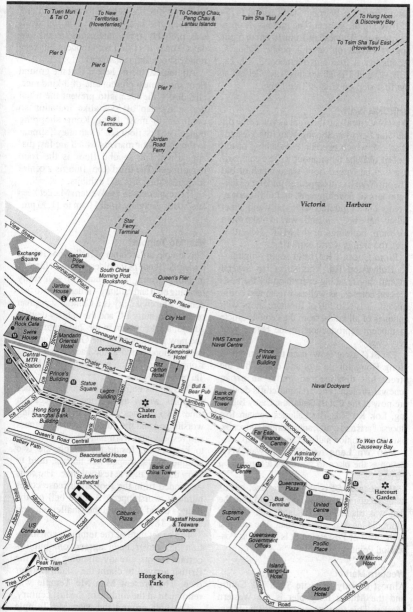

dating from the Warring States period (475-221 BC) to the present. The museum is open daily except Wednesday, from 10 am to 5 pm and is closed on several public holidays. Admission is free. Bus Numbers 3, 12, 23, 23B, 40 and 103 all go this way. Get off at the first stop on Cotton Tree Drive.

SHEUNG WAN

West of Central (on the right as you come off the Star Ferry) is Sheung Wan (the Western District), which once had something of the feel of old Shanghai about it. The comparison is a bit forced now, since much of old Sheung Wan has disappeared under the jackhammers of development, and old stairway streets once cluttered with stalls and street sellers have been cleared away to make room for more buildings or the MTR. Nevertheless, the area is worth exploring.

From Queen's Rd, head south – uphill – to **Hollywood Rd**. This street has several funeral shops, selling everything for the best-dressed corpses, as well as wreath and coffin makers. It is also full of furniture shops with antiques of all kinds, from the genuine article to modern reproductions made before your very eyes.

Cat St (Lascar Row) used to be famous in Hong Kong for its arts and crafts, but the street has disappeared under an urban renewal project. The arts and crafts dealers are now at the **Cat St Galleries**, Casey Building, Lok Ku Rd. The galleries contain five floors of arts and crafts, antiques and souvenirs, plus an exhibition hall and auction room.

Man Wa Lane near Sheung Wan MTR station is the place to go to get a name chop carved.

Possession St is an obscure lane, but its name recalls that somewhere around here the flag was planted for England after Captain Elliot did his deal with Qi Shan. The area just to the west of Possession St is known as Possession Point.

Western Market

Almost directly opposite Shun Tak Centre and the Macau ferry pier is the Western Market. This four-storey red brick building,

built in 1906, has been fully renovated and was reopened in 1991. Nice as it sounds, it was probably more interesting in the old days. Today it's filled with modern but very trendy shops and restaurants.

An unusual theme here is that the ground floor shops must present one-of-a-kind merchandise – the idea is to prevent the usual boring overlap of look-alike imitation so common in most Hong Kong shopping malls. The first floor is a 'cloth alley', similar to those outdoor markets which are fast disappearing. The second floor is the food department. The third (top) floor is a centre for performing arts and exhibits.

The restaurants in the Western Market keep late hours, generally from 11 am to 11.30 pm.

Man Mo Temple

This temple, at the corner of Hollywood Rd and Ladder St, is one of the oldest and most famous in Hong Kong. The Man Mo – literally meaning civil and military – is dedicated to two deities. The civil deity is a Chinese statesman of the 3rd century BC and the military deity is Kuanti, a soldier born in the 2nd century AD and now worshipped as the God of War. (See the Religion section in the Facts about Hong Kong chapter.) Kuanti is also known as Kwan Tai or Kwan Kung.

Outside the entrance are four gilt plaques on poles which are carried at procession time. Two plaques describe the gods being worshipped and the others request quietness and respect, and warn menstruating women to keep away. Inside the temple are two antique chairs, shaped like houses, used to carry the two gods at festival time. The coils suspended from the roof are incense cones burnt by worshippers. A large bell on the right is dated 1846 and the smaller ones on the left, 1897.

The exact date of the temple's construction has never been agreed on, but it's certain it was already standing when the British arrived to claim the island as their own. The present Man Mo Temple was renovated in the middle of the last century.

The area around the Man Mo Temple

Fung Ping Shan Museum

This museum (☎ 2859-2114) houses collections of ceramics and bronzes, plus a lesser number of paintings and carvings. The bronzes are in three groups: Shang and Zhou dynasty ritual vessels; decorative mirrors from the Warring States period to the Tang, Song, Ming and Qing (Ching) dynasties; and Nestorian crosses from the Yuan dynasty (the Nestorians were a Christian sect which arose in Syria, and at some stage found their way to China, probably during the Tang dynasty).

A collection of ceramics includes Han dynasty tomb pottery and recent works from the Chinese pottery centres of Jingdezhen and Shiwan in the People's Republic.

The museum is in Hong Kong University, 94 Bonham Rd. Take bus No 3 from Edinburgh Place (adjacent to city hall), or bus Nos 23 or 103 coming from Causeway Bay, and get off at Bonham Rd, opposite St Paul's College. The museum is open Monday to Saturday, 9.30 am to 6 pm, and is closed on Sunday and several public holidays. Admission is free.

VICTORIA PEAK

If you haven't been to the Peak, then you haven't been to Hong Kong. Every visitor tries to make the pilgrimage, and for good reason – the view is one of the most spectacular in the world. It's also a good way to get Hong Kong into perspective. It's worth repeating the Peak trip at night – the illuminated view is something else. Bring a tripod for your camera for some sensational night photos.

The Peak has been *the* place to live ever since the British moved in. The taipans built their summer houses here to escape the heat and humidity (it's usually about 5°C cooler than down below), although they spent three months swathed in mist for their efforts. It's still the most fashionable place to live in Hong Kong, but the price of real estate is astronomical. Ditto for the prices charged in some of the cafes on the Peak – check the menu to avoid indigestion later.

At the top of the tram line at 400m elevation is the three-level Peak Galleria, a type of scenic shopping mall. The place is designed to withstand winds of more than

Man Mo temple is one of Hong Kong's oldest and most famous landmarks. The temple is dedicated to two deities, one civilian and one military.

was used extensively for location shots in the film *The World of Suzie Wong*. The building to the right of the temple was used as Suzie's hotel; the hotel in the novel (the Luk Kwok, alias the Nam Kok) was in Wan Chai, several km to the east.

The extremely steep flight of steps next to the temple belong to Ladder St. Once it was crammed with stalls and shops selling everything, but the stalls were cleared away. Ladder St is well over 100 years old and probably the best example of old Hong Kong.

HONG KONG UNIVERSITY

West of Sheung Wan takes you through Sai Ying Pun and Shek Tong Tsui districts to Kennedy Town, a residential and harbour district at the end of the tram line. The chief attraction of Shek Tong Tsui is Hong Kong University's Fung Ping Shan Museum.

270 km/h, hopefully more than the theoretical maximum that can be generated by typhoons. High-powered binoculars on the lower balcony cost HK$1 for a few minutes – worth every cent. Inside the tower you can find all sorts of overpriced shops peddling everything from T-shirts to dim sum.

When people refer to the Peak, this generally means the Peak Galleria and surrounding residential area. Victoria Peak is actually the summit – about ½ km to the west and 140m higher. You can walk around Victoria Peak easily without exhausting yourself. Harlech and Lugard Rds encircle it: Harlech Rd is on the south side while Lugard Rd is on the north slope and together they form a loop. For those who would rather run, not walk, this makes a spectacular jogging route.

You can walk from the restaurant to the remains of the old governor's mountain lodge near the summit (550m elevation). The lodge was burnt to the ground by the Japanese during WWII, but the gardens remain and are open to the public. The views are particularly good and there is a toposcope identifying the various geographical features you can see.

For a downhill hike you can walk about two km from the Peak to Pok Fu Lam Reservoir Rd, which leaves Peak Rd near the car park exit. This goes past the reservoir to the main Pok Fu Lam Rd, where you can get the No 7 bus to Aberdeen or back to Central.

Another good walk is down to Hong Kong University. First walk to the west side of Victoria Peak by taking either Lugard or Harlech Rd. After reaching Hatton Rd on the west side of Victoria Peak, follow it down. The descent is very steep but the path is obvious.

If you're going to the Peak, you should go by the Peak tram – at least one way. The tram terminal is in Garden Rd, Central, just opposite the US consulate or 650m from the Star Ferry terminal. The tram trip takes about eight minutes and costs HK$14 one way, or HK$21 round trip (for children under 12, HK$4 one way and HK$7 return). The tram operates every day from 7 am to midnight, and runs about every 10 minutes with three stops along the way. Avoid going on a Sunday, when there tends to be long queues. A free shuttle bus between the Peak tram and the Star Ferry pier runs every 20 minutes from 10 am to 8 pm (every 10 minutes after 11 am on Sunday and public holidays).

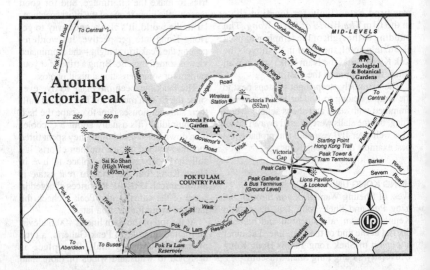

Running for more than a century, the tram has never had an accident – a comforting thought if you start to have doubts about the strength of the cable. In 1885 everyone thought the Honourable Phineas Kyrie and William Kerfoot Hughes were quite crazy when they announced their intentions of building a tramway to the top, but it opened three years later, wiping out the scoffers and the sedan-chair trade in one go. Since then the only occurrences which have stopped the tram have been WWII, and the violent rainstorms of 1966 which washed half the track down the hillside.

Alternatively, bus No 15 from Central bus terminal (the ground floor of Exchange Square) will take you on a 40-minute trip around the perilous-looking road to the top. Bus No 15B runs from Causeway Bay (Yee Wo St) to the Peak. Minibus No 1 leaves from the HMS Tamar building, eastern side of City Hall.

HONG KONG TRAIL

For those who like a challenge, it is possible to walk the entire length of Hong Kong Island. The Hong Kong Trail starts from the Peak Tram terminus, follows Lugard Rd to the west, drops down the hill to Pok Fu Lam Reservoir near Aberdeen before turning east and zigzagging across the ridges. The trail traverses the four country parks of Hong Kong Island – **Pok Fu Lam Country Park** on the south side of Victoria Peak; **Aberdeen Country Park** on the east side of the Peak; **Tai Tam Country Park** on the east side of the island; and **Cape D'Aguilar Country Park** in the south-east near Shek O. It's not likely that you'll want to hike the entire length of the trail in one day, since it's a rugged 50 km. There are no designated camping sites along the trail.

Tai Tam is the largest of the country parks on Hong Kong Island, and arguably the most beautiful. The Hong Kong Trail skirts along the northern side of **Tai Tam Reservoir**, the largest lake on the island.

If you intend to do this hike, it would be wise to purchase the map *Hong Kong Trail* published by the Country Parks Authority

(CPA) or the *Countryside* series map for Hong Kong Island. Both maps are available from the Government Publications Centre in the Government Offices Building, 66 Queensway, Admiralty.

There is a map with no English name but the Chinese name translates as *Hong Kong Hiking Trails*. Despite the lack of an English title, the map is bilingual. It's available from many bookstores in Hong Kong.

WAN CHAI

Heading east from Central brings you to Hong Kong's famed Wan Chai district. In all the tourist-brochure hype, Wan Chai is still inseparable from the name of Suzie Wong – not bad considering that the book dates back to 1957 and the movie to 1960. Although Wan Chai had a reputation during the Vietnam War as a seedy red-light district, these days you can bring grandma and the kids.

Instead of brothels and girlie bars Wan Chai is being taken over by high-rise office blocks spreading out from Central, but a walk down Lockhart Rd will give you a wisp of what it was like when the place was really jumping. You can still find plenty of topless bars, massage parlours and tattooists, but you don't need an appointment any more. Further along Lockhart Rd towards Causeway Bay, the area turns into a tourist shopping district that rivals Tsim Sha Tsui in Kowloon.

Central Plaza

Shaped like a giant ballpoint pen, the 78-storey Central Plaza is Hong Kong's tallest structure. The building was completed in 1992. Some of the tourist literature you'll see will still claim that this is Asia's tallest building, but it was in fact surpassed in 1996 by the 112-storey Petronas Towers in Kuala Lumpur, Malaysia.

It's possible to visit the Sky Lobby on the 46th floor, from where you get a sweeping view of Hong Kong Island and lower Kowloon. Unfortunately, there's no cafe or anything similar and it's forbidden to sit on the floor, so you probably won't want to linger too long.

HONG KONG

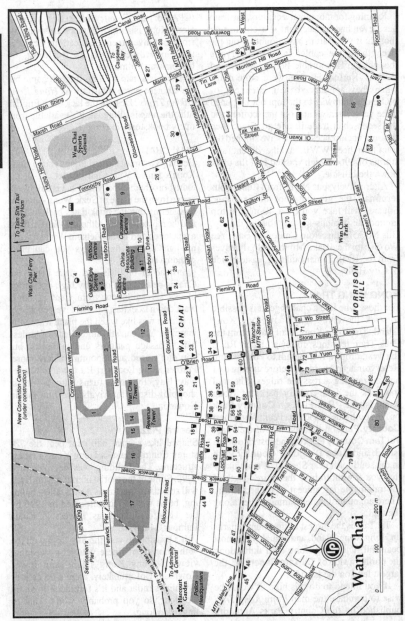

Wan Chai

PLACES TO STAY

1	Grand Hyatt Hotel
2	New World Harbour View Hotel
15	Harbour View International House
20	Luk Kwok Hotel
24	Harbour Hotel
32	Century Hotel
40	Wharney Hotel
48	Wesley Hotel
49	Empire Hotel
50	New Harbour Hotel
65	Charterhouse Hotel
67	South Pacific Hotel

PLACES TO EAT

22	3 6 9 Restaurant
23	Oliver's Super Sandwiches
26	Carriana Chiu Chow Restaurant
29	Late Night Food Stalls/Noodle Shops
34	Kublai's
37	Yin King Lau Restaurant
45	Bacchus Bar & Restaurant
46	Yoshinoya Beef Bowl
53	Saigon Beach Vietnamese Restaurant
54	Brett's Seafood Restaurant
60	Doner Kebab
63	Oliver's Super Sandwiches
66	Ichibantei Ramen Shop
71	Lung Moon Restaurant
72	Sheung Hai Teahouse
73	Johnston Mess
75	Jo Jo Mess Club
76	Thai Delicacy Restaurant
78	Steam & Stew Inn
82	3 6 9 Restaurant
83	Harry Ramsden's

OTHER

3	HK Convention & Exhibition Centre
4	Bus Terminus
5	Columbia Classics Cinema
6	Harbour Road Indoor Games Hall
7	Training Swimming Pool
8	Cine Art
9	Sun Hung Kai Centre

10	Museum of Chinese Historical Relics
11	Visa Office of People's Republic of China
12	Central Plaza
13	Immigration Tower
14	Shui On Centre
16	Hong Kong Arts Centre
17	Academy for the Performing Arts
18	Joe Bananas
19	Big Apple Pub & Disco
21	KPS Video Express
25	Wan Chai Police Station
27	Hong Kong Sauna
28	New Paradise Health Club
30	Sunny Paradise Sauna
31	New Tonnochy Night Club
33	Horse & Groom
35	Horse & Carriage
36	Neptune Disco II
38	Delaney's
39	Flying Pig & Ridgeways
41	Rick's Cafe
42	Carnegie's
43	New Pussycat
44	The Wanch
47	Post & Telecom Office
51	Neptune Disco
52	Royal Arms
55	Country Club 88
56	New Makati
57	Old China Hand
58	Alliance Française
59	BB's
61	Lockhart Road Market
62	British Council
64	New Imperial Cinema
68	Morrison Hill Swimming Pool
69	Imperial Cinema
70	Cathay Cinema
74	Southorn Stadium
77	Cosmos Books
79	Tai Wong Temple
80	Hopewell Centre
81	Post Office
84	Sikh Temple
85	Queen Elizabeth Stadium
86	New China News Agency

High Time

The Central Plaza Building is notable for being Hong Kong's tallest structure (78 storeys). Less well known is that the lights at the top indicate the time – making the building the world's biggest clock.

The system, which is only in effect from 6 pm until midnight, is based on colour codes. The bottom light indicates the hour: red = 6 pm; white = 7 pm; purple = 8 pm; yellow = 9 pm; pink = 10 pm; green = 11 pm. When all four lights are the same colour, it's right on the hour. When the top light is different from the bottom ones, it's 15 minutes past the hour. If the top two and bottom two are different, it's half-past the hour. If the top three match, it's 45 minutes past the hour. ■

The Central Plaza building is at Gloucester and Fleming Rds, one block south-east of the Convention & Exhibition Centre.

Hong Kong Arts Centre

Also in the Wan Chai district is the Arts Centre (☎ 2823-0200) on Harbour Rd. The Pao Sui

Loong Galleries (☎ 2582-0256) are on the 4th and 5th floors of the centre and international and local exhibitions are held year round with an emphasis on contemporary art. Opening hours are 10 am to 8 pm daily. Admission is free. To get there take the MTR to Wan Chai station and follow the signs.

Police Museum
This museum (☎ 2849-7019) at 27 Coombe Rd relates the history of the Royal Hong Kong Police Force, which was formed in 1844. Intriguingly, the museum also houses a Triad Societies Gallery.

Operating hours are Wednesday to Sunday, 9 am to 5 pm, and Tuesday from 2 pm to 5 pm. Closed on Mondays. Admission is free.

You can get there on bus No 15 from Central. Get off at the intersection of Peak Rd and Stubbs Rd.

Hong Kong Convention & Exhibition Centre
This enormous building on the harbour (Seafront Rd) boasts the world's largest 'glass curtain': a window seven storeys high. I sure wouldn't want to be the one to wash it. You can ride the escalator to the 7th floor for a superb harbour view. There are plans to build an artificial island just off the coast here with yet more high-rises.

Museum of Chinese Historical Relics
This musem (☎ 2827-4692) houses cultural treasures from China unearthed in archaeological digs. Two special exhibitions each year focus on artefacts from specific provinces.

The museum is on the 1st floor, Causeway Centre, 28 Harbour Rd, Wan Chai. Enter from the China Resources Building. Operating hours are 10 am to 6 pm weekdays and Saturdays, 1 to 6 pm Sundays and holidays. From Central, take bus Nos 10A, 20, 21 or 104. Admission is free.

CAUSEWAY BAY
Catch the tram that goes through Wan Chai and let it take you to Causeway Bay. The old Causeway Bay – Tung Lo Wan (meaning 'Copper Gong Bay' in Chinese) – has almost disappeared through reclamation. This area was the site of a British settlement in the 1840s and was once a *godown* (warehouse) area for merchants and a harbour for fishermen. One of Hong Kong's top shopping and nightlife areas, this area was reclaimed from swamp and the bottom of the harbour. Many of the big Japanese department stores are here, mostly clustered around the Hotel Excelsior and Park Lane Radisson.

Typhoon Shelter
The waterfront used to be a mass of junks and sampans huddling in the Causeway Bay Typhoon Shelter, but these days it's nearly all *gwailo* ('foreign devil') yachts. This should come as no surprise, since the Royal Hong Kong Yacht Club has its headquarters here.

The land jutting out is Kellett Island – which has been a misnomer ever since a causeway was built to it in 1956, and further land reclamation turned it into a peninsula. The cross-harbour tunnel comes up here.

Noonday Gun
Satirist Noël Coward made the noonday gun famous with his 1924 song *Mad Dogs and Englishmen* about colonists who brave the heat of the noonday sun while the natives stay indoors:

In Hong Kong they strike a gong, and fire off a noonday gun, to reprimand each inmate, who's in late.

The best-known landmark in Causeway Bay, this recoil-mounted three-pounder built in 1901 stands in a small garden in front of the Excelsior Hotel on Gloucester Rd. It's fired daily at noon, but exactly how this tradition started is unknown.

One story goes that Jardine Matheson (one of Hong Kong's largest companies) fired it either to wish bon voyage to a departing managing director or to welcome an incoming ship. The navy got so enraged that their function had been usurped (or because an ordinary person got a salute reserved for officials) that they told Jardine's to fire the gun every day as punishment.

Jardine's executives stand around the gun on New Year's Eve and fire it off at midnight, to the applause of a colonial gathering. But it could well be that the firing on 1 January 1997 turns out to be the last.

Victoria Park

Victoria Park, between Causeway Bay and Victoria Park Rd, is a large playing field built on reclaimed land. Football matches are played on weekends and the Urban Services League puts on music and acrobatic shows. Early in the morning it's a good place to see the slow-motion choreography of t'ai chi practitioners.

Victoria Park becomes a flower market a few days before the Chinese Lunar New Year. Other New Year goods on display include peach and kumquat trees (symbols of good luck). The park is also worth a visit during the evening of the Mid-Autumn (Moon) Festival, when people turn out en masse carrying lanterns. Other events in the park include the Hong Kong Tennis Classic and the Hong Kong International Kart Grand Prix.

Causeway Bay Sports Ground

This is the most popular sports ground in Hong Kong and home of the Chinese Recreation Club. The sports ground is on the south side of Causeway Rd, just south of Victoria Park. Among the public facilities are areas to play football, volleyball, badminton and tennis.

Tin Hau Temple

One more thing worth a look in Causeway Bay is a tiny Tin Hau temple on Tin Hau Temple Rd (at the junction with Dragon Rd), on the east side of Victoria Park (near Tin Hau MTR station). Before reclamation, the temple to the seafarers' goddess stood on the waterfront. An old bell inside dates back to the 15th century. The temple itself is about 200 years old.

Tiger Balm Gardens

Not actually in Causeway Bay but in the adjacent Tai Hang district are the famous (infamous?) Tiger Balm Gardens, officially known as the Aw Boon Haw Gardens. A pale relative of the better-known park of the same name in Singapore, Hong Kong's Tiger Balm Gardens are three hectares of grotesque statuary in appallingly bad taste. These concrete gardens were built at a cost of HK$16 million (and that was in 1935!) by Aw Boon Haw, who made his fortune from the Tiger Balm cure-everything medication. Aw is widely described as having been a philanthropist, though perhaps his millions could have been put to a more philanthropic use.

The gardens are just off Tai Hang Rd near **Jardine's Lookout**. It would be a rather long trudge from Happy Valley. It's best to take bus No 11 which you can catch at Exchange Square, Admiralty MTR station or Yee Wo St (Causeway Bay). The gardens are open daily from 9.30 am to 4 pm and admission is free.

HAPPY VALLEY

There are two neighbourhoods on the north side of Hong Kong Island that have been colonised by gwailos with expense accounts. One is the Mid-Levels and the other is Happy Valley.

However, gwailo-watching is not the main reason for coming here. There are two horse-racing tracks in Hong Kong – one at Shatin in the New Territories and the other at Happy Valley. The racing season is from late September to May. For details, see the Activities section in the Facts for the Visitor chapter.

Besides losing your money at the track, the other main activity in Happy Valley is taking advantage of some fine restaurants which have sprouted in the neighbourhood. See Places to Eat for details.

Getting there is easy: a tram marked Happy Valley runs from Central.

QUARRY BAY

The main attraction of Quarry Bay is the Cityplaza Shopping Centre, one of Hong Kong's finest. Although not normally considered a tourist attraction, it has much to recommend it. For one thing, shopping is

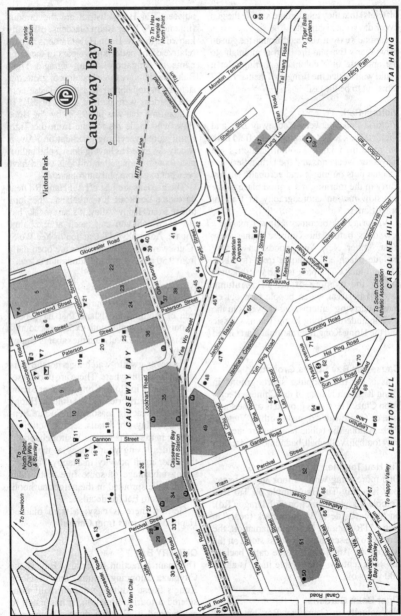

PLACES TO STAY

9	Excelsior Hotel
18	Central Building
19	Payless Inn & Jetvan Traveller's House
20	Wang Fat Hostel
22	Park Lane Hotel
25	Noble Hostel
56	Regal Hong Kong Hotel
57	New Cathay Hotel
64	Phoenix Apartments
68	Causeway Bay Guesthouse & The Barn Pub
72	Leishun Court

PLACES TO EAT

2	King Heung Peking Restaurant
4	Vegi Food Kitchen
7	Martino Coffee Shop
15	Yuet Hing Yuen Vietnamese Restaurant
16	Fairwood Fast Food
21	Kirin Plaza/Haagen Dazs
26	TCBY
27	Snake King Two
32	Sze Chuan Lau Restaurant
33	Tai Woo Seafood Restaurant
37	Café De Coral (in basement)
43	Kung Tak Lam Vegetarian Restaurant
46	McDonald's, Wendy's & KFC
47	Fat Mun Lam Vegetarian Restaurant
53	Red Pepper Restaurant
54	Ichiban
55	Night Market (Dai Pai Dong)
60	Kublai's
63	Queen's Cafe
65	Chinese Delights
66	Genroku Sushi
67	Indonesian Restaurant
69	Fortune Vegetarian & Korea Restaurants
70	Forever Green Taiwanese Restaurant

OTHER

1	Noonday Gun
3	Brewery Tap Pub
5	Daimaru Household Square & Supermarket
6	Vogue Alley
8	Post Office
10	World Trade Centre
11	Shakespeare Pub
12	Royal's Pub
13	Green Peace Boutique
14	Wellcome Supermarket & 7 Eleven
17	President Cinema
23	Wellcome Supermarket
24	Pearl & Jade Cinemas
28	The Jump (pub)
29	Causeway Bay Plaza II
30	New York Cinema
31	HongkongBank
34	Causeway Bay Plaza
35	Sogo Department Store
36	Daimaru Department Store
38	Matsuzakaya Department Store
39	HMV CD Store
40	Windsor House/Windsor Cinema
41	7 Eleven
42	CRC Department Store
44	The Commercial Press (bookstore) & Standard Chartered Bank
45	HongkongBank
48	Watson's & KPS CD Store
49	Mitsukoshi Department Store
50	UA Times Square Cinema
51	Times Square
52	Lee Theatre Plaza
58	Bus Terminal
59	St Paul's Hospital
61	Brecht's Circle Pub
62	Dao Heng Bank
71	King's Arms Pub

much more pleasant once you get out of the tourist zones. Shops have price tags on merchandise and there is no bargaining, yet prices are generally lower than you could bargain for in Tsim Sha Tsui.

At least Cityplaza has clean public toilets – even toilet paper is provided.

Tom Steiger

Even if you don't need to use the toilet, Cityplaza has other amenities: it's the only shopping mall in Hong Kong with an ice skating rink; its Tivoli Terrace cafe is one of the nicest in town; and it has a good dim sum place, the Cityplaza Palace Restaurant.

To get to Cityplaza, take the MTR to Tai Koo station, from where there is an exit which leads directly into the shopping mall.

CHAI WAN

Out at the east end of Hong Kong Island's MTR is Chai Wan, a region of nondescript office buildings, warehouses and workers' flats. Gwailos in this neighbourhood are rare, and if you have a Western face you may even be a local tourist attraction yourself. However, other than seeing what's at the end of the MTR line, there is one small museum out here that might be worth tracking down.

Jardine Matheson

For a long time Jardine Matheson was Hong Kong's largest and most powerful *hong* (big company). It set up shop in Causeway Bay in 1844, after moving its headquarters from Macau. Now Jardine's Hong Kong residence is in the World Trade Centre, next to the Hotel Excelsior.

The area is still full of company names and memorials. Percival St, which crosses Hennessy Rd, is named after Alexander Percival, a relative of Sir James Matheson who joined the firm in 1852 and ended up a partner. Matheson St leads off Percival. Hennessy Rd becomes Yee Wo St, Yee Wo being the name under which Jardine traded in Shanghai. Jardine's Corner is just south of Victoria Peak and Jardine's Lookout is to the south-east, in the hills overlooking the harbour.

Jardine Matheson bought heavily in the first land sale in the colony in 1841. It bought a large tract of land on what was then the waterfront at Causeway Bay and hewed a whole township out of the rock. It built *godowns* (warehouses), offices, workshops, a slipway, homes and messes for employees. All that remains of the East Point establishment is an old gateway with a couple of plaques. You'll find it on a side street from Yee Wo St. It's still owned by Jardine Matheson but is now full of modern warehouses.

Two streets to the right behind Yee Wo St you'll find Jardine's Bazaar and Jardine's Crescent, names which recall the old firm. A Chinese bazaar was once on the first street. A hint of the past is still visible – the area has Chinese provision stores, herb stores and cooked-food stalls. Jardine's Crescent is still one big street market, which nowadays sells mostly clothes. Between Jardine's Bazaar and the crescent is the short Fuk Hing Lane, an interesting shopping alley with leather handbags, silk scarves, Chinese padded jackets and designer jeans.

The handover of Hong Kong to China has heralded Jardine's decline as top business dog in Hong Kong. The company fell into disfavour with the Chinese government shortly after the 1984 Sino-British Joint Declaration was signed. Sensing that a communist government was bad business, Jardine's moved its headquarters to Bermuda. In the 1990s, it further angered China by backing efforts to introduce democracy in Hong Kong. China retaliated by refusing to approve construction of Container Terminal Nine because it was to be built by a consortium headed by Jardine's.

While other hongs such as Swire and Hutchison Whampoa have entered into potentially lucrative joint-venture deals with the Chinese government, Jardine's has found itself on the outer. Nevertheless, the firm's management is unrepentant, and has indicated that the other hongs may yet rue the day they decided to let China's state-run firms into their business. But at least for some harried British executives, Bermuda is looking better all the time. ∎

Law Uk Folk Museum

This is Hong Kong's newest museum, even if it is over 200 years old. The Law Uk Folk Museum (☎ 2896-7006) is a restored Hakka village house. The Hakka (or 'guest people') migrated from the north in the 1200s. The museum was dressed up with a few wax figures of Chinese in traditional Hakka dress. Furniture and farming tools are also on display. It's open from Tuesday through Saturday from 10 am to 1 pm, and 2 to 6 pm. On Sunday and public holidays it opens from 1 to 6 pm. It's closed on Monday and some public holidays. The address is 14 Kut Shing St – take the MTR to Chai Wan station. Admission is free.

SHEK O

Shek O, on the south-east coast, has one of the best beaches on Hong Kong Island. All around Shek O are homes that belong to Hong Kong's wealthy entrepreneurial class; many of the best homes are protected by walls which are cleverly hidden by landscape gardening. Shek O is a prestigious place to live, though the Peak still ranks as number one in terms of snob appeal.

To get to Shek O, take the MTR or tram to Shau Kei Wan and from Shau Kei Wan take bus No 9 to the last stop.

Big Wave Bay, another excellent beach, is two km to the north of Shek O, but there is no public transportation. It makes a nice walk, passing the **Shek O Country Club & Golf Course** along the way.

Shek O is one of the few places in Hong Kong where you can hire a bicycle to explore the coast.

STANLEY

This is the trendy, suburban gwailo place to live. It's on the south-east side of the island just 15 km as the crow flies from Central. Once the village was indeed a village. About 2000 people lived here when the British took over in 1841, making it one of the largest settlements on the island at the time. The British built a prison near the village in 1937 – just in time to be used by the Japanese to intern the expatriates.

Now it's used as a maximum-security prison. Hong Kong's contingent of British troops was housed in Stanley Fort at the southern end of the peninsula, which is off-limits to the public at the time of writing.

There is an OK beach (not as crowded as the one at Repulse Bay) at Stanley Village. It's also possible to rent windsurfers here. The **Stanley Market** dominates the town. It's open all week, but on weekends it's wall-to-wall tourists. The market runs roughly from 10 am to 7 pm, selling clothes, furniture, household goods, hardware, foodstuffs and imitation designer jeans.

Stanley has a **Tin Hau temple** which dates back to 1767. On one of the walls hangs the skin of a tiger killed by Japanese soldiers outside the temple. The temple is on a corner of Stanley Main St, approaching Ma Hang Village.

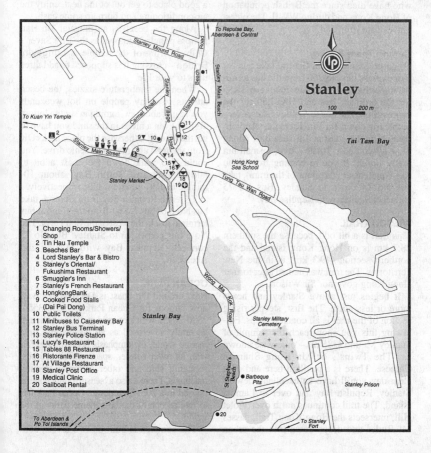

Stanley

0   100   200 m

To Repulse Bay, Aberdeen & Central

To Kuan Yin Temple

Stanley Mound Road

Stanley Beach Road

Stanley Main Beach

Carmel Road

Stanley Village Road

Stanley Main Street

Stanley Market

Tai Tam Bay

Hong Kong Sea School

Tung Tau Wan Road

Stanley Bay

Wong Ma Kok Road

Stanley Military Cemetery

Stanley Prison

St Stephen's Beach

Barbeque Pits

To Aberdeen & Po Toi Islands

To Stanley Fort

1   Changing Rooms/Showers/ Shop
2   Tin Hau Temple
3   Beaches Bar
4   Lord Stanley's Bar & Bistro
5   Stanley's Oriental/ Fukushima Restaurant
6   Smuggler's Inn
7   Stanley's French Restaurant
8   HongkongBank
9   Cooked Food Stalls (Dai Pai Dong)
10 Public Toilets
11 Minibuses to Causeway Bay
12 Stanley Bus Terminal
13 Stanley Police Station
14 Lucy's Restaurant
15 Tables 88 Restaurant
16 Ristorante Firenze
17 At Village Restaurant
18 Stanley Post Office
19 Medical Clinic
20 Sailboat Rental

Further up from the Tin Hau temple is the **Kuanyin (Kwun Yum) Temple** in Ma Hang Village. Kuanyin is a goddess of mercy and the temple contains a six-metre statue of her. The statue is sheltered by a pavilion specially built in 1977 following a claim by a woman and her daughter that they saw the statue move and a bright light shine from its forehead...maybe Stanley isn't such a dull place after all.

From Stanley you can take bus No 73A to **St Stephen's Beach** a bit further down the coast. Both Stanley and St Stephen's beaches have all the usual facilities. The cemetery at St Stephen's Beach is for military personnel who have died since the British occupation of Hong Kong and during WWII. The oldest graves date from 1843.

Getting There & Away

To get to Stanley from Central take bus No 6 or express bus No 260 from the bus terminal under Exchange Square. Fares are HK$5 for the ordinary bus and HK$7.50 for the express bus. The bus to Stanley takes a very scenic trip down Tai Tam Rd to the reservoir, then along the coast at Tai Tam Bay. Along the way you pass **Turtle Cove**, a small but pretty beach. If you're coming from Shau Kei Wan (eastern terminus of the tram), take bus No 14 down to Stanley. Bus No 73 connects Stanley with Repulse Bay.

WILSON TRAIL

This trail is a bit odd, because the southern 28.7 km is on Hong Kong Island and the northern section (49.3 km) is in the New Territories. The trail was named after former Hong Kong governor Sir Wilson.

It begins just above Stanley and heads more or less north. The first, steeply rising section of the trail is all concrete steps. Following this you soon reach the summit of Stanley Mound (385 m) – otherwise known as 'The Twins', or Ma Kong Shan in Chinese. There is a pavilion here and on a clear day you'll have an excellent view of Stanley, Repulse Bay and over to Lamma Island. The trail continues north over Violet Hill, intersects the Hong Kong Trail, passes Mt Butler and drops down into the urban

chaos and terminates at Quarry Bay MTR station. Actually, the 'trail' becomes a road and goes straight through the Eastern Cross-Harbour Tunnel to Lam Tim MTR station in the New Territories. Forget about walking through the tunnel, just take the MTR. For details on the northern section of this trail, see the New Territories chapter.

REPULSE BAY

The prime attraction is the beach and, on weekends and holidays, the **flea market** on Beach Rd. Also, the posh **Repulse Bay Shopping Arcade** at 109 Repulse Bay Rd is a good place to get out of the heat, enjoy the air-conditioning and burn up some cash.

Along the beach is an unusual **Tin Hau temple** popularly known as the Life Saver's Club. In front of the temple is **Longevity Bridge** – crossing it is supposed to add three days to your life.

When the temperature sizzles, the beach attracts so many people on hot weekends you're just about swimming in suntan lotion. To find even a niche in the sand you have to get there early. Otherwise the place looks OK from the road and makes a scenic drive. You could also walk down the coast a bit to **Middle Bay** and **South Bay**, about 10-minute and 30-minute walks, respectively.

To reach Repulse Bay from Central, take bus No 6 or bus No 61 from the Central bus terminal just to the west of the Star Ferry. The No 6 bus carries on to Stanley. Bus No 73 connects Repulse Bay with Stanley and Aberdeen.

OCEAN PARK

Next around the coast is Deep Water Bay, now famous for Ocean Park (☎ 2555-3554; 2580-2495), which opened in 1976. Although generally advertised as an oceanarium or a marine world, the emphasis is on the fun fair with its roller coaster, space wheel, octopus, swinging ship and other astronaut-training machines. There's also a 'sensurround' cinema housed in a 20m-high dome. Ocean Park has to rate as one of the best theme parks in the world.

The complex is built on two levels, connected by a seven-minute cable-car ride, and looks down on Deep Water Bay. At the park entrance are landscaped gardens with a touch-and-feed section where kids can pet llamas, goats, calves and kangaroos. I never saw such cooperative kangaroos in Australia, not even in a zoo, and I wonder how the Chinese managed this. Perhaps the kangaroos were given prefrontal lobotomies.

Chinese arts like kungfu (*gongfu*), opera and so on are often staged in the gardens. There's an exotic bird section too. There are several theatres where penguins, whales, sea lions, monkeys and other animals perform. Bring a pen and paper to write down the various show times – these are displayed on a noticeboard at the entrance, but there is no handout available.

Right at the rear entrance to Ocean Park is the Middle Kingdom, a sort Chinese cultural village representing 13 dynasties. The village has temples, pagodas, traditional street scenes and Middle Kingdom employees sporting the fashions of ancient China.

Entrance fees are HK$150 for adults, or HK$75 for kids age three to 11. Opening hours are 10 am to 6 pm daily. Get there early because there's much to see. It's best to go on weekdays since weekends are very crowded.

Getting There & Away

The cheapest way to get to Ocean Park from Central is to take bus No 70 from the Central bus terminal (under Exchange Square, near Star Ferry) and get off at the first stop after the tunnel. From there it's a 10-minute walk. Slightly more expensive is minibus No 6 from the Central bus terminal, but it does not run on Sundays and holidays. Most expensive is the air-conditioned Ocean Park Citybus which leaves from the ground floor of Exchange Square or from underneath Bond Centre (Admiralty MTR station) every half-hour from 8.45 am. You can also buy your admission tickets for Ocean Park from the Citybus kiosks.

Bus No 73 connects Ocean Park with Aberdeen to the west and Repulse Bay and Stanley to the east.

WATER WORLD

Adjacent to the front entrance of Ocean Park is Water World, a collection of swimming pools, water slides and diving platforms. Water World is open from June to October. During July and August, operating hours are from 9 am to 9 pm. During June, September and October it is open from 10 am to 6 pm. Admission for adults/children costs HK$60/30 during the day, but in the evenings falls to HK$40/20.

From the Central bus terminal in Exchange Square, take bus No 70 and get off at the first stop after the tunnel, then follow the signs to Ocean Park. Alternatively, take minibus No 6 from the Central bus terminal, although it does not run on Sundays and holidays. You can also take the Ocean Park Citybus from the Bond Centre, Admiralty, but it's very important that you get off at the first stop, which is the front entrance of Ocean Park. The second stop is the rear entrance of Ocean Park, which is far away from Water World.

ABERDEEN

For many years Aberdeen Harbour was one of Hong Kong's top tourist attractions because of the large number of people (estimated at over 6000) who lived and worked on junks moored here. Over the years the number of boats has dwindled as more and more of the 'boat people' have moved into high-rises or abandoned fishing as a career. The harbour is still worth a look, but these days the best fishing harbour is on Cheung Chau Island (see the Outlying Islands chapter for details).

Also moored in Aberdeen Harbour are three palace-like floating restaurants, sightseeing attractions in themselves. Sampan tours of the harbour are inexpensive and popular with visitors. The price should run at about HK$40 per person and the boat operators will usually wait until they have four persons before going. A little bit of bargaining is in order. Watertours of Hong Kong does a 20-minute trip around the harbour for HK$40 per person, but it's more fun to charter a sampan: if you're with a

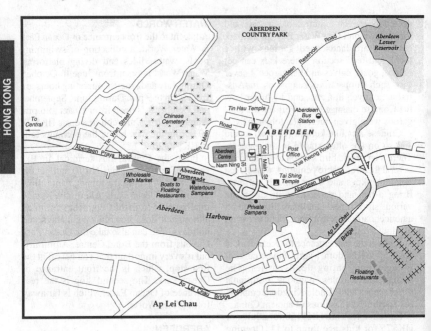

group it should cost about HK$120 for 30 minutes. The price goes down the further away from the bus stop you get. If you are by yourself, just hang out by the harbour as the old women who operate the boats will leap on you and try to get you to join a tour. Some travellers take a free harbour tour by riding the boat out to the Jumbo Floating Restaurant then riding back.

On one side of the harbour is the island of Ap Lei Chau. The island used to be not much more than a junk-building centre, but now it's covered with housing estates. The walk across the bridge to Ap Lei Chau affords good views of the harbour.

At the junction of Aberdeen Main Rd and Aberdeen Reservoir Rd is a **Tin Hau temple** built in 1851.

Getting There & Away

A tunnel linking Aberdeen with the northern side of Hong Kong Island provides rapid access to the town. From the Central bus terminal in Exchange Square, take bus No 7 or No 70 to Aberdeen. No 7 goes via Hong Kong University, and No 70 goes via the tunnel. Bus No 73 from Aberdeen will take you along the southern coast to Ocean Park, Repulse Bay and Stanley.

PLACES TO STAY – BOTTOM END

Hong Kong Island has far less budget accommodation than Kowloon. This probably reflects the higher cost of property in this more desirable part of the city. Nevertheless, a few very good places are well worth considering, especially in Causeway Bay.

Youth Hostels

On top of Mount Davis, not far from Kennedy Town is the *Ma Wui Hall* (☎ 2817-5715), the only dormitory accommodation on Hong Kong Island. The advantage of this place is that it's very clean and quiet and has great views of the harbour. Dorm beds cost

HONG KONG

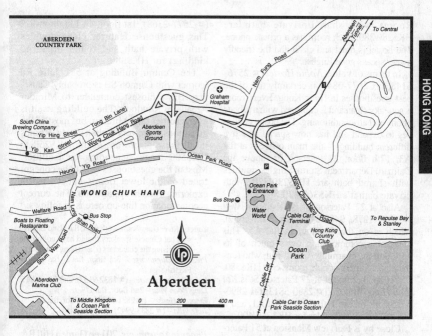

Aberdeen

only HK$50 per night if you belong to the IYHA (HK$70 for nonmembers). Family rooms are available (four beds maximum) for HK$200. There are 112 beds, cooking facilities, secure lockers and air-conditioning in summer. It's open seven days a week from 7 am to 11 pm. Camping is not permitted at this hostel.

The only problem with this place is in getting to it. Its position effectively isolates

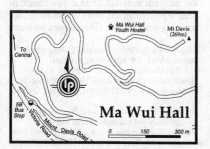

Ma Wui Hall

you from much of Hong Kong's nightlife. Take bus No 5B, 44 or 77 and get off at Felix Villas (the 5B terminus) on Victoria Rd. From the bus stop walk back 100m. Look for the YHA sign and follow Mt Davis Path (don't confuse it with Mt Davis Rd). The walk from the bottom up to the hostel takes from 20 to 30 minutes.

If you come from the airport, take the A2 bus to Central, then change to the 5B or 47 bus. Bus No 5B runs from Paterson St in Causeway Bay to Felix Villas. Bus No 47 starts at the Central bus terminal, under Exchange Square near the Star Ferry. You're least likely to use bus No 77, which runs from the Western District to Aberdeen. If you can't handle climbing the hill with your luggage, you can take a taxi to the hostel.

Guesthouses

The excellent *Wang Fat Hostel* (☎ 2895-1015) is on the 3rd floor, flat A2, 47 Paterson St, just above the Daimaru Department Store.

Rooms with shared/private bath are HK$280/380. Each room has a private phone. The hostel is quiet and clean and the friendly owner speaks good English.

In terms of value, *Noble Hostel* (☎ 2576-6148; fax 2577-0847) is certainly one of the best guesthouses in Hong Kong. Every room is squeaky clean and is equipped with a private phone and air-conditioning. The hostel continues to expand and has now spread into five different buildings – the main office is at flat A3, 17th floor, 27 Paterson St (above the Daimaru Department Store). Singles/doubles with shared bath are HK$230/320. With private bath it's HK$360/420.

Also at 27 Paterson St is *Wonderful Well* (☎ 2577-1278, 9480-6481; fax 2577-6639), which is on the 4th floor in flat A5. This pleasant accommodation owes much of its appeal to the charming Angela Hui, who runs the place. Superb double rooms cost HK$380.

Yet another hostel at 27 Paterson St is *Kai Woo Hung Wan Co* (☎ 2890-5813; fax 2890-5725). It's on the 11th floor in flat A1, and it has good singles/doubles for HK$380/400.

Close by is Fairview Mansion at 51 Paterson St. On the 5th floor in flat A you'll find *Payless Inn* (☎ 2808-1030) which has singles/doubles without bath for HK$250/300, or doubles with attached bath for HK$500. Down on the 4th floor of the same building is *Jetvan Travellers' House* (☎ 2890-8133), which has singles/doubles sans bath for HK$300/400.

A small (just four rooms) but friendly guesthouse is *Hong Mei Trading Company* (☎ 2894-8066) in Towning Mansion, 50-56 Paterson St, 2nd floor, flat C2. All rooms cost HK$350.

The *Causeway Bay Guest House* (☎ 2895-2013; fax 2895-2355), is a good one. It's very clean and all rooms come with private bath, phone, air-conditioning and (rarest of all in Hong Kong) a window. The friendly owner speaks good English, and rates for singles/doubles/triples are HK$350/450/600. It's at flat B, 1st floor, 44 A-D Leighton Rd (enter the building from Leighton Lane just around the corner).

Almost adjacent is *Emerald House* (☎ 2577-2368), 1st floor, 44 Leighton Rd. This guesthouse features clean doubles with private bath and round beds (no kidding) for HK$380.

The Central Building at 531 Jaffe Rd (corner with Cannon St) is probably Causeway Bay's closest contender to Mirador Arcade in Kowloon. The building itself is even grottier than Mirador, but most of the guesthouses are very stylish inside. Rooms in all these places are in the HK$250 to HK$500 range, depending on facilities. Most of the guesthouses tend to be concentrated on the lower floors, but it's worth exploring further upstairs too. The current accommodation line-up here is as follows:

Yangtze River Guesthouse – 6th floor, flat N, no English sign but Chinese speakers should have no trouble recognising the characters (*chángjiāng bìnguǎn*)
President Guesthouse – 3rd floor, flat F, has a huge English sign
Lung Tin Guesthouse – (☎ 2832-9133), 2nd floor, flat F
Lung Poon Villa – 2nd floor, flat L
Empress House – (☎ 2831-9809), 1st floor, flat A
Jade Villa – (☎ 2833-9942), 1st floor, flat L

Phoenix Apartments, 70 Lee Garden Hill Rd, Causeway Bay, has a number of elegant and reasonably priced guesthouses. The catch here is that most are short-time love hotels where rooms are rented by the hour. Still, provided that they've changed the sheets recently, it's not a bad place to stay. Some of these places are quite plush, with brass rail beds and mirrors on the ceiling. One oddity is that the price may be determined by what time you check in. For example, you could be charged HK$500 if you check in early in the day, but only HK$200 if you check in after 9 pm (when the short-timers have presumably gone home). Guesthouses include:

Manor Inn – 1st floor, advertises '24-hour service'
Baguio Motel – (☎ 2890-5868), 1st floor
Hoi Wan Guesthouse – (☎ 2577-7970), 1st floor
Wonderful Garden – (☎ 2577-7306), 2nd floor
Garden House – (☎ 2577-7391), 2nd floor, '24-hour service'
Kai King House – 4th floor, advertises 'avoidance of publicity and reasonable rental rate'
Wah Lai Villa Guesthouse – (☎ 2576-2768), 4th floor, one of the cheaper options at HK$200

Full Art Villa – 4th floor, '24-hour service' (☎ 2881-0632)
The Elegant House – 4th floor
Fu Lai Villa – (☎ 2577-0649), 5th floor

Leishun Court at 116 Leighton Rd, Causeway Bay, is another option. The building houses a number of reasonably priced guesthouses and love hotels, mostly on the lower floors.

Fuji House – (☎ 2577-9406), 1st floor, is good value at HK$290 for a room with private bath.
Lisboa Villa – (☎ 2577-3911), 1st floor
Sam Yu Apartment – (☎ 2881-8887), 2nd floor
VIP House – (☎ 2577-7127), 2nd floor

The *Pak Sha Guesthouses* are a collection of hostelries in a small six-storey building at 14-20 Pak Sha Rd. The building is undergoing major renovation at the time of writing and all but one of the guesthouses is closed for repairs. Presumably it will all look pretty good when the building reopens. Guesthouses to be found here include the *Hei Lok Garden*, *Berlin Guest House* and *Famous Villa*, but after renovation they could change names.

PLACES TO STAY – MIDDLE

Wan Chai is now pretty tame and you're unlikely to accidentally find yourself checking into a brothel as did the lead character in Richard Mason's novel *The World of Suzie Wong*. The hotel mentioned in that novel, the *Nam Kok*, was in fact the *Luk Kwok*, a real hotel at 67 Gloucester Rd, Wan Chai. The original *Luk Kwok* has long since been demolished, but there is now a modern highrise hotel of the same name.

In terms of mid-range hotels (defined here as having double rooms costing between HK$500 and HK$1000), there isn't much available on Hong Kong Island. The following is about all you can expect to find in this decidedly lean category:

New Cathay – (☎ 2577-8211; fax 2576-9365), 17 Tung Lo Wan Rd, Causeway Bay, 223 rooms, singles HK$650, doubles HK$900 to HK$1180, suites HK$1700 to HK$1900. Facilities: coffee shop and Cantonese restaurant. Near Causeway Bay MTR station.
Harbour View International House – (☎ 2802-0111; fax 2802-9063), 4 Harbour Rd, Wan Chai, 320 rooms, doubles HK$950 to HK$1400. Facilities: bar, coffee shop, hotel doctor and American restaurant. Three stars. Near Wan Chai MTR station.
New Harbour – (☎ 2861-1166; fax 2865-6111), 41-49 Hennessy Rd, Wan Chai, 173 rooms, doubles HK$980 to HK$1480, suites HK$1780 to HK$1980. Facilities: business centre, coffee shop and in-house video. Three stars. Near Wan Chai MTR station.
South China – (☎ 2503-1168; fax 2512-8698), 67-75 Java Rd, North Point, 204 rooms, doubles HK$680 to HK$1580. Facilities: conference room, disabled rooms, hotel doctor, in-house video and Cantonese restaurant. Three stars. Near North Point MTR station.
YWCA – Garden View International House – (☎ 2877-3737; fax 2845-6263), 1 MacDonnell Rd, Central, 130 rooms, doubles HK$800 to HK$900, suites HK$1375 to HK$1650. Facilities: business centre, coffee shop, conference room, exercise centre, outdoor swimming pool and of course YWCA classes (recreation & Chinese arts). The closest MTR station is Central, but from there it's a steep walk uphill – the hotel is on the uphill side of the Zoological & Botanic Gardens.

PLACES TO STAY – TOP END

Hotels in this category have price tags that start from HK$1000 and rise rapidly towards the moon. Obviously, all of these places have excellent facilities. Hotels in this category include:

Bishop Lei International House – (☎ 2868-0828; fax 2868-1551), 4 Robinson Rd, Mid-Levels, 227 rooms, singles HK$980, doubles HK$1380, suites HK$1880 to HK$3800. Facilities: business centre, coffee shop, conference room, disabled room, exercise centre, outdoor swimming pool and international restaurant.
Century Hong Kong – (☎ 2598-8888; fax 2598-8866), 238 Jaffe Rd, Wan Chai, 516 rooms, doubles HK$1750 to HK$2250, suites HK$3400 to HK$7000. Facilities: bar, business centre, coffee shop, conference room, disabled rooms, exercise centre, hotel doctor, outdoor swimming pool and Italian restaurant. Three stars. Near Wan Chai MTR station.
Charterhouse – (☎ 2833-5566; fax 2833-5888), 209-219 Wan Chai Rd, Wan Chai, 237 rooms, singles HK$1200 to HK$2200, doubles HK$1550 to HK$1650, suites HK$1900 to HK$2800. Facilities: bar, business centre, coffee shop, conference room, disabled rooms, nightclub, in-house video

and restaurants (Cantonese & Western). Near Causeway Bay or Wan Chai MTR stations.

City Garden – (☎ 2887-2888; fax 2887-1111), 9 City Garden Rd, North Point (Fortress Hill MTR station), 615 rooms, doubles HK$1450 to HK$1950, suites HK$3100. Facilities: bar, business centre, coffee shop, conference room, exercise centre, hotel doctor, in-house video, outdoor swimming pool and restaurants (Cantonese & international). Near Fortress Hill MTR station.

Conrad International – (☎ 2521-3838; fax 2521-3888), Pacific Place, 88 Queensway, Admiralty, 513 rooms, doubles HK$2550 to HK$3500, suites HK$6000 to HK$20,000. Facilities: bar, business centre, coffee shop, conference room, disabled rooms, exercise centre, hotel doctor, in-house video, outdoor swimming pool and restaurants (Cantonese, French & Italian). Near Admiralty MTR station.

Empire – (☎ 2866-9111; fax 2861-3121), 33 Hennessy Rd, Wan Chai, 341 rooms, doubles HK$1150 to HK$1700, suites HK$2200 to HK$5300. Facilities: bar, business centre, coffee shop, conference room, disabled rooms, exercise centre, hotel doctor, in-house video, outdoor swimming pool and restaurants (Cantonese & international). Three stars. Near Wan Chai MTR station.

Excelsior – (☎ 2894-8888; fax 2895-6459), 281 Gloucester Rd, Causeway Bay, 885 rooms, doubles HK$1600 to HK$2700, suites HK$3200 to HK$7500. Facilities: bar, hairdresser-barber shop, business centre, coffee shop, conference room, exercise room, hotel doctor, in-house video, tennis courts and restaurants (Western & Chinese). Four stars. Near Causeway Bay MTR station.

Furama Kempinski – (☎ 2525-5111; fax 2845-9339), 1 Connaught Rd, Central, 517 rooms, doubles HK$1850 to HK$3000, suites HK$3200 to HK$9000. Facilities: bar, hairdresser-barber shop, business centre, coffee shop, conference room, exercise room, hotel doctor, in-house video and restaurants (Cantonese, Western, Japanese & international buffet). Near Central MTR station.

Grand Hyatt – (☎ 2588-1234; fax 2802-0677), 1 Harbour Rd, Wan Chai, 572 rooms, doubles HK$2800 to HK$3850, suites HK$5300 to HK$25,000. Facilities: bar, hairdresser-barber shop, business centre, coffee shop, conference room, disabled rooms, night club, golf putting green, exercise centre, hotel doctor, in-house video, outdoor swimming pool, tennis court and restaurants (Cantonese, Western & Japanese). Near Wan Chai MTR station.

Grand Plaza – (☎ 2886-0011; fax 2886-1738), 2 Kornhill Rd, Quarry Bay, 248 rooms, doubles HK$1250 to HK$2100, suites HK$2350 to HK$3600. Facilities: bar, business centre, coffee

shop, conference room, disabled rooms, golf putting green, exercise centre, hotel doctor, indoor swimming pool, squash courts and international restaurant. Four stars. Near Tai Koo MTR station.

Island Shangri-La – (☎ 2877-3838, 2521-8742), Pacific Place, Supreme Court Rd, Admiralty, 565 rooms, doubles HK$2400 to HK$3450, suites HK$5500 to HK$25,000. Facilities: bar, hairdresser-barber shop, business centre, coffee shop, conference room, exercise centre, hotel doctor, in-house video, outdoor swimming pool and restaurants (Cantonese, Japanese & French). Near Admiralty MTR station.

JW Marriot – (☎ 2810-8366; fax 2845-0737), Pacific Place, 88 Queensway, Admiralty, 604 rooms, doubles HK$2450 to HK$3400, suites HK$5000 to HK$15,000. Facilities: bar, hairdresser-barber shop, business centre, coffee shop, conference room, disabled rooms, exercise centre, hotel doctor, in-house video, outdoor swimming pool and restaurants (American & Cantonese). Near Admiralty MTR station.

Luk Kwok – (☎ 2866-2166; fax 2866-2622), 72 Gloucester Rd, Wan Chai, 198 rooms, singles HK$1350 to HK$1550, twins HK$1500 to HK$1700, suites HK$3200. Facilities: bar, business centre, conference room, disabled rooms, hotel doctor and restaurants (Cantonese & Western). Near Wan Chai MTR station.

Mandarin Oriental – (☎ 2522-0111; fax 2810-6190), 5 Connaught Rd, Central, 538 rooms, doubles HK$2400, suites HK$5000 to HK$22,000. Facilities: bar, hairdresser-barber shop, business centre, coffee shop, conference room, exercise centre, hotel doctor, indoor swimming pool, in-house video and restaurants (Cantonese & Western). Near Central MTR station.

New World Harbour View – (☎ 2802-8888; fax 2802-8833), 1 Harbour Rd, Wan Chai, 862 rooms, singles HK$2030 to HK$3350, doubles HK$2280 to HK$3600, suites HK$4500 to HK$14,000. Facilities: bar, hairdresser-barber shop, business centre, coffee shop, conference room, golf putting green, exercise centre, hotel doctor, in-house video, outdoor swimming pool, tennis court and restaurants (Cantonese, Western & international). Four stars. Near Wan Chai MTR station.

Newton – (☎ 2807-2333; fax 2807-1221), 218 Electric Rd, North Point (Fortress Hill MTR station), 362 rooms, doubles HK$1250 to HK$2200, suites HK$3700. Facilities: bar, business centre, coffee shop, conference room, disabled rooms, exercise centre, hotel doctor, in-house video, outdoor swimming pool and international restaurant. Three stars. Near Fortress Hill MTR station.

Park Lane – (☎ 2890-3355; fax 2576-7853), 310 Gloucester Rd, Causeway Bay, 807 rooms, doubles HK$1980 to HK$3380, suites HK$3380 to HK$16,880. Facilities: bar, barber shop, business centre, coffee shop, conference room, exercise centre, hotel doctor, in-house video and restaurants (American, Cantonese, French & Western). Near Causeway Bay MTR station.

Regal Hongkong – (☎ 2890-6633; fax 2881-0777), 88 Yee Wo St, Causeway Bay, 425 rooms, doubles HK$2200 to HK$2500, suites HK$4000 to HK$18,000. Facilities: bar, business centre, coffee shop, conference room, disabled rooms, exercise centre, hotel doctor, in-house video and restaurants (Cantonese, Chaozhou, international & Western). Five stars. Near Causeway Bay MTR station.

Ritz-Carlton – (☎ 2877-6666; fax 2877-6778), 3 Connaught Rd, Central, 216 rooms, doubles HK$2400 to HK$3800, suites HK$5200 to HK$15,000. Facilities: bar, hairdresser-barber shop, business centre, conference room, disabled rooms, exercise centre, in-house video, outdoor swimming pool and restaurants (Cantonese, Japanese & Western). Near Central MTR station.

South Pacific – (☎ 2572-3838; fax 2893-7773; Email hinfo@southpacifichotel.com.hk; http://www.southpacifichotel.com.hk), 23 Morrison Hill Rd, Wan Chai, 293 rooms, singles HK$1300 to HK$1900, doubles HK$1450 to HK$1900, suites HK$3300 to HK$4800. Facilities: bar, coffee shop, conference room, disabled rooms, hotel doctor, in-house video and restaurants (Chaozhou & international). Four stars. Near Causeway Bay MTR station.

Wesley – (☎ 2866-6688; fax 2866-6633), 22 Hennessy Rd, Wan Chai, 251 rooms, singles HK$1000 to HK$1800, doubles HK$1200 to HK$2200. Facilities: business centre, coffee shop, disabled rooms, hotel doctor and international restaurant. Three stars. Near Admiralty MTR station.

Wharney – (☎ 2861-1000; fax 2865-6023), 57-33 Lockhart Rd, Wan Chai, 332 rooms, doubles HK$1350 to HK$1750, suites HK$2800 to HK$3000. Facilities: bar, business centre, conference room, exercise centre, hotel doctor, indoor swimming pool, in-house video and restaurants (Cantonese & international). Near Wan Chai MTR station.

The Island Shangri-La Hotel has a wonderful atrium on the 41st floor: there are some bubble elevators from one of the 41st to the 56th floor. Gliding up, one can see one of the biggest paintings in the world (around 60m high!) – a wonderful picture of a very mountainous Chinese landscape.

Gunter Quaisser

PLACES TO EAT

Besides what is listed here, please refer to the Nightlife section in this chapter to find pub grub and other assorted late-night munchies.

All the places to eat in Lan Kwai Fong are also listed in the Nightlife section.

Central

Breakfast To save time and money, there are food windows opposite the Star Ferry that open shortly after 6 am. It's standard commuter breakfasts, consisting of bread, rolls and coffee, with no place to sit except on the ferry itself. As you face the ferry entrance, off to the right is a *Maxim's* fast food outlet, also with no seats.

If you'd prefer something better, *Jim's Eurodiner* (☎ 2868-6886), Paks Building, 5-11 Stanley St, does outstanding morning meals between 8 and 10.30 am for around HK$30. From noon until 10 pm it's standard Western fare.

The most central branch of *Delifrance* is in Pacific House, Zetland St. There is another small branch in the arcade at Queensway Plaza (next to Admiralty MTR station).

American *Dan Ryan's Chicago Grill* (☎ 2845-4600), unit 114, The Mall, Pacific Place, 88 Queensway, is an international chain with outstanding food. This place features a big-screen video showing sports shows, and packs out during the American World Series baseball games. Operating hours are from 8.30 am until midnight and it's not terribly cheap.

Chinese Dim sum is relatively cheap, but it's usually served for breakfast/lunch only. In the evening they drag out more pricey Cantonese fare like pigeon, snake and shark-fin soup. You can easily find expensive Cantonese restaurants in big hotels. The following places are in the middle to low price range:

Tai Woo – (☎ 2524-5618), 15-19 Wellington St, Central, dim sum served from 11 am to 4.30 pm
Luk Yu Tea House – (☎ 2523-5464), 26 Stanley St, Central, dim sum served from 7 am to 6 pm; this restaurant has lots of traditional character
Zen Chinese Cuisine – (☎ 2845-4555), LG 1, The Mall, Pacific Place Phase I, 88 Queensway, Admiralty, dim sum served from 11.30 am to 3 pm

European At the top end of the price scale is *Jimmy's Kitchen* (☎ 2526-5293), ground floor, South China Building, 1 Wyndham St. Expect to pay up to HK$700 for steak dinners for two persons, though you can rest assured that it's the best steak in town. It opens at noon and latest orders are at 11 pm.

Fast Food *Domino's Pizza* (☎ 2521-1300), 9 Glenealy St, has no restaurant facilities but delivers to any address within a two km radius. Delivery is supposedly guaranteed within 30 minutes, even in Hong Kong's horrendous traffic.

Famous fast-food chains have the following outlets in Central:

Café de Coral – 10 Stanley St; 18 Jubilee St; 88 Queen's Rd
Fairwood – Ananda Tower, 57-59 Connaught Rd
Hardee's – Grand Building, 15 Des Voeux Rd
KFC – 6 D'Aguilar St
Maxim's – Sun House, 90 Connaught Rd
McDonald's – basement, 37 Queen's Rd; Sanwa Building, 30-32 Connaught Rd; shop 124, Level 1, The Mall, Pacific Place, 88 Queensway
Pizza Hut – B38, basement 1, Edinburgh Tower, The Landmark, 17 Queen's Rd
Spaghetti House – lower ground floor, 10 Stanley St

French Wine, cheese, the best French bread and bouillabaisse can be found at *Papillon* (☎ 2526-5965), 8-13 Wo On Lane. This narrow lane intersects D'Aguilar St (around No 17) and runs parallel to Wellington St.

Cafe Gypsy (☎ 2521-0000), 29 Shelley St, is in the Mid-Levels right below the travelator. Prices are not cheap, but where else in Hong Kong can you buy goat's cheese marinated in olive oil and herbs?

Indian Indian food is plentiful and popular, but like on the Kowloon side some restaurants maintain their idiotic 'members only' rule. One which does *not* is the ever-popular *Ashoka* (☎ 2524-9623), 57 Wyndham St.

Just next door to Ashoka, in the basement at 57 Wyndham St, is *Village Indian Restaurant* (☎ 2525-4117). On request the cook will adjust the level of spiciness to suit your tastes – anything from almost bland to fiery hot is permissible.

Greenlands (☎ 2522-6098), 64 Wellington St, is another superb Indian restaurant offering all-you-can-eat buffets for HK$68.

Club Sri Lanka (☎ 2526-6559) in the basement of 17 Hollywood Rd (at the Wyndham St end) has great Sri Lankan curries. Their fixed-price all-you-can-eat meals are good value – HK$70 for lunch and HK$78 for dinner.

OK, it's not exactly Indian, but the food at *Nepal* (☎ 2869-6212), 14 Staunton St, comes close. It's just off the travelator in the Mid-Levels and its spicy takeaways have satisfied many commuters on their way home.

Italian What better name for an Italian restaurant than *Tony's* (☎ 2544-6346). Prices are good and so is the food. It's at 46 Cochrane St, very close to the travelator.

Japanese Eating Japanese cuisine can quickly lead to bankruptcy, so if you don't have deep pockets, eat elsewhere.

If you can afford it, try the excellent *Ichizen* restaurant (☎ 2523-6031), Seibu Food Court, Level LG1, Pacific Place, 88 Queensway (near Admiralty MTR station). Teppanyaki beef dinners go for HK$200 and an Asahi beer is HK$60.

Kosher The *Shalom Grill* (☎ 2851-6300), 2nd floor, Fortune House, 61 Connaught Rd, serves up kosher and Moroccan cuisine. If you're in the mood for a Jerusalem felafel or a Casablanca couscous, this is the place.

Malaysian If you like Malaysian food, try *Malaya* (☎ 2525-8823), 15B Wellington St, Central.

Portuguese If you acquired a taste for Portuguese cuisine on your last trip to Macau, you can satisfy this urge in Hong Kong at *Casa Lisboa* (☎ 2869-9631). It's at 20 Staunton St, in the Mid-Levels (right off the travelator). Staunton St is two travelator stops downhill from Caine Rd.

Spanish *Rico's* (☎ 2840-0937), 44 Robinson Rd, is located in the high-rent Mid-Levels yet serves reasonably-priced Spanish food. The tapas (from HK$35 up) and gazpacho (HK$38) go down well with a jug of sangria.

Thai *Phukets* (☎ 2868-9672), shop D, 30-32 Robinson Rd, is in the Mid-Levels and has the usually spicy but excellent Thai dishes. The chicken with green curry paste is recommended.

Vegetarian If you crave curry dishes of the Indian and Sri Lankan variety, check out *Club Lanka II* (☎ 2545-1675) in the basement at 11 Lyndhurst Terrace, Central. The all-you-can-eat luncheon buffet costs HK$70 (all drinks free), and dinner is HK$75 (includes one drink).

Other The *Rickshaw Club* (☎ 2525-3977), 22 Robinson Rd (at the intersection with Mosque St), is spread out over three floors. This unconventional restaurant offers up such dishes as Greek salad on pita bread, and the set lunch at HK$50 is a bargain. The 'Rickshaw Pizza' is truly superb.

Self-Catering Perhaps the best health-food store in Hong Kong is *Healthgate* (☎ 2545-2286), Hung Tak Building, 8th floor, 106 Des Voeux Rd, Central.

For imported delicacies, check out *Oliver's Delicatessen*, shop 233-236, Prince's Building, 10 Chater Rd (at Ice House St).

USA & Company sells Americana cuisine, everything from tortilla chips to Cheese Whiz. The Central branch is in Printing House, 18 Ice House St. Another branch is up on Victoria Peak in the Peak Galleria.

The largest stock of imported foods is found at the Seibu Department Store, Level LG1, Pacific Place, 88 Queensway (near Admiralty MTR station). Besides the imported cheeses, breads and chocolates, tucked into one corner is the Pacific Wine Cellar. This is *the* place to get wine, and there are frequent sales on wine by the case. It's open from 11 am until 8 pm.

Of special interest to chocolate addicts is *See's Candies* with two stores in Central: B66 Gloucester Tower, The Landmark, 11 Pedder St; and shop 245, Pacific Place, Phase II, Queensway (near Admiralty MTR station).

The Central Market on Queen's Rd, between Jubilee and Queen Victoria Sts, has three floors of meat, vegetables, fish and poultry. The daily prices are posted on a large noticeboard. If you really want to rub elbows with the proletariat, this is the place to do it.

Ice Cream *Haagen-Dazs*, the American ice-cream outlet with the Scandinavian name, is in World Wide House on Pedder St (between Des Voeux and Connaught Rds). There is another branch at 1 Lan Kwai Fong (see the Lan Kwai Fong map).

Sheung Wan

There are a few good places to try for dim sum here. One of these is *Diamond* (☎ 2544-4708), 267-275 Des Voeux Rd, Sheung Wan. Dim sum is served from 6.30 am to 4 pm, and the restaurant closes at 11 pm. It's an excellent place with moderate prices but very few tourists.

Wan Chai

Aussie & British While the cuisine of Oz and the UK have not taken the world by storm, Hong Kong has a dedicated following of expat fish & chips lovers. *Brett's Seafood* (☎ 2866-6608), 72-86B Lockhart Rd and 71-85B Hennessy Rd, is the Aussie fast-food hang-out that gets fine reviews.

Most of the Brits congregate at *Harry Ramsden's* (☎ 2832-9626), Wu Chung House, Queen's Rd East (near Spring Garden Lane). A very full meal in this place will set you back around HK$80.

Chinese Restaurants doing Chinese cuisine tend to be expensive in Wan Chai. A few dim sum places to try include:

Broadway Seafood – (☎ 2529-9233), Hay Wah Building, 73-85B Hennessy Rd, Wan Chai, dim sum served from 11 am to 5 pm, other food to midnight, reasonable prices

Dynasty – (☎ 2584-6971), 3rd floor, New World Harbour View Hotel, 1 Harbour Rd, good food and impressive harbour views, dim sum hours are brief at 11.30 am to 3 pm

East Ocean Seafood – (☎ 2827-8887), 3rd floor, Harbour Centre, 25 Harbour Rd, dim sum hours 11 am to 6 pm

The *Round Dragon Chinese Restaurant*, Hopewell Centre, 183 Queen's Road East, is rather special. It's on the 60th (!!) floor and the food is very good. Prices are surprisingly moderate.

Fast Food Wan Chai's contribution to fast-food cuisine can be found at the following locations:

Café De Coral – 76 Johnston Rd; 13 Fleming Rd; 151 Lockhart Rd

Domino's Pizza – (☎ 2833-6803), Canal Rd East, no sit-down restaurant but delivers to any address within two km, which in this case means Causeway Bay too

Ka Ka Lok – 10E Canal Rd West

Fairwood Fast Food – 165 Wan Chai Rd

Hardee's – 101 Wan Chai Rd

McDonald's – CC Wu Building, 302-308 Hennessy Rd

Spaghetti House – 1st floor, 68 Hennessy Rd; 1st floor, 290 Hennessy Rd

Filipino *Cinta* (☎ 2529-9752), 41 Hennessy Rd, does excellent Filipino and Indonesian food. There is also a newer branch, *Cinta-J* (☎ 2529-4183), Malaysia Building, 50 Gloucester Rd. Both are fairly expensive – figure HK$300 per person. Both of the Cintas also offer late-night cocktail-lounge entertainment. Operating hours are 11 am to 2 am.

Greek *Bacchus* (☎ 2529-9032), Hop Hing Centre, 8-12 Hennessy Rd, has the best Greek food in Wan Chai.

Indian *Jo Jo Mess Club* (☎ 2527-3776) 86 Johnston Rd, has great Indian food, including vegetarian dishes. There are also numerous vegetarian places nearby.

Ashoka (☎ 2891-8981) is on the ground floor, shop 1, Connaught Commercial Building, 185 Wan Chai Rd, Wan Chai. Prices are

reasonable for big luncheon and dinner buffets. Also reasonably priced is the *Maharaja* (☎ 2891-2302) at 222 Wan Chai Rd.

Italian You can try the pleasantly relaxed *Rigoletto's* (☎ 2527-7144) at 16 Fenwick St in Wan Chai. Pizza and lasagne is tantalising at *La Bella Donna* (☎ 2802-9907), 1st floor, Shui On Centre, 6-8 Harbour Rd, Wan Chai.

Vietnamese A very nice Vietnamese restaurant is *Saigon Beach* (☎ 2529-7823), at 66 Lockhart Rd, Wan Chai.

Causeway Bay

Breakfast *Delifrance* is located in 'The Marketplace', in the basement of Times Square shopping mall (near the MTR station entrance). Of course, you can eat lunch or dinner here too, but the emphasis is on croissants, pastry, soup, sandwiches and coffee.

Burmese Hong Kong has only one place to sample Burmese food, *Rangoon Restaurant* (☎ 2893-0778), ground floor, 265 Gloucester Rd.

Chinese A brilliant Sichuan restaurant is *Sze Chuen Lau* (☎ 2891-9027), 466 Lockhart Rd. Specialities include orange beef, smoked duck and chilli prawns. This place is open from noon until midnight and is always full of expats.

Some places that do dim sum and other Chinese delights include:

Maxim's Chinese – (☎ 2894-9933), 1st & 2nd floors, Hong Kong Mansion, 1 Yee Wo St, dim sum served from 7.30 am to 5 pm

Chiuchow Garden – (☎ 2882-2232), Windsor House, 311 Gloucester Rd (at Great George St and just above HMV music store); there's another branch (☎ 2577-3391) on the 2nd & 3rd floors, Hennessy Centre, 500 Hennessy Rd

Fast Food The line-up of well-known fast-food chains is as follows:

Café De Coral – basement, Matsuzakaya Department Store, 6 Paterson St; 50 Leighton Rd; 483 Jaffe Rd; 19 Jardine's Bazaar

Fairwood Fast Food – 9 Cannon St

Jack in the Box – 53 Paterson St

KFC – 40 Yee Wo St
McDonald's – 46 Yee Wo St, in the McDonald's Building (no kidding); basement 2, Mitsukoshi Department Store, 500 Hennessy Rd
Oliver's Super Sandwiches – World Trade Centre (opposite the Excelsior Hotel)
Pizza Hut – 482 Hennessy Rd, upstairs above the Dahsing Bank. The entrance is on Percival St.
Spaghetti House – 1st floor, 483 Jaffe Rd
Wendy's – 42 Yee Wo St

Indonesian Most popular is the Indonesia Padang Restaurant (☎ 2576-1828), 85 Percival St.

There is also the Indonesian Restaurant (☎ 2577-9981) at 28 Leighton Rd, which does a mean satay.

Japanese Causeway Bay caters to a large number of Japanese tourists and is perhaps the best area in Hong Kong to look for this type of food. Japanese food is never cheap, but you can save a bit by looking in the basements of Japanese department stores. Daimaru Household Square on Kingston St and Gloucester Rd has takeaway Japanese food but no place to sit.

Tomokazu (☎ 2833-6339) is in shop B, Lockhart House, 441 Lockhart Rd. For Japanese food, consider it a bargain. The set lunches for two persons cost HK$200 and the amount of food is more than most people can finish.

Korean Korea Restaurant (☎ 2577-9893), 58 Leighton Rd, is a good place for an authentic Korean barbecue. Other spots for Korean food include Koreana (☎ 2577-5145), Vienna Mansion, 55 Paterson St, and Myong Dong Chong (☎ 2836-3877), 1st floor, 500 Jaffe Rd.

Malaysian Banana Curry Leaf (☎ 2573-8187), 440 Jaffe Rd, is notable for serving up Malaysian cuisine on a banana leaf.

Cafe Malaya (☎ 2577-3277), 1st floor, B4 Dragon Rise, 9-11 Pennington St, has magnificent Malaysian food, including an elaborate vegetarian menu.

Thai The Chili Club (☎ 2527-2872), 88 Lockhart Rd, does outstanding Thai food. There is another branch (☎ 2520-2318) at Hennessy Rd.

Baan Thai (☎ 2831-9155) is on the 4th floor at Causeway Bay Plaza I, 489 Hennessy Rd. The food is stunning.

Vegetarian Vegi Food Kitchen (☎ 2890-6660), ground floor, Highland Mansions, 8 Cleveland St, has a sign warning you not to bring meat or alcohol onto the premises. If you're carrying a meat loaf in your backpack, you'd better check it in at the door.

Fat Mun Lam Vegetarian Kitchen, 41-43 Jardine's Bazaar, is small, reasonably priced and has very good Chinese-style veggie dishes.

Fortune Vegetarian Restaurant (☎ 2881-1697), 50 Leighton Rd, is a relatively upscale venue for Chinese-style veggie food.

Vietnamese Also excellent is the reasonably priced Yin Ping (☎ 2832-9038), 24 Cannon St.

Mixed Asian The top three floors of the Times Square shopping mall is designated the 'Food Forum', and dedicated entirely to restaurants (expensive ones!). From the 9th floor of the shopping mall you can catch the escalator up. There is also a lift, but it's just not the same. There are two or three restaurants on each floor. The 10th floor is where you'll find the Chrysanthemum Seafood Restaurant (☎ 2506-3033) and Elegant Banyan Restaurant (☎ 2506-2866). The 11th floor specialises in mixed Asian dishes, and here you'll find the Golden Elephant Thai Restaurant (☎ 2506-1333), Arirang Korean Restaurant (☎ 2506-3298) and Roy's at the New China Max (☎ 2506-2282). This last one (Roy's) is arguably the most interesting. The motif is 'tropical island'. There is often live music and on Friday and Saturday after 10 pm there is a cover charge of HK$100 unless you've had dinner here, in which case you just pay for the food and brew. Happy hour is fairly brief – from 5 to 7.30 pm.

The top floor of Times Square is home to the Golden Bull Vietnamese Restaurant,

HONG KONG

Nam Garden Chinese Restaurant and *Yunnan Kitchen*.

Ice Cream *Haagen-Dazs* plugs its cones at a small shop in 'The Marketplace', which is the arcade in the basement of the Times Square shopping mall.

Self-Catering Besides the ubiquitous supermarkets, there's a Western specialty food store called *USA & Company* (☎ 2923-7920) in the Times Square shopping mall.

Happy Valley

Perhaps someone will suggest I get my head examined, but one of the biggest bargains in Hong Kong is the vegetarian cafeteria on the 6th floor of the *Adventist Hospital* at 40 Stubbs Rd. Opening hours are short: breakfast 6 to 7.30 am, lunch noon to 1.30 pm and dinner 5 to 6.30 pm.

Stanley

Ristorante Firenze (☎ 2813-9090) is an Italian restaurant near the Stanley post office at 126 Stanley Main St. It's a relative of the famed *Il Mercato Restaurant* in Lan Kwai Fong and the food is equally good.

The Curry Pot (☎ 2899-0811), 6th floor, 90B Stanley Main St, is absolutely the best Indian restaurant in the village.

Pepperoni's (☎ 2813-8605), 64 Stanley Main St, is right in the bustling market area. The pizza here is outstanding.

Also excellent, but definitely upmarket, is *Stanley's Oriental Restaurant* (2813-9988), 90B Stanley Main St. Check out the exquisite colonial decor (will China permit this after 1997?).

Also upper crust is *Stanley's French Restaurant* (☎ 2813-8873), 86 Stanley Main St. Aside from the food, the charming rooftop garden is worth visiting.

Tables 88 (☎ 2813-6262), 88 Stanley Village Rd, is notable not only for its fine Western food but also its location in the old Stanley police station. The interior decoration is a knock-out.

Domino's Pizza (☎ 2813-9239) has established a beachhead at 30A Stanley Main St.

Repulse Bay

While there aren't any restaurants of special interest in Repulse Bay, travellers are often pleased to find two of Hong Kong's best delicatessens. *Oliver's* (☎ 2812-7739) is at 109 Repulse Bay Rd. *USA & Company* (☎ 2812-1958) is in the Dairy Farm Shopping Centre, which is right on the beach at 35 Beach Rd.

Aberdeen

The *Aberdeen Marina Club* on Shum Wan Rd was recently renovated and has a beautiful collection of restaurants doing everything from dim sum to prime rib. Dim sum hours are generally from noon to about 5 pm, but late-night feasting continues until nearly midnight.

Floating Restaurants There are three floating restaurants moored in Aberdeen Harbour, all specialising in seafood. Dinner in such a place will cost about HK$200 and up. My opinion is that the food is average, prices are high – you're paying for the atmosphere.

Top of the line is the *Jumbo Floating Restaurant* (☎ 2553-9111), which also serves relatively cheap dim sum from 7.30 am to 5 pm. The adjacent *Floating Palace Restaurant* (☎ 2554-0513) also does dim sum but is more expensive. Nearby is the *Tai Pak Floating Restaurant* (☎ 2552-5953) which has no dim sum but plenty of seafood. Another alternative is to take an evening *kaido* from Aberdeen to Sok Kwu Wan on Lamma Island (see Outlying Islands chapter) where seafood is somewhat cheaper.

ENTERTAINMENT

Central

Cinema There are only a couple of cinemas in Central geared towards English-language films. One is *Queen's* (☎ 2522-7036), Luk Hoi Tung Building (rear entrance), 31 Queen's Rd.

UA Queensway (☎ 2869-0372) is the plushest cinema in Hong Kong and has the best sound system. It's at Pacific Place One in Admiralty.

Lan Kwai Fong Running off D'Aguilar St is

a narrow L-shaped alley closed to cars. This is Lan Kwai Fong, and along with neighbouring streets and alleys it is Hong Kong's No 1 eating and drinking venue. The street has changed over the years – refugees from Chungking Mansions can no longer afford the pricey food, and many of the bars and discos have moved to Wan Chai. The clientele tends to be upwardly mobile, sporting cellular phones (pagers are no longer chic). Nevertheless, the people you see walking the street are mixed: businessmen in suits hand-in-hand with Filipino bar girls; fashionably dressed Western women in slit gowns and high heels; backpackers in sandals and T-shirts; African traders, Russian sailors and Chinese yuppies (invariably called 'chuppies'). There is no place quite like it in the world; disco music thumps in the background everywhere, the alleys are packed with people and everybody is there to see and be seen. Just how Lan Kwai Fong ever got started is a mystery. Equally uncertain is how it will end – high rents and 1997 keep Lan Kwai Fong proprietors awake at night.

Some night spots in this stratified part of town have a dress code, which basically means no shorts, sandals or T-shirts. Many travellers have run afoul of this rule, particularly during the scorching summer months. If you demand to be comfortable, you'll just have to forego the most chic clubs. Otherwise, carry a fancy set of clothes and change in the nearest rest room or phone booth.

Lan Kwai Fong became world famous (or rather, infamous) on New Years' Eve, 31 December, 1992. The street was so thoroughly mobbed with drunken revellers that 21 people were trampled to death and many others were injured. Since then, the authorities have instituted 'crowd control' – the number of customers permitted inside a business establishment is supposedly limited, sidewalk cafes have theoretically been banned (some continue to resist), the authorities are getting very tough with liquor licences, and so on. Some places were judged unsafe and closed, and business is definitely down compared to what it used to be. Oddly, the bars have retorted by moving even further upmarket – squeezing more dollars out of a smaller crowd.

One of the least expensive and most popular drinking spots is *Club 64* (☎ 2523-2801), 12-14 Wing Wah Lane, D'Aguilar St. This used to be a spot where you could sit outside and drink under the stars, but the bureaucrats have said that this is a no-no. Nevertheless, for the backpacker set this is *the* place to be in Lan Kwai Fong.

As you face the entrance of Club 64, off to your left are some stairs (outside the building, not inside). Follow the stairs up to a terrace to find *Le Jardin* (☎ 2526-2717), 10 Wing Wah Lane. This is an excellent place to drink, relax and socialise, but it's certainly more upscale than Club 64.

Facing Club 64 again, look to your right to find *Bon Appetit* (☎ 2525-3553), 14B Wing Wah Lane, a Vietnamese restaurant serving up cheap but scrumptious meals.

Top Dog (☎ 2801-4377), 7 Lan Kwai Fong, produces every kind of hot dog imaginable. Opening hours are late and the management's policy is to stay open 'until nobody is left in the street'.

As the name implies, late-night hours are kept at *Midnight Express* (☎ 2525-5010), 3 Lan Kwai Fong. This place has a combination menu of Greek, Indian and Italian food, with deliveries available from Monday through Saturday. The kebabs are outstanding and cost around HK$35 to HK$45. Opening hours are 11.30 am to 3 am the next day except on Sundays, when it opens at 6 pm.

While glasnost is already yesterday's buzzword, you can still find it at *Yelt's Inn* (☎ 2524-7796), 17-22 D'Aguilar St. This place boasts Russian vodka, a bubbly party atmosphere and extremely loud music.

If it's fine Lebanese food, beer and rock music you crave, what better place to find it than in *Beirut* (☎ 2804-6611)? It's at 27 D'Aguilar St.

Club Yes (☎ 2877-8233), 19 Lan Kwai Fong, has such loud music that you can enjoy the performance from out on the street. Members of the audience are invited to sing along – think of it as disco karaoke. This place enforces a dress code.

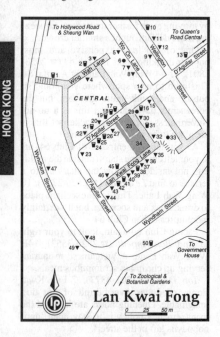

Lan Kwai Fong

0   25   50 m

Post 97 (☎ 2810-9333), 9 Lan Kwai Fong, is a very comfortable eating and drinking spot. During the daytime it's more of a coffee shop, and you can sit for hours to take advantage of the excellent rack of Western magazines and newspapers. It can pack out at night, and the lights are dimmed to discourage reading at that time, but it's a fine place to take a date.

Next door in the same building and under the same management is *Club 1997* (☎ 2810-9333), known for really fine Mediterranean food. This place has recently become 'members only' and the policy is strictly enforced, so short-termers can forget it. There is a small (read 'puny') dance floor.

Another near neighbour is *F-Stop* (☎ 2868-9607), a small place at 14 Lan Kwai Fong. Live music is on offer on Thursday, Friday and Saturday nights.

The *Cactus Club* (☎ 2525-6732), 13 Lan Kwai Fong, does passable Mexican food but people complain about the stingy portions. It seems like more of a pub than a restaurant, with top-grade beer and tequila imported from Mexico. Their Mescal, brewed from the peyote cactus, is pretty strong stuff – tastes like it still has the needles in it.

Supatra's (☎ 2522-5073), 50 D'Aguilar, is Lan Kwai Fong's top venue for Thai food.

Al's Diner (☎ 2521-8714), 39 D'Aguilar St, Lan Kwai Fong, is a Hong Kong institution. The place looks like it was lifted lock, stock, burgers and French fries from a New York diner of the 1930's. Delectables on the menu include eggs with hash-brown potatoes and chilli with toast, but none of this comes cheaply.

A Japanese restaurant popular with Westerners is *Yorohachi* (☎ 2524-1251), 5-6 Lan Kwai Fong. Not far away, *Kiyotaki* (☎ 2877-1772), at 19 D'Aguilar St, does a mean teppanyaki. In the fancy California Entertainment Building is *Hanagushi* (☎ 2521-0868). The latest addition to the scene is a sushi bar and Japanese restaurant with the off-colour name of *Tokio Joe* (☎ 2525-1889) at 16 Lan Kwai Fong.

Schnurrbart (☎ 2523-4700) in the Winner Building on D'Aguilar St, Lan Kwai Fong, is a Bavarian-style pub.

Hardy's Folk Club (☎ 2522-4448), 35 D'Aguilar St, is a rowdy watering hole where some of the patrons occasionally get up on stage to demonstrate their talent (or lack of it).

Oscar's (☎ 2804-6561), 2 Lan Kwai Fong, is a very posh cafe and bar combination. Specialties include pizza, pasta and sandwiches on pita bread. Food is available from noon until 11 pm and the place stays open until 2 am. Bring lots of money.

La Dolce Vita (☎ 2810-8098), 9 Lan Kwai Fong, is another upper-crust establishment, but the Italian brandy and customers in their chic pinstripes make it better than watching TV.

A number of other elegant Italian restaurants have recently spring up in Lan Kwai Fong. The selection includes: *Va Bene* (☎ 2845-5577), 58-62 D'Aguilar St; *Tutto Meglio* (☎ 2869-7833), 33 D'Aguilar St; and *Tutta Luna* (☎ 2869-0099), 12 Lan Kwai Fong.

Dillingers (☎ 2521-2202), at 38-44 D'Aguilar St, is a plush steak house and saloon bar.

Pomeroy's (☎ 2810-1162), 1-9 On Hing Terrace, packs out with suits after 5 pm when the office set gets off work. The bistro-style food includes vegetarian dishes and there is an extensive wine list. Open daily from 11 am to midnight, happy hour from 5 to 7 pm.

Also at 1-9 On Hing Terrace but on the 3rd floor is *Tandoor Indian Restaurant* (☎ 2845-2299), which offers lunch and dinner buffets. The betel-nut desserts are unique in Hong Kong and musicians perform live Indian music (also most unusual in Hong Kong).

The *Milk Bar* (☎ 2521-2202), Commercial Building, 38-44 D'Aguilar St, is one of the newest and fanciest additions to the Lan Kwai Fong scene. The outdoor terrace and long bar make for a good atmosphere to enjoy the pizza, salad and sandwiches. And no, you don't have to drink milk.

The *California Entertainment Building* is at the corner of Lan Kwai Fong and D'Aguilar St. There are numerous places to eat here at varying price levels, but it tends to be upmarket. Note that the building has two blocks with four separate entrances. The entrance adjacent to McDonald's is 34-36 D'Aguilar St, while the one at the corner of Lan Kwai Fong is 30-32. This creates some confusion, so if you don't find a place mentioned in this book be sure to check out the other block.

Koh-I-Noor (☎ 2877-9706), an Indian restaurant on the 1st floor of the California Entertainment Building, has a mixed menu of meat and meatless dishes. In the same building is *Il Mercato* (☎ 2868-3068) which steals the show for Italian food.

The *California* (☎ 2521-1345), ground floor, California Entertainment Building, is perhaps the most expensive bar mentioned in this book. Open from noon to 1 am, it's a restaurant by day, but there's disco dancing and a cover charge Wednesday through Sunday nights from 5 pm onwards. A friend of mine from California was once refused admission because he 'was dressed like a Californian'. Leave the beach clothes behind – it's long trousers, 'proper' footwear and collared shirts only. Skirts are acceptable, but only for women.

The *Jazz Club* (☎ 2845-8477), 2nd floor, California Entertainment Building, has a great atmosphere. Bands playing blues and reggae are a feature here, as well as friendly management and customers. Beer is reasonable at HK$40 a pint, but a cover charge is tacked on for special performances, sometimes up to HK$250 (half-price for members). Many consider this Lan Kwai Fong's best venue for live music.

The American Pie (☎ 2877-9779) is *the* locale for desserts in Hong Kong. Not only pies, but all sorts of killer desserts like cakes, tarts, puddings and everything else containing sinful amounts of sugar. There's also superb coffee and tea. If you're on a diet, don't even go near the place. It's very upmarket and the sweets are priced accordingly. This shop is on the 4th floor of the California Entertainment Building.

Sherman's Bar & Grill (☎ 2801-4946), ground floor, California Entertainment Building, doesn't have any special entertainment but the cosy woody interior seems to keep patrons lingering until midnight.

Cafe des Artistes (☎ 2526-3880), is the newest addition to the California Entertainment Building. The decor is French and so is most of the menu.

Food by Fone (☎ 2868-6969), 25 D'Aguilar St, brings home the bacon if you live in Central or Mid-Levels. There is no service charge – the catch is that they only deliver food from the most expensive restaurants in Lan Kwai Fong. This service operates daily, but hours are short – 6.30 to 10.30 pm.

Other Central Pubs & Grub The *Hard Rock Cafe* (☎ 2377-8168), Swire House, 11 Chater Rd, Central, does its happy hour from 3 to 7 pm.

The *Fringe Club* (☎ 2521-7251), 2 Lower Albert Rd, is an excellent pub known for cheap beer and an avant-garde atmosphere. Live music is provided nightly by various local folk and rock musicians.

The *Mad Dogs Pub* (☎ 2810-1000), 1 D'Aguilar St, is just off trendy Lan Kwai Fong. It's a big Australian-style pub serving pub grub and drinks.

LA Cafe (☎ 2526-6863), ground floor, shop 2, Lippo Centre, 89 Queensway (near Admiralty MTR station) has a large, loyal following of late-night revellers. The mostly-Mexican luncheons are not to be overlooked either – great guacamole, burritos and other Tex-Mex delights, but it isn't cheap.

La Bodega (☎ 2877-5472), at 31C Wyndham St, is an unusual place. It's a comfortable bar with a Mediterranean flavour. Although moderately expensive, drinks are half-price on Friday until somebody goes to the toilet! A Spanish-style band (with Filipino musicians) provides the entertainment.

The *Bull & Bear* (☎ 2525-7436), ground floor, Hutchison House, 10 Harcourt Rd, sounds like a place for Wall St stockbrokers, but is in fact the most British-style pub in Hong Kong. It dishes up everything from lagers to meat pies and gets pretty lively in the evenings. Its open from 8 am to midnight.

Portico (☎ 2523-8893), lower ground floor, Citibank Plaza, 3 Garden Rd, is an early-opener that is even suitable for breakfast. On weekdays it's basically muffins, salad and pizza, but the atmosphere dramatically changes on Saturday night from around 10 pm onwards, when bands give rave performances. This place claims to have the longest bar in Hong Kong. Open Monday to Saturday, 7 am until midnight, closed on Sunday.

Just above Lan Kwai Fong, where Lower Albert Rd joins Wyndham St, you'll find Glenealy St. This is the location of *Afrikan* (☎ 2868-9299), 7 Glenealy St. This cafe and wine bar is open from noon until midnight.

It's hard to explain just what the theme is at *Judgement AD* (☎ 2521-0309). Some of the patrons seem to be dressed in feathers and various costumes that would go down well at a voodoo ritual. You be the judge – it's located in the basement of the Bank of America Tower on Lambeth Walk, Admiralty.

The basement of the Ritz-Carlton Hotel is where you'll find *Cossack's* (☎ 2869-0328), a Russian-motif bar that serves over 30 different kinds of vodka.

Drifters (☎ 2522-6562), 32 Robinson Rd, is in the Mid-Levels and is known for its outstanding pub grub. Pig out on pizza, burgers, fish & chips, steak & kidney pie, meatball submarine or a ploughman's sandwich. Prices are quite reasonable.

If you need to get high when you drink, take the lift up to the 56th floor of the Island Shangri-La Hotel to visit *Cyrano's* (☎ 2820-8591). The bartenders here are highly-skilled – a necessity given some of the fussy corporate types who hang out here. Good views and live jazz are a feature here and given all this, prices are not too outrageous. It's open from 6 pm to around 2 am.

Wan Chai

Cinema For movie fanatics, some cultural organisations show films occasionally. *Alliance Française* (French Institute) (☎ 2527-7825; fax 2865-3478) at 123 Hennessy Rd, is one place to try. Also contact the *Goethe Institut* (German Cultural Centre) (☎ 2802-0088; fax 2802-4363), 14th floor, Hong Kong Arts Centre, 2 Harbour Rd.

Wan Chai has other cinemas specialising in English-language features, as follows:

Cathay – (☎ 2833-5677), 125 Wan Chai Rd
Cine-Art House – (☎ 2827-5015), Sun Hung Kai Centre, 30 Harbour Rd
Columbia Classics – (☎ 2827-8291), Great Eagle Centre, 23 Harbour Rd
Imperial – (☎ 2573-7374), 29 Burrows St
New Imperial – (☎ 2893-9612), 220A Wan Chai Rd
South Pacific – (☎ 2575-7363), South Pacific Hotel, 23 Morrison Hill Rd

Discos, Pubs & Parties The name 'Wan Chai' has for so long been associated with *The World of Suzie Wong*, sailors, bar girls and brothels that the neighbourhood has an unseemly reputation. The image of sleazy bars crowded with drunken sailors and nearly naked Filipino and Thai women dancing on the tables is part of the Wan Chai legend, but this form of entertainment has declined sharply. Just what will happen to the naughty shows and pick-up joints after 1997 remains to be seen, but Wan Chai has already evolved into a very upscale neighbourhood with fashionable pubs, deluxe restaurants,

five-star hotels, raging discos, quiet folk-music lounges and trendy coffee shops.

Needless to add, prices have moved upscale – there are few bargains around. However, Wan Chai can still claim to be the drinking and disco capital of Hong Kong – it has now left Lan Kwai Fong in the dust. Most of the action concentrates around the intersection of Luard and Jaffe Rds.

Joe Bananas (☎ 2529-1811), 23 Luard Rd, Wan Chai, has become a trendy disco nightspot but you may have to queue to get in. Admission is HK$100 for men on Friday and Saturday, though women have to pay too after 1 am. The place stays open until around 5 am.

Neptune Disco (☎ 2528-3808), basement of Hong Kong Computer Centre, 54-62 Lockhart Rd, is pure disco and heavy metal from 4 pm until 5 am. To say this place is popular is an understatement. To survive the night, spend the previous week doing aerobic exercises, and bring your dancing shoes and earplugs.

To accommodate the spillover crowd, there is now *Neptune Disco II* (☎ 2865-2238), 98-108 Jaffe Rd. This place has live bands and a weekend cover charge of HK$80.

Westworld (☎ 2824-0523), also known as *The Manhattan*, is known for its late-night dancing music. This place draws mostly a Cantonese crowd. Admission is HK$80 except on Fridays and Saturdays, when it costs HK$140 (one drink included). It's on the 4th floor of the New World Harbour View Hotel – ask at the front desk where to find the lift.

JJ's (☎ 2588-1234 ext 7323), Grand Hyatt Hotel, 1 Harbour Rd, Wan Chai, is known for its excellent rhythm & blues bands. There is a steep cover charge after 8.30 pm – HK$120, and it rises to HK$170 on Friday and Saturday nights.

When you've had enough of JJ's, try *BB's* (☎ 2529-7702), ground floor, 114-120 Lockhart Rd. This place is home to the South China Brewing Company, Hong Kong's only microbrewery, which produces such ales as Crooked Island, Dragon's Back and Breen's Brew. Happy hour here is from 4 to 8.30 pm.

The Big Apple Pub & Disco (☎ 2529-

3461), basement, 20 Luard Rd, is a thumping disco. There is a weekend cover charge of HK$60 for men, HK$40 for women. From Monday through Friday it operates from noon until 5 am, and on weekends and holidays it's open from 2 pm until 6 am.

Old Hat (☎ 2861-2300), 1st floor, 20 Luard Rd, keeps some of the latest hours around – it's open 24 hours on Friday and Saturday, so you can stay up all evening and have breakfast there. There are daily set lunches Monday through Friday from noon until 2.30 pm, happy hours, crazy hours, satellite TV and take-away burgers, French fries, pizza and satay.

Crossroads (☎ 2527-2347), 42 Lockhart Rd, Wan Chai, is a loud disco that attracts a young crowd. Dancing is from 9 pm to 4 am. There is a cover charge, but one drink is included.

At 54 Jaffe Rd just west of Fenwick Rd is the *Wan Chai Folk Club* (☎ 2861-1621), better known as *The Wanch*. It stands in sharp contrast to the more usual Wan Chai scene of hard rock and disco. This is a very pleasant little folk-music pub with beer and wine at low prices, but it can pack out.

If you've got an ID card or other proof that you are a member of the journalistic community, you should drop into the *Hong Kong Press Club* (☎ 2511-2626), 3rd floor, 175 Lockhart Rd, Wan Chai. Besides the good food and congenial company, it's one of the few places in Hong Kong where you can play pool.

Delaneys (☎ 2804-2880), 2nd floor, One Capital Place, 18 Luard Rd, serves excellent Irish food and has Irish music. This exceedingly popular place features its own house brew, Delaney's Irish Ale (which is made in Hong Kong, not Ireland). Open noon to about 2 am.

The *Flying Pig* (☎ 2865-3730), 2nd floor, 81-85 Lockhart Rd, is a fun place with an aviation memorabilia theme including chic aircraft lounge seats. Fasten your seat belt and enjoy the long happy hour from 11.30 am to 9 pm.

On the 1st floor of the same building is *Ridgeways* (☎ 2866-6608) where you can play billiards if you don't mind queuing. Happy hour is 11 am to 10 pm.

If you want to meet the Filipinos, *New Makati* (☎ 2866-3928), 100 Lockhart Rd, is their lively hang-out. Cover charge is HK$70 for men and HK$40 for women.

The *Old China Hand* (☎ 2527-9174), 104 Lockhart Rd, is usually filled with old China hands reminiscing on how it used to be back in the days of Suzie Wong.

Dali's (☎ 2528-3113), 78 Jaffe Rd, is a lively Spanish bar-cafe scene. Tapas, the Spanish-speciality bar snack, goes down just right with the imported Spanish wines.

Rick's Cafe (☎ 2528-1812), 78-82 Jaffe Rd, is a new adjunct to the legendary original in Tsim Sha Tsui. Happy hour here is long, from 11 am to 10 pm. A HK$100 cover charge is imposed on men only on Friday and Saturday nights after 10 pm.

Hostess Clubs If your idea of a good time is paying HK$2000 to a topless waitress for a simple conversation, you should either a) have your head examined, or b) visit a hostess bar in Wan Chai. Assuming you can find a place to park the Rolls, places to check out include: the *Mandarin Palace* (☎ 2575-6551), 24 Marsh Rd; and the *New Tonnochy* (☎ 2575-4276), 1 Tonnochy Rd.

Causeway Bay

Compared to the raging atmosphere of Lan Kwai Fong and Wan Chai, Causeway Bay is relatively tame at night. However, it's an up and coming neighbourhood – expect big changes here in the near future.

One place to enjoy a rendezvous in subdued settings is the very pleasant *Martino Coffee Shop* (☎ 2576-7666), ground floor, Prospect Mansion, 66 Paterson St. This place can boast some of the fanciest name cards in Hong Kong (or the world) – they're shaped like a coffee pot.

The atmosphere is a little more raucous at the *Hot Shot Cafe* (☎ 2805-7001), 1st floor, 2-4 Kingston St.

For the suits looking to relax after a hard day at Exchange Square, there's the *Wall St*

Bar (☎ 2891-4222) on the 11th floor, Kyoto Plaza, 491-499 Lockhart Rd.

A reliable expat hang-out in this neighbourhood is *The Jump* (☎ 2832-9007), 7th floor, Causeway Bay Plaza II, 463 Lockhart Rd. The food is basically California-style, featuring spicy chicken, nachos, fajitas, burgers and cheesecake. Open from noon to 2 am most days, but to 4 am on Friday and Saturday night when there's a HK$100 cover charge. It's great for a late-night rendezvous, but tends toward the expensive side.

The Barn (☎ 2504-3987), ground floor, 44-48 Leighton Rd, has recently emerged as another late-night contender. It's popularity has given rise to *The Barn II* (☎ 2591-0354), 1st floor, Cigna Tower, 484 Jaffe Rd.

Brecht's Circle (☎ 2576-4785), at 123 Leighton Rd, is relatively quiet and a good place for an intimate conversation with your partner rather than raging revelry. The decor is Swiss-German, but the busts of Hitler and Mao don't go down well with everyone. Happy hour is from 4 to 8 pm.

Dubliner Bar (☎ 2890-8830), Lee Theatre Plaza, basement 2, 99 Percival St, has an obvious Irish theme. Happy hour is from noon to 9 pm.

The *Brewery Tap Pub* (☎ 2576-2075), is in fashionable Vogue Alley, shops A-D, 66-72 Paterson St. It has British decor, right down to the brass rail bar and billiard-felt-green walls. Don't forget to try the steak & kidney pie. It's open from noon to 2 am.

King's Arms (☎ 2895-6557), Sunning Plaza (corner of Sunning Rd and Hysan Ave) is an indoor-outdoor pub that appeals to expats.

Nearby on the 1st floor of Eight Plaza (8 Sunning Rd) is *Piccadilly Tavern* (☎ 2882-8912). It's not quite Piccadilly Circus, but it is one of Causeway Bay's better attempts at a British-style pub.

Royal's Pub (☎ 2832-7879), 21 Cannon St, is a Tudor-style pub. Like most such pubs in Hong Kong, it appeals more to the Chinese than to Westerners.

Cinema Causeway Bay is packed with cinemas, which include the following:

Isis – (☎ 2577-2296), 7 Moreton Terrace

Jade – (☎ 2882-1805), Paterson & Great George Sts
New York – (☎ 2838-7380), 475 Lockhart Rd
Pearl – (☎ 2822-1805), PJ Plaza, Paterson St between Kingston & Great George Sts
President – (☎ 2833-1937), 517 Jaffe Rd
Windsor – (☎ 2882-2621), Windsor House, Gloucester Rd & Great George St

North Point

While this neighbourhood is a bit out of the way, it's just starting to be explored by gwailos. The English-language cinemas in the neighbourhood include:

Park – (☎ 2570-4646), 180 Tunglowan Rd
State – (☎ 2570-6241), 291 King's Rd
Sunbeam – (☎ 2586-0154), 423 King's Rd

Stanley

There are a number of gwailo pubs that get raging in the late afternoon and continue until after midnight. A large share of this market belongs to *The Smugglers' Inn* (☎ 2813-8852), 90-A Main St.

Lord Stanley's Bar & Bistro (☎ 2813-1876), 92A Main St, offers a similar atmosphere of loud music and good food. The same management owns the adjacent *Beaches* (☎ 2813-7313) at No 92B.

Repulse Bay

Close to McDonald's and KFC is *Popeye Bar* (☎ 2592-7960) at 16 Beach Rd.

Deep Water Bay

The drinking and food scene is supplied by a single restaurant right on the beach called *Sampan East* (☎ 2812-1618). It's open from noon until 10.30 pm.

Shek O

The two nightlife hot spots are *Village Too* (☎ 2809-2129) and *Black Sheep* (☎ 2809-2021).

THINGS TO BUY

Central is the big tourist shopping district on Hong Kong Island, closely followed by Wan Chai and Causeway Bay, but prices are slightly lower in the non-touristy neighbourhoods. The most glitzy tourist shopping mall in Hong Kong is at Pacific Place, 88 Queensway, by Admiralty MTR station, which is also the venue of the Seibu Department Store. The World Trade Centre and Times Square in Causeway Bay are those sorts of places with everything under one roof. Many of the locals shop at Cityplaza and the adjacent Kornhill Plaza, two big shopping malls in Quarry Bay at Tai Koo MTR station.

Antiques & Auctions Serious antique buyers should check out the auction houses. Three good ones are:

Christie's Swire
(☎ 2521-5396), room 2806, 28th floor, Alexandra House, 16-20 Chater Rd, Central
Lammert Brothers
(☎ 2522-3208), 9th floor, Malahon Centre, 10 Stanley St, Central;
Sotheby's Hong Kong
(☎ 2524-8121), room 502, Tower Two, Exchange Square, Central.

Wyndham St has a number of antique shops that are worth exploring.

Backpacking & Camping The place to go is Sunmark Camping Equipment (☎ 2893-8511), 141 Wan Chai Rd, Wan Chai.

Clothing In Central the clothing alleys run between Queen's Rd and Des Voeux Rd. One alley sells only buttons and zips. Li Yuen St sells costume jewellery, belts, scarves and shoes. Another street is devoted almost exclusively to handbags and luggage, and yet another to sweaters, tights, underwear and denims. However, high rents are starting to push out these shops and the cloth vendors have already relocated to the Western Market in Sheung Wan.

Johnston Rd in Wan Chai is perhaps the best place on Hong Kong Island to search for cheap clothes. If you like the relatively low-priced stuff at Giordano's, you can find branches at 541 Lockhart Rd and 22 Paterson St, both in Causeway Bay.

One well-known upscale boutique is Vogue Alley, in Causeway Bay, and within a block there are more than 30 others catering to the travellers'-cheque crowd. The area was once known as Food St, but the restaurants are being pushed out by pricey boutiques. Vogue Alley is at the intersection of Paterson and Kingston Sts.

The British chain Marks & Spencer also plugs the latest fashions. Branches can be found at shops 120 & 229, The Mall, Pacific Place Two, Central; ground to 2nd floors, Excelsior Plaza, East Point Rd, Causeway Bay;

Lais, Damned Lais

China has a tendency to politicise everything – a point made perfectly clear to a Hong Kong entrepreneur, Jimmy Lai. He founded Giordano (named for a New York pizza parlour), which has become one of the most successful clothing retailers in the world. The chain has spread quickly across Asia and beyond. It also seems to have inspired a close competitor, Bossini.

Giordano clothing is made in China, and in recent years Giordano outlets have opened in most major Chinese cities. One would think the Chinese authorities would be pleased with Giordano's success. After all, the jobs created in the clothing factories go to Chinese workers and the foreign exchange earned by exporting the clothes goes into China's coffers.

But unfortunately for Giordano shareholders, founder Jimmy Lai also decided to start a Chinese-language newspaper in Hong Kong. Unlike most Hong Kong newspapers, which kowtow to Beijing, Lai's paper made some very unflattering remarks about the Chinese Premier, Li Peng. The Chinese authorities swooped on Giordano outlets in China, shutting down stores and harassing the employees. For the good of the company, Lai stepped down. However, the Chinese police have continued their campaign against the company. Giordano shareholders have tried unsuccessfully to convince the authorities that Lai no longer has a financial interest in the company.

Lai has many supporters in Hong Kong – both expat gwailos and Hong Kong locals flock to Giordano stores, partially as an act of defiance against China. But it's hard to be optimistic about Lai's future, unless he emigrates. His newspaper is certainly a target for China, as are Giordano stores in Hong Kong. And as it is, Lai needs continuous protection against Hong Kong's Triads, who have put a contract out on him. ■

basement, The Landmark, Pedder St, Central; and shops 100 & 217, Cityplaza I, Quarry Bay.

For silk clothing, you might do better in the shopping malls. However, one specialty place to try is *The Silkwear House* (☎ 2877-2373), shop 207, Pedder Building, 12 Pedder St, Central. There is another branch (☎ 2576-9228) at shop 29E, Paterson Plaza, Paterson St, Causeway Bay.

Another special-interest clothing shop is *Festival & Party Accessories* (☎ 2529-2956), shop 73, 1st floor, Admiralty Centre Tower II, 18 Harcourt Rd, Central.

Cameras & Photoprocessing Stanley St in Central is one of the best spots in Hong Kong for buying photographic equipment – there are seven camera shops in a row and competition is keen. Everything carries price tags, though some low-level bargaining might be possible.

Photo Scientific (☎ 2522-1903), 6 Stanley St, is the favourite of Hong Kong's resident professional photographers. You *might* find equipment somewhere else for less, but Photo Scientific has a rock-solid reputation – labelled prices, no bargaining, no arguing and no cheating.

Almost next door is *Color Six* (☎ 2526-0123), 18A Stanley St, which has the best photoprocessing in town. Colour slides can be professionally processed in just three hours. Many special types of film which are on sale here can be bought no where else in Hong Kong, and all film is kept refrigerated.

Stanley St has about six other camera shops in close proximity. Most are reputable, but if you don't find labelled prices on all the equipment then it's a shop to avoid.

Union Photo Supplies (☎ 2526-6281), 13 Queen Victoria St (next to Central Market) is excellent for colour slide processing. However, I have found camera prices to be higher here than on Stanley St so do some comparisons before buying anything expensive.

CDs & Music Tapes HMV (☎ 2869-6936), Swire House, 9 Connaught Rd, Central, has an immense collection of CDs at good prices.

The other branch of HMV (☎ 2504-3669) is in Windsor House, 311 Gloucester Rd (at Great George St), Causeway Bay.

Tower Records (☎ 2506-0811), 7th floor, shop 701, Times Square, Matheson St, Causeway Bay, is also a good place to look for recorded music. Prices are about the same as HMV.

KPS is another place to go for discounted CDs and music tapes. It's also a good place to buy (legal) computer software. In Central, there is a branch in the Prince's Building (☎ 2868-2020), 9-25 Chater Rd. There is another on the 3rd floor of the Capitol Centre (☎ 2890-8709), 5-19 Jardine's Bazaar, Causeway Bay (hidden above a Watson's and a Park 'N' Shop supermarket).

Chinese Emporiums The Chinese Arts & Crafts chain is owned by the PRC and offers a wide selection. The locations are as follows:

Shell House
    (☎ 2522-3621), 24-28 Queen's Rd, Central; ground & 1st floors, lower block
China Resources Building
    (☎ 2827-6667), 26 Harbour Rd, Wan Chai; unit 230,
The Mall
    Pacific Place, (☎ 2523-3933), 88 Queensway, Admiralty
Prince's Building
    ground floor, (☎ 2845-0092), 3 Des Voeux Rd, Central

CRC Department Stores (also known as China Products) give a 15% discount to foreign passport holders. This is not to say that their goods are really cheap, but any discount is better than none. There are three branches:

Chiao Shiang Building
    92 Queen's Rd, Central
Lok Sing Centre
    31 Yee Wo St, Causeway Bay; and 488-500 Hennessy Rd, Causeway Bay.

CRC is my favourite department store. The Central and Hennessy Rd branches sell almost anything you can imagine, from herbal medicine to electric transformers. And the help there is sometimes friendly, unusual for Hong Kong and even more unusual for a mainland China store.

John Harkness

Department Stores These are not very cheap, so if you're looking for bargains look elsewhere. Hong Kong's original Western-style department store is Lane Crawford, which has branches as follows:

Lane Crawford House
    70 Queen's Rd, Central
The Mall
    One Pacific Place, 88 Queensway, Admiralty
Windsor House
    311 Gloucester Rd, Causeway Bay
Times Square
    Matheson and Russel Sts, Causeway Bay.

Hong Kong Chinese department stores in the Central district include Wing On, with branches at 26 and 211 Des Voeux Rd; Sincere at 173 Des Voeux Rd; and Dragon Seed, 39 Queen's Rd.

Japanese department stores are heavily concentrated in Causeway Bay. The main branch of Daimaru is at the corner of Paterson and Great George Sts. Personally I find the smaller Daimaru Household Square (cnr Kingston St & Gloucester Rd) to be more interesting – among other things it houses the Asahiya Japanese Bookstore. Matsuzakaya is at 6 Paterson St and Sogo is at 545 Hennessy Rd. Another good one is Mitsukoshi at 500 Hennessy Rd.

Computers Hong Kong Computer Centre, 298 Hennessy Rd, Wan Chai, has the largest selection of computer stores on Hong Kong Island. Times Square, the multi-level shopping mall in Causeway Bay, has a few computer shops on the 7th floor.

Jewellery King Fook and Tse Sui Luen are two chain stores which guarantee to buy back any jewellery they sell to you at fair market value. Branches are located as follows:

King Fook
    King Fook Building, 30-32 Des Voeux Rd, Central (☎ 2523-5111); shop 216-217, The Mall, Pacific Place, 88 Queensway, Admiralty (☎ 2848-6766);

ground floor, Hong Kong Mansion, 1 Yee Wo St, Causeway Bay (☎ 2576-1032); ground floor, 458-568 Hennessy Rd, Wan Chai (☎ 2892-0068)
Tse Sui Luen
    ground floor, Commercial House, 35 Queen's Rd, Central (☎ 2524-0094); Factory outlet, ground floor, Wah Ming Building, 34 Wong Chuk Hang Rd, Aberdeen (☎ 2878-2618); shop B, ground floor, Kin Tak Fung Commercial Building, 467-473 Hennessy Rd, Causeway Bay (☎ 2838-6737); ground floor, Hong Chiang Building, 141-143 Johnston Rd, Wan Chai (☎ 2893-2981); shops G10 & A7, Tai On Building, 57-87 Shau Kei Wan Rd, Shau Kei Wan (☎ 2569-7760)

Pharmaceuticals Watson's stores are all over the place, but a slightly more economical chain store is Mannings. There is one in shop B, 22-23, 1st basement, The Landmark, 12-16A Des Voeux Rd, Central; and shop J1-J8, Queensway Plaza, Queensway, Admiralty.

Toys Toys R Us is the big American-owned chain at 3rd floor, Windsor House, corner Great George St and Gloucester Rd, Causeway Bay. Another large toy store on Hong Kong Island is Wise Kids (☎ 2868-0133), shop 134, Phase II, Pacific Place, 88 Queensway, Admiralty.

Sporting Goods The largest selection of sporting-goods shops is found in Mongkok on the Kowloon side. Nevertheless, Hong Kong Island chips in with the following:

Bike Boutique (bicycles)
    (☎ 2836-0547), ground floor, 3 Wood Rd, Wan Chai
Bunn's Diving Equipment
    (☎ 2572-1629), ground floor, shop E & G, Kwong Sang Hong Building, 188 Wan Chai Rd, Wan Chai
Mountain Services International
    (mountaineering equipment)
    shop 106, Vicwood Plaza, 199 Des Voeux Rd, Central
Po Kee Fishing Tackle
    (☎ 2543-7541), 6 Hillier St, Central

The New Territories

Not many tourists take the time to visit the New Territories. This is a shame since it has a character very different from the bustling commercial districts of Kowloon and Hong Kong Island. The New Territories is large – larger than Hong Kong Island, Kowloon and Lantau Island combined. You can see much of it in one day, though certainly not all, and any effort you make will be very rewarding.

The New Territories is Hong Kong's bedroom – about one-third of the population lives here, mostly in appropriately named 'new towns'.

Everything north of Boundary St on the Kowloon Peninsula up to the mainland China border is the New Territories. This land was leased from China in 1898 for 99 years. The lease covers all the Outlying Islands except Stonecutters Island, on the west coast of Kowloon, which is now no longer an island because of land reclamation. Excluding the Outlying Islands, the New Territories makes up 70% of Hong Kong's land area.

Since its inception, the New Towns Programme in this area has consumed more than half of the government's budget, with a lot of that money spent on land reclamation, sewage, roads and other infrastructure projects. About 60% of the new housing units have been built by the government.

The population of the New Territories has mushroomed from less than half a million in 1970 to the present 2.5 million, and it's expected to reach 3.5 million by the year 2000.

The biggest impediment to growth in the New Territories has been the lack of good transportation. This changed dramatically in 1982 with the opening of the Mass-Transit Railway (MTR) Tsuen Wan line.

In the same year, the Kowloon-Canton Railway (KCR) underwent a major expansion and the system was electrified and double-tracked.

The Light Rail Transit (LRT) system opened in 1988 and hoverferries now connect Tuen Mun to Central, reducing commuting time to just 30 minutes.

However, fewer people need to commute to Kowloon and Hong Kong Island because many industries are moving into the New Territories.

The most northerly part of the New Territories, within one km of the mainland China border, is a closed area which is fenced and well-marked with signs. With the 1997 hand-over, it marks the boundary of the Special Administration Region (better known as Hong Kong), but it's a boundary nonetheless. Don't be tempted to walk inside the closed area just to have a look, even briefly. You may not see any police around, but the area is staked out with the latest in high-technology motion detectors. There is a heavy fine for entering this forbidden zone.

If you want to avoid public transport, take a tour to the New Territories. The Hong Kong Tourist Association (HKTA) can book you on the 'Land Between' Tour, which takes six hours and costs HK$295.

The Getting Around chapter of this book has a map and a table of bus routes which includes the New Territories – you'd do well to study it before venturing out. The HKTA has a useful information sheet with a map of New Territories bus routes.

Do yourself a favour and pick up the *Countryside* series of maps; four maps are needed to cover the New Territories: *North-West New Territories*, *Central New Territories*, *Sai Kung & Clearwater Bay* and *North-East New Territories*. These are available from the Government Publications Centre. See the Maps section in the Facts for the Visitor chapter.

TSUEN WAN

The easiest place to reach in the New Territories, Tsuen Wan is an industrial and residential area north-west of Kowloon. Simply take the MTR to Tsuen Wan station,

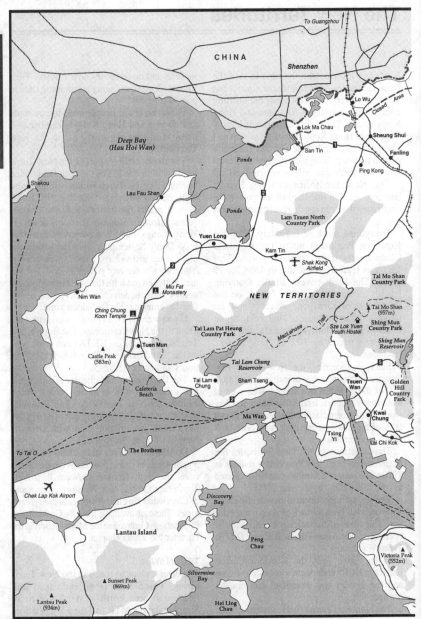

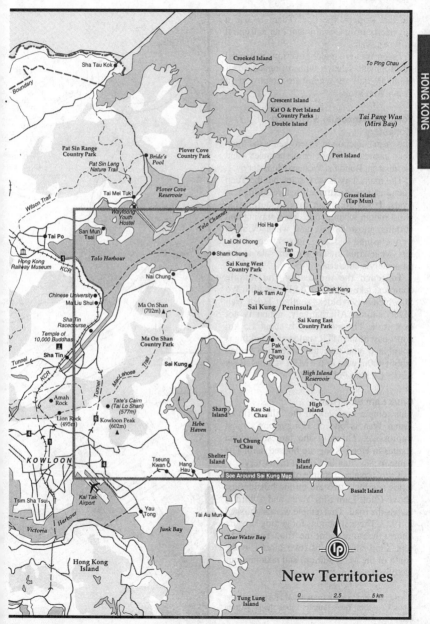

New Territories

the last stop on the line. There is also a hoverferry from Government Pier in Central to Tsuen Wan.

Tsuen Wan is a major government-backed development scheme with a population of 900,000, half of whom are employed in Tsuen Wan itself.

Yuen Yuen Institute & Western Monastery

The main attraction in Tsuen Wan is the Yuen Yuen Institute – a Taoist temple complex – and the adjacent Buddhist Western Monastery.

The monastery is very quiet, but the Yuen Yuen Institute is extremely active during festivals. I was fortunate to visit during the ghost month when people were praying and burning ghost money, and when cymbals were crashing and worshippers were chanting. Vegetarian meals are for sale at the monastery's cafeteria.

To reach the monastery and temple complex, take minibus No 81 from Shiu Wo St, which is two blocks south of Tsuen Wan MTR station. Alternatively, a taxi is not expensive. The monastery is about 1.5 km north-east of the MTR station and walking is possible if you take the pedestrian bridge (about 400m west of the MTR station) to get across Cheung Pei Shan Rd.

Chuk Lam Sim Yuen

This temple complex in the hills north of Tsuen Wan is one of Hong Kong's most impressive. Three of the largest Buddha statues in Hong Kong are housed here. The name means 'bamboo forest monastery'.

There are also a couple of smaller monasteries nearby – two are on the hillside just above Chuk Lam Sim Yuen, and a third is across the road. This temple was established in 1927. The instructions for getting here are almost the same as for the Yuen Yuen Institute. Find Shiu Wo St (two blocks to the south of the MTR station) and take minibus No 85.

It's no problem to walk from the MTR station to the Chuk Lam Sim Yuen Temple. I took the pedestrian bridge west of the station and from there followed the

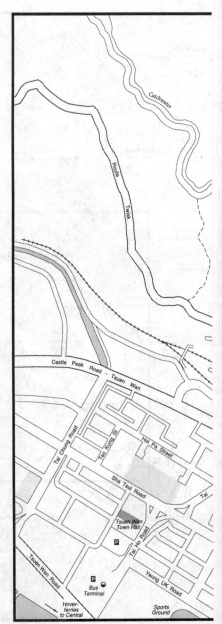

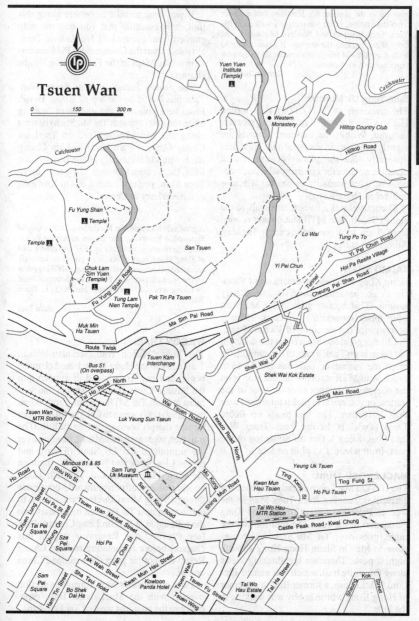

Tsuen Wan

0   150   300 m

Yuen Yuen Institute (Temple)

Western Monastery

Hilltop Country Club

Hilltop Road

Catchwater

Catchwater

Fu Yung Shan Temple

Temple

Lo Wai

Tung Po To

San Tsuen

Yi Pei Chun

Yi Pei Chun Road

Hoi Pa Resite Village

Chuk Lam Sim Yuen (Temple)

Fu Yung Shan Road

Tung Lam Nien Temple

Pak Tin Pa Tsuen

Cheung Pei Shan Road

Tunnel

Muk Min Ha Tsuen

Ma Sim Pai Road

Route Twisk

Tsuen Kam Interchange

Shek Wai Kok Road

Shek Wai Kok Estate

Bus 51 (On overpass)

Tai Ho Road North

Shing Mun Road

Wai Tsuen Road

Texaco Road North

Tsuen Wan MTR Station

Luk Yeung Sun Tsuen

Yeung Uk Tsuen

Ting Kwok St

Ting Fung St

Ho Road

Minibus 81 & 85

Shu Wo St

Sam Tung Uk Museum

Sai Lau Kok Road

Mei Kong

Shing Mun Road

Kwan Mun Hau Tsuen

Ho Pui Tsuen

Chuen Lung Street

Hoi Pa St

Chung On Street

Tsuen Wan Market Street

Tai Pei Square

Sze Pei Square

Hoi Pa

Yan Chau St

Tai Wo Hau MTR Station

Castle Peak Road - Kwai Chung

Sam Pei Square

Ham Tin Street

Sha Tsui Road

Tak Wah Street

Kwun Hau Street

Tsuen Wah

Kowloon Panda Hotel

Tsuen Fu Street

Tsuen Wing

Tai Wo Hau Estate

Tai Ha Street

Cheung Kok Street

Bo Shek Dai Ha

path up to the temple. It's less than half an hour from the station. From the temple I walked to the Yuen Yuen Institute and Western Monastery, and from there back to the station. It's interesting to walk from the old religious monuments to the new (commercial) monuments.

Gunter Quaisser

Sam Tung Uk Museum

The museum (☎ 2411-2001) is a walled Hakka village founded in 1786 and recently restored. Within the museum grounds are eight houses plus an ancestral hall. Travellers generally like the place because it's all genuine, not like the commercial representations of what normally passes for 'Chinese culture' in Hong Kong.

The museum is a five-minute walk to the east of Tsuen Wan MTR station and is open from 9 am to 4 pm daily except Tuesday. Admission is free.

TAI MO SHAN

Hong Kong's highest mountain is not Victoria Peak, as many tourists mistakenly assume. That honour goes to Tai Mo Shan ('big misty mountain'), which at 957m is nearly twice the elevation of Victoria Peak.

Climbing Tai Mo Shan is not too difficult, but there is no Peak Tram to the summit. To reach the mountain, take bus No 51 from Tsuen Wan MTR station – the bus stop is on the overpass that goes over the roof of the station, or you can also pick it up at the Tsuen Wan ferry pier. The bus heads up Route Twisk (Twisk is derived from 'Tsuen Wan Into Shek Kong'). Get off at the top of the pass, from where it's uphill on foot.

MACLEHOSE TRAIL

The 100-km MacLehose Trail spans the New Territories, running from Tuen Mun in the west to Pak Tam Chung (on the Sai Kung Peninsula) in the east. The trail follows the ridge, goes over Tai Mo Shan and passes close to Ma On Shan, Hong Kong's fourth highest peak. There are breathtaking views along the entire trail, which was named after Lord MacLehose, a former British governor of Hong Kong whose hobby was walking in the hills.

If you want to hike anywhere along this trail, it is essential that you buy the map entitled (you guessed it) *MacLehose Trail*, available from the Government Publications Centre (see Maps in the Facts for the Visitor chapter).

The easiest access is from Tsuen Wan. Take bus No 51 to the top of Route Twisk. From here you have the choice of heading off to the east (towards Tai Mo Shan) or west along the MacLehose Trail to Tai Lam Chung Country Park, the Tai Lam Chung Reservoir and eventually all the way to Tuen Mun, the western terminus of the trail. From Tuen Mun, you can catch a bus to Kowloon or a hoverferry to Central.

A good side hike from the MacLehose Trail is around Shing Mun Reservoir, also known as Jubilee Reservoir. The reservoir was built in 1937 and is now part of Shing Mun Country Park. It's a good five-km walk around on paved roads and there are good hiking paths for the more adventurous. You can reach the trail head by taking minibus No 82 from Shiu Wo St in Tsuen Wan.

Julia Tsai

WILSON TRAIL

The 78-km Wilson Trail (see also Wilson Trail entry in the Hong Kong Island chapter) begins on Hong Kong Island, disappears into the Eastern Cross-Harbour Tunnel and surfaces at Lam Tin MTR station. From there, the path zigzags south to Lei Yue Mun before turning sharply north again into the hills. The trail then takes a westward turn, heading over the summit of Tai Lo Shan (577m), and passes Lion Rock and Beacon Hill (both on the north side of Kowloon). The path makes another sharp turn northward, continues through Shing Mun Country Park, returns to civilisation near Tai Po, then disappears into the hills again at Pat Sin Leng Country Park (see Plover Cove Reservoir section this chapter) before terminating at Nam Chung Reservoir, not far from the mainland China border.

Parts of the trail's New Territories section overlap with the MacLehose Trail, especially in the area just west of Tai Lo Shan.

TUEN MUN

This is the main new town in the north-west of the New Territories. And despite the endless rows of high-rise housing estates, there are interesting things to see.

If you have the slightest interest in shopping, be sure to visit **Tuen Mun Town Plaza**, easily reached by taking the LRT line to Town Centre station. This gigantic shopping mall is Hong Kong's largest. It's dominated by the Yaohan Department Store, a Japanese-owned chain.

The **Ching Chung Koon Temple** ('green pine' temple) is just to the north of Tuen Mun. It's a huge Taoist temple which is very active during festivals. From Tuen Mun, you can easily get to the temple by taking the LRT to Ching Chung station.

Castle Peak Monastery is interesting, but it's very hard to reach. From Tuen Mun you would need to take a taxi, but returning may be awkward unless you have the taxi wait for you (a privilege you'll pay for). The Chinese name for the monastery is pronounced 'ching sharn miu'.

Getting There & Away

Bus Nos 53, 60M and 68M start from Tsuen Wan and follow the coast from Tsuen Wan to Tuen Mun. Or you can take bus Nos 60X or 68X, both of which start from Jordan Rd ferry pier in Kowloon. Sit upstairs on the left side for spectacular views. En route you pass another Hong Kong high-tech wonder – the world's largest seawater desalination plant at Lok An Pai.

The fastest and most fun way to get to Tuen Mun is by hoverferry. These depart from the Central Harbour Services pier in Central, Hong Kong Island. The ride takes 30 minutes and lets you off at the LRT terminal.

MIU FAT MONASTERY

Head a few km to the north from Tuen Mun to Lam Tei to find the Miu Fat Buddhist Monastery. The top floor has three large golden statues of Buddha plus thousands of little images clinging to the walls. Often there are monks inside the temple chanting.

Try not to disturb them by taking photographs with a flash.

The temple is easily reached by taking the LRT to Lam Tei. The monastery is on Castle Peak Rd, between Tuen Mun and Yuen Long, a five minute walk along Castle Peak Rd from Lam Tei LRT station.

YUEN LONG

There isn't anything special here, but it's the last stop on the LRT line so you have to get off. It's not a bad place to eat lunch. Other than that, there isn't any reason to linger.

LAU FAU SHAN

If you love oysters, and fancy washing them down with a little local history, Lau Fau Shan is the place to go. Many of the shellfish are turned into oyster sauce, a basic ingredient in Chinese cooking. A large portion of the oysters are also dried and exported. Take the LRT to Yuen Long and get off at Ping Shan station. From the station it's an out-and-back trip to Lau Fau Shan on bus No 655.

Just how long Lau Fau Shan retains its rural charm remains to be seen. Right next to Lau Fau Shan is the oyster-raising community of Tin Shui Wai, the site of a 35-storey housing estate. Enjoy the oysters while you still can.

The **Ping Shan Heritage Trail** is also good for a day's outing. Again, take the LRT to Ping Shan Station (Nos 610, 614 or 615). At Ping Shan station, backtrack about 30m and turn right up Ping Ha Rd. The trail is signposted (not prominently) after about 10 minutes' walk, opposite a bus stop. Guide pamphlets are available free at various points along the way.

MAI PO MARSH

If you're a birdwatcher, the 300-hectare Mai Po Marsh in the north-west part of the New Territories is one of the best places in Hong Kong to see your feathered friends (besides on the dinner plate at the Temple St night market). The majority of the birds are migratory, which means the marsh is at its best in spring and autumn. Winter is also not too bad, but the birds

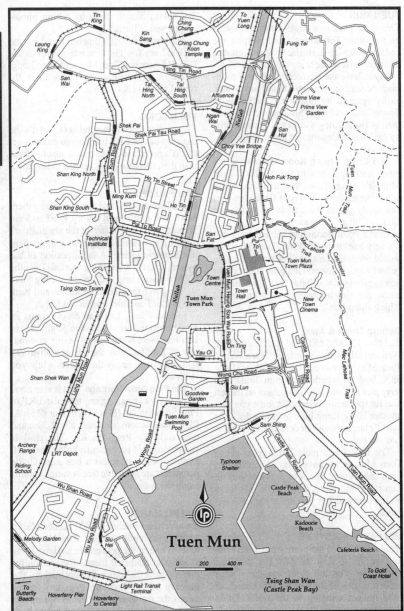

Tin King

Kin Sang

Leung King

Ching Chung

To Yuen Long

Fung Tei

Ching Chung Koon Temple

Tsing Tin Road

San Wai

Tai Hing North

Tai Hing South

Affluence

Prime View

Prime View Garden

Ngan Wai

Shek Pai

San Hui

Shek Pai Tau Road

Choy Yee Bridge

Hoh Fuk Tong

Ming Kum Road

Shan King North

Ho Tin Street

Ho Tin

Tuen Mun Trail

Ming Kum

Shan King South

Pui To Road

San Fat

Pui To

MacLehose Trail

Technical Institute

Town Centre

Tuen Mun Heung Sze Wui Road

Tuen Mun Town Plaza

Tsing Shan Tsuen

Tuen Mun Town Park

Tuen Mun Town Hall

New Town Cinema

Nullah

Castle Peak Road

MacLehose Trail

Yau Oi

On Ting

Shan Shek Wan

Wong Chu Road

Siu Lun

Leung Mun Road

Goodview Garden

Sam Shing

Ho Wong Road

Tuen Mun Swimming Pool

Castle Peak Road

Archery Range

LRT Depot

Typhoon Shelter

Castle Peak Beach

Riding School

Wu Shan Road

Kadoorie Beach

Melody Garden

Wu King Road

Siu Hei

Tuen Mun

0   200   400 m

Cafeteria Beach

To Gold Coast Hotel

To Butterfly Beach

Hoverferry Pier

Light Rail Transit Terminal

Hoverferry to Central

Tsing Shan Wan (Castle Peak Bay)

are scarcest during summer. Over 250 species have been identified.

The good news is that this is a protected area. The bad news is that you must have an authorised guide to be allowed in. This means you must go with a group and pay HK$50 per person (transport *not* included) and you can only go when there are sufficient numbers to make the tour economically feasible. Individual tours may be possible for a much higher fee, so enquire if interested. The place to contact for bookings is the World Wide Fund for Nature (☎ 2526-4473), 1 Tramway Path, Central (adjacent to the Peak Tram entrance). This is also a good place to pick up the *Birds of Hong Kong* guide and other useful publications.

Visitors are advised to bring binoculars, cameras, walking shoes or boots, and not to wear bright clothing.

KAM TIN

The small town of Kam Tin contains two walled villages, Kat Hing Wai and Shui Tau. Most tourists go to Kat Hing Wai. Shui Tau is larger and less touristy, but don't expect to find ancient China here. The area around the villages is a bit messy, having a rather uncharming collection of scrap yards and dumps.

Most other walled villages in Hong Kong have vanished under the jackhammers, though there is a good one at Ping Kong (see below). The walled villages are one of the last reminders that Hong Kongers were once faced with marauding pirates, bandits and soldiers. Of course, 1997 may change all that.

Kam Tin is the home of the Tang clan who have lived here for centuries. They were high-ranking public servants in the imperial court of China in the 19th century.

To reach Kam Tin take bus No 64K, which runs from Yuen Long to Tai Po and passes Kam Tin along the way. Another option is bus No 77K between Yuen Long and Sheung Shui. Bus No 54 also goes from Yuen Long to Kam Tin. You can reach Kam Tin from Tsuen Wan by taking bus No 51 over scenic Route Twisk. Whatever bus you take, sit on the top deck to enjoy the view and witness the massive desecration of the New Territories.

Kat Hing Wai

This tiny 500-year-old village was walled some time during the Ming dynasty (1368 - 1644). Just off the main road, it's really one small street with a maze of dark alleys leading off it. The high street is packed with souvenir sellers. Just to remind you that this is indeed Hong Kong, you are expected to give a 'donation' of HK$5 when you enter the village. Put the money in the coin slot by the entrance.

You can take photographs of the Hakka women in their traditional black dress. Most of them are anxious to model as long as you pay. Agree on a price beforehand – between HK$5 and HK$10 is usually sufficient.

Shui Tau

This 17th-century village is famous for its carved roofs, which are ship-prow shaped and decorated with sculpted fish and dragons. Tiny traditional houses huddle inside Shui Tau's walls.

The ancestral hall in the middle of the village is used as a school in the mornings, but was originally built for the clan to worship its forebears. Their ancestors' names are listed on the altar in the inner hall and on the long boards down the side. The sculpted fish on the roof of the entrance hall represent husband and wife and are there for good luck. Soldiers painted on the doors guard the entrance. To reach Shui Tau get off the bus on the outskirts of Kam Tin and walk down the road leading north.

The **Tin Hau temple** on the outskirts of the town was built in 1722. Its enormous bell weighs 106 kg.

SHEK KONG AIRFIELD

No, this isn't an insider's tip on how to avoid the crowds at Kai Tak airport. This small airfield has been used for military training, but it's also the venue for aerial sports and helicopter flights. Information about parachuting can be found in the Activities section in the Facts for the Visitor chapter. To rent a helicopter, see the Getting Around chapter.

SHEUNG SHUI

This is where you can get on the Kowloon-Canton Railway (KCR). From Yuen Long or Kam Tin, take bus No 77K. Buy a ticket and take the train just one station south to Fanling. A stored-value ticket or tourist ticket from the MTR can be used on the KCR.

PING KONG

This is another walled village, but it gets few tourists. It's far more authentic than Kam Tin and you can take a walk into the farming area behind the village compound.

Getting here is a little tricky. There's a minibus in Sheung Shui but it's hard to find. The easiest way is to take a taxi from Sheung Shui to Ping Kong (about HK$30). Finding the minibus for the trip back into town is no problem.

FANLING

The main attraction in this town is the Fung Ying Sin Koon Temple, a Taoist temple for the dead. The ashes of the departed are deposited here in what might be described as miniature tombs with a photograph on each one. It's an interesting place to look around, but be respectful of worshippers.

Easy to find, the temple is across from Fanling KCR station.

TAI PO

Another of the residential and industrial new towns, Tai Po is home to many of Hong Kong's high-tech industries (including the offices of the *South China Morning Post* newspaper). There isn't much special about the town, but one worthwhile activity is to hire a bicycle and ride to Plover Cove Reservoir on the east side of Tolo Harbour, or to the Chinese University on the west side of the harbour (in Ma Liu Shui). Allow half a day for either trip. There is an inland route to the university, but the coastal route has the best views.

Bicycle rentals are easy to find around Tai Po Market KCR station. Definitely do this trip on a weekday – on weekends and holidays thousands of people descend on the place with the same idea. At these times, bikes are scarce, the rates are higher and the road is crowded with cyclists.

Hong Kong Railway Museum

The Railway Museum (☎ 2653-3339), an old railway station built in 1913 and recently restored, is also at Tai Po. It features trains dating back to 1911 and exhibits detailing the history of local railway development.

Reach the museum from Tai Po Market KCR station by following the railway tracks to the north-west for about 10 minutes. The museum is on On Fu Rd and there are a few signs pointing the way. The museum is open daily (except Tuesdays) from 9 am to 4 pm. Admission is free.

Man Mo Temple

Like the Man Mo Temple in Sheung Wan, Hong Kong Island, this place is dedicated to two Taoist deities representing the pen and the sword. The temple is on Fu Shin St, about 200m from the Railway Museum.

SAN MUN TSAI

San Mun Tsai is a small village by the sea that gets few visitors. It's a charming place though, a floating mix of homes belonging to fishing families. Note the power cables and phone lines strung precariously between rafts.

Figuring out how to get here by bus can be confusing, so the best bet is to take a taxi (about HK$30) from Tai Po Market KCR station. You can then return to Tai Po by minibus.

PLOVER COVE RESERVOIR

If you're trying to see the New Territories in one day, you won't have time for this place. Plover Cove Reservoir is good hiking and cycling country, and if you make the effort to come here you'll probably want to spend a full day.

The reservoir was completed in 1968. Before that Hong Kong often faced critical

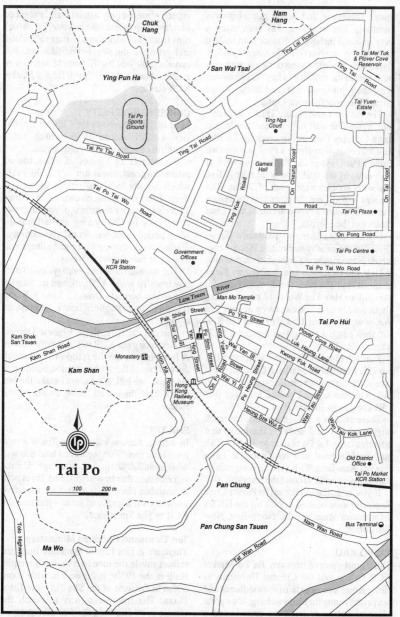

Tai Po

water shortages and water rationing was common. The reservoir was built using a very unusual technique. Rather than build a dam across a river (Hong Kong has few rivers that amount to anything), a dam was built across the mouth of a bay. The seawater was then pumped out and fresh water pumped in, mostly from China.

The Pat Sin Leng Nature Trail is an excellent walk. The trail begins near the Pat Sin Leng Country Park visitor centre at Tai Mei Tuk and ends near Bride's Pool and the two Bride's Pool Waterfalls. Public transport is at both ends of the trail. The walk is only five km with an elevation gain of 300m. The scenery is good, but the place gets packed on weekends unless a typhoon comes along and clears out the tourists.

If you want to do more strenuous walking, detour to the nearby summit of Wong Leng, which is more than 600m high, then continue to Hok Tau Reservoir and the Country Parks centre at Hok Tau Wai. The distance from Tai Mei Tuk to Hok Tau Wai is 12 km and takes about four hours. You can camp at Hok Tau Wai or walk another 1.5 km to Shau Tau Kok Rd, then catch a bus to Fanling and a KCR train to Kowloon.

To reach Plover Cove Reservoir, catch bus No 75K from Tai Po Market KCR station and take it all the way to the last stop at Tai Mei Tuk. On Sunday and public holidays Bus 75R goes on to Bride's Pool.

There is also a village bus (a blue truck with a canopy and seats on the back) that operates from Tai Po market to Tai Mei Tuk and Bride's Pool and terminates at Leng Pui/Wu Kau Tang. This service is especially useful if you walk around the reservoir.

If you're going to hike in the Plover Cove Reservoir area be sure to pick up the HKTA information sheet on the North-East New Territories.

TAI PO KAU

This forest reserve between Tai Po Market KCR station and the Chinese University is Hong Kong's most extensive woodlands and is a prime venue for birdwatching. It's a great place to get away from the crowds and a

superb place to enjoy a quiet walk, except on Sunday. To get there take bus No 72A, which runs from Tai Po Industrial Estate to Tai Wai, and get off at the stop before Sha Tin. You can also take bus No 72 from Mong Kok or a taxi (about HK$20) from Tai Po Market KCR station.

CHINESE UNIVERSITY

Ma Liu Shu is home to the Chinese University, established in 1963, which has a beautiful campus and is worth a visit.

Its Institute of Chinese Studies has an interesting **art museum** (π 2609-7416) which houses local collections as well as those from museums elsewhere in China. There's an enormous exhibit of paintings and calligraphy by Guangdong artists from the Ming period to modern times; a collection of 2000-year-old bronze seals; and a large collection of jade flower carvings.

The museum is open weekdays and Saturday from 10 am to 4.30 pm, and on Sunday and public holidays from 12.30 to 4.30 pm (closed on some public holidays). Admission is free.

You can easily reach the Chinese University by taking the KCR to University station. A free bus outside the station runs through the campus to the administration building at the top of the hill. It's easiest to take the bus uphill and then walk back down to the station.

SHA TIN

In a long, narrow valley, Sha Tin is a new town built mostly on reclaimed land that was a big mudflat just a few years ago. Unlike some of the other new towns, Sha Tin is both a desirable place to live and an attractive town to visit. It's easy to get to – just take the KCR to Sha Tin station.

Ten Thousand Buddhas Monastery

There are in fact 12,800 miniature Buddhist statues inside the monastery's main temple. Built in the 1950s, it sits on a hillside about 500m to the west of the Sha Tin New Town Plaza. The traditional way to reach the temple is by climbing the 400-odd steps on

PAUL STEEL

RICHARD I'ANSON

RICHARD I'ANSON

Top Left: Aberdeen Harbour, Hong Kong Island.
Top Right: Life with a harbour view in Aberdeen.
   Bottom: Boats are a way of life for many Hong Kongers, providing
           transport, entertainment, a livelihood and even a home.

GLENN BEANLAND

ROBERT STOREY

ROBERT STOREY

Top: Jumbo Restaurant, Aberdeen, Hong Kong Island.
Bottom Left: The statue of Tin Hau, Repulse Bay, protects all seafarers.
Bottom Right: Good fungshui. A carefully constructed apartment block at Repulse Bay, Hong Kong Island, allows dragons to follow meridian lines to the sea.

the hillside. However, a recent renovation has added an escalator (covered by a transparent red plastic roof) and a sort of lift-cum-funicular railway. The trail starts from Sha Tin KCR station – just ask anyone to point the way. The temple complex is open from 8 am to 6.30 pm.

From the main monastery area, walk up some more steps to find a smaller temple housing the body of a monk who died in 1965 at the age of 87. He was the founder of the monastery. His body was encased in gold leaf and is now on display behind a glass case. It is considered polite to put a donation in the box next to the display case to help pay for the temple's upkeep.

Che Kung Temple

This is a small, active Taois temple between Sha Tin and Tai Wai KCR stations. It's dedicated to Che Kung, a Sung dynasty general. The temple is interesting, but not as imposing as some of the larger Taoist temples (Wong Tai Sin in Kowloon, for example). However, it is very popular with the Chinese, especially on holidays.

As you enter the temple grounds, be prepared to be mugged by little old ladies who excitedly stuff red pieces of paper with Chinese characters into your hands and then demand money for them. With the help of a Chinese friend, I was able to discern that the papers are a type of blessing. The old women will insist that 'the more money you give, the more blessing you will receive'. Unfortunately, they prove to be insatiable, as the more you give, the more they want.

From Tai Wai KCR station, you can walk to the temple. Bus No 80K from Sha Tin KCR station also stops near the temple, or you can catch a cab.

Sha Tin Racecourse

Sha Tin is the site of Hong Kong's second racecourse, opened in 1980 after seven years in the making at a cost of HK$500 million. It was financed by the introduction of night racing at Hong Kong Island's Happy Valley racecourse (see under Spectator Sports in the Facts for the Visitor chapter).

In the centre of the race track is the interesting eight-hectare **Penfold Park**, open to the public most days except on race days, Monday and the day following public holidays. It can pack out on weekends, an indication of just how desperate Hong Kongers are to find a bit of greenery among the concrete housing estates.

You can get to the racecourse by taking the KCR to either Fo Tan or Racecourse stations.

Amah Rock

It may just be a rock, but like many Chinese landmarks, a local legend has grown up around it. The story goes that for many years a fisherman's wife, with her baby on her back, stood on this spot to watch for her husband's return. The husband never came back and the gods took pity on her and transported her to heaven with a lightning bolt – which left a rock in her place. In Hong Kong, an amah is a servant or maid.

As you take the train south towards Kowloon, Amah Rock is on the left side up on the hillside after Tai Wai KCR station but before the train enters the tunnel.

Sha Tin New Town Plaza

Hong Kongers flock to Sha Tin on weekends to shop at one of the biggest shopping malls in Hong Kong. In addition to the plethora of shops and restaurants, there is a huge indoor swimming pool.

Adjacent to the New Town Plaza is a well-stocked **public library**, the largest in the New Territories. Many cultural events are held in the adjoining **Sha Tin Town Hall**. There is also **Bun's Amusement Centre** which offers bowling and roller skating. The whole complex is adjacent to Sha Tin KCR station.

CLEARWATER BAY

Clearwater Bay is in the south-eastern corner of the New Territories and, as the name implies, has brilliant, clear water. It certainly stands in sharp contrast to nearby Junk Bay which, as the name implies, has plenty of junk floating in it.

Clearwater Bay is beautiful and has one of

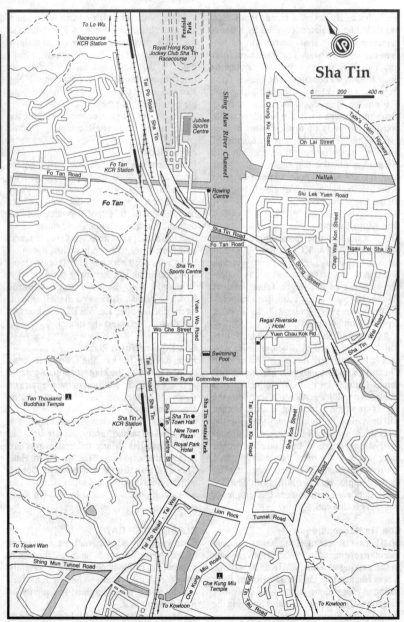

Sha Tin

To Lo Wu
Racecourse KCR Station
Penfold Park
Royal Hong Kong Jockey Club Sha Tin Racecourse
Jubilee Sports Centre
Shing Mun River Channel
Rowing Centre

Tai Chung Kiu Road
Tate's Cairn Highway
On Lai Street
Nullah

Fo Tan Road
Fo Tan KCR Station
Fo Tan
Fo Tan Road

Sha Tin Road
Fo Tan Road
Siu Lek Yuen Road
Chap Wai Kon Street
Ngau Pei Sha St

Sha Tin Sports Centre
Nam Shing Street

Wo Che Street
Yuen Wo Road
Regal Riverside Hotel
Yuen Chau Kok Rd
Sha Tin Wai Road

Swimming Pool
Tai Chung Kiu Road

Sha Tin Rural Committee Road

Ten Thousand Buddhas Temple
Tai Po Road - Sha Tin
Sha Tin KCR Station
Sha Tin Centre St
Sha Tin Town Hall
New Town Plaza
Royal Park Hotel
Sha Tin Central Park
Sha Kok Street
Sha Tin Tau Road

Lion Rock Tunnel Road
Sha Tin Road

To Tsuen Wan
Tai Po Road - Tai Wai
Shing Mun Tunnel Road
Che Kung Miu Road
Che Kung Miu Temple
To Kowloon
Sha Tin Tau Road
To Kowloon

the best beaches in Hong Kong. It's very popular, in fact too popular, as on a hot summer weekend it's standing room only.

Naturally the beauty of Clearwater Bay has not gone unnoticed by Hong Kong's well-to-do class. Mediterranean-style villas have sprouted on the hillsides and there is now a **Clearwater Bay Country Club**, complete with golf course, squash and tennis courts, jacuzzi, badminton, etc.

Neighbouring Junk Bay is to be the site of another huge upmarket project built on reclaimed land. A tunnel is to be built across Junk Bay and the MTR will probably be extended to here. All this will no doubt make Clearwater Bay much more accessible, but it could also lead to the sort of development which will make it not worth visiting at all.

There are some country parks on the peninsula and some decent trails, but serious hikers should look elsewhere in the New Territories.

One of Hong Kong's leading movie companies is Shaw Brothers which has its huge **Movietown studios** on Clearwater Bay Rd. To visit the studios, phone the company's public relations office (☎ 2719-1551)

Clearwater Bay is easily accessible. Take the MTR to Choi Hung station and look for exit B. From there, walk to the nearby bus terminus and catch bus No 91, which goes all the way to Clearwater Bay.

SAI KUNG PENINSULA

This is the garden spot of the New Territories. The Sai Kung Peninsula is the last chunk of Hong Kong besides the Outlying Islands that remains a haven for hikers, campers, swimmers and boating enthusiasts. Pirates and tigers are no longer a problem, but hikers sometimes encounter unpleasant dogs – carry a stick, dog repellent, grenades or whatever you deem necessary.

Some of Hong Kong's best swimming beaches are on the Sai Kung Peninsula, where windsurfing equipment can also be hired. Just keep in mind that sharks make a yearly pilgrimage to this area and attacks are not uncommon.

The peninsula is largely undeveloped, and

those who care about Hong Kong's environment would like to keep it that way. Meanwhile, real estate agents are eyeing those virginal beaches and licking their chops.

Sai Kung Town

A number of slick tourist brochures refer to Sai Kung as a 'picturesque fishing village', but I'd have to disagree. In the not-too-distant past, Sai Kung was mainly a marketplace for farmers and fishing families to tout their wares, but the town's charms have eroded considerably with the arrival of motor vehicles and mass tourism. The ugly concrete structures are not particularly charming, and the 'quaint' Old Town is positively a dump. However, the town is still blessedly free of high-rise buildings.

Sai Kung's saving grace is its waterfront, which is lined with seafood restaurants overlooking the fishing fleet moored in the small harbour. Hong Kongers are absolutely loony about seafood, and during all holidays the restaurants overflow with visitors. There are also a few restaurants and pubs which cater to the *gwailo* ('foreign devil') minority. See Places to Eat in this chapter.

The great attraction of Sai Kung town is its boat services to the nearby islands, most of which are protected from development by Kiu Tsui Country Park. You'll have plenty of offers from little old ladies wanting you to rent a sampan, but most people prefer the *kaidos* (small boats) which are considerably cheaper. One clearly marked kaido makes frequent trips over to the **Jockey Club golf course** on Kau Sai Chau, the largest island in the area. Kiu Tsui Chau (Sharp Island) is a popular tourist destination; there's a sandy beach with a campsite at Hap Mun Bay near the southern end of the island. Less visited but also worthwhile is Yim Tin Tsai, a tiny isle connected to Kau Sai Chau by a sand spit during low tide (the island also boasts an old Catholic church). The tiny sandy islets of Pak Sha Chau (White Sand Island) and Cham Tau Chau (Reclining Head Island) can be visited by sampan. On summer weekends kaidos go as far as High Island (in fact, no longer an island), stopping at the beaches of

HONG KONG

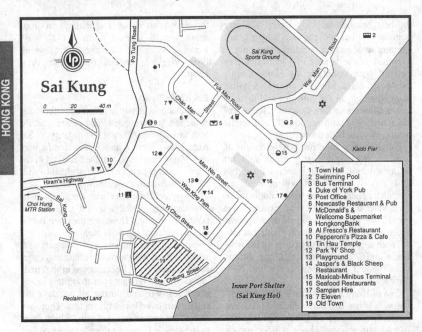

Sai Kung

0   20   40 m

To
Choi Hung
MTR Station

Hiram's Highway

Po Tung Road

Chan Man Street

Fuk Man Road

Wai Man Road

Sai Kung Sports Ground

Man Nin Street

Wan King Path

Yi Chun Street

See Cheung Street

Sai Kung Rd

Reclaimed Land

Inner Port Shelter
(Sai Kung Hoi)

Kaido Pier

1 Town Hall
2 Swimming Pool
3 Bus Terminal
4 Duke of York Pub
5 Post Office
6 Newcastle Restaurant & Pub
7 McDonald's &
   Wellcome Supermarket
8 HongkongBank
9 Al Fresco's Restaurant
10 Pepperoni's Pizza & Cafe
11 Tin Hau Temple
12 Park 'N' Shop
13 Playground
14 Jasper's & Black Sheep
   Restaurant
15 Maxicab-Minibus Terminal
16 Seafood Restaurants
17 Sampan Hire
18 7 Eleven
19 Old Town

Tai She Wan (Big Snake Bay) and Pak Lap Wan (White Wax Bay).

To get to Sai Kung, take the MTR to Choi Hung station. Head out through exit B where signs say 'Clearwater Bay Road North' or 'Ngau Chi Wan Civic Centre'. From here you can catch bus No 92 to Sai Kung town, or the No 1 minibus which is faster and definitely more frequent. The ride from Choi Hung to Sai Kung town takes about 30 minutes on the big bus, or about 20 minutes by minibus. The ride back tends to be slower, and the town's bus terminus gets extremely busy on weekends.

Hebe Haven

Bus No 92 (or preferably minibus No 1) from Choi Hung MTR station to Sai Kung town passes the small bay of Hebe Haven (or Pak Sha Wan, meaning 'white sand bay'), home of the **Hebe Haven Yacht Club**. You won't have a hard time recognising the place – the yacht fleet practically chokes the harbour, which is itself surrounded by luxury villas. Without a doubt, Hebe Haven holds its own against other prestigious gwailo ghettos such as the Peak and Discovery Bay.

If you're not a yachting buff, catch a sampan to the tiny peninsula (Ma Lam Wat) across the bay to swim at **Trio Beach**. The beach is excellent and the sampan trip should be only a few dollars. Alternatively, walk out to the peninsula from Sai Kung town, a distance of about 2.5 km one way.

Ma On Shan

At 702m, Ma On Shan is the fourth-highest peak in Hong Kong, only surpassed by Tai Mo Shan in the New Territories and two peaks on Lantau Island (Lantau and Sunset peaks).

Ma On Shan the mountain is not to be confused with Ma On Shan the village. Ma On Shan village is another new town, com-

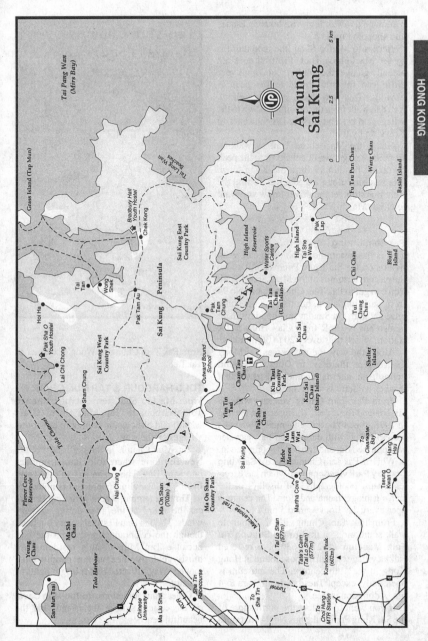

Around Sai Kung

plete with a row of high-rise housing estates and shopping malls.

Access to Ma On Shan (the mountain) is by the MacLehose Trail. The trail does not actually go over the summit, but comes very close and the spur route to the peak is obvious. This is a steep, strenuous climb. You can walk from the mountain down to the village and get a bus to Sha Tin, then back to Kowloon by train.

Get to the MacLehose Trail by walking from Sai Kung town or get closer to the peak by taking bus No 99 from Sai Kung town. The bus runs along Sai Sha Rd. To find the right bus stop, let the driver know you want to climb Ma On Shan.

Pak Tam Chung

This is the easternmost point you can reach by bus on the Sai Kung Peninsula. It's also the eastern terminus of the MacLehose Trail. You can get to Pak Tam Chung on bus No 94 from Sai Kung town, but this bus runs only once an hour. On Sunday and holidays there is also bus No 96R from Choi Hung MTR station, which runs every 20 to 30 minutes.

Along the way, the bus passes Tai Mong Tsai where there is an **Outward Bound school**, an international organisation that teaches wilderness survival.

From Pak Tam Chung you can walk to High Island Reservoir. The reservoir, opened in 1978, used to be a sea channel. Both ends were blocked with dams, then the seawater was pumped out and fresh water pumped in.

While in Pak Tam Chung, visit the **Sai Kung Country Park visitor centre**, which has excellent maps, photographs and displays of the area's geology, fauna and flora. The centre is open every day from 9 am to 5 pm.

From Pak Tam Chung, it's a 25-minute walk south along a trail to the **Sheung Yiu Folk Museum** (☎ 2792-6365), a restored Hakka village typical of those found in Hong Kong in the 19th century. The museum is open daily, except Tuesday, from 9 am to 4 pm. Admission is free.

If you want to explore the north shore of the Sai Kung Peninsula, bus No 94 continues

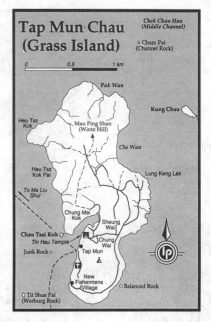

from Pak Tam Chung to Wong Shek pier in Tai Tan.

TOLO HARBOUR & TAP MUN CHAU

From Ma Liu Shui, ferries cruise through Tolo Harbour to Tap Mun Chau (Grass Island) and back again, calling in at various villages on the way.

Tap Mun Chau is in the north-east of the New Territories where Tolo Harbour empties into Mirs Bay. The island has an old-world fishing village atmosphere and is noted for its **Tin Hau temple**, where whistling sounds can be heard at the altar during easterly winds. The Tin Hau Festival is very big here, though the celebrants come from the city because Tap Mun Chau's residents are mostly elderly. The young people have moved away, attracted by the bright lights of the city.

Other main attractions are **Tap Mun Cave**, on the eastern side of the island, and the beautiful beaches.

Many visitors claim that Tap Mun Chau is the most interesting island of all those around Hong Kong. Unfortunately, the beach is carpeted with beer cans, plastic bags and other detritus, plus getting there is a bit of a hassle. It's worth it for the seafood though. There is no accommodation on the island.

The Tolo Harbour ferry is operated by the Polly Ferry Company (☎ 2771-1630). Ferries begin the journey at Ma Liu Shui, which is about a 15-minute walk from University KCR station. The HKTA can supply you with the current ferry schedule, but at the time of writing it is as follows:

Monday – Saturday		
	1st class	*2nd class*
Ma Liu Shui	8.30am	3.15pm
Sham Chung	9.00am	3.45pm
Lai Chi Chong	9.15am	4.00pm
Tap Mun Chau	9.45am	4.30pm
Ko Lau Wan	9.50am	4.35pm
Chek Keng	10.05am	4.45pm
Tai Tan	10.20am	5.00pm
Tap Mun Chau	10.40am	5.20pm
Lai Chi Chong	11.10am	5.50pm
Sham Chung	11.25am	6.05pm
Ma Liu Shui	12.05pm	6.45pm

Sundays & Holidays			
	1st class	*2nd class*	*3rd class*
Ma Liu Shui	8.30am	3.15pm	
Sham Chung	9.00am	3.45pm	
Lai Chi Chong	9.15am	4.00pm	
Tap Mun Chau	9.45am	4.30pm	
Ko Lau Wan	9.50am	4.35pm	
Chek Keng	10.05am	1.15pm	4.45pm
Tai Tan	10.20am	1.30pm	5.00pm
Tap Mun Chau	10.40am	1.45pm	5.20pm
Lai Chi Chong	11.10am	2.15pm	5.50pm
Sham Chung	11.25am	2.30pm	6.05pm
Ma Liu Shui	12.05pm	3.00pm	6.45pm

As an alternative to the Tolo Harbour ferry, an easy way to reach Tap Mun Chau is to take a kaido from Wong Shek pier in Tai Tan, which is the last stop of bus No 94. The kaidos run once hourly. This route is particularly scenic because it cruises through narrow Tai Tan Hoi Hap (Long Harbour), which is more reminiscent of a fjord in Norway than a harbour in Hong Kong.

PING CHAU

This small island is in Mirs Bay in the far north-east of the New Territories. It's very close to the coast of China and used to be one of the most popular destinations for people who wanted to leave China by swimming – braving the sharks and Chairman Mao's patrol boats.

At one time the island supported a population of 3000, but now it is uninhabited. The exodus started in the 1960s when everyone suddenly decided that life in a Hong Kong factory was preferable to life on a peaceful fishing isle. There are several abandoned buildings on the island, but visitors are advised to bring camping equipment.

The island's highest point is only about 30m, but it has unusual rock layers in its cliffs which glitter after a night of rain. The island is also good for swimming: there are some beautiful white sand beaches, especially at Lai Tau Wan.

Getting to Ping Chau is quite an expedition. Unless you have your own yacht, you must take the ferry from Ma Liu Shui (near the Chinese University) in the New Territories. The ferry only runs on weekends, departing on Saturday

and returning on Sunday, so a visit to Ping Chau involves a mandatory camping trip.

Ferries depart from Ma Liu Shui on Saturday at 11.15 am and return on Sunday from Ping Chau at 1.10 pm. Check these times since the schedule can change and you certainly don't want to miss the boat back to Hong Kong. Only round-trip tickets are sold.

Tickets for this ferry can be bought at the head office of the Hong Kong and Yau Ma Tei Ferry Company (☎ 2542-3081), 1st floor, Central Harbour Services pier, Pier Rd, Central, or at the pier in Ma Liu Shui on the day of travel. They only sail if the weather is good.

PLACES TO STAY
YHA Hostels

There are four hostels in the New Territories, and three of them permit camping. Don't forget to bring your IYHF membership card when checking in.

Bradbury Lodge (☎ 2662-5123) is the HKYHA's premier hostel in the New Territories. Beds cost HK$35, plus an additional HK$10 in summer if the air-conditioning is turned on. Family rooms for four persons are available at HK$200. Camping is *not* permitted. The hostel is at the base of Plover Cove Reservoir on Ting Kok Rd, just a few hundred metres south of Tai Mei Tuk. Bicycles can be rented in Tai Mei Tuk and rowboats are for hire alongside the bay. There are some easy hiking possibilities in the area, plus a fairly strenuous hike up into the Pat Sin Leng mountains. Take the KCR to Tai Po Market station, then bus No 75K to Tai Mei Tuk and follow the access road with the sea on your right side (less than five minutes walking).

Don't confuse the above hostel with *Bradbury Hall* (☎ 2328-2458) in Chek Keng (on the Sai Kung Peninsula). This place has 100 beds costing HK$25 each, and camping is permitted (also for HK$25). Take the MTR train to Choi Hung station and head for exit B, which leads you to Clearwater Bay Rd North. This is where you'll find the Choi Hung Estate bus terminus – take bus No 92 (or a green minibus) to the Sai Kung town

terminus. From Sai Kung, take bus No 94 (runs only once hourly between 8 am and 7 pm) to Yellow Stone pier, but get off at Pak Tam Au (it's the fourth bus stop after the County Park entrance, near the top of a hill). There's a footpath at the side of the road (going east) leading to Chek Keng village. The hostel is right on the harbour facing the Chek Keng pier. An alternative route is to take the ferry from Ma Liu Shui (adjacent to University KCR station) to Chek Keng pier. This ferry departs at 8.30 am and 3.15 pm, with an extra run at 1.15 pm on Sunday and public holidays.

Pak Sha O Hostel (☎ 2328-2327) is also on the Sai Kung Peninsula. It charges HK$25 a bed (112 beds available) and camping is permitted. Get to Sai Kung town as above; from there take Bus No 94 (hourly service between 8 am and 7 pm) towards Wong Shek pier and get off at Ko Tong Village. From there, find Hoi Ha Rd and a road sign 30m ahead showing the way to Pak Sha O. Note that from Wong Shek pier you can take a boat trip to Tap Mun Chau.

Sze Lok Yuen (☎ 2488-8188) is on Tai Mo Shan Rd. Beds cost HK$25 and tent camping is permitted. This is a good place from which to climb Tai Mo Shan, Hong Kong's highest peak. Because of the high elevation, it can get amazingly cold at night, so be prepared. Take the No 51 bus (Tsuen Wan Ferry Pier to Kam Tin) at Tsuen Wan MTR station and alight at Tai Mo Shan Rd. Follow Tai Mo Shan Rd for about 45 minutes, then turn on to a small concrete path on the right-hand side which leads directly to the hostel. You should buy food in Tsuen Wan before getting on the bus. The hostel is only open on Saturday night and evenings before a public holiday.

Camping

Aside from the camping grounds mentioned above, there are a few other designated camping spots in the New Territories. In the Plover Cove area, there are campsites at Sam A Chung and Hok Tau. The Sai Kung Peninsula has many camping grounds (see the Around Sai Kung map for details).

Hotels

Tsuen Wan The *Kowloon Panda Hotel* (☎ 2409-1111; fax 2409-1818), 3 Tsuen Wah St, Tsuen Wan. There are 1026 rooms (no kidding) and doubles cost HK$990 to HK$1650; suites are HK$2100 to HK$6000. Facilities: bar, business centre, coffee shop, conference room, exercise centre, hotel doctor, in-house video, outdoor swimming pool and restaurants (Cantonese, Italian & Japanese). Take the MTR to Tai Wo Hau station.

Sha Tin The *Regal Riverside* (☎ 2649-7878; fax 2637-4748), Tai Chung Kiu Rd, is a huge three-star hotel with 830 rooms – doubles from HK$1750 to HK$2100 and suites for HK$3000 to HK$8000. Facilities: bar, barber shop, business centre, coffee shop, conference room, exercise centre, hotel doctor, in-house video, outdoor swimming pool and restaurants (Cantonese, Asian, Western & international).

The *Royal Park* (☎ 2601-2111; fax 2601-3666), 8 Pak Hok Ting St, has 448 rooms with doubles priced from HK$1380 to HK$1980 and suites for HK$3200 to HK$4800. Facilities: bar, business centre, coffee shop, disabled rooms, exercise centre, hotel doctor, in-house video, outdoor swimming pool, tennis courts and restaurants (Chaozhou, Japanese, Western & Asian).

Tuen Mun The *Gold Coast Hotel* (☎ 2452-8888; fax 2440-7368), 1 Castle Peak Rd, Castle Peak Bay, is to the south-east of town overlooking the waterfront and yacht club. There are 450 rooms, doubles cost HK$1300 to HK$1950, suites are HK$2300 to HK$8800. Facilities: bar, business centre, coffee shop, conference room, golf putting green, exercise centre, in-house video, outdoor swimming pool, tennis courts, Cantonese & international restaurants.

PLACES TO EAT
Sha Tin

The multi-level Sha Tin New Town Plaza has more restaurants than you can shake a chopstick at – everything from Big Macs and pizzas to Peking duck and shark's fin soup. A notable place for Indian food is *Koh-I-Noor* (☎ 2601-

4969) on the ground floor of New Town Plaza Phase III.

If you want to escape the shopping-mall cuisine, an interesting change of pace is the *Treasure Floating Restaurant* (☎ 2637-7222). It's moored in the river at 55 Tai Chung Kiu Rd. Dim sum hours are from 8 am to 5 pm, and the restaurant dishes up pricier seafood until 11.30 pm.

Also of special interest is *Yucca De Lac Restaurant* (☎ 2691-1630) in Ma Liu Shui, where outdoor tables afford a view of Tolo Harbour. No dim sum here, but standard Chinese dishes are served (the roast pigeon is a house speciality).

Yuen Long

If you're looking for dim sum in Yuen Long, it's served from 7 am to 3 pm at the *Kar Shing Restaurant* (☎ 2476-3228) in room 333, 3rd floor, Yuen Long Plaza, 249 Castle Peak Rd.

Sai Kung

The *Duke of York* (☎ 2792-8435), 42-56 Fuk Man Rd, is OK for pub grub. Specialties are the baked fish and salad, washed down with a Foster's or Carlsberg.

The *Black Sheep* cafe (☎ 2792-6662), at 9 Sha Tsui Path (directly facing the playground in the centre of town) has some stylish cuisine on offer.

Jasper's (☎ 2792-6388), 13 Sha Tsui Path, is also alongside the playground. The speciality here is French and Italian food. Open from 9 am to 11 pm, but closed on Monday.

Pepperoni's Pizza & Cafe (☎ 2792-2083), 1592 Po Tung Rd, is a favourite with expats in the area. Just across the street and under the same management is *Al Fresco's* (☎ 2792-5296), 183-D Po Tung Rd, which specialises in steaks, ribs and seafood. Both places are open from 9 am to 11 pm.

New Castle Restaurant & Pub (☎ 2792-5225) is near *McDonald's*. Steaks, fish & chips and snacks monopolise the menu. This place opens at noon but only gets busy in the evening. The kitchen stays open until 9 pm.

Don't overlook the excellent seafood restaurants on the waterfront, some of which are hidden away in the old town section.

Outlying Islands

Sure, there's Hong Kong Island – but what about the 234 other islands that make up Hong Kong? Together, the Outlying Islands make up about 20% of its total land area. Officially they are part of the New Territories – except for Stonecutters Island, which has become part of Kowloon thanks to land reclamation.

The tiny islands of Tap Mun Chau and Ping Chau are covered in the New Territories chapter because they are best reached from there; the islands in this chapter are all easily accessible from Hong Kong Island.

While many are little more than uninhabited rocks occasionally seen above sea level, Lantau is actually larger and higher than Hong Kong Island. Nevertheless, in all the Outlying Islands put together there are fewer than 100,000 people, which is less than 2% of Hong Kong's total.

Just a few decades ago, almost all of the habitable islands had permanent settlements supported mostly by the fishing industry. Now many of these villages are ghost towns, their inhabitants lured away by the promise of wealth in the nearby glittering metropolis.

But if Chinese fishing families have been lured off the islands, foreigners have been moving in the opposite direction. Expats are among the most staunch defenders of traditional island ways of life, fiercely opposing proposals to build high-rises and introduce cars to the islands.

In an ironic twist, the influx of foreigners helps developers justify more building projects. Since few Chinese are moving to the islands, it's the *gwailos* ('foreign devils') who are driving up the rents and spurring new housing developments that make the rural atmosphere a little less rural every year. Developments such as Lantau's Discovery Bay – where matchbox high-rises now compete for a view of the sea – could be an indication of the way the islands are heading. Foreigners talk about instituting a building moratorium, but it seems unlikely. The problem is that every new resident wants to be the last.

The one factor that has kept these islands unspoilt has been inconvenient transport. Discovery Bay only developed into suburbia thanks to the introduction of high-speed ferries which cut commuting time to 20 minutes. Elsewhere, it takes nearly an hour each way. Unfortunately for conservationists, plans are afoot to introduce high-speed ferries to *all* the major islands. When that happens, Cheung Chau, Lamma and Lantau could all be headed the same way as Kowloon. But at least for the moment, the Outlying Islands remain tranquil backwaters free of motor vehicles, noise and crowds.

Cars are prohibited on all of the Outlying Islands except Lantau. On Lantau, a special vehicle permit is required and not easily obtained, though this may change soon with the opening of the new airport.

One chronic hazard on all the islands is the dogs. Although it's illegal to have an unleashed and unmuzzled mutt in high-rise Hong Kong, the rules are largely ignored here. The island dogs are mostly friendly but some are fond of taking a bite out of tourism. If you are attacked, get a good look at the dog that bit you and then call the police – they may be able to track down the owner, who will have to pay your medical expenses plus a fine.

The large number of stray dogs is in part because of thoughtless foreigners who come to Hong Kong for a brief time to work. They take on a dog and when they depart give it to a friend, who sooner or later abandons it.

Only those islands which are accessible by public ferry are included in this chapter. You probably won't get to visit the numerous other islands unless you can afford to charter a boat. Many of the remote islands are popular destinations for Hong Kong's fleet of yachts, where boat owners often indulge in such prohibited pastimes as nude swimming.

ORIENTATION & INFORMATION

If you intend to do a major hike, it would be wise to equip yourself with the excellent *Countryside* series of maps produced by the Crown Lands and Surveys Office. The essential map for the Outlying Islands is called *Countryside Series Map No 3: Lantau and Islands*. Another useful map is *Lantau Trail*. The maps are cheap and can be bought at the Government Publications Centre in the Government Offices Building, 66 Queensway, Admiralty.

ACCOMMODATION

Individual hostels, guesthouses and hotels are listed in the Places to Stay sections for each island in this chapter. However, leasing a flat in the islands (even just for a weekend) is handled differently.

You can book flats in the city before your arrival at the islands. The cost for leasing a flat can be amazingly low, especially if you're staying a week or longer. In the not-so-distant past there was an Outlying Islands holiday-flat booking office next to the ferry pier in Central, but this has been wiped out (perhaps only temporarily) by a major construction project. In the meantime there are two places in Hong Kong where you can book island flats. Probably most convenient is the Jubilee International Tour Centre (☎ 2530-0530; fax 2845-2469), room 302-303, Man Yee Building, 60 Des Voeux Rd, Central. This office also books yachts, tour buses and even Rolls-Royces.

The other place is the Sino Centre, 582 Nathan Rd, Mong Kok. The centre houses numerous competing booking offices housed under one roof. None can be recommended over the others, so you just have to go there and sort it out.

On Cheung Chau there are numerous booking offices for flats right near the ferry pier (see the Cheung Chau section for details). Lantau Island has one such office, but it only seems to function during weekends and public holidays. The other islands do not have any booking offices for flats, though there are some individual guesthouses and estate agents.

GETTING THERE & AWAY

The main islands are linked to Hong Kong by regular ferry services – not just for tourists but also for locals who work in the city and live on the islands. The ferries are comfortable and cheap, and many have an air-conditioned top deck which costs extra. They all have a basic bar serving drinks and snacks. Smoking is prohibited on all the ferries and the rules are enforced.

There are two classes on the large ferries: ordinary and de luxe (de luxe is air-conditioned). Prices are raised significantly higher on weekends and holidays. For definition purposes, a weekend includes Saturday from noon onwards. There are discounts for children aged under 12. Seniors over 65 can also get a discount but only in ordinary class, not de luxe.

If you're staying on the islands and want to make a day trip into the city, definitely buy a round-trip ticket (holidays only). The ticket is only good on the day you bought it, but comes with a 50% discount. However, no such discount is given on weekdays and it is not available on tickets sold in the city.

Hoverferries also connect the islands – they cost over twice as much and go twice as fast as the normal ferries. They're fun, but definitely not for those prone to seasickness! Eat lightly or bring a plastic bag. There is only one deck on the hoverferries, and thus only one class.

The timetables are pretty stable but they are subject to slight change. You can pick up the latest timetable from the Hong Kong Tourist Association (HKTA).

If you want to catch breakfast on Hong Kong Island while waiting for the ferry, the *Seaview Restaurant*, upstairs on the Outlying Islands ferry pier, does a mean dim sum.

The islands are popular holiday destinations for Hong Kongers – in fact too popular! On weekends the ferries become so crowded it's a wonder they don't sink. As soon as business offices close on Saturday afternoon there is a mad rush for the boats, the islands' more accessible beaches are practically standing room only and most hotels charge double rates – if you can find a room!

Try to keep at least HK$20 worth of change with you and a small wad of HK$10 notes. You can buy the ticket from a booth, but you'll save time by putting exact change into a turnstile as you enter the pier. On some of the smaller ferries they run out of change, so it helps to have small coins. Under no circumstances will the ticket offices change bills larger than HK$100.

If your time is limited, Watertours (☎ 2525-4808) runs trips to the islands.

Cheung Chau

Only 2.5 sq km, Cheung Chau is 10 km west of Hong Kong Island, off the south-east tip of Lantau. Despite the small size, it's the most populous of the Outlying Islands. Cheung Chau means 'long island' in Cantonese.

Archaeological digs have shown that Cheung Chau, like Lamma and Lantau, was inhabited in prehistoric times. The island had a thriving fishing community 2500 years ago and a reputation for piracy from the year dot – probably started by the earliest Cantonese and Hakka settlers who supplemented their incomes with piracy and smuggling.

When Guangzhou and Macau opened up to the West in the 16th century the island was a perfect spot from which to prey on passing ships stacked with goodies. The infamous and powerful pirate Cheung Po Tsai is said to have had his base here during the 18th century.

The piracy and smuggling have gone, but fishing is still an important industry for a large number of the island's inhabitants. About 22,000 people now live on the island – about 10% on junks and sampans anchored offshore.

There are several interesting temples on the island, the most important being the Pak Tai temple, which hosts the annual Cheung Chau Bun Festival.

There are a couple of OK beaches on the island. Overlooking the largest beach is Cheung Chau's tallest building, the six-storey Warwick Hotel, which may be a portent of abominations to come. The island is getting crowded, but there are still a few unspoilt headlands where you can escape the claustrophobia of Hong Kong Island. Because of the crowded situation, the island can no longer supply its own drinking water, so it's brought in by an undersea pipeline from Lantau.

While Cheung Chau is not for serious walkers, it's ideal if you enjoy an easy stroll among butterflies and lush vegetation. The island is packed with missionary schools, churches, retreats and youth centres of every denomination, and has built up a fair-sized community of gwailos who have fled the rat race.

There is no traffic noise on the island. In fact, there is no motorised transport other than a few tiny cargo tractors powered by lawn-mower engines. Cheung Chau is extremely popular with the Hong Kong locals who come to pig out on seafood, but on weekends and holidays it tends to become a circus.

CHEUNG CHAU VILLAGE
No longer really a village but a small town, the main built-up area on the island is along the narrow strip at the centre of the two headlands that make up the dumb-bell-shaped island. The waterfront is a bustling place any time of day and late into the night.

CHEUNG CHAU TYPHOON SHELTER
This is the second largest typhoon shelter in Hong Kong, only surpassed by Aberdeen. As in Aberdeen, touring the typhoon shelter by boat is a must. Chartering a sampan for 20 minutes costs around HK$50 (subject to negotiation). Virtually any small boat you see in the harbour is a water taxi and can be hired for a tour. Simply wave to the boats and two or three will likely stop to offer a ride. Agree on the fare first.

PAK TAI TEMPLE
There are several temples on the island and two of the most interesting are on the water-front. To find them, turn to your left as you get off the ferry and walk up Kwok Man Rd.

You will come to the Pak Tai temple, dedicated to the god Pak Tai – see the Religion section in Facts about Hong Kong. The temple is the oldest on the island and is the focus of the famous annual Bun Festival.

The story goes that the first settlers from Guangdong Province in China brought Pak Tai, protector of fisherfolk (among other things) with them to Cheung Chau. Carrying the god through the village in the year 1777 is supposed to have scared away a plague. The temple was built six years later.

The temple has several historic relics. A large iron sword said to have been forged in the Sung dynasty (960 – 1279 AD) stands here. It was recovered from the sea by a local fisherman more than 100 years ago and presented to the god by the islanders. The sword is regarded as a symbol of good luck and its disappearance from the temple several years ago caused great consternation on the island. The person who took it was kind enough to return it when he realised the concern he had caused. There is also a wooden sedan chair, made in 1894, which was used to carry Pak Tai around the island on festival days, and two pillars depicting dragons, hewn from hunks of granite at the turn of the century.

BUN FESTIVAL
The festival takes place in May and is famous for its bun towers – bamboo scaffolding covered with holy buns. The towers can be up to 20m high.

If you go to Cheung Chau a week or so before the festival you'll see these towers being built in the courtyard of the Pak Tai temple.

In previous times, at an appointed hour, hundreds of people would scramble up the towers to fetch one of the buns for good luck. It was believed that the higher the bun the better the luck, so naturally it got to be something of a riot as everyone headed for the top. This sounds like a recipe for disaster and indeed, a serious accident occurred in 1978 when a tower collapsed. Now the buns are handed out and no one is allowed to climb up to fetch their own.

The third day of the festival (a Sunday) is the most interesting, with a procession of floats, stilt walkers and people dressed as legendary characters.

Most fascinating are the colourfully dressed 'floating children' who are carried through the streets on poles, cleverly strapped to metal supports hidden under their clothes. The supports include built-in footrests and a padded seat. On Pak She St, a few doors down from the Pak Tai temple, there is a photo exhibition of the floating children. One of the supports for carrying them is displayed.

During the celebrations several deities are worshipped, including Tin Hau, Pak Tai and Hung Hsing (the god of the south) – all significant to people who make their living from the sea. Homage is also paid to Tou Tei, god of the earth, and Kuanyin, goddess of mercy.

Offerings are made to the spirits of all fish and other animals whose lives have been sacrificed to provide food. During the four days of worship no meat is eaten and a priest reads a decree calling on the villagers to abstain from killing any animals during festival time.

The festival is unique to Cheung Chau and its origins are not really known. One popular theory is that the ceremony is to appease the ghosts of those who were killed by pirates, otherwise they would bring disasters such as typhoons to the island.

The bun festival is held over four days. Accommodation in Cheung Chau is heavily booked at this time. The stacks of extra ferries laid on for the festival are always packed. Still, it's worth making the journey if you can.

TIN HAU TEMPLES
Cheung Chau's Tin Hau temples, dedicated to the patron goddess of fishermen, indicate the important role fishing has played on the island. One Tin Hau temple is at the southern end of Cheung Chau village waterfront. Another is at Sai Wan on the south-west tip of the island – walk here or take a *kaido* (small boat) near the pier. A third temple is to the north of the Pak Tai temple.

TUNG WAN BEACH

From the ferry pier, follow Tung Wan Rd to the east side of the island. This is where you'll find Tung Wan Beach, the biggest and most popular, but not necessarily the prettiest beach on Cheung Chau. The best part of Tung Wan is the far southern end. It's possible to hire windsurfers here.

OTHER BEACHES

Most of the northern headland is uninhabited, with not much more than a reservoir on it. At the north-west corner of the island is Tai Kwai Wan, which has a sandy beach. On the north-east corner is another beach, the more isolated Tung Wan Tsai.

The southern part of Cheung Chau is perhaps the most interesting. South of Tung Wan Beach, past the six-storey Warwick Hotel, there's Kwun Yam Wan Beach. At the end of the beach a footpath takes you uphill past the small Kwun Yam Temple, dedicated to the goddess of mercy. Continue up the footpath and look for the sign pointing the way to the Fa Peng Knoll. The concrete footpath takes you past quiet, tree-shrouded villas.

From the knoll you can walk down to Don Bosco Rd (again look for the sign); it leads to rocky Nam Tam Wan, where swimming is possible. If you ignore Don Bosco Rd and continue straight down you will come to the intersection of Peak and Kwun Yam Wan Rds. Kwun Yam Wan Rd will take you back to Cheung Chau village.

Peak Rd is the main route to the island's cemetery. You'll pass several pavilions on the road, built for coffin bearers who have to sweat their way along the hilly climb to the cemetery.

Once at the cemetery it's worth dropping down to Pak Tso Wan (Italian Beach), a sandy, isolated spot which is good for swimming.

Peak Rd continues to Sai Wan (West Bay) on the south-west bulge of the island. There's a ferry pier here and a Tin Hau temple.

CHEUNG PO TSAI CAVE

This cave in the south-west corner of the island is said to have been the hiding place of the infamous pirate, Cheung Po Tsai, who used Cheung Chau as a base.

The cave area has become a tourist attraction and there is a nearby Cheung Po Tsai Cave picnic area. The glorification of Cheung Po Tsai seems ironic, considering that he had a reputation for extreme brutality, and ruthlessly robbed, murdered and tortured many people. One of the island's Tin Hau temples is near the cave and picnic area.

Reach the cave by walking almost two km from Cheung Chau village, or take a kaido to the pier at Sai Wan. From Sai Wan the walk is less than 200m.

PLACES TO STAY

There are several good places to stay, but prices escalate dramatically on weekends unless you make a long-term booking, like a month.

As you exit the ferry pier, in front of you and a little to the left there are numerous tables and booths displaying photographs of various rooms for rent. Practically none of the people who operate these booths speak English, but if you can make yourself understood, it's possible to find a cheap room. Some of these people are renting out rooms in their own flat, while others will rent you a whole flat or villa. Prices vary wildly, but you can negotiate cheaper rates for a longer term.

The best cheap place to stay is the *Star House Motel* (☎ 2981-2186) at 149 Tai San Back St. Double rooms start at HK$200 on weekdays and run to between HK$600 and HK$700 a night on weekends.

The *Warwick Hotel* (☎ 2981-0081; fax 2981-9741) is a six-storey, two-star eyesore on the beach with 70 rooms. Doubles cost HK$620 on a weekday and HK$1050 on a weekend, plus a 10% service charge and 5% tax. There are four suites renting for HK$2120. The hotel has a good Cantonese and Western restaurant.

PLACES TO EAT

As on most islands around Hong Kong seafood is the local speciality, but you won't have any trouble finding other types of Chinese food. In the morning many restaurants along the waterfront serve dim sum.

As you get off the ferry, turn to your left and head about 200m up the street. Here you'll find numerous cafes where you can sit by the waterfront and watch the world go by as you eat.

Two restaurants offering good food and low prices are *Bor Kee* and *East Lake*, on Tung Wan Rd just east of the *Garden Cafe/Pub*. These places are popular with local expats. During summer evenings, they set up outdoor tables and the place takes on the atmosphere of an open-air party.

There are a couple of restaurants on the eastern waterfront overlooking Tung Wan Beach.

From the cargo pier, you can take a free sampan (the one with the flag) to the *Float-ing Restaurant*. Fishing families hold their wedding parties there.

ENTERTAINMENT
There is only one real nightlife spot, the *Garden Cafe/Pub* (☎ 2981-4610), 84 Tung Wan Rd, just to the west of the Bor Kee Restaurant. It's a friendly place and always packed with gwailos. This is the only place on the island which serves European food.

There's a bar at the Warwick Hotel, but it's high-priced and hasn't attracted much of a following among the expat community.

GETTING THERE & AWAY
The ferry schedules for Cheung Chau are listed below. Cheung Chau's fishing harbour makes for a dramatic entrance – keep your camera handy. See facing page 241 for the Inter-island ferry schedule.

Central – Cheung Chau Ferry Schedule

Monday – Saturday		Sunday & Holidays	
From Central	*From Cheung Chau*	*From Central*	*From Cheung Chau*
6.25am	5.35am*	6.25am	5.35am*
7.30	6.00	7.30	6.00
8.00	6.40	8.40	6.40
9.00	7.25	9.15!	7.30
10.00	7.45	10.00	8.45
11.00	8.00	10.45!	10.00
noon	8.40	11.15	11.15
1.00pm	9.15	noon!	12.10pm!
2.00	10.15	12.30pm	12.30
3.00	11.15	1.20!	1.20!
4.15	12.15pm	2.00	1.45
5.15	1.15	3.00	2.45!
5.45	2.15	4.30	3.15
6.20	3.15	5.45	4.00!
6.45	4.15	6.25	4.30
7.30	5.20	7.05	5.15!
8.15	6.20	8.20	5.40
9.30	7.00	9.30	6.50
10.30	7.45	10.30	8.00!
11.30	8.30	11.30	8.20
12.30am	9.30	12.30am	9.30
–	10.30	–	10.30
–	11.30	–	11.30

* Via Peng Chau & Mui Wo   ! Optional
Journey time: one hour

Fares:	Class	Week days	Weekends
	deluxe	adult HK$16	adult HK$30
		child HK$16	child HK$16
	ordinary	adult HK$8.50	adult HK$11.50
		child/senior HK$4.30	child/senior HK$6

Hoverferries

Monday – Friday except Holidays

From Central	From Cheung Chau
9.00am	9.40am
10.15	10.50
12.15pm	12.50pm
2.15	2.50
4.05	4.50

Journey time: 35 minutes

Fares: adult HK$22, child & senior HK$11.50

Tsim Sha Tsui – Cheung Chau

Saturday Only	*Sunday & Holidays*	
From Kowloon	*From Kowloon*	*From Cheung Chau*
4.00pm	8.00am	12.45 pm
–	10.00am	–

Fares: same as those from Hong Kong Island

Inter-island Ferry Schedule

Monday to Saturday

Peng Chau	Mui Wo	Chi Ma Wan	Cheung Chau
6.30am	6.10am	5.35am	–
–	5.40	6.05	6.25am
8.15	7.55	7.30	7.00
8.20	8.40	9.00	9.30
10.40	10.20	10.00	9.30
10.45	11.10	11.30	noon
1.10pm	12.50pm	12.30pm	noon
1.20	1.40	2.00	2.30pm
3.25	3.05	2.30	–
3.25	3.45	4.05	4.30
5.40	5.20	5.00	4.30
–	5.45	6.05	6.40
7.45	7.25	7.05	6.40
7.50	8.10	8.30	9.00
–	9.35	9.00	–
–	9.35	–	10.10
11.10	10.50	10.35	10.10

Sundays & Public Holidays

Peng Chau	Mui Wo	Chi Ma Wan	Cheung Chau
6.30am	6.10am	5.35am	–
6.00	6.25	6.45	7.10
8.15	7.55	7.35	7.10
8.20	8.45	9.05	9.30
10.30	10.10	9.55	9.30
10.45	11.10	11.30	noon
1.10pm	12.50pm	12.30pm	noon
1.20	1.40	2.00	2.30pm
3.30	3.10	2.50	2.30
3.40	4.10	4.30	5.00
6.10	5.50	5.30	5.00
6.20	6.40	7.00	7.25
–	8.10	7.45	7.25
–	8.10	8.30	9.00
–	9.40	9.20	9.00
–	9.40	10.15	–
11.15	10.55	10.35	10.15

Fares: adult HK$6.50, children & seniors HK$3.30

GETTING AROUND

Walking is not the only way to get about Cheung Chau: you can hire bikes on the island, though you'll have a few big hills to tackle outside the built-up areas. Bicycles can be hired from the shop on the western waterfront, near the north end of Pak She Praya Rd.

Lamma

Also known as Pok Liu Chau, Lamma is the large island (13 sq km) clearly visible from Victoria Peak as you look to the south-west. Lamma is believed to have been settled before Hong Kong Island, yet it's now the least developed of the large islands.

There is a devoted Western community on Lamma which has fled Hong Kong's sky-high rents and urban congestion. Lamma officially supports a population of about 3000; unofficially, it's three times that – largely because of the resident expats who don't have Hong Kong ID cards.

Although low in population, archaeological evidence indicates that Lamma had the oldest settlement in all southern China. A team of 14 archaeologists doing a routine dig at Tai Wan San Tsuen unearthed evidence that there was a small village on the island 5000 to 6000 years ago.

Plans to build an oil refinery on Lamma were dropped in 1973 after a lot of heated opposition. Instead, Hongkong Electric constructed a huge coal-fired power station on the north-west coast of the island; the two enormous smoke stacks are clearly visible from Hong Kong Island. Meanwhile, on the south-east side of the island, the hillsides around Sok Kwu Wan are slowly being quarried away. Patrons at the bayside seafood restaurants can admire the quarry and adjacent cement plant while dining on crabs and prawns.

Vigorous objections were raised by local residents at the time these schemes were proposed, but 'progress' won out over environmental concerns. Given the fact that there are more than 200 uninhabited islands around Hong Kong which could have been reduced to rubble without anyone complaining, just why Lamma was singled out for such development is a mystery to many.

Despite all this seemingly bleak news, enough of Lamma is still unspoilt enough to make it worth visiting. The island is good for walking and swimming, and is a favourite weekend mooring spot for gwailo junks. It's also a fishing port and the few small towns all have a good assortment of seafood restaurants.

YUNG SHUE WAN

The larger of the two main townships on Lamma, Yung Shue Wan (Banyan Tree Bay) is still a pretty small place. Plastic was the big industry here a few decades ago, when people in almost every house sprayed a vast assortment of plastic parts for toys and other goods. The plastics sweatshops have vanished and now restaurants and other tourist-related businesses are the main employers. There is a small Tin Hau temple here.

Without a doubt, Yung Shue Wan has Hong Kong's largest hippie community. It also has lots of late-night partying, plenty of stray dogs, lots of unemployment and an increasing amount of theft. The locals are appalled by this and relations between the gwailos and Chinese are generally poor. However, the community includes quite a few Chinese hippies – it's not just gwailos who live on banana muesli and sit by the beach playing flutes.

HUNG SHING YE

The most interesting way to see Lamma Island is to walk between Yung Shue Wan and Sok Kwu Wan, which takes a little over an hour. At the southern end of Yung Shue Wan there's a sign pointing to the Lamma Youth Hostel (the hostel is for Chinese only and is mainly used as a summer camp for school kids).

Follow the signs and you will soon find yourself in the countryside on a paved track. The first developed place you reach is Hung Shing Ye Beach, which is very nice although the view of the nearby power station takes some getting used to. The beach has lifeguards, a small restaurant and a few hotels. It would be a pleasant place to stay on weekdays, though on weekends the crowds multiply rapidly.

Continuing south from Hung Shing Ye, the path climbs steeply until it reaches a Chinese-style pavilion near the top of the

HONG KONG

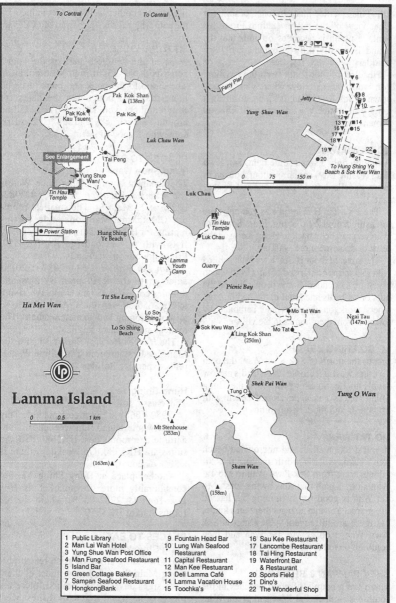

Lamma Island

0   0.5   1 km

1 Public Library	9 Fountain Head Bar	16 Sau Kee Restaurant
2 Man Lai Wah Hotel	10 Lung Wah Seafood	17 Lancombe Restaurant
3 Yung Shue Wan Post Office	Restaurant	18 Tai Hing Restaurant
4 Man Fung Seafood Restaurant	11 Capital Restaurant	19 Waterfront Bar
5 Island Bar	12 Man Kee Restuarant	& Restaurant
6 Green Cottage Bakery	13 Deli Lamma Café	20 Sports Field
7 Sampan Seafood Restaurant	14 Lamma Vacation House	21 Dino's
8 HongkongBank	15 Toochka's	22 The Wonderful Shop

hill. This is a nice place to relax, despite the clear view of the power station. From this vantage point, it becomes obvious that the island is mostly hilly grassland and large boulders, with very few trees.

Heading further south from the pavilion, you soon come to a ridge where you can look down at Sok Kwu Wan. It's a beautiful sight until you notice the quarry and adjacent cement works.

SOK KWU WAN
Although only a small settlement, Sok Kwu Wan (Picnic Bay) supports about a dozen or more excellent waterfront seafood restaurants.

There's a Tin Hau temple as you enter the township from Lo So Shing. From Sok Kwu Wan you can head back to Hong Kong on the ferry or do some more walking.

The small harbour at Sok Kwu Wan is filled with fish farms comprised of rafts from which cages are suspended. Some people live on the rafts or on boats anchored in the harbour, but others work on the rafts and commute by rowboat from their homes in the village.

LO SO SHING BEACH
Just to the north of Sok Kwu Wan, the path diverges west and crosses the island's narrow saddle to Lo So Shing Beach. Like Hung Shing Ye, this is a developed beach with lifeguards and modern amenities.

MO TAT WAN
If you'd like a clean and uncrowded beach (on weekdays), it's worth making the 20-minute walk from Sok Kwu Wan to Mo Tat Wan along a path that runs by the coast. Mo Tat Wan is good for swimming but has no lifeguards. You can also get there on a kaido, but these are infrequent – they start at Sok Kwu Wan, stop at Mo Tat Wan and then continue on to Aberdeen.

SHEK PAI WAN & SHAM WAN
There are a couple of good beaches in the south-east – Shek Pai Wan and Sham Wan. They're relatively isolated and do not have lifeguards or other facilities. Get to them by the path which leads south from Mo Tat Wan.

MT STENHOUSE
Most of the southern part of the island consists of the 353m-high Mt Stenhouse. The climb to the peak and back takes no more than two hours, but the paths are rough and not well defined. The coastline around here is rocky and it's hard to find somewhere good to swim.

PLACES TO STAY
Yung Shue Wan
The cheapest hotel in Yung Shue Wan is the *Lamma Vacation House* (☎ 2982-0427) at 29 Main St. The smallest rooms are Chungking Mansions-style coffins renting for HK$150, but reasonably cushy flats with private bath go for HK$350. Prices double on weekends.

Man Lai Wah Hotel (☎ 2982-0220) is adjacent to the ferry pier. Singles and doubles cost HK$350 on weekdays, rising to HK$650 on weekends. All rooms have air-conditioning and an attached bath. The management speaks English.

The *Hoi Yee Holiday Resort* is inside the Man Kee Restaurant in Yung Shue Wan; it rents expensive holiday flats.

Hung Shing Ye
The classy and expensive *Concerto Inn* (☎ 2982-1668) is the nicest place to stay on the whole island. On weekends, standard/deluxe rooms cost HK$680/880 and suites are HK$980. On weekdays there is a 30% discount.

Another place at Hung Shing Ye, but considerably more downmarket, is *Han Lok Yuen* (☎ 2982-0608) where double rooms start at HK$350.

PLACES TO EAT
Yung Shue Wan
The town has a string of good restaurants along Main St, and though most of them have signs advertising seafood, there are plenty of meat and vegetable dishes. Most of these places have English menus if you

ask for them. Because of the large expat community, Western food is readily available.

If it's cheap eats you're looking for, the bottom of the market belongs to *Man Kee Restaurant*. Sandwiches start at HK$8, with spaghetti and noodle dishes for around HK$18 and up.

Deli Lamma (☎ 2982-1583), just south of Man Kee Restaurant, is a great place catering to the gwailo market. It's open daily except Tuesdays from 8.30 am to 12.30 am.

Dino's is a new and trendy place that does great snacks and Thai takeaways.

Close to the ferry pier is the *Man Fung Seafood Restaurant* (☎ 2982-1112) which has a nice view of the harbour. If you're here in the morning (6 to 11 am), this is Lamma's prime dim sum shop: trolleys are stacked to overflowing with trays of delectables. By noon this place evolves into a standard seafood and noodle restaurant.

A favourite of the expat community is the *Lung Wah Seafood Restaurant* (☎ 2982-0791) at 20 Main St, next to the HongkongBank. This place also does a fine morning dim sum from 6 to 11 am (until noon on weekends), though it's not immediately obvious – the dim sum is kept covered in steaming baskets.

Lancombe Restaurant is the best in the mid-range. Outstanding specialities include fried squid, sweet & sour pork and scallops with broccoli and garlic.

Sampan Seafood Restaurant (☎ 2982-2388), 16 Main St, is the fanciest and most expensive in Yung Shue Wan.

Further down Main St are the *Capital*, *Lee Garden*, *Sau Kee* and *Tai Hing* restaurants.

Just on the edge of town is *The Wonderful Shop*, which features tasty ice cream and fruit milk shakes.

Sok Kwu Wan

An evening meal at Sok Kwu Wan is the most fun, and a good way to end a trip to the island. The restaurants are in a row along the waterfront. Some have names like *Lamma Hilton* and *Lamma Regent*. A few years ago these were little more than shacks, but now they are modern buildings, an indication of the money that the island has since come by.

If you haven't noticed it by now, Hong Kong people like to eat, and they are particularly fond of seafood. A steady convoy of kaidos brings customers to Sok Kwu Wan every evening from Hong Kong Island.

Mo Tat Wan

Mo Tat Wan has a superb by-the-water dining spot, *Coral Seafood Restaurant* (☎ 2982-8328). While the food is similar to what you get at Sok Kwu Wan, the prices are lower and the surroundings better.

ENTERTAINMENT
Yung Shue Wan

The large number of expats in Yung Shue Wan supports four pubs which become quite busy from about 6 pm until midnight. The *Island Bar* (☎ 2982-1376) is where the real old-timers hang out. The *Fountain Head* (☎ 2982-2118) next to HongkongBank is the most popular bar. *Toochka's* (☎ 2982-0159) is another favourite. The *Waterfront Bar* (☎ 2982-0914) is the yuppie pub – beer is expensive, but this place has the best Western food on the island (check out the pizza) and pretty good Indian food too.

The *Man Loon*, a 10-minute walk from Yung Shue Wan on the path to Hung Shing Ye beach, is a store, rather than a pub, with picnic tables set up outside. On Sunday it becomes an impromptu all-day drinking party.

GETTING THERE & AWAY

Ferries run from Central to Lamma's two main villages, Yung Shue Wan and Sok Kwu Wan. The journey between Central and Yung Shue Wan takes 40 minutes, and between Central and Sok Kwu Wan it's 50 minutes.

There is also a smaller ferry (kaido) running between Sok Kwu Wan and Aberdeen on the south side of Hong Kong Island. The kaido makes a brief stop at Mo Tat Wan along the way. The journey between Sok Kwu Wan and Mo Tat Wan takes 10 minutes; from Mo Tat Wan to Aberdeen it's 25 minutes.

HONG KONG

Hong Kong – Lamma Island Ferry Schedule (Hong Kong Ferry Company Ltd)
Central – Yung Shue Wan

Monday – Saturday		Sunday & Holidays	
from Central	from Yung Shue Wan	from Central	from Yung Shue Wan
6.45am	6.20am	8.15am	6.50am
8.30	7.20	8.45	7.50
10.30	8.00	9.45	9.00
noon	9.30	10.45	10.30
12.50pm	11.30	11.15	noon
2.00	12.50pm	12.45pm	1.30pm
3.50	1.40	2.15	3.00
4.35*	3.00	3.45	4.30
5.30	4.40	5.15	5.55
6.40	5.20*	6.45	6.15
7.40	6.20	7.30	7.45
8.20	7.30	9.30	8.30
9.50	9.05	11.20	10.35
11.20	10.35	12.30am	–
12.30am	–	–	–

* Optional except Saturday
Journey Time: 40 minutes

Fares:	Class	Week days	Weekends
	deluxe	adult HK$16	adult HK$30
		child HK$16	child HK$16
	ordinary	adult HK$8.50	adult HK$11.50
		child/senior HK$4.30	child/senior HK$6

Central – Sok Kwu Wan

Monday – Saturday		Sunday & Public Holidays	
from Central	from Sok Kwu Wan	from Central	from Sok Kwu Wan
8.00am	6.50am	7.30am	8.20am
10.00	9.00	9.15	10.05
2.30pm	11.00	11.00	noon
4.15	3.30pm	1.00pm	2.00pm
7.10	5.20	3.00	4.00
9.00	8.05	4.50	5.45
11.00	10.00	6.35	7.30
–	–	9.00	10.00
–	–	11.00	–

Journey time: 50 minutes
Fares: same as Yung Shue Wan

Aberdeen – Mo Tat Wan – Sok Kwu Wan
Doesn't stop at Mo Tat Wan

Monday – Saturday		Sunday & Holidays	
from Aberdeen	from Sok Kwu Wan	from Aberdeen	from Sok Kwu Wan
6.45am	6.05am	8.00am	6.15am
8.00	7.25#	8.45	7.30
9.30	8.45	9.30	8.45
11.15	10.15	10.15	9.30
2.00pm	12.45pm	11.00	10.15
4.00	3.00	11.45	11.00
6.00	5.00	12.30pm	11.45
7.25	6.45	2.00	12.30pm
–	–	2.45	2.00
–	–	3.30	2.45
–	–	4.15	3.30
–	–	5.00	4.15
–	–	5.45	5.00
–	–	6.30	5.45
–	–	7.15	6.30
–	–	7.55	7.15

Gwailos attending late-night parties in the city often miss the last ferry back to the island. The solution in that case is to charter a sampan or kaido from Aberdeen. Depending on how late it is, the boat crew may want HK\$200 or more for the service. Fortunately, it's often not difficult to round up 10 other inebriated late-night revellers at the pier to split the cost!

A proposal to add a new high-speed ferry to Lamma might throw the schedule completely out of whack, but for the moment refer to the table opposite.

GETTING AROUND

Like Cheung Chau, the island has very little motorised traffic apart from some carts used to haul seafood to the restaurants. Lamma's one road was built to service the power station, but you could spend a whole day here and not see a single vehicle go by. A concrete path links the two main villages, Yung Shue Wan in the north and Sok Kwu Wan in the south, but elsewhere there are mostly overgrown dirt trails. You can walk from Yung Shue Wan to Sok Kwu Wan and there is a kaido service between Sok Kwu Wan and Mo Tat Wan (see Getting There & Away).

Lantau

Lantau means 'broken head' in Cantonese, but it also has a more appropriate name: Tai Yue Shan ('big island mountain'). And big it is – 142 sq km, almost twice the size of Hong Kong Island. Amazingly, only abut 30,000 people live here, compared to Hong Kong Island's 1.5 million. Most of those 30,000 are concentrated in just a couple of centres along the coast, mainly because the interior is so mountainous.

Lantau is believed to have been inhabited by primitive tribes before being settled by the Han Chinese. The last Sung dynasty emperor passed through here in the 13th century during his flight from the Mongol invaders. He is believed to have held court

in the Tung Chung Valley, which takes its name from a hero said to have given his life for the emperor. He's still worshipped on the island by the Hakka people, who believe he could predict the future.

Like Cheung Chau, Lantau had a reputation as a base for pirates, and is said to have been one of the favourite haunts of the 18th-century pirate Cheung Po Tsai. The island was also important to the British as a trading post long before they became interested in Hong Kong Island.

Lantau is the home of several important monasteries, including the Trappist Monastery and the Buddhist Po Lin Monastery. The Po Lin was rebuilt several years ago but lately it's become a Disneyland in miniature rather than a place of quiet retreat. On a hill above the monastery is the Tiantan Buddha Statue, the largest outdoor Buddha statue in the world. Let's hope they don't add a Ferris wheel.

MUI WO

Mui Wo ('five petal flower') is on Silvermine Bay, so named for the silver mines which were once on the outskirts of the settlement.

This is where the ferries from Hong Kong Island land. There's a swimming beach, but the waters are frequently choked with plastic bags. However, the views are fine, there are opportunities for walking and the township's not a bad place for seafood restaurants. About a third of Lantau's population lives in the township of Mui Wo and surrounding hamlets.

PUI O BEACH

A little less than five km by road from Mui Wo is the small township of Pui O. This place has recently become the overflow bedroom community for gwailos who want to get away from it all. Pui O has a decent beach.

TRAPPIST HAVEN MONASTERY

To the north-east of Mui Wo is the Trappist Monastery. The Trappist order was established by a clergyman in La Trappe, France, in 1644 and gained a reputation as one of the most austere orders of the Roman Catholic

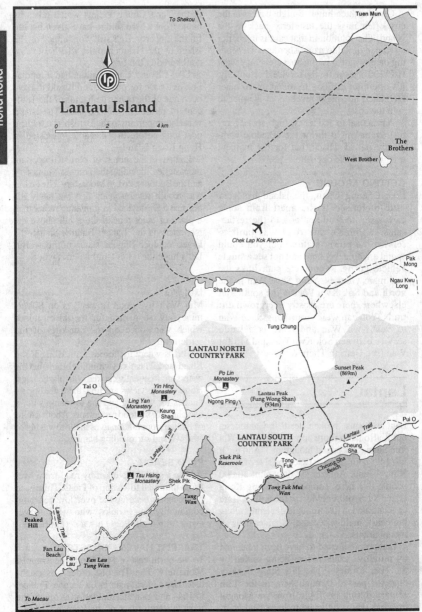

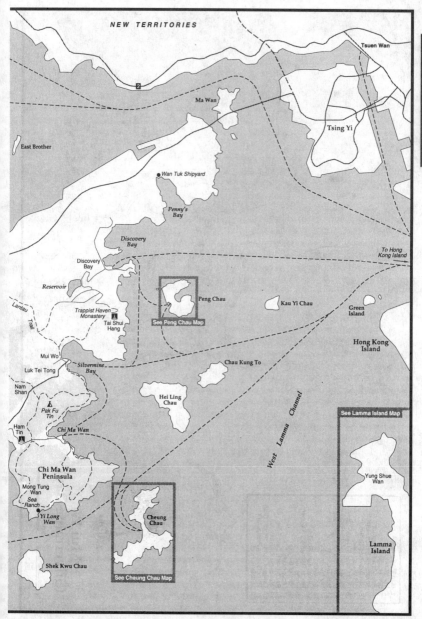

NEW TERRITORIES

Tsuen Wan

Ma Wan

Tsing Yi

East Brother

Wan Tuk Shipyard

Penny's Bay

Discovery Bay

To Hong Kong Island

Discovery Bay

Reservoir

Lantau Trail

Trappist Haven Monastery

Tai Shui Hang

Peng Chau

See Peng Chau Map

Kau Yi Chau

Green Island

Hong Kong Island

Mui Wo

Silvermine Bay

Chau Kung To

Luk Tei Tong

Nam Shan

Pak Fu Tin

Hei Ling Chau

Ham Tin

Chi Ma Wan

Chi Ma Wan Peninsula

See Lamma Island Map

Mong Tung Wan

Sea Ranch

Yi Long Wan

Cheung Chau

West Lamma Channel

Yung Shue Wan

Shek Kwu Chau

See Chaung Chau Map

Lamma Island

HONG KONG

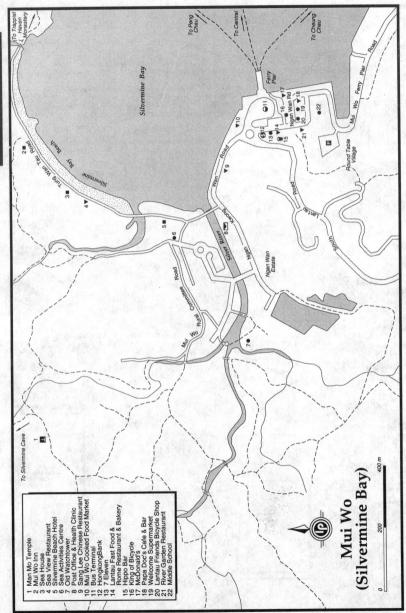

Silvermine Bay

Tung Wan Tau Road

Silvermine Bay Beach

To Trappist Haven Monastery

To Silvermine Cave

Mui Wo Rural Committee Road

Silver River

Ngan

Wan Road

Ngan Wan Estate

To Peng Chau

To Central

To Cheung Chau

Ferry Pier

Ngan Wan Rd

Mui Wo Ferry Pier Road

Lantau South Road

Round Table Village

Mui Wo
(Silvermine Bay)

0   200   400 m

1 Man Mo Temple
2 Mui Wo Inn
3 Sea House
4 Sea View Restaurant
5 Silvermine Beach Hotel
6 Sea Activities Centre
7 Old Watchtower
8 Post Office & Health Clinic
9 Sang Lee Chinese Restaurant
10 Mui Wo Cooked Food Market
11 Bus Terminal
12 HongkongBank
13 7 Eleven
14 Lantau Fast Food &
   Rome Restaurant & Bakery
15 Hippo Bar
16 King of Bicycle
17 McDonald's
18 Papa Doc's Cafe & Bar
19 Wellcome Supermarket
20 Lantau Friends Bicycle Shop
21 River Garden Restaurant
22 Middle School

church. The Lantau order was established in Beijing. The Lantau monks run a dairy farm and sell the milk locally.

The monastery is not for those who like wild nightlife as the monks have all taken a vow of silence; there are signs asking visitors to keep their radios and cassette players turned off and to speak in low tones. If it's a carnival you're after then try the Po Lin Monastery on a weekend.

You can get to the monastery by taking a ferry to Peng Chau then crossing over on a kaido for HK$3; the kaidos leave from a small pier just to the south of the main ferry pier on Peng Chau. En route to Discovery Bay, *they only stop at the monastery if you ask them to.* There is no extra charge, but if you don't say anything the kaidos will probably go directly to Discovery Bay. From the monastery you can easily walk to Discovery Bay (the coastal walk takes about one hour). You can also walk between the monastery and Mui Wo, but the trail is very steep in parts.

NGONG PING

Perched 500m up in the western hills of Lantau is the Ngong Ping region, the major

drawcard for Hong Kong day-trippers and foreign tourists.

Po Lin Monastery

The original temple was built in 1921, but the place has undergone considerable renovation since then. Today, Po Lin ('precious lotus') is a Buddhist retreat-cum-fairground. It's a large temple complex of mostly new buildings with the simpler, older buildings tucked away behind them. From here the warm hand of friendship is offered not just to tourists but also to local film and television companies, who frequently use it as a set.

On a hill above the monastery is the largest outdoor **Buddha statue** in the world. The statue is 22m high – 34m if you include the pedestal. The current statue replaces an earlier one on the same site – the one you see now was dedicated on 29 December, 1993, after more than 10 years of construction. There has been at least one concession to good taste – the statue is not the fat, jolly Buddha often portrayed in tacky souvenir shops. The Birthday of Buddha, around May, is a good time to be here.

Whatever you do, try to avoid visiting on a weekend. The place is flooded with day-

Po Lin, on Lantau Island, is Hong Kong's largest Buddhist monastery and features an impressive statue of Buddha.

Ready for Takeoff

It's amazing that Lantau has more or less escaped the development schemes which turned Hong Kong Island into a skyscraper jungle. More than 50% of Lantau is made up of country parks. Unfortunately, this tranquillity is severely threatened by the new airport on Chek Lap Kok Island, just off the north coast of Lantau.

The airport is built on reclaimed land, which meant chopping off the tops of nearby mountains and using the rubble to fill in the sea, and will link Lantau to the New Territories with bridges, a six-lane highway and a high-speed train to Hong Kong Island via a third cross-harbour tunnel. With that much infrastructure in place, high-rise housing developments are expected to follow fast.

China originally opposed the project, mostly to harass Hong Kong as punishment for accepting the democratic reforms introduced by Governor Chris Patten. However, with the approach of 1997, Hong Kong's new landlords finally figured out that the construction delays were adding to the project's total cost – which ultimately comes out of China's pocket.

Given its negative impact on Lantau's largely unspoilt surroundings, the airport project had its local opponents. However, Hong Kong has never been strong on Green politics and the northern side of Lantau will develop regardless of what the environmentalists think.

The early stages of construction were carried out, quite literally, by the British. That is, most of the blue-collar labour was supplied by young British construction workers. With considerable smug satisfaction, *Wen Wei Po* (China's mouthpiece newspaper in Hong Kong) has noted the use of British 'coolie labour' to do the dirty work. More ominously, Beijing decried the introduction of so much British 'filth' into the colony, and expressed concern that all these gwailo workers might not ever leave. For their part, the 'filth' did not made themselves popular with the locals – keeping to themselves and earning a reputation for hard drinking and occasional fighting. This led many of the old-timers to express their gratitude that at least Lantau doesn't have a soccer stadium. ∎

trippers with their radios and families, and consequently you're more likely to trip over a toy than a meditating monk.

Since this is a monastery, visitors are requested to observe some decorum in dress and behaviour. Also, it is prohibited to bring meat into the grounds.

You can also spend the night here, though one traveller had a nasty early-morning encounter:

I was attacked by three dogs near Po Lin Monastery while walking around at sunrise. The stable manager was there and did nothing to call off the dogs. I just began to holler at them very loudly and backed off while they stood there, teeth bared and growling. So be careful of all the dogs!

Johanna Polsenberg

Lantau Tea Gardens

Beside the Po Lin Monastery are the Lantau Tea Gardens (☎ 2985-5718), the only tea gardens in Hong Kong. The tea bushes are in sad shape, but that hardly matters – the emphasis is on commercial tourism. There are horses for hire, and sitting on one for 10 minutes to get your photo taken costs HK$50; 30 minutes of riding is HK$150; one hour is HK$250, and you are supposed to

ride with a minimum group size of three persons. Riding lessons are also available. The tea plantation also operates an outdoor skating rink which is in incredibly bad condition and is deserted on weekdays, but can be noisy with screaming kids on weekends. Skate rental costs HK$25 per hour.

Lantau Peak

Also known as Fung Wong Shan, this mountain, at 934m, is the second-highest peak in Hong Kong. Only Tai Mo Shan in the New Territories is higher. The views from the summit of Lantau Peak are stunning and on a clear day it is possible to see Macau. Unfortunately, a number of cretins have trashed the summit with plastic wrappers, styrofoam lunch boxes and drink cans.

The easiest way to make the climb is to spend the night at the Po Lin Monastery, tea gardens or the SG Davis Youth Hostel. Get up at the crack of dawn and head for the summit. Many climbers get up earlier and try to reach the summit to see the sunrise. The trail begins just to the east of the tea plantation and there is an information board there.

LANTAU TRAIL

This footpath, 70 km long, runs the length of the island along the mountain tops and then doubles back along the coast. At a normal pace, the estimated walking time for the entire trip (not allowing for rests) is 23.5 hours. Unless you're a marathon runner you probably won't cover it in one day, though no doubt someone will try.

A more realistic approach is to do the middle section of the trail (the highest and most scenic part), which goes over Lantau Peak and is easily accessible from the Po Lin Monastery at Ngong Ping. From Ngong Ping to Mui Wo, via Lantau and Sunset Peaks, it is 17.5 km and it is estimated to take at least seven hours.

The western part of the trail – along the south-western coast of Lantau – is also very scenic. Note that the first section of the Lantau Trail is all along South Lantau Rd. There's an alternative path from Mui Wo to Nam Sham, via Luk Tei Tong.

Equip yourself with food, water, rain gear and UV (sunblock) lotion. Shops are few and far between along the trail. Cool drinks are available at Fan Lau in the south-west corner of the island. The next opportunity occurs three hours later at Tai O. Other refreshment spots are Ngong Ping, Pui O and Mui Wo. Start out early, allowing yourself plenty of time to reach civilisation or a campsite.

If you're going to walk on this route, it would be wise to pick up the *Lantau Trail* map, published by the Country Parks Authority and available from the Government Publications Centre in the Government Offices Building, 66 Queensway, Admiralty (see Maps in the Facts for the Visitor chapter).

TAI O

For many years this village was the largest settlement on the island, but it's now in decline. A hundred years ago, along with Tung Chung village, Tai O was an important trading and fishing port, exporting salt and fish to China. The salt pans are still there but are almost unused. The locals make a living from duck farming, fishing, rice growing, making shrimp paste and processing salt

fish. However, young people disdain these professions and the population is declining. Processing tourists has in recent years become a major contributor to the economy.

Tai O is built partly on Lantau and partly on a tiny island a few metres from the shore – two women pull a rope-drawn boat across the creek. This ferry service could easily be replaced with a modern bridge but no one wants this as the ferry is one of the most photographed things in town. The cost for the ferry is HK$1. For HK$10 you can take a sampan tour of the village.

A few of the old-style village houses still stand, but most are being replaced by modern concrete houses. There are still many stilt houses on the waterfront as well as other shanties, including houseboats that haven't set sail for years and have been extended in such a way that they never could again. But many of these old structures have been abandoned and are slowly decaying. It's an interesting place all the same, but there are some pretty powerful odours from the fish-processing industry. The local temple is dedicated to the god of war, Kuanti.

FAN LAU

Fan Lau on the south-west tip of Lantau has a couple of very good beaches and an old fort, very overgrown but with a good view. From Tai O village, it's a couple of hours clamber along the coastal section of the Lantau Trail.

CHEUNG SHA BEACH & TONG FUK

Buses head to the Po Lin Monastery from Mui Wo along the road that hugs the southern coast. There are long stretches of good beaches (with occasional good surf) from Cheung Sha to Tong Fuk on the south coast of Lantau. Both are major tourist-beach centres. There is also a prison in Tong Fuk – but at least it's a scenic prison.

SHEK PIK RESERVOIR

At Tong Fuk the bus starts to go inland around the Shek Pik Reservoir (completed in 1963), which provides Lantau with its drinking water. Underwater pipes also supply

Cheung Chau and parts of Hong Kong Island with fresh water from this reservoir. It's considered a pretty place with forest plantations and picnic spots, but the prison spoils the view. If you're feeling fit, you can walk down from Ngong Ping.

CHI MA WAN

Chi Ma Wan, the peninsula in the south-east, takes its name from the large prison here. You can walk down through the Chi Ma Wan Peninsula to the beaches at Yi Long and Tai Long, but arm yourself with a map. You can also get there by kaido from Cheung Chau, though it stops at the prison and you may be asked what you're doing around there.

At the southern end of the peninsula is Sea Ranch, an upscale residential area which might be described as a 'weekend Discovery Bay'. It's not really geared towards tourism – more towards well-to-do Hong Kongers whose villas here mostly get used on weekends.

A ferry runs from Central twice daily on weekdays but much more frequently on weekends. It costs HK$25 on weekdays, HK$30 on weekends, and special bookings (☎ 2989-2128) can be made by ringing up the office between 9.30 am and 9 pm daily.

TUNG CHUNG

This relatively flat farming region is centred around the village of Tung Chung, on the northern shore of Lantau. There are several Buddhist establishments in the upper reaches of the valley, but the main attraction is the 19th-century Tung Chung Fort, which still has its old cannon pointing out to sea. The fort dates back to 1817, when Chinese troops were garrisoned on Lantau, and the area was also used as a base by the infamous pirate Cheung Po Tsai. The Japanese briefly occupied it during WWII, but found it of little military use and soon abandoned the neighbourhood. The fort was completely restored in 1988.

About one km to the north is the much smaller Tung Chung Battery, another fort built around the same town. All that remains is a wall, the rest of it having fallen down.

Currently, there are no plans for restoration. These ruins were only discovered in 1980, having been hidden for about a century by vegetation.

Relatively few tourists come here because of the poor transportation. This will change with the completion of the new Chek Lap Kok airport as Tung Chung becomes another Kowloon-style housing estate. In the meantime, it's a peaceful place. You can walk from the Lantau Tea Gardens in Ngong Ping down to Tung Chung (five km) in two hours and then take the bus back. Otherwise hike from Mui Wo to Tung Chung – this takes about 4.5 hours and meanders through old Hakka villages before reaching the coast and the farming settlement. Hiking from Tai O to Tung Chung takes about five hours.

DISCOVERY BAY

Discovery Bay was discovered by real estate developers around 1975. Nearly everyone thought they were crazy trying to build luxury condominiums in a remote corner of Lantau. To make the long commutation tolerable, high-speed ferries were introduced. A massive advertising campaign had to be launched to draw in buyers and renters for the condos – 'Discover Discovery Bay' was the slogan. The cynics laughed and predicted early bankruptcy for the whole project.

Now it's the developers who are laughing all the way to the bank. The massive building boom is continuing at a feverish pace and rents are just as high as Mid-Levels on Hong Kong Island.

The bay is definitely a gwailo community, and the gwailos live high. The Chinese minority that lives here is definitely in the upper-income bracket. The golf course and yacht club make it pretty clear that it's no place for the Chungking Mansions budget crowd. Tourists are not particularly welcomed, and there's a distinct lack of hotels (though renting a holiday flat might be possible).

Law and order is maintained by a private security force, and even the leash laws for controlling dogs are strictly enforced. There is no rubbish on the ground and the beautiful beach is so spotless you'd swear they employ

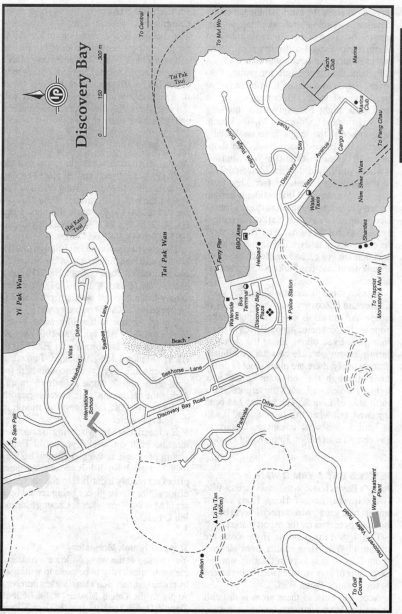

Discovery Bay

servants to wash the sand. All the necessary cleaning, sweeping and polishing is performed by a crew of Filipinos, many of whom live in a small collection of squatters' shacks hidden in a cove south of town.

Perhaps the main reason for visiting Discovery Bay is to compare it with the rest of the Outlying Islands. When you step off the ferry, you might be forgiven for thinking you've landed at California's Malibu Beach. Appropriately, the locals have unofficially renamed the place 'Disco Bay'. The shopping mall has the best from the West, and this is where you'll find the first McDonald's in all the Outlying Islands. In fact, Discovery Bay is so Westernised that residents hop on the ferry to nearby Peng Chau to eat Chinese food, shop at a traditional market and remind themselves that they are indeed living just off the coast of China. Heading in the opposite direction are Peng Chau residents, in search of junk food and the Park 'N' Shop supermarket.

Besides some pleasant walks in the steep hills around Discovery Bay, the other way to escape the crowd is on a mountain bike. None are for rent here, so you'll need to bring your own. Even biking along the streets is fairly pleasant because cars are prohibited. Unfortunately, there are plans afoot to drill a tunnel through the mountain to the new highway which will reach the airport on the north side of Lantau. The project has been approved, but when this is completed it will be hard to see what advantage Discovery Bay can offer to life on Hong Kong Island.

PENNY'S BAY & YAM O WAN

Penny's Bay is home to the main yard of Wan Tuk shipyard, one of Hong Kong's most famous boat yards, which specialises in building sailing cruisers for the export market.

The biggest log ponds in Hong Kong are at Yam O Wan. Here timber from all over South-East Asia is kept in floating storage. Large rafts of logs are often seen being towed by tug towards Tsuen Wan.

Access to both of these areas is difficult unless you have your own boat.

PLACES TO STAY

Camping

The cheapest accommodation on Lantau is the government-run campsites at Pak Fu Tin and near Pui O, Nam Shan and many places along the south coast. The *Countryside* map or the HKTA *Hostels, Campsites and Other Accommodation in Hong Kong* leaflet will tell you where they are. There is no camping charge at most of these sites.

Mui Wo

At Mui Wo, turn to your right as you exit the ferry pier – the beach and all places to stay are in this direction along Tung Wan Tau Rd. One of the best deals around is the *Mui Wo Inn* (☎ 2984-1916), with doubles from HK$243 to HK$435 on weekdays, and HK$435 to HK$565 on weekends.

There's a place with no English sign, but it's No 23 Tung Wan Tau Rd and offers beachside accommodation starting from HK$250 for a double. *Sea House* (☎ 2984-7757) has rather dumpy-looking rooms starting from HK$200 on weekdays, HK$400 on weekends.

Top of the line is the *Silvermine Beach Hotel* (☎ 2984-8295; fax 2984-1907) which has 135 rooms. Doubles go for HK$860 to HK$1200 plus a 15% surcharge. Two stars. There are some very good discounts here for long-term rentals (one month or more) during the off season. One traveller negotiated a rate of HK$7500 for a full month in the dead of winter.

If you arrive at Mui Wo during the summer months, even on weekdays, you'll find a swarm of people at the pier renting holiday flats. Not much English is spoken, but these places are readily identified by the photos on display. Not all the places being rented here are in Mui Wo – many are at Cheung Sha and Pui O beaches.

Trappist Haven Monastery

You can stay at the vow-of-silence monastery, but applications have to be made in writing or by phone (no, they don't have a silent number). Apply to the Grand Master (☎ 2987-6286), Trappist Haven, Lantau Island, PO Box 5, Peng

RICHARD I'ANSON

RICHARD I'ANSON

RICHARD I'ANSON

Top: The Ten Thousand Buddhas Monastery, Sha Tin, is reached after climbing over 400 stairs through a pleasant wood of trees and bamboo.
Bottom Left: Ten Thousand Buddhas Monastery, Sha Tin.
Bottom Right: Statues of Buddha's followers surround the monastery.

ROBERT STOREY

TONY WHEELER

NICKO GONCHAROFF

Top Left: Trappist Haven Monastery, Lantau, is a quiet refuge.
Top Right: Po Lin Monastery, also on Lantau Island, features a huge Buddha statue.
Bottom: Room at the top. A shade pavilion on Lamma Island offers sanctuary from the noise and confusion of Hong Kong.

Chau, Hong Kong. Men and women must sleep in separate dorms.

Ngong Ping

People who stay at Ngong Ping normally do so to climb nearby Lantau Peak in time to catch the sunrise.

A 10-minute walk to the east of the Lantau Tea Gardens is the YHA's *SG Davis Youth Hostel* (☎ 2985-5610), which has dormitory beds (52 beds available) and a campsite (a YHA card is required for camping too). Dorm beds cost HK$25. The hostel is often closed on weekdays. If you visit in winter be sure to bring warm clothing – evenings can be amazingly chilly at this elevation. To get there from Mui Wo, catch bus No 2. From the bus stop in Ngong Ping, it's a 10-minute walk (facing the giant Buddha statue, take the paved path to your left, walk past the horse stables and turn left at the hostel sign). Although vegetarian food is available at the monastery, if you need additional munchies you'd best bring them from Mui Wo.

Also at Ngong Ping is the *Tea Garden Hotel* (☎ 2985-5161) which has some truly grotty single rooms with shared bath for HK$170 on weekdays. Slightly better rooms for two persons on week days/weekends cost HK$200/300.

Chi Ma Wan

The HKYHA and Jockey Club jointly operate the beach-side *Mong Tung Wan Hostel* (☎ 2984-1389) in the south-east corner of the island on the Chi Ma Wan Peninsula. Beds cost HK$25 and camping is permitted.

From Mui Wo, take the bus to Pui O, then walk along the road to Ham Tin. At the junction of Chi Ma Wan Rd and the temple, take the footpath to Mong Tung Wan, about a 45-minute walk. An alternative route is to take a ferry to Cheung Chau island, and hire a sampan to the jetty at Mong Tung Wan – a sampan carries about 10 people.

PLACES TO EAT
Mui Wo

As you exit the ferry, just to your right is the *Mui Wo Cooked Food Market* which harbours a large number of food stalls. Unfortunately, the food isn't all that great; the restaurants are not too clean; English menus are lacking; and foreigners are frequently overcharged.

If you continue past the market towards the beach, you'll soon come to *San Lee Chinese Restaurant*. The food here is good, the staff speak some English, they can provide you with an English menu and prices are reasonable. They can do vegetarian cooking too.

The most expat-oriented pub/restaurant in town is *Papa Doc's Bar & Cafe* (☎ 2984-9003) at 3 Ngan Wan Rd. It's just beyond the Wellcome supermarket.

Hippo Bar & Cafe (☎ 2984-9876) is another Western-style bar/restaurant combination, but this one attracts far more local Chinese than expats. This place is hidden in a narrow alley just behind the *Rome Restaurant & Bakery*.

Pui O

This mini-town can boast one Australian-owned pub & grub spot, *Charlie's* (☎ 2984-8329), where you can dine outdoors under sun umbrellas. The extensive menu includes Cantonese, Indian and Western food. Business here seems to be booming – on weekends you might need a reservation. Open from 11 am to 3 pm, and from 5 to 11 pm; closed on Wednesday.

The *Thai Restaurant* has excellent food and has become a major expat hang-out – many say it's the best restaurant on the island, and it would be hard to disagree. Prices are reasonable.

At the time of writing, a South African-style restaurant called *The Gallery* is planning to open in Pui O (the owners are just waiting for their liquor licence). One of these restaurants is already established in nearby Tong Fuk (see below).

Tong Fuk

The Gallery has a theme unique in Hong Kong: a South African barbecue. You can fill up on sausage, steak and salad for between HK$75 and HK$90. At HK$25, beer here is cheaper than elsewhere on Lantau. This very

Hong Kong – Lantau Island Ferry Schedule

Central – Mui Wo

Monday to Saturday		Sunday & Holidays	
from Central	*from Mui Wo*	*from Central*	*from Mui Wo*
7.00am*	6.10am*	7.00am*	6.10am*
8.30	7.00	8.00#	7.00*
9.30	7.15*	8.30	8.15*
10.30	8.30	9.00#	9.30
11.30	9.30	9.30	10.30
12.30pm	10.30	10.00#	11.30
1.30	11.30	10.30	12.30pm
2.00!	12.30pm	11.00#	1.30
2.30	1.30	11.30	2.30
3.00!	2.30	12.30pm	3.00#
3.30	3.30	1.30	3.30
4.30	4.30	2.30	4.00#
5.30	5.30	3.30	4.30
6.30	6.30	4.30	5.00#
7.30	7.30	5.30	5.30
8.30	9.00*	6.30	6.00#
9.00*	10.00*	7.45*	6.30
10.00*	11.10*	8.50*	7.30
11.15*	–	10.00*	9.00*
12.20am	–	11.15*	10.00*

* *Via Peng Chau*
! *Optional sailing on Saturday only*   # *Optional sailing*
Journey time: Mui Wo – Hong Kong Island one hour, via Peng Chau 70 minutes

Fares:	Class	Week days	Weekends
	Deluxe	adult HK$16	adult HK$30
		child HK$16	child HK$16
	ordinary	adult HK$8.50	adult HK$11.50
		child/senior HK$4.30	child/senior HK$6

Hoverferries: Central – Mui Wo

Monday – Friday except Holidays	
from Central	*from Mui Wo*
9.40am	10.20am
11.20	12.10pm
2.25pm	3.10
4.25	5.10

Journey time: 30 minutes
Fares: adult HK$22, child & senior HK$11.50

popular place is only open on Friday, Saturday, Sunday and public holidays.

Ngong Ping

Po Lin Monastery has a good reputation for its vegetarian food. In the monastery's large canteen HK$60 gets you a big plate of spring rolls, mushrooms, vegetables and rice. There is also a 'de luxe lunch' for HK$100. You'll get more variety in the dishes if you bring some friends along to share the meal with you.

If you'd prefer to eat meat, the place to go is the *Tea Gardens Restaurant*. Facing the giant Buddha, take the paved footpath to your left and continue past the horse stables. The restaurant is on your left, close to the SG Davis Youth Hostel.

Central – Discovery Bay
From Central: 6.50 am - 12.30 am, every 10-30 minutes, 1, 2, 3.30, 5 & 6.30 am
From Discovery Bay: 6.20 am - 12.20 am, every 10-30 minutes, 1.20, 2.50, 4.20 & 5.50 am
Fares: adults HK$23, child HK$12

New Territories – Lantau

Saturdays

from Central	*from Tuen Muen*	*from Sha Lo Wan*	*from Tai O*
9.15am	10.40am	11.20am	11.50am
3.00pm	4.25pm	5.05pm	5.35pm

Saturdays

from Tai O	*from Sha Lo Wan*	*from Tuen Muen*
11.50am	12.20pm	1.00
5.45pm	6.15	6.55

Sunday & Holidays

from Central	*from Tuen Muen*	*from Sha Lo Wan*	*from Tai O*
8.15am	9.40am	10.20am	10.50am
–	4.15pm	4.55pm	5.25pm

from Tai O	*from Sha Lo Wan*	*from Tuen Muen*	*from Central*
3.00pm	3.30pm	4.10pm	–
5.30	6.00	6.40	8.20pm

from Tsuen Wan	*from Tuen Mun*	*from Sha Lo Wan*	*from Tai O*
8.00am	8.45am	9.15am	9.45am

from Tai O	*from Sha Lo Wan*	*from Tuen Mun*	*from Tsuen Wan*
4.45pm	5.15pm	5.45pm	6.30pm

Central – Sea Ranch

Monday to Friday		Saturday		Sunday & Holidays	
from Central	*from Sea Ranch*	*from Central*	*from Sea Ranch*	*from Central*	*from Sea Ranch*
8.15am	7.30am	8.15am	7.30am	10.00am	9.00am
6.30pm	5.15pm	12.30pm	11.45	12.45pm	noon
–	–	2.00	1.15pm	2.15	1.30pm
–	–	5.45	5.00	5.45	5.00
–	–	7.15	6.30	8.15	7.30

Tai O

This village is famous for its seafood restaurants, which are mostly unnamed. There is a decent Chinese restaurant with no English sign – to get there, cross the creek on the hand-pulled boat, then go straight up to the end of the road. The restaurant is directly in front of you at the T-intersection.

Discovery Bay

The *Waterside Inn* (☎ 2987-0063), shop G01, is in the commercial plaza near the ferry pier. It's a restaurant and pub with a terrace overlooking the scenic waterfront and is chock- a-block with gwailos on a Saturday night.

The other trendy place in town for pub grub is *Ebeneezer's* (☎ 2987-0036) which is in the commercial plaza at shop G06.

McDonald's needs no introduction, but right next to it is *Cajun's*, offering spicy takeaway fried chicken (eat it at the picnic tables in the centre of the mall).

Upstairs from McDonald's is *Siam Palace Thai Food*, *Jojo's Indian Food*, *Lunch Box* (Italian) and the *Discovery Bay Restaurant* (dim sum and other Chinese).

Lantau Bus Schedule

Route No 1: Mui Wo – Tai O
Departs: Mui Wo about every 30 minutes between 6 am and 1.30 am.
Departs: Tai O about every 30 minutes between 5.15 am and 10.15 pm.
Journey time: 40 minutes.

Fares:	Class	Monday – Saturday	Sunday & Holidays
	air-con	adult HK$11	adult HK$17.50
		child HK$5.50	child HK$8.80
	ordinary	adult HK$7.50	adult HK$12
		child/senior HK$3.80	child/senior HK$6

Route No 2: Mui Wo – Ngong Ping

Monday to Saturday

from Mui Wo	from Ngong Ping
8.20am	7.00am
9.35	8.30
10.35	9.30
11.35	10.30
12.35pm	11.30
1.35	12.30pm
2.35	1.30
3.35	2.30
4.35	3.30
5.35	4.30
6.35	5.30
–	6.30
–	7.30

Sunday & Public Holidays
Departs: Mui Wo about every 30 minutes between 8.20 am and 6.30 pm.
Departs: Ngong Ping about every 30 minutes between 7 am and 7.30 pm.
Journey time: 45 minutes.

Fares:	Class	Monday – Saturday	Sunday & Holidays
	air-con	adult HK$14.50	everyone HK$23
		child/senior HK$7.30	
	ordinary	adult HK$9.50	adult HK$16
		child/senior HK$4.80	child HK$8

Route No 3: Mui Wo – Tung Chung

Monday to Saturday		Sunday & Holidays	
from Mui Wo	from Tung Chung	from Mui Wo	from Tung Chung
6.40am	6.00am	6.40am	6.00am
7.45	7.20	7.50	7.20
7.50	8.35	9.35	8.35
9.35	10.30	10.35	10.30
10.35	11.30	11.35	11.30
11.35	1.30pm	1.35pm	1.30pm
1.35pm	2.30	2.35	2.30
2.35	3.30	3.35	3.30
3.35	4.30	4.35	4.00*
4.35	5.30	6.35	4.30
6.35	6.15	–	5.30
–	7.30	–	6.30
–	7.15	–	7.15

* Optional
Journey time: 45 minutes.

Fares:	Monday – Saturday	Sunday & Holidays
	adult HK$6.60	adult HK$10.50
	child/senior HK$3.30	child/senior HK$5.30

Route No 4: Mui Wo – Tong Fuk
Approximately once hourly during daytime.

Route No 5: Mui Wo – Shek Pik
Approximately once hourly during daytime.

Route No 7: Mui Wo – Pui O
Weekdays: Depart Mui Wo 8.15 am, 9.30 am
then once hourly until 5.30 pm
(optionally until 9.30 pm).
Departs: Pui O 6.40 am, 8.10 am, 8.45 am,
10 am then once hourly until 5 pm.

Sunday & Holidays:
Departs: Mui Wo 8.15 am, 9 am then once
every 30 minutes until 7 pm.
Departs: Pui O 8.30 at, 9.15 am, 9.45 am
then once every 30 minutes until 5.45 pm
(6.15 pm optional).

Route No 21: Tai O – Ngong Ping

from Tai O	from Ngong Ping
7.45am	7.30am
10.00	10.15
11.00	11.15
noon	12.15 pm
1.00pm	1.15
2.00	2.15
3.00	3.15
–	4.15*
–	5.00

* *Sunday & Holidays only*
Journey time: 18 minutes

Fares:

Class	Monday – Saturday	Sunday & Holidays
air-con	adult HK$5.80 child/senior HK$2.90	everyone HK$12
ordinary	adult HK$4 child/senior HK$2	adult HK$8.30 child HK$4.20

Route No 23: Tung Chung – Ngong Ping
Sunday & Holidays only

from Tung Chung	from Ngong Ping
10.15am	11.20am
11.15	12.20pm
12.15pm	1.20
1.15	2.20
2.15	3.20

Journey time: 45 minutes
Fare: HK$16, no discounts for
children or seniors.

On the ground level is *Seoul Garden*
(☎ 2987-0073), a Korean restaurant. The *New
Garden Food Court* does cafeteria-style Chinese
fast food and Western breakfasts. Buried within
the shopping mall is *Mövenpick*, known for its
premium Swiss ice cream.

Uncle Russ is a Hong Kong chain of stand-
up coffee bars with good muffins, cakes and
brownies.

GETTING THERE & AWAY
Most frequent are the Hong Kong-Mui Wo ferries
and Discovery Bay ferries. It's easy to imagine
that there will be a major change in the Discovery
Bay ferry schedule when the new bridge and
tunnel open, which will allow a direct bus service
between Discovery Bay and Kowloon.

The inter-island ferry connects Lantau with
Peng Chau and Cheung Chau. There is also a
small ferry between Peng Chau and Discovery
Bay, as well as some late-night 'water taxis' for
about HK$150.

There are boats sailing on Saturday,
Sunday and public holidays to Tai O on the
west end of the island. The boats run from
either Tuen Mun or Tsuen Wan, in the New
Territories, to Tai O via Sha Lo Wan on the
northern side of Lantau. One of the boats begins at Central (see timetables on pages 258 and
259 for details).

GETTING AROUND
Bus
Services run by the New Lantau Bus Company all leave from the car park by the ferry
pier in Mui Wo. On most routes the schedule
is increased during weekends and public holidays to handle the flood of tourists, and bus
No 23 runs on weekends and public holidays
only. For bus routes and schedules see pages
260 and 261.

Taxi
If you think the bus service is lacking, just wait
until you try Lantau taxis. In supposedly free-
market Hong Kong, Lantau taxi drivers are a
protected lot. The number of taxis is inade-
quate, they will not pick you up along country
roads where you desperately need them and are

generally hostile to customers. It's easiest to find taxis in Mui Wo and occasionally in Tong Fuk – elsewhere, they are a rare item indeed.

Bicycle

The best place by far to hire is Lantau Friends Bicycle Shop (☎ 2984-8385), opposite the Park 'N' Shop in the centre of Mui Wo.

During summer, bikes can also be hired on weekends from stalls in front of the Silvermine Bay Beach Hotel in Mui Wo, and from stalls in Pui O.

Hitching

Forget it. I even tried it accompanied by a Chinese girl who looked totally harmless – we didn't have a crumb of success.

Peng Chau

Shaped like a horseshoe, tiny Peng Chau is just under one sq km in area. It is inhabited by around 8000 souls, making it far more densely populated than nearby Lantau.

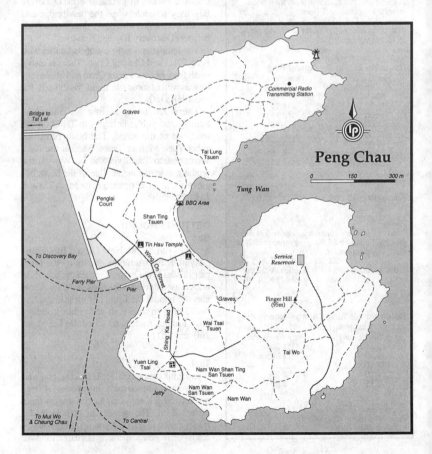

The island is not especially beautiful, but it still has its charms. Of all the islands mentioned in this chapter, Peng Chau is perhaps the most traditionally Chinese – narrow alleys, crowded housing, a good outdoor market (near the ferry pier) and heaps of closet-sized restaurants and shops. There are a couple of small temples. Island residents claim that this is the last bit of traditional Hong Kong that remains. Indeed, the main reminder that you are still in modern-day Hong Kong is the 7-Eleven store.

Unfortunately, the government recently built the 'modern' yellow and green Penglai Court Housing Estate on Peng Chau, an abomination deplored more by the island's few gwailos than by the Chinese majority. And the new Monterey Villas are going up right near the ferry pier. Furthermore, on a clear day you can easily see the rapidly-growing skyscraper forest across the water in Discovery Bay.

Until recently, the island's economy was supported by fishing and some tiny cottage industries (notably the manufacture of furniture, porcelain and metal tubes). However, the manufacturing industries are all but dead, having moved to China where cheap labour is plentiful and no one worries much about industrial safety or pollution. Nowadays, weekend tourists contribute significantly to Peng Chau's coffers – Hong Kongers head straight for the seafood restaurants and spend a small fortune on banquet-sized meals. The waitresses are as likely as not to be Filipinas, as young Hong Kong women prefer working in the air-conditioned office towers of Central.

There are no cars on Peng Chau and you can walk around it with ease in an hour. Climbing the island's highest point, Finger Hill (95m), will give you some light exercise and excellent views when the weather is clear. Unfortunately, most of Peng Chau's sewage, plastic bags and styrofoam wind up in the sea, making the otherwise pleasant beach on the east side of the island too dirty for swimming.

PLACES TO EAT

Two popular pub/restaurant combinations are a big hit with the gwailos. The larger of the two, the *Sea Breeze Club* (☎ 2983-8785), at 38 Wing Hing St, is known for its fine T-bone steak dinners. The food is good and reasonably priced that residents from nearby Discovery Bay take the ferry across just to eat here. It packs out on Sunday, especially in the afternoon.

The *Forest Pub* (☎ 2983-8837) is just next door at No 38C. It's a small but cosy place with good pub grub. It owes much of its ambience to the friendly owner, an expat New Zealander.

GETTING THERE & AWAY

The interesting thing about Peng Chau is that you have a lot of options. Most people arrive by the regular ferries from Central, but there are also hoverferries on that route. Additionally, there is the inter-island ferry which can take you to Mui Wo and Cheung Chau, or a smaller ferry to the Trappist Haven Monastery and Discovery Bay. You can also hire water taxis to Discovery Bay.

Tung Lung Chau

Guarding the eastern entrance to Victoria Harbour is remote Tung Lung Chau ('east dragon island'). The island's position was at one time considered strategic to protect the harbour, but in this age of jet aircraft and missiles it hardly matters. Tung Lung Fort on the north-east corner of the island was eventually abandoned and is now preserved as a historical site. Pirates no doubt used the island as a staging post, but there is little remaining evidence of their presence.

Humans have apparently been on Tung Lung Chau for a long time. The north-west corner of the island has some ancient rock carvings, the largest ever found in Hong Kong. No one knows who the original artists were and the carvings are simply classified as dating back to the Bronze Age. They are believed to represent a dragon, which may be another way of saying nobody really knows what kind of animal it is. Except for nomadic bands of weekend tourists, the island is now uninhabited.

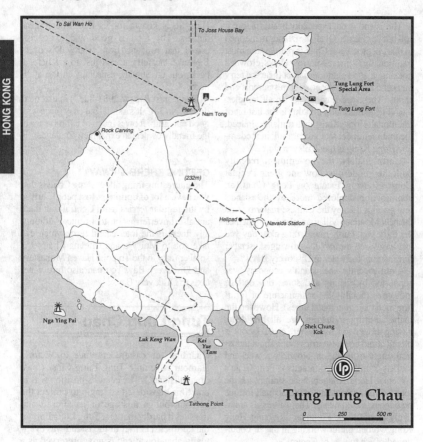

Tung Lung Chau

0   250   500 m

Unless you have your own boat or charter one, the only time you can visit Tung Lung Chau is on weekends. The one-way fare is HK$10. Kaidos depart from Sai Wan Ho just east of Quarry Bay on Hong Kong Island, stop at Tung Lung Chau and then continue to Joss House Bay in the New Territories. The ride to Joss House Bay is significantly shorter than the trip from Sai Wan Ho, and you could go by one route and return by the other. From Joss House Bay you can get buses to Choi Hung MTR station in Kowloon. Service is offered by Lam Kee Kaido (☎ 2560-9929), and if you want to charter a boat then get a Cantonese speaker to

ring them up. A minimum of 30 persons is usual when chartering a kaido, though you can have fewer people if you pay more. The weekend schedule is as follows:

Sai Wan Ho – Tung Lung Chau

	Saturday		Sunday & Holidays	
	from Sai Wan Ho	from Tung Lung	from Sai Wan Ho	from Tung Lung
	8.30am	4.00pm	8.15am	2.00pm
	3.30pm	–	9.40am	3.00pm
	–	–	4.00pm	–

Po Toi

Po Toi is a rocky island off the south-east coast of Hong Kong Island. There is a small number of permanent residents, but who knows how much longer before they finally give up their peaceful outpost and migrate to the sin and glitter of the city just beyond their shores.

This is one of the least visited islands, and that fact alone may make it worth the trip. From Monday to Saturday tourists are scarce to nonexistent, but on Sunday there is the usual migration of city-bound Hong Kongers looking for a day in the countryside and a seafood dinner.

Ferries to Po Toi depart from Aberdeen on Tuesday, Thursday and Saturday at 9 am. They return from Po Toi at 10.30 am, which means that if you want to explore the island, you must stay overnight. However, on Sunday, there are three boats, so you can go and return the same day. The earliest Sunday boat departs from Aberdeen at 8 am. There are two Sunday boats departing from Stanley at 10 am and 11.30 am. Going the other way, there are Sunday departures from Po Toi at 9.15 and 10.45 am, and 3, 4.30 and 6 pm.

A reservation is needed for all these boats. This can be booked by phone (☎ 2554-4059), but they don't speak English. Locals pay HK$15 for a one-way journey, but non-residents of Po Toi pay HK$30 for the round-trip if returning the same day. If staying overnight, the fare is HK$50 for the round-trip. The Aberdeen-Po Toi trip takes 70 minutes, but only 35 minutes from Stanley.

Ma Wan

Ma Wan is a flat and forested island off the north-eastern tip of much larger Lantau Island. It was once famous as the Gate to

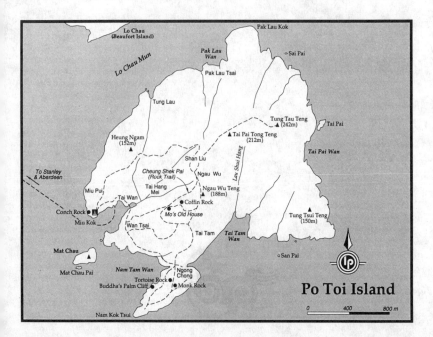

Po Toi Island

Kowloon, where foreign ships would collect before entering Chinese waters.

Ma Wan was once charming, but these days it's hardly worth a visit. The two beaches where swimming is possible – Tung Wan and Tung Wan Tsai – have become polluted. However, swimming is still allowed and a lifeguard is present. The view on the eastern side of Ma Wan has been marred by the construction of oil storage tanks on nearby Tsing Yi Island.

Ma Wan has been strongly affected by the new airport development project, and two enormous road and rail bridges now connect Ma Wan to both Lantau and the mainland. Having already been colonised by the British, the island is now destined to be Kowloonised.

As if all this wasn't enough, there are plans to build a big Ocean Park-style amusement centre on Ma Wan.

MACAU

澳門

Facts about Macau

Only 65 km from Hong Kong but predating it by 300 years, Macau is the oldest and only remaining European colony in Asia. It's also the last of Portugal's colonies.

Soon to be swallowed up by China, Macau for the moment retains an interesting mix of cultures. It is a city of cobbled side streets, baroque churches, Portuguese fortresses and exotic street names. There are several Chinese temples and restored colonial villas, and Macau is the final resting place of many European seamen and soldiers. You will also find casinos, discos, high-rises and five-star hotels.

Tourism has had a shot in the arm in recent years, with several large luxury hotels being built on the mainland and on the islands. Yet apart from the Chinese gamblers, most tourists who go to Macau spend just a few whistle-stop hours there. Many who visit Hong Kong don't bother going to Macau at all – a pity, because it is one of those curious places where something new can be found on every visit.

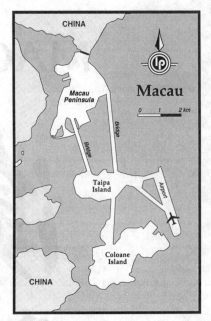

HISTORY

Macau means the City of God and takes its name from A-Ma-Gau, the Bay of A-Ma. At Barra Point stands the A-Ma Temple, which dates back to the early 16th century. According to legend, A-Ma, a poor girl looking for a passage to Guangzhou, was turned away by the wealthy junk owners, so a fisherman took her on board. A storm blew up and wrecked all the junks except the boat carrying the girl. When it landed in Macau the girl disappeared, only to reappear later as a goddess on the spot where the fisherman built her temple.

Portuguese Colonisation

Macau is an oddity which has managed to cling to the Chinese coast since the mid-16th century, despite attempts by the Chinese, Spanish and Dutch to brush it off. For more than a hundred years previously, the Portu-

guese had been pushing down the west African coast in their search for a sea route to the Far East. But they were delayed by the attractions of slaves and gold from Guinea, which brought immediate material rewards, and by their ambition to find the mysterious Christian king Prester John, who would join them in a crusade against the Muslims.

When, in 1498, Vasco da Gama's ships rounded the southern cape of Africa and arrived in Calicut (now known as Kozhikode) in India, the Portuguese suddenly got a whiff of the enormous profits to be made from the Asian trade. And because the trade was almost exclusively in the hands of Muslims, they had the added satisfaction (and excuse) that any blow against their commercial rivals was a blow against the infidels.

There had never been any real intention to conquer large tracts of territory, colonise foreign lands or convert the native populations to Christianity en masse. Trade was always first and foremost in Portuguese minds. To this end, a vague plan was devised to bring all the important Indian Ocean trading ports under Portuguese control and to establish the necessary fortifications to protect their trade.

Thus, the Portuguese captured Goa on the west coast of India in 1510, and then Malacca on the Malay Peninsula in 1511 (their first ships had arrived there in 1509). They then attempted to subdue the Spice Islands of the Moluccas (Maluku), in what is now Indonesia, and thus control the lucrative spice trade.

The Portuguese never did manage to monopolise the trade. As the years rolled by their determination and ability to do so declined. By the end of the 16th century their efforts were curtailed by the arrival in Indonesia of powerful Dutch fleets also bent on wresting control of the spice trade.

More encouraging for the Portuguese was the trade with China and Japan. On their earliest voyages to India the Portuguese had heard of a strange, light-skinned people called the Chin, whose huge ships had once visited India but whose voyages had suddenly ceased. (From 1405 to 1433 the second Ming emperor, Yong Le, had dispatched several enormous maritime expeditions which had made contact with many parts of Asia and Africa.)

When the Portuguese arrived in Malacca in 1511 they came upon several junks with Chinese captains. Realising that the Chins were not a mythical people and concluding that they had come from the 'Cathay' of Marco Polo's travels, a small party of Portuguese were sent northwards to find out what they could and possibly open trade with the Chinese.

The first Portuguese set foot on Chinese soil in 1513 at the mouth of the Pearl River, near what is now Macau and Hong Kong. They reached Japan by accident in 1542, their ship having been blown off course.

By and large, initial Portuguese contact with China did not go well, and for years their attempts to gain a permanent trading base on the China coast met with little success. But in the early 1550s they reached some sort of agreement with Cantonese officials to settle on Sanchuang, a small island about 80 km south-west of the mouth of the Pearl River. Sanchuang's exposed anchorage led the Portuguese to abandon the island in 1553, moving to another island closer to the Pearl River.

To the north-east was a peninsula where the Portuguese also frequently anchored. It had two natural harbours – an inner harbour on the West River and an outer harbour in a bay facing the Pearl River – and to its south were some sheltering islands. In 1556 or 1557 the Portuguese and some Guangzhou officials made an agreement which allowed the Portuguese to rent this peninsula – known variously as Amagao, Amacon, Aomen and Macau – apparently in return for ridding the area of marauding pirates who plagued this stretch of coast. However, the peninsula was never formally ceded to the Portuguese.

Macau grew rapidly as a trading centre, largely because the Chinese wanted to trade with foreign countries but were forbidden to go abroad on penalty of death. The most lucrative trade route for the Portuguese was the long circuit from the west of India to Japan and back, with Macau as the essential link. Acting as agents for Chinese merchants, they took Chinese goods to the west coast of India, exchanged them for cotton and textiles which they took to Malacca to trade for spices and aromatic woods. The Portuguese then continued to Japan, where they sold their Malacca cargo for Japanese silver, swords, lacquerware and fans, and returned to Macau to exchange them for more Chinese goods.

The Japanese were forbidden to enter Chinese ports and China's trade with other Asian nationals was insignificant. The Portuguese displaced the Arabs and, with no other Europeans yet on the scene, they became the carriers of all large-scale international commerce with China and Japan.

17th-Century Macau
By the start of the 17th century Macau supported

several thousand permanent residents, including about a thousand Portuguese. The rest were Chinese Christian converts, mixed-race Christians from Malacca, Japanese Christians and a large number of African, Indian and Malay slaves. Large numbers of Chinese citizens worked in the town as hawkers, labourers and servants. There were many Chinese traders too.

Trade was the most important activity of the new town, but Macau also fast became a centre of Christianity in the Far East. Priests and missionaries accompanied Portuguese ships, though the attack was not jointly planned and the interests of traders and missionaries frequently conflicted. Among the earliest missionaries was Francis Xavier (later canonised) of the Jesuit order, who had spent from 1549 to 1551 in Japan attempting to convert heathens, before turning his attention to China. Xavier was stalled by Portuguese who feared the consequences of his meddling in Chinese affairs, but he made it as far as Sanchuang, where he died in December 1552. In the years to follow it was Jesuit missionaries, not traders, who were able to penetrate China beyond Macau and Canton (Guangzhou).

The Portuguese who stayed in Macau, along with their Macanese (mixed-blood) descendants, created a home away from home: their luxurious rococo houses and splendid baroque churches were paid for with the wealth generated by their monopoly on trade with China and Japan. These structures included the Basilica of St Paul, hailed as the greatest monument to Christianity in the East.

Apart from traders and priests, this odd little colony attracted some colourful adventurers, madmen, artists and poets. Among them was the 16th-century poet Luis de Camões, who was banished from Portugal to Goa and then to Macau, although some say he was never in the colony. In Macau, he is said to have written at least part of his epic poem *Os Lusiadas*, which recounts the voyage of Vasco da Gama to India. British artist George Chinnery spent a quarter of a century in Macau, from 1825 until his death in 1852, and is remembered for his paintings of the place and its people.

Portuguese Decline

The Portuguese decline was as rapid as its success. In 1580 Spanish armies occupied Portugal and in the early years of the 17th century the Dutch began making their presence felt in the Far East. In response, the Portuguese at Macau began building fortresses in anticipation of Dutch attacks. Dutch attempts to take Macau included major but unsuccessful attacks in 1607 and 1627.

Next, the Japanese became suspicious of Portuguese (and Spanish) intentions. They began persecuting Japanese Christians and eventually closed the country to foreign trade in 1637. In 1640 the Dutch took Malacca by force. Although Portugal regained its independence in 1640, all trade connections with China and Japan were cut off. The Portuguese could no longer provide the Chinese with the Japanese silver they wanted in exchange for their silk and porcelain, nor with spices, since the spice trade was now in the hands of the Dutch. Macau was no longer of any use to the Chinese and by 1640 they had closed the port of Canton (Guangzhou) to the Portuguese, leaving Macau to deteriorate rapidly into an impoverished settlement in danger of extinction.

But Macau managed to survive by other means. From the mid-18th century – as the French, Dutch, Danes, Swedes, Americans and Spanish all profited from trading with China via Guangzhou – restrictions and regulations concerning non-Portuguese residing in Macau were lifted. The colony in effect became an outpost for all of Europe in China, a position which it held until the British took possession of Hong Kong in 1841 and other Chinese ports were forced open to foreign trade in the years following.

Until the middle of the 19th century the history of Macau was a long series of incidents – incitements, stand-offs, threats, disputes and attacks, involving the Portuguese, Chinese and British – as the Portuguese attempted to maintain their grasp. Around 1850, the Portuguese even made plans to attack Canton (Guangzhou) as the British had done during the opium wars, in order to dictate a Chinese-Portuguese treaty. A series of disasters, including the intended flagship of the fleet blowing up off Taipa

Island, meant this plan never came to fruition. The Portuguese were once again forced to settle their differences with China through negotiation, though it was not until 1887 that a treaty was signed in which China effectively recognised Portuguese sovereignty over Macau. As for the problem of keeping Macau solvent, that had been more or less solved by Isidoro Francisco Guimaraes, the colony's governor between 1851 and 1863, who introduced what has become Macau's best-known feature – licensed gambling.

20th-Century Macau

Macau had turned into something of a decaying backwater by the late 19th century, though it continued to serve as a refuge for Chinese fleeing war and famine in the north.

When the Sino-Japanese War erupted in the 1930s, the population swelled to 500,000. Europeans also took refuge in Macau during WWII because the Japanese honoured Portuguese neutrality and did not take Macau as they did Hong Kong. More people came in 1949 when the communists took power in China, and from 1978 until about 1980 Macau was a destination for Vietnamese boat people. Somehow the tiny place managed to contain them all.

Macau's last great convulsion occurred in 1966, when China's Cultural Revolution spilled over into the colony. Macau was stormed by Red Guards and there were violent riots in which a few Red Guards were shot dead by Portuguese troops. The then governor reportedly proposed that the troubles could be ended if Portugal simply left Macau forever, but fearing the loss of foreign trade through Macau and Hong Kong, the Chinese backed off.

In 1974 a military coup in Portugal brought a left-wing government to power, which proceeded to divest Portugal of the last remnants of its empire (including Mozambique, Angola and East Timor). But the Chinese told the Portuguese that they preferred to leave Macau as it was.

Until 1975, Portugal maintained a 'touch-base' policy regarding Chinese immigrants.

That is, any Chinese reaching Macau could obtain residency, even if they reached it by swimming. After 1975 the policy was changed and all Chinese sneaking into Macau are now regarded as illegal immigrants.

Macau Today

Once the Joint Declaration over Hong Kong was signed by Britain and China in 1948, it was inevitable that China would seek a similar agreement with Portugal on Macau's future. That agreement was finally inked in March 1987.

Under the Sino-Portuguese pact, Macau will become a Special Administrative Region (SAR) of China for 50 years after 20 December 1999. Like Hong Kong, Macau is to enjoy a 'high degree of autonomy' in all matters except defence and foreign affairs.

An important change occurred in 1982 regarding the status of Macau's Chinese majority. Before 1982, any person born in Macau could have full Portuguese citizenship. Partly due to pressure from China, and partly due to a scandal involving the selling of Portuguese passports to Hong Kongers, the rules were changed. Now, one parent must be a Portuguese citizen, though he or she need not be of Portuguese descent. Less than 20% of Macau's ethnic Chinese population holds a Portuguese passport. Nevertheless, China continues to raise objections, claiming that anyone of Chinese descent is a Chinese citizen. In other words, race should be the deciding factor, not place of birth. China does not permit dual citizenship, and has threatened to revoke the Portuguese citizenship of Macau's ethnic Chinese; this has caused much anxiety. However, so far there has not been a massive flight of people and capital as there has been from Hong Kong. The reason may have more to do with the fact that few Chinese have the financial resources to leave Macau.

The pro-democracy demonstrations in 1989 that swept through China – before being brutally suppressed – also caught on in Macau. Shortly before the tanks started rolling over students in Beijing, a pro-democracy rally that was held in Macau attracted over 100,000 participants – more than 20% of the population.

All in all, 1990 was not a good year for Macau. Tourism was already down because of the Beijing massacre, but China's wheelchair leadership shook everyone's confidence even further by interfering in Macau's internal affairs. Lu Ping, Deputy Director of China's Hong Kong & Macau Affairs Office, launched a verbal barrage against the Macau government. Lu insisted that they tear down the statue of former Governor Joao Ferreira do Amaral because it was 'too colonial'. The statue, which was only erected in 1940, was shipped off to Portugal in 1992.

Lu went on: he condemned the opening of a Taipei Trade & Tourism Office in Macau, and insisted that the government should move faster to make Chinese (Putonghua) the official language of Macau, and that all Portuguese laws should be translated into Chinese. He also wanted Macau's civil service to be controlled by local Chinese, rather than Portuguese and Macanese as is presently the case.

Macau's governor Carlos Melancia launched a verbal counterattack, but he soon had serious problems of his own. He was forced to resign after a scandal involving kickbacks for construction contracts on Macau's new airport. The evidence against him was weak and many believe the accusations were politically motivated.

The aftershock of the 1989 Beijing massacre has gradually worn off. Tourism and foreign investment are both picking up again, but Macau enters its final decade under Portuguese rule with a bad case of the jitters. China's increasingly bellicose threats against Hong Kong have not gone unnoticed in Macau. On the other hand, Macau has not been subjected to the barrage of verbal abuse that China has levelled at Hong Kong for the simple reason that the Portuguese have not attempted to introduce any democratic reforms in Macau. Nevertheless, many in Macau are preparing to emigrate if they can.

China, of course, has its defenders. There are those who claim that China's increasing prosperity will eventually build a society that is as prosperous and free as Macau is now. As for the illegal immigrants, they have no doubts – despite the official policy of returning them to China, they continue to swim to what they hope will be a better life.

GEOGRAPHY

Macau is divided into three main sections – the Macau Peninsula, which is attached to China at the northern tip, and the two islands of Taipa and Coloane. Taipa is directly to the south of Macau and is attached by two bridges, each two km in length. Coloane is south of Taipa and connected to it by a causeway.

Macau is a tiny place. It has a total land area of 23.5 sq km, including the peninsula and the two islands, but it is gradually getting bigger because of land reclamation.

The northern tip of the Macau Peninsula, near the China border, is the newer part of town. Many high-rise apartments have been built here, mostly on reclaimed land.

Most of the interesting historical buildings are in the central and southern parts of the peninsula. The southern part (near the Penha Church) is the most high-class area of town, and has expensive homes perched on the hillsides overlooking the sea.

CLIMATE

Macau's climate is almost the same as Hong Kong's, with one minor difference – the cool sea breeze is delightful on summer nights and acts as natural air conditioning.

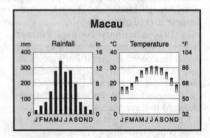

GOVERNMENT & POLITICS

Officially, Macau is not considered a colony. Instead, the Portuguese government regards Macau as a piece of Chinese territory under Portuguese administration. The difference is largely a matter of semantics.

The colony/Chinese territory has a governor who is appointed by the president of Portugal. The governor appoints five undersecretaries, each with a specific field of administration. There is also a legislative assembly with 23 members: eight are directly elected, another eight are elected by various 'economic interest groups', and seven are appointed by the governor. The assembly then elects its own president. There are three mayors: one for the Macau Peninsula and one each for the two islands, Taipa and Coloane.

ECONOMY

For many years gambling was Macau's *raison d'être*, and although that's no longer as true as in the recent past, it's still the number one cash cow. The 'gaming industry' (as it prefers to be called) is monopolised by a small but wealthy Chinese business syndicate which trades under the name of STDM – Sociedade de Turismo e Diversoes de Macau (Macao Travel & Amusement Co). It was STDM that introduced the hydrofoils (later replaced with jetfoils) from Hong Kong to Macau and built the Lisboa Hotel. This group won monopoly rights on all licensed gambling in Macau in 1962.

Although Macau has had a reputation for centuries as a gambling centre, casino gambling only got under way in 1934, when a Chinese syndicate called the Tai Hing obtained monopoly rights from the colonial government. Monopoly rights were renewed every five years and went to whichever company was willing to pay the most tax. The story goes that the original owners of the Tai Hing were able to pay a puny tax sum, but held on to the monopoly by paying off competitors. It wasn't until after the death of the two founders of the Tai Hing that the STDM gained a monopoly on the gambling industry.

About one third of government revenue comes from gambling, another third from direct and indirect taxes and the rest from land rents and service charges.

Macau entertains almost six million tourists a year, or more than 12 times the local population. Over 80% of the tourists come from Hong Kong, with most of the remainder from Japan, the UK, Taiwan, USA, Thailand and South Korea. Gambling and tourism provide about 25% of GDP. The colony has various light industries, such as fireworks, textile and garment production – and wages are much lower than in Hong Kong. The main reason wages have remained low, despite a labour shortage, is that Macau has an agreement with China which allows a large number of Chinese workers to cross the border daily from Zhuhai. The agreement is controversial, since it weakens the position of Macau's workers so they cannot demand better wages, but it also greatly benefits workers living in Zhuhai. The cheap supply of labour is attracting foreign investment. Taiwan, which suffers from its own labour shortage, is reportedly keen to invest heavily in Macau.

Macau closely follows the economic success formula employed in Hong Kong. It is a duty-free port and the maximum rate of taxation is around 15%, as in Hong Kong.

The last few years have enormous public works projects come on line. The completion of Macau's US$625 million airport was by far the most important.

Another biggie was the construction of a deep-water port on the north-east side of Coloane Island. In order to develop export-oriented industries like electronics, some way had be found to accommodate container ships. But keeping the port open will be a challenge – Macau's shallow harbour is constantly choked with mud flowing down from China's Pearl River. Nearby Hong Kong has one of the finest natural deep-water harbours in the world.

The third major project is the construction of Taipa City, a large high-rise housing development on Taipa Island. This is an ongoing project – but the rural charm that existed into the 1980s is well and truly gone.

In order to handle an expected increase in motor vehicle traffic, a second bridge was

MACAU

built between Taipa and the Macau Peninsula. And on the Chinese side of the border a new freeway is being built between Zhuhai and Guangzhou. This will connect with the freeway being built from Hong Kong to Guangzhou. There is even talk of extending the railway from Guangzhou down to Zhuhai and maybe into Macau as well.

Another scheme underway is a massive land reclamation project right on the Praia Grande, Macau's historic waterfront. Known as the Nam Van Lakes project because it will create two artificial freshwater lakes, the project has stirred considerable controversy; despite opposition from conservationists, construction is proceeding apace.

In view of all the foregoing, you'd be right to conclude that Macau's former image as a peaceful, colonial backwater is rapidly changing. Old-timers are appalled at the traffic and new high-rise buildings, but there is no denying that these projects will benefit the economy. The question for visitors is whether Macau will really be any different from Hong Kong in 10 years' time.

POPULATION & PEOPLE

Macau's population is approximately 500,000, but increasing rapidly at 3.8% a year. The sharp growth rate is due less to births than to a steady trickle of immigration from China.

About 98% of the people live on the Macau Peninsula, making it one of the most crowded areas in the world. The two islands have remained essentially rural, but this will change with the construction of Taipa City, a high-rise development on Taipa Island.

The population consists of about 95% Chinese, and about 3% Portuguese and Machines (Macau-born Portuguese and Eurasians).

EDUCATION

Macau University (☎ 831622) on Taipa Island is the main institute of higher learning. The school was once the small, privately-owned University of East Asia, but has been renamed, taken over by the government and opened as a public university with a student body of 5000. The school is still rapidly

expanding and even attracts students from Hong Kong and overseas.

Macau Polytechnic Institute (☎ 578722) at Avenida da Sidonio Pais 1 offers industrial and technical training.

ARTS

Chinese art is partially covered in the Facts about Hong Kong chapter of this book. As for the Portuguese, their art is most apparent in the old churches and cathedrals which grace Macau's skyline. It's here that you'll see some fine examples of painting, stained-glass windows and sculpture.

Music

Canto-pop from Hong Kong is of course the rage in Macau too, but the Portuguese minority does their bit to liven up the cultural milieu. You can get a good feel for Portuguese music by visiting Portuguese bookshops around town; they also sell CDs.

SOCIETY & CONDUCT
Traditional Culture

About 95% of the population is Chinese and is culturally indistinguishable from Hong Kong. See the Hong Kong chapter of this book for details.

Of course, the Portuguese minority has a vastly different culture which they have kept largely intact. Although mixed marriages are not uncommon in Macau, there has been surprisingly little assimilation between the two ethnic groups – most Portuguese cannot speak Chinese and vice versa.

Dos & Don'ts

The casinos have a dress code. Men cannot wear shorts, even if the shorts are relatively long and stylish-looking. Men also cannot wear vests unless they have a shirt on under the vest. During the summer, many male travellers run afoul of these rules and are refused admission.

Women *can* wear shorts and vests into casinos. Indeed, women can get away with wearing very skimpy outfits – apparently the casinos consider it good for business.

Neither men nor women are permitted to

wear thongs (flip-flop sandals) into casinos. Many restaurants will also not permit this. Thongs are basically only for wearing inside your hotel room or at the beach. Sandals with a strap across the back of the ankle are generally OK, though.

RELIGION

For the Chinese majority, Taoism and Buddhism are the dominant religions. However, nearly 500 years of Portuguese influence has definitely left an imprint, and the Catholic church is very strong in Macau. Many Chinese have been converted and you are likely to see Chinese nuns.

LANGUAGE

Portuguese is the official language, though Cantonese is the language of choice for about 95% of the population. English is regarded as a third language, even though it's more commonly spoken than Portuguese. Mandarin Chinese, or Putonghua, as it's officially called, is understood by more than half the Chinese population.

Within the Macau educational system, English is now the main language of instruction and starts at elementary school. So if you're having trouble communicating, your best bet is to ask a young person.

Although there is no compelling reason for you to learn Portuguese while in Macau, there are a few words which are fun to know for reading street signs and maps. The most useful ones are:

admiral
  almirante
avenue
  avenida
alley
  beco
bay
  baía

beach
  praia
bridge
  ponte
bus stop
  paragem
church
  igreja
district
  bairro
friendship
  amizade
guesthouse
  hospedaria or vila
hill
  alto or monte
island
  ilha
library
  biblioteca
lookout point
  miradouro
money changer
  casa de cambio
of
  da, do
pier
  ponte-cais
post office
  correios
path
  caminho
rock, crag
  penha
small hill
  colina
square (small)
  largo
street
  rua

big
  grande
building
  edificio
cathedral
  sé
courtyard
  pátio
fortress
  fortaleza
garden
  jardim
guide
  guia
hotel
  pousada
lane
  travessa
lighthouse
  farol
market
  mercado
museum
  museu
pawn shop
  casa de penhores
police
  polícia
restaurant (small)
  casa de pasto
road
  estrada
school
  escola
square
  praça
steep street
  calçada
teahouse
  casa de chá

Facts for the Visitor

PLANNING
When to Go
Hong Kongers account for over 90% of tourist arrivals in Macau. What this means is that all weekends and public holidays in Hong Kong generate a flood tide of tourists pouring into Macau. You'd be wise to avoid these times, since hotels double their prices and rooms of any sort can be hard to find.

For Western tourists, summer tends to be the peak travel season. There's no reason why it should be though, because the most delightful weather comes in October and November. However, the Macau Grand Prix (third week of November) is a real crunch time.

Maps
One of the most detailed maps available is the *Map of Macau & Zhuhai* published by Universal Publications. It is easily obtained in Hong Kong and Macau for about HK$20. The map has a complete street index on the back, shows the bus routes and has streets labelled in both Chinese characters and Portuguese.

You can get a free *Macau Tourist Map* from the Macau Government Tourist Office. It includes all the major streets and tourist sights, labelled in both Portuguese and Chinese characters – useful for navigating by taxi when the driver doesn't speak English.

What to Bring
Macau is a perfectly modern place and you'll be able to buy whatever you need.

HIGHLIGHTS
Although gambling is what draws most people to Macau, the fine colonial architecture makes it unique. Highlights include the Ruins of St Paul, Monte Fortress, Guia Fortress, Leal Senado and the Penha Church. St Michael Cemetery is a fascinating place to walk through, and many visitors are impressed by A-Ma Temple. Taipa Village on Taipa Island is interesting, and there is no better way to round

off a trip to Macau than with a fine meal at a Portuguese restaurant.

TOURIST OFFICES
Local Tourist Offices
The Macau Government Tourist Office, or MGTO (☎ 315566), is well organised and very helpful. It's at Largo do Senado, Edificio Ritz No 9, next to the Leal Senado building in the square in the centre of Macau. This office is open daily from 9 am to 6 pm.

There is a small but very helpful tourist information counter right at the Macau Jetfoil Pier. They can answer questions and issue maps and other brochures.

Tourist Offices Abroad
On Hong Kong Island there's a useful branch of the MGTO (☎ 2540-8180; 2559-6513) at room 3704, Shun Tak Centre, 200 Connaught Rd, next to the Macau Jetfoil Pier. If you're taking the jetfoil or ferry to Macau, you can collect all the MGTO literature and read it while you're on the boat. The MGTO is closed for lunch from 1 to 2 pm.

Macau also has overseas tourist representative offices, most of which are called Macau Tourist Information Bureaus (MTIB). They are as follows:

Australia
> MTIB, 449 Darling St, Balmain, Sydney, NSW 2041 (☎ (02) 9555-7548; (008) 252448; fax (02) 9555-7559)

Belgium
> Tourism Delegation, Avenue Louise, 375 Bte 9, 1050 Brussels (☎ (02) 647-1265; fax 640-1552)

Canada
> MTIB, Suite 157, 10551 Shellbridge Way, Richmond, BC V6X 2W9
> (☎ (604) 231-9040; fax 231-9031)
> 13 Mountalan Ave, Toronto, Ontario M4J IH3
> (☎ (416) 466-6552)

France
> MTIB Consultant, Atlantic Associates, SARL, 52 Champs-Elysées, 75008 Paris
> (☎ (01) 4256-4551; fax 4651-4889)

Germany
    Macau Tourism Representative, Shafergasse 17,
    D-60313, Frankfurt-am-Main
    (☎ (069) 234094; fax 231433)
Japan
    MTIB, 4th floor, Toho Twin Tower Building, 5-2
    Yuraku-cho 1-chome, Chiyoda-ku, Tokyo 100
    (☎ (03) 3501-5022; fax 3502-1248)
Malaysia
    MTIB, 10.03 Amoda, 22 Jalan Imbi, 55100
    Kuala Lumpur (☎ (03) 245-1418; fax 248-6851)
New Zealand
    MTIB, PO Box 42-165, Orakei, Auckland 5
    (☎ (09) 575-2700; fax 575-2620)
Philippines
    MTIB, 664 EDSA Extension, Pasay City, Metro
    Manila (☎ (02) 521-7178; fax 831-4344)
Portugal
    Macau Tourist Representative, Avenida 5 de
    Outubro 115, 5th floor, 1000 Lisbon
    (☎ (01) 793-6542; fax 796-0956)
Singapore
    MTIB, 11-01A PIL Building, 140 Cecil St, Sin-
    gapore 0106 (☎ 225-0022; fax 223-8585)
South Korea
    MGTO Representative, Glocom Korea, 1006
    Paiknam Building, 188-3 Ulchiro 1-ga, Chung-
    gu, Seoul 100-191
    (☎ (02) 778-4401; fax 778-4404)
Taiwan
    MGTO Representative, Compass Public Rela-
    tions, 11th floor, 65 Chienkuo North Rd, Section
    2, Taipei (☎ (02) 516-3008; fax 515-1971)
Thailand
    MTIB, 150/5 Sukhumvit 20, Bangkok 10110, or
    GPO Box 1534, Bangkok 10501
    (☎ (02) 258-1975; fax 258-1975)
UK
    MTIB, 6 Sherlock Mews, Paddington St, London
    W1M 3RH (☎ (0171) 224-3390; fax 224-0601)
USA
    MTIB, 3133 Lake Hollywood Drive, Los
    Angeles, CA, or PO Box 1860, Los Angeles, CA
    90078 (☎ (213) 851-3402, (800) 331-7150; fax
    (213) 851-3684)
    Suite 2R, 77 Seventh Ave, New York, NY 10011
    (☎ (212) 206-6828; fax 924-0882)
    PO Box 350, Kenilworth, IL 60043-0350
    (☎ (708) 251-6421; fax 256-5601)
    999 Wilder Ave, Suite 1103, Honolulu, HI 96822
    (☎ (808) 538-7613)

VISAS & DOCUMENTS
Visas
For most visitors, all that's needed to enter
Macau is a passport. Everyone gets a 20-day
stay on arrival except Hong Kongers, who
get 90 days (and Portuguese, who can stay

until China boots them out). Visas are not
required for the following nationalities: Aus-
tralia, Austria, Belgium, Brazil, Canada,
Denmark, Finland, France, Germany,
Greece, Hong Kong, India, Ireland, Italy,
Japan, Luxembourg, Malaysia, Mexico,
Netherlands, New Zealand, Norway, Philip-
pines, Singapore, South Africa, South
Korea, Spain, Sweden, Switzerland, Taiwan,
Thailand, UK and USA.

All other nationalities must have a visa,
which can be obtained on arrival in Macau.
Visas cost M$175 for individuals, M$350 for
married couples and families and M$88 per
person in a bona fide tour group (usually 10
persons minimum). People holding passports from countries which do not have
diplomatic relations with Portugal must
obtain visas from an overseas Portuguese
consulate before entering Macau. In Hong
Kong, the Portuguese Consulate (☎ 2802-
2587) is in Harbour Centre, 25 Harbour Rd,
Wan Chai, but there is also a Macau Consulate, care of the British Trade Commission
(☎ 2523-0176), Bank of America Tower,
Lambeth Walk, Admiralty.

Visa Extensions After your 20 days are up,
you can obtain a one-month extension. A
second extension is not possible, though it's
easy enough to cross the border to China then
come back again. The Immigration Office
(☎ 577338) is on the 9th floor, Macau
Chamber of Commerce Building, 175 Rua
de Xangai, which is one block to the north-
east of the Hotel Beverly Plaza.

Driving Licences & Permits
Drivers must be at least 21 years of age. An
international driver's licence is required –
these cannot be issued in Macau unless you
already have a Macau driver's licence.

CUSTOMS
Customs formalities are few and it's unlikely
you'll be bothered by them. You're allowed
to bring in a reasonable quantity of tobacco,
alcohol and perfumes. Like Hong Kong,
Macau customs takes a very dim view of

drugs. Weapons aren't allowed, so leave your AK-47 behind. There are no export duties on anything bought in Macau. You aren't supposed to bring fireworks bought in Macau back to Hong Kong – many Hong Kongers do just that, which is why they get searched.

When heading back to Hong Kong, you are supposedly only permitted to bring one litre of alcohol and a miserly 50 cigarettes.

BAGGAGE STORAGE

Many travellers want to leave their heavy luggage in Hong Kong while they zip over to Macau for a couple of days. If you search hard, you'll find a few lockers in Shun Tak Centre (Macau Jetfoil Pier) in Hong Kong. Some Hong Kong hotels (and even some guesthouses) will allow you to store a bag for a few days; the cost varies, but is typically about HK$10 or more per bag per day.

It's easier to store bags in Macau: there are lockers at the Jetfoil Pier which cost M$30-40 for 24 hours; there is a luggage storage room at the Jetfoil Pier on the 1st floor (departure level, at the end of the passenger corridor); and another option are hotels in Macau – most will have a baggage storage room. They will generally allow you to store a bag when you check out, a big convenience if you must check out by noon but don't want to return to Hong Kong until the evening.

MONEY
Costs

As long as you don't go crazy at the roulette wheel or slot machines, Macau is cheaper than Hong Kong. To help keep costs down, avoid weekends.

ATMs

Some (but not all) Jetco ATMs will work with American Express or Visa cards. This is particularly true of the Jetco machines in the casinos – you'll find one on the 2nd floor of the Lisboa Hotel arcade.

You'll probably have better luck at the HongkongBank branch at Avenida da Praia Grande and Rua Palha. There is an Electronic Teller Card (ETC) machine here which accepts Visa and other ATM cards which use Plus, GlobalAccess and Electron. HongkongBank ATMs are also found in the arcade on the 2nd floor of the Lisboa Hotel and on the ground floor of the Macau Jetfoil Pier.

Credit Cards

Major credit cards are readily accepted at Macau's hotels and casinos. Theft or loss of a credit card should be reported to the company's representative office in Hong Kong. MasterCard (☎ 832738) has a representative office in Macau and American Express has a representative office inside the Lisboa Hotel.

International Transfers

As in Hong Kong, international telegraphic transfers are quick and efficient. Some banks which handle wire transfers are Banco Nacional Ultramarino and Banco Comercial de Macau.

Pawn Shops

You can literally lose your shirt gambling in Macau – these pawnbrokers sell everything. Of course, a second-hand shirt is worth peanuts. Even for a fancy gold watch or camera, you'll be lucky to get enough to pay for your jetfoil ticket back to Hong Kong.

Currency

Macau's currency is called the pataca, normally written as M$, and one pataca is divided into 100 avos. Coins come as 10, 20 and 50 avos and one and five patacas. Notes are 5, 10, 50, 100, 500 and 1000 patacas. Commemorative gold M$1000 and silver M$100 coins have been issued, though it's hardly likely you'll see them used as currency. There are no exchange control regulations and money can be freely transferred in and out of Macau. All major credit cards are accepted in big hotels, car rental agencies, etc.

Currency Exchange

Because Macau's pataca is pegged to the Hong Kong dollar (give or take a few cents), exchange rates are virtually the same as for Hong Kong (see Exchange Rates in the Hong Kong Facts for the Visitor chapter).

Changing Money

Hong Kong dollars, including coins, are readily accepted everywhere in Macau just as if they were patacas. You might save a few cents by converting into patacas, but then changing surplus patacas back is more trouble than it's worth. Patacas are not so well received in Hong Kong, where money changers often refuse the currency. Even worse, most Hong Kong banks won't take your patacas either! The only place I know of that will change patacas for Hong Kong dollars is the main branch of the Hang Seng Bank, at 18 Carnarvon Rd, Tsim Sha Tsui. You lose a little bit by changing them in Hong Kong rather than in Macau, and even Hang Seng Bank doesn't want the coins. You would be wise to use all your patacas before departing Macau.

Black Market

No currency black market exists in Macau.

Tipping & Bargaining

Classy hotels and restaurants will automatically hit you with a 10% service charge, which is supposedly a mandatory tip. Just how much of this money actually goes to the employees is a matter of speculation.

You can follow your own conscience, but tipping is not customary among the Chinese. Of course, porters at expensive hotels have become accustomed to handouts from well-heeled tourists.

Most stores have fixed prices, but if you buy clothing, trinkets and other tourist junk from the street markets, there is some scope for bargaining.

Macau is noticeably friendlier than Hong Kong, and therefore you should be too. Bargain politely – the rough manners of Hong Kong don't go down well in Macau, and if you're nasty you'll get nowhere in a bargaining session. Smile, tell them you don't have much money and would like a discount, then see what they say.

It's a different story at the pawn shops. Bargain ruthlessly! See the section on Things to Buy at the end of this chapter for more details.

POST & COMMUNICATIONS

Postal Rates

Domestic letters cost M$1 for up to 20g. For international mail, Macau divides the world into zones: Zone 1 is east Asia, including Korea, Taiwan, etc; Zone 2 is everything else. There are special rates for China and Portugal. The rates in M$ for airmail letters, postcards and aerogrammes are as follows:

Grams	China	Portugal	Zone 1	Zone 2
10	2.00	3.00	3.50	4.50
20	3.00	4.50	4.50	6.00
30	4.00	6.00	5.50	7.50
40	5.00	7.50	6.50	9.00
50	6.00	9.00	7.50	10.50

Printed matter receives a discount of about 30% off these rates. Registration costs an extra M$12.

Sending Mail

The postal service is efficient and the clerks can speak English. Besides a few main post offices, there are also numerous mini-post offices throughout Macau. These are little red booths that sell stamps from vending machines. Large hotels like the Lisboa also sell stamps and postcards and can post letters for you. Speedpost (EMS) is available at the GPO.

Receiving Mail

Poste restante service is available at the GPO on Avenida de Almeida Ribeiro in Leal Senado. It's open from 9 am to 8 pm, Monday to Saturday.

Telephone

Macau's telephone monopoly is Companhia de Telecomunicacoes (CTM). There is a useful CTM office next to Leal Senado, but the main CTM office (for applying for phone service and paying bills) is on Avenida do Dr Rodrigo Rodrigues, just up from the Lisboa Hotel.

The phone service is good – you'll seldom have trouble with broken public phones and noisy lines. Unfortunately, public pay phones can be hard to find, being mostly

MACAU

concentrated around the Leal Senado. Most large hotels have a phone in the lobby, but you may have to stand in line.

Local calls are free from a private or hotel telephone (there is a courtesy phone at the MGTO). At a public pay phone, local calls cost M$1 for five minutes. All pay phones permit international direct dialling (IDD). The procedure for dialling Hong Kong is different to all other countries. You first dial 01 then the number you want – you must *not* dial the country code.

The international access code for every country *except* Hong Kong is 00, after which you must dial the country code, the area code and finally the number you wish to reach. If the area code begins with a zero, omit the first zero. To call Macau from abroad, the country code is 853.

You can call home reverse charges (collect) or with a credit card by using the 'home direct' system. This method doesn't work for every country. You need to dial an access code, and then an operator from your home country will come on the line and ask which number you want to reach and how you want to charge the call. For details on international access codes see under Telephone in the Hong Kong Facts for the Visitor chapter.

Remember you'll need a big pocket full of change to make an IDD call unless you buy a telephone card from CTM. These are sold in denominations of M$50, M$100 and M$200. Phones which accept these cards are numerous around Leal Senado, the Jetfoil Pier and at a few large hotels.

Yet another way is to make a call from the telephone office at Leal Senado, next to the GPO. The way to do it is to leave a deposit with a clerk and they will dial your number. When your call is completed the clerk deducts the cost from the deposit and refunds the balance. The clerks speak English and the office is open from 8 am until midnight Monday through Saturday, and from 9 am until midnight on Sundays. There is another telephone office north of the Lisboa Hotel on Avenida do Dr Rodrigo Rodriques, but this one is open only from 9 am to 8 pm, Monday through Saturday.

Useful Phone Numbers

Emergency	☎ 999
Police	☎ 573333
Directory Assistance (Macau)	☎ 181
Directory Assistance (Abroad)	☎ 101
Time	☎ 140
Fire	☎ 572222

Residents of Macau who wish to obtain a pager can contact Kong Seng Paging (☎ 555555), Avenida do Conselheiro Ferreira de Almeida 71.

Fax, Telegraph & Email

Unless you're staying at a hotel that has its own fax, the easiest way to send and receive fax is at the GPO (not the telephone office) on Leal Senado. You can also receive a fax at this office (fax (853) 550117). The person sending the fax must put your name and hotel telephone on top of the message so the postal workers can find you. The cost for receiving a fax is M$7.50, regardless of the number of pages.

The telephone office *(not* the post office) handles telegrams.

Email services are not well developed in Macau. If you belong to a service like Compuserve or America Online, you'll have to call Hong Kong. Residents of Macau can apply for an Internet account through the main CTM office on Avenida do Dr Rodrigo Rodrigues.

BOOKS

Books about Macau are scarce. Much of what's been published is in Portuguese, but there are a few good books in English.

Guidebooks

Travellers to the Middle Kingdom should get Lonely Planet's comprehensive guide to *China* (which includes a chapter on Hong Kong and Macau). Macau is also briefly covered in Lonely Planet's *Hong Kong city guide* and *South-East Asia on a shoestring*.

If you can track down a copy it's worth getting the *Macau AOA Gambling Handbook*. This comes as part of a set which includes the *Macau Pictorial Guide* and an excellent map of Macau. The whole package costs only HK$25 and is available from most of the main bookshops in Hong Kong. If not, you could try the MGTO in Hong Kong or go directly to the publisher, AOA (☎ 2389-0352), 10th floor, 174 Wai Yip St, Kwun Tong, Hong Kong.

Behind the service counter at the MGTO on the Leal Senado there is a small collection of books and other goods for sale. Check the list to see what is currently available.

Travel

There are several pictorial coffee-table books about Macau. One is simply called *Macau*, written by Jean-Yves Defay. Another, also called *Macau*, is by Leong Ka Tai & Shann Davies. It's an excellent hardbound pictorial and written history of the colony.

A good coffee-table sketchbook of the colony is *Old Macau* by Tom Briggs & Colin Crisswell.

A Macao Narrative is by Austin Coates, a well-known Hong Kong magistrate, who also wrote *City of Broken Promises*.

Another good book with the title of *Macau* is by Cesar Guillen-Nuñez.

History & Politics

Historic Macao by CA Montalto de Jesus was first published in 1902 as a history of the colony. In 1926 the author added extra chapters in which he suggested that the Portuguese government cared so little about the colony and did so little to meet its needs that it would be better if Macau was administered by the League of Nations. The Portuguese government was outraged and copies of the book were seized and destroyed. The book can be bought at the Luis de Camões Museum in Macau.

General

Novels set in Macau are rare but there is at least one – *Macau*, by Daniel Carney.

Bookshops

Few shops in Macau carry English-language books, and those few only have a limited selection. The easiest to find is Livraria Sao Paulo (☎ 323957) on Rua do Campo (near McDonald's). Many of the books are in Portuguese and oriented towards the Catholic church, but they have some general-interest English books and good maps of Macau. The CD collection here includes some rare recordings from Africa and remote corners of Asia – nowhere else this side of Kabul will you find such an assortment of Afghanistani folk music! This is also one of the only bookshops in Macau that stocks Lonely Planet guides.

For Portuguese-language publications, check out Livraria Portuguesa (☎ 566442), 18-20 Rua de Sao Domingos. This place also has a good assortment of Portuguese music CDs.

A general-interest bookshop is inside the Plaza Cultural, basement, 32 Avenida do Conselheiro Ferreira de Almeida (close to Lou Lim Ioc Gardens).

ONLINE SERVICES

Macau has an almost unique system of 'computerised city guides'. This is a simple online service consisting of computer terminals placed at strategic locations around the city. Here you can find information about transport, hotels, sightseeing and even daily events.

You'll find the computer terminals at the Jetfoil Pier, the lobby of the Leal Senado, the Lisboa Hotel, Hyatt Regency Hotel, Yaohan Department Store, Plaza Cultural and Livraria Portuguesa. If the service proves popular, no doubt more terminals will be installed.

As for sites on the World Wide Web, http://www.macau.net is a good place to start a search. And http://www.lonelyplanet.com will steer you to Lonely Planet's award-winning site.

NEWSPAPERS & MAGAZINES

Other than the free monthly tourist newspaper *Macau Travel Talk*, English-language newspapers are published in Macau. However, both the *South China Morning Post* and *Hong Kong Standard* are readily available from big hotels and some bookshops. It's also easy to buy major foreign news magazines.

Foreign residents of Macau can subscribe to English-language magazines through

MACAU

World Book Company Macau, Rua dos Mercadores 68.

RADIO & TV

Macau has three radio stations, two of which broadcast in Cantonese and one in Portuguese. There are no local English-language radio stations, but you should be able to pick up Hong Kong stations.

Teledifusao de Macau (TdM) is a government-run station which broadcasts on two channels. Shows are mainly in English and Portuguese, though there are some Cantonese programmes. It's easy to pick up Hong Kong stations in Macau (but not vice versa) and you can also receive stations from China. Hong Kong newspapers list Macau TV programmes.

Hong Kong's famous satellite TV system, STAR TV, is readily available in Macau at any hotel with a cable or satellite dish hookup.

VIDEO SYSTEMS

Like Hong Kong, Macau uses the PAL standard for TV broadcasting and video tapes.

PHOTOGRAPHY & VIDEO

You can find most types of film, cameras and accessories in Macau, and photo-processing is of a high standard. The most complete store in town for all photographic services is Foto Princesa (☎ 555959), 55-59 Avenida de Infante D'Henrique, one block east of Avenida da Praia Grande. This place sells professional (refrigerated) film, video equipment, video tapes and binoculars, and also does quickie visa photos. One-hour photoprocessing is available here at about M$65 for a 36-exposure roll, though some other places around town are *slightly* cheaper. For example, Oasis Colour Photo Processing Centre (☎ 551933), Avenida Praia Grande 77, offers the same thing for M$58.

TIME

Like Hong Kong, Macau is eight hours ahead of GMT/UTC and does not observe daylight savings.

ELECTRICITY
Voltage & Cycle

Macau's electricity system is the same as in Hong Kong and China – 220V AC, 50 Hz. There are still a few old buildings wired for 110V, but as long as you see three round holes on the outlets you can be assured it's 220V.

Plugs & Sockets

The electric outlets are the same as Hong Kong's older design, that is three round pins.

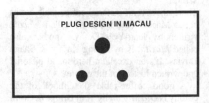

PLUG DESIGN IN MACAU

WEIGHTS & MEASURES

Macau uses the international metric system. As in Hong Kong, street markets and medicine shops sell things by the *leung* (37.5g) and the *catty* (600g).

LAUNDRY

Hidden in the alleys are many hole-in-the-wall laundry services that charge reasonable prices. The trick is finding them: most only display Chinese characters on their advertisements. One which is relatively easy to find is Lavandaria Macau, in the same building as San Va Hospedaria, Rua de Felicidade 67.

Almost all hotels do laundry, but check prices first before handing over your clothes.

TOILETS

Macau has far more public toilets per capita than Hong Kong. Good venues to find toilets include the tourist office, parks, temples, museums, casinos, fast-food restaurants, the Macau Jetfoil Pier and shopping plazas.

WOMEN TRAVELLERS

Wearing a skimpy bikini at the beach will elicit some stares, but Macau is almost as open as Hong Kong when it comes to fashion. You can get away with wearing just about anything.

TRAVEL WITH CHILDREN

On the 3rd floor of the Lisboa Hotel is Children's World, where kids can play video games for hours while mum and dad lose their life savings at the blackjack tables. Teenagers can also occupy themselves here playing snooker. Leave the kids here all day and they probably won't even miss you.

If you want to get rid of the kids for five days, the Hyatt Regency Hotel on Taipa Island has a modest proposal. For HK$4380, the hotel's summer camp will keep the kids constructively occupied with such activities as camping, scuba diving, water polo, tennis, windsurfing, ice skating, canoeing and rock climbing. Less strenuous activities include theatre, picnics, barbecues and sing-around-the-campfire social activities. The five-day camps run every week from early July to late August, and children must be aged between nine and 14. The hotel can arrange to pick up the kids in Hong Kong and return them there, which gives parents a few extra days to do their Tsim Sha Tsui shopping routine. If staying at the hotel, parents are entitled to a 25% discount by signing up the kids, though you can get the same discount by booking through Hong Kong travel agents.

USEFUL ORGANISATIONS

The International Ladies Club of Macau (ILCM) invites English-speaking women of all nationalities to join. However, it's geared towards expats living in Macau – not the short-term tourist. Activities include simply making friends, helping newcomers settle into Macau, organising fundraisers for charity, publishing a monthly newsletter and whatever else the membership wishes to do. There are usually several meetings a month, mostly informal get-togethers over coffee, tea or lunch. If interested, write to PO Box 1370, Macau.

DANGERS & ANNOYANCES

In terms of violent crime, Macau is pretty safe, but residential burglaries and pick-pocketing are problems. Most hotels are well guarded, and reasonable care with your valuables should be sufficient to avoid trouble.

Traffic is heavy and quite a few tourists have been hit while jaywalking. Macau police have been cracking down on this, and though they go light with foreigners you can still get fined. Be especially careful at rush hour when the traffic (and the police) come out in force.

Cheating at gambling is a serious criminal offence, so don't even think about it.

BUSINESS HOURS

The operating hours for most government offices in Macau are Monday to Thursday from 9 am to 1 pm and 2.30 to 5.45 pm. On Friday, business hours are the same except that they close at 5.30 pm. Private businesses keep longer hours and some casinos are open 24 hours a day, including (especially!) weekends.

Banks are normally open Monday to Saturday from 9 am to 4.30 pm.

PUBLIC HOLIDAYS & SPECIAL EVENTS

The Chinese in Macau celebrate the same religious festivals as their counterparts in Hong Kong, but there are several Catholic festivals and some Portuguese national holidays too. The tourist newspaper *Macau Travel Talk*, available from the MGTO, has a regular listing of events and festivals. Here are some of the more important holidays in Macau – see the Hong Kong chapters for details about Chinese holidays.

New Year's Day – The first day of the year is a public holiday.
Chinese Lunar New Year – As in Hong Kong, this is a three-day public holiday in late January or early February.
Lantern Festival – Not a public holiday, but a lot of fun, this festival occurs two weeks after the Chinese Lunar New Year. See the Hong Kong Facts for the Visitor chapter.
Procession of Our Lord of Passion – Not a public holiday, but interesting to watch. The procession begins in the evening from St Augustine's Church and goes to the Macau Cathedral. The statue is kept in the cathedral overnight and the procession returns to St Augustine's the following day.

Feast of the Earth God Tou Tei – A minor holiday for the Chinese community in March or April.

Ching Ming Festival – A major public holiday in April. See the Hong Kong Facts for the Visitor chapter.

Easter – A four-day public holiday starting on Good Friday and lasting through to Monday.

Anniversary of the 1974 Portuguese Revolution – This public holiday on 25 April commemorates the overthrow of the Michael Caetano regime in Portugal in 1974 by a left-wing military coup.

Procession of Our Lady of Fatima – Celebrated on 13 May, this commemorates a miracle that took place at Fatima, Portugal in 1917. It is not a public holiday. The procession begins from Santa Domingo Church and ends at Penha Church.

A-Ma Festival – This is the same as the Tin Hau Festival in Hong Kong and occurs in May. It's not a public holiday.

Festival of Tam Kong – A relatively minor holiday usually celebrated in May.

Camões and Portuguese Communities Day – Held on 10 June, this public holiday commemorates 16th-century poet Luis de Camões.

Dragon Boat Festival – As in Hong Kong, this is a major public holiday held in June.

Procession of St John the Baptist – The procession for the patron saint of Macau is held on 10 June.

Feast of St Anthony of Lisbon – This June event celebrates the birthday of the patron saint of Lisbon. A military captain, St Anthony receives his wages on this day from a delegation of city officials, and a small parade is held from St Anthony's Church. This is not a public holiday.

Battle of 13 July – Celebrated only on the islands of Taipa and Coloane, this holiday commemorates the final defeat of pirates in 1910.

Ghost Month – This festival, in August or September, is an excellent time to visit temples in Macau. See the Hong Kong Facts for the Visitor chapter.

Mid-Autumn Festival – A major public holiday in September. See the Hong Kong Facts for the Visitor chapter.

Portuguese Republic Day – A public holiday on 5 October.

Cheung Yeung Festival – A public holiday in October. See the Hong Kong Facts for the Visitor chapter.

All Saints' Day – Held on 1 November. Both All Saints' Day and the following day (All Souls' Day) are public holidays.

Portuguese Independence Day – Celebrated on 1 December, a public holiday.

Winter Solstice – Not a public holiday, but an interesting time to visit Macau. Many Macau Chinese consider the winter solstice more important than Chinese Lunar New Year. There is plenty of feasting and temples are crammed with worshippers.

Christmas – Both the 24th and 25th of December are public holidays.

Rock Around the Clock

There were musical programmes on New Year's Eve in the plaza next to the main post office – I heard some old ladies doing karaoke (in Cantonese) and a fledgling rock band playing 'Hotel California'. Little if any Portuguese influence as far as music is concerned.

New Year's Eve in the Lisboa casino seemed only slightly more packed than usual. At midnight, no announcement, no music, nothing – just the usual frenzied gambling.

Bill Rubens

Find out about cultural events, concerts, art exhibitions and other such activities from the tourist newspaper *Macau Travel Talk*. Free copies are available from the tourist office.

The Dragon Boat Festival is a Chinese holiday well known for its exciting dragon-boat races. Macau's races are usually held at the tip of the Macau Peninsula (Barra Fortress), but check with the MGTO to be certain. Similar races are held in Hong Kong and Taiwan. The Dragon Boat Festival is scheduled according to the lunar calendar, but usually falls sometime in June.

The Miss Macau Contest is held every August. Whether this a cultural or anti-cultural event depends on one's point of view.

The International Music Festival is held during the third week of October.

Bull fights have occasionally been staged during the Chinese New Year in the sports field across from the Lisboa Hotel.

Grand Prix

The biggest event of the year is undoubtedly the Macau Grand Prix. As in Monaco, the streets of the town make up the race track. The six-km circuit starts near the Lisboa Hotel and follows the shoreline along Avenida da Amizade, going around the reservoir and back through the city.

The Grand Prix consists of two major races – one for cars and one for motorcycles. Both races attract many international contestants. Pedicab races are included as a novelty event.

The race is a two-day event held on the third weekend in November. More than 50,000 people flock to see it and accommodation – a problem on normal weekends – becomes as rare as a three-humped camel. Be sure to book a return ticket on the jetfoil if you have to get back to Hong Kong. If you don't book, you may still be able to squeeze on board one of the ferries. Otherwise, if you have a China visa, you might consider making your exit through the People's Republic and staying at a hotel in Zhuhai. Ferries connect Zhuhai to Shenzhen and Hong Kong.

Certain areas in Macau are designated as viewing areas for the races. Streets and alleyways along the track are blocked off, so it's unlikely you'll be able to get a good view without paying. Prices for seats in the reservoir stand are M$175 for adults, M$88 for children; Lisboa stand, M$520; Mandarin Oriental stand, M$520; Grand stand, M$575.

If, one week after the Grand Prix, you still haven't managed to get out of Macau (a possibility), you can join the Macau Marathon. Like the Grand Prix, this race attracts a lot of international attention. It's held in the first week of December.

ACTIVITIES

Future Ice Skating Rink (☎ 989-2318) is on Praca de Luis Camões, just on the south side of Camões Grotto & Gardens. The same place also features a bowling alley.

Up around the Guia Lighthouse is the best track for jogging. It's also the venue for early-morning t'ai chi.

There is a public swimming pool on Estrada da Vitoria near the Royal Hotel. Adjacent to the swimming pool is a gymnasium where local clubs get together to practice martial arts, t'ai chi, basketball and other activities. Foreigners are a rarity here, but if you approach the locals in a friendly way you are likely to be invited to participate in their activities. The clubs have a schedule of their events tacked up in the hall of the gymnasium.

Coloane Island features two decent swimming beaches: Cheoc Van Beach, which has a yacht club, and nearby Hac Sa Beach, which has a horse-riding stable and tennis courts. Hac Sa also has a number of sea toys

for rent, including windsurfers and water scooters.

In the hills of Coloane there's a hiking trail over eight km in total length. Bicycles are available for hire on Taipa but not on the Macau Peninsula.

A few hotels have exercise facilities which non-guests can use by paying a fee. The Westin Resort on Coloane features billiards, table tennis and a golf course. The health spa in the Kingsway Hotel offers hourly rates for use of the facilities: one hour M$163, 1½ hours M$208, two hours M$278 or a half day for M$300.

WORK

Unless you hold a Portuguese passport, finding employment is difficult. Most Portuguese speak excellent English, so there is little need to import foreign English teachers. However, there are growing opportunities for work with foreign joint-ventures, and people with specialised technical skills are always in demand.

Nearly 1% of Macau's population are young foreign females from such diverse places as Thailand, the Philippines and Russia. Some are employed in restaurants and hotels but the rest work in what is loosely called the 'entertainment industry'.

Unskilled labour is supplied by Chinese workers from nearby Zhuhai, who are paid a pittance.

ACCOMMODATION

There's good and bad news. The bad news is that hotel prices in Macau continue to rise – the old dumps are being torn down and replaced with comfortable hotels, which usually charge uncomfortable prices. Nor are there dormitories like those in Hong Kong which cater to the backpacker market.

But don't close the book yet, there is good news. Macau's hotels are cheaper than those in Hong Kong. For the same price that you'd pay in Hong Kong for a dormitory bed, you'll be able to find a private room (though without private bath). For about the same that you'd pay for a dumpy room in Hong Kong's Chungking Mansions, you can get a comfortable room in Macau with air-conditioning, private bath, TV and fancy carpeting. In other words, staying in Macau will probably wind up costing you the same as Hong Kong – you won't live cheaply, but you'll live better.

The all-important factor is that you must avoid weekends and holidays. At such times, room prices double and accommodation of any kind is difficult to get. For definition purposes, 'weekend' means both Saturday and Sunday nights. Friday night is usually not a problem unless it's also a holiday. Also, during special events, like the Grand Prix, rooms can be impossible to obtain.

Another way to save money is to avoid the peak season (summer). Peak-season prices are quoted in this book because that's when most travellers visit, but be aware that you can get substantial discounts in winter (except during Chinese New Year).

Camping

It seems hard to believe that in tiny, crowded Macau there could be a camping area. But there is a small one in *Seac Pai Van Park*, which is on Coloane Island south of the city. Whether it's worth the trouble to go this far to save some money on a night's accommodation is something you'll have to decide. See the section on Coloane Island in the Macau Islands chapter for details on how to reach this park by bus.

Hostels

There is only one hostel in all of Macau, and like the camping ground it's also on Coloane Island. The problem is that you can't simply show up at the hostel and ask if they have an empty bed. You must first go to the Youth Hostel Booking Office (☎ 344340; fax 960115), which is near the A-Ma Temple on Macau Peninsula. The office is only open during business hours, which means you can forget about it after 5.45 pm (or on weekends and holidays). The office will sell you a voucher for M$35 which you bring to the hostel when you check in.

See the section on Coloane Island in the Macau Islands chapter for the exact location of the hostel.

Guesthouses

By government edict, all guesthouses must have signs in both Chinese and Portuguese. Guesthouses usually call themselves *vila*, but sometimes they are called *hospedaria* or *pensão*.

There are a few old classic (dumpy) guesthouses still remaining in Macau – dirt cheap prices and plenty of dirt, not to mention cockroaches and other things that crawl in the night. However, these are becoming difficult to find – the dumps are being torn down (sometimes burned down). Many old guesthouses are being renovated and now offer luxurious rooms with air-conditioning, shag carpeting, etc, though the prices are about the same as the mid-range hotels. Prices at the old dumps can be as cheap as M$50, but the usual bottom-end at guesthouses is now about M$120 and many want M$200 or more. While this compares favourably to Hong Kong, it's not exactly a budget travellers' heaven.

Hotels

Macau has an incredible variety of hotels. Some are architectural museum pieces which have been fully renovated, while others are the modern high-rise glass-and-concrete cylinders like you see in Hong Kong. Then there are the really luxurious resorts – the type with swimming pools, saunas, tennis courts and carpeting around the toilet.

Most hotels in the middle to upper price range charge a 5% government room tax plus a 10% service charge.

One way to receive a substantial discount (up to 30%) is to book rooms through a travel agency, but this only applies to three-star and above hotels. If you're staying at a two-star or lower place, you'll have to bargain your own discount. Agents offering this service can be readily found at the Shun Tak Centre (Macau Jetfoil Pier) in Hong Kong and also in Macau at the Jetfoil Pier. You *cannot* get these discounts simply by showing up at the hotel and asking – only travel agents can arrange it.

FOOD

For some travellers, eating is the most rewarding part of a trip to Macau. Given its cosmopolitan past, it's not surprising that the food is an exotic mixture of Portuguese and Chinese cooking. There is also a little influence from other European countries and Africa. The English-speaking waitresses are invariably from the Philippines.

The most famous local speciality is African chicken – chicken baked with peppers and chillies. Other specialities include *bacalhau*, which is cod, served baked, grilled, stewed or boiled. The cod is imported and rather salty. Sole, a tongue-shaped flatfish, is another Macanese delicacy. There's also ox tail and ox breast, rabbit prepared in various ways, and soups like *caldo verde* and *sopa a alentejana* made with vegetables, meat and olive oil. The Brazilian contribution is *feijoadas*, a stew made of beans, pork, potatoes, cabbage and spicy sausages. The contribution from the former Portuguese enclave of Goa on the west coast of India is spicy prawns.

Apart from cod, there's other seafood aplenty – shrimp, prawns, crab, squid and white fish. You won't find Macau's baked crab or huge grilled and stuffed king prawns anywhere else. There are lots of little seafood restaurants where you can pick your meal from the tank at the front of the shop.

If you're going out for a meal, it's worth remembering that people eat early in Macau – in many places the dining room is clear and the chef has gone home by 9 pm.

DRINKS
Nonalcoholic Drinks
Macau doesn't produce any local specialities. The soft-drink market is dominated by imported brands from the West and Hong Kong. Chinese tea predominates in the restaurants, but Macau's supermarkets can supply you with a quick fix of Twinings and Lipton.

Alcoholic Drinks
The Portuguese influence is most visible in the many fine imported Portuguese red and white wines, port and brandy. Mateus Rosé is the most famous Portuguese wine and sells for a mere M$44. Even cheaper are bottles of red or white wine. Most are considerably more drinkable than the Chinese firewater.

Wine, spirits and beer are cheaper in Macau than in Hong Kong – even cheaper than at so-called 'duty-free stores'. Part of the reason has to do with Hong Kong's 90% import tax on alcoholic beverages. In Macau, Portuguese wine carries no import duty, and other imported brews are taxed at 22%.

Wine prices vary in the restaurants but are usually not too expensive. Many people leave Macau with a bottle of Mateus tucked under their arm. You can buy wine from supermarkets or Macau's duty-free shops at the airport and the Jetfoil Pier.

There is no minimum drinking age in Macau. If you're old enough to get the bottle open, you can drink whatever is inside.

ENTERTAINMENT
Gambling
I once worked in a Las Vegas casino as a slot machine mechanic and later as a floorman (slot machine attendant). During that time I saw humanity at its worst.

Although the games in Macau are somewhat different from Las Vegas, the same basic principles apply. The most important one to remember is this – if you want to win at gambling, own a casino. In every game, the casino enjoys a built-in mathematical advantage. The casinos don't cheat the players because they don't have to. In the short-term, anyone can hit a winning streak and get ahead, but the longer you play, the more certain it is that the odds will catch up with you. There is no system that can help you win. I know of one Las Vegas casino that caught a woman with a portable computer in her handbag; they let her go because, as the manager said, 'a computer won't help'.

Your best bet is to gamble for fun only. Don't bet more than you can afford to lose and don't think you can 'make up your losses' by gambling more. If you win, consider yourself lucky – this time.

The most popular form of gambling in Macau is mahjong, played not in the casinos but in private homes. You can hear the rattle of mahjong pieces late into the night if you walk through any side street.

The legal gambling age in Macau is 18 for

foreigners and 21 for residents. Photography is absolutely prohibited inside the casinos.

If you want to play casino games which are more sophisticated than the slot machines, it's essential that you track down a copy of the *Macau AOA Gambling Handbook*.

Slot Machines These are the classic sucker games in any casino. Maybe the reason why slot machines are so popular is because it takes no brains to play – just put the coin in the slot and pull the handle. Some machines allow you to put in up to five coins at a time, which increases your chance of winning by five times (but costs you five times as much, so you're no better off). Contrary to popular belief, how hard or gently you pull the handle has no influence on the outcome. There are many small pay-offs to encourage you to keep playing, but the goal of every slot player is to hit the grand jackpot (or megabucks as it is called in Macau).

The odds for winning on a slot machine are terrible. Machines are usually designed to give the casino a 25% advantage over the player. It's easy to win small pay-offs, but the odds of hitting the grand jackpot are very small indeed. It's like spinning five roulette wheels at once and expecting them to all land on number seven. The more reels on the machine, the more unlikely it is they will line up for the ultimate pay-off. Three-reel machines give you one chance in 8000 of hitting the jackpot. You have one chance in 160,000 of lining up four reels. If you play a five-reel machine, your chances of lining up all five winning numbers is one in 3.2 million.

Contrary to popular belief, slot machines are not controlled by computers, magnets or any other sophisticated device. The machines are as dumb as a pair of dice. Another popular myth is that the machines will eventually fill up with money and then must pay out. Neither is this true. When the machine is full, coins overflow down a tube into a bucket placed under the machine. The buckets are inside the cabinets that the machines rest on. The cabinets are unlocked and the buckets are emptied at about 4 am, when the casino is nearly deserted. Buckets filled with coins are heavy – one was dropped on my foot and broke my big toe. To this day, the toenail has not grown back.

If you do hit a jackpot, don't move away from the machine. Bells will ring, lights will flash, and a floorman will come running over to pay you in bills because the machine cannot possibly hold enough coins to pay a large jackpot.

People have tried all sorts of methods to cheat slot machines, but the machines have been designed to counter these efforts. Attempts to influence the spinning reels with magnets doesn't work because they are made from anti-magnetic materials. More professional thieves try to pick the lock on the machine's door to gain access to the cash box – the machines are equipped with alarms and various anti-theft devices to thwart this. Less professional thieves attempt to cheat the machines by inserting metal wires or pouring Coca-Cola into the coin slot, hoping that the machine will malfunction and pay out. This doesn't work but it creates employment for slot machine mechanics. Back in the early days of Las Vegas, when the casinos were owned by the Mafia (some say they still are), cheating at gambling could earn the cheater a pair of 'cement shoes'. These days, the penalty is more likely to be a free holiday behind bars. As with all other casino games, the slots are carefully watched by the famed 'eye-in-the-sky' – video cameras constantly monitored by security personnel.

Blackjack Also known as 21, this card game is easy to play, though it requires a little skill. The dealer takes a card and also gives one to the player. Each card counts for a particular number of points. The goal is to get enough cards to add up as close as possible to 21 without going over. If you go over 21, then you 'bust', which means you lose. If both you and the dealer go bust at the same time, the dealer still wins and this is what gives the casino the edge over the player. If the dealer and player both get 21, it's a tie and the bet is cancelled. If the player gets 21 (blackjack) then he or she gets even money plus a 50% bonus.

Dealers must draw until they reach 16 and stand on 17 or higher. The player is free to decide when to stand or when to draw.

You may occasionally see a book or newspaper article describing a system for beating the casinos at blackjack. Such a system does exist and is called card counting. To do it you need a good memory and a quick mind. Basically, if you can remember which cards have been dealt from the deck you will know which cards remain: as the dealer nears the end of the deck you can make very good guesses about which cards remain to be dealt. Therefore, you can estimate your chances of going bust, and know when to stand and when to draw. When you're sure you can beat the dealer's hand, you bet heavily.

It sounds great. The problem is it no longer works because to defeat card counters the casino dealers play with multiple decks and reshuffle the cards frequently.

Roulette This is a very easy game to play and I don't know why it isn't more popular in Macau. At the moment, the only roulette

wheel remaining in all of Macau is at the Lisboa Hotel, and who knows how long before it gets retired?

The dealer simply spins the roulette wheel in one direction and spins a ball in the opposite direction. Roulette wheels have 36 numbers plus a zero, so your chance of hitting any given number is one in 37. The pay-off is 35 to one, which is what gives the casino its advantage.

Rather than betting a single number, it's much easier to win if you bet odd or even, or red versus black numbers. If the ball lands on zero, everyone loses to the house (unless you also bet the zero). If you bet red or black, odd or even, the casino's advantage is only 2.7%.

Very similar to roulette is boule. In fact it's identical except that it's played with a large ball about the size of a billiard ball. There are fewer numbers too. Boule has 24 numbers plus a star. The pay-off is 23 to one on numbers. On all bets (numbers, red or black, odd or even) the casino has a 4% advantage over the players.

Craps This game is extremely popular in the West and I don't know why it's rare in Macau. In fact, on my last trip to Macau I didn't see a single craps table and I wonder if they've been done away with. Maybe the casinos prefer not to have this game because the house has such a small advantage – only about 1.4%.

Craps is played by tossing a pair of dice down a long, narrow table. The dice are thrown by the players, not the dealers, so there is more of a feeling of participation. The person tossing the dice, the shooter, is permitted to shoot until he or she loses, then the dice are passed to the next player at the table in a counter-clockwise direction.

This game is more complicated than most. On the first roll (the 'come-out' roll) the shooter automatically wins if he or she throws a seven or 11. If a two, three or 12 is thrown on the first roll, it's an automatic loss. Any other number results in a point. The shooter must continue to toss the dice until the point is thrown again. However, if a seven is rolled before the point is made, then it's a loss. This method of betting is called betting the 'come' or 'front line'.

There are other ways to play. You can also bet that the shooter will lose (don't come) or that a pair of fours (a hard eight) will be thrown before other combinations adding up to eight (a soft eight). The complexity of the game is one of its attractions. If a shooter gets hot (wins several rolls in succession) the game gets exciting, with lots of players jumping up and down and yelling. The exhilaration probably explains why craps is a favourite with compulsive gamblers.

Baccarat Also known as *chemin de fer*, this has become the card game of choice for the upper crust. Baccarat rooms are always the most classy part of any casino and the minimum wager is high – at least M$50, and up to M$1000 in some casinos.

Two card hands are dealt at the same time – the player hand and the bank hand. The hand which scores closest to nine is the winner. Players can bet on either their own hand or the bank hand. Neither is actually the house hand. The casino deducts a percentage if the bank hand wins, which is how the house makes its profit.

If the player understands the game properly, the house only enjoys slightly better than a 1% advantage over the player.

Fan Tan This is an ancient Chinese game practically unknown in the West. The dealer takes an inverted silver cup and plunges it into a pile of porcelain buttons, then moves the cup to one side. After all bets have been placed, the buttons are counted out in groups of four. You have to bet on how many will remain after the last set of four has been taken out. You can bet on numbers one, two, three or four, as well as odd or even.

Dai Siu This is Cantonese for 'big-small'. The game is also known as Sik Po ('dice treasure') or Cu Sik ('guessing dice'). It's extremely popular in Macau.

The game is played with three dice which are placed in a covered glass container. The container is then shaken and you bet that the total of the toss will be from three to nine (small) or from 10 to 18 (big). However, you lose on combinations where all three dice come up the same, like 2-2-2, 3-3-3, etc, unless you bet directly on three of a kind.

For betting 'big-small' the house advantage is 2.78%. Betting on a specific three of a kind gives the house a 30% advantage – a sucker bet.

Pai Kao This is Chinese dominoes and reminds me a lot of mahjong. One player is designated the role of banker and the others individually compare their hands against the banker. The casino doesn't play, but deducts a 3% commission from the winnings for providing the gambling facilities.

Keno Although keno is played in Las Vegas and other Western casinos, it's believed to have originated in China more than 2000 years ago. Keno was introduced to America by Chinese railroad workers in the 19th century.

Keno is basically a lottery. There are 80 numbers, of which 20 are drawn in each game. You are given a keno ticket and the object is to list the numbers you think will be drawn. You can bet on four numbers and if all four are among those drawn in the game, you're a winner. You can play five numbers, six, seven and so on. You have about one chance in nine million of guessing all 20 winning numbers. With only about two drawings per hour, it's a slow way to lose

---

Chipping In

Want to visit Macau for free? All you've got to do is buy HK$5000 worth of gambling chips and the Lisboa Hotel will provide you with a free jetfoil ticket. Buy HK$30,000 worth of chips and they'll give you a free night's accommodation as well. It doesn't stipulate that you actually have to lose the chips although I guess they'd like it if you did. The proliferation of pawn shops around the casinos would seem to indicate that some people lose the lot. ■

your money. I consider keno to be the most boring game in the casino.

SPECTATOR SPORT

The *Taipa Stadium* next to the Macau Jockey Club on Taipa Island seats 20,000 fans. At certain times of year there are international soccer meets and track and field competitions.

The *Macau Forum* is where you can see volleyball games, roller hockey, table tennis and other team sports.

Dog Racing

Macau has a *Canidrome* – yes, that's what they call it – for dog racing. It's off Avenida General Castelo Branco, not far from the Barrier Gate. Greyhound races are held three times a week on – Tuesday, Thursday and either Saturday or Sunday – starting at 8 pm. You can call (☎ 574413) to check the schedule. There are 14 races per night with six to eight dogs per race. Admission to the Canidrome costs M$2, or M$5 in the members' stand; there are boxes for six persons costing M$80 for the whole group and a VIP room for M$25.

Off-Course Betting Centres will accept bets from 5 pm onwards. The centres are in the Lisboa Hotel, Floating Casino and Jai Alai Casino.

Once a year (usually at the end of summer) the Macau Derby is held at the Canidrome. This is the year's biggest race and the winner's purse is currently M$80,000.

Horse Racing

Horse racing has a long history in Macau. In the early 1800s horse races were held outside the city walls on an impromptu course. You may notice on the Macau map that there is a street called Estrada Marginal do Hipodromo in the extreme north-east corner of town, near the Barrier Gate. This was a popular racecourse in the 1930s, but the area has now been taken over by flats and factories.

A trotting track was opened on Taipa Island, but closed in 1989. This has given way to the fancy *Macau Jockey Club*, where regular horse races are held. For more details on horse racing, see the Macau Jockey Club section in the Taipa Island chapter.

THINGS TO BUY

Pawnshops are ubiquitous in Macau. It's possible to get good deals on cameras, watches and jewellery, but you must be prepared to bargain without mercy.

The St Dominic Market is in the alley just behind the Hotel Central and next to the MGTO. It's a good place to pick up cheap clothing.

If you've got the habit, Macau is a bargain for booze and tobacco (including cigars and pipe tobacco). Check out the supermarkets for the best prices.

The largest department store in Macau is the well-known Japanese retailer Yaohan. The store is near the Jetfoil Pier.

Macau is proud of its unusual stamps, which include portraits of everything from colonial architecture to the roulette tables and the jetfoil. Collectors' sets are on sale at the GPO.

A Pawn Loser

In Macau pawn shops, it's no holds barred. These guys would sell their own mother to a glue factory. I saw a nice camera – a Ricoh KR-5 – in a pawnshop window with a M$850 price tag. That's about how much it cost new, and this camera was eight years old! I examined it and found the automatic timer was broken. After an exhaustive bargaining session, I got the price down to M$600. I bought the camera and the next day had it appraised at a camera shop. They told me I shouldn't have paid more than M$200. Just for fun, I took it over to another pawnshop and asked how much they would give me for it. They said it was worth M$50.

James Whitham

Getting There & Away

AIR
Airports & Airlines
Macau's airport opened in December 1995. It's one of the least busy airports in Asia, and as a result immigration, customs and baggage-handling procedures are fast and efficient. Airlines serving Macau include:

Air Macau
    Edificio Tai Wah 9-12 Andar, Avenida da Praia Grande 693
    (☎ 396-6888; fax 396-6866, airport 898-3388)
Air Portugal (TAP)
    ground floor, Edificio Dynasty Plaza (adjacent to Mandarin Oriental Hotel) (☎ 750408, 750410; fax 713782; airport 898-2288)
Asiana
    room 22-24, mezzanine floor, Passengers' Terminal, Macau airport (☎ 861400; fax 861404)
CSA
    TTS Travel Service, Bank of China Building, Avenida Dr Mario Soares (☎ 787877)
EVA Airways
    room 6, mezzanine floor, Passengers' Terminal, Macau airport (☎ 861330; fax 861324)
Korean Air
    room 15-18, mezzanine floor, Passengers' Terminal, Macau airport (☎ 861482; fax 861485)
Malaysia Airlines
    18th floor, Bank of China Building, Avenida Dr Mario Soares
    (☎ 787898; fax 787883; airport 886-1253)
Sabena
    shares an office with Air Portugal on the ground floor, Edificio Dynasty Plaza (adjacent to Mandarin Oriental Hotel) (☎ 750412)
Singapore Airlines
    room 1001, 10th floor, Luso International Building, 1-3 Rua Dr Pedro Jose Lobo
    (☎ 711728; fax 711732 airport 861321)
TransAsia
    11th floor, block B-C, Macau Financial Centre, Beijing St 244-246, New Coast
    (☎ 688-6455, 701777; fax 862200)

Buying Tickets
The situation for buying tickets to or from Macau is much the same as in Hong Kong. As always, better deals on discount fares will be found through travel agencies rather than purchased from the airlines directly. With new airlines entering the Macau market, there are some great promotional fares on offer, but these tend to be short-lived. Some airlines even throw in a free boat ticket between Macau and Hong Kong to sweeten the deal.

Travel Agencies A few travel agencies in Macau which offer discounted tickets include:

Amigo Travel
    ground floor, new wing in the Lisboa Hotel
    (☎ 337333; fax 378383)
Estoril Tours
    ground floor, New Wing, Lisboa Hotel
    (☎ 710361; fax 710353; HK 2540-8028)
Hong Kong Student Travel Macau
    Rua do Campo 13 (☎ 311100)

China
Air Macau connects Macau with Beijing, Shanghai and Xiamen. CSA flies from Macau to Changsha, Chongqing, Dalian, Shenyang, Qingdao, Xi'an, Yantai and Wenzhou.

Europe
Air Portugal (TAP) and Sabena of Belgium have made a joint venture to do a direct Macau-Brussels flight with a stopover in Lisbon. At present there are two flights weekly, but more flights will no doubt be added if demand picks up.

Hong Kong
For Hong Kongers in a hurry to lose their money, East Asia Airlines runs a helicopter service. Flying time from Hong Kong is 20 minutes at a cost of HK$1206 on week days, HK$1310 on weekends – quite an expense just to save the extra 30 minutes required by boat. There are up to 17 flights daily between 9.30 am and 10.30 pm. In Hong Kong, departures are from the Jetfoil Pier at the Shun Tak Centre (☎ 2859-3359), 200 Connaught Rd, Sheung Wan; in Macau, departures are from the Jetfoil Pier (☎ 725939).

Japan

No regularly scheduled direct flights exist between Macau and Japan yet, but All Nippon Airways and Japan Air System have both been running charters. Negotiations are under way to establish regular air services.

Korea

Asiana Airlines and Korean Air offer direct Macau-Seoul flights.

Singapore

Malaysia Airlines and Singapore Airlines fly between Macau and Singapore.

Taiwan

You can fly from either Taipei or Kaohsiung to Macau on EVA Air, TransAsia or Air Macau. Round-trip tickets cost US$250.

Thailand

Air Macau offers direct Macau-Bangkok flights three times weekly. THAI will soon begin service on this route too.

LAND
China

Just across the border from Macau is the town of Gongbei in the Zhuhai Special Economic Zone. The border crossing is open from 7.30 am until 11.30 pm.

There is a bus from Macau to Guangzhou via Gongbei, but it's more hassle than it's worth. The bus stops at the border for over an hour while all the passengers go through immigration and customs formalities. It would be easier to take a bus to the border, walk across, and catch a minibus to Guangzhou from the other side. However, if you prefer the 'direct' bus, tickets are sold at Kee Kwan Motors (☎ 572264) across the street from the Floating Casino. Buses leave daily at 7 am and noon and take about six hours.

SEA
Hong Kong

Although Macau is separated from Hong Kong by 65 km of water, the journey can be made in as little as one hour. There are frequent departures throughout the day. The schedule is somewhat reduced between 10 pm and 7 am, but boats run virtually 24 hours.

You have four types of vessels to choose from. There are jetfoils (single-hull jet-powered hydrofoils), turbocats (jet-powered catamarans), foil-cats (catamaran-jetfoils) and HK Ferries (433-passenger two-deck ferries). The journey takes 55 minutes on the jetfoils and foil-cats, 65 minutes by turbocat and 95 minutes on HK Ferries. It's fun to take one sort of boat going to Macau, and a different one when returning.

A wide variety of small craft use Macau's harbour, but you won't see any huge cruise ships simply because the harbour isn't deep enough to accommodate them.

Most of the boats depart from the huge Macau Jetfoil Pier next to the Shun Tak Centre at 200 Connaught Rd, Sheung Wan, Hong Kong Island – this is easily reached by taking the MTR to Sheung Wan station. A few boats also depart from the China-Hong Kong City ferry terminal on Canton Rd in Tsim Sha Tsui.

On weekends and holidays, you'd be wise to book your return ticket in advance because the boats are sometimes full. On week days the boats are not even half full and you'll have no problem getting a seat.

In Macau, you can book tickets on all boats at the Jetfoil Pier. You can also book tickets for all boats in the lobby of the Lisboa Hotel.

Luggage space on the jetfoils and turbocats is limited – there is no room under the seat and no overhead racks, so you have to sit on your bag or it sits on your lap. You are theoretically limited to 10 kg of carry-on luggage (you can probably get away with more if it's not bulky), but oversized or overweight bags can be taken as checked luggage. On the HK Ferries there is a little more luggage space. There are a small number of lockers at the Shun Tak Centre.

You need to arrive at the pier at least 15 minutes before departure, but from my experience you'd be wise to allow 30 minutes because of occasional long queues at the immigration checkpoint, especially on the

Hong Kong side (immigration works faster in Macau).

Jetfoil tickets can be purchased up to 28 days in advance in Hong Kong at the pier (Shun Tak Centre) or at a MTR Travel Services Centre (☎ 2859-6569) in the following MTR stations: Admiralty, Causeway Bay, Central, Kwun Tong, Mong Kok, Tai Koo, Tsim Sha Tsui and Tsuen Wan. Telephone bookings can be made if you have a credit card.

Turbocat bookings can be made 28 days in advance, but no phone bookings are available. You can buy tickets at the Shun Tak Centre, or at China-Hong Kong City in Kowloon.

HK Ferries can be booked 28 days in advance at the Shun Tak Centre or any Ticketmate outlet.

Most boats offer two classes (economy and first). The turbocats have a VIP cabin which seats up to six persons, and the cost per ticket is the same whether one or six persons occupy the cabin. Boat tickets cost M$4 less in Macau than in Hong Kong – the following prices (in HK$) are what you pay in Hong Kong:

Vessel	Weekday	Weekend	Night
Turbocat	123/223/	134/234/	146/246/
	1336	1396	1476
Foil-Cat	133/147	145/190	165/190
HK			
Ferries	111	126	144
Jetfoil	123/136	134/146	152/166

Shekou

There is a once-daily ferry connecting Macau to Shekou in the Shenzhen Special Economic Zone (north of Hong Kong). The boat departs Macau at 2.30 pm and arrives in Shekou at 4 pm. The fare is M$100 and tickets can be bought up to three days in advance. Note that this ferry does not depart from the main Jetfoil Pier in Macau – it departs from a pier behind the Peninsula Hotel (next to the Floating Casino).

DEPARTURE TAX

Airport departure tax is M$130, payable in either Macau patacas or Hong Kong dollars.

There are also departure taxes on boats. The Hong Kong government charges a HK$26 departure tax which is included in the price of your boat ticket. Macau charges M$22, also included in the ticket price.

ORGANISED TOURS

Tours offer a fast way to see everything with minimum hassle and can easily be booked in Hong Kong or Macau after arrival. Tours booked in Macau are generally much better value because those booked in Hong Kong usually cost considerably more (though they include transportation to and from Macau and a side-trip across the border to Zhuhai in China). These are usually one-day whirlwind tours, departing for Macau in the morning and returning to Hong Kong the same evening. A full-day whirlwind tour from Hong Kong typically costs about HK$600.

There is an exhausting one-day tour that departs Hong Kong at 7 am, takes you to Shekou (in the Shenzhen Special Economic Zone north of Hong Kong), then by boat to Zhuhai Special Economic Zone north of Macau, then to the home of Dr Sun Yatsen in Zhongshan County, then by bus to Macau, then by jetfoil back to Hong Kong by 7.30 pm. This trip costs HK$800, not including the medical treatment you might need for seasickness or cardiac arrest.

If you'd like a slower pace, a three- to four-day tour from Hong Kong to Macau, Zhuhai, Cuiheng (home of Dr Sun Yatsen), Shiqi, Foshan, Guangzhou and then back to Hong Kong by train, costs about HK$1700.

Finding these tours is not difficult. In Hong Kong, the ubiquitous money changers often have a collection of free pamphlets offering tours to Macau. The MGTO at the Shun Tak Centre (Macau Jetfoil Pier) has piles of information on tours and this is probably the best place to go. Most Hong Kong travel agencies can also book tours.

For booking a tour after arrival in Macau, see the following Getting Around chapter.

Getting Around

THE AIRPORT

Airport bus AP1 leaves the airport and first zips around Taipa passing the Jockey Club, Hyatt and New Century hotels, then crosses the bridge and stops at the Lisboa Hotel, then takes in some other hotels in the centre, the China border crossing and terminates at the Jetfoil Pier. The fare is M$5 and the bus runs from 6.15 am until 1.20 am.

Numerous taxis meet all incoming flights. Drivers use their meters without argument. Expect to pay roughly M$30 for a ride into town.

BUS

There are minibuses and large buses, and both offer air-conditioning and frequent service. They operate from 7 am until midnight. You need exact change, but either Macau or Hong Kong coins are acceptable. Long-termers can buy a monthly bus pass for M$165. For questions, complaints, etc, call Transmac (☎ 271122).

Macau's bus routes change so frequently that the mapmakers have given up – most maps of the city do not show bus routes. Nevertheless, a detailed map (preferably bilingual) will be of some help in navigation.

Macau Peninsula

Buses on the Macau peninsula cost M$2. Arguably, the two most useful buses to travellers are No 3 and 3A which run between the Jetfoil Pier and the central area near the GPO. No 3 also goes to the China border, as does No 5. There are numerous other routes. The following are the current bus routes:

No 1
  Fai Chi Kei, Avenida do Almirante Lacerda, Rua do Almirante Sergio, Barra Hill
No 1A
  Jai Alai Casino, Rua dos Pescadores, Estrada de Areia Preta, Avenida do Almirante Lacerda, Barra Hill
No 2
  Praca Serenidade, Avenida de Venceslau de Morais, Macau Electric Company, Rua do Campo, Avenida Almeida Ribeiro, Barra Hill, Avenida Almeida Ribeiro, Rua do Campo, Avenida Conselheiro Ferreira de Almeida, Avenida do Coronel Mesquita, Macau Electric Company, Estrada da Areia Preta, Praca Serenidade
No 3
  Jetfoil Pier, Jai Alai Casino, Kingsway Hotel, Lisboa Hotel, Avenida Almeida Ribeiro, Avenida do Almirante Lacerda, Avenida de Artur Tamagnini Barbosa, Barrier Gate
No 3A
  Jetfoil Pier, Jai Alai Casino, Kingsway Hotel, Lisboa Hotel, Avenida Almeida Ribeiro, Praca Ponte E Horta
No 4
  Fai Chi Kei, Lin Fung Miu (Lotus Temple), Avenida Horta e Costa, Rua do Campo, Avenida Almeida Ribeiro, Avenida do Almirante Lacerda, Fai Chi Kei
No 5
  Barra Hill, Avenida Almeida Ribeiro, Avenida Conselheiro Ferreira de Almeida, Avenida Horta e Costa, Avenida do Almirante Lacerda, Barrier Gate, Lin Fung Miu (Lotus Temple), Avenida Horta e Costa, tunnel, Jai Alai Casino, Avenida do Dr Rodrigo Rodrigues, Jai Alai Casino, Avenida Almeida Ribeiro, Barra Hill
No 6
  Praca Serenidade, Iao Hon Market, Avenida de Venceslau de Morais, Macau Electric Company, Avenida Horta e Costa, Rua da Ribeira do Patane, Barra Hill, Avenida da Republica, Avenida da Praia Grande, Lisboa Hotel, Government Hospital, Rua Nova a Guia, Avenida do Dr Rodrigo Rodrigues, Avenida Almeida Ribeiro, Avenida do Almirante Lacerda, Avenida Horta e Costa, Avenida Conselheiro Ferreira de Almeida, Macau Electric Company, Avenida de Venceslau de Morais, Iao Hon Market, Praca Serenidade
No 7
  Rua 1 de Bairro Iao Hon, Rua Francisco Xavier Pereira, Avenida do Ouvidor Arriaga, Rua do Campo, Avenida Almeida Ribeiro, Barra Hill, Avenida da Republica, Rua Afonso Albuquerque, Avenida do Ouvidor Arriaga, Fai Chi Kei, Rua 1 de Bairro Iao Hon
No 8
  Ihla Verde, Lin Fung Miu (Lotus Temple), Avenida Horta e Costa, Rua Carlos da Maia, Rua de Sacadura Cabral, Estoril Hotel, Avenida Almeida Ribeiro, Barra Hill, Avenida Almeida Ribeiro, Rua do Campo, Estrada do Cemiterio, Estrada do Repouso, Rua da Barca, Rua Fran-

cisco Xavier Pereira, Estrada da Areia Preta, Ihla Verde

No 8A

Ihla Verde, Lin Fung Miu (Lotus Temple), Avenida Horta e Costa, Rua do Almirante Costa Cabral, Estrada de Adolfo Loureiro, Rua do Campo, Avenida Almeida Ribeiro, Rua do Tarrafeiro, Kiang Wu Hospital, Rua da Barca, Rua Francisco Xavier Pereira, Estrada da Areia Preta, Ihla Verde

No 9

Barrier Gate, Lin Fung Miu (Lotus Temple), Avenida do Ouvidor Arriaga, Estoril Hotel, Rua do Campo, Avenida da Praia Grande, Lisboa Hotel, Central Hotel, Rua do Chunambeiro, Barra Hill, Rua de Inacio Baptista, Bela Vista Hotel, Avenida da Praia Grande, Lisboa Hotel, Rua do Campo, Avenida Horta e Costa, Avenida do Almirante Lacerda, Avenida de Artur Tamagnini Barbosa, Barrier Gate

No 9A

Barrier Gate, Lin Fung Miu (Lotus Temple), Avenida do Ouvidor Arriaga, Estoril Hotel, Rua do Campo, Avenida da Praia Grande, Lisboa Hotel, Central Hotel, Rua do Chunambeiro, Avenida da Praia Grande, Lisboa Hotel, Rua do Campo, Avenida Horta e Costa, Avenida do Almirante Lacerda, Avenida de Artur Tamagnini Barbosa, Barrier Gate

No 16

Rua Marginal do Canal das Hortas, Barrier Gate, Avenida do Almirante Lacerda, Rua do Almirante Sergio, Rua de Inacio Baptista, Avenida da Praia Grande, Rua do Campo, Avenida do Ouvidor Arriaga, Fai Chi Kei, Rua Marginal do Canal das Hortas

No 28B

Ihla Verde, Avenida de Venceslau de Morais, Rua dos Pescadores, Jetfoil Pier, Jai Alai Casino, Kingsway Hotel, Lisboa Hotel, Avenida da Praia Grande, Travessa do Padre Narciso, Barra Hill, Avenida da Praia Grande, Kingsway Hotel, Rua dos Pescadores, Avenida de Venceslau de Morais, Ihla Verde

No 28B

(partial route) Ihla Verde, Estrada da Areia Preta, Avenida de Venceslau de Morais, Jetfoil Pier, Jai Alai Casino, Kingsway Hotel, Lisboa Hotel

No 28C

Jai Alai Casino, Kingsway Hotel, Lisboa Hotel, Government Hospital, Avenida Conselheiro Ferreira de Almeida, Avenida Horta e Costa, Rua do Bosco, Iao Hon Market, Avenida de Artur Tamagnini Barbosa, Barrier Gate, Lin Fung Miu (Lotus Temple), Avenida do Ouvidor Arriaga, Royal Hotel, Lisboa Hotel, Jai Alai Casino

No 32

Fai Chi Kei, Lin Fung Miu (Lotus Temple), Avenida Horta e Costa, tunnel, Jetfoil Pier, Jai Alai Casino, Macau Forum, Lisboa Hotel, Macau Forum, Jai Alai Casino, tunnel, Avenida Horta e Costa, Lin Fung Miu (Lotus Temple), Fai Chi Kei

The Islands

Buses to Taipa cost M$2.50, to Coloane Village it's M$3.20 and to Hac Sa Beach (on Coloane) it's M$4. Taipa-Hac Sa costs M$2.50, Coloane-Hac Sa is M$1.70. The complete bus routes to the islands are as follows:

No 11

Praca Ponte e Horta, Floating Casino, Avenida Almeida Ribeiro, GPO, Lisboa Hotel, bridge, Hyatt Regency Hotel (Taipa), Macau University, Taipa Village, Jockey Club, Hyatt Regency Hotel, Avenida Almeida Ribeiro (Macau Peninsula), Praca Ponte e Horta

No 26

Fai Chi Kei, Avenida do Almirante Lacerda, Rua da Ribeira do Patane, Avenida Almeida Ribeiro, Lisboa Hotel, Hyatt Regency Hotel (Taipa), Coloane Village, Cheoc Van Beach, Hac Sa Beach, Coloane Village, Taipa, Avenida do Infante D'Henrique, Avenida Almeida Ribeiro, Rua do Tarrafeiro, Kiang Wu Hospital, Avenida Horta e Costa, Avenida do Almirante Lacerda, Fai Chi Kei

No 26A

Fai Chi Kei, Lin Fung Miu (Lotus Temple), Avenida Almeida Ribeiro, Lisboa Hotel, Hyatt Regency Hotel (Taipa), Coloane Village, Cheoc Van Beach, Hac Sa Beach

No 28A

Jetfoil Pier, Jai Alai Casino, Kingsway Hotel, Lisboa Hotel, Hyatt Regency Hotel (Taipa), Macau University, Taipa Village, Jockey Club, Macau University, Hyatt Regency Hotel, Lisboa Hotel (Macau Peninsula), Jetfoil Pier

No 33

Fai Chi Kei, Lin Fung Miu (Lotus Temple), Avenida Almeida Ribeiro, Lisboa Hotel, Hyatt Regency Hotel (Taipa), Macau University, Taipa Village, Hyatt Regency Hotel, Lisboa Hotel (Macau Peninsula), Avenida Almeida Ribeiro, Avenida do Almirante Lacerda, Fai Chi Kei

No 38

Special bus running from the city centre to the Jockey Club on Taipa one hour before the races

TAXI

Macau taxis all have meters and drivers are required to use them. Flagfall is M$8 for the first 1.5 km, thereafter it's M$1 every 250m. There is a M$5 surcharge to go to Taipa, and M$10 to go to Coloane, but there is no surcharge on return trips. Taxis can be dispatched by radio if you ring up Vang Lek Radio Taxi

Company (☎ 519519). Not many taxi drivers speak English, so it would be helpful to have a map with both Chinese and English or Portuguese.

You can hire a taxi and driver for a whole day or a half day. The price as well as the itinerary should be agreed on in advance. Large hotels can usually help arrange this.

CAR & MOTORCYCLE

While plenty of people in Macau buy cars, they do so mainly for prestige. As for practical transportation, cars are a disaster on the Macau peninsula. Apart from the bumper to bumper traffic, there is really no place to park a car in the city. To stop to look at something or go shopping, it's entirely possible that you'll spend more than 30 minutes or more searching for a parking place and wind up parking several hundred metres from your destination.

While driving on the Macau peninsula cannot be recommended, a rented car (or moke) can be a convenient way to explore the islands.

Motorcycles are not available for rent.

Rental

Happy Rent-A-Car (☎ 726868) is across from the Jetfoil Pier in Macau, and also in the New Century Hotel (☎ 831212) on Taipa Island. A Moke can be rented for M$380. This rate is for 24 hours (same rate weekends or weekdays). The Moke is originally British, but the ones in Macau are custom-made Portuguese clones.

You can also rent Mokes from Avis Rent-A-Car (☎ 336789, 567888 ext 3004) which is located at the Mandarin Oriental Hotel. It's probably not necessary on weekdays, but you can book in advance at the Avis Hong Kong office (☎ 2541-2011).

Road Rules

An international driver's licence is required theoretically, and these cannot be issued in Macau unless you already have a Macau driver's licence – arrange it before arrival. Drivers must be 21 years of age or over. As in Hong Kong, driving is on the left-hand side of the road. Another local driving rule is that motor vehicles must always stop for pedestrians at crossings if there is no traffic

light. It's illegal to beep the horn (if only Hong Kong had this rule!).

If you happen to be a resident of Macau, local driver's licences are applied for at the Leal Senado. However, international licences are applied for at the Edificio do Apoio do Grande Premio (☎ 726578), near the Jetfoil Pier on Avenida da Amizade.

Police in Macau are strict and there are stiff fines for traffic violators, so obey the rules unless you want to contribute even more to Macau's economy.

PEDICABS

These are three-wheeled bicycles, known as *triciclos* in Portuguese. In many third world countries, pedicabs (or cyclos) are used as cheap taxis. In Macau, which is hardly the third world, pedicabs are a tourist novelty which are actually more expensive than taxis. As pedicabs don't have meters, agree on the fare before getting in. A short ride will cost perhaps M$20, while an hour of sightseeing is anywhere from M$50 to M$100. As pedicabs cannot negotiate hills, you'll be limited to touring the waterfront and some of the narrow alleys.

It's easiest to find the pedicabs near the Lisboa Hotel and to a much lesser extent at the Jetfoil Pier. You won't have to solicit the drivers. If you so much as look their way they'll come chasing after you.

BICYCLE

Bicycle rentals are available in Taipa Village. The machines are available in a wide variety of classes from light ten-speeds to heavyweight clunkers.

At one time they were available in Coloane, but at present nobody is pursuing this business. Conceivably, Coloane might some day have bikes for rent again.

Walking is permitted on the older Macau-Taipa Bridge, but bicycles are prohibited. The only way to take a bike across to the islands is in the boot of a taxi. However, bikes are allowed on the Taipa-Coloane Causeway, but it's not very safe as the causeway is narrow and traffic can be heavy. One false move and you may wind up staying in Macau a lot longer than you intended.

WALKING

Macau is certainly small enough to visit many areas on foot. However, it's going to be a long and exhausting day if you don't take to motorised transport, so at least start early if you're going to rely on foot power alone.

TOUR MACHINE

If you want to do something really touristy, you can ride the 'Tour Machine', a replica of a 1920s English bus equipped with leather upholstery. It's painted fire-engine red and has bright yellow letters declaring it the 'Tour Machine'. The bus seats nine people and runs on a few fixed routes – you need to get the little brochure to figure out the routes and times. The machine can be chartered for M$200 per hour in Macau, or M$300 for trips across the border into China.

If this interests you, contact Avis Rent-A-Car (☎ 336789, 567888 ext 3004) which is located at the Mandarin Oriental Hotel.

ORGANISED TOURS

It's cheaper to book tours after arrival in Macau as opposed to doing it in Hong Kong.

A typical city tour (booked in Macau) of the peninsula takes three to four hours and costs about M$100 per person, often including lunch. Bus tours to the islands run from about M$40 per person. You can also book a one-day bus tour across the border into Zhuhai in China, which usually includes a trip to the former home of Dr Sun Yatsen in Zhongshan County.

In Macau, contact the tourist office or go directly to one of these tour agencies:

Able Tours
    5-9 Travessa do Padre Narciso
    (☎ 566939; fax 566938; HK 2545-9993)
Asia
    25-B Avenida da Praia Grande
    (☎ 593844; fax 565060; HK 2548-8806)
China Travel Service
    Xinhua Building, Rua de Nagasaki
    (☎ 705506; fax 606611; HK 2540-6333)
Feliz
    14th floor, Rua de Xangai 175
    (☎ 781697; fax 781699; HK 2541-1611)
Gongbei
    Rua Leoncio Ferreira 8
    (☎ 552355; fax 569954; HK 2850-6891)

Gongfei
    Avenida da Praia Grande 101-5
    (☎ 344696; fax 312-2386; HK 2541-7393)
Guangdong
    Avenida da Praia Grande 37-E
    (☎ 588807; fax 323771; HK 2832-9118)
Heaven
    Nam Fong Building, block 1-6,
    Avenida da Amizade
    (☎ 706648; fax 566622; HK 2368-6781)
Hi-No-De Caravela
    Rua de Sacadura Cabral 6A-4C
    (☎ 333-8338; fax 566622; HK 2368-6781)
International
    Travessa do Padre Narciso 9, Loja B
    (☎ 975183; fax 974072; HK 2541-2011)
Lotus
    Edificio Fong Meng, Rua de Sao Lourenco
    (☎ 972977)
Macau
    Avenida Dr Mario Soares 35
    (☎ 710003; fax 710004; HK 2542-2338)
Macau Chu Kong Tours
    ground floor, Tai Fung Bank,
    Avenida da Praia Grande 31
    (☎ 371327; fax 371326; HK 2581-0022)
Macau Mondial
    Avenida do Conselheiro Ferreira de Almeida
    74-A (☎ 566866; fax 574531)
Macau Star
    room 511, Tai Fung Bank Building, Avenida
    Almeida Ribeiro 34
    (☎ 558855; fax 586702; HK 2922-3013)
Macau Zhuhai
    room 406, Hotel Presidente, Avenida da Amizade
    (☎ 552739; fax 552735)
Mirada
    ground floor, Rua do General Castelo Branco 9
    (☎ 261582; fax 261-1583)
Peninsula
    Rua das Lorchas 14 (☎ 316699; fax 362944)
Presidente
    Avenida da Amizade 355
    (☎ 781334; fax 781335)
Sintra
    room 135, Lisboa Hotel, Avenida da Amizade
    (☎ 710361; fax 710359; HK 2540-8028)
South China
    5th floor, flat O, Nam Fong Building, Avenida da
    Amizade
    (☎ 706620; fax 710353; HK 2540-8028)
TKW
    apartment 408, 4th floor, Rua Formosa 27-31
    (☎ 591122; fax 576200; HK 2723-7771)
Vacations International
    shopping arcade, Mandarin Oriental Hotel,
    Avenida da Amizade
    (☎ 567888 ext 3004; fax 314112)

Macau Peninsula

CENTRAL MACAU

Avenida de Almeida Ribeiro is the main street of Macau and is as good a place to start your tour as any. It crosses Avenida da Praia Grande just up from the waterfront and effectively divides the narrow southern peninsula from the rest of Macau. It continues down to the Lisboa Hotel under the name of Avenida do Infante D'Henrique (Macau's streets may not be very big but their names certainly are). A good place to start is the Lisboa Hotel, that grotesquely distinctive building which dominates the old waterfront of Macau.

Jorge Alvares Statue

The monument is on the Avenida da Praia Grande. Alvares was credited with being the first Portuguese to set foot on Chinese soil when he and his party landed on the island of Lingding, halfway between Macau and Hong Kong.

Leal Senado

Across the street from the GPO on Avenida de Almeida Ribeiro is the Leal Senado, which houses the municipal government offices.

The Leal Senado (Loyal Senate) is the main administrative body for municipal affairs, but it once had much greater powers and dealt on equal terms with Chinese officials during the last century. It's called the Loyal Senate because it refused to recognise Spanish sovereignty when the Spanish marched into Portugal in the 17th century, and during the subsequent 60 years' occupation. When Portuguese control was re-established, the city of Macau was granted the official name of Cidade do Nome de Deus de Macau, Nao ha Outra Mais Leal or 'City of the Name of God, Macau. There is None More Loyal.'

Above the wrought-iron gates leading to the garden, inside the main building, is an interesting bas-relief which is the subject of

some dispute. Some say the woman depicted is the Virgin Mary sheltering all those in need of mercy. Others hold that it represents the 16th century Portuguese Queen Leonor.

Also inside the Leal Senado is the public library, open on week days from 9 am to noon and from 2 to 5.30 pm, and on Saturdays from 9 am to 12.30 pm. In front of the Leal Senado is the Largo do Senado, the Senate Square.

St Dominic's Church

The most beautiful of Macau's baroque churches is St Dominic's (Sao Domingo) Church. The huge 17th-century building has an impressive tiered altar with images of the Virgin & Child and of Our Lady of Fatima, which is carried in procession during the Fatima Festival. There is a small museum at the back which is full of church regalia, images and paintings. The church is only open in the afternoon. To get in, ring the bell by the iron gates at the side. It is on Rua do Sao Domingos, at the northern end of Largo do Senado.

Luis de Camões Museum

A few blocks to the north of St Dominic's (Sao Domingo) Church is the modern Church of St Anthony. The church is memorable for having been burnt to the ground three times.

To the left is the entrance to the Luis de Camões Museum, a historically interesting building and once the headquarters of the British East India Company in Macau. The museum has an extensive collection that includes early Chinese terracotta, enamel ware and pottery, paintings, old weapons, religious objects and a collection of sketches and paintings of old Macau and Canton (Guangzhou). However, the building itself (which dates back to the 18th century) is of the most interest. It's open from 11 am to 5

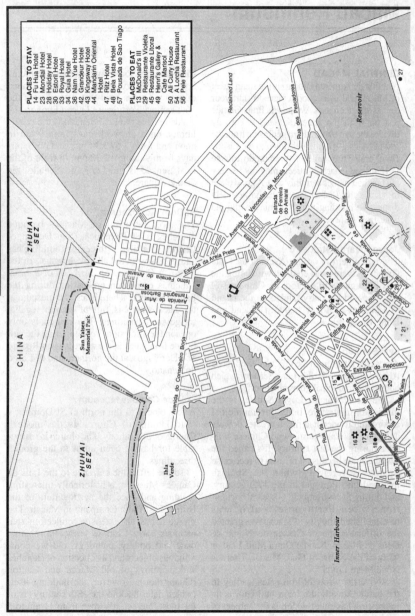

MACAU

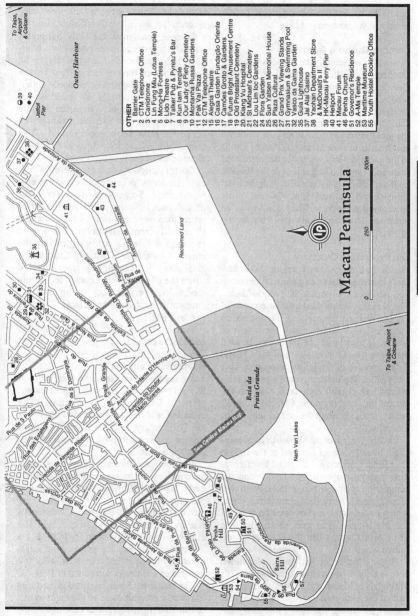

Macau Peninsula

OTHER
1 Barrier Gate
2 CTM Telephone Office
3 Canidrome
4 Lin Fung Miu (Lotus Temple)
5 Mong-Ha Fortress
6 Lido Theatre
7 Talker Pub & Pyretu's Bar
8 Kun Iam Temple
9 Our Lady of Piety Cemetery
10 Montanha Russa Gardens
11 Pak Vai Plaza
12 CTM Telephone Office
13 Alegria Theatre
15 Alegria Theatre
16 Casa Garden Fundação Oriente
17 Camões Grotto & Gardens
18 Future Bright Amusement Centre
19 Old Protestant Cemetery
20 Kiang Vu Hospital
21 St Michael's Cemetery
22 Lou Lim Ioc Gardens
24 Flora Gardens
25 Sun Yatsen Memorial House
26 Plaza Cultural
27 Grand Prix Viewing Stands
31 Gymnasium & Swimming Pool
32 Vasco da Gama Garden
35 Guia Lighthouse
37 Jai Alai Casino
38 Yaohan Department Store
   & McDonald's II
39 HK-Macau Ferry Pier
40 Heliport
41 Macau Forum
46 Penha Church
51 Governor's Residence
52 A-Ma Temple
53 Maritime Museum
55 Youth Hostel Booking Office

Outer Harbour

To Taipa, Airport & Coloane

Jetfoil Pier

Reclaimed Land

Baia da Praia Grande

Nam Van Lakes

See Central Macau Map

To Taipa, Airport & Coloane

Penha Hill

Barra Hill

0   250   500m

pm daily, except Wednesdays and public holidays. Admission is M$1.

Camões Grotto & Gardens

Behind the museum in the Camões Grotto & Gardens is another memorial to Luis de Camões, the 16th-century Portuguese poet who has become something of a local hero, though his claim is not all that strong. He is said to have written his epic *Os Lusiadas* by the rocks here, but there is no firm evidence that he was ever in Macau. A bust of him is in the gardens – looking rather better than the man, so it is said. The gardens are a pleasant, cool and shady place popular with the local Chinese and you may find old men sitting here playing checkers. They don't mind an audience. There are good views from the top of the hill.

Old Protestant Cemetery

Beside the Camões Museum is the Old Protestant Cemetery – the resting place of numerous non-Portuguese who made their way to Macau. The cemetery was needed because ecclesiastical law forbade the burial of Protestants on Catholic soil – which meant the whole of Macau, at least inside the city walls. Beyond the walls was Chinese soil, and the Chinese didn't approve of foreigners desecrating their pitch either. The unhappy result was that Protestants had to bury their dead either in the nearby hills and hope the Chinese wouldn't notice, or else beneath the neutral territory of the city walls.

Finally, the governor allowed a local merchant to sell some of his land to the British East India Company – despite a law forbidding foreign ownership of land – and the cemetery was established in 1821. A number of old graves were then transferred there, which explains the earlier dates on some of the tombstones. The gate shows the date 1814, which was when the cemetery committee was set up.

Among the better known people buried here is artist George Chinnery, noted for his portrayals of Macau and its people in the first half of the 19th century. Also buried here is Robert Morrison, the first Protestant mis-

sionary to China, who, as his tombstone records, 'for several years laboured alone on a Chinese version of the Holy Scriptures which he was spared to see completed'. Morrison is buried beside his wife Mary, who became one of the cemetery's first burials after dying in childbirth – 'erewhile anticipating a living mother's joy suddenly, but with a pious resignation, departed this life after a short illness of 14 hours, bearing with her to the grave her hoped-for child'. Also buried here is Lord John Spencer Churchill, an ancestor of Sir Winston Churchill.

Other inscriptions on the tombstones indicate that ships' officers and crew are well represented. Some died from accidents aboard, such as falling off the rigging, while others died more heroically, like Lieutenant Fitzgerald 'from the effects of a wound received while gallantly storming the enemy's battery at Canton'. Captain Sir Humphrey Le Fleming Stenhouse died 'from the effects of fever contracted during the zealous performance of his arduous duties at the capture of the Heights of Canton in May 1841'.

Fortune-tellers have set up shop just outside the cemetery.

Ruins of St Paul

Some say the ruins (Ruinas de Sao Paulo) of St Paul's Cathedral are the greatest monument to Christianity in the East. The cathedral was finished in the first decade of the 17th century, and the crowned heads of Europe competed to present it with its most prestigious gift.

Built on one of Macau's seven hills, it was designed by an Italian Jesuit and built by early Japanese Christian exiles. All that remains is the facade, the magnificent mosaic floor and the impressive stone steps leading up to it. The church caught fire during a disastrous typhoon in 1835. For a while it seemed like the whole thing might eventually fall apart, but renovation work was undertaken and finally completed in 1991.

The facade has been described as a sermon in stone, recording some of the main events of Christianity in the various carvings. At the top is the dove, representing the Holy Spirit, surrounded by stone carvings of the sun, moon and stars. Beneath the dove is a statue of the Infant Jesus surrounded by stone carvings of the implements of the crucifixion. In the centre of the third tier stands the Virgin Mary, with angels and two types of flowers – the peony representing China and the chrysanthemum representing Japan. The fourth tier has statues of four Jesuit saints.

In 1996, **St Paul's Museum** was opened just behind the ruined church. The museum houses a number of recently unearthed artefacts, including the tomb of Father Alessandro Valignano, the Jesuit who was responsible for building St Paul's Cathedral and the Jesuit College in Macau. Father Alessandro is also given credit for establishing Christianity in Japan.

St Paul's Museum is also home to a piece of the right arm bone of St Francis Xavier. Other bits of St Francis can be found in southern India.

Monte Fort

The fort (Fortaleza do Monte) is on a hill overlooking the St Paul's ruins and was built by the Jesuits around the same time. The first Portuguese settlers in Macau built their homes in the centre of the peninsula, and the fort once formed the strong central point of the old city wall. The cannons on the fort are the very ones that dissuaded the Dutch from further attempts to take over Macau: in 1622 a cannon ball hit a powder keg on one of the invader's ships, which exploded, blowing the Dutch out of the water. It's the only time these cannons were ever fired in combat. Since this event occurred on St John the Baptist's Day, 24 June, he was promptly proclaimed the city's patron saint.

Now the old building is used as an observatory and a museum. From it there are sweeping views across Macau. Enter the fort from a narrow cobbled street leading off Estrada do Repouso near Estrada do Cemiterio. There is also a path from the fortress down to the St Paul's ruins.

St Michael's Cemetery

This beautiful Catholic cemetery is almost exactly in the centre of the Macau Peninsula, on Estrada do Cemiterio. Although a few of the tombs are plain to look at, most are stunning works of art. The whole cemetery is adorned with statues of angels. This is the largest cemetery on the peninsula, though there is an even bigger Chinese cemetery on Taipa Island.

Lou Lim Ioc Gardens

The restful Lou Lim Ioc Gardens are on Avenida do Conselheiro Ferreira de Almeida. The gardens and ornate mansion, with its columns and arches (now the Pui Ching School), once belonged to the wealthy Chinese Lou family. The gardens are a mixture of European and Chinese plantings, with huge shady trees, lotus ponds, pavilions, bamboo groves, grottos and strangely-shaped doorways. The twisting pathways and ornamental mountains are built to represent a Chinese painting and are said to be modelled on those in the famous gardens of Suzhou in eastern China.

Sun Yatsen Memorial Home

Around the corner from the Lou Lim Ioc Gardens, at the junction of Avenida da Sidonio Pais and Rua de Silva Mendes, is a memorial house dedicated to Dr Sun Yatsen. Sun practised medicine in Macau for some years before turning to revolution and seeking to overthrow the Qing dynasty. A rundown on Sun's involvement with the anti-Qing forces and later with the Kuomintang and communist parties is in the Facts about Guangzhou chapter.

The memorial house in Macau was built as a monument to Sun and contains a collection of flags, photos and other relics. It replaced the original house, which blew up while being used as an explosives store. The house is open every day except Tuesday. It's open from 10 am to 1 pm Wednesday to Friday and from 10 am to 1 pm and 3 to 5 pm on the weekend.

Guia Lighthouse

This was once a fortress occupying the highest point on the Macau Peninsula. The 17th-century chapel here is the old hermitage

MACAU

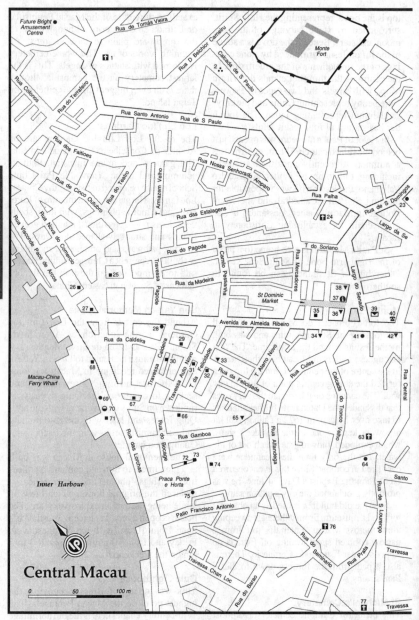

MACAU

Future Bright
Amusement
Centre

Rua de Tomás Vieira

Rua D Belchior Carneiro

Calçada de S Paulo

Monte
Fort

🏨 1

2

Rua Colonos

Rua do Terraleiro

Rua Santo Antonio   Rua de S Paulo

Rua dos Faitioes

Rua de Cinco Outubro

Rua do Teatro

T Armazem Velho

Rua Nossa Senhora do Amparo

Rua Palha

Rua de S Domingos
23

🏨 24

Largo da Se

Rua das Estalagens

Rua Nova do Comercio

Rua Visconde Paço de Arcos

Rua do Pagode

Travessa Pagode

Rua Camilo Pessanha

Rua da Madeira

Rua Mercadores

T do Soriano

Largo do Senado

St Dominic
Market

38 ▼
37 ℹ️

39 📧
40 ☎️

■ 25

26 ■

27 ■

35 ■   36 ▼

28 ●

Rua da Caldeira

Avenida de Almeida Ribeiro

34 ▼

41 ●

42 ▼

Rua Central

29 ■

▼ 33

Rua Cules

30 ■

Travessa Caldeira

Travessa Auto Novo

T da Felicidade

31 ■
32 ■

Rua da Felicidade

Rua Aterro Novo

Calçada do Tronco Velho

Macau-China
Ferry Wharf

68 ■

69 ●
70 ◐
71 ■

67 ●

66 ■

65 ▼

63 🏨

64 ●

Santo

Rua do Bocage

Rua das Lorchas

Rua Gamboa

Rua Alfandega

Rua de S Lourenço

72 ■ 73 ●

74 ■

Inner Harbour

Praça Ponte
e Horta

75 ●

Rua Prata

Travessa

Patio Francisco Antonio

76 🏨

Rua do Seminario

🟦 WP

Central Macau

0   50   100 m

Travessa Chan Loc

Rua do Barao

77 🏨

Travessa

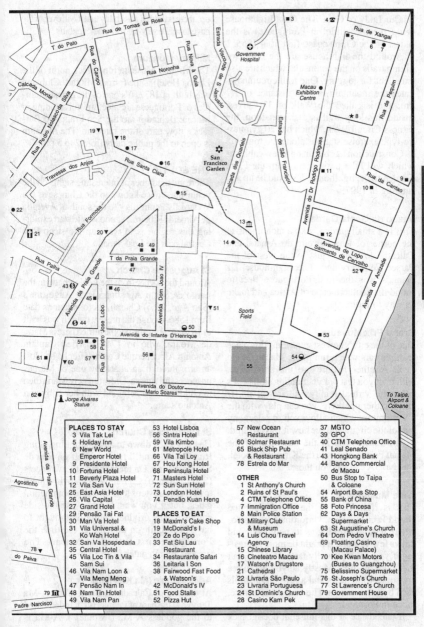

MACAU

PLACES TO STAY
3 Vila Tak Lei
5 Holiday Inn
6 New World
   Emperor Hotel
9 Presidente Hotel
10 Fortuna Hotel
11 Beverly Plaza Hotel
12 Vila San Vu
25 East Asia Hotel
26 Vila Capital
27 Grand Hotel
29 Pensão Tai Fat
30 Man Va Hotel
31 Vila Universal &
   Ko Wah Hotel
32 San Va Hospedaria
35 Central Hotel
45 Vila Loc Tin & Vila
   Sam Sui
46 Vila Nam Loon &
   Vila Meng Meng
47 Pensão Nam In
48 Nam Tin Hotel
49 Vila Nam Pan

53 Hotel Lisboa
56 Sintra Hotel
59 Vila Kimbo
61 Metropole Hotel
66 Vila Tai Loy
67 Hou Kong Hotel
68 Peninsula Hotel
71 Masters Hotel
72 Sun Sun Hotel
73 London Hotel
74 Pensão Kuan Heng

PLACES TO EAT
18 Maxim's Cake Shop
19 McDonald's I
20 Ze do Pipo
33 Fat Siu Lau
   Restaurant
34 Restaurante Safari
36 Leitaria I Son
38 Fairwood Fast Food
   & Watson's
42 McDonald's IV
51 Food Stalls
52 Pizza Hut

57 New Ocean
   Restaurant
60 Solmar Restaurant
60 Black Ship Pub
   & Restaurant
78 Estrela do Mar

OTHER
1 St Anthony's Church
2 Ruins of St Paul's
4 CTM Telephone Office
7 Immigration Office
8 Main Police Station
13 Military Club
   & Museum
14 Luis Chou Travel
   Agency
15 Chinese Library
16 Cineteatro Macau
17 Watson's Drugstore
21 Cathedral
22 Livraria São Paulo
23 Livraria Portuguesa
24 St Dominic's Church
28 Casino Kam Pek

37 MGTO
39 GPO
40 CTM Telephone Office
41 Leal Senado
43 Hongkong Bank
44 Banco Commercial
   de Macau
50 Bus Stop to Taipa
   & Coloane
54 Airport Bus Stop
55 Bank of China
58 Foto Princesa
62 Days & Days
   Supermaket
63 St Augustine's Church
64 Dom Pedro V Theatre
69 Floating Casino
   (Macau Palace)
70 Kee Kwan Motors
   (Buses to Guangzhou)
75 Belissimo Supermarket
76 St Joseph's Church
77 St Lawrence's Church
79 Government House

of Our Lady of Guia. The Guia Lighthouse (*guia* means 'guide' in Portuguese) is the oldest on the China coast, first lit in 1865.

Around the lighthouse are the only two hiking trails on the peninsula, which are also excellent for jogging. One trail circumnavigates the mountain, a total distance of 1.7 km, and is called the Walk of 33 Curves. Inside this loop trail is a shorter loop, the Fitness Circuit Walk, which has 20 gymnastic-type exercise stations along the route.

Construction has begun on a new cable car which will take passengers from the Flora Garden to the lighthouse. It should be up and running in 1997.

Vasco da Gama Garden

This is a small garden, with a monument, at the corner of Rua Ferreira do Amaral and Calcada do Gaio – just to the west of the Parsee Cemetery and Guia Lighthouse. Da Gama's was the first Portuguese fleet to round the southern cape of Africa and make its way to India.

Grand Prix Museum

One of the city's newest museums, this place features cars which run in the Macau Grand Prix. Another feature are the simulators, which let you test out your racing skills – it's not quite virtual reality, but it will do. If you'd rather not drive, you can play with the TV monitors which allow you to select any part of the circuit and see how it was covered.

The museum is in the basement of the Macau Forum opposite the Kingsway Hotel. Bus No 3A can get you there.

Wine Museum

This is right next to the aforementioned Grand Prix Museum. Unfortunately, it's nowhere near as exciting as its neighbour and draws few visitors. It might be more interesting if you could actually taste the wine, but that's not on offer. Mostly all you get to see are some wine racks and a few simple tools used by winemakers. The wine is, of course, made in Portugal.

If attendance at this museum doesn't pick

up, there is the real possibility that it will eventually have to make way for some other exhibit.

Military Museum

The Military Museum (one block north of the Lisboa Hotel) is the former Military Club and was built in 1872. It's one of the oldest examples of Portuguese architecture still standing in Macau. Behind it are the Sao Francisco Barracks, now part of the museum. The museum is open to the public daily from 2 to 5 pm.

THE SOUTH

There are a number of interesting sights on the peninsula – once known to the Chinese as the Water Lily Peninsula – to the south of Avenida de Almeida Ribeiro. A good way to start exploring this region is to walk up the steep Rua Central near the Leal Senado.

St Augustine Church

Around the corner from the Leal Senado in the Largo de Santo Agostinho is St Augustine's (Sao Agostinho) Church. Its foundations date from 1586, though the present church was built in 1814. Among the people buried here is Maria de Moura, who in 1710 married Captain Antonio Albuquerque Coelho after he had lost an arm through an attack by one of Maria's unsuccessful suitors. Unfortunately Maria died in childbirth and is buried with her baby and Antonio's arm.

St Lawrence's Church

Heading back down to and continuing along Rua Central, you'll find yourself on Rua de Sao Lourenno. On the right is St Lawrence's (Sao Lourenno) Church with its twin square towers. Stone steps lead up to the ornamental gates, but if you want to go in use the side entrance. The original church is thought to have been built on this site at the time the Portuguese first settled in Macau. The present church dates from 1846.

A-Ma Temple (Ma Kok Miu)

At the end of Calcada da Barra is the A-Ma Temple at the base of Penha Hill. It is dedicated to the goddess A-Ma ('Mother'). A-Ma is

Dedicated to the Queen of Heaven, the original A Ma temple was already standing when the Portuguese arrived.

more commonly known by her Hong Kong synonym Tin Hau ('Queen of Heaven').

The original temple on this site was probably already standing when the Portuguese arrived, although the present building may only date back to the 17th century.

A-Ma became A-Ma-Gao to the Portuguese and they named their colony after it. The temple consists of several shrines dating from the Ming dynasty. The boat people of Macau come here on pilgrimage each year in April or May. The temple is actually a complex of temples, some dedicated to A-Ma and others to Kun Iam.

There are several stories about A-Ma, one of which is related in the Hong Kong Religion section, but in Macau the tale goes that she was a beautiful young woman whose presence on a Guangzhou-bound ship saved it from disaster. All the other ships in the fleet, whose rich owners had refused to give her a passage, were destroyed in a storm.

The A-Ma Temple is one of the venues in Macau where fortune-tellers ply their trade.

Maritime Museum

This museum, opposite the A-Ma Temple, is really world class and not to be missed. It has a collection of boats and other artefacts related to Macau's seafaring past. There is also a dragon boat which is used in races held during the Dragon Boat Festival, plus a flower boat, a tugboat and a Chinese fishing vessel.

A motorised junk moored next to the museum offers 30-minute rides around the harbour on Saturday, Sunday and Monday. Departures are at 10.30 and 11.30 am, 3.30 and 4.30 pm. The fare is M$15, which includes the admission fee (M$5) to the museum.

The Maritime Museum is open from 10 am until 5.30 pm, Wednesday through Monday. It's closed on Tuesdays.

Barra Hill

From the A-Ma Temple you can follow Rua de Sao Tiago da Barra around to Barra Hill at the end of Avenida da Republica. At one time the hill was topped by a fortress which had great strategic importance when it was built in 1629, as ships entering the harbour had to come very close to the shore. The Pousada de Sao Tiago hotel has been built within the walls of the fortress and is worth seeing even if you can't afford to stay there. The hilltop is now a park, and you can circumnavigate it and enjoy the views by walking along Calcada da Penha, which is closed to motorised traffic.

Governor's Residence

On the east side of the tip of the Macau Peninsula is Avenida da Praia Grande, one of the most scenic streets in the city. Here you find the pink Governor's Residence, built in the 19th century as a residence for a Macanese aristocratic family. The building is not open to tourists, but you can admire the architecture from outside. Slightly further to the north is the **Bela Vista Hotel**, Macau's equivalent to Singapore's Raffles, built at the end of the 19th century.

Penha Church

On a hill above the Bela Vista is the Bishop's Residence and Penha Church. From here you get an excellent view of the central area of Macau. You can also see across the Pearl River into China. In front of the church is a replica of the Grotto of Lourdes.

Government House

The Government House on Avenida da Praia Grande is pink like the Governor's Residence. Originally built for a Portuguese noble in 1849, it was acquired by the government at the end of the 19th century.

THE NORTH

The northern part of the peninsula has been more recently developed than the southern and central areas. Nevertheless, there are a few interesting historical sites in this region of Macau.

Kun Iam Temple

The Kun Iam Temple on Avenida do Coronel Mesquita is really a complex of temples, the most interesting in Macau, and is dedicated to the goddess Kun Iam (Guanyin) – the Queen of Heaven and the Goddess of Mercy. The temple dates back about 400 years, though the original temple on the site was probably built more than 600 years ago.

This is also where the first treaty of trade and friendship between the USA and China was signed in 1844. These days it's a place for fortune-telling rather than treaties and gets quite a lot of visitors.

Lin Fong Miu (Lotus Temple)

Near the Canidrome is Estrada do Arco, where you'll find Lin Fong Miu (the Lotus Temple). The main hall of this temple is dedicated to Kun Iam. Another shrine is for A-Ma, the Goddess of Seafarers, and another is for Guanti (Kuanti in Hong Kong), the God of War, Literature and Pawnshops. The temple complex probably predates the arrival of the Portuguese in Macau.

Barrier Gate

Once a popular tourist spot, the Barrier Gate (Portas do Cerco) is the gate between Macau and China. In Portuguese, Portas do Cerco literally means 'Gate of Siege'. Before 1980, when 'China-watching' was meant literally, Macau's Barrier Gate and Hong Kong's Lok Ma Chau attracted many curious visitors simply because it was the border, and that was as close as any foreigner ever got to the People's Republic. These days the Barrier Gate is just a busy border crossing, but if you want to see it, head straight up Istmo Ferreira do Amaral from Lin Fong Miu (the Lotus Temple).

PLACES TO STAY

Hotels on the Macau Peninsula are most densely concentrated in two areas – near the Floating Casino, or near the waterfront by the Avenida da Praia Grande and the Jetfoil Pier. The ones near the Floating Casino tend to be slightly cheaper, though not by much.

For definition purposes, 'budget' in Macau is anything costing up to M$200. Over M$200 but under M$500 is 'mid-range' and over M$500 is the top end. Realise though that prices change with the season, and there is some room for bargaining. You might be able to do much better than the prices quoted here.

Places to Stay – bottom end

The key to finding a good, cheap room is patience. If one place charges too much, then try another. As long as you haven't arrived on a weekend, you should find something acceptable within half an hour or so of beginning your search. All places listed are on the Central Macau map unless otherwise noted.

A few blocks from the Floating Casino is *San Va Hospedaria* (☎ 573701), Rua de Felicidade 67. A double with shared bath costs M$70.

Two blocks to the south of the Floating Casino, on Rua das Lorchas, is a large square (now buried beneath an indoor market) called Praca Ponte e Horta. Around the square are several places to stay. On the east end of the square is *Pensao Kuan Heng* (☎ 573629, 937624), 2nd floor, block C, Rua Ponte e Horta. Singles/doubles are M$150/250 and it's very clean and well-managed.

The *Vila Tai Loy* (☎ 937811) is at the corner of Travessa das Virtudes and Travessa Auto Novo. At M$200, it's barely in the budget class, but the rooms are attractive and the manager is friendly.

Also in this vicinity is *Pensao Tai Fat*, 41-45 Rua da Caldeira, where rooms cost M$200.

Moving to the east side of the peninsula, the area between the Lisboa Hotel and Rua da Praia

Grande has some budget accommodation. Intersecting with Rua da Praia Grande is a small street called Rua Dr Pedro Jose Lobo where there's a cluster of guesthouses, including *Vila Meng Meng* (☎ 710064) on the 3rd floor at No 24. If you don't mind a shared bathroom, you can get an air-conditioned room for M$130. Next door is the *Vila Nam Loon*, where rooms start at M$150.

Just above Foto Princesa (a camera shop) at Avenida Infante D'Henrique 55-59 is *Vila Kimbo* (☎ 710010) where singles go for M$130 and up.

On Rua Dr Pedro Jose Lobo, the *Vila Sam Sui* (☎ 572256) seems very nice and barely qualifies as budget, with rooms for M$200. Its neighbour, *Vila Loc Tin* has moved upmarket – rooms are M$250.

Running off Avenida D Joao IV is an alley called Travessa da Praia Grande. At No 3 you'll find *Pensao Nam In* (☎ 710024), where singles with shared bath are M$110, or M$230 for a pleasant double with private bath. On the opposite side of the alley is the *Nam Tin Hotel* (☎ 711212), which looks cheap but isn't – singles are M$330! *Vila Nam Pan* (☎ 572289) on the corner has also gotten too pricey, with singles for M$250, but you could try polite bargaining.

Behind the Lisboa Hotel on Avenida de Lopo Sarmento de Carvalho is a row of pawnshops and a couple of guesthouses. The *Vila San Vu* is friendly and has good rooms for M$200.

The *Jai Alai Hotel* (☎ 725599; fax 726105), is inside a sleaze circus known as China City Nightclub. It's adjacent to Yaohan Department Store (see the Macau Peninsula map) and close to the Jetfoil Pier, but other than that has little to recommend it. Rooms here are overpriced at M$575.

Places to Stay – middle

A personal favourite is the excellent *East Asia Hotel* (☎ 922433), Rua da Madeira 1-A. This is one of the city's classic colonial buildings – the outside maintains its traditional facade, but it's been remodelled on the inside. Spotlessly clean singles/twins are M$320/360 with private bath and fierce air-conditioning. The dim sum restaurant on the 2nd floor does outstanding breakfasts.

Almost next door to the East Asia Hotel is the *Vila Capital* (☎ 920154) at Rua Constantino Brito 3. Singles/twins are M$250/300.

The *Central Hotel* (☎ 373888) is centrally located at Avenida de Almeida Ribeiro 26-28, a short hop west of the GPO. Singles/doubles with private bath cost from M$250/300.

The *London Hotel* (☎ 937761) on Praca Ponte e Horta (two blocks south of the Floating Casino) has singles for M$200. Rooms are comfortable and clean.

The *Sun Sun Hotel* (☎ 939393; fax 938822), Praca Ponte e Horta 14-16, offers rooms for much less than its advertised price. Regular price is supposedly M$600, but on week days this drops to M$360 and on weekends to M$480.

A few doors to the south of the Floating Casino you'll find an alley called Travessa das Virtudes. On your left as you enter the alley is the *Hou Kong Hotel* (☎ 937555; fax 338884) which has singles/doubles for M$220/280. Official address is Rua das Lorchas 1.

Just a block to the north of the Floating Casino, at Avenida de Almeida Ribeiro 146, is the *Grand Hotel* (☎ 921111) where singles/twins cost M$380/480.

One block to the east of the Floating Casino is a street called Travessa Caldeira, where you'll find the *Man Va Hotel* (☎ 388655), Rua da Caldeira 32. Doubles cost M$280 but this place is perpetually full.

In the same neighbourhood is the very clean and very friendly *Vila Universal* (☎ 573247) at Rua de Felicidade 73. The manager speaks good English and doubles/twins cost M$200/252.

Next door at Rua de Felicidade 71, close to Travessa Auto Novo, is *Ko Wah Hotel* (☎ 375599) which has doubles for M$202 to M$212. Reception is on the 4th floor – check out the ancient lift.

Just on the north side of the Floating Casino on Rua das Lorchas is the *Peninsula Hotel* (☎ 318899). Singles/twins are M$350/400. This hotel is large, clean and popular.

One more place to look around is the area north of the Lisboa Hotel on a street called Estrada Sao Francisco. You have to climb a steep hill to get up this street, but the advantage is that the hotels have a little sea breeze and it's quiet. Up here at Estrada Sao Francisco 2A is *Vila Tak Lei* (☎ 577484), where doubles go for M$200, but try bargaining. Next door are the grottier *Vila Mikado* and *Vila Empress*.

Places to Stay – top end

During the summer travel season, many of the top-end places are solidly booked, even during week days. Wherever these rich high-rollers come from, there seem to be plenty of them.

Most upmarket hotels in Macau have telephone numbers in Hong Kong where you can book rooms, and these numbers are indicated below. However, you'll get a better deal if you book through a travel agency at Hong Kong's Shun Tak Centre or Macau's Jetfoil Pier.

The current selection of three-star and above hotels includes:

Bela Vista – (☎ 965333; fax 965588; HK 2881-1688), on Rua Comendador Kou Ho Neng, eight rooms. This grand colonial building is more than 100 years old and overlooks the waterfront on the south-east corner of the peninsula. This is Macau's answer to Hong Kong's Peninsula Hotel. Prices at the Bela Vista are M$1500 to M$4000. Five stars.

Beverly Plaza – (☎ 782288; fax 780684; HK 2739-9928), Avenida do Dr Rodrigo Rodrigues, 300 rooms, doubles M$740 to M$900, suites M$1600 to M$1800. Three stars.

Fortuna – (☎ 786333; fax 786363; HK 2517-3728), Rua da Cantao, 368 rooms, doubles M$780 to M$980, suites M$1800. Three stars.

Fu Hua – (☎ 553838; fax 527575; HK 2559-0708), Rua de Francisco Xavier Pereira 98, 140 rooms. Doubles M$680, triples M$730. Three stars.

Grandeur – (☎ 781233; fax 785896; HK 2857-2846), Rua de Pequim, 350 rooms, doubles M$850 to M$1050, suites M$1400 to M$5500. Four stars.

Guia – (☎ 513888; fax 559822;), Estrada do Eng Trigo 1-5, 89 rooms. Doubles M$470 to M$570, triples M$650, suites M$750 to M$950. Three stars.

Holiday Inn – (☎ 783333; fax 782321; HK 2810-9628), Rua Pequim, 410 rooms, doubles M$700 to M$1200, suites M$2400 to M$9600. Four stars.

Kingsway – (☎ 702888; fax 702828), Rua de Luis Gonzaga Gomes, 410 rooms, doubles M$730 to M$930, suites M$1180 to M$3580. Three stars.

Lisboa – (☎ 377666; fax 567193), Avenida da Amizade, 1050 rooms. This is Macau's most famous landmark, but it's difficult to find the right adjective to describe the unique architecture (orange background with white circles). Regardless of what you think of the external design, the interior is first rate. The Lisboa has the best arcade in Macau, and it is filled with shops, restaurants, banks, a billiard room and bowling alley. Other facilities include a bar, hairdresser-barber shop, conference room, disabled rooms, exercise centre, hotel doctor and outdoor swimming pool. Double rooms cost M$600 to M$1100, and suites are M$1650 to M$7000. Four stars.

Mandarin Oriental – (☎ 567888; fax 594589; HK 2881-1688), Avenida da Amizade, 435 rooms, doubles M$1150 to M$1700, suites M$3500 to M$18,800. Facilities: bar, hairdresser-barber shop, business centre, coffee shop, conference room, exercise centre, hotel doctor, indoor and outdoor swimming pools, in-house video, tennis courts, squash courts and restaurants (Cantonese, Italian & Portuguese). Five stars.

Masters – (☎ 937572; fax 937565; HK 2598-7808), Rua das Lorchas 162 (next to the Floating Casino), 75 rooms, singles M$440, doubles M$550 to M$1000. Three stars.

Metropole – (☎ 388166; fax 330890; HK 2833-9300), Avenida da Praia Grande 493-501, 112 rooms, singles M$460, doubles M$600, suites M$1050 to M$1150. Facilities: bar, coffee shop and restaurants (Cantonese & Portuguese). Three stars.

Mondial – (☎ 566866; fax 514083; HK 2540-8180), Rua de Antonio Basto (east side of Lou Lim Ioc Gardens), 141 rooms. Old wing: doubles M$360 to M$480, suites M$850; new wing: doubles M$580 to M$630, suites M$1050 to M$2300.

Nam Yue – (☎ 726288; fax 726726; HK 2559-0708), Avenida do Dr Rodrigo Rodrigues, 388 rooms, doubles M$680 to M$880, suites M$1680 to M$3380. Three stars.

New World Emperor – (☎ 781888; fax 782287; HK 2724-4622), Rua de Xangai, 405 rooms, doubles M$870 to M$990, suites M$1480 to M$4680. Four stars.

Pousada de Sao Tiago – (☎ 378111; fax 552170; HK 2803-2015), Avenida da Republica, 23 rooms. This is the best hotel in town. The location at the southern tip of the peninsula is dramatic enough, but the traditional architecture is nothing short of stunning. It's worth coming here to have a drink at the bar and take a look. Originally the hotel was a fortress, the Fortaleza da Barra, which was built in 1629. Doubles are M$1180 to M$1490 and suites M$1650 to M$3000. Facilities: bar, coffee shop, conference room, hotel doctor, outdoor swimming pool and restaurants (Cantonese, Macanese & Portuguese). Despite the upmarket prices, this place is frequently booked solid. Five stars.

Presidente – (☎ 553888; fax 552735; HK 2857-1533), Avenida da Amizade, 340 rooms, doubles M$620 to M$850, suites M$2800 to M$3800. Facilities: bar, hairdresser-barber shop, coffee shop, conference room, exercise centre, hotel doctor, in-house video and restaurants (American, Cantonese, Korean & Portuguese). Four stars.

Ritz – (☎ 339955; fax 317826; HK 2739-6993), Rua da Boa Vista 2, 163 rooms, doubles M$1180 to M$1280, suites M$1680 to M$8880. Five stars.

Royal – (☎ 552222; fax 2543-6426), Estrada da Vitoria 2-4 (across from the Vasco da Gama Monument), 380 rooms, doubles M$750 to M$880, suites M$1850 to M$2980. Facilities: bar, hairdresser-barber shop, coffee shop, conference room, exercise centre, indoor swimming pool, in-house video and restaurants (Cantonese, French, Japanese & Portuguese). Four stars.

Sintra – (☎ 710111; fax 510527; HK 2546-6944), Avenida Dom Joao IV, 240 rooms, doubles M$560 to M$820, suites M$1180. Facilities: bar, coffee shop, hotel doctor, exercise centre and restaurants (Chinese & Western). Three stars.

PLACES TO EAT
Cheap Eats
Street Stalls As in other Chinese cities, the evening street markets are about as cheap as cooking for yourself.

Seafood is the local speciality. Eating the sea snails takes a little practice. The idea is to use two toothpicks to roll the organism out of its shell, then dip it in sauce and devour.

Food stalls are conveniently located in Rua da Escola Commercial, a tiny lane one block west of the Lisboa Hotel, just next to a sports field. There are also many cheap but grotty Chinese restaurants (called casa-pasto in Portuguese – look for the signs) setting up chairs outdoors at night near the Floating Casino on Rua das Lorchas.

In the somewhat unlikely event that you find yourself near the Barrier Gate at night, there is a good dai pai dong (food stall) on Estrada do Arco, a small street in front of Lin Fong Miu (the Lotus Temple).

Fast Food Just to the north side of the tourist office in the plaza fronting Leal Senado is the Food Plaza. Here you'll find a Fairwood Fast Food joint, which sounds much more appetising in Portuguese: Comidas Rapido Fairwood.

There is another Food Plaza on the 3rd floor of the Yaohan Department Store (and yes, there's another Fairwood there too). The Pokka Cafe on the 1st floor does a mixed Chinese-Western menu, but is notable for its fine harbour view and banana splits.

At M$9.20, Macau's Big Macs are the second cheapest in the world (China is slightly cheaper). Macau's first McDonald's is at Rua do Campo 17-19. A second McDonald's (informally called McDonald's II) is upstairs in the Yaohan Department Store near the Jetfoil Pier. And a third (McDonald's III?) is at Praca de Luis de Camoes 6-8. The fourth is in Central Plaza on Avenida de Almeida Ribeiro.

Opposite McDonald's is Maxim's Cake Shop, a good place to grab a quick takeaway breakfast.

Pizza Hut is on Avenida de Lopo Sarmento de Carvalho, just behind the Lisboa Hotel. You can enter through the Lisboa Hotel shopping arcade – it's in the basement.

For superb yoghurt and milkshakes, try Leitaria I Son close to the MGTO. Chinese-style yoghurt is served in a rice bowl. You can put together a decent breakfast here too.

Self-Catering There are lots of small grocery stores scattered around town. There are few supermarkets in the tourist zone – they tend to be in the residential neighbourhoods. Belissimo Supermarket is the main supermarket near the budget hotels in the Floating Casino area. The largest supermarket in Macau is on the second floor of Yaohan Department Store close to the Jetfoil Pier.

Portuguese & Macanese
Henri's Galley (☎ 556251) is right on the waterfront at Avenida da Republica 4 G-H, the south end of the Macau Peninsula. The food is OK though not special by Macau's standards, and prices are high. You could check out Henri's near neighbour, Cafe Marisol (☎ 565198), at Avenida da Republica 4D.

Just a stone's throw south of Henri's is Ali Curry House (☎ 555865), Avenida da Republica 4K. This place features outdoor tables and fine curry dishes.

For relatively cheap Portuguese and Macanese food, the *Estrela do Mar* (☎ 322074), at Travessa do Paiva 11, off the Avenida da Praia Grande, is the place to go.

Solmar (☎ 574391) at Avenida da Praia Grande 512 is famous for its African chicken and seafood.

Restaurante Litoral (☎ 967878), Rua do Almirante Sergio 261, is a short walk north of the Maritime Museum.

Fat Siu Lau (☎ 573580) – or 'House of the Smiling Buddha' – serves Portuguese and Chinese food. It's at Rua da Felicidade 64, once the old red-light Street of Happiness. It's supposed to be the oldest Macanese restaurant in the colony, dating back to 1903. The speciality is roast pigeon.

An excellent place to eat is *Restaurante Safari* (☎ 322239) at Patio do Cotovelo 14 near the Leal Senado. It has good coffee shop dishes as well as spicy chicken, steak and fried noodles. This is a good place to eat breakfast.

A Lorcha (☎ 313193), Rua do Almirante Sergio 289, is near the A-Ma Temple at the south-west tip of the peninsula. It's reputed to have some of the best food in Macau. Just next door at No 287A is another fine Portuguese restaurant, *Barra Nova* (☎ 512287). Just a bit to the south is *Pele* (☎ 965624), Baco Ancora 3.

Ze do Pipo (☎ 374047), Avenida da Praia Grande 95A (near Rua do Campo) is a two-storey splashy Portuguese restaurant with all the trimmings.

Black Ship Restaurant (☎ 934119), in the basement at Rua do Gamboa 10AA, is a fine pub-style Portuguese restaurant. It's on the west side of Macau not far from the Floating Casino.

Café a Bica (☎ 391-0168), Avenida do Dr Rodrigo Rodrigues 223-225, boasts a quaint atmosphere. It's actually inside the Macau Exhibition Centre – take the escalator up to the 1st floor. This place is open for breakfast.

If you can afford the ticket, outstanding Portuguese food is served at the restaurant balcony of the *Bela Vista Hotel* (☎ 965333), Rua Comendador Kou Ho Neng. Opening hours are from 7 am until 3 pm, and from 7 to 11 pm.

If you'd like to try something different, the *Military Club* (☎ 714009), Avenida da Praia

Grande 795, serves Portuguese food in one of Macau's distinguished colonial buildings.

If you want a place that's easy to find, you can't beat the *New Terminal Restaurant* at the Jetfoil Pier terminal on the 3rd floor. It's open 24 hours a day. From 11 am to 10 pm it features Portuguese and other Western dishes. From 10 pm to 8 am you can enjoy dim sum snacks. Don't confuse this place with its neighbour, the *Restaurante Chines New Terminal* which does seafood and other Cantonese dishes (including dim sum).

Also easy to find is *Great Fortune BBQ Portuguese Restaurant* on the 3rd floor above the Watson's on the Leal Senado square.

The *Sintra Hotel Coffeeshop* offers an all-you-can-eat Portuguese luncheon buffet for M$38, but the catch is that the only items on the menu are soup, salad and desserts, and the offer is only valid on week days. The sumptuous dinner buffet on Saturday evening is a more substantial M$138, but on Sunday it's reduced to M$88.

Italian
Mezzaluna (☎ 783-3871), inside the Mandarin Oriental Hotel, advertises itself as a 'Cucina Italiana' and dishes up everything from pasta to pizzas.

The Holiday Inn chips in with its *Frascati Restaurant* (☎ 783333).

Vegetarian
Bodhi Vegetarian Restaurant (☎ 726116) is in the Food Plaza on the 3rd floor of the Yaohan Department Store.

Chinese
All hotel Chinese restaurants do a breakfast and lunch dim sum, which can be amazingly cheap in the mid-range hotels. A good dim sum meal can be had for M$40.

The *Restaurant Long Kei* (☎ 573970) is right in the centre on the Leal Senado square, No 7B. It's a straightforward Cantonese place with bright overhead lights and sparse surroundings, but it also has top notch Cantonese food and amiable waiters. It's open from 11 am to 11 pm.

Jade Restaurant (☎ 375125), Avenida de

Almeida Ribeiro 26, does morning and afternoon dim sum, plus delicious Cantonese food in the evening. It's a good place for breakfast, and is open from 7 am to midnight.

Han Court Chiu Chow Restaurant (☎ 373311) is on the 1st floor of the food court just above Watson's chemist in the Leal Senado square.

Other Asian Cuisine
Korean If you have a craving for bulgogi and kimchi, good Korean food can be found at *Restaurante Korean* (☎ 569039) in the Presidente Hotel.

Japanese You can expect to pay Japanese prices for your sushi regardless of whether you buy it in Tokyo or Macau. Perhaps for this reason, Japanese restaurants tend to be inside the upmarket hotels. The Lisboa Hotel is where you'll find *Edo Sushi* (☎ 713888) and *Furusato Nippon* (☎ 388568).

Miscellaneous
Buffets Many hotels offer all-you-can-eat luncheon specials, though these aren't really all that cheap. By way of example, the *Royal Hotel* offers one from noon to 2 pm for M$110. Dinner buffets are offered on Saturday evenings.

ENTERTAINMENT
Cinemas
The *Cineteatro Macau* (☎ 572050) is on Rua Santa Clara, down the street from Watson's Drugstore. The main theatre often has good quality films in English, as well as some Hong Kong movies. Other cinemas include:

Guohua Cinema – Rua de Pedro Nolasco da Silva
Jai Alai Cinema (United Artists) – China City Nightclub (adjacent to Yaohan Department Store)
Lido Theatre – (☎ 210224), Avenida do Almirante Lacerda 178K-L
Pak Vai Cinema – (☎ 331374), Pak Vai Plaza
Teatro Alegria – (☎ 311636), Estrada do Repouso

On rare occasions, there might be a French film showing at the *Alliance Française* (☎ 965342), Veng Fu San Chun.

Theatre
Teatro Dom Pedro V on Largo St Augustine is a beautiful old theatre used for occasional special events (music festivals, drama performances, etc).

Shows are irregular. There is no schedule and you'll have to do some checking to see what's on. The MGTO might have some information, but most likely you'll have to check with the theatre itself (☎ 939646). This place is geared towards the local and expat community rather than foreign tourists.

Billiards & Pinball
The *shopping arcade* at the Lisboa Hotel includes a video games centre to keep the kids busy, and a billiards room for grown-up kids.

Discos
The most popular with the locals is the *Mondial Disco* at the Hotel Mondial, Rua de Antonio Basto. There is no cover charge, but you are obligated to buy two drinks for M$70.

The Hotel Presidente is home to the *Skylight Disco* (☎ 780923). There is no cover charge here, but you must buy one drink for M$80.

Other hotels have their discos; cover charges vary from M$60 to M$150, with one or two free drinks thrown in.

Karaoke
These are everywhere and the music is mostly Canto-pop. Every hotel of any size has a karaoke bar. To find one, just look for the sign saying 'OK'.

Nightclubs
These places tend to appeal more to the Hong Kongers than the Westerners. The *Savoy Nightclub* in the Lisboa Hotel is a huge, brightly-lit place with a M$200 cover charge. The club features a Filipino band and floor show.

The *Crazy Paris Show* is performed nightly in the Mona Lisa Hall of the Lisboa Hotel and is similar to the revue-style shows in Las Vegas. Shows scheduled from Sunday through Friday are at 8.30 and 10 pm. On Saturday, shows are at 8.30, 10 and 11 pm. Admission is M$90 on week days or M$100

MACAU

on weekends. There is no admittance for anyone under 18.

The *China City Nightclub* is near the Jetfoil Terminal. This is basically a male-oriented girlie club, with hostesses who circulate and keep the clientele smiling. There is even a scantily-clad hostess in the men's washroom who hands paper towels to the customers. Admission is M$200 and there may be additional charges for time simply talking with the hostesses. The whole building gives the impression of being an absolute sleaze pit. The edifice is home to the Jai Alai Casino, Jai Alai Hotel, several pawnshops, a movie theatre, the Darling Thai Massage & Sauna, the Taipan Health Spa and the Show Palace, which features Russian strippers who dance on the tables. Single male travellers who go anywhere near the place will almost certainly be accosted by pushy touts explaining the virtues of their particular establishment's services.

Pubs

Near the Kun Iam Temple at Rua de Pedro Coutinho 104 is *Talker Pub* (☎ 550153, 528975). Just next door at No 106 is *Pyretu's Bar* (☎ 581063). Both of these places open around 8 pm but don't get moving until after 9 pm and often don't close until the sun is up. These two pubs draw young expats from as far as Hong Kong.

The *Jazz Club*, Rua da Alabardas 9, lives up to its name in large part because of an annual jazz festival which is staged here. On Friday and Saturday nights live bands usually perform, and on other evenings they do excellent recorded music. The Jazz Club is just behind St Lawrence's (Sao Lourenno) Church.

As you might guess from the name, the *Billabong Bar* is run by an Aussie expat. Beers from Oz are a feature here, as well as cricket and footy on TV. You'll find this cozy place at Beco do Goncalo 2C, just off Rua Central.

Oskar's Pub inside the Holiday Inn draws a large number of local expats.

Bar da Guia in the Mandarin Oriental Hotel is decorated in a Grand Prix motif. There is live music every night, with jazz a speciality every Wednesday. A big-screen TV broadcasts sporting matches.

Bar da Montanha Russa (☎ 302731), Estrada Ferreira de Amaral, is popular with the locals as both a bar and a Portuguese restaurant. It's easy to find, being right inside Montanha Russa Gardens.

Casinos

None of the casinos in Macau offer the atmosphere or level of service considered minimal in Las Vegas. There are no seats for slot machine players and no cocktail waitresses offering free drinks to gamblers. Incredibly, they don't even have 'change girls' who walk the casino floor giving change to slot players so they can keep playing. The most obnoxious custom is that the dealers will tip themselves 10% of your winnings without asking! Any dealer doing this in Las Vegas would be immediately fired, and possibly subject to criminal prosecution. The casinos have no windows, the dealers don't talk to the customers and no one smiles. Perhaps smiling is against the rules?

Nevertheless, the casinos have no trouble attracting customers. Indeed, they are jam-packed. One thing they do have in common with Las Vegas is that there are no clocks or windows – no sense letting people know how late it is, lest they be tempted to stop playing and go to bed. With the exception of the tiny Casino Victoria on Taipa Island, all casinos in Macau stay open daily, 24 hours, unless a major typhoon blows in. Here is a rundown of the casino battlefield:

Lisboa Casino Although it's by no means the newest casino in town, the Lisboa is still the largest and liveliest. When typhoon signal eight is hoisted and all the other casinos shut down, only this one stays open.

There are four storeys of gambling halls. The Lisboa has a more comfortable feel about it than the other casinos – maybe this is because it's just so much more spacious. The adjacent hotel offers the comforts of a good but overpriced shopping arcade, fine restaurants and a video arcade to keep the kids busy while mum and dad lose their life savings at the blackjack tables. There is a big meter in the casino which shows how much will be paid if you hit the grand jackpot on the five-reel slot machines. The total shown on the meter increases until someone hits 'megabucks', then the meter is reset to zero and starts again. Of all the gambling halls in Macau, this one comes closest to matching the grandeur of a Las Vegas casino.

Floating Casino Officially, the name is *Macau Palace*, but everyone calls it the Floating Casino. Built in an old, converted ferry anchored on the west side of Macau, the concept conjures up romantic images of riverboat gambling, but the reality is somewhat different. Apart from being earthquake-proof, the casino has little to recommend it. Inside, it's a crowded, windowless, smoke-filled box where players climb over each other to get at the tables. It's one of Macau's oldest casinos and looks it. The players look very serious and oblivious to all else but the next roll of the dice.

Kam Pek Casino The original Kam Pek Casino used to look like a Salvation Army soup kitchen, but the new one near the Floating Casino has been considerably improved. However, it still leaves me cold – the casino hardly looks like a place to enjoy a holiday. The Kam Pek is known as a 'neighbourhood casino' – it appeals mainly to the locals and foreign tourists are made to feel unwelcome. The slot machines here are the only ones in Macau to work with Macau patacas (the other casinos require Hong Kong dollars).

Mandarin Oriental Hotel Casino This place appeals to the upper crust and has a very stuffed-shirt atmosphere. Men often wear neckties and the women dress in formal gowns. Even the hotel lobby looks like a museum. I could swear the toilet paper was perfumed. The Mandarin Hotel is to the south of the Jetfoil Pier.

Jai Alai Casino Known as the *Palacio de Pelota Basca* in Portuguese, this casino once distinguished itself as the venue for *jai alai* (pronounced 'hi-a-lie') games. Jai alai is reputed to be the world's fastest ball game and is popular in many Latin American countries, particularly Cuba and Mexico. The game is similar to handball, racquetball or squash. The ball is three-quarters the size of a baseball and harder than a golf ball. Each player alternatively catches it and throws it with his *pletora* – an elongated wicker basket with an attached leather glove that is strapped to his wrist. As with horse racing and dog racing, jai alai is something else for gamblers to wager on.

Sadly, the jai alai games are no more. The game just never caught on with Hong Kongers, and the present-day Jai Alai Casino just has the standard table games and slots. Nevertheless, this casino remains popular, partially because it's close to the Jetfoil Pier, thus giving arriving visitors their first chance to gamble (or departing visitors their last chance).

Kingsway Hotel Casino Close to the Jai Alai Casino is the Kingsway. This is Macau's newest casino and aspires to be the best, with fancy decor. Games are the same as elsewhere, but the minimum bets at some tables are too high for many players.

Macau Islands

The quiet environment and sandy beaches of Coloane and Taipa Islands stand in sharp contrast to Macau's glittering casinos and jam-packed streets. Before the islands were a haven for tourists, they were a haven for pirates – the last raid took place in 1910.

Once known as a peaceful paradise, the islands are now coming under intense development pressure. Taipa now has two major hotels, a university, horse racing track, high-rise apartments and an almost-finished airport. A golf course and deepwater port on Coloane heralds the new era of change at any cost. A massive land reclamation project to connect Taipa and Coloane could be the final nail in the coffin. Still, these islands have a way to go before reaching the level of intense development seen on the peninsula.

TAIPA ISLAND

When the Portuguese first saw Taipa (Tamzai in Chinese) it was actually two islands, but during the past few hundred years the east and west halves have joined – one of the more dramatic demonstrations of the power of siltation. Tiny Macau is one part of the huge Pearl River Delta. The siltation process continues and, if the mudflats to the south of Taipa Village are any indication, Taipa and Coloane are destined to become one island unless the greenhouse effect submerges everything but the high-rises.

Casinos

Hyatt Regency When you come over the bridge, the first large building you encounter is the Hyatt Regency. Aside from being the only hotel on the island, it has one of Macau's upper crust casinos. Apparently the out-of-the-way location has not hurt business.

Casino Victoria It's hard to take this casino seriously. It's basically just a gaming room at the Macau Jockey Club on Taipa Island. It's only open on race days from 11 am to 3 pm.

Macau University

Just a few hundred metres to the east of the Hyatt is a set of large modern buildings on a hill overlooking the sea. This is Macau University, the only university in this tiny enclave. It's worth dropping in for a quick look around and the cafeteria is a cheap place to eat. The vast majority of the students are from Macau and Hong Kong, but making conversation with them should be no problem since the language of instruction is English. The university is open seven days a week throughout the year, except for public holidays.

Kun Iam Temple

Walking downhill from the university (back towards the Hyatt Regency) you should find some stone steps off to your right going down towards the sea. Follow these a short distance and you'll soon reach the Kun Iam Temple. The temple is very small, and it's by the sea because Kun Iam is a goddess who protects sailors.

Pou Tai Un Temple

Less than 200m to the west of the Hyatt Regency is the Pou Tai Un Temple, the largest temple on the island. It overlooks the tennis courts of the Hyatt. If you're around during lunch time, the temple operates a vegetarian restaurant – the vegetables are said to be grown in the temple's own garden.

From the temple you can walk back to the Hyatt and catch a bus to Taipa Village at the south end of the island, or you could walk the 1.5 km to Taipa Village.

Taipa Village

This is the only settlement on the island large enough to be called a village. The chief attraction is a street at the south-east corner of town called **Avenida da Praia**. This means 'Avenue of the Beach', but as you'll see, siltation has overwhelmed the beach and it has become a mudflat extending almost all the way to Coloane at low tide. Nevertheless,

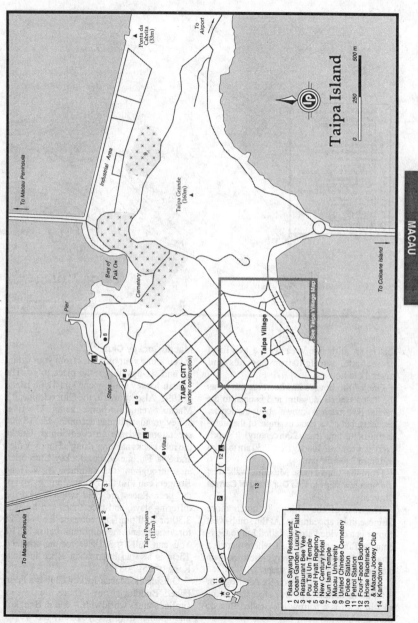

MACAU

Taipa Island

0   250   500 m

Ponta da Cabrita (33m)

To Airport

To Macau Peninsula

Industrial Area

Taipa Grande (160m)

Bay of Pak On

Cemetery

Pier

Steps

See Taipa Village Map

Taipa Village

TAIPA CITY (under construction)

To Macau Peninsula

Villas

Taipa Pequena (112m)

To Coloane Island

1 Rasa Sayang Restaurant
2 Ocean Garden Luxury Flats
3 Restaurant Bee Vee
4 Pou Tai Un Temple
5 Hotel Hyatt Regency
6 New Century Hotel
7 Kun Iam Temple
8 Macau University
9 United Chinese Cemetery
10 Police Station
11 Petrol Station
12 Four-Faced Buddha
13 Horse Racetrack
    & Macau Jockey Club
14 Kartodrome

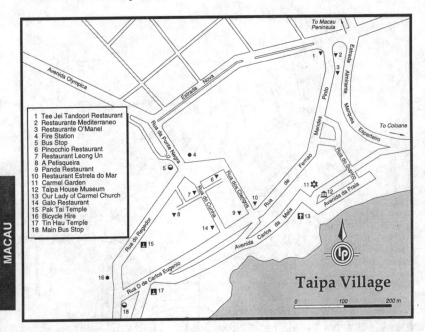

1 Tee Jei Tandoori Restaurant
2 Restaurante Mediterraneo
3 Restaurante O'Manel
4 Fire Station
5 Bus Stop
6 Pinocchio Restaurant
7 Restaurant Leong Un
8 A Petisqueira
9 Panda Restaurant
10 Restaurant Estrela do Mar
11 Carmel Garden
12 Taipa House Museum
13 Our Lady of Carmel Church
14 Galo Restaurant
15 Pak Tai Temple
16 Bicycle Hire
17 Tin Hau Temple
18 Main Bus Stop

Taipa Village

this is an attractive area with a tree-lined promenade, wrought-iron benches and several old houses.

One of the houses has been preserved as the **Taipa House Museum** and is open to the public. Not much is known about the former residents, but it's a good example of the architecture of the time (early 20th century). It's open every day except Monday from 9.30 am to 1 pm and from 3 to 5.30 pm.

From the Taipa House Museum, walk west and up a few steps to find **Our Lady of Carmel Church**.

The rest of the village is much more Chinese in its appearance. At the south-west corner is a divided street, called Largo Governador Tamagnini Barbosa, where there is a small **Tin Hau temple**. It's very close to the main bus stop and bicycle rental shops.

Just around the corner on Rua do Regedor is a **Pak Tai temple**. The only other sightseeing spot in town is a narrow alley called **Rua do Cunha**, which has many tiny shops.

Macau Jockey Club
If you know your quinellas from your trifectas and six-ups, this is the place to go. The Macau Jockey Club opened on Taipa Island in 1991. Also known as the Hippodrome, it's Macau's venue for horse racing. The five-storey grandstands can accommodate 18,000 spectators and are air-conditioned. Unlike the race tracks at Hong Kong's Happy Valley and Sha Tin, the Macau Jockey Club operates throughout the summer. Now Hong Kongers can lose their money any season of the year. Races are held twice weekly on differing days, and race times can be at 2, 3.30 or 7.30 pm. The entrance fee is M$20 for visitors and the minimum bet is M$10. You can call (☎ 321888) for the schedule. There is also an information office in Hong Kong (☎ 2517-0872).

Outside the Macau Jockey Club is a Four-Faced Buddha shrine. There are several similar statues worldwide – one in Bangkok and another in (brace yourself) Las Vegas.

Praying to the Buddha is supposed to bring good fortune, which is what one undoubtedly needs in Macau's casinos.

Kartodrome

You may have heard of the Canidrome, well now there's the kartodrome. This venue is for go-cart racing. Officially, it's called the Karting School (or Escola de Karting), but locals prefer to call it the Kartodromo. Just why anyone would need to go to school to learn how to operate a go-cart is something I haven't determined. The Karting School is open from 10 am to 6 pm.

United Chinese Cemetery

The cemetery on the north-east corner of the island is worth a look. Among the graves is a 30m-high statue of Tou Tei, the Earth god. Some say Tou Tei is a bit perturbed by the newly constructed Macau airport nearby. No telling what kind of bad fungshui is being stirred up by all those aircraft.

Places to Stay

There's nothing on Taipa for budget travellers. The *Hyatt Regency* (☎ 831234; fax 830195; HK 2559-0168) has 326 rooms and everything you'd expect in a five-star hotel. Facilities include a bar, barber shop, business centre, coffee shop, conference room, disabled rooms, exercise centre, hotel doctor, in-house video, outdoor swimming pool, tennis courts, squash courts, and restaurants dishing up Cantonese, Macanese and Portuguese food. Doubles range from M$990 to M$1380, suites M$2800 to M$10,000. The hotel operates its own shuttle bus to the Macau Peninsula. Five stars.

The *New Century Hotel* (☎ 831111; fax 832222; HK 2581-9863), 600 rooms, is just across the street from the Hyatt Regency. Doubles are M$1100 to M$1650 and suites cost M$3000 to M$20,000. However, this place does offer one 'bargain' – apartments available for rent by the month. These cost M$20,500 to M$22,500 per month for two bedrooms, or M$27,000 to M$29,000 per month for three bedrooms. Five stars.

Places to Eat

Taipa Village has several good medium-priced restaurants. The best known for excellent Portuguese food is *Restaurante Panda* (☎ 827338) at No 4-8 Rua Direita de Carlos Eugenio. At Rua dos Clerigos 45 is *Galo* (☎ 827318), easily recognised by the picture of a rooster above the door. Also nearby is *Pinocchio* (☎ 827128) at Rua do Sol 4, an obscure alley near the fire station. *Mocambique* (☎ 827471), 8 Rua dos Clerigos does good African chicken. Also in an obscure alley is the excellent *A Petisqueira* (☎ 825354), Rua de Sao Joao 15. An exquisite, reasonably priced little place is *Restaurante Mediterraneo* (☎ 825069) on Rua de Fernao Mendes Pinto. Just next door at No 88 is *O'Manel* (☎ 827571), and across the street is one of Macau's few Indian restaurants, *Tee Jei Tandoori Restaurant* (☎ 320203).

At the northern end of Taipei, near the bridge to the Macau Peninsula, is *Bee Vee Restaurant* (☎ 812288), which also does excellent Portuguese food.

For those on a budget, the best deal is the *student cafeteria* at Macau University.

Entertainment

The Hyatt Regency Hotel is the centre of Taipa's upscale nightlife. *The Bar* has an American theme and is decked out with photos of Hollywood stars. Drinks are pricey but there is a happy hour from 5 to 7 pm.

As you might imagine, the Hyatt Regency has an upmarket *casino*. It's also fairly small and doesn't radiate that atmosphere of chaos that many gamblers enjoy. On the other hand, if you're attracted by high-stakes gambling this is the place.

COLOANE ISLAND

Of the two islands, Coloane (Luhuan in Chinese) is larger and known for its beautiful beaches. While Coloane is free of high-rises, a number of hotels, villas and even a golf course have sprouted near the previously pristine beaches. The new deep-water port has the potential to turn north-east Coloane into a jumble of factories, wharfs and warehouses. Still, for the moment the island is largely unspoilt and

MACAU

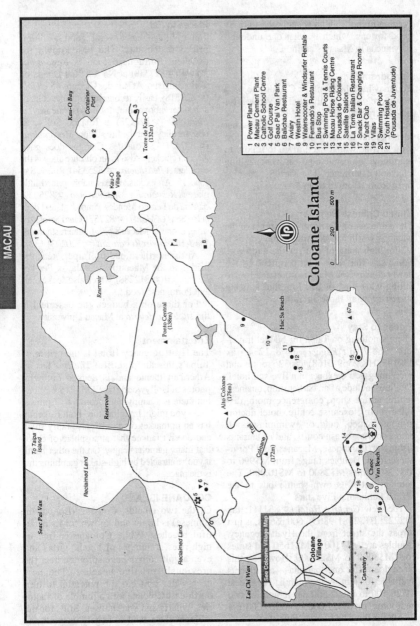

Coloane Island

1   Power Plant
2   Macau Cement Plant
3   Catholic School Centre
4   Golf Course
5   Seac Pai Van Park
6   Balichao Restaurant
7   Aviary
8   Westin Hotel
9   Waterscooter & Windsurfer Rentals
10 Ferando's Restaurant
11 Bus Stop
12 Swimming Pool & Tennis Courts
13 Macau Horse Riding Centre
14 Pousada de Coloane
15 Satellite Station
16 La Torre Italian Restaurant
17 Snack Bar & Changing Rooms
18 Yacht Club
19 Villas
20 Swimming Pool
21 Youth Hostel,
    (Pousada de Juventude)

ROB FLYNN

GLENN BEANLAND

RICHARD I'ANSON

RICHARD I'ANSON

Top Left: Monte Fort's cannons were fired only once in anger – with deadly effect.
Top Right: The facade of Macau's Monte Fort shows Portuguese influence.
Bottom Left: Colourful neon at Lisboa Casino lures gamblers like moths to a flame.
Bottom Right: The dragon dance is performed on festive occasions in Macau.

ROB FLYNN

ROB FLYNN

Top: Saving face. The restored facade is all that remains of St Paul's Cathedral – once described as the greatest monument to Christianity in the east.
Bottom: Largo do Senado is Macau's central square. Fine examples of colonial architecture can be seen here and throughout Macau.

will probably remain that way for a few years yet.

Seac Pai Van Park

About one km south of the causeway, Seac Pai Van Park covers 20 hectares. There is a fountain and well-tended gardens, but the most notable feature is the aviary behind Balichao Restaurant.

The park is open from 9 am to 7 pm daily, and admission costs M$5. It costs another M$5 to visit the aviary, and M$20 if you want to rent a table in the picnic area. The park has a camping area.

Hiking Trails

Behind Seac Pai Van Park are two hiking trails. The longest is simply called the Coloane Trail (Trilho de Coloane) and the entire loop walk is 8.6 km. The shorter North-East Coloane Trail (Trilho Nordeste de Coloane) is near Kau-O, and the total length is 6.2 km.

Coloane Village

The only real town on the island, this is largely a fishing village, although in recent years tourism has given the local economy a big boost. At the northern end of town are numerous **junk-building sheds**. Just how long this business can last is debatable – siltation threatens to make the harbour a mudflat within a decade. You can walk to the sheds and see how the junks are built, but take along a big stick as several of the sheds are guarded by vicious xenophobic dogs!

If you arrive by bus, you'll be dropped off near the village roundabout. If you walk one short block to the west you'll see the waterfront. Here you'll get a good view of China. It's so close one could easily swim across the channel. In fact, many people used to do just that to escape from China.

A sign near the waterfront points towards a **Sam Seng temple**. This temple is very small – not much more than a family altar. Just past the temple is the village pier.

Walking south along Avenida de Cinco de Outubro, you'll soon come to the main attraction in this village – the Chapel of St

Francis Xavier. This interesting chapel was built in 1928 to honour St Francis Xavier, who died on nearby Shang Ch'an Island in 1552. He had been a missionary in Japan and to this day Japanese come to Coloane to pay their respects.

A fragment of arm bone which once belonged to St Francis Xavier used to be kept in the chapel, along with several boxes of bones of the Portuguese and Japanese Christians who were martyred in Nagasaki in 1597; Vietnamese Christians killed in the early 17th century; and Japanese Christians killed in a rebellion in Japan in the 17th century. In 1978, all these bones were shipped from St Joseph's seminary to the Chapel of St Francis Xavier, but they were returned in 1995. In 1996, the bones of St Francis got moved to the new St Paul's Museum (see Macau Peninsula chapter).

Near the chapel is a **monument** surrounded by cannon balls to commemorate the successful final battle against pirates in these islands in 1910. The battle is celebrated locally on July 13.

South of the chapel is a library and a sign pointing towards the Kun Iam temple. This temple is tiny – not much more than an altar inside a little walled compound. Although there are no signs to indicate the path, if you walk just a little further past the stone wall you'll find a considerably larger and more interesting **Tin Hau temple**.

At the very southern end of Avenida de Cinco de Outubro is a **Tam Kong Temple**. Inside is a whale bone, more than a metre long, which has been carved into a model of a ship – complete with a dragon's head and a crew of men in pointed hats. The temple custodian enthusiastically welcomes foreigners and then holds up a little placard in English soliciting donations for the maintenance of the temple. Such donations are voluntary, so let your conscience be your guide.

Cheoc Van Beach

About 1.5 km down the road from Coloane Village is Cheoc Van Beach. The name means Bamboo Bay. You can swim in the ocean for free (there are public changing

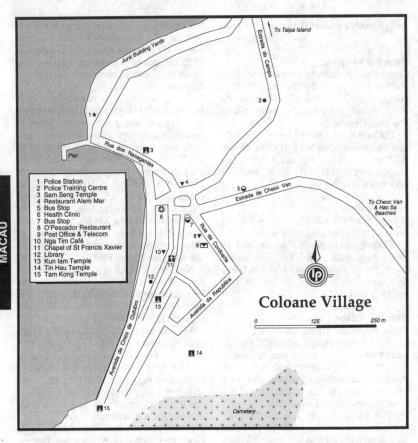

```
1   Police Station
2   Police Training Centre
3   Sam Seng Temple
4   Restaurant Alem Mar
5   Bus Stop
6   Health Clinic
7   Bus Stop
8   O'Pescador Restaurant
9   Post Office & Telecom
10  Nga Tim Café
11  Chapel of St Francis Xavier
12  Library
13  Kun Iam Temple
14  Tin Hau Temple
15  Tam Kong Temple
```

Coloane Village

rooms) or at the pool in Cheoc Van Park (for a fee). The pool is open from 9 am to 10 pm. Cheoc Van Beach also has a yacht club where you can inquire about boat rentals.

Hac Sa Beach

The largest and most popular beach in Macau, the name Hac Sa means 'Black Sand'. The sand does indeed have a grey to black colour and this makes the water look somewhat polluted, but actually it's perfectly clean and fine for swimming. The area is beautiful and on a clear day you can see the mountains on Hong Kong's Lantau Island.

Just near the bus stop is **Hac Sa Sports & Recreation Park**. Within the park is a large swimming pool, roller skating rink, playground and miniature golf course. It's open 9 am to 9 pm daily, and admission costs M$5. Use of the pool costs an additional M$15.

Behind Fernando's Restaurant is the Macau Horse Riding Centre (☎ 328303). It costs M$250 per hour, with a two-hour and two-person minimum. The horses are retired runners from the Macau Jockey Club on Taipa Island.

At the far end of Hac Sa Beach is a place to rent windsurfers and – if you can stand the noise – water scooters.

The golf course at the Westin Hotel is open to non-guests as well, but you have to pay. Green fees for 18 holes are M$600 on a week day and M$800 on weekends, topped off by a 5% tax.

Bus No 21A provides frequent service to Hac Sa. On weekends the buses are even more frequent.

Kau-O Village
At the eastern end of Coloane is Kau-O Village, but it's not likely that you'll want to go there. It's not very attractive because of the neighbouring cement and power plants. There is also a leprosarium here. In the past, there was a Vietnamese refugee camp, but this was long since closed and demolished.

Following the tradition of putting things here that Macau's government would rather the tourists didn't see, a deep-water container port is being built.

Perhaps the most interesting sight in town is the church called Our Lady of Sorrows, which has a large bronze crucifix above the north door.

Places to Stay
Youth Hostels The *Pousada de Juventude* (☎ 882050), also known as *Vila Dom Bosco*, youth hostel is at Cheoc Van Beach. Off season (basically winter) it's pretty easy to get in here, but during peak season (summer and holidays) competition for beds is keen. Big youth groups tend to book this place out during school holidays. There are only 30 beds, 15 each for men and women.

Another complication is that you can't simply show up at the hostel and ask to check in. You must first visit the Youth Hostel Booking Office (☎ 344340), which is near the A-Ma Temple on the Macau Peninsula. This office is only open Monday to Friday from 9 am to 1 pm and 2.30 to 5.45 pm. The booking office will book your bed and sell you a voucher which you then take to the hostel when you want to check in.

An International Youth Hostel Federation (IYHF) card is needed. The hostel is closed from 10 am to 3 pm and lights are out from 11 pm until 7 am. The cost for a dormitory bed is M$35 for foreigners and M$20 for Macau residents.

Hotels Very close to the beach at Cheoc Van Beach is a luxury hotel with 22 rooms, the *Pousada de Coloane* (☎ 882143; fax 882251; HK 2540-8180). It has perhaps the most relaxing atmosphere of any hotel in Macau. Doubles range from M$600 to M$680. The hotel has its own sauna and swimming pool and is well known for its excellent Sunday lunch buffet.

The *Westin Hotel* (☎ 871111; fax 871122; HK 2803-2015) is a luxury resort complex with 208 rooms on the east side of Hac Sa Beach. The emphasis is on villas and a country club atmosphere, as indicated by the 18-hole golf course and eight tennis courts, swimming pools, sauna and gymnasium. Doubles are M$1300 to M$1650, and suites cost M$4000 to M$16,000. Five stars.

Places to Eat
Right near the roundabout at Coloane Village is *Restaurant Alem Mar*, which serves Cantonese food. The best Portuguese restaurant in town is near the post office, *O'Pescador* (☎ 880197), Rua da Cordoaria 87-91. Right next to the St Francis Chapel is the small and cheap *Nga Tim Café*.

Next to the swimming pool at Cheoc Van is a fine Italian restaurant, *La Torre* (☎ 880156). Much cheaper is the *Snack Bar* (☎ 328528) just above the changing rooms by the beach. There are also two Portuguese restaurants, *Coloane* (☎ 882143) and *A Nau* (☎ 882725).

At Hac Sa Beach, *Fernando's* (☎ 328264) deserves honorable mention for some of the best food in Macau. The atmosphere is also pleasant and it can get crowded in the evening. Beware, there is no sign above the door and it's possible to wander around for quite a while looking for it. The restaurant is at the far end of the car park, close to the bus stop. The menu is in Portuguese and Chinese only, but Fernando himself (the manager) will gladly translate for you; he recommends the clams.

Balichao (☎ 870098) is in Seac Pai Van Park and serves fine Portuguese food from noon until 11 pm.

GUANGZHOU

Facts about Guangzhou

Hong Kong and Macau are mere specks on the map within the huge political entity known as Guangdong Province. 'Canton' is the traditional Western name for both the Chinese province of Guangdong, and also its capital city, Guangzhou. In recent years, the Chinese have been most insistent that the official pinyin Romanisation system be applied to geographical names. Thus, 'Peking' is now 'Beijing', 'Nanking' is 'Nanjing', and so on. Nevertheless, English speakers are much happier with the adjective 'Cantonese' rather than 'Guangdongnese' when describing the food, the people and the language.

Guangzhou has burnt its image into the Western consciousness. The image of 'Chinatown' that most Westerners now have is based on the Cantonese version of China. In Chinatowns from Melbourne to Toronto to London, Cantonese food is eaten and the Cantonese dialect predominates.

HISTORY

China is a sleeping giant. Let her sleep, for when she awakes, she will astonish the world.

Napoleon

It was the people of Guangdong who first made contact (often unhappy) with both the merchants and the armies of the modern European states, and it was these people who spearheaded the Chinese emigration to North America, Australia and South Africa in the mid-19th century. The move was spurred by gold rushes in those countries, but it was mainly wars and growing poverty which induced the Chinese to leave in droves.

The history of Guangdong Province over the past 2000 years is only known to us in outline. While the Chinese were carving out a civilisation centred on the Yellow River region in the north, the south remained a semi-independent tributary peopled by native tribes, the last survivors of which are now minority groups.

It was not until the Qin dynasty (221 – 207 BC), when the Chinese states of the north were first united under a single ruler, that the Chinese finally conquered the southern regions. However, revolts and uprisings were frequent and the Chinese settlements remained small and dispersed among a predominantly aboriginal population.

Chinese emigration to the region began in earnest around the 12th century AD. The original native tribes were killed by Chinese armies, isolated in small pockets or pushed further south – like the Li and Miao peoples who now inhabit the mountainous areas of Hainan Island off the southern coast of China.

By the 17th century the Chinese had outgrown Guangdong. The pressure of population forced them to move into adjoining Guangxi Province and into Sichuan, which had been ravaged and depopulated after rebellions in the mid-17th century.

As a result of these migrations, the people of Guangdong are not a homogeneous group. The term Cantonese is sometimes applied to all people living in Guangdong Province, but there are significant minorities – such as the Hakka people – who started moving southward from the northern plains around the 13th or 14th centuries.

What the migrants from the north found beyond the mountainous areas of northern and western Guangdong was the Pearl River Delta, cutting through a region which is richer than any in China, except for around the Yangzi and Yellow Rivers. Because of their fertility, the delta and river valleys could support a huge population. The abundant waterways, heavy rainfall and warm climate allowed wet-rice cultivation of two crops a year.

The first town to be established on the site of present-day Guangzhou dates back to the Qin dynasty, coinciding with the conquest of southern China by the north. Close to the sea, Guangzhou became an outward-looking

326

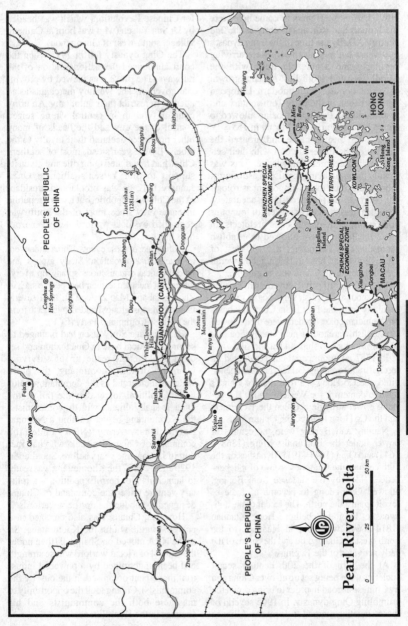

Pearl River Delta

city. The first foreigners to come here were the Indians and Romans as early as the 2nd century AD. By the time of the Tang dynasty 500 years later, Arab traders were arriving regularly and a sizeable trade with the Middle East and South-East Asia had grown.

Initial contact with modern European nations began in the early 16th century and resulted in the Portuguese being allowed to set up base downriver at Macau in 1557.

Next the Jesuits came and aroused the interest of the imperial court with their scientific and technical knowledge. This was mainly through their expertise in astronomy, which permitted the all-important astrological charts to be produced more accurately, though others worked as makers of fountains and curios, or as painters and architects. In 1582 the Jesuits were allowed to establish themselves at Zhaoqing, a town west of Guangzhou, and later in Beijing, but overall their influence on China was negligible.

In 1685 the imperial government opened Guangzhou, and British ships began to arrive regularly from the East India Company bases on the Indian coast. Traders were then allowed to establish warehouses near Guangzhou as a base from which to ship out tea and silk.

In 1757 a new imperial edict restricted all foreign trade to a single Guangzhou merchants' guild, the Co Hong – a reflection of China's relative contempt for Western trade. The ensuing power struggle between the Westerners and the Co Hong sparked the Opium Wars.

Nanjing and Beijing were the centres of power under the isolationist Ming (1368 – 1644) and Qing (1644 –1911) dynasties. In the 19th century the Cantonese sense of independence, aided by the distance from Beijing, allowed Guangdong to become a cradle of revolt against the north. The leader of the anti-dynastic Taiping Rebellion, Hong Xiuquan (1814-1864), was born in Huaxian, to the north-west of Guangzhou and the centre of the early activities of the Taipings.

At the turn of the 20th century secret societies were being set up all over China and by Chinese abroad in order to bring down the crumbling Qing dynasty. In 1905 several of these societies merged to form the Alliance

for Chinese Revolution, which was headed by Dr Sun Yatsen (who was born at Cuiheng village, south-west of Guangzhou).

The Qing dynasty fell in 1911 when the court announced the nationalisation of the railways. The move was viewed by provincial governors and wealthy merchants as an attempt to restrict their autonomy. An army coup in Wuhan in central China seized control of the city and the heads of many other provinces declared their loyalty to the rebels. By the year's end, most of southern China had repudiated Qing rule and given its support to Sun Yatsen's alliance. On 1 January 1912 he was proclaimed president of the Chinese Republic, but it was a republic in name only since most of the north was controlled by local warlords left over from the Qing era.

In the wake of these events, China underwent an intellectual revolution. Study groups and other political organisations sprang up everywhere and included as members people such as Zhou Enlai and Mao Zedong. In 1921 several Chinese Marxist groups banded together to form the Chinese Communist Party (CCP).

By this stage Sun Yatsen had managed to secure a political base in Guangzhou and set up a government made up of surviving members of the Kuomintang, the party which had emerged as the dominant revolutionary political force after the fall of the Qing. In shaky alliance with the communists, the Kuomintang began training a National Revolutionary Army (NRA) under the command of Chiang Kaishek, who had met Sun in Japan some years before. Sun died in 1925 and by 1927 the Kuomintang was ready to launch its Northern Expedition – a military venture under the command of Chiang designed to subdue the northern warlords.

However, Chiang was also engaged in a power struggle within the Kuomintang. So as the NRA moved on Shanghai (then under the control of a local warlord whose strength had been undermined by a powerful industrial movement organised in the city by the communists), Chiang took the opportunity to massacre both the communists and his enemies in the Kuomintang.

By mid-1928 the Northern Expedition had reached Beijing and a national government was established, with Chiang holding the highest political and military positions. Those communists who survived the massacres made their famous Long March to the Jinggang Mountains, on the Hunan-Jiangxi border and other mountainous areas of China, From there they began a war against the Kuomintang, which lasted just over 20 years and ended in victory for the communists in 1949. Mao Zedong became chairman of the CCP and essentially the country's leader until his death in 1976. During his reign, Mao presided over numerous crises, including the Korean War in 1950-1953, the economically disastrous Great Leap Forward, a traumatic split with the Soviet Union and the chaotic Cultural Revolution.

In the middle of 1977 Deng Xiaoping, an accused 'capitalist roader' who had twice been purged for his views, returned to power and was appointed to the positions of vice-premier, vice-chairman of the party and chief of staff of the PLA. Final power now passed to the collective leadership of the six-member Standing Committee of the CCP, which included Deng. The China they took over was racked with problems – a backward country in desperate need of modernisation. Deng adopted what have become known as 'pragmatic economic policies' – China remains officially socialist while 'temporarily' adopting capitalist economic incentives in order to modernise the country.

In 1978 China embarked on its Four Modernisations (agriculture, industry, national defence, and science and technology) in earnest. The Deng Xiaoping years have seen a slow but sure freeing up of the Chinese economy, and by the early '90s it had become the fastest growing in the world. This achievement itself points to major changes not just in economic policy but in the outlooks of the ordinary Chinese that have brought about this success. The early '70s saw the Chinese people dispirited and psychologically scarred by the events of the Cultural Revolution, most of them employed in state enterprises that doled out pay cheques whether workers did anything or not. The Chinese system was one in which politics were in command, the philosophy of which is well summed up in the Cultural Revolution saying: 'a socialist train running late is better than a revisionist train running on time'.

The assimilation of southern China was a slow process, reflected in the fact that the southerners referred to themselves as men of Tang (of the Tang dynasty 618 – 907), while the northerners referred to themselves as men of Han (of the Han dynasty 206 BC – 220 AD). The northerners regarded their southern compatriots with disdain, or as one 19th-century northern account put it:

The Cantonese ... are a coarse set of people ... Before the times of Han and Tang, this country was quite wild and waste, and these people have sprung forth from unconnected, unsettled vagabonds that wandered here from the north.

Despite the nasty rhetoric, the Cantonese are widely admired for their entrepreneurial skills. Of all the Chinese, the Cantonese have probably been the most influenced by the outside world. Almost everyone in southern Guangdong has relatives in Hong Kong who for years have been storming across the border loaded down with the latest fashions, and gifts of electronic appliances, music tapes (legal), smuggled video tapes (illegal) and even motorcycles.

Free enterprise, private business and individualism is the path that Guangdong took. And despite repeated interference by Beijing's bureaucrats, it is Guangdong that continues to drag China – kicking and screaming – into the capitalist era.

GEOGRAPHY

Guangdong Province lies on the south-east coast of China and occupies just 1.8% of China's total land area. The dominant feature is the Pearl River Delta, a fertile plain which supports a huge population and provides a natural harbour. The river provides a natural transport system and is a chief reason for Guangzhou's existence as an economic hub. Not surprisingly, the Cantonese have a much closer affection for Hong Kong than Beijing

GUANGZHOU

– Guangzhou is a mere 120 km north-west of Hong Kong but 2300 km from the national capital. Guangzhou is the sixth largest city in China and the capital of Guangdong Province.

Guangzhou was originally three cities. The inner city was enclosed behind sturdy walls and was divided into the new and old cities. The outer city was everything outside these walls. The building of the walls began during the 11th century and was completed in the 16th century. The walls were 15 km in circumference, eight metres high and between five and eight metres thick. Not surprisingly, the walls have since come down to make way for roads, flats and fast-food barns.

Foreigners tend to gravitate towards two main parts of town: Shamian Island in the west, which attracts tourists and business travellers; and The Greenery in the east, a complex of expensive expat apartments which has, among other things, the American School and a computer shopping arcade.

GEOLOGY

Except for a few eroded granite hills, Guangzhou is built on the alluvial plain created by the immense Pearl River. The city and most of the surrounding region is as flat as a billiard table.

CLIMATE

Most of Guangdong Province has a subtropical climate, but temperatures tend to be more extreme further inland. Winter tends to be dreary – chilly, damp and overcast, but temperatures are not extreme. Average monthly temperatures and rainfall for Guangzhou are as follows:

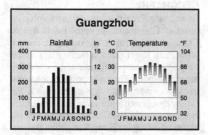

ECOLOGY & ENVIRONMENT

If you think Hong Kong could do with a little more green space, wait until you see Guangzhou and its environs. Most of what's left of Guangdong's flora and fauna is found to the north of Guangzhou. From Guangzhou southwards to Hong Kong and Macau, what was farmland 20 years ago is now a hellscape of roads, dockyards, factories, chimneys and workers' flats. The environment is particularly blighted along waterways, which means most of the Pearl River Delta. The most wildlife you are likely to see in this area can be found at the Guangzhou Zoo and Qingping Market.

GOVERNMENT & POLITICS

Every revolution evaporates, leaving behind only the slime of a new bureaucracy.
Franz Kafka

Precious little is known about the inner workings of the Chinese government, but Westerners can make educated guesses.

The highest authority rests with the Standing Committee of the Communist Party Politburo.

Apocalypse Mao. Mao Zedong was the architect of a Cultural Revolution that propelled China into a spasm of chaos and violence during the 1960s.

Playing Favourites

In 1989, the massacre and brutal suppression of the pro-democracy movement in Beijing had a huge impact on China's economy. Tourism, foreign aid and investment all fell off sharply. Many feared that China would revert to its xenophobic past and close off to the outside world. This, at least, has not happened, and China's economy has been booming since 1991.

But concern about human rights remains a sore spot, and when it was revealed that prison labour was being used to produce cheap manufactured goods, some of China's trading partners suggested an economic embargo. Recent revelations of a gruesome new trade has not helped China's image – Chinese prisoners in Guangzhou are executed after being tissue-matched to Hong Kongers in need of organ transplants.

The United States has criticised China's human rights record, and as a result relations between the two powers have become very tense. Harry Wu – a US citizen of Chinese descent who exposed China's use of prison labour – was arrested when trying to re-enter China. His arrest nearly led the US to revoke China's status as a Most-Favoured Nation (MFN). Having MFN status is crucial to China's export industries, which have become greatly dependent on the US market. Loss of MFN status would be a crippling blow to Guangdong's economy, as well as to Hong Kong.

The Chinese government eventually released Wu, but the US and China nearly came to blows again in March 1996, when China tried to intimidate the Taiwanese during their presidential election. China fired live missiles just off the coast of Taiwan and amassed a huge army in what looked like preparation for an invasion. The US reacted by stationing its fleet of aircraft carriers just off the coast of Taiwan, and the presidential election went on as scheduled.

Although MFN status has so far been renewed every year, some US representatives have vowed to revoke it if human-rights violations continue unchecked. China responds that such issues involving Chinese citizens (including Hong Kongers and Taiwanese) are part of China's 'internal affairs', and foreigners have no right to interfere.

So far, Beijing has gambled correctly – knowing that the US values its trade with China too much to impose widespread economic sanctions. ∎

Below it is the 210-member Central Committee, made up of younger party members and provincial party leaders. At the grassroots level the party forms a parallel system to the administrations in the People's Liberation Army (PLA), universities, government, and industries. Real authority is exercised by the party representatives at each level in these organisations. They, in turn, are responsible to the party officials in the hierarchy above them, thus ensuring strict central control. Although elections are held for the lowest level positions, democracy in the Western sense simply does not exist.

Throughout the system, there are various antagonistic factions. Governing the country seems to involve a delicate balance between these rivals, and as a result the government is often too paralysed to make any significant policy decisions.

Things are somewhat different in Guangdong Province. While paying lip service to the official line taken by geriatric socialists in Beijing, Guangdong officials from the governor down have continued to push their own programmes of economic liberalisation.

Although political liberalisation is not presently possible, officials have a relaxed attitude and are much less interested in controlling people's lives than making money.

The basic unit of government organisation is the work unit, or *danwei*. Every Chinese is a member of one. Nothing can proceed without the work unit. It decides if a couple may marry or divorce, and when they can have a child. It assigns housing, sets salaries, handles mail, recruits party members, keeps files on each unit member, arranges transfers to other jobs or other parts of the country, and gives permission to travel abroad. Work unit members are also compelled to attend propaganda meetings which the government calls 'political education'.

Through it's 5000-year history, China has been plagued by the lack of a system for orderly succession. China's patriarch Deng Xiaoping has officially retired from all positions of power, yet as long as he (allegedly) lives, no one person or faction can emerge as China's new leader. Deng is over 90 years old and reported to be critically ill. It is widely believed that his demise would usher

GUANGZHOU

in a traumatic period of political struggle, which could have far-reaching effects (either good or bad) on China's economic and political system.

ECONOMY

China's economic policies have undergone a radical change since the death of Mao Zedong. Under Mao, it had largely isolated itself from other nations, apprehensive that economic links with would make China dependent.

This has all changed. Foreign investment, most of it funnelled into China via Hong Kong, has transformed the country. Not surprisingly, Guangdong has benefited more than any other province, and Guangzhou has become one of China's biggest boom towns.

While capitalist-style reforms have undeniably boosted growth to record levels in China, the country still claims to be a socialist state. This is at least partially true – the economy is littered with state-run enterprises which do nothing but lose money and drink up subsidies. Privatising the state sector has been suggested numerous times, but is politically unpalatable to the leadership because it would essentially mean the death of communist ideology. Still, if any place in China is likely to dissolve or diminish the state sector, it would be Guangdong.

POPULATION & PEOPLE

China's population is over 1.2 billion people, and with a national growth rate of 1.2% annually it is expected to hit 1.3 billion by the year 2000. According to the last official census, Guangdong Province's population is about 63 million. More than 98% of the inhabitants are Han Chinese; the rest belong to small minority groups, such as the Miao and Li.

EDUCATION

According to official figures 81.5% of China's population is literate.

ARTS

Basically it's the same as for Hong Kong, but there are a few differences. Politics invades every aspect of life in China, and much of what Hong Kongers see in the movies or even in museums is considered inappropriate for China's masses. This includes everything from nude paintings to films about politically sensitive subjects.

Music & Dance

Love songs and soft rock from Taiwan and Hong Kong are in vogue in Guangzhou. Tastes run more towards heavy metal and punk elsewhere, and there are clubs in all the major cities to cater for the craze – often with live bands featuring batteries of horns and electric violins.

Attempts to tailor Chinese classical music, song and dance to Western tastes have resulted in a Frankenstein's monster of Broadway-style spectaculars and epic theatre film scores. One Chinese rock star, Cui Jian, released a big hit called 'Rock for the New Long March'. And in an attempt to show that China's geriatric leaders are also hip, government officials authorised a disco version of 'The East is Red'. There are orchestras organised on Western lines which substitute Chinese for Western instruments. Exactly where all this is leading no one knows.

SOCIETY & CONDUCT
Traditional Culture

Traditional culture has taken a beating in China since the communists came to power in 1949. Much of what was traditional Chinese culture was supplanted by politics in a series of campaigns and sometimes bloody purges. Indeed, the whole point of the cultural revolution of the 1960s was to erase Chinese culture and start out with a clean slate.

Nonetheless, traditional Chinese culture is staging a comeback in large part, thanks to the influence of Hong Kong, Taiwan and overseas Chinese communities in the West. This revival comes in many forms – religion, architecture, classic books (which were once banned), music, re-establishing festivals and resurrecting nearly forgotten practices such as *qigong* (kungfu meditation).

The government has even dusted off Confucianism, long distained by the communists as a feudalistic practice. This, however, may have much to do with politics, as Confucius em-

The Dying Rooms

It has long been the case in China that couples prefer boys over girls. Boys are cherished largely because young men have a moral duty in Chinese society to support their elderly parents. By contrast, a woman joins her husband's family when she gets married, and her moral duty is to support her in-laws when they get old. For many Chinese couples, a baby girl represents a financial liability. All this is nothing new – for centuries, the only way for Chinese couples to recoup their investment in raising a girl has been to sell her (either to a brothel or to an older man who needs a wife). Other Chinese couples have solved the 'problem' by murdering their newborn female babies.

Ever since China adopted a one-child family policy in 1979, the situation has been worsening. All estimates are crude guesses, but a number of sources have suggested that about 15 million female babies have 'disappeared' since 1979. The figure is based on the (skewed) official birth statistics which show a lot more boys being born than girls. While many girls are being aborted before birth, there is some disturbing evidence to indicate that they are being 'aborted' months or years later.

Even China's supporters were shocked by a documentary called *The Dying Rooms*, which was released in early 1996. Using a hidden video camera, a documentary team funded by Britain's Channel Four posed as members of an American charity group and managed to film the inside of four Chinese orphanages. Unlike the showcase orphanages shown to foreigners wishing to adopt Chinese children, the four orphanages in the documentary looked more like concentration camps.

The children in the video were tied up with ropes and clearly starving to death. The video also revealed that all the children – with the exception of a few handicapped boys – were girls. Informal interviews with the caretakers at the orphanage, again secretly filmed, indicated that most of the children were abandoned by their parents. The staff implied that they fully expected all these children to die, not from disease but from sheer neglect and starvation.

Kate Blewett, who led the documentary team, took care not to attack the one-child family policy, which for all its flaws may be the only way for China to tackle its severe overpopulation problem.

'We don't want to criticise the one-child policy, but we do want to focus on the problems it is causing which can be solved,' said Blewett.

The documentary also featured a tour of a privately funded orphanage where the children were well treated. 'We were very keen to show what could be done with the right attitude,' Blewett added.

Before the documentary was shown, the Chinese government was asked to give a response to the allegations of neglect and death in the orphanages. The government's shrill response became the final sequence to the documentary when it was publicly shown:

'The so-called dying rooms do not exist in China at all. Our investigations confirm that those reports are vicious fabrications made out of ulterior motives. The contemptible lie about China's welfare work in orphanages cannot but arouse the indignation of the Chinese people, especially the great numbers of social workers who are working hard for children's welfare.'

The Chinese government later rolled out stage-managed happy smiling couples showing off their well-cared-for 'adopted' children.

Whether or not the Chinese government knowingly starves unwanted children to death can be debated, but the government did little to help its image when the Philip Hayden Charitable Foundation came to China's aid a few weeks later. Perhaps naively, the foundation thought the problem might simply be a lack of cash, and decided to launch a fundraising dinner for the orphans at a luxury hotel in Beijing. Lots of important people were invited to the fundraiser, including the US ambassador to China Jim Sasser, American-Chinese author Amy Tan, prominent American business people and about half the American Chamber of Commerce in Beijing. All up, about 450 people bought tickets at US$720 apiece, raising more than US$30,000. But before Tan could deliver the opening speech, the Beijing police showed up and declared the fundraiser an illegal gathering. The guests were ordered to leave. ∎

phasised the importance of obedience to the established powers.

Dos & Don'ts

Clothing After Hong Kong, which resembles one big fashion show, you may actually find Guangzhou to be a relief. Most people in China dress casually, partly because of poverty and partly because communist ideology glorifies peasants and workers. Foreigners can get away with wearing almost anything as long as it isn't overly revealing.

In summer, shorts are OK and many Chinese men walk around outdoors bare-chested. However, shy Western men with a lot of body hair should not try this, as displaying a hairy chest in public will attract a large crowd of enthusiastic onlookers. Men with hairy chests should wear a T-shirt when swimming. Children may actually pull your body hair to test if it's real!

RELIGION

The situation is similar to Hong Kong and Macau, the basic difference being that all forms of religion were harshly suppressed during the Cultural Revolution. Priests, nuns and monks were imprisoned, executed or sent to labour in the countryside while temples and churches were ransacked and converted into factories and warehouses. Since the early 1980s, temples have been restored, at least for the sake of tourism. There has been a religious revival of sorts, but the main feature you will note about temples in China is that they are usually devoid of worshippers. Communist Party members are not permitted to belong to any religious organisation.

Catholics have a particularly hard time – loyalty to the Pope is regarded as treason and priests are still rotting in prison for refusing to denounce the Holy See. The government has set up a Catholic church which does not recognise the Vatican.

LANGUAGE

What a difference a border makes. Cantonese is still the most popular dialect in Guangzhou and the surrounding area, but the official language of the People's Republic is the Beijing dialect, usually referred to in the West as 'Mandarin'. In China it's referred to as *putonghua* or 'common speech' and the Chinese government set about popularising it in the 1950s. A large percentage of foreigners living and working in China manage to gain a reasonable level of fluency in the spoken language, but the written form is another story. Most foreigners are more successful at learning Mandarin than Cantonese.

Pinyin

In 1958 the Chinese officially adopted a system known as *pinyin* as a method of writing their language using the Roman alphabet. Since the official language of China is the Beijing dialect, this pronunciation is used. The original idea was to eventually do away with characters completely and just use pinyin. However, tradition dies hard and the idea has gradually been abandoned.

Pinyin is often used on shop fronts, street signs and advertising billboards. The popularisation of this spelling is still at an early stage, so don't expect Chinese to be able to use pinyin. In the countryside and the smaller towns you may not see a single pinyin sign anywhere, so unless you speak Chinese you'll need a phrasebook with Chinese characters. Though pinyin is helpful, it's not an instant key to communication, since Westerners usually don't get the pronunciation and intonation of the Romanised word correct.

Since 1979 all translated texts of Chinese diplomatic documents and Chinese magazines published in foreign languages have used the pinyin system of spelling names and places. The system replaces the old Wade-Giles and Lessing systems of Romanising Chinese script. Thus under pinyin, 'Mao Tse-tung' becomes *Mao Zedong*; 'Chou En-lai' becomes *Zhou Enlai*; and 'Peking' becomes *Beijing*. The name of the country remains as it has been generally written: 'China' in English and German; 'Chine' in French; and 'Zhongguo' in pinyin.

Tones

Mastering tones is tricky for the untrained Western ear, but with practise it can be done. Four basic tones are used in Mandarin, which makes it easier for foreigners to learn than Cantonese. As in Cantonese, changing the tone changes the meaning. For example, in Mandarin the word *'ma'* can have four distinct meanings depending on which tone is used:

high tone	*mā* is mother
rising tone	*má* is hemp or numb
falling-rising tone	*mǎ* is horse
falling tone	*mà* is to scold or swear

Technically there is a fifth, the so-called 'neutral' tone. It can be indicated by a dot over the vowel, as in *mȧ*, but it is usually not indicated at all. A neutral tone does not need to be pronounced and does not affect the meaning.

The following is a description of the sounds produced in spoken Mandarin Chinese. The letter **v** is not used in Chinese. For beginners, the trickiest sounds in pinyin are **c, q** and **x** because their pronunciation isn't remotely similar in English. Most letters are pronounced as in English, except for the following:

Vowels

a   like the 'a' in 'father'
ai   like the 'i' in 'I'
ao   like the 'ow' in 'cow'
e   like the 'u' in 'blur'
ei   like the 'ei' in 'weigh'
i   like the 'ee' in 'meet' or the 'oo' in 'book'*
ian   like in 'yen'
ie   like the English word 'yeah'
o   like the 'o' in 'or'
ou   like the 'oa' in 'boat'
u   like the 'u' in 'flute'
ui   like 'way'
uo   like 'w' followed by an 'o' like in 'or'
yu   like German umlaut 'ü' or French 'u' in 'union'
ü   like German umlaut 'ü'

Consonants

c   like the 'ts' in 'bits'
ch   like in English, but with the tongue curled back
h   like in English, but articulated from the throat
q   like the 'ch' in 'chicken'
r   like the 's' in 'pleasure'
sh   like in English, but with the tongue curled back
x   like the 'sh' in 'shine'
z   like the 'ds' in 'suds'
zh   like the 'j' in 'judge' but with the tongue curled back

*The letter **i** is pronounced like the 'oo' in 'book' when it occurs after c, ch, r, s, sh, z, zh.

Consonants can never appear at the end of a syllable except for **n, ng**, and **r**.

In pinyin, apostrophes are occasionally used to separate syllables. So, you can write *(ping'an)* to prevent the word being pronounced as *(pin'gan)*.

Body Language

Hand signs are well-used in China. The 'thumbs-up' sign has a long tradition as an indication of excellence or, in Chinese, *guā guā jiào*.

The Chinese have a system for counting on their hands. If you can't speak the language, it would be worth your while to at least learn Chinese finger counting. The symbol for number 10 is to form a cross with the index fingers, but in many locations the Chinese just show a fist.

Useful Phrases

Lonely Planet's *Mandarin Chinese Phrasebook* includes common words, useful phrases and word lists in English, simplified Chinese characters and pinyin. Over the page you will find some survival phrases to get you started.

GUANGZHOU

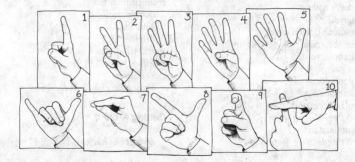

Pronouns

I
  wǒ 我
you
  nǐ 你
he, she, it
  tā 他
we, us
  wǒmen 我们
you (plural)
  nǐmen 你们
they, them
  tāmen 他们

Greetings & Civilities

hello
  nǐ hǎo 你好
goodbye
  zàijiàn 再见
thank you
  xièxie 谢谢
you're welcome
  búkèqì 不客气
I'm sorry/excuse me
  duìbùqǐ 对不起
name card
  míngpiàn 名片

Negotiation

I want...
  wǒ yào... 我要
I want to buy...
  wǒ yào mǎi... 我要买..
No, I don't want it
  búyào 不要
yes, have
  yǒu 有
no, don't have
  méiyǒu 没有
How much does it cost?
  duōshǎo qián? 多少钱
too expensive
  tài guì 太贵
Do you understand?
  dǒng bùdǒng? 懂不懂
I don't understand
  wǒ tīng bùdǒng 我听不懂
I do understand
  wǒ tīngde dǒng 我听得懂

Necessities

bathroom (washroom)
  xǐshǒujiān 洗手间
mosquito incense coils
  wénxiāng 蚊香
mosquito mats
  diàn wénxiāng 电蚊香
sanitary pads (Kotex)
  wèishēng mián 卫生棉
sunscreen (UV) lotion
  fáng shài yóu 防晒油
tampons
  wèishēng mián tiáo 卫生棉条
toilet paper
  wèishēng zhǐ 卫生纸
toilet (restroom)
  cèsuǒy 厕所
wash clothes
  xǐyīfú 洗衣服

Air Transport

airport
  fēijīchǎng 飞机场
boarding pass
  dēngjì kǎ 登记卡
CAAC
  zhōngguó mínháng 中国民航
cancel
  qǔxiāo 取消
reserve a seat
  dìng wèizǐ 定位子
ticket
  piào 票
buy a ticket
  mǎi piào 买票
one-way ticket
  dānchéng piào 单程票
reconfirm air ticket
  quèrèn 确认
refund a ticket
  tuìpiào 退票
round-trip ticket
  láihuì piào 来回票
ticket office
  shòu piào chù 售票处

Getting Around

bicycle hire
  zìxíngchē chūzū 自行车出租

bus
   gōnggòng qìchē 公共汽车
1st-class waiting room
   tóuděng hòuchē lóu 头等候车楼
hard-seat
   yìngxí, yìngzuò 硬席/硬座
hard-sleeper
   yìngwò 硬卧
I want to get off (bus/taxi)
   xià chē 下车
long-distance bus station
   chángtú qìchē zhàn 长途汽车站
luggage
   xínglǐ 行李
luggage storage room
   jìcúnchù 寄存处
pier
   mǎtóu 码头
platform ticket
   zhàntái piào 站台票
railway station
   huǒchē zhàn 火车站
soft-seat
   ruǎnxí, ruǎnzuò 软席/软座
soft-sleeper
   ruǎnwò 软卧
taxi
   chūzū chē 出租车
train
   huǒchē 火车
upgrade ticket (on train)
   bǔ piào 补票
Which platform?
   dìjǐ hào zhàntái 第几号站台

Directions
alley
   nòng 弄
boulevard
   dàdào 大道
Go straight
   yìzhí zǒu 一直走
I'm lost
   wǒ mí lù 我迷路
lane
   xiàng 巷
No 21
   21 hào 21号

road
   lù 路
section
   duàn 段
street
   jiē, dàjiē 街/大街
Turn around
   xiàng huí zǒu 向回走
Turn left
   zuǒ zhuǎn 左转
Turn right
   yòu zhuǎn 右转
Where is the...?
   ...zài nǎlǐ? ...在那里

Accommodation
bed
   chuángwèi 床位
big hotel
   jiǔdiàn, bīnguǎn 酒店/宾馆
book the whole room
   bāofáng 包房
check-in (register)
   dēngjì 登记
deposit
   yājīn 押金
dormitory
   duōrénfáng 多人房
double room (2 beds)
   shuāngrénfáng 双人房
economy room
   jīngjì fáng 经济房
economy room with bath
   jīngjì tàofáng 经济套房
hostel
   zhāodàisuǒ 招待所
hotel (all kinds)
   lǚguǎn 旅馆
luxury room with bath
   háohuá tàofáng 豪华套房
reserve a room
   dìng fángjiān 定房间
room
   fángjiān 房间
single room (1 bed)
   dānrénfáng 单人房
standard room with bath
   biāozhǔn tàofáng 标准套房

Post

aerogramme
hángkōng yóujiǎn 航空邮简
airmail
hángkōng xìn 航空信
envelope
xìnfēng 信封
GPO
zǒng yóujú 总邮局
international express mail (EMS)
kuàijié 快捷
package
bāoguǒ 包裹
post office
yóujú 邮局
postcard
míngxìn piàn 明信片
poste restante
cún jú hòu lǐng lán 存局候领栏
registered mail
guà hào 挂号
stamp
yóupiào 邮票
surface mail
píngyóu 平邮
telegram
diànbào 电报

Telecommunications

collect call
duìfāng fùqián 对方付钱
direct dial
zhí bō diànhuà 直拨电话
fax
chuánzhēn 传真
international call
guójì diànhuà 国际电话
telephone card
diànhuà kǎ 电话卡
telephone office
diànxùn dàlóu 电讯大楼
telephone
diànhuà 电话
telex
diànchuán 电传

Visas & Documents

Foreign Affairs Branch
wàishìkē 外事科
passport
hùzhào 护照
Public Security Bureau
gōng ān jú 公安局
visa extension
yáncháng qiānzhèng 延长签证
visa
qiānzhèng 签证

Emergencies

antibiotics
kàngjūnsù 抗菌素
Fire!
huǒ zāi! 火灾
Help!
jiùmìng a! 救命啊
hospital
yīyuàn 医院
I'm a diabetic
wǒ yǒu tángniào bìng 我有糖尿病
I'm allergic to...
wǒ duì...hěn guòmǐn 我对.. 很过敏
I'm injured
wǒ shòushāng 我受伤
I'm sick
wǒ shēng bìng 我生病
penicillin
qīngméisù 青霉素
pickpocket
páshǒu 勒贼
rapist
qiángjiānfàn 强奸犯
Thief!
xiǎo tōu! 小偷

Time

What is the time?
jǐ diǎn? 几点
hour
diǎn 点
minute
fēn 分
now
xiànzài 现在
today
jīntiān 今天
tomorrow
míngtiān 明天

yesterday
zuótiān 昨天
Wait a moment
děng yī xià 等一下

Numbers

0	*líng*	零
1	*yī*	一
2	*èr, liǎng*	二, 两
3	*sān*	叁
4	*sì*	四
5	*wǔ*	五
6	*liù*	六
7	*qī*	七
8	*bā*	八
9	*jiǔ*	九
10	*shí*	十
11	*shíyī*	十一
12	*shí'èr*	十二
20	*èrshí*	二十
21	*èrshíyī*	二十一
100	*yìbǎi*	一百
200	*liǎngbǎi*	两百
1,000	*yìqiān*	一千
2,000	*liǎngqiān*	两千
10,000	*yíwàn*	一万
20,000	*liǎngwàn*	两万
100,000	*shíwàn*	十万
200,000	*èrshíwàn*	二十万

Useful Expressions

bill (cheque)
zhàngdān 帐单
chopsticks
kuàizi 筷子
fork
chāzi 叉子
I can't eat spicy food
wǒ bùnéng chī là 我不能吃辣
I'm a vegetarian
wǒ shì chīsùde 我是吃素的

Facts for the Visitor

PLANNING

When to Go

Since the weather is tolerable almost any time of year, your main consideration will be avoiding the crowds. One rule to remember is to avoid travelling on weekends and (even more so) at public holiday times, such as Easter and Chinese Lunar New Year. At these times everything is booked out as herds of Hong Kongers stampede across the border, leaving trampled foreign tourists in their wake. Accommodation in Guangzhou is also somewhat difficult to find during the Guangzhou Fair, held in April and October. At this time it's best to visit other places in the province if you want to avoid the crowds.

Maps

Finding maps of Guangzhou and other Chinese cities is easy enough – if you can read Chinese characters. To find one in English, look in the gift shops of the major hotels. Especially recommended are the maps of *Guangzhou* and *Shenzhen* by Universal Publications of Hong Kong, which show both Chinese and English place names. You can't buy these in China, but they are available at most Hong Kong bookshops.

What to Bring

While you can now buy almost everything you need in China, certain things are difficult to find. This is doubly true if you can't speak Chinese. To preserve your sanity, bring some reading material. Due to the State's heavy-handed censorship, good books in English are scarce in China.

But the biggest problem is finding pharmaceutical items. Expats living in Guangzhou were much relieved when the first Watson's chemist opened in the city. Unfortunately, there are many everyday pharmaceuticals which you may suddenly need when no Watson's is in sight. And don't expect to find a convenience store on every corner as you do in Hong Kong.

With this in mind, you'd best bring enough of your everyday pharmaceutical needs to last your entire trip in Guangzhou and beyond. See the What to Bring section in the Hong Kong Facts for the Visitor chapter.

HIGHLIGHTS

Guangzhou is an interesting city and a worthwhile place to visit, but it would be dishonest to describe it as beautiful. The main attraction is the feeling of being in China – the street markets, temples, the food, the chaos, surprising prosperity amid crushing poverty, etc. The same could be said for most of the area around Guangzhou, known as the Pearl River Delta. While many tourists take one look and conclude that this area is extremely poor, it's actually quite the opposite. The delta's ravaged environment is the price paid for rapid economic growth unencumbered by planning or organisation.

That having been said, there are some major attractions in and around Guangzhou. Within the city itself are a few charming diversions like Yuexiu Park, the Pearl River Cruise and Shamian Island. The Qingping Market is morbidly fascinating – but not recommended for animal lovers. The Southern Yue Tomb Museum and Chen Clan Academy get good reviews from travellers.

Scenic beauty can be found outside the city. Highlights include: Zhaoqing and Dinghushan to the west; Luofushan to the east; Xiqiao Hills to the south-west; Lotus Mountain to the south-east; and the White Cloud Hills in the near north.

TOURIST OFFICES

Local Tourist Offices

China doesn't have any equivalent to the Hong Kong Tourist Association or the Macau Government Tourist Office. What China does have are mammoth government-owned travel agencies with branch offices all over the country and abroad. In recent years there has been a proliferation of government-owned travel agencies, but the biggies have always been China International Travel Service (CITS) and China Travel Service (CTS).

There is an enormous CITS office (☎ 8666-6271; fax 8667-8048) at 179 Huanshi Lu next to the Guangzhou railway station, but they have little information. It's one big ticket office and the only thing the overworked clerks are likely to say to you is 'next please'. You can buy tickets here for trains, planes, hovercraft and ships.

CTS (☎ 8333-6888; fax 8333-2247) is at 10 Qiaoguang Lu, Haizhu Square (next to the Hotel Landmark Canton).

Overseas Representatives

CITS and CTS in Hong Kong and abroad are under separate management and are therefore more efficient than the China-based ones. You really can get some useful information from them.

CITS Outside China and Hong Kong, CITS is usually known as China National Tourist Office (CNTO). CITS in Hong Kong and CNTO offices overseas are located as follows:

Australia
    CNTO, 19th floor, 44 Market St, Sydney NSW 2000 (☎ (02) 9290-4057; fax (02) 9290-1958)
France
    CNTO, 116 Avenue des Champs-Elysées, 75008, Paris (☎ (01) 4296-9548; fax (01) 4261-5468)
Germany
    CNTO, Ilkenhans Strasse 6, 6000, Frankfurt M 50 (☎ (069) 528465; fax (069) 528490)
Hong Kong
    Main Office, New Mandarin Plaza, Tower A, 12th floor, 14 Science Museum Rd, Tsim Sha Tsui East (☎ 2725-5888); Central Branch, 18th floor, Wing On House, 71 Des Voeux Road, Central (☎ 2810-4282; fax 2868-1657)
Israel
    CNTO, 19 Frishman St, PO Box 3281, Tel-Aviv 61030 (☎ 522-6272; fax 522-6281)
Japan
    CNTA, 6th floor, Hamamatsu Cho Building, 1-27-13 Hamamatsu-Cho, Minato-Ku, Tokyo (☎ (03) 3433-1461; fax 3433-8653)

Singapore
    CNTO, 1 Shenton Way, No 17-05 Robina House, Singapore 0106 (☎ 221-8681; fax 221-9267)
Spain
    CNTO, Gran Via 88, Grupo 2, Planta 16, 28013 Madrid (☎ (1) 548-0011; fax 548-0597)
UK
    CNTO, 4 Glenworth St, London NW1 (☎ (0171) 935-9427; fax 487-5842)
USA
    CNTO, Los Angeles Branch, 333 West Broadway, Suite 201, Glendale CA 91204 (☎ (818) 545-7504; fax 545-7506)
    New York Branch, 350 Fifth Avenue, Suite 6413, New York, NY 10118 (☎ (212) 760-9700; fax (212) 760-8809)

CTS Overseas representatives include the following:

Australia
    ground floor, 757-759 George St, Sydney, NSW 2000 (☎ (02) 9211-2633; fax (02) 9281-3595)
France
    32 Rue Vignon, 75009, Paris (☎ (01) 4451-5566; fax (01) 4451-5560)
Germany
    Düsseldorfer Strasse 14, 6000, Frankfurt M1 (☎ (69) 250515; fax (69) 232324)
Hong Kong
    Head Office, 4th floor, CTS House, 78-83 Connaught Rd, Central (☎ 2853-3533; fax 2541-9777); Central Branch, China Travel Building, 2nd floor, 77 Queen's Rd, Central (☎ 2525-2284; fax 2868-4970) Kowloon Branch, 1st floor, Alpha House, 27-33 Nathan Rd, Tsim Sha Tsui (☎ 2315-7188; fax 2721-7757)
Indonesia
    PT Cempaka Travelindo, Jalan Hayam Wuruk 97, Jakarta-Barat (☎ (21) 629-4452; fax 629-4836)
Japan
    103 Buyoo Building, 3-8-16, Nihombashi, Chuo-Ku, Tokyo (☎ (03) 3273-5512; fax 3273-2667)
Macau
    Xinhua Building, Rua de Nagasaki (☎ 705506; fax 706611)
Malaysia
    ground floor, 112-114 Jalan Pudu, 55100, Kuala Lumpur (☎ (03) 201-8888; fax 201-3268)
Philippines
    801-803 Gandara St (corner Espeleta St), Santa Cruz, Manila (☎ (02) 733-1396; fax (02) 733-1431)
Singapore
    1 Park Rd, No 03-49 to 52, People's Park Complex, Singapore, 0105 (☎ 532-9988; fax 535-4912)

GUANGZHOU

Thailand
559 Yaowaraj Rd, Sampuntawang, Bangkok
10100 (☎ (02) 226-0041; fax (02) 226-4712)
UK
CTS House, 7 Upper St Martins Lane, London
WC2H 9DL
(☎ (0171) 836-9911; fax (0171) 836-3121)

VISAS & DOCUMENTS
Visas
The visa requirements for visiting China are totally different from Hong Kong and Macau (even if they are officially part of China): virtually all foreigners need a visa to visit China.

You'll normally be issued a one-month single-entry visa for HK$90. The visa is only good for one month from the date of entry you specify on your application. It is possible to get three-month visas, but only if you apply through a travel agent.

You can also obtain a dual-entry visa for HK$180, a three-month multiple-entry visa for HK$500 or a six-month multiple-entry visa for HK$700. The multiple-entry visa is in fact a business visa – it permits you to stay for 30 days at a time but cannot be extended inside China.

It normally takes two days to process a visa application, but if you're in a hurry, you can obtain an express visa in one day for an extra charge.

Heaps of travel agencies and even some guesthouses can get visas for you. This saves you the hassle of queuing, but you'll pay an extra service charge.

If you don't mind queuing, the cheapest visas can be obtained from the Visa Office of the Ministry of Foreign Affairs of the PRC, 5th floor, low block, China Resources Building, 26 Harbour Rd, Wan Chai, Hong Kong Island (☎ 2893-9812). Open Monday to Friday, 9 am to 12.30 pm and 2 to 5 pm; Saturdays 9 am to 12.30 pm.

Visas can be obtained at the China border crossing at Lo Wu. However, this costs a whopping HK$360 for a single-entry visa, and you might not even get the usual 30-day stay.

Visa applications require one photo. You're advised to have one entire blank page in your passport. You'll have to part with your passport while your visa application is processed, so be sure you have enough money because you need the passport for cashing travellers' cheques.

Visa Extensions Visa extensions are handled by the Foreign Affairs Section of the local Public Security Bureaus (the police force). Extensions cost US$3 for most nationalities, but some pay US$6 and others get it free. The general rule is that you can get one extension of one month's duration. At an agreeable Public Security Bureau you may be able to wangle more, especially with cogent reasons like illness (except AIDS), transport delays or a pack of Marlboros, but second extensions are usually only granted for one week with the understanding that you are on your way out of China.

Re-Entry Visas Most foreign residents of China have multiple-entry visas and don't need a re-entry visa. However, there might be other requirements (tax clearance, vaccinations, etc) – if in doubt, check with Public Security before departing.

Photocopies
Married couples should have a copy of their marriage certificate with them. This is especially true if the wife is ethnic Chinese or looks like she could be – the authorities are hyper-sensitive about foreign males 'insulting Chinese women'.

Driving Licence
Visitors to China are not allowed to drive, so there is no need to bring an international driver's licence. However, foreign residents can obtain a Chinese driving permit. To obtain this, you need your *original* driver's licence from your home country. This can be exchanged for a Chinese driver's licence. When you leave China, you get your original driver's licence back.

Other Documents
Given the Chinese preoccupation with official bits of paper, it's worth carrying around a few

business cards, student cards and anything else that's printed and laminated in plastic.

Chinese bicycle-renters often want a deposit or other security for their bikes – sometimes they ask you to leave your passport, but you should insist on leaving some other piece of ID or a deposit instead. It's most useful if you have an old expired passport for this purpose. Some hotels also require you to hand over your passport as security, even if you've paid in advance – again, an old passport is handy.

Foreigners who live, work or study in China will be issued with a number of documents. The most important of these documents is the so-called 'green card' or residence permit. Foreigners living in China say that if you lose your green card, you might want to leave the country rather than face the music. Resembling a small passport, the card is issued for one year and must be renewed annually.

EMBASSIES
Chinese Embassies Abroad
Australia
15 Coronation Drive, Yarralumla, ACT, 2600 (☎ (06) 273-4780, 273-4781)
Austria
Metterrichgasse 4, 1030 Vienna (☎ (06) 713 67 06)
Belgium
21 Blvd Général Jacques 19, 1051 Bruxelles (☎ (02) 640 40 06)
Canada
515 St Patrick St, Ottawa, Ontario, KIN 5H3 (☎ (613) 234-2706, 234 2682)
Denmark
12 Oregaards alle, DK 2900 Hellerup, Copenhagen 2900 (☎ 31 61 10 13)
France
21 Rue de L'amiral D'Estaing, 75016 Paris (☎ (01) 47 20 86, 47 20 63 95)
Germany
Freidrich-Ebert Strasse 59, 53177 Bonn (☎ (0228) 35 36 54, 35 36 22)
Italy
00135 Roma Via Della Camilluccia 613 (☎ (06) 3630-8534, 3630-3856)
Japan
3-4-33 Moto-Azabu, Minato-ku, Tokyo 106 (☎ (03) 3403-3380, 3403-3065)
Netherlands
Adriaan Goekooplaan 7, 2517 JX The Hague (☎ (070) 355 15 15, 355 92 09)

New Zealand
104 Korokoro Rd, Petone, Wellington (☎ (04) 587-0407)
Spain
Arturo Soria 111, 28043 Madrid (☎ (341) 413-5892, 413-2776)
Sweden
Ringwvagen 56, 18134 Lidings (☎ (08) 767 87 40, 767 40 83)
Switzerland
7 JV Widmannstrasse, 3074 Muri Bern (☎ (031) 951 14 01, 951 14 02)
UK
Cleveland Court, 1-3 Lenister Gardens, London W2 6DP (☎ (0171) 723-8923, 262-0253)
USA
2300 Connecticut Ave NW, Washington, DC 20008 (☎ (202) 328-2500, 328-2517)

Consulates in Guangzhou
Depending on what passport you hold, the Polish embassy can be useful if you want to do the Trans-Siberian. These days most Western nationalities do not require a visa for Poland.

The US consulate might better be called the 'Emigration Information Centre'. If you go there with some other intention besides emigrating to the USA, the staff will be so happy to see you they might throw a party.

Australia
GITIC Plaza, main building, room 1503-4, 15th floor, 339 Huangshi Donglu (☎ 8331-2738; fax 8331-2198)
Canada
room 1563, China Hotel Office Tower, Liuhua Lu (☎ 8666-0569; fax 8666-2401)
Germany
Shamian Dajie, Shamian Island
Japan
Garden Hotel Tower, 368 Huanshi Donglu (☎ 8333-8999 ext 7365; fax 8333-8972)
Malaysia
3rd floor, Ramada Pearl Hotel, 9 Mingyue 1-Lu, Dongshan district (☎ 8739-5660; fax 8739-5669)
Poland
63 Shamian Dajie, Shamian Island (☎ 8186-1854; fax 8186-2872)
Thailand
room 316, White Swan Hotel, 1 Shamian Nanjie, Shamian Island (☎ 8188-6968 ext 3312; fax 8187-9451)

GUANGZHOU

USA
   1 Shamian Nanjie, Shamian Island
    (☎ 8188-8911; fax 8186-4001)
Vietnam
   13 Taojin Beilu
    (☎ 8358-0555 ext 601 & 604; fax 8358-1000)

CUSTOMS

Chinese border crossings have gone from being severely traumatic to exceedingly easy. While there seems to be lots of uniformed police around, the third degree at customs seems to be reserved for pornography-smuggling Hong Kongers rather than the stray foreigner.

You'll note that there are clearly marked 'green channels' and 'red channels', the latter reserved for those with such everyday travel items as refrigerators, motorcycles and TV sets.

You're allowed to import 600 cigarettes or the equivalent in tobacco products, two litres of alcohol and one *pint* of perfume. You're allowed to import 900m of movie film, and a maximum of 72 rolls of still film. Importation of fresh fruit is prohibited.

It's illegal to import any printed material, film, tapes, etc 'detrimental to China's politics, economy, culture and ethics'. But don't be too concerned about what you take to read. As you leave China, any tapes, manuscripts, books, etc 'which contain state secrets or are otherwise prohibited for export' can be seized. Cultural relics, handicrafts, gold and silver ornaments, and jewellery purchased in China have to be shown to customs on leaving. You'll also have to show your receipts; otherwise the stuff may be confiscated. Don't get paranoid – they seldom search foreigners.

BAGGAGE STORAGE

Most hotels in Guangzhou and elsewhere in China have luggage storage rooms where you can safely leave your bags for a small fee. This service is always available to guests at the hotel, even after you've checked out (save your check-in receipt). This service is sometimes offered to non-guests, but don't always count on it. The word for 'luggage storage room' is *jìcúnchù*.

There are also luggage storage rooms at all railway stations. At Guangzhou station there's a den of thieves, so you'd be wise to use the facilities at Guangzhou East station.

MONEY
Costs

China is experiencing rapid inflation, and for that reason most of the prices quoted hereafter are in US$. China devalues its currency periodically, and prices in US$ terms have remained relatively stable.

Although China is cheaper than Hong Kong or Macau, it's not as cheap as you would expect given the low wage levels. The main reason is the deliberate government policy of squeezing as much money as possible out of foreign tourists. Foreigners must pay triple for train fares and about 30% more than locals for airfares. Accommodation is usually the biggest expense. If you get into a dormitory, then China is cheap – otherwise, your daily living expense could be higher than in Hong Kong.

Hotel restaurants in Guangzhou have grown accustomed to charging high prices for food, but you can get around this by eating at hole-in-the-wall restaurants. You should live comfortably on US$30 per day in Guangzhou.

Cash

The easiest foreign currencies to exchange are US dollars and Hong Kong dollars. Forget about Macau patacas.

Travellers' Cheques

You actually get a much better exchange rate on travellers' cheques than you do for cash. US-dollar cheques are easiest to exchange.

ATMs

At the present time, ATMs in Guangzhou only work with the Chinese banking system and foreign cards will just be rejected. Of course, this could change overnight, but at the moment ATMs in China are only useful if you're a resident and have a Chinese-issued ATM card.

Credit Cards

Credit cards are not nearly so readily accepted in Guangzhou as in Hong Kong or Macau. Major hotels will accept them, but elsewhere don't expect to get much use out of your card.

American Express (☎ 8331-1888 ext 70111; fax 8331-3535) is in room C1, ground floor, central lobby, Guangdong International Hotel, 339 Huanshi Donglu.

International Transfers

China's decrepit banking system is notoriously slow when it comes to doing telegraphic transfers. In some cases you may wait weeks for your money. It you really need money transferred to you, it would be much better to do it through Hong Kong or Macau.

If you must do an international transfer in China, talk to some of the representative offices of foreign banks. They are not authorised to do international transfers, but can advise you on the best way. Some foreign bank representatives include: HongkongBank (☎ 8667-7061 ext 1363), Sumitomo Bank (☎ 8778-4988), Standard Chartered Bank (☎ 8778-8813), Societe Generale (☎ 8778-2688), Citibank (☎ 8332-1711) and ANZ Bank (☎ 8331-1490).

Currency

The basic unit of Chinese currency is the *yuan* – designated in this book by a capital 'Y'. In spoken Chinese, the word *kuai* is often substituted for yuan – in spoken Chinese, it's pronounced *mao*. Ten *fen* make up one jiao, but these days fen are becoming rare because they are worth so little – most people will not accept them.

China has another name for its currency, the renminbi (RMB) which means 'people's money'. It's issued by the Bank of China. Paper notes are issued in denominations of one, two, five, 10, 50 and 100 yuan; one, two and five jiao; and one, two and five fen. Coins are in denominations of one yuan; five jiao; and one, two and five fen. The one-fen note is small and yellow, the two-fen note is blue, and the five-fen note is small and green – all are next to worthless.

Be careful – there are plenty of fake bills about, especially of larger denominations

(Y50 and Y100 notes). If you get the money from a bank, it will presumably be OK.

Currency Exchange

Australia	A$1	=	Y6.55
Canada	C$1	=	Y6.07
Hong Kong	HK$1	=	Y1.07
France	Ffr1	=	Y1.65
Germany	DM1	=	Y5.63
Japan	¥100	=	Y7.72
Korea (South)	W100	=	Y1.01
Netherlands	G1	=	Y4.86
New Zealand	NZ$1	=	Y5.76
Philippines	P1	=	Y0.32
Singapore	S$1	=	Y5.90
Switzerland	Sfr1	=	Y6.98
Taiwan	NT$1	=	Y0.30
Thailand	1B	=	Y0.33
UK	UK£1	=	Y12.94
USA	US$1	=	Y8.31

Changing Money

Foreign currency and travellers' cheques can be changed at the main centres of the Bank of China, the tourist hotels, some big department stores, at the airport, border crossings and international ferry wharfs. If you want to change money at the airport on departure from China, it's important to remember that you have to do it *before* entering the immigration queue. Of course, if your next stop is Hong Kong, you can easily unload your excess Chinese currency there.

Unlike in Hong Kong, the exchange rates are pretty much the same all over and no hidden commissions are charged. One annoyance is that a few five-star hotels only change money for their own guests – you can always make up a room number.

Always be sure to keep enough money on you to last for at least a few days. Public holidays can pose a big problem: even hotels don't want to do business because they can't call up the bank to get the latest official rates.

Whenever you change foreign currency into Chinese currency you'll be given a money-exchange voucher recording the transaction. If you've got any leftover RMB when you leave the country and want to reconvert it to hard currency you *must* have some of those vouchers – 50% of what you originally exchanged can be re-exchanged on departure. The government is saying that you must spend the rest while in China.

You can ignore the preceding if your next stop is Hong Kong, since Hong Kong money changers are willing to exchange RMB. However, if you're flying directly from Guangzhou to another country, you'd better get rid of all your RMB at the airport.

Black Market
In every edition of this book we warn people not to use the black market. Nevertheless, we get a constant stream of letters from people telling us how they got ripped off changing money on the street. Certainly, if you look like a foreigner and hang around Guangzhou for long, you will be approached by the 'change money' people. If you deal with them you will get robbed. It's that simple.

Tipping & Bargaining
Tipping is not normally a custom. Bribery is another matter. Don't be blatant about it, but if you need some special service, it's customary to offer someone a cigarette and just tell them 'Go ahead and keep the pack – I'm trying to quit'. In China, a 'tip' is given before you receive the service, not after.

Since foreigners are so frequently overcharged in China, bargaining becomes essential. You can bargain in shops, hotels, with taxi drivers, with most people – but not everywhere. In large stores where prices are clearly marked, there is usually no latitude for bargaining. In small shops and street stalls, bargaining is expected, but there is one important rule to follow – be polite. There is nothing wrong with asking for a discount, if you do so with a smile. In 'face-conscious' China, any nastiness or intimidation on your part is likely to make the vendor more recalcitrant and you'll be overcharged.

You should keep in mind that entrepreneurs are in business to make money. Your goal should be to pay the Chinese price, as opposed to the foreigners' price – if you can do that, you've done well.

Guangzhou was different bargaining-wise. Even official-looking shops on the tourist trail with marked prices were prepared to offer huge discounts. Most people in our tour party didn't ask. I looked at a tea set in the souvenir shop attached to the Sun Yatsen Memorial Middle School for which they were asking Y1200. The sales assistant was pressing me to buy it – I said no, too expensive, much cheaper in Hong Kong. She asked how much in Hong Kong – I had forgotten the exact figure, but told her I thought it was about Y400. She said OK!

Cilla Taylor

Consumer Taxes
Although big hotels and fancy restaurants may add a tax or 'service charge' of 10% or more, all other consumer taxes are included in the price tag.

POST & COMMUNICATIONS
Postal Rates
With China's rapid inflation, postal rates can escalate suddenly, so use the following only as a general guide. Rates per kg are of course cheaper for printed matter, small packets and parcels:

Letters (up to 20g) Local city Y0.10; elsewhere in China Y0.20; Hong Kong, Macau & Taiwan surface mail Y0.60; Hong Kong, Macau & Taiwan airmail Y0.80; international surface mail Y2.20; international airmail Y2.90.

Postcards Local city Y0.10; elsewhere in China Y0.15; Hong Kong, Macau & Taiwan surface mail Y0.40; Hong Kong, Macau & Taiwan airmail Y0.60; international surface mail Y1.60; international airmail Y2.30.

Aerogrammes Hong Kong, Macau and Taiwan Y0.60; other countries Y2.80.

EMS (Speedpost) Domestic EMS parcels up to 200g cost Y12; each additional 200g costs Y3. For international EMS, rates vary according to country. For nearby Asian countries (Japan, Korea, etc) it's Y105 for up to 500g, Y30 for each additional 500g. EMS to eastern Europe is Y382 for the first 500g, Y120 for each additional 500g.

Registration Fees The registration fee for letters, printed matter and packets posted to

Hong Kong, Macau and Taiwan is Y2.20; elsewhere in the world it costs Y4.50.

Sending Mail

The international postal service seems efficient, and air-mailed letters and postcards will probably take around five to 10 days to reach their destinations. If possible, write the country of destination in Chinese, as this should speed up delivery. Domestic post is amazingly fast, perhaps one or two days from Guangzhou to Beijing. Within a city it may be delivered the same day it's sent.

As well as the local post offices there are branch post offices in most major tourist hotels and you can send letters, packets and parcels (the contents of packets and parcels are checked by post office staff). Even at cheap hotels you can usually post letters from the front desk – reliability varies but in general it's OK. In some places, you may only be able to post printed matter from these branch offices. Other parcels may require a Customs form to be attached at the town's main post office, where their contents will be checked.

Large envelopes are a bit hard to come by – try the department stores. If you expect to be sending quite a few packets, stock up when you come across such envelopes. A roll of strong tape is a useful item to bring along and serves many purposes. String, glue and sometimes cloth bags may be supplied at post offices, but don't count on it. Department stores will sometimes package and mail purchases for you, but only goods actually bought at the store.

For tourists staying on Shamian Island, the nearest major post office is at 43 Yanjiang West Lu near the riverfront. This is one of the post offices authorised for sending parcels overseas.

Postcards are hard to find in Guangzhou. If you don't want to bring some from Hong Kong or Macau, try the shopping arcades in the large hotels (the bookshop in the White Swan Hotel has them).

Courier Service Private couriers offering express document and parcel service include:

DHL
   37 Xiaobei, Xiatangxi Lu
   (☎ 8335-5034; fax 8335-1647)
Federal Express
   room 1356-1357, Garden Tower, Garden Hotel,
   368 Huanshi Donglu
   (☎ 8386-2026; fax 8386-2012)
United Parcel Service
   room 2103, South Tower, Guangzhou World Trade
   Centre, 371-375 Huanshi Donglu (☎ 8775-5778)

Receiving Mail

Adjacent to Guangzhou railway station is the GPO, locally known as the Liuhua Post Office (☎ 8666-2735) (liúhuā yóu jú). You can collect poste restante letters here, although there is no poste restante window. Names are written on a notice board and you are supposed to see if your name is there and then find someone (but who?) to get the letter for you.

Some major tourist hotels will hold mail for guests, but this doesn't always work. Try writing instructions on the envelope.

It's worth noting that some foreigners living in China have had their mail opened or parcels pilfered before receipt – and some have their outgoing mail opened and read. This seems to affect tourists less, although letters with enclosures will almost certainly be opened. Your mail is less likely to be opened if it's sent to cities that handle high volumes of mail, like Guangzhou.

Officially, the People's Republic forbids several items from being mailed to it – the regulations specifically prohibit 'reactionary books, magazines and propaganda materials, obscene or immoral articles'. You also cannot mail Chinese currency abroad, or receive it by post. Like elsewhere, mail-order hashish and other recreational chemicals will not amuse the authorities.

Telephone

China's creaky phone system is being overhauled, at least in major cities. Whereas just a few years ago calling from Guangzhou to Shanghai could be an all-day project, now you can just pick up a phone and dial direct. International calls have also become much easier.

You can place both domestic and international long-distance phone calls from

GUANGZHOU

telecommunications offices. However, dealing with these offices can be a nuisance – you have to fill out forms in Chinese, pay for the call in advance, wait for perhaps 30 minutes and finally someone gestures to you indicating that you've been connected so pick up the phone and start talking. The Guangzhou telephone office is across from the Guangzhou railway station on the east side of Renmin North Lu. However, there is little need to go there as you can most likely make your call from your hotel.

Most hotel rooms are equipped with phones from which local calls are free. Local calls can be made from public pay phones (there are some around but not many). China's budding entrepreneurs try to fill the gap – people with private phones run a long cord out the window and stand on street corners, allowing you to use their phone to place local calls for around Y1 each – long-distance domestic and international calls are not always possible on these phones, but ask. In the lobbies of many hotels, the reception desks have a similar system – free calls for guests, Y1 for non-guests, and long-distance calls are charged by the minute.

Domestic long-distance rates in China vary according to distance, but are ridiculously cheap. International calls are relatively expensive. Calls to Hong Kong and Macau are considered international calls.

Rates for station-to-station calls to most countries in the world are Y16 per minute, but Hong Kong is half price at Y8 per minute. Some hotels might bill you at a higher rate than this, so ask first. There is no discount for calling late at night and there is a minimum charge of three minutes. Collect (reverse-charge) calls are sometimes cheaper than calls paid for in China. Time the call yourself – the operator will not break in to tell you that your minimum period of three minutes is approaching. After you hang up, the operator will ring back to tell you how much it cost. There is no call cancellation fee.

If you are expecting a call – either international or domestic – try to advise the caller beforehand of your hotel room number. The operators frequently have difficulty understanding Western names, and the hotel receptionist may not be able to locate you.

Direct Dialling Domestic direct dialling (DDD) and international direct dialling (IDD) calls are cheapest if you can find a phone which accepts magnetic cards. These phones are usually available in the lobbies of major hotels, at least in big cities, and the hotel's front desk should also sell the phone cards. These cards come in two denominations, Y20 and Y100 – for an international call, you'll need the latter.

If card phones aren't available, you can usually dial direct from the phones in the business centres found in most luxury hotels. You do not have to be a guest at these hotels to use these facilities.

If your hotel lacks card phones or a business centre, you should be able to dial direct from your hotel room. You'll have to ask the staff at your hotel what the dial-out code for a direct line is (it's '7' on most switchboards, but sometimes it's a combination like '78'). Once you have the outside line, dial '00' (the international access code – always the same throughout China) followed by the country code, area code and the number you want to reach. If the area code begins with zero (like '03' for Melbourne, Australia) omit the first zero.

There are a few things to be careful of. The equipment used on most hotel switchboards is not very sophisticated – it's often a simple timer and it begins charging you 30 seconds after you dial '7' (or '78' or whatever) – the timer does not know if your call succeeds or not so you get charged if you stay on the line over 30 seconds, even if you just let the phone ring repeatedly or get a busy signal.

After you make the call, someone usually comes to your room to collect the cash. If the hotel does not have IDD, you can usually book calls from your room through the switchboard and the operator can call you back.

With domestic direct dialling, it's useful to know the area codes of China's cities. These all begin with zero, but if you're dialling China from abroad, omit the first zero from each code. China's country code is 86. Some important area codes in Guangdong province include: Foshan 0757; Guangzhou 020; Shenzhen 0755; Zhaoqing 0758; Zhongshan 07654; Zhuhai 0756.

Some useful telephone numbers are the same in every Chinese city (not including Hong Kong and Macau). Some examples include:

local & international directory assistance	☎ 114
domestic long-distance directory assistance	☎ 116
operator assistance – domestic long-distance	☎ 113
operator assistance – international	☎ 103
AT&T Service (English)	☎ 10811
ambulance	☎ 120
fire hot line	☎ 119
phone repair	☎ 112
police hot line	☎ 110
time enquiries	☎ 117
weather forecast	☎ 121

Telecommunication for Expats Short-term visitors needn't bother reading this, but those planning to do business, work or study in China have several telecommunication options not available to tourists.

Getting a private telephone installed in your hotel room or apartment is possible in large cities like Guangzhou, but there is a waiting period of up to six months. To install a telephone, no matter if it is IDD or not, costs Y5115. The price is the same for foreigners or local people. If a company has a non-IDD line, a deposit of Y5000 must be made to upgrade to IDD. For a personal line this deposit is not needed. For a mobile telephone (analog system) the cost is Y13,000. Digital phones are available and cost more – Y15,000. Mobile phones are available immediately – no queue for them.

Those living on a budget, such as foreign students, may well find pagers a more realistic option. Pagers are more common than telephones in China, making it the world's second largest pager market after the USA. Those with a residence permit can obtain a pager in just a couple of weeks.

Pagers for use in Guangzhou only cost Y15 a month. For a pager useable throughout

China, the price rises to Y80 per month. The paging market was opened to free competition in 1993 – there are now more than 1700 paging operators in China so it's difficult to say which company is best.

The market for cellular phones and pagers is dominated by the US's Motorola and Sweden's Ericsson. The Chinese don't yet manufacture cellular phones, but they do make pagers which even the locals will tell you are junk.

Fax, Telegraph, Email & Telex
Major hotels usually operate a business centre complete with telephone, fax and telex service, not to mention photocopying and perhaps the use of typewriters and word processors. As a rule, you do not have to be a guest at the hotel to use these services, but you certainly must pay. Prices seem to be pretty uniform regardless of how fancy the hotel is, but it's still not a bad idea to ask the rates first.

International fax and telexes (other than those to Hong Kong or Macau) cost Y20 per minute, with a three-minute minimum charge. International telegram rates are usually around Y3.20 per word, and more for the express service. Rates to Hong Kong and Macau are less.

Guangzhou is not well-organised for Email. If you don't have a resident's visa, then you'll have to do your Email by calling long-distance to Hong Kong at about Y8 per minute. If you do have residency, then you have two options for getting on the Internet. The best one is GITICNet, offered by the Guangdong International Trade & Investment Corporation (GITIC). Enquire at the GITIC Plaza Building on Huanshi Donglu. The sign-up fee is Y500, and the Y100-per month charge gets you five hours' use (Y10-per hour thereafter).

The other Internet option is available from the post office – sign up at the GPO near the Guangzhou railway station. The sign-up fee is Y600.

BOOKS
Rare Finds
There are numerous books about China but

rather few dealing specifically with Guangzhou or Guangdong Province. One of the few is *Kwangtung or Five Years in South China* by the English Wesleyan minister Reverend John Arthur Turner, who worked as a missionary in China from 1886 to 1891. His book was originally published in 1894.

Another early account of Western contact with China comes from the Jesuit priest and missionary Matteo Ricci, who was permitted to take up residence at Zhaoqing near Guangzhou in the late 16th century, and in Beijing in 1601. An English translation of his diaries has been published under the title *China in the 16th Century – the Journals of Matteo Ricci 1583-1610*. This book is not easy to find.

Other rare books about Guangzhou include *Canton in Revolution – The Collected papers of Earl Swisher, 1925-1928*. Also, Ezra Vogel's *Canton Under Communism* covers the history of the city from 1949 to 1968.

The Classics
The best known English fiction about China is *The Good Earth* by Pearl Buck.

If you want to read a weighty Chinese classic, you could try *Journey to the West*, available in English in a four-volume set in China and some Hong Kong bookshops. Condensed versions are available in paperback.

The Dream of the Red Chamber (also known as *The Story of the Stone*) by Cao Xueqin, is a Chinese classic written in the late 18th century. It's not an easy read. Again, look for the condensed version.

The third great Chinese classic is *Outlaws of the Marsh*. This is also available in abridged form.

History & Politics
The Search for Modern China by Jonathan Spence is the definitive work, often used as a textbook in college courses. If you want to understand the People's Republic, this is the book to read.

A dimmer view of China under Deng Xiaoping is taken by Italian journalist Tiziano Terzani in *Behind the Forbidden Door*. Terzani, once an avid socialist, became

disillusioned after living in China from 1980 to 1984, when he was finally booted out for his critical reporting.

An intriguing and popular book is *The New Emperors* by Harrison Salisbury. The 'emperors' he refers to are Mao Zedong and Deng Xiaoping.

Seeds of Fire: Chinese Voices of Conscience is an anthology of blistering eloquence from authors such as Wei Jingsheng, Liu Qing, Wang Xizhe and Xu Wenli (imprisoned for their roles in the Democracy Movement) and the poet Sun Jingxuan. Wei Jingsheng's description of Q1, China's top prison for political detainees, is utterly horrific.

The issue of human rights is covered in Amnesty International's *China: Violations of Human Rights* – a grim aspect of the country that should not be ignored.

Cultural Revolution
The best seller seems to be *Life and Death in Shanghai* by Nien Cheng. The author was imprisoned for six years, and this is her gripping story of survival.

Other stories from this period include *Born Red* by Gao Yuan and *Son of the Revolution* by Liang Heng and Judith Shapiro.

The Chinese People Stand Up by Elizabeth Wright examines China's turbulent history from 1949 up to the brutal suppression of pro-democracy demonstrators in 1989.

The Soong Dynasty by Sterling Seagrave is one of the most popular books on the corrupt Kuomintang period. Unfortunately, the author severely damaged his credibility when he later published *The Marcos Dynasty* which contains more rumour than fact.

The Private Life of Chairman Mao is banned in China. The author, Dr Li Zhisui, was the personal physician to Mao Zedong. Despite the Communist Party's attempts to depict Mao as a paragon of virtue, Dr Li asserts that the old chairman in his later years spent nearly all his free time in bed with teenage girls.

General
A moving and popular book is *Wild Swans* by Jung Chang. The author traces the lives of three Chinese women – the author's grandmother

(an escaped concubine with bound feet), her mother and herself.

The Joy Luck Club and *The Kitchen God's Wife* by Amy Tan have also become bestsellers.

ONLINE SERVICES

As big as China is, it's a disappointment for Net surfers. At the time of writing, there are only 60,000 Internet users in China. That figure sounds particularly dismal when you realise that there are over 300,000 Net nerds in Hong Kong alone! At present, there are only two authorised Internet providers in China (compared to 33 in Hong Kong). Internet users have to register with the government, and content is carefully monitored. Obviously, the authorities fears they can't control all that dangerous information being tossed around on the Internet.

If you're seeking online information about China, you'll do better to check out some of the Usenet groups in Western countries where there are large overseas Chinese communities. Also keep your eye out for the *China News Digest*, a summary of Chinese news and views which appears on many BBSs.

NEWSPAPERS & MAGAZINES
Chinese-Language Publications

There are nearly 2000 national and provincial newspapers in China. The main one is *Renmin Ribao* (the People's Daily), with nationwide circulation. It was founded in 1946 as the official publication of the Central Committee of the Communist Party. Most of these tend to be exceedingly boring, though they do provide a brief rundown of world events.

At the other end of the scale there is China's version of the gutter press – several hundred 'unhealthy papers' and magazines hawked on street corners and bus stations in major cities with nude or violent photos and stories about sex, crime, witchcraft, miracle cures and UFOs. These have been severely criticised by the government for their obscene and racy content – they are also extremely popular. There are also about 40 newspapers for the minority nationalities.

Foreign-Language Publications

China publishes various newspapers, books and magazines in a number of European and Asian languages. The only English-language newspaper is the *China Daily*, first published in June 1981. It now has two overseas editions (Hong Kong and USA). Overseas subscriptions can be obtained from the following sources:

Hong Kong
    Wen Wei Po, 197 Wan Chai Rd
    (☎ 2572-2211; fax 2572-0441)
USA
    China Daily Distribution Corporation, Suite 401, 15 Mercer St, New York, NY 10013
    (☎ (212) 219-0130; fax (212) 210-0108)

Although you might stumble across some of the English-language magazines in luxury hotels and Friendship Stores, they are most readily available by subscription. These can be posted to you overseas. The place to subscribe is not in China itself, but in Hong Kong. If interested, contact the Peace Book Company (☎ 2804-6687), Wing On House, 26 Des Voeux Rd, Central, Hong Kong. You can write or drop by the office for their catalogue. Here's a rundown of what's available in English and other non-Chinese languages:

Beijing Review
    a weekly magazine on political and current affairs. Valuable for learning about China's latest half-baked political policies. The magazine is published in English, French, Spanish, German and Japanese.
China Medical Abstracts
    a special-interest quarterly magazine in English.
China Philately
    a magazine in English for stamp collectors.
China Pictorial
    a monthly large-format glossy magazine with photos, and cultural and historical stuff. Available in English, French, Spanish, German and Japanese.
China Screen
    a quarterly magazine in English or Chinese with a focus on the Chinese film industry.
China Sports
    an English-language monthly which helps demonstrate the superiority of Chinese athletes over foreigners.
China Today
    a monthly magazine. The magazine was founded in 1952 by Song Qingling (the wife of Sun Yatsen) and used to be called *China Recon-*

structs. The name was changed in 1989 because as one official said '37 years is a hell of a long time to be reconstructing your country'.

China's Foreign Trade
a monthly publication in English, French, Spanish or Chinese, with a self-explanatory title.

China's Patents & Trademarks
a quarterly magazine in Chinese and English. The title is self-explanatory.

China's Tibet
a quarterly magazine in Chinese or English. It's chief purpose is to convince overseas readers that China's historical claim to Tibet is more than just hot air. Some of the articles about Tibetan culture and religion might prove interesting.

Chinese Literature
a quarterly magazine in English or French. Topics include poetry, fiction, profiles of Chinese writers and so on.

El Popola Cinio
a monthly magazine in Esperanto – good if you want to familiarise yourself with this language.

Kexue Tongbao
a monthly publication in English with a focus on the sciences.

Nexus
a quarterly magazine in English. It is claimed that this is China's first privately funded magazine in English. Articles cover various aspects of Chinese culture and society.

Shanghai Pictorial
a magazine available in Chinese or English. Photos of fashionable women dressed in the latest, as well as container ships, cellular telephones and other symbols of Shanghai's developing economy.

Social Sciences in China
a quarterly publication in English. The magazine covers topics like archaeology, economics, philosophy, literature and a whole range of academic pursuits by Chinese scholars.

Women of China
a monthly magazine in English designed to show foreigners that Chinese women are not treated as badly as they really are.

The government also publishes impressive glossy magazines in minority languages such as Tibetan. These appear to be strictly for foreign consumption – they are not available in China.

Imported Publications In large cities like Guangzhou, it's fairly easy to find copies of popular imported English-language magazines like *Time*, *Newsweek*, *Far Eastern Economic Review* and *The Economist*. A censored edition of Hong Kong's *South China Morning Post* is also available. You can find these publications at major hotels.

A different set of rules applies to Chinese-language publications from Hong Kong and Taiwan – essentially, these cannot be brought into China without special permission.

News Agencies

China has two news agencies, the New China (Xinhua) News Agency and the China News Service. The New China News Agency is a national organisation with its headquarters in Beijing and branches in each province, as well as in the army, Hong Kong and many foreign countries. It provides news for the national, provincial and local papers and radio stations; transmits radio broadcasts abroad in foreign languages; and is responsible for making contact with and exchanging news with foreign news agencies. In Hong Kong, this agency acts as the unofficial embassy.

The main function of the China News Service is to supply news to overseas Chinese newspapers and journals, including those in Hong Kong and Macau. It also distributes Chinese documentary films abroad.

RADIO & TV

Chinese TV is broadcast in either Cantonese or Mandarin. The only English-language programmes are occasional subtitled foreign movies or educational shows that attempt to teach English.

However, the situation is not hopeless. After years of attempts to tear down their TV antennas and jam foreign broadcasting, many Cantonese now have access to satellite dishes and receive Hong Kong's transmission of the latest bourgeois and subversive episodes of Western programmes which the authorities believe have ruinous influences on their moral and ideological uprightness.

Nevertheless, what you get to see on satellite is also sanitised. The Chinese government forced Hong Kong's STAR TV to delete the BBC World News. In China, you are only supposed to watch good, wholesome movies like *Fatal Attraction* and *Natural Born Killers*.

In the border areas of Shenzhen and Zhuhai

GLENN BEANLAND

ROBERT STOREY   TONY WHEELER

Top: A cruise along the Pearl River offers views of Guangzhou.
Bottom Left: Sentry duty, Nanhu Amusement Park, Guangzhou.
Bottom Right: The Year of the Rat race. Despite Guangzhou's growing affluence,
bicycles still compete with motor vehicles for road space.

ROBERT STOREY

GLENN BEANLAND

GLENN BEANLAND

Top: Lotus Mountain, Guangzhou, was once a quarry.
Bottom Left: The Zhenhai Tower in Yuexia Park now houses the City Museum.
Bottom Right: The Flower Pagoda, in the Temple of the Six Banyan Trees, is the oldest
and tallest in Guangzhou.

it is easy to pick up uncensored English-language broadcasts from Hong Kong.

VIDEO SYSTEMS
Like Hong Kong, China uses the PAL video system.

PHOTOGRAPHY & VIDEO
In China you'll get a fantastic run for your money; for starters there are 1.2 billion portraits to work your way through. Religious reasons for avoiding photographs are absent among the Han Chinese – some guy isn't going to stick a spear through you for taking a picture of his wife and stealing part of her soul – though you probably won't be allowed to take photos of statues in many Buddhist temples.

Some Chinese shy away from having their photo taken, and even duck for cover. Others are proud to pose and will ham it up for the camera – and they're especially proud if you're taking a shot of their kid. Nobody expects any payment for photos – so don't give any or you'll set a precedent. What the Chinese would go for, though, is a copy of a colour photo, which you could mail to them. People tend also to think that the negative belongs to the subject as well, and they'll ask for both the negative and the print – but through the post there's no argument.

There are three basic approaches to photographing people. One is the polite 'ask for permission and pose it' shot, which is sometimes rejected. Another is the 'no-holds barred and upset everyone' approach. The third is surreptitious, standing half a km away with a metre-long telephoto lens. Many Chinese will disagree with you on what constitutes good subject matter; they don't really see why anyone would want to take a street scene, a picture of a beggar or a shot of butchered dogs on display in the market.

Another objection often brought up is that the subject is not 'dignified' – be it a labourer straining down the street with a massive load on his hand-cart, or a barrel of excrement on wheels. The official line is that peasants and workers are the glorious heroes of China, but you'll have a tough time convincing your photo subject of this.

A lot of Chinese still cannot afford a camera and resort to photographers at tourist places. The photographers supply dress-up clothing for that extra touch. The subjects change from street clothing into spiffy gear and sometimes even bizarre costumes and make-up for the shot. Others use cardboard props such as opera stars or boats.

The standard shot is one or more Chinese standing in front of something significant. Temples, waterfalls, heroic statues or important vintages of calligraphy are considered suitable backgrounds. At amusement parks, Mickey Mouse and Donald Duck get into nearly every photo – Ronald McDonald and the Colonel of Kentucky Fried fame are favourite photo companions at these prestigious restaurants. If you hang around these places you can sometimes click off a few portrait photos for yourself, but don't be surprised if your photo subjects suddenly drag you into the picture as an exotic prop!

Imported film is relatively expensive, but Japanese companies like Fuji and Konica now have factories in China – this has brought the price of colour print film down to what you'd pay in the West, sometimes less. While colour print film is available almost everywhere, it's almost always 100 ASA (21 DIN). Video cassettes are becoming increasingly easy to find.

Black & white film can be found in Guangzhou's larger department stores, but in general it's hard to buy in China – colour photos are now all the rage.

In general, colour slide film is also hard to find – check out major hotels, department stores and Friendship Stores if you get caught short. When you do find slide film, it's usually expensive and sometimes out-of-date, though last year's slide film is still better than none. Ektachrome and Fujichrome can be found in Guangzhou – Kodachrome and Agfachrome are close to non-existent in China or Hong Kong.

Polaroid film is rumoured to exist, but if you need the stuff you'd better bring your own supply from Hong Kong.

Finding special lithium batteries used by many cameras is pretty easy in large cities like Guangzhou. Some cameras have a manual mode which allows you to continue shooting with a dead battery, though the light meter won't work. Fully automatic cameras just drop dead when the battery goes.

Video cameras were once subject to shaky regulations but there seems to be no problem now. The biggest problem is recharging your batteries off the strange mutations of plugs in China – bring all the adaptors you can, and remember that it's 220V.

You're allowed to bring in 8 mm movie cameras, but 16 mm or professional equipment may raise eyebrows with Customs. Motion picture film is hard enough to find in the West these days, and next to impossible in China where it is tightly controlled.

Photoprocessing Major cities like Guangzhou and Shenzhen are equipped with the latest Japanese photoprocessing machines. Quality colour prints can be turned out in one or two hours at reasonable cost.

It's a different situation with colour slides. Ektachrome and Fujichrome can be processed in Guangzhou but this can be expensive and quality is not assured. If you don't want your slides scratched, covered with fingerprints or over-developed, save the processing until you get home or to Hong Kong. Kodachrome film cannot be processed in China.

Undeveloped film can be sent out of China and, going by personal experience only, the dreaded X-ray machines do not appear to be a problem.

Prohibited Subjects Photography from planes and photographs of airports, military installations, harbour facilities and railroad terminals are prohibited; bridges may also be a touchy subject.

Taking photos is not permitted in most museums, at archaeological sites and in many temples, mainly to protect the postcard and colour slide industry. These rules are enforced if the enforcers happen to be around. If you plan to photograph something that is prohibited, at least take the precaution of starting with a new roll of film. That way,

if the film gets ripped out your camera, you haven't lost too much.

TIME
Time throughout China is set the same as Hong Kong, eight hours ahead of GMT/ UTC. China experimented with daylight savings time but has now dropped it.

ELECTRICITY
As in Hong Kong, China uses AC 220V, 50 Hz. The only difference is in the design of the electrical outlets. There are at least four permutations of electric outlet designs.

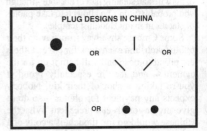

PLUG DESIGNS IN CHINA

Conversion plugs are easily purchased in Hong Kong but are damn near impossible to find in Guangzhou. Battery chargers are widely available, but these are generally the bulky style which are not suitable for travelling – buy a small one in Hong Kong.

Power failures occasionally happen, especially during summer when everyone turns on their air-conditioner. Given this situation, a torch (flashlight) is essential survival gear. Chinese torches are indeed torturous – half the time they don't work and the bulbs seldom last as long as the batteries. Bring a small but good-quality torch from Hong Kong or elsewhere.

WEIGHTS & MEASURES
The international metric system is in use. Local Chinese units of weight are still used in markets: the *leung* (37.5g) and the *catty* (600g).

LAUNDRY
Most hotels have a laundry service, but check the prices first – some places charge

so much you could buy new clothes cheaper. Many travellers wind up washing their clothes by hand. If you plan on doing this, dark clothes are better since the dirt doesn't show up so clearly.

Hospitals

If you get sick you can go to one of the hospitals or to the medical clinic for foreigners – Guangzhou People's Hospital No 1 (☎ 8333-3090) *(dìyī rénmín yīyuàn)*, 602 Renmin North Lu.

Guangzhou is *the* place to go if you want to be treated with acupuncture and herbs. Just next to Shamian Island and the Qingping Market is the Traditional Chinese Medicine Hospital (☎ 8188-6504; *zhōngyī yīyuàn*) at 16 Zhuji Lu. Another option is the Liwanqu Traditional Chinese Medicine Hospital (☎ 8181-8679), 32 Zhoumen Xijie, Zhongshan 8-Lu (in the east end of town).

Resident foreigners may be interested in the health services offered by SOS International (☎ 8759-5357) at The Greenery, 55-79 Huayang Jie, Tiyu Donglu.

TOILETS

Toilet paper is never provided in the toilets at bus and railway stations or other public buildings (mainly because people steal it), so you'd be wise to keep a stash of your own with you at all times. Only in big modern hotels can you hope to find toilet paper.

In hotels, the toilets are clearly labelled in English, but in most public buildings only Chinese is used. To avoid embarrassment, try to remember:

男　女

Men　　　Women

In Guangzhou you may encounter squat toilets – basically, a hole in the floor that *usually* flushes. A variation on the theme is a ditch with water running through it. Both the hole and the ditch take some getting used to. The Chinese, though, appear to have difficulty adapting to Western toilets. In big hotels or fast-food restaurants where Western-style toilets are available, you'll often find big black footprints and urine on the seats.

In many places, the plumbing system cannot adequately handle toilet paper. In that case, you should toss the paper into a waste basket provided for just that purpose.

WOMEN TRAVELLERS

Western women report relatively little sexual harassment in China. The biggest complaints come from women with Asian features – indeed, some have been raped. All women visitors should take the precaution of dressing conservatively.

What to Wear

Shorts are acceptable for women, though it's better to wear the longish variety rather than the fashionable 'hot pants' favoured by young Hong Kong women.

Beach wear should be conservative and women should wear one-piece swimsuits. Bikinis will attract spectators and public nudity will get you arrested.

You can wear thongs (flip flops) inside your hotel room or in a youth hostel, but if you set foot outside with them on you can expect stares and rude remarks. You may see some Chinese wearing thongs outdoors, but don't think that means it's OK – it's considered an extremely low-class thing to do, like begging. As in Hong Kong, sandals are OK if they have a strap across the back of the ankle.

GAY & LESBIAN TRAVELLERS

In 1992 the Chinese government caught up with the rest of the world and declared that homosexuality was not illegal. The authorities instructed police to cease detaining men who confined their sexual activities to their

GUANGZHOU

home and ruled that there was no legal reason to separate cohabiting lesbian couples.

USEFUL ORGANISATIONS
Public Security Bureau (PSB)

Not everyone will agree that they are useful, but the Public Security Bureau *(gōng'ān jú)* is the name given to China's police, both uniformed and plain-clothes. Its responsibilities include suppression of political dissidence, crime detection, preventing foreigners and Chinese from having sex with each other (no joke), mediating family quarrels and directing traffic. The Foreign Affairs Branch *(wài shì kē)* of the Public Security Bureau (PSB) deals with foreigners. This branch is responsible for issuing visa extensions.

In Guangzhou, the Public Security Bureau (☎ 8333-1060) is at 863 Jiefang North Lu, opposite the road which leads up to Zhenhai

Tower in Yuexi Park, a 15-minute walk from the Dongfang Hotel.

The United States Information Service, usually just called USIS (☎ 8335-4269), is on the restaurant floor of the Garden Hotel.

The American Chamber of Commerce (☎ 8331-1888) is in the Guangdong International Hotel next to the GITIC Plaza.

DANGERS & ANNOYANCES

Visiting any country involves hassles and some culture shock. China is not the worst for this, but there are certain aspects of the culture that set Westerners on edge. It does little good to get overly upset and lose your temper. The best advice is to learn to laugh it off. Among the things you will have to learn to live with are:

Theft

Guangzhou is far more dangerous than either

Killing the Rooster to Frighten the Monkey

It's hard to say how China's crime rate compares with those in other countries, though the country has its share of rapists and murderers. White-collar crime is also a big problem and the Chinese newspapers regularly report arrests and even the occasional execution of frauds and embezzlers.

The crackdown on corruption has been given extensive coverage in the official press. In Shanghai the sons of three senior cadres were executed for attacks on women. A Shanghai party official was also jailed for life for accepting over Y30,000 in bribes. Although such sentences were intended to show that all are equal before the law, the centuries-old system of privilege for high officials and their relatives is unlikely to receive more than a dent.

When the minister and vice-minister of astronautics embezzled US$46 million in foreign exchange they were rebuked with 'serious disciplinary warnings within the party'. Meanwhile, local pickpockets get the death penalty.

Juvenile crime is a growing problem in China's cities. The types of crime committed include murder, rape and theft of large sums of money. The official view is that they are victims of 'spiritual pollution' – influenced by images of foreign criminal cliques portrayed in mass media. Other factors such as unemployment and disillusionment are rarely blamed.

Justice in China seems to be dispensed entirely by the police, who also decide the penalty. The ultimate penalty is execution, which serves the purpose of 'killing the rooster to frighten the monkey' or, to phrase this in official terms, 'It is good to have some people executed so as to educate others'. With no independent judiciary, people charged with a crime have little chance of beating a conviction unless they're well connected.

China has become famous for its periodic crackdown campaigns. When official word comes down that it's time to get tough on crime, the newspapers routinely report impressive-sounding figures – thousands of people arrested, many executions. To judge from official figures, these anti-crime campaigns are a resounding success. The police seem to have little difficulty filling their quota. How many of these people really committed the crimes in question is another matter.

The standard manner of dispatching convicted criminals is with a bullet in the back of the head. Afterwards, a mug shot and maybe even a photo of the extinguished body appears in the newspapers or even gets pinned up on a public noticeboard. Such executions are generally performed at mass gatherings, often at a stadium but sometimes in front of bus or railway stations. The railway station routine has become less popular in recent years, mainly because some foreign tour groups would occasionally disembark from their train just in time to see someone get their head blown off. Should you by chance happen upon such a spectacle, taking photos may be a bad idea. ■

Hong Kong or Macau. As one of China's boom towns, the city has attracted a large number of immigrants from the countryside in search of the proverbial pot of gold. Needless to say, most become disillusioned when they find themselves camped out on the pavement with no prospects for employment. Many turn to begging and theft. Guangzhou taxis have plastic shields or wire screens separating the driver from the passengers. Before these became mandatory, many drivers were attacked and some were killed.

For foreigners, there is little physical danger in walking the streets but pickpockets are a problem, especially on crowded buses. You should also be cautious of bag snatchers, especially around the railway station. Some thieves use bicycles as their getaway vehicles. Another tactic is to slit your bag or pocket open with a razor blade and remove the contents. The police are worthless in such cases.

Violent crime is also increasing. Knife-wielding gangs attack passengers on trains and jump off as the train approaches a station. So far, the criminals have shown a preference for robbing Chinese and leaving foreigners alone, but this is starting to change too.

The police often show a stunning lack of interest in getting involved when someone reports a crime. Rather than respond to individual complaints, the situation is handled collectively with periodic high-profile crackdown campaigns.

Spitting
Clearing your throat and discharging the phlegm on the floor or out the window (to the peril of those below) is perfectly acceptable in China. Everyone does it – any time, any place. It's not so bad in summer, but in winter – when many people are afflicted by the notorious 'China Syndrome' – you'll have a hard time trying to keep out of the crossfire!

Littering
The environmental movement has not reached China. Rather than carry the garbage down the stairs once a day, many Chinese find it more convenient to dump it out the window. (You get a hint of this in Hong Kong at Chungking Mansions – just look in the light-wells in the centre of the building). Sewer grates are also convenient garbage dumps. Restaurants and street vendors usually dump all uneaten food down the sewer, much to the joy of the rats who inhabit the underworld.

If you take a boat cruise on the Pearl River, sit on the lower deck – you can watch in astonishment as it rains garbage from the upper deck. Of course, every boat has a rubbish bin and some people use it – which is why a shipmate comes along about once an hour and dumps the contents overboard.

Nevertheless, the streets in China are reasonably clean, but not because civic-minded citizens are careful with their rubbish. The government employs a small army of people who do nothing all day but sweep up the continual mess – otherwise the country would be quickly buried in it.

Push & Shove
When Mao was alive, leftists in Western countries pointed to China as a model of harmony and happiness, where smiling peasants joined hands and worked together in a cooperative effort to build a better society.

Undoubtedly, many of them were dismayed when they finally did get to visit the People's Republic and saw what the Chinese go through to get on a bus. No cooperative effort here, just panicked mobs frantically pushing, shoving and clawing. Those who want to get off are shoved right back inside by those who want to get on. In a few notorious incidents (mostly involving overcrowded ferries) people have actually been trampled to death.

Price Gouging
Overall, Nathan Rd in Hong Kong is worse when it comes to price gouging, but Guangzhou is hardly a hotbed of honesty. It probably wouldn't matter if they only charged us double, but you might be charged five times the going rate for some simple service such as doing laundry or a shoe

repair. Needless to say, it's always wise to negotiate the price beforehand.

LEGAL MATTERS

The PSB is responsible for introducing and enforcing regulations concerning foreigners. So, for example, they bear responsibility for exclusion of foreigners from certain hotels. If this means you get stuck for a place to stay, they can offer advice.

There are a few ways you can inadvertently have an unpleasant run-in with the PSB. The most common way is to overstay your visa. Foreign males who are suspected of being 'too friendly' with Chinese women could have trouble with the PSB. Foreign missionaries who enter China on a tourist visa and proceed to proselytise are routinely arrested.

If you do have a run-in with the bureau, you may have to write a confession of your guilt and pay a fine. In more serious cases, you can be expelled from China (at your own expense). But in general, if you aren't doing anything particularly nasty like smuggling suitcases of dope or weapons through Customs, the PSB will probably not throw you in prison.

If you do get arrested, you should insist on the right to contact your country's embassy.

BUSINESS HOURS

In 1995, the Chinese work week was reduced to five days (it had previously been six) – so the residents of Guangzhou actually work fewer days than their more affluent counterparts in Hong Kong and Macau.

Banks, offices and government departments are open Monday to Friday. As a rough guide only, they open around 8 to 9 am, close for two hours in the middle of the day, and reopen until 5 or 6 pm.

Many parks, zoos and monuments have similar opening hours, and are also open on weekends and often at night. Shows at cinemas and theatres end at about 9.30 or 10 pm.

Restaurants are open for early-morning breakfast (sometimes as early as 5.30) until about 7.30 am, then open for lunch and again for dinner around 5 pm to 9 pm. Chinese eat early and go home early – by 9 pm you'll probably find the chairs stacked and the cooks heading home. Privately run restaurants are usually open all day, and often late into the night, especially around railway stations.

Long-distance bus stations and railway stations open their ticket offices around 5 or 5.30 am before the first trains and buses pull out. Apart from a one or two-hour break in the middle of the day, they often stay open until about 11 or 11.30 pm.

PUBLIC HOLIDAYS & SPECIAL EVENTS

The Chinese have nine national holidays during the year, as follows:

New Year's Day – 1 January

Chinese Lunar New Year – the first day of the first lunar month. This holiday usually falls in the first half of February, but sometimes occurs during the last week of January. Also known as the Spring Festival, the actual holiday lasts three days but many people take a week off. It's a bad time to travel as all accommodation and transport is chock-a-block. Most businesses are closed as this is a family holiday. If you have to be in China at this time, settle down in a nice quiet place with some books and try not to go anywhere until the chaos ends.

International Working Women's Day – 8 March

International Labour Day – 1 May

Youth Day – 4 May commemorates the Beijing student demonstrations of 4 May 1919 when the Versailles Conference gave Germany's 'rights' in the city of Tianjin to Japan.

Children's Day – 1 June

Anniversary of the founding of the Communist Party of China – 1 July

Anniversary of the founding of the Chinese People's Liberation Army (PLA) – 1 August

National Day – 1 October, celebrates the founding of the People's Republic of China in 1949.

ACTIVITIES

T'ai chi

If you don't mind getting up at the crack of dawn, you can join the Chinese in any park for an early morning t'ai chi exercise session.

Fitness Clubs

Swimming pools, gymnasiums, weightlifting rooms, etc, are popular ways to keep fit and enjoy yourself. While swimming pools and gymnasiums exist for the Chinese public, they are generally overcrowded and in poor condition. You'll find better facilities at the tourist hotels. Most hotels in big cities like Guangzhou permit non-guests to use the gyms, pools, saunas, tennis courts, etc, on a fee basis. This is not a bad idea if you're staying for a month or more – monthly fees typically start at around US$50.

Massage
Legitimate massage has traditionally been performed by blind people in China. The Chinese can take credit for developing many of the best massage techniques which are still employed today.

One place in which blind men perform excellent massage is the Hongde Weisheng Yuan (☎ 8430-1805). It's in the basement at No 28 Lane 5, Hongde Lu. It's almost opposite a Christian church and very close to the Zhoutouzui Wharf (see map). The place is popular with expats. The cost is Y50 for 1.5 hours.

Upmarket hotels also have sauna and massage facilities which non-guests can use for a fee.

Golf
The Guangzhou Luhu Golf and Country Club (☎ 8359-5516; fax 8359-6401) boasts an 18-hole golf course and fitness complex. It's within the grounds of Luhu Park on the southern slope of the White Cloud Hills. Non-members can use the facilities for a fee.

The Guangzhou International Golf Club (☎ 8332-1609) also has facilities and members have access to several courses outside Guangzhou, including some in Hong Kong and Shenzhen.

Educational Courses
As China continues to experiment with capitalism, universities have found it increasingly necessary to raise their own funds and not depend so much on state largesse. For this reason, most universities welcome fee-paying foreign students. Most of the courses offered are Chinese language study, but other possibilities include Chinese medicine, acupuncture, painting,

music, etc. If you've got the cash, almost anything is possible.

There is considerable variation in the quality of instruction and the prices charged. Tuition alone typically runs from US$1000 to US$3000 per year, sometimes double that, and it may depend on your nationality. The university is supposed to arrange your accommodation (no, it's not free) – living conditions vary from reasonably comfortable to horrific.

If possible, don't pay anything in advance – show up at the school to assess the situation, and talk to other foreign students to see if they're satisfied. Once you've handed over the cash, don't expect a refund.

Language The Chinese Language Centre of Zhongshan University in Guangzhou, at 135 Xingang Xilu, offers a language course in Chinese. This is an excellent place to study Chinese, either Mandarin or Cantonese. Courses are typically four hours per day, five days weekly and cost Y6650 per semester. Dormitory accommodation for students is approximately Y25 to Y35 per day.

Traditional Medicine Acupuncture and herbal medicine classes also attract foreign students. The most popular venue for this by far is the Traditional Chinese Medicine Hospital (☎ 8188-6504) (*zhōngyī yīyuàn*) at 16 Zhuji Lu (near Shamian Island).

WORK
There are opportunities to teach English and other foreign languages, or even other technical skills if you're qualified. Teaching in China is not a way to get rich – pay is roughly US$180 a month, payable in RMB rather than foreign currency. While this is about four times what the average urban Chinese worker earns, it won't get you far after you've left China. There are usually some fringe benefits like free or low-cost housing and special ID cards that get you discounts on trains and flights. As a worker in China, you will be assigned to a 'work unit', but unlike the locals you'll be excused from political meetings and the God-like controls

GUANGZHOU

The Point of it All

Can you cure people by sticking needles into them? The Chinese think so, and they've been doing it for thousands of years. Now the technique of acupuncture is gaining popularity in the West. In recent years, many Westerners have made the pilgrimage to China either to seek treatment or to study acupuncture. Guangzhou is a particularly popular place both for patients, and for students who want to learn more about this ancient medical technique.

Getting stuck with needles might not sound pleasant, but if done properly it doesn't hurt. Knowing just where to insert the needle is crucial. Acupuncturists have identified more than 2000 insertion points, but only about 150 are commonly used.

The exact mechanism by which acupuncture works is not fully understood. The Chinese talk of energy channels or meridians which connect the needle insertion point to the particular organ, gland or joint being treated. The acupuncture point is sometimes quite far from the area of the body being treated. Acupuncture is even used to treat impotence, but where, one wonders, should the needle be inserted?

Among acupuncturists there are several schools of thought. The most common school in China is called the Eight Principles School. Another is the Five Elements School.

As with herbal medicine, the fundamental question asked by potential acupuncture patients is: 'Does it work?' The answer has to be: 'That depends.' It depends on the skill of the acupuncturist and the condition being treated. Like herbal medicine, acupuncture tends to be more useful for those who suffer from long-term conditions (like chronic headaches) rather than sudden emergencies (like acute appendicitis).

However, there are times when acupuncture can be used for an immediate condition. For example, surgical operations have been performed using acupuncture as the only anaesthetic (this works best on the head). In this case, a small electric current (from batteries) is passed through the needles. This is a good example of how Western medicine and Chinese medicine can be usefully combined.

While some satisfied patients give glowing testimonials about the prowess of acupuncturists, others are less impressed. The only way to find out is to try it yourself.

While acupuncture itself is relatively harmless, one should not forget that AIDS and hepatitis B can be spread easily by contaminated needles. In Western countries, the use of disposable acupuncture needles has become routine. This is also the case in Hong Kong, but not necessarily elsewhere in China. Back-alley acupuncturists who reuse needles are still common in many parts of Asia. If you're going to experiment with acupuncture outside Hong Kong, first find out if the doctor has disposable needles. If not, you can buy your own needles and bring them to the doctor. Of course, you must find out if the doctor is willing. Also, you need to consult with the doctor to find out what size and gauge of needles you should buy.

Loosely related to acupuncture is massage. The Chinese variety is somewhat different from the popular techniques practised by people in the West. One traditional Chinese method employs cups placed on the patient's skin. A burning piece of alcohol-soaked cotton is briefly put inside the cup to drive out the air before it is applied. As the cup cools, a partial vacuum is produced, leaving a nasty-looking but harmless mark on the skin. The mark goes away after a few days. Other methods include bloodletting and scraping the skin with coins or porcelain soup spoons – this leaves marks that look like the patient indeed has some dreaded disease.

Moxibustion is a variation on the theme. Various types of herbs, rolled into what looks like a ball of fluffy cotton, are held near the skin and ignited. This method can be spiced up by placing the herb on a slice of ginger and then igniting it. The idea is to apply the maximum amount of heat possible without burning the patient. This heat treatment is supposed to be good for diseases such as arthritis. ■

over your life that the typical Chinese has to endure.

It's become fairly typical for universities to pressure foreigners into working excessive hours. A maximum teaching load should be 20 hours per week, and even this is a lot – you can insist on no more than 15. Chinese professors teach far fewer hours than this – some hardly show up for class at all since they often have outside business interests.

Two topics which cannot be discussed in

the classroom are politics and religion. Foreigners teaching in China have reported spies being placed in their classrooms. Other teachers have found microphones hidden in their dormitory rooms (one fellow we know took revenge by attaching his stereo to the microphone wires and blasting the snoops with punk music!).

People with technical skills and the ability to speak Chinese can sometimes land lucrative jobs with large foreign companies, but this is not accomplished so easily. Such jobs are often advertised in the *China Daily*.

Foreigners who have gone to work for Chinese companies have complained about cheating on wages. One group of Americans was hired by a disco in Guangzhou to set up an elaborate sound and lighting system. When they finished the job (which took three weeks), the Chinese simply refused to pay. The Chinese court system proved useless when the Americans tried to recover their money. Such tales of woe are not uncommon in China.

Doing Business

At one time, China was the world's most advanced nation. The Chinese invented gunpowder, rockets, the printing press and paper currency. How did such an advanced nation fall so far behind? Probably because the Chinese also invented bureaucracy.

In bureaucratic China, even simple things can be made difficult – renting property, getting a telephone installed, hiring staff, paying taxes, etc, can generate mind-boggling quantities of red tape. Many foreign businesspeople who have worked in China say that success is usually the result of dogged persistence.

If you have any intention of doing business in China, it's worth knowing that most towns and – in large cities – many neighbourhoods, have a Commerce Office (*shāngyè jú*). If you approach one of these offices for assistance, the reaction you get can vary from enthusiastic welcome to bureaucratic inertia. In case of a dispute (the goods you ordered are not what was delivered, etc), the Commerce Office could assist you.

Buying is simple, selling is more difficult, but setting up a business in China is a whole different can of worms.

If yours is a high-technology company, you can go into certain economic zones and register as a wholly foreign-owned enterprise. In that case you can hire people yourself without going through the government, enjoy a three-year tax holiday, obtain long-term income tax advantages, and import duty-free personal items for corporate and expat use. The alternative is listing your company as a representative office, which does not allow you to sign any contracts in China – these must be signed by the mother company. The Foreign Service Company (FESCO) is where you hire employees. FESCO currently demands around US$325 per month per employee, 75% of which goes to the government.

It's easier to register as a representative office. First find out where you want to set up (a city or special economic zone), then go through local authorities (there are no national authorities for this). Go to the local Commerce Office, Economic Ministry, Foreign Ministry, or any ministry that deals with foreign economic trade promotion. Setting up in a 'high-technology zone' is recommended if you can qualify, but where you register depends on what type of business you're doing. Contact your embassy first – they can advise you.

The most important thing to remember when you go to register a company is not to turn away when you run into a bureaucratic barrier. Bureaucrats will tell you that everything is 'impossible'. In fact, anything is possible – it all depends on your *guanxi* (relationships). Whatever you have in mind is negotiable – the rules are not necessarily rules at all.

Tax rates vary from zone to zone, authority to authority – it seems to be negotiable, but 15% is fairly standard from economic zones. Every economic zone has a fairly complete investment guide in English and Chinese – your embassy's economic council might have one of these, and these investment guides are getting to be very clear (but even all these printed 'rules' are negotiable!).

Red tape is not the only obstacle foreign investors have to face. It's very common that once a foreign-owned business gets up and running successfully, the military or the police suddenly move in Mafia-style and demand to become your 'joint-venture partner'. That is to say, they demand 50% of your earnings. If you don't agree to this, you'll simply be harassed out of business. Many (if not most) expat-owned pubs and restaurants have fallen into this trap. Indeed, it's one of the thing that most worries Hong Kong – already several large Hong Kong businesses have been forced to take on Chinese state-run companies as 'partners'.

ACCOMMODATION

Public Security prohibits foreigners from staying in the dirt-cheap Chinese hotels. Private guesthouses, such as Hong Kong's Chungking Mansions, are also forbidden. At present, there is only one real budget hotel remaining in Guangzhou, the Guangzhou Youth Hostel on Shamian Island, and this place often fills up.

Fortunately, there are a few tricks to keeping the hotel bill down. The simplest way is to share a room – usually a second person can stay in the room for no extra cost. Also be aware that there is some confusion in terms – what most Chinese hotels call a 'single room' is a room with one bed. If two people sleep in a single room in the same bed, it's still a single room (and priced accordingly). A 'double room' is in fact a room with twin beds – (up to four people could stay in a 'double room' for the same price as a single traveller. The vast majority of China's hotel rooms are actually doubles, and you pay for that second bed whether you use it or not. Rooms with three and four beds can also be found.

Discounts If you're a foreign student in the People's Republic you can get a discount on room prices. Students usually have to show their government-issued 'green card', though sometimes a fake 'white card' will do the trick. Foreign experts working in China usually qualify for the same discounts as students.

If you are really stuck for a place to stay, it sometimes helps to phone or visit the local PSB and explain your problem. Just as the PSB makes the rules, the PSB can break them – a hotel not approved for foreigners can be granted a temporary reprieve by the PSB and all it takes is a phone call from the right official. Unfortunately, getting such an exemption is not a usual practice.

Hotel Etiquette Most hotels have an attendant on every floor. The attendant keeps an eye on the hotel guests. This is partly to prevent theft and partly to stop you from bringing locals back for the night.

To conserve energy, in many cheaper hotels hot water for bathing in only available in the evening – sometimes only for a few hours a night or once every three days! It's worth asking when/if the hot water will be turned on.

The policy at every hotel in China requires that you check out by noon to avoid being charged extra. If you check out between noon and 6 pm there is a charge of 50% of the room price – after 6 pm you have to pay for another full night.

Almost every hotel has a left-luggage room (*jìcún chù* or *xínglǐ bǎoguǎn*), and in many hotels there is such a room on every floor. If you are a guest in the hotel, use of the left-luggage room might be free (but not always).

The trend in China over the last few years has been to equip every room – even in the cheap hotels – with TV sets permanently turned to maximum volume. The Hong Kong-style ultra-violent movies are noisy enough, but the introduction of Nintendo-style video games and karaoke microphones (which can be attached to TV sets) has added a new dimension to the cacophony. The combination of screams, screeches, shootings, songs, rings, gongs, beeps and buzzers which reverberate through the vast concrete corridors could force a statue to run away.

The Chinese method of designating floors is the same as used in the USA, but different from that used in Hong Kong, Australia or the UK. What would be the 'ground floor' in Hong Kong is the '1st floor' in China, the 1st is the 2nd, and so on. However, there is some inconsistency – a few Hong Kong-owned hotels in southern China use the British system!

Rental

Most Chinese people live in government-subsidised housing – the price is almost always dirt cheap. For foreigners, the situation is totally different.

If you're going to be working for the Chinese government as a teacher or other type of foreign expert, then you'll almost certainly be provided with cheap or low-cost housing. Conditions probably won't be luxurious, but should be inexpensive.

The news is not good for those coming to China to do business or work for a foreign company. The cheap apartments available to the Chinese are off-limits to foreigners, which leaves you with two choices – a hotel, or a luxury flat in a compound specifically designated for foreigners.

If you live in a hotel, you might be able to negotiate a discount for a long-term stay, but that's not guaranteed. As for luxury flats and villas, prices start at around US$2000 and reach US$5000 or more. Even at these prices, there is a shortage of flats available for foreigners.

Considering the sky-high rents, buying a flat or villa might seem like a good idea for companies with the cash. It's actually possible, but the rules vary from city to city. In some cities, only overseas Chinese are permitted to buy luxury villas – real estate speculators from Taiwan do a roaring trade. Shenzhen has long been in the business of selling flats to Hong Kongers, who in turn rent them out to others. Foreigners can buy flats in some cities (at astronomical prices), and doing this can actually gain you a residence permit.

As for simply moving in with a Chinese family and paying them rent, forget it – Public Security will swoop down on you (and the hapless Chinese family) faster than ants at a picnic.

FOOD

Chinese food is similar to what you'll find in Hong Kong, except that there's a good deal of wildlife on the menu. Snake, monkey, pangolin (an armadillo-like creature), bear, giant salamander and raccoon are among the tastes that can be catered for, not to mention the more mundane dog, cat and rat dishes.

One look at the people fishing in the sewage canals around Guangzhou might dull your appetite for Pearl River trout.

Western food is a rarity, and is mostly limited to fast-food cuisine of the Big Mac variety. Hong Kong fast-food chains like Fairwood have entered the Chinese market.

Useful Expressions
bill (cheque)
  zhàngdān 帐单
chopsticks
  kuàizi 筷子

fork
  chāzi 叉子
I can't eat spicy food
  wǒ bùnéng chī là 我不能吃辣
I'm a vegetarian
  wǒ shì chīsùde 我是吃素的
knife
  dāozi 刀子
menu
  càidān 菜单
restaurant
  cāntīng 餐厅
spoon
  tiáogēng 调羹

Rice 饭
plain white rice
  mǐfàn 米饭
rice noodles
  mǐfěn 米粉
watery rice porridge
  xīfàn 稀饭

Bread, Buns & Dumplings 麦类
boiled dumplings
  jiǎozi 饺子
fried bread stick
  yóutiáo 油条
fried roll
  yínsī juǎn 馒头
prawn cracker
  lóngxiā piàn 龙虾片
steamed buns
  mántóu 银丝卷
steamed meat buns
  bāozi 包子

Vegetable Dishes 菜类
assorted hors d'oeuvre
  shíjǐn pīnpán 什锦拼盘
assorted vegetarian food
  sù shíjǐn 素什锦
bean curd & mushrooms
  mógū dòufǔ 磨菇豆腐
bean curd casserole
  shāguō dòufǔ 沙锅豆腐
black fungus & mushroom
  mù'ěr huákǒu mó 木耳滑口磨
broiled mushroom
  sù chǎo xiānme 素炒鲜麽

Chinese salad
jiācháng liángcài 家常凉菜
fried bean curd in oyster sauce
háoyóu dòufǔ 蚝油豆腐
fried beansprouts
sù chǎo dòuyá 素炒豆芽
fried cauliflower & tomato
fānqié càihuā 炒蕃茄菜花
fried eggplant
sùshāo qiézi 素烧茄子
fried garlic
sù chǎo dàsuàn 素炒大蒜
fried rape in oyster sauce
háoyóu pácài dǎn 蚝油扒菜胆
fried rape with mushrooms
dōnggū pácài dǎn 冬菇扒菜胆
fried green beans
sù chǎo biǎndòu 素炒扁豆
fried green vegetables
sù chǎo qīngcài 素炒青菜
fried noodles with vegetables
shūcài chǎomiàn 蔬菜炒面
fried peanuts
yóuzhà huāshēng mǐ 油炸花生米
fried rice with vegetables
shūcài chǎofàn 蔬菜炒饭
fried white radish patty
luóbo gāo 萝卜糕
garlic & morning glory
dàsuàn kōngxīn cài 大蒜空心菜
spiced cold vegetables
liángbàn shíjǐn 凉拌什锦
spicy hot bean curd
mápó dòufǔ 麻婆豆腐
spicy peanuts
wǔxiāng huāshēng mǐ 五香花生米

Egg Dishes
egg & flour omelette
jiān bǐng 煎饼
fried rice with egg
jīdàn chǎofàn 鸡蛋炒饭
fried tomatoes & eggs
xīhóngshì chǎo jīdàn 西红柿炒鸡蛋
preserved egg
sōnghuā dàn 松花蛋

Beef Dishes
beef braised in soy sauce
hóngshāo niúròu 红烧牛肉

beef curry & noodles
gālí jīròu miàn 咖哩牛肉面
beef curry & rice
gālí jīròu fàn 咖哩牛肉饭
beef platter
niúròu tiěbǎn 牛肉铁板
beef with green peppers
qīngjiāo niúròu piàn 青椒牛肉片
beef with oyster sauce
háoyóu niúròu 蚝油牛肉
beef with tomatoes
fānqié niúròu piàn 蕃茄牛肉片
beef with white rice
niúròu fàn 牛肉饭
fried noodles with beef
niúròu chǎomiàn 牛肉炒面
fried rice with beef
niúròusī chǎofàn 牛肉丝炒饭
noodles with beef (soupy)
niúròu tāng miàn 牛肉汤面
spiced noodles with beef
niúròu gān miàn 牛肉干面

Chicken Dishes
chicken braised in soy sauce
hóngshāo jīkuài 红烧鸡块
chicken curry & noodles
gālí jīròu miàn 咖哩鸡肉面
chicken curry & rice
gālí jīròu fàn 咖哩鸡肉饭
chicken curry
gālí jīròu 咖哩鸡肉
chicken leg with white rice
jītuǐ fàn 鸡腿饭
chicken pieces in oyster sauce
háoyóu jīdīng 蚝油鸡丁
chicken slices & tomato sauce
fānqié jīdīng 蕃茄鸡丁
fried noodles with chicken
jīsī chǎomiàn 鸡丝炒面
fried rice with chicken
jīsī chǎofàn 鸡丝炒饭
fruit kernel with chicken
guǒwèi jīdīng 果味鸡丁
mushrooms & chicken
cǎomó jīdīng 草蘑鸡丁
noodles with chicken (soupy)
jīsī tāng miàn 鸡丝汤面
sauteed chicken with green peppers
jiàngbào jīdīng 酱爆鸡丁

GUANGZHOU

sauteed chicken with water chestnuts
  nánjiè jīpiàn 南芥鸡片
sauteed spicy chicken pieces
  làzi jīdīng 辣子鸡丁
sliced chicken with crispy rice
  jīpiàn guōbā 鸡片锅巴
spicy hot chicken & peanuts
  gōngbào jīdīng 宫爆鸡丁
sweet & sour chicken
  tángcù jīdīng 糖醋鸡丁

Duck Dishes
Beijing Duck
  běijīng kǎoyā 北京烤鸭
duck with fried noodles
  yāròu chǎomiàn 鸭肉炒面
duck with noodles
  yāròu miàn 鸭肉面
duck with white rice
  yāròu fàn 鸭肉饭

Pork Dishes
boiled pork slices
  shuǐzhǔ ròupiàn 水煮肉片
Cantonese fried rice
  guǎngzhōu chǎofàn 广州炒饭
fried black pork pieces
  yuánbào lǐjī 芫爆里肌
fried noodles with pork
  ròusī chǎomiàn 肉丝炒面
fried rice (assorted)
  shíjǐn chǎofàn 什锦炒饭
fried rice with pork
  ròusī chǎofàn 肉丝炒饭
golden pork slices
  jīnyín ròusī 金银肉丝
noodles, pork & mustard greens
  zhàcài ròusī miàn 榨菜肉丝面
pork & fried onions
  yángcōng chǎo ròupiàn 洋葱炒肉片
pork & mustard greens
  zhàcài ròusī 榨菜肉丝
pork chop with white rice
  páigǔ fàn 排骨饭
pork cubes & cucumber
  huángguā ròudīng 黄瓜肉丁
pork fillet with white sauce
  huáliū lǐjī 滑溜里肌
pork with crispy rice
  ròupiàn guōbā 肉片锅巴

pork with oyster sauce
  háoyóu ròusī 蚝油肉丝
pork, eggs & black fungus
  mùxū ròu 木须肉
sauteed diced pork & soy sauce
  jiàngbào ròudīng 酱爆肉丁
sauteed shredded pork
  qīngchǎo ròusī 清炒肉丝
shredded pork & bamboo shoots
  dōngsǔn ròusī 冬笋肉丝
shredded pork & green beans
  biǎndòu ròusī 扁豆肉丝
shredded pork & green peppers
  qīngjiāo ròusī 青椒肉丝
shredded pork & hot sauce
  yúxiāng ròusī 鱼香肉丝
shredded pork fillet
  chǎo lǐjī sī 炒里肌丝
soft pork fillet
  ruǎnzhá lǐjī 软炸里肌
spicy hot pork pieces
  gōngbào ròudīng 宫爆肉丁
spicy pork cubes
  làzi ròudīng 辣子肉丁
sweet & sour pork fillet
  tángcù lǐjī 糖醋里肌
sweet & sour pork fillet
  tángcù zhūròu piàn 糖醋猪肉片

Seafood Dishes
braised sea cucumber
  hóngshāo hǎishēn 红烧海参
clams
  gé 蛤
crab
  pángxiè 螃蟹
deep-fried shrimp
  zhá xiārén 炸虾仁
diced shrimp with peanuts
  gōngbào xiārén 宫爆虾仁
fish braised in soy sauce
  hóngshāo yú 红烧鱼
fried noodles with shrimp
  xiārén chǎomiàn 虾仁炒面
fried rice with shrimp
  xiārén chǎofàn 虾仁炒饭
fried shrimp with mushroom
  xiānmó xiārén 鲜蘑虾仁
lobster
  lóngxiā 龙虾

GUANGZHOU

sauteed shrimp
qīngchǎo xiārén 清炒虾仁
squid with crispy rice
yóuyú guōbā 鱿鱼锅巴
sweet & sour squid roll
suānlà yóuyú juàn 酸辣鱿鱼卷

Soup

bean curd & vegetable soup
dòufǔ cài tāng 豆腐菜汤
clear soup
qīng tāng 清汤
corn & egg thick soup
fènghuáng lìmǐ gēng 凤凰栗米羹
cream of mushroom soup
nǎiyóu xiānmó tāng 奶油鲜蘑汤
cream of tomato soup
nǎiyóu fānqié tāng 奶油蕃茄汤
egg & vegetable soup
dànhuā tāng 蛋花汤
fresh fish soup
shēng yú tāng 生鱼汤
mushroom & egg soup
mógu dànhuā tāng 蘑菇蛋花汤
pickled mustard green soup
zhàcài tāng 榨菜汤
squid soup
yóuyú tāng 鱿鱼汤
sweet & sour soup
suānlà tāng 酸辣汤
three kinds seafood soup
sān xiān tāng 三鲜汤
tomato & egg soup
xīhóngshì dàn tāng 西红柿蛋汤
vegetable soup
shūcài tāng 蔬菜汤
wanton soup
húndùn tāng 馄饨汤

Miscellanea & Exotica

deermeat (venison)
lùròu 鹿肉
dogmeat
gǒu ròu 狗肉
eel
shàn yú 鳝鱼
frog
qīngwā 青蛙
goat, mutton
yáng ròu 羊肉

kebab
ròu chuàn 肉串
Mongolian hotpot
huǒguō 火锅
pangolin
chuānshānjiǎ 穿山甲
ratmeat
lǎoshǔ ròu 老鼠肉
snake
shé ròu 蛇肉
turtle
hǎiguī 海龟

Condiments

black pepper
hújiāo 胡椒
butter
huáng yóu 黄油
garlic
dàsuàn 大蒜
honey
fēngmì 蜂蜜
hot pepper
làjiāo 辣椒
hot sauce
làjiāo jiàng 辣椒酱
jam
guǒ jiàng 果酱
ketchup
fānqié jiàng 蕃茄酱
MSG
wèijīng 味精
salt
yán 盐
sesame seed oil
zhīmá yóu 芝麻油
soy sauce
jiàng yóu 酱油
sugar
táng 糖
vinegar
cù 醋

Desserts & Snacks

biscuits
bǐnggān 饼干
cake
dàngāo 蛋糕
ice cream
bīngqílín 冰淇淋
yoghurt
suānnǎi 酸奶

DRINKS
Nonalcoholic Drinks

Aside from the ubiquitous tea, China has come up with a few surprisingly good local soft drinks. A local speciality is the orange and honey flavoured *Jianlibao*. Oddities include lychee-flavoured carbonated drinks and orange drinks with strange pieces of something floating in them.

Alcoholic Drinks

Most Chinese firewater has little appeal to Western tastes. Famous brews like *Shaoxing* and *Maotai* taste like they could take the paint off a car. Rice wine *(mǐ jiǔ)* is meant for cooking, but it's also a cheap drink – the next morning you'll feel like your brain is made of cottage cheese.

By contrast, most Chinese beers are excellent. The most popular is *Tsingtao*, now a major export item. It's actually a German beer – the town where it is made, Tsingtao (now spelled 'Qingdao') was once a German concession. The Chinese inherited the brewery when the Germans were kicked out. Guangzhou is also known for it's local *Zhujiang* ('Pearl River') brand. San Miguel has a brewery in Guangzhou.

The Chinese also do a few sweet grape wines. The stuff is drinkable, but isn't likely to leave French winery owners shaking in their boots.

Drinks Vocabulary

hot
  rè 热
ice cold
  bīngde 冰的
ice cubes
  bīngkuài 冰块

Alcoholic Drinks

beer
  píjiǔ 啤酒
San Miguel Beer
  shēnglì pí 生力啤
Tsingtao Beer
  qīngdǎo píjiǔ 青岛啤酒
Zhujiang Beer
  zhūjiāng píjiǔ 珠江啤酒
vodka
  fútèjiā jiǔ 伏特加酒
whiskey
  wēishìjì jiǔ 威士忌酒

Non-Alcoholic Drinks

Coca-Cola
  kěkǒu kělè 可口可乐
Sprite
  xuěbì 雪碧
coffee
  kāfēi 咖啡
fizzy drink (soda)
  qìshuǐ 汽水
mineral water
  kuàng quán shuǐ 矿泉水
red grape wine
  hóng pútáo jiǔ 红葡萄酒
rice wine
  mǐ jiǔ 米酒
tea
  chá 茶
black tea
  hóng chá 红茶
jasmine tea
  mòlìhuā chá 茉莉花茶
oolong tea
  wūlóng chá 乌龙茶
tea with milk
  nǎichá 奶茶
water
  kāi shuǐ 开水
white grape wine
  bái pútáo jiǔ 白葡萄酒

ENTERTAINMENT

Overall, Guangzhou is not renowned for its nightlife. Karaoke bars at the big hotels dominate the scene, while discos have a small but dedicated following. There are some fledgling Western-style pubs and restaurants in Guangzhou, but nothing to compete with the raging nightlife in Hong Kong. China's English-language newspaper, the *China Daily*, has a reasonably good entertainment section which covers the major cities favoured by tourists.

GUANGZHOU

Warning Besides any mental damage you may suffer from listening to karaoke, these places can be ruinous to your budget. There have been disturbing reports that the 'Tokyo Nightclub Syndrome' has hit Guangzhou. Basically, foreigners (chiefly male) sitting in a karaoke bar are suddenly joined by an attractive young woman (or maybe several women) who 'just want to talk'. A few drinks are ordered – maybe just Coke or orange juice – and at the end of an hour's conversation a bill of perhaps US$500 or so is presented to the hapless foreigner. The drinks might only cost US$10, but the other US$490 is a 'service charge' for talking to the women, who are in fact bar hostesses.

Even more sinister is that these women even approach foreigners on the street, ostensibly just to 'practise their English'. Somewhere in the conversation they suggest going to a 'nice place', which happens to be a karaoke bar. What they fail to mention is that they work for the bar and get a percentage of the profits for every sucker they bring in.

It needs to be mentioned that the victims of these schemes are not only Western foreigners. Overseas Chinese, Hong Kongers, Taiwanese and even mainland Chinese who appear to have money are also targeted. This rip-off system seems to be spreading.

SPECTATOR SPORT
Horse Racing

That most bourgeois of capitalist activities, gambling, has staged a comeback in Guangzhou with the opening of the Guangzhou Horse Racing Track *(pǎo mǎ chǎng)*. Chairman Mao is no doubt doing somersaults in his tomb. Gambling is actually still illegal throughout China, but the Guangdong government gets around this by calling it an 'intelligence competition'.

Races are held in the evening twice weekly during the racing season, which is winter, but the exact times are subject to change.

THINGS TO BUY

The Chinese produce some interesting items for export – tea, clothing, Silkworm missiles – the latter not generally for sale to the public.

Gone are the ration cards and the need for connections to buy TV sets and refrigerators – the consumer sboom has arrived. Chinese department stores are like Aladdin's caves stocked to the rafters with goodies – tourist attractions in themselves.

Unfortunately, quality has not kept pace with quantity. There is an awful lot of junk on sale – zippers which break the first time you use them, music cassette players which last a week, electric appliances that go up in smoke the first time they're plugged in, etc. Given this state of affairs, you might wonder how China manages to successfully export so much – the simple fact is that export items are made to a much higher standard while junk is dumped on the local markets. Always test zippers, examine stitching and, in the case of electrical appliances, plug it in and

---

Ad Nauseam

Advertising for the foreign market is one area the Chinese are still stumbling around in. A TV advertisement in Paris for Chinese furs treated viewers to the bloody business of skinning and cadavers in the refrigerator rooms before the usual parade of fur-clad models down the catwalk.

It would be fun to handle the advertising campaigns for their more charming brands. There's Pansy underwear (for men) or you can pamper your stud with Horse Head facial tissues. Wake up in the morning with a Golden Cock alarm clock (since renamed Golden Rooster). You can start your breakfast with a glass of Billion Strong Pulpy C Orange Drink, or finish your meal with a cup of Imperial Concubine Tea. For your trusty portable radio it may be best to stay away from White Elephant batteries, but you might try the space-age Moon Rabbit variety. Long March car tyres should prove durable, but what about the ginseng product with the fatal name of Gensenocide?

Rambo toilet paper must be the toughest stuff around, but its rival Flying Baby seems to have vanished. Smokers can pick up a pack of Puke cigarettes.

The characters for Coca-Cola translate as 'tastes good, tastes happy' but the Chinese must have thought they were really on to something when the 'Coke adds life' slogan was mistranslated and claimed the stuff could resurrect the dead. And as a sign of the times, one enterprising food vendor has started a chain store named Capitalist Road. ∎

make sure it won't electrocute you before handing over the cash. Chinese sales clerks expect you to do this – they'll consider you a fool if you don't.

The intersection of Beijing Lu and Zhongshan Lu is the top shopping area in the city. Here many excellent shops spread out along both streets. Another street that demands your attention is the bottom part of that long loop (see map) in the south-west part of the city. I can't tell you the name of the street because it changes every few blocks. The section north of Shamian Island (near the Guangzhou Restaurant) is called Dishipu Lu. As you walk east from there the name changes to Xiajiu Lu, then Shangjiu Lu and finally Dade Lu. Whatever you want to call it, it's an excellent street for walking and shopping. The downtown section of Jiefang Lu is also good.

Department Stores Guangzhou's department stores have certainly changed over the past decade. Visitors from the 1980s recall finding everyday consumer goods for sale such as jackhammers, lathes, anti-aircraft spotlights and 10,000-volt transformers. These days, you're more likely to find video tape players, electric guitars and Nintendo games.

Guangzhou's main department store is the Nanfang (nánfáng dàshà) at 49 Yanjiang 1-Lu, just to the east and opposite the main entrance to the Cultural Park. You can also enter the store from the Yanjiang Lu side by the Pearl River.

At the corner of Beijing Lu and Xihu Lu is the Guangzhou Department Store (guǎngzhōu bǎihuò dàlóu). The other main store in town is the Dongshan Department Store (dōngshān bǎihuò dàlóu), just south of Zhongshan 1 Lu and north of Dongshanhu Park.

Friendship Stores There are two Friendship Stores in Guangzhou. The main one is next to the Baiyun Hotel on Huanshi Lu. It's adjacent to the Friendship Cafe. This store has a particularly good supermarket, so if you have a craving for Cadbury chocolate bars or Swiss cheese, this is the place.

The other Friendship Store is near the China Hotel on the corner of Liuhua Lu and Jiefang North Lu. Both Friendship Stores accept all main credit cards and can arrange shipment of goods back to your country.

Shopping Malls Guangzhou's first true shopping mall is Nam Fong International Plaza (nánfāng guójì guǎngchǎng) immediately to the east of the Friendship Store on Huanshi Lu. There is a decent Hong Kong-style supermarket here, but the mall is heavily geared towards luxury items like jewellery, perfume, lipstick and the latest fashions.

Down Jackets If you're heading to north China in winter and don't already have a good down jacket, get one in Guangzhou. Your life will depend on it!

Down jackets are a bargain in China. With all the ducks and geese that the Cantonese eat, they have to do something with all those feathers. You can pick up a decent down jacket for around US$25 at 310 Zhongshan 4 Lu, on the north side of the street and east of Beijing Lu and the Children's Park. This store also sells top-quality down sleeping bags.

Always check zippers when you buy clothing in China. Good down jackets should have some sort of elastic around the inside of the sleeves near the wrists. Otherwise the cold will travel up to your armpits. Make sure the jacket has a hood.

Antiques Guangzhou has its antique market in the alleys off Daihe Lu (see the West Guangzhou map). It's very informal and consists mostly of people peddling wares from their windows or the back of a truck. It can be very interesting, but be aware that few of these 'antiques' are very old and many may be fake. Still, it's good fun to come here.

The Friendship Stores have antique sections, but don't expect to find a bargain. Only antiques which have been cleared for sale to foreigners may be taken out of the country. When you buy an item which is more than 100 years old it will come with an official red wax seal attached – this seal does not necessarily indicate that the item is an antique!

You'll also get a receipt of sale which you must show to Customs when you leave the country, otherwise the antique will be confiscated. Imitation antiques are sold everywhere. Some museum shops sell replicas of pieces on exhibit.

Another place that plugs these wares is the touristy Guangzhou Antique Shop (☎ 8333-4229) at 146 and 162 Wende Beilu.

Arts & Crafts Brushes, paints and other art materials may be worth checking: a lot of this stuff is being imported by Western countries, so you should be able to pick it up cheaper at the source.

Scroll paintings are sold everywhere and are invariably expensive, partly because the material on which the paintings are done is expensive. There are many street artists in China who sit on the sidewalk making on-the-spot drawings and paintings and selling them to passers-by.

Beautiful kites are sold in China and are worth getting just to hang on your wall. Paper rubbings of stone inscriptions are cheap and make nice wall hangings when framed. Papercuts are sold everywhere and some are exquisite. Jade and ivory jewellery is commonly sold in China, but watch out for fakes. Remember that every ivory item bought brings the African elephant closer to extinction, and that countries such as Australia and the USA prohibit the importation of ivory.

The Jiangnan Native Product Store at 399 Zhongshan 4 Lu has a good selection of bamboo and baskets and the Guangzhou Arts and Crafts Market is convenient at 284 Changdi Dama Lu, near the Aiqun Hotel.

No prizes for guessing the speciality at the Guangzhou Pottery Store, 151 Zhongshan 5 Lu.

Books, Posters & Magazines The gift shops at major hotels might seem like a strange place to shop for books, but they have a decent collection of English-language maps, books and foreign magazines such as *Time, Newsweek, Far Eastern Economic Review* and the *Economist*. You can find lower prices in Guangzhou's Chinese bookshops, but the foreign magazines are priced the same everywhere. The Holiday Inn seems to have one of the better bookshops in town.

The Foreign Language Bookstore at 326 Beijing Lu has mostly textbooks and some notable English classics, but it's slim pickings if you'd like some contemporary blockbusters.

The Classical Bookstore at 338 Beijing Lu specialises in pre-1949 Chinese string-bound editions.

The Xinhua Bookstore at 336 Beijing Lu is the main Chinese bookshop in the city. It has a good collection of maps, which are often better than those you can buy on the street; most are in Chinese characters though some maps have both Chinese characters and pinyin. It also has lots of wall posters and reproductions of Chinese paintings.

Stamps Some travellers seem to think they can buy stamps cheaply in China and sell them for a profit at home, but it rarely works out that way. Nevertheless, China produces some beautiful stamps, and if you're a collector, they're worth checking out. The Guangzhou Stamp Company is at 151 Huanshi Xilu, west of the railway station.

Getting There & Away

AIR

While Hong Kong is a great place to find cheap airfares, Guangzhou is not – tickets purchased within China are invariably more expensive (usually much more) than those purchased elsewhere. For example, buying a Melbourne-Guangzhou ticket will be cheaper if you purchase the ticket in Melbourne rather than Guangzhou. In China, there is almost no such thing as discounting – you pay the full fare. This is in sharp contrast to Hong Kong, where cut-throat competition and discounting are the norm.

For this reason, prices quoted in this chapter are what you'd pay in China. If you're after the cheapest flights you can get from outside China, see the Hong Kong Getting There & Away chapter.

Aside from being more expensive, flights into Guangzhou are not at all numerous. Only a handful of airlines fly into the city, mostly from neighbouring Asian countries. The situation will probably improve, but for now the easiest way to reach Guangzhou by air is to fly into Hong Kong then change flights.

On the other hand, Guangzhou is a major hub for domestic flights to other parts of China.

Airports & Airlines

To give pilots a challenge, Guangzhou's Baiyun airport is right next to the White Cloud Hills, Guangzhou's only mountains. It's 12 km north of the city centre. The facilities are pretty grotty, but the city's new airport is expected to open in 1997.

On domestic and international flights the free baggage allowance for an adult passenger is 20 kg in economy class and 30 kg in 1st class. You are also allowed five kg of hand luggage, though this is rarely weighed.

For years, CAAC (Civil Aviation Administration of China) was China's only domestic and international carrier. It has now been broken up and private carriers have been allowed in. CAAC is now the umbrella organisation for the numerous subsidiaries. Under the CAAC umbrella, you can find airlines including: Air China, China Eastern, China Southern, China Northern, China Southwest, China Northwest, Great Wall, Shanghai, Shenzhen, Sichuan, Xiamen, Xinjiang and Yunnan airlines.

CAAC still publishes a combined international and domestic timetable in both English and Chinese in April and November each year. These can be obtained for free in Hong Kong, but can be hard to find in Guangzhou (or indeed, anywhere in China). It's important to realise that many of CAAC's flights are technically charters, even if they do run according to a regular schedule. If you purchase one of these 'charter' tickets, there will be no refund for cancellations and no changes are permitted. Don't count on the CAAC staff to tell you this.

It is possible to buy all of your domestic CAAC tickets from some non-Chinese airlines that have reciprocal arrangements with CAAC. However, this is generally *not* a good idea. First of all, it saves you no money whatsoever. Secondly, the tickets issued by travel agencies need to be exchanged for a proper stamped ticket at the appropriate CAAC offices in China – these offices have at times gotten their wires crossed and refused to honour 'foreign' tickets. Furthermore, CAAC flights sometimes cancel – and you'll have to return the ticket to the seller to get a refund. Your best bet is to buy your tickets directly from a CAAC office.

While CAAC's service has improved, some of its affiliated airlines fly pretty dodgy-looking old Russian jets which will make you sorry you didn't purchase extra life insurance. Fortunately, on major routes such as Hong Kong-Guangzhou you'll likely be flying on a new Boeing or Airbus. All the CAAC-affiliated airlines are listed in the CAAC timetable and sell tickets through

CAAC offices – some even have the CAAC logo on the tickets.

In Guangzhou, you'll find the following airline offices:

Air China,
917 Renmin Lu (☎ 8668-1319; fax 8668-1286)
China Eastern,
1st floor, Leizhou Hotel, 88 Zhanqian Lu
(☎ 8668-1688 ext 3362; fax 8667-1104)
China North-West,
197-199 Dongfeng Xilu
(☎ 8330-8058, 8330-9212; fax 8330-9212)
China Northern
(☎ 8668-2488)
China South-West
(☎ 8667-3747)
China Southern, Baiyun airport
(☎ 8657-8901; fax 8664-4623)
Garuda Indonesia
(☎ 8332-5424, 8332-5484)
Hainan,
99 Zhanqian Lu (☎ 8669-9999)
Malaysia,
shop M04-05, Garden Hotel, 368 Huanshi Lu
(☎ 8335-8828, 8335-8868)
Shanghai
(☎ 8668-1149)
Singapore,
mezzanine floor, Garden Hotel, 368 Huanshi Lu
(☎ 8335-8999, 8335-8886)
Vietnam
(☎ 8382-7187)

Australia

There are flights directly between Guangzhou and either Melbourne or Sydney. The non-discounted airfares (in US$) that you would pay in China are as follows:

Class	One-Way	Return
Economy	1302	2480
Business	1498	2855
First	1915	3646

Hong Kong

There are at least four daily flights between Hong Kong and Guangzhou on China Southern Airlines. A one-way airfare is US$64 and a return ticket costs exactly double. The flight takes 35 minutes.

Indonesia

Garuda and CAAC fly between Guangzhou

and both Jakarta and Surabaya. Airfares (in US$) are as follows:

Class	One-Way	Return
Economy	609	1158
Business	701	1336
First	790	1506

Malaysia

Kuala Lumpur is connected directly with Guangzhou on Malaysia Airlines. Airfares (in US$) are:

Class	One-Way	Return
Economy	445	846
Business	511	974
First	580	1103

Philippines

There are direct Guangzhou-Manila flights on CAAC. Airfares (in US$) are:

Class	One-Way	Return
Economy	163	311
Business	188	359
First	236	448

Singapore

Both Singapore Airlines and CAAC fly the Guangzhou-Singapore route. The airfares (in US$) are:

Class	One-Way	Return
Economy	505	961
Business	581	1109
First	651	1241

Thailand

CAAC offers Guangzhou-Bangkok flights at the following airfares (in US$):

Class	One-Way	Return
Economy	320	610
Business	385	735
First	444	844

USA

Northwest Airlines has been discussing the possibility of linking Guangzhou directly with the US west coast, but these flights will possibly be routed via Beijing or Shanghai. At present, it's still much easier to fly via Hong Kong.

Vietnam

The only direct flight between Ho Chi Minh City (Saigon) and China is to Guangzhou. All other Vietnam-China flights are via Hanoi. The Guangzhou-Hanoi flight (US$140 one-way) takes 1.5 hours; Guangzhou-Ho Chi Minh City (Saigon) (US$240 one-way) takes 2.5 hours.

BUS

Guangzhou Bus Stations

There are several long-distance bus terminals in Guangzhou. Different terminals serve different routes, though there is some overlap.

The Provincial bus station (adjacent to Guangzhou railway station) serves many long-distance destinations such as Guilin, Macau, Zhanjiang and Zhongshan.

The Guangzhou City bus station is another major terminal, just across the street from Guangzhou railway station. Buses here serve Conghua, Shekou, Shenzhen, Foshan, Taiping, Zhaoqing, Zhuhai and many other places.

Guangfo bus station serves Foshan, Taiping, Zhongshan and Zhuhai. Nearby is the Xijiao bus station, which is also useful for getting to towns in the Pearl River Delta. Places served from here include Shenzhen, Zhongshan and Zhuhai.

The small Dashatou bus station is near the Dashatou Wharf and serves Taiping, Zhanjiang and Zhongshan. It's not much used and foreigners should probably avoid dealing with it.

The Panyu bus station is also called the Shayuan bus station and serves Lianhuashan and Panyu.

The Baiyun Lu bus station is one place where you can get buses to Conghua Hot Springs, but most people use the Guangzhou City bus station.

The Yuexiunan bus station is a remote one that you aren't likely to use – all of its routes are better served by the larger stations. Ditto for the Sanyuanli bus terminal.

Hong Kong

The big news is the partial completion of a six-lane super highway from Hong Kong to Guangzhou. This has reduced the bus journey to around three hours. The expressway will eventually be extended to make a 240-km loop from Hong Kong to Guangzhou to Macau.

Citybus operates express buses on the Hong Kong-Guangzhou route. The bus journey takes about three hours and costs HK$160. Departures in Kowloon are from the Guangdong bus station on Canton Rd (between Austin and Jordan Roads). There are also departures from Admiralty MTR station on Hong Kong Island and City One in Sha Tin (New Territories). Departures from Hong Kong are mostly in the morning, and buses leave Guangzhou in the afternoon. In Guangzhou, you catch these buses from major hotels, popular spots being the Garden Hotel and the Victory Hotel (on Shamian Island). Schedules change frequently – in Hong Kong you can ring Citybus (☎ 2736-3888) for the latest information.

Shenzhen

In Shenzhen, air-conditioned minibuses line up near the Hong Kong border at the Luohu bus station (opposite Shenzhen railway station). The fares are posted on a sign where they line up, and at the time of writing it is Y80. The drivers in Shenzhen often ask for Hong Kong dollars but will accept RMB. Most minibuses take the expressway, which reduces travel time to about 2.5 hours.

From Guangzhou to Shenzhen, minibuses operate from several locations. They're most numerous at the Guangzhou city bus station in front of the Liuhua Hotel. But there are numerous other departure points, such as other hotels and at the airport.

Macau

If you want to go directly from Macau, Kee Kwan Motors, across the street from the Floating Casino, sells bus tickets to Guangzhou. One bus takes you to the border at Zhuhai and a second takes you to Guangzhou four hours later. The trip takes about five hours in all. On week days, buy your ticket in the evening before departure.

This international bus is not necessarily

GUANGZHOU

the best way to make this journey. Having to get off the Macau bus, go through immigration and customs, wait for all your fellow passengers (and their enormous luggage), and then reboard another bus is a time-wasting and confusing exercise. It's usually faster to cross the Macau-Zhuhai border by foot and catch a minibus from Zhuhai to Guangzhou. In Macau, bus No 3 runs between the Jetfoil Pier and the China border via the Lisboa Hotel, Avenida Almeida Ribeiro and the Floating Casino.

Zhuhai

From the Zhuhai bus station (next to the Yongtong Hotel), you can catch minibuses to Guangzhou. Some of the buses discharge passengers at Guangzhou's Xijiao bus station (near to the Guangfo bus station), which is just a short taxi ride from Shamian Island.

Going in the other direction, most of the minibuses to Zhuhai depart from the Guangzhou city bus station, though a few also go from the Xijiao bus station. There are also buses direct from Guangzhou's Baiyun airport to Zhuhai. The journey takes about three hours and costs Y50.

Guilin & Yangshuo

You can get a bus ticket without problems from a booth in the forecourt to the left of the Guangzhou railway station. A sleeper costs Y150 and leaves at 6 pm. A free minibus will take you from the railway station area to the long-distance bus station, which is slightly out of town. You get a tour of bus stations until the bus is full. The trip is not very comfortable and takes 15 hours, but you can get off at Yangshuo if you don't want to go all the way to Guilin.

TRAIN

Guangzhou is blessed with extensive international and domestic train services. But in socialist China, trains do not have classes – instead you have hard seat, hard sleeper, soft seat and soft sleeper.

Except on the trains which serve some of the branch or more obscure lines, hard seat is not in fact hard but padded. But it is hard

on your sanity, and if you're travelling long distance you'll get little sleep on the upright seats. Hard seat carriages get packed to the gills, the lights stay on all night, passengers spit on the floor, you can asphyxiate from cigarette smoke and the carriage speakers endlessly drone news, weather, information and music. Hard seat is OK for a day trip; some foreigners can't take more than five hours of it, while others have a threshold of 12 hours or even longer. A few brave, penniless souls have even been known to travel *long-distance* this way – some roll out a mat on the floor under the seats and go to sleep on top of the gob, chicken bones and peanut shells.

Hard sleepers are comfortable and only a fixed number of people are allowed in the sleeper carriage. The carriage is made up of doorless compartments with six bunks in three tiers, and sheets, pillows and blankets are provided. It does very nicely as a budget hotel. The best bunk to get is a middle one since the lower one is invaded by all and sundry who use it as a seat during the day, and the top one has little headroom. The top bunks are also where the cigarette smoke floats about and it's usually stinking hot up there in summer, even with the fans on full blast. The worst possible bunks are the top ones at either end of the carriage or right in the middle – they're right up against the speakers and you'll get a rude shock at about 6 in the morning. Lights and speakers in hard sleeper go out at around 9.30 to 10 pm. Competition for hard sleepers has become keen in recent years, and you'll be lucky to get one on short notice.

On short journeys (such as Shenzhen to Guangzhou) some trains have soft-seat carriages. The seats are comfortable and overcrowding is not permitted. Smoking is prohibited, a significant advantage unless you enjoy asphyxiation. If you want to smoke in the soft-seat section, you can do so only by going out into the corridor between cars. Soft seats cost about the same as hard sleepers, but it's well worth it. Unfortunately, soft-seat cars are a rarity.

Soft sleeper is the luxury class. Softies get the works, with four comfortable bunks in a

Up in Smoke

China has the world's largest number of smokers, a fact you'll be pointedly reminded of if you travel in the hard-seat section on trains. A typical Chinese smoker puffs away three packs or more daily.

Some Westerners speculate that cigarette smoking is a more effective means of reducing China's population than the one-child family policy. Although the government launched an anti-smoking campaign in 1996, there is little indication that this is being taken seriously. Nor is it likely to be, since tax revenue from tobacco sales is a major source of income for the government. It also seems that few are heeding the warnings to be careful with lit cigarettes – in hotel rooms note the burns in the carpets, bed sheets and furniture. Perhaps it's a good thing that Chinese hotels are made from bricks and concrete rather than wood.

As with drinking hard liquor, smoking in public is largely a male activity – a young woman who smokes in public may be regarded as morally corrupt. This is not to say that no Chinese women smoke, but most who have the habit prefer to light up in private. Conversely, men tend to smoke like chimneys in public and frequently ignore 'no smoking' signs in public places.

If you're the sort of person who gets upset by people smoking in places like buses and restaurants, either change your attitude, leave the country or buy a gas mask – the Chinese typically laugh off any attempts to tell them not to smoke.

The Chinese place considerable prestige value on smoking foreign cigarettes. Brands such as Marlboro, Dunhill and 555 are high-priced and widely available – the ultimate status symbol for aspiring Chinese yuppies. Not surprisingly, the counterfeiting of foreign cigarettes has become a profitable cottage industry. As for rolling your own, you occasionally see the older Chinese doing this, but young people sneer at this proletarian activity – much better to spend a full day's pay on a pack of imported cigarettes.

Many foreigners consider Chinese tobacco to have the gentle aroma of old socks, but some good-quality stuff is grown, mostly in Yunnan Province. Chinese-made Red Pagoda Mountain *(hóng tǎ shān)* smokes cost more than Marlboros. Many foreigners are familiar with Double Happiness *(shuāngxǐ)* cigarettes, the only brand so far that has been developed for export. ■

closed compartment – complete with straps to stop the top fatso from falling off in the middle of the night, wood panelling, potted plants, lace curtains, tea set, clean washrooms, carpets (so no spitting), and often air-con. As for those speakers, not only do you have a volume control, you can turn the bloody things off! Soft sleeper costs twice as much as hard sleeper, and almost the same price as flying (on some routes even *more* than flying!). It's relatively easy to get soft sleeper because few Chinese can afford it. However, the growing class of *nouveaux riches* plus high-ranking cadres (who charge it to their expense accounts) have upped the demand for soft sleepers, so you might wind up in a hard seat no matter how much cash you've got. Travelling in soft sleeper should be experienced once – it gives you a good chance to meet the ruling class.

Guangzhou railway station is a nightmare – mobs of people do battle for a limited number of seats and only the fit survive. Add to that an army of thieves and pickpockets, and it's not hard to see why many foreigners opt for the bus. However, if you want to go

by train, there is a way to be spared all this. Many trains (but not the international train, unfortunately) depart from Guangzhou East station *(guǎngzhōu dōng zhàn)*. This station is newer, considerably cleaner and definitely safer. There is also a special foreigners' ticket window.

Hong Kong

The express train between Hong Kong and Guangzhou is comfortable and convenient. It covers the 182-km route in 2.5 hours.

Departures are from the Kowloon KCR station. You must complete immigration exit formalities at the station before boarding. Therefore, you'd best arrive about 45 minutes before train departure time – the gate closes 20 minutes before the train departs.

When returning to Hong Kong, the toilets on the train close once you cross the border so if you need to use them think about it early. There's a long wait to get through immigration in Hong Kong, and then there are crowds lining up for the loo!

To reach the Kowloon KCR station from Tsim Sha Tsui, take green minibus No 6 from

GUANGZHOU

Hankow Rd (south side of Peking Rd opposite the HMV CD store).

Train No	Depart Kowloon	Arrive Guangzhou
96	8.45am	10.40am
98	9.25am	noon
92	12.45pm	3.10pm
94	3.05pm	5.00pm
100	5.45pm	8.10pm

Train No	Depart Guangzhou	Arrive Kowloon
91	8.30am	11.05am
93	11.30am	1.25pm
95	4.50pm	6.45pm
97	6.15pm	8.45pm
99	1.45pm	4.10pm

The fares vary significantly depending on whether you take the express or normal train, travel in peak or low season and/or ride in first or second class. Nevertheless, the spread isn't very much – bottom-end fares are HK$200 while the priciest ticket costs HK$290. Children's tickets are half price.

In Hong Kong, tickets can be booked up to seven days before departure at CTS or the Kowloon KCR station. Return tickets are also sold, but only seven to 30 days before departure.

In Guangzhou, CITS or CTS both sell train tickets but *not* for same-day departure. Same-day tickets can be bought on the first floor of the Express Departure Area, to your right as you enter Guangzhou railway station.

You're allowed to take bicycles on the express train, and these are stowed in the freight car.

The train ticket in first class includes two free cans of orange drink – the lady clips the corner off your ticket in exchange for the drinks. All the other food being offered on the train must be purchased. It's confusing because there's nothing really to differentiate the freebie drinks from all the others – the cart comes along the aisle and the lady calls out what she's got. I thought at first she was a drink vendor doubling as a ticket collector, so I produced the ticket to oblige and was amazed to receive two free drinks!

Cilla Taylor

Shenzhen

The local hard-seat train from Shenzhen to Guangzhou is cheap and reasonably fast, but there are often long queues for tickets and seats can be difficult to come by at peak times. Hard seats (rock-bottom class) are Y58. Soft seats (de luxe class) cost Y80 and are only available on the express train. There are dozens of trains every day from Shenzhen to Guangzhou, but the schedule changes so often that it's hardly worth quoting here. The trip takes about three hours.

Most local hard-seat trains from Shenzhen terminate at Guangzhou East station. Although the station is far from the centre, it's much cleaner and safer than Guangzhou station where the express trains stop. Buses and minibuses connect the two stations.

In Guangzhou, you can buy train tickets from CITS or hotel service desks several days in advance. Otherwise, you can join the queues at the railway station.

Other

Trains head north from Guangzhou to Beijing, Shanghai and everywhere else in the country except Hainan Island and Tibet. Sleepers can be booked several days in advance at CITS in Guangzhou (east side of Guangzhou station). You can also book domestic railway tickets at CTS in Hong Kong at a steep premium.

In Future A high-speed railway line is being constructed between Hong Kong and Guangzhou which should reduce the trip to perhaps an hour or so. A new line is also under construction from Guangzhou to the Zhuhai Special Economic Zone near Macau. Yet another line is being built up the east coast with the goal of connecting Guangzhou to Fujian Province. Don't expect to be making use of all these marvellous additions to the Chinese railway system for a long while.

BOAT

Travel to China by boat is usually less stressful than the trains or buses. There are fast jet-powered catamarans and slow overnight ferries to major destinations in the Pearl River Delta region. The overnight boats have beds and are generally preferred to fast boats since you sleep through most of the trip and save one night's accommodation in a hotel.

The most popular boat is the overnight ferry to Guangzhou, but another one to consider is the overnight ferry to Zhaoqing. Some travellers make use of the fast catamarans plying the route from Hong Kong to Shenzhen, Huangtian airport (also in Shenzhen), Zhuhai and Zhongshan. For details, see the Getting There & Away sections for these cities in the Around Guangzhou chapter.

CTS is the main booking agent for boats and charges HK$25 for the service. You can get tickets cheaper at the China Hong Kong City terminal on Canton Rd in Kowloon, but the level of English spoken there is low. The ferry company also has a booking office (☎ 2885-3876) at 24 Connaught Rd West, but the language of business there is Cantonese.

Hong Kong

There are two types of ships plying the route between Hong Kong and Guangzhou: jetcat (jet-powered catamaran) and a slow, overnight ferry.

The jetcat (named *Liwanhu*) takes three hours from Hong Kong to Guangzhou. It departs Hong Kong once daily from the China Hong Kong City terminal, Tsim Sha Tsui at 8.15 am and costs HK$208 on week days or HK$183 on weekends and public holidays. In Guangzhou, departures are from Zhoutouzui Wharf at 1 pm. Tickets can be bought at the wharf and some major hotels if you give them enough notice. There are discounts for children. You must pay in Hong Kong dollars even when buying the ticket in Guangzhou!

The Pearl River Shipping Company runs two overnight ferries between Hong Kong and Guangzhou – the *Tianhu* and the *Xinghu*. This is an excellent way to get to Guangzhou from Hong Kong. The ships are clean, fully air-conditioned and have comfortable beds. One ship departs Hong Kong daily from the China Hong Kong City terminal in Tsim Sha Tsui at 9 pm and arrives in Guangzhou the following morning at 6 am (though you cannot disembark until 7

am). In Guangzhou, the other ship departs at 9 pm and arrives in Hong Kong at 6 am. There is no service on the 31st day of the month. The ships have good restaurants, and especially recommended are the dim sum breakfasts available from 6 am onwards.

In Hong Kong, ferry tickets to Guangzhou can be bought at the pier or from CTS. In Guangzhou you can buy tickets at the pier, but you must pay in Hong Kong dollars.

Second class has dormitory beds, which are quite comfortable – the biggest problem might be noisy neighbours. A first-class ticket gets you a bed in a four-person cabin with private bath. Special class is a two-person cabin with bath. VIP class is like your own little hotel room.

The rates (in HK$) for these boats are as follows:

Class	Status	Rates
Special-A	2-bed cabin	470
Special-B	2-bed cabin	265
First	2-bed cabin	230
Second-A	4-bed cabin	195
Second-B	4-bed cabin	185
Third	dormitory	155
Child		91

Bus No 31 (not trolleybus No 31) will drop you off near Houde Lu in Guangzhou, which leads to Zhoutouzui Wharf (see the West Guangzhou map). To get from the wharf to Guangzhou railway station, walk up to the main road, cross to the other side and take bus No 31 all the way to the station.

Wuzhou-Yangshuo

You can purchase a combination boat/bus ticket to make an overnight trip from Guangzhou to Yangshuo via Wuzhou. The boat has dormitory accommodation and is reasonably comfortable. The boat departs from Dashatou Wharf (see the East Guangzhou map) daily at 12.30 pm and terminates at Wuzhou, where you pick up the bus. The combination ticket costs Y75.

From Wuzhou you can return to Hong Kong directly by ship. These depart Wuzhou at 7.30 am on odd-numbered dates and take 10 hours.

Don't pay more than Y50 for the cab ride from Zhoutouzui Wharf to Dashatou Wharf. The drivers ask for Y130 but their meter doesn't go over Y20 for the trip! The boat trip to Wuzhou took a little longer than expected (25 hours) because it became quite foggy after midnight. Nevertheless, the trip was excellent. By sailing west, there was a spectacular sunset that we could see from the front deck. Also, the plate of green peppers and beef that was served at dinner for Y14 was absolutely delicious!

Scott Kerwin

Hainan Island

Boats to Haikou, the capital of Hainan Island, depart daily at 9 am from Guangzhou's Zhoutouzui Wharf at 9 am. The trip takes 25 hours. Starting from second class and moving down-market, prices are Y203, Y157, Y137 and Y115.

ORGANISED TOURS

If time and convenience are more important than money, then the brief tours to Guangzhou from Hong Kong are worth considering. Although expensive, you will never be able to complain about not being shown enough. Itineraries are invariably jam-packed with as much as can possibly be fitted into a day, and the Chinese expect stamina from their guests.

There are innumerable variations on the theme. A tour could just take in Guangzhou, but it could be expanded to include Shenzhen, Zhuhai and Macau. The best information on tours is available from Hong Kong travel agents, CITS or CTS. They all keep a good stock of leaflets and information on a range of tours to China. You usually have to book tours one or two days in advance. Essentially, the same tours can be booked from CTS in Macau.

Judging by the mail we receive at Lonely Planet, many people who have booked extended tours through CTS and CITS have been less than fully satisfied. Although the one-day tours seem to be OK, tours further afield frequently go awry. Most complaints have been about overcharging, substandard accommodation and tours being cut short. No refunds are given if you cancel – you forfeit the full amount.

DEPARTURE TAX

If leaving China by air, the departure tax is Y90. The domestic airport departure tax is Y15. There is no departure tax if you leave by boat.

Getting Around

THE AIRPORT

In Guangzhou, CAAC is at 181 Huanshi Lu, to your left as you come out of Guangzhou railway station. The office is open from 8 am to 8 pm daily. There is an airport bus costing Y10 that runs directly from the CAAC office to Baiyun airport and back again.

Finding a taxi is hardly a problem. Indeed, you'll have to fight off the mass of drivers who greet arriving passengers. In an attempt to create some order, the authorities at Baiyun airport are trying (not always successfully) to get the drivers (and passengers) to line up at a taxi stand. As you'll soon learn, the Chinese are not particularly fond of standing in line.

If you get into a taxi and the driver doesn't turn on the meter immediately, either insist that he does or get out. Negotiating a fixed fare in advance is also possible, though it seldom works out in your favour.

BUS

Guangzhou has an extensive network of buses and trolleybuses which will get you just about anywhere you want to go. The problem is that they are almost always packed. Once an empty bus pulls in at a stop, a battle for seats ensues and a passive crowd suddenly turns into a stampeding herd.

Even more aggravating is the tedious speed at which buses move, accentuated by the drivers' peculiar habit of turning off their motors and letting the bus roll to the next stop. You just have to be patient. Never expect anything to move rapidly and allow lots of time to get to the railway station to catch your train. Sometimes you may find it's best to give up and walk.

When boarding a bus, point to where you want to go on a map so that the conductor (who is seated near the door) will be able to sell you the right ticket. They usually tell you where you have to get off. In the early days of individual travel to China it was common for Chinese to offer their seats to foreigners.

Sorry, but the novelty has worn off and these days you'll stand like everybody else.

Good Chinese maps of the city with bus routes are sold by hawkers outside the railway stations, and at some of the tourist hotel bookshops. Get one! There are too many bus routes to list here, but a few of the important ones are:

No 31
Runs along Gongye Dadao Bei, east of Zhoutouzui Wharf, crosses Renmin Bridge and goes straight up Renmin Lu to Guangzhou railway station at the north of the city.

No 30
Runs from Guangzhou station eastwards along Huanshi Lu before turning down Nonglin Xia Lu to terminate in the far east of the city. This is a convenient bus to take if you want to go from the railway station to the Baiyun or Garden Hotels.

No 5
Starting from Guangzhou railway station, this bus takes a similar route to No 31, but instead of crossing Renmin Bridge it carries on along Liu'ersan Lu, which runs by the northern side of the canal separating the city from Shamian Island. Get off here and walk across the small bridge to the island.

Giving Some Stick

At one bus stop near the Guangzhou railway station I noticed that the company running the buses employs a big guy with a bamboo pole to make sure nobody jumped the queue. When I was there, everyone lined up as they were supposed to. Then someone pulled the usual trick of shoving their way to the front. The big guy yelled 'pai dui!' ('stand in line'). The other guy continued to shove, so was promptly knocked halfway across the car park! I like this bus company.

Chiu Miaoling

TRAIN

Guangzhou is constructing a subway and officially a small section of Line 1 will be opened on 1 July 1997 to coincide with China's takeover of Hong Kong. More realistically, the line won't be fully operational until at least the end of 1998. When completed, it will be 18.5 km long and will have 16 stations. Line 1 will certainly be very useful to visitors; it starts out from Guangdong East railway station, passes major shopping areas along Zhongshan Lu and stops near the popular Shamian Island before terminating on the south side of the Pearl River.

Work has started on Line 2. It will also have 16 stations, but there are already proposals to extend it. It will probably not be opened before the year 2000.

Still on the drawing board is a surface train (light rail transit system) which will run towards east Guangzhou.

TAXI

Taxis are available from the main hotels 24 hours a day. You can also catch a taxi outside the railway stations or hail one in the street – a first for China. Demand for taxis is great, particularly during the peak hours: from 8 to 9 am and during lunch and dinner hours.

Taxis are equipped with meters and drivers use them unless you've negotiated a set fee in advance. The cost depends on what type of vehicle it is. The cost per km (after flagfall) is displayed on a little sticker on the right rear window. For the cheapest taxis, the sticker displays the number 2.00. Flagfall for these taxis is Y7.80, which takes you one km, after which you are charged at the rate of Y2 for every additional km (the meter clicks Y1 for every 500m). The taxis marked Y2.40 cost Y9 at flagfall and Y2.40 per km. Taxis marked Y2.80 cost Y10.20, and thereafter Y2.80 per km.

Taxis can be hired for a single trip or chartered on an hourly or daily basis. The latter is worth considering if you've got the money or if you're in a group which can split the cost. If you hire for a set period of time, negotiate the fee in advance and make it clear which currency you will pay with.

MINIBUS

Minibuses seating 15 to 20 people ply the streets on set routes. If you can find out where they're going, they're a good way to avoid the crowded buses. The front window usually displays a sign with the destination written in Chinese characters.

MOTORBIKE TAXI

A fine example of China's budding free-enterprise reforms, people who own motorcycles hang around railway stations and bus stops to solicit passengers. It is required that passengers wear a safety helmet, and the drivers will supply one. There are no meters on motorcycles, so get the fare established in advance. In general, a ride on a motorcycle will be at least 30% cheaper than a regular taxi.

CAR & MOTORCYCLE

In spite of numerous optimistic rumours and predictions, self-drive rental cars of the Avis and Hertz genre have still not made their debut in Guangzhou. On the other hand, renting a car with a driver is rapidly developing into a cottage industry. Prices are highly negotiable and depend on type of vehicle and distance travelled. In reality, this isn't much different than booking a taxi for a whole day (or several days). Large hotels charge high prices for arranging vehicle rentals. Small hotels charge less, or just try asking a porter or waitress – everyone in Guangzhou seems to have a friend or relative who is doing business.

Resident expats with a Chinese driver's licence can purchase a car and drive it themselves, but there are restrictions on travel outside the city. In general, foreigners are permitted to drive their own vehicles almost anywhere in the Pearl River Delta, but not beyond. This basically means you can drive from Guangzhou to Hong Kong, Macau and all points in between. As for going elsewhere, the rules are ill-defined – trips to Zhaoqing by car seem to be permissible. Foreigners who have gotten in trouble for this particular offence have mostly been caught when checking into hotels far from Guangzhou.

Under certain circumstances, expats can get permission to import a foreign-made vehicle into China duty free.

Driving is on the right side of the road, the opposite to Hong Kong and Macau.

Resident foreigners can also purchase a motorbike, either with or without a sidecar. In China, both driver and passenger are required to wear a safety helmet.

BICYCLE

While China has more bicycles than any other country in the world, they are regarded with disdain. Chinese who ride bicycles do so because it's the only transportation they can afford. The idea of riding for fun mystifies the Chinese. Affluent foreigners who insist on riding a bike simply for pleasure are regarded as loonies.

For this reason, you won't find many bike rental shops in Guangzhou. Shamian Island, which caters to loonies, still has one place that rents bicycles: the Happy Bike Rental Station, opposite the White Swan Hotel and across the road from the Guangzhou Youth Hostel.

A Y200 deposit is required unless you leave your passport. Bicycle theft is a problem, so you'd be wise to buy a cable lock (widely available) and try to leave the bike only in designated bicycle parks where it will be watched by attendants.

WALKING

Guangzhou proper extends for 60 sq km, with most of the interesting sights scattered throughout, so seeing the place on foot is impractical. Just the walk from Guangzhou railway station to the youth hostel on Shamian Island is about six km – good exercise but not recommended for beginning each day's sightseeing.

Guangzhou City

Peasant Movement Institute
(nóngmín yùndòng jiǎngxí suǒ)

Guangzhou's Peasant Movement Institute was built on the site of a Ming dynasty Confucian temple in 1924. In the early days of the Communist party, its members (from all over China) were trained at the Institute. It was set up by Peng Pai, a high-ranking communist leader who believed that if a communist revolution was to succeed in China then the peasants had to be its main force. Mao Zedong – of the same opinion – took over as director of the institute in 1925 or 1926. Zhou Enlai lectured here and one of his students was Mao's brother, Mao Zemin. Peng was executed by the Kuomintang in 1929, and Mao Zemin was executed by a warlord in Xinjiang Province in 1942.

The buildings were restored in 1953 and they're now used as a revolutionary museum. There's not a great deal to see: just a replica of Mao's room, the soldiers' barracks and rifles, and old photographs. The institute is at 42 Zhongshan 4 Lu.

Memorial Garden to the Martyrs
(lièshì língyuán)

This memorial is within walking distance of the Peasant Movement Institute, east along Zhongshan 4 Lu to Zhongshan 3 Lu. It was officially opened in 1957 on the 30th anniversary of the December 1927 Guangzhou uprising.

In April 1927, Chiang Kaishek ordered his troops to massacre communists in Shanghai and Nanjing. On 21 May the communists led an uprising of peasants on the Hunan-Jiangxi border, and on 1 August they staged another in Nanchang. Both uprisings were defeated by Kuomintang troops.

On 11 December 1927 the communists staged another uprising in Guangzhou, but this was also bloodily suppressed by the Kuomintang. The communists claim that over 5700 people were killed around the time of the uprising. The memorial garden is laid out

on Honghuagang ('Red Flower Hill'), which was one of the execution grounds.

There's nothing of particular interest here, though the gardens themselves are attractive. You'll also see the Pavilion of Blood-Cemented Friendship of the Sino-Soviet Peoples and the Pavilion of Blood-Cemented Friendship of the Sino-Korean Peoples.

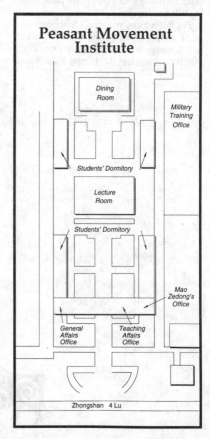

Peasant Movement Institute

Dining Room

Military Training Office

Students' Dormitory

Lecture Room

Students' Dormitory

Mao Zedong's Office

General Affairs Office

Teaching Affairs Office

Zhongshan 4 Lu

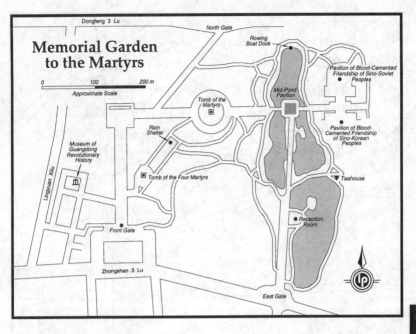

Memorial Garden
to the Martyrs

Dongfeng 3 Lu

North Gate

Rowing
Boat Dock

0   100   200 m
Approximate Scale

Pavilion of Blood-Cemented
Friendship of Sino-Soviet
Peoples

Mid-Pond
Pavilion

Tomb of the
Martyrs

Rain
Shelter

Pavilion of Blood-
Cemented Friendship
of Sino-Korean
Peoples

Museum of
Guangdong
Revolutionary
History

Langyuan Xilu

Tomb of the Four Martyrs

Teahouse

Front Gate

Reception
Room

Zhongshan 3 Lu

East Gate

Mausoleum of the 72 Martyrs & Memorial of Yellow Flowers

(huánghuā gāng qīshí'èr lièshì mù)

This memorial was built in memory of the victims of the unsuccessful Guangzhou insurrection of 27 April 1911. (It was not until October 1911 that the Qing dynasty collapsed and a Republic of China was declared in the south of the country.) The uprising had been planned by a group of Chinese organisations which opposed the Qing and which had formally united at a meeting of representatives in Tokyo in August 1905, with Sun Yatsen as leader.

The memorial was built in 1918 with funds provided by Chinese from all over the world, and was the most famous revolutionary monument of pre-communist China. It's a conglomeration of architectural symbols of freedom and democracy used worldwide, since the outstanding periods of history in the rest of the world were going to be used as guidelines for the new Republic of China.

What that really means is that it's an exercise in architectural bad taste. In front, a small Egyptian obelisk carved with the words 'Tomb of the 72 Martyrs' stands under a stone pavilion. Atop the pavilion is a replica of the Liberty Bell in stone. Behind stands a miniature imitation of the Trianon at Versailles, with the cross-section of a huge pyramid of stone on its roof. Topping things off is a miniature replica of the Statue of Liberty. The Chinese influence can be seen in the bronze urns and lions on each side.

The monument stands on Huanghuagang ('Yellow Flower Hill') on Xianlie Lu, east of the Baiyun and New Garden Hotels.

Sun Yatsen Memorial Hall

(sūn zhōngshān jìniàn táng)

This hall on Dongfeng Lu was built in honour of Sun Yatsen, with donations from overseas Chinese and from Guangzhou citizens. Construction began in January 1929 and finished in November 1931. It stands on

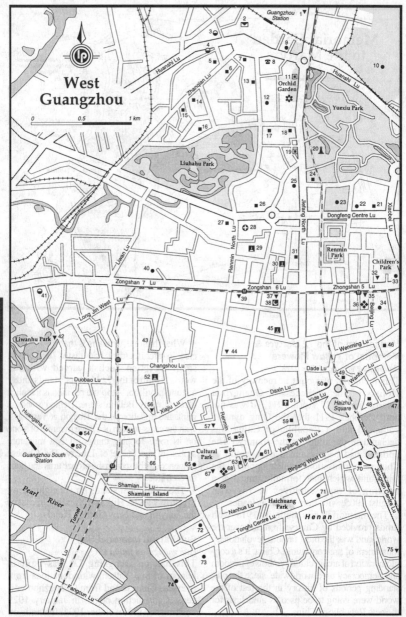

West Guangzhou

0   0.5   1 km

Guangzhou Station

Huanshi Lu

Zhanqian Lu

Liuhahu Park

Renmin North Lu

Orchid Garden

Yuexiu Park

Huanshi Lu

Jiefang North Lu

Dongfeng Centre Lu

Renmin Park

Children's Park

Xiaobei Lu

Zhongshan 5 Lu

Zhongshan 7 Lu

Zongshan 6 Lu

Beijing Lu

Liwan Lu

Long Jin West Lu

Liwanhu Park

Wenming Lu

Changshou Lu

Daxin Lu

Dade Lu

Wanfu Lu

Yide Lu

Haizhu Square

Duobao Lu

Huangsha Lu

Xiajiu Lu

Renmin

Guangzhou South Station

Cultural Park

Yanjiang West Lu

Binjiang West Lu

Shamian Lu

Shamian Island

Pearl River

Tunnel

Huati Lu

Fangcun Lu

Nanhua Lu

Tongfu Centre Lu

Haichuang Park

Henan

Jiangnan Centre Lu

PLACES TO STAY

5 Zhanqian Hotel
站前酒店
6 New Mainland Hotel
新大地宾馆
7 Liuhua Hotel
流花宾馆
13 Hotel Equatorial
贵都酒店
14 Overseas Chinese Hotel
华侨酒店
15 Leizhou Hotel
雷州酒店
16 China Merchants Hotel
招商宾馆
17 Dongfang Hotel
东方宾馆
18 China Hotel & Hasty Tasty Fast Food
中国大酒店
21 Guangdong Building
广东大厦
24 Parkview Square
越秀天安大厦
26 Financial Hotel
金融酒店
27 Hutian Hotel
湖天宾馆
31 Guangdong Guesthouse
广东迎宾馆
46 Lido Hotel
丽都大酒店
48 Hotel Landmark Canton & CTS
华厦大酒店, 中国旅行社
49 Guangzhou Hotel
广州宾馆
58 New Asia Hotel
新亚酒店
59 Furama and GD hotels
富丽华大酒店, 广东大酒店
61 Aiqun Hotel
爱群大厦
63 Xinhua Hotel & Datong Restaurant
新华酒店, 大同饭店
64 White House Hotel
白宫酒店
70 Haizhu Hotel
海珠酒店

PLACES TO EAT

1 Fairwood Fast Food
大快活
32 Taipingguan
太平馆餐厅
35 McDonald's
麦当劳
37 Caigenxiang (Veg) Restaurant
菜根香素菜馆
39 Muslim Restaurant
回民饭店
42 Banxi Restaurant
泮溪酒家

44 McDonald's, Pizza Hut, Watson's
& Park 'n' Shop·
麦当劳, 必胜客, 屈臣氏, 百佳超市
55 Taotaoju Restaurant
陶陶居酒家
56 Guangzhou Restaurant
广州酒家
57 Snake Restaurant
蛇餐馆
60 KFC
肯德基家乡鸡
62 Timmy's Fast Food
添美食
67 Buddhist World Vegetarian
Restaurant
佛世界素食社
75 Pizza Hut & KFC
必胜客, 肯德基家乡鸡

OTHER

2 GPO
邮政总局 (流花邮局)
3 Provincial Bus Station
广东省汽车客运站
4 Guangzhou City Bus Station
广州市汽车客运站
8 Telephone Office
国际电话大楼
9 CAAC & CITS
中国民航, 中国国际旅行社
10 Guangzhou TV Tower
广州电视台
11 Mohammedan Tomb
穆罕默德墓
12 Guangzhou Fair
广州出口商品交易会
19 Southern Yue Tomb Museum
南越王汉墓
20 Sculpture of the Five Rams
五羊石像
22 Provincial Government
省政府
23 Sun Yatsen Memorial Hall
孙中山纪念堂
25 PSB
公安局外事科
28 Guangzhou People's
Hospital No 1
第一人民医院
29 Bright Filial Piety Temple
光孝寺
30 Temple of the Six Banyan Trees
六榕寺花塔
33 Down Jacket & Sleeping
Bag Store
工农服装场
34 Xinhua Bookstore
新华书店
36 Guangzhou Department Store
广州百货大厦

GUANGZHOU

38 Huaisheng Mosque
怀圣寺光塔
40 Chen Clan Academy
陈氏书院, 陈家词
41 Guangfo Bus Station
广佛车站
43 Antique Market
古玩市场
45 Five Genies Temple
五仙观
47 Tianzi Pier
天字码头
50 Guangdong Trade Centre
广东贸易中心
51 Sacred Heart Church
石室教堂
52 Jade Market & Hualin Temple
玉市场, 华林寺
53 The `Dollar Store' 2
谊园
54 The `Dollar Store' 1
谊园
65 Small Antique Market
小古玩市场
66 Qingping Market
清平市场
68 Nanfang Department Store
& Rock Disco
南方大厦, 滚石俱乐部
69 Xidi Pier
西堤码头
71 Guangzhou Daily Supermarket
广州市天天超级商场
72 The Swan Club (bowling alley)
天鹅会俱乐部
73 Massage Service
洪德卫生院, 洪德路洪德五巷
28号地下
74 Zhoutouzui Wharf
洲头嘴码头

the site of the residence of the governor of Guangdong and Guangxi during the Qing dynasty, later used by Sun Yatsen when he became president of the Republic of China. The Memorial Hall is an octagonal Chinese monolith some 47m high and 71m wide; seating capacity is about 4000. The hall is on Dongfeng Centre Lu, opposite Renmin Park.

Temple of the Six Banyan Trees
(liù róng sì huā tǎ)
The temple's history is vague, but it seems that the first structure on this site, called the Precious Solemnity Temple, was built during the 6th century AD, and was ruined by fire in the 10th century. The temple was rebuilt at the end of the 10th century and renamed the Purificatory Wisdom Temple because the monks worshipped Hui Neng, the sixth patriarch of the Zen Buddhist sect. Today it serves as the headquarters of the Guangzhou Buddhist Association.

The temple was given its name by Su Dongpo, a celebrated poet and calligrapher of the Northern Song dynasty who visited the temple in the 11th or 12th century. He was so enchanted by the six banyan trees growing in the courtyard (no longer there) that he contributed two large characters for 'Six Banyans'.

Within the temple compound is the octagonal Flower Pagoda, the oldest and tallest in the city at 55m. Although it appears to have only nine storeys from the outside, inside it has 17. It is said that Bodhidharma, the Indian monk considered to be the founder of the Zen sect, once spent a night here, and owing to the virtue of his presence the pagoda was rid of mosquitoes forever.

The temple stands in central Guangzhou, on Liurong Lu just to the west of Jiefang Beilu. Until a few years ago the three large Buddha statues stood in the open courtyard. The main hall was rebuilt in 1984. The Buddhas have been painted and several other shrines opened. One shrine houses a statue of Hui Neng. The temple complex is now a major tourist attraction.

I would like to suggest that you make a point of reminding readers that many of the temples listed are 'working', they're not there for tourists. At Liu Rong Si...some Americans and French were happily snapping shots of the kneeling worshippers; some even snuck up in front of the altar to do so. My Chinese friend said her blood was close to boiling...she did indeed seem awfully close to losing her temper.

Bright Filial Piety Temple
(guāngxiào sì)
This temple is one of the oldest in Guangzhou. The earliest Buddhist temple on this site possibly dates as far back as the 4th century AD. The place has particular significance for Buddhists because Hui Neng was a novice monk here in the 7th century. The temple buildings are of much more recent

construction, the original buildings having been destroyed by fire in the mid-17th century. The temple is on Hongshu Lu, just west of the Temple of Six Banyan Trees. A section of the complex now houses the Guangdong Antique Store.

Five Genies Temple
(wǔ xiān guān)
This Taoist temple is held to be the site of the appearance of the five rams and celestial beings in the myth of Guangzhou's foundation (see the section on Yuexiu Park).

The stone tablets flanking the forecourt commemorate the various restorations that the temple has undergone. The present buildings are comparatively recent, as the earlier Ming dynasty buildings were destroyed by fire in 1864.

The large hollow in the rock in the temple courtyard is said to be the impression of a celestial being's foot; the Chinese refer to it as the 'Rice-Ear Rock of Unique Beauty'. The great bell, which weighs five tonnes, was cast during the Ming dynasty – it's three metres high, two metres in diameter and about 10 cm thick. It's known as the 'calamity bell', since the sound of the bell, which has no clapper, is a portent of calamity for the city.

At the rear of the main tower stand life-size smiling stone figures which appear to represent four of the five genies. In the temple forecourt are four statues of rams, and inside the temple are inscribed steles.

The temple is south of the Temple of Six Banyan Trees, at the end of an alleyway off Huifu Xilu. Huifu Xilu runs westwards off Jiefang Zhonglu. Hours are from 8.30 to 11.30 am and 2.30 to 5.30 pm daily. Next door is Tom's Gym, whose equipment dates back to the Stone Age.

Sacred Heart Church
(shí shì jiàotáng)
This impressive edifice is known to the Chinese as the 'House of Stone', as it is built entirely of granite. Designed by the French architect Guillemin, the church is an imitation of a European Gothic cathedral. Four bronze bells in a building to the east of the church were cast in France; the original coloured glass was also made in France, but almost all of it is gone.

The site was originally the location of the office of the governor of Guangdong and Guangxi Provinces during the Qing dynasty, but the building was destroyed by British and French troops at the end of the Second Opium War in the 19th century. The area was leased to the French following the signing of the Sino-French Tianjin Treaty. Construction of the church began in 1863 and was completed in 1888. It's on Yide Lu, not far from the riverfront, and is normally closed, except on Sundays when masses are held. All are welcome.

Another church you may find interesting is the Zion Christian Church at 392 Renmin Lu. The building is a hybrid, with traditional European Gothic outlines and Chinese eaves. It's an active place of worship.

Huaisheng Mosque
(huáishèng sì guāng tǎ)
The original mosque on this site is said to have been established in 627 AD by the first Muslim missionary to China, possibly an uncle of Mohammed. The present buildings are of recent construction. The name of the mosque means 'Remember the Sage', in memory of the prophet. Inside the grounds there's a minaret, which because of its flat, even appearance is known as the Guangta or 'Smooth Tower'. The mosque stands on Guangta Lu, which runs eastwards off Renmin Lu.

Mohammedan Tomb & Burial Ground
(mùhǎn mò dé mù)
Situated in the Orchid Garden at the top of Jiefang North Lu, this is thought to be the tomb of the Muslim missionary who built the original Huaisheng Mosque. There are two other Muslim tombs outside the town of Quanzhou on the south-east coast of China, thought to be the tombs of other missionaries sent by Mohammed.

The Guangzhou tomb is in a secluded bamboo grove behind the Orchid Garden; continue past the entrance to the garden, walk through the narrow gateway ahead and take the

GUANGZHOU

GUANGZHOU

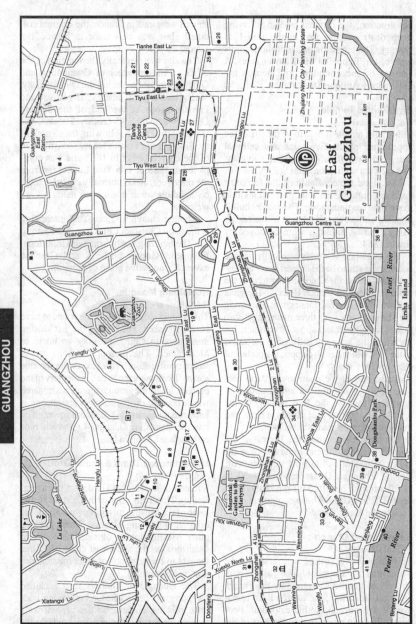

PLACES TO STAY
3 Shahe Hotel
沙河大饭店
4 Star Hotel
景星酒店
5 Zhejiang Building (Fuchun Hotel)
浙江大厦 (富春宾馆)
6 Unic Internatonal Hotel
黄花岗国际酒店
8 Holiday Inn
文化假日酒店
10 Baiyun Hotel
白云宾馆
12 Guangdong International Hotel,
GITIC Plaza & McDonald's
广东国际大厦, 麦当劳
14 Garden Hotel
花园酒店
15 Cathay Hotel
国泰宾馆
16 Huatai Hotel
华泰酒店
17 Ocean Hotel
远洋宾馆
18 Hakkas Hotel
嘉应宾馆
25 Overseas Chinese Friendship Hotel
华侨友谊大厦
28 Tianhe Guesthouse
天河宾馆
30 Dongshan Guesthouse
东山宾馆
35 Foreign Businessmen's Club (hotel)
广东外商活动中心
36 Ramada Pearl Hotel
凯旋华美达酒店
37 Zhujiang Hotel
珠江宾馆
41 GITIC Riverside Hotel
广信江湾大酒店

PLACES TO EAT
2 Luming Restaurant
麓鸣酒家

11 Hill Bar
小山酒吧
13 KFC
肯德基家乡鸡
23 Guangzhou Restaurant Building
广州酒家

OTHER
1 Luhu Golf & Country Club
麓湖高尔夫乡村俱乐部
7 Mausoleum of the 72 Martyrs
黄花岗七十烈士墓
9 Friendship Store & Kathleen's Cafe
友谊商店
19 Meilihua Plaza
美丽华广场
20 Guangzhou Book Centre
广州购书中心
21 American School
美国学校
22 The Greenery
名雅苑
24 Computer Shopping Arcade
广州电脑城
26 Electronics Market
电子品市场
27 Tianhe Shopping Mall
天河城
29 One Love Disco
红风车酒吧
31 Peasant Movement Institute
农民运动讲习所
32 Guangdong Provincial Museum
广东省博物馆
33 Baiyun Lu Bus Station
白云路汽车站
34 Dongshan Department Store
东山百货大楼
38 Clock Market
时钟市场
39 Electronics Market
电子品市场
40 Dashatou Wharf
大沙头码头

GUANGZHOU

narrow stone path on the right. Behind the tomb compound are Muslim graves and a monumental stone arch. The tomb came to be known as the 'Tomb of the Echo' or the 'Resounding Tomb' because of the noises that reverberate in the inner chamber.

Pearl River
(zhūjiāng)
The northern bank of the Pearl River is one

of the most interesting areas of Guangzhou; filled with people, markets and dilapidated buildings. Before the communists came to power, the waterfront on the south side of the Pearl River was notorious for its gambling houses and opium dens. It's fair to say that things have changed a bit.

One of the best ways to see the river is to take the Pearl River Cruise (hǎishàng lèyuán), which is actually a restaurant ship.

There is a lunch cruise from 11 am to 2 pm and a dinner cruise from 5 to 8 pm. The trip is popular with both Chinese and foreigners. Departures are from the Xidi ferry pier near the Nanfang Department Store.

Liu'ersan Lu
(liù'èrsān lù)
Just before you reach the south end of Renmin Lu, Liu'ersan Lu heads west. 'Liu' er san' means '6 2 3', referring to 23 June 1925, when British and French troops fired on striking Chinese workers during the Hong Kong-Guangzhou Strike.

Qingping Market
(qīngpíng shìchǎng)
A short walk east on Liu'ersan Lu takes you to the second bridge connecting the city to the north side of Shamian Island. Directly opposite the bridge, on the city side, is the entrance to Qingping Market on Qingping Lu – Guangzhou's largest and most interesting market.

The market came into existence in 1979. Although such private markets are a feature of all Chinese cities today, it was one of Deng Xiaoping's more radical economic experiments at that time. Deng probably did not realise that he was also creating one of Guangzhou's more radical tourist attractions – if you want to buy, kill or cook it yourself, this is the place to come since the market is more like a takeaway zoo. Near the entrance you'll find the usual selection of medicinal herbs and spices, dried starfish, snakes, lizards, deer antlers, dried scorpions, leopard and tiger skins, bear paws, semi-toxic mushrooms and bark.

Further up you'll find death row, where sad-eyed monkeys rattle at the bars of their wooden cages; tortoises crawl over each other in shallow tin trays; owls sit perched on boxes full of pigeons; and fish paddle around in small tubs. Here you can get bundles of frogs, live scorpions (some people like them fresh), giant salamanders, pangolins, dogs, cats and raccoons, alive or contorted by recent violent death – which may just swear you off meat for the next few weeks.

The market spills out into Tiyun Lu, which cuts east-west across Qingping Lu. Further north is another area supplying vegetables, flowers, potted plants and goldfish. There are small food stalls in the streets on the perimeter of the market – very cheap.

Shamian Island
(shāmiàn)
Liu'ersan Lu runs parallel to the north bank of Shamian Island. The island is separated from the rest of Guangzhou by a narrow canal on one side and the Pearl River on the other. Until recently, five bridges connected the island to the city. Now, land reclamation on the west side has made the island part of the mainland.

Shamian means 'Sand Surface', which is all the island was until the 18th century, when foreigners were permitted to set up their warehouses here. Land reclamation gradually increased the area to its largest pre-reclamation size: 900m from east to west, and 300m from north to south. With the defeat of the Chinese in the Opium Wars in 1861, Shamian became a British and French concession, essentially making it a free-trade zone. The European presence left its mark – Shamian is covered with decaying colonial buildings which housed trading offices and residences. The Europeans got the boot when Japan invaded China during WWII and Shamian returned to Chinese control in 1946.

The French Catholic church has been restored and stands on the main boulevard. The old British church at the western end of the island has been turned into a workshop, but is betrayed by bricked-up, Gothic-style windows. Today most of the buildings are used as offices or apartment blocks and the area retains a quiet residential atmosphere, detached from the bustle across the canals.

Another 30,000 sq metres of land was added to the south bank of the island for the site of the 35-storey White Swan Hotel, which was built in the early 1980s. It's worth a walk along the north bank of Shamian Island to get a view of the houses on Liu'ersan

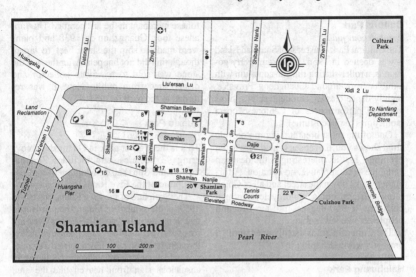

Shamian Island

0   100   200 m

Pearl   River

1 Hospital of Traditional   Chinese
  Medicine
  中医医院
2 Qingping Market
  清平市场
3 Silver Palace Restaurant
  银宫大酒楼
4 Victory Hotel (new annex)
  胜利宾馆 (新楼)
5 Post Office
  邮局
6 Hot Gossip Bar & Coffee Shop
  嘉宾廊西餐厅
7 Victory Hotel
  胜利宾馆
8 Victory Bakery
  胜利饼屋
9 German Consulate
  德国领事馆
10 Kiu Mei Restaurant
  侨美食家
11 Li Qin Restaurant
  利群饮食店

12 Polish Consulate
   波兰领事馆
13 Shamian Bar
   沙面吧
14 Happy Bike Rental Station
   租自行车店
15 US Consulate
   美国领事馆
16 White Swan Hotel
   白天鹅宾馆
17 Guangzhou Youth Hostel
   广州青年招待所
18 Shamian Hotel
   沙面宾馆
19 New Litchi Bay Restaurant
   新荔枝湾酒楼
20 Lucy's Bar & Cafe
   露丝咖啡室
21 Bank of China
   中国银行
22 Chicago Coffee Shop
   芝加哥咖啡馆

GUANGZHOU

across the canal – the dilapidated three- and four-storey terrace houses, probably dating to the 1920s and 1930s, make a pretty sight in the morning or evening sun. A few buildings of much the same design survive in the back streets of Hong Kong Island.

Just near the island, by the riverbank on Yanjiang West Lu near the Renmin Bridge overpass, stands the Monument to the Martyrs of the Shaji Massacre (as the 1925 massacre was known).

Cultural Park

(wénhuà gōngyuán)

The Cultural Park – just east of Shamian Island – was opened in 1956. Inside are merry-go-rounds, a roller-skating rink, an aquarium with exhibits from around Guangdong Province, nightly dance classes, acrobatic shows, films and live performances of Cantonese opera (sometimes in full costume).

One of the most breathtaking motorcycle stunt shows you'll ever see is held here in the evenings. Just as interesting is the deadpan audience – no applause, no reaction. A foreigner walks down the street and all of China turns to stare, but a motorcycle stuntman performs a 360-degree mid-air flip and people act like it's nothing.

The Cultural Park is usually open until 10 pm – it's worth dropping in.

Haichuang Park

(hǎichuáng gōngyuán)

Renmin Bridge stands just east of Shamian Island and connects the north bank of the Pearl River to the area of Guangzhou known as Henan, the site of Haichuang Park. This would be a nondescript park but for the remains of what was once Guangzhou's largest monastery, the Ocean Banner Monastery. It was founded by a Buddhist monk in 1662, and in its heyday the monastery grounds covered 2.5 hectares. After 1911 the monastery was used as a school and army barracks. It was opened to the public as a park in the 1930s. Though the three colossal images of the Buddha have gone, the main hall remains and is now used at night as a dance hall. During the day the grounds are full of old men chatting, playing cards and chequers, and airing their pet birds.

The large stone which decorates the fish pond at the entrance on Tongfu Centre Lu is considered by the Chinese to be a tiger struggling to turn around. The stone came from Lake Tai in Jiangsu Province. During the Qing dynasty the wealthy used these rare, strangely shaped stones to decorate their gardens. Many are found in the gardens of the Forbidden City in Beijing. This particular stone was brought back by a wealthy Cantonese merchant in the last century. The Japanese took Guangzhou in 1938 and plans were made to ship the stone back to Japan, though this did not happen. After the war the stone was sold to a private collector and disappeared from public view. It was returned to the park in 1951.

Yuexiu Park

(yuèxiù gōngyuán)

This is the biggest park in Guangzhou, covering 93 hectares, and includes Zhenhai Tower, the Sun Yatsen Monument and the Sculpture of the Five Rams.

The Sculpture of the Five Rams, erected in 1959, is the symbol of Guangzhou. It is said that long ago five celestial beings wearing robes of five colours came to Guangzhou riding through the air on rams. Each carried a stem of rice, which they presented to the people as an auspicious sign from heaven that the area would be free from famine forever. Guangzhou

The Sculpture of the Five Rams, erected in 1959, is the symbol of Guangzhou.

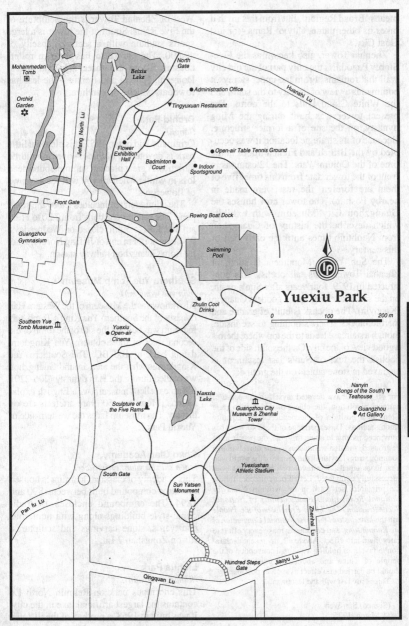

Mohammedan Tomb

Orchid Garden

Beixiu Lake

North Gate

Administration Office

Tingyuxuan Restaurant

Huanshi Lu

Jiefang North Lu

Flower Exhibition Hall

Open-air Table Tennis Ground

Badminton Court

Indoor Sportsground

Front Gate

Rowing Boat Dock

Guangzhou Gymnasium

Swimming Pool

Zhulin Cool Drinks

Yuexiu Park

0   100   200 m

Southern Yue Tomb Museum

Yuexiu Open-air Cinema

Nanxiu Lake

Nanyin (Songs of the South) Teahouse

Sculpture of the Five Rams

Guangzhou City Museum & Zhenhai Tower

Guangzhou Art Gallery

South Gate

Yuexiushan Athletic Stadium

Sun Yatsen Monument

Zhenhai Lu

Pan fu Lu

Hundred Steps Gate

Jiaoyu Lu

Qingquan Lu

GUANGZHOU

means 'Broad Region', but from this myth it takes its other name, City of Rams – or just Goat City.

Zhenhai Tower, also known as the Five-Storey Pagoda, is the only part of the old city wall that remains. From the upper storeys it commands a view of the city to the south and the White Cloud Hills to the north. The present tower was built during the Ming dynasty, on the site of a former structure. Because of its strategic location it was occupied by the British and French troops at the time of the Opium Wars. The 12 cannons in front of the tower date from this time (five of them are foreign, the rest were made in nearby Foshan). The tower now houses the Guangzhou City Museum with exhibits which describe the history of Guangzhou from Neolithic times until the early part of this century.

The Sun Yatsen Monument is south of Zhenhai Tower. This tall obelisk was constructed in 1929, four years after Sun's death, on the site of a temple to the goddess Guanyin (Kuanyin). The obelisk is built of granite and marble blocks. There's nothing to see inside, though a staircase leads to the top where there's a good view of the city. On the south side of the obelisk the text of Sun's last testament is engraved in stone tablets on the ground:

For 40 years I have devoted myself to the cause of national revolution, the object of which is to raise China to a position of independence and equality among nations. The experience of these 40 years has convinced me that to attain this goal, the people must be aroused, and that we must associate ourselves in a common struggle with all the people of the world who treat us as equals. The revolution has not yet been successfully completed. Let all our comrades follow the principles set forth in my writings *Plans for National Renovation*, *Fundamentals of National Reconstruction*, *The Three Principles of the People* and the *Manifesto of the First National Convention of the Kuomintang*, and continue to make every effort to carry them into effect. Above all, my recent declaration in favour of holding a national convention of the people of China and abolishing unequal treaties should be carried into effect as soon as possible.

This is my last will and testament.

(Signed) Sun Wen
11 March, 1925

West of Zhenhai Tower is the Sculpture of the Five Rams. South of the tower is a large sports stadium with a seating capacity of 40,000. The park also has its own roller-coaster. There are three artificial lakes: Dongxiu, Nanxiu and Beixiu – the last has rowboats which you can hire.

Orchid Park
(lánpǔ)

Originally laid out in 1957, this pleasant little park is devoted to orchids – over a hundred varieties. A great place in summer, but a dead loss in winter when all you will see are rows of flowerpots.

The admission fee includes tea by the small pond. The park is open daily from 7.30 to 11.30 am and 1.30 to 5 pm; closed on Wednesdays. It's at the northern end of Jiefang North Lu, not far from Guangzhou railway station.

Southern Yue Tomb Museum
(nán yuè wáng mù)

Also known as the Museum of the Western Han dynasty of the Southern Yue King's Tomb, this museum was built on the site of the tomb of the second ruler of the Southern Yue Kingdom, dating back to 100 BC. The Southern Yue Kingdom is what the area around Guangzhou was called during the Han dynasty (206-220). It's an excellent museum with English explanations. More than 500 rare artefacts are on display. The museum faces the western side of Yuexiu Park.

Chen Clan Academy
(chén shì shū yuàn; chén jiā cí)

This academy of classical learning is housed in a large compound built between 1890 and 1894. The compound encloses 19 traditional-style buildings along with numerous courtyards, stone carvings and sculptures. It's on Zongshan 7 Lu.

Liuhua Park
(liúhuā gōngyuán)

This enormous park on Renmin North Lu contains the largest artificial lake in the city. It was built in 1958, a product of the ill-fated

Great Leap Forward. The entrance to the park is on Renmin North Lu.

Guangzhou Zoo
(guăngzhōu dòngwùyuán)
The zoo was built in 1958 and is one of the better zoos you'll see in China, which is perhaps not saying much. It's on Xianlie Lu, east of the Mausoleum of the 72 Martyrs.

Guangdong Provincial Museum
(guăngdōng shĕng bówùguăn)
The museum houses exhibitions of archaeological finds from around Guangdong Province, but overall isn't too good. You'll find it at the corner of Yuexiu North Lu and Wenming Lu, one big block south of the Peasant Movement Institute.

Zhongshan University
(zhōngshān dàxué)
On Yan'an 2 Lu, the university houses the Lu Xun Museum *(lŭ xùn bówùguăn)*. Lu Xun (1881-1936) was one of China's great modern writers; he was not a Communist though most of his books were banned by the Kuomintang. He taught at the university in 1927.

Sanyuanli
(sānyuánlĭ)
In the area north of Guangzhou railway station is the nondescript neighbourhood of Sanyuanli. Today, it's an area of factories and apartment blocks, which obscures the fact that this place was notable for its role in the first Opium War. A Chinese leaflet relates that:

In 1840, the British imperialists launched the opium war against China. No sooner had the British invaders landed on the western outskirts of Guangzhou on 24 May 1841 than they started to burn, slaughter, rape and loot the local people. All this aroused Guangzhou people's great indignation. Holding high the great banner of anti-invasion, the heroic people of Sanyuanli together with the people from the nearby 103 villages took an oath to fight against the enemy at Sanyuan Old Temple. On 30 May, they lured the British troops to the place called Niulangang where they used hoes, swords and spears as weapons and annihilated over 200 British invaders armed with rifles and cannons. Finally the British troops were forced to withdraw from the Guangzhou area.

A little-visited monument *(kàngyīng jìniàn bēi)* commemorates the struggle that took place at Sanyuanli. You pass Sanyuanli on your way from Guangzhou to Baiyun airport.

Guangzhou Fair
(zhōngguó chūkŏu shāngpĭn jiāoyì huì)
Apart from the Chinese Lunar New Year, this is the biggest event in Guangzhou. The name implies that this is a fair with circus acts, clowns and balloons for the kiddies. In fact, it's nothing of the sort. The Guangzhou Fair is otherwise known as the Chinese Export Commodities Fair and is mostly of interest to businesspeople who want to conduct foreign trade with China. The fair aims to promote China's exports, although it is a good place to make business contacts which could be helpful later in China. The fair is held twice a year, during the last 20 days in April and October.

The fair takes place in the large exhibition hall across the street from the Dongfang Hotel, near the intersection of Liuhua Lu and Renmin North Lu. During the rest of the year, when there is no fair, the building sits unused. Unfortunately, the fair is not open to everybody who would like to attend. You must first receive an invitation from one of China's national foreign trade corporations (FTC).

Getting an invitation takes some effort. Those who have previously done business with an FTC should automatically receive an invitation. Those who have never done business with China should apply to China Travel Service (CTS) in Hong Kong. They need several days to process an application.

There are some very interesting goods on display at the fair – everything from electric fans to AK-47s. While it's occasionally possible to buy samples, prospective shoppers are liable to feel frustrated since most of these items are not for retail sale. On the other hand, if you'd like to purchase 40 container loads of Chinese-made silk stockings, this is the place to do it.

The Guangzhou Fair is important to travellers for one reason – this is the traditional time for hotels to double and even triple their

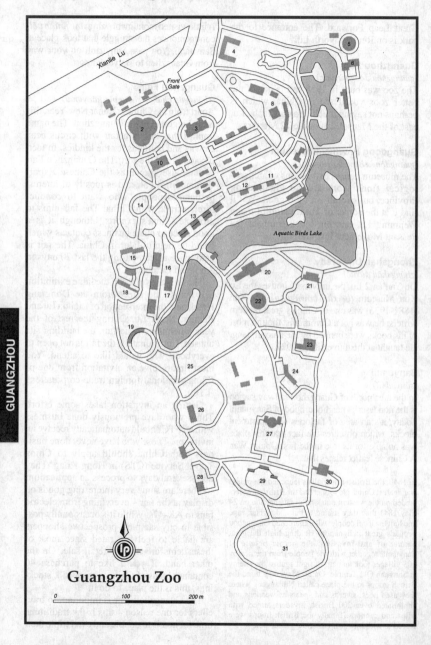

Xianlie Lu

Front Gate

Aquatic Birds Lake

GUANGZHOU

Guangzhou Zoo

0   100   200 m

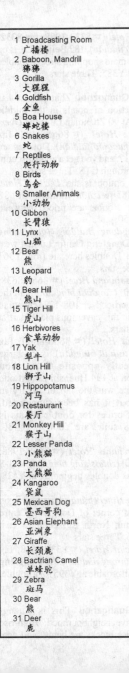

1 Broadcasting Room
　广播楼
2 Baboon, Mandrill
　狒狒
3 Gorilla
　大猩猩
4 Goldfish
　金鱼
5 Boa House
　蟒蛇楼
6 Snakes
　蛇
7 Reptiles
　爬行动物
8 Birds
　鸟舍
9 Smaller Animals
　小动物
10 Gibbon
　长臂猿
11 Lynx
　山猫
12 Bear
　熊
13 Leopard
　豹
14 Bear Hill
　熊山
15 Tiger Hill
　虎山
16 Herbivores
　食草动物
17 Yak
　犁牛
18 Lion Hill
　狮子山
19 Hippopotamus
　河马
20 Restaurant
　餐厅
21 Monkey Hill
　猴子山
22 Lesser Panda
　小熊猫
23 Panda
　大熊猫
24 Kangaroo
　袋鼠
25 Mexican Dog
　墨西哥狗
26 Asian Elephant
　亚洲象
27 Giraffe
　长颈鹿
28 Bactrian Camel
　单峰驼
29 Zebra
　斑马
30 Bear
　熊
31 Deer
　鹿

prices. Even the Guangzhou Youth Hostel charges double prices while the fair is on. The excuse for overcharging is the alleged 'shortage' of hotel rooms, but I've been in Guangzhou during the fair and had no difficulty obtaining accommodation. Upmarket restaurants also raise prices during the fair. But if you don't mind paying the rip-off rates, there is no particular reason to avoid Guangzhou during the fair.

PLACES TO STAY
Places to Stay – bottom end
South-West Guangzhou Shamian Island remains a popular place to look for cheapish hotels in reasonably pleasant and quiet surroundings. To get to there, take bus No 5 from Huanshi Lu; the stop is on the opposite side of the road and just to the west of Guangzhou railway station. The bus runs along Liu'ersan Lu on the northern boundary of the canal which separates Shamian Island from the rest of Guangzhou. Four footbridges connect Shamian Island to the city.

Near the massive White Swan Hotel is the *Guangzhou Youth Hostel* (☎ 8188-4298) *(guǎngzhōu qīngnián zhāodàisuǒ)* at 2 Shamian 4-Jie. By default, this place wins the title of 'backpackers' headquarters' in Guangzhou since there is almost nothing else in this price range open to foreigners. The hostel was gutted by a fire in 1992 but has now been reopened with fancy decor. The dormitories have just three beds per room and cost Y60 per person. Double rooms are Y120 to Y190.

North-West Guangzhou Near Guangzhou railway station is the *Zhanqian Hotel* (☎ 8667-0348) *(zhànqián jiǔdiàn)*, 81 Zhanqian Lu. This place is a bargain (for Guangzhou at least) with twin rooms costing Y200.

Places to Stay – middle
South-West Guangzhou The *Shamian Hotel* (☎ 8191-2288; fax 8191-0268) *(shāmiàn bīnguǎn)*, 52 Shamian Nanjie, is only a few steps to the east of the Guangzhou Youth Hostel on Shamian Island. Doubles with twin beds start at Y280. Two stars.

GUANGZHOU

At 53 Shamian Beijie is the *Victory Hotel* (☎ 8186-2622; fax 8186-2413) *(shènglì bīnguǎn)*. There's a lack of English signs, but the hotel is easily identified – it looks like a seafood restaurant with big fish tanks outside. Doubles are Y300 to Y350, suites are Y420. Rooms in the luxurious new annex are Y375. Three stars.

The *Aiqun Hotel* (☎ 8186-6668; fax 8188-3519) *(aìqún dà jiǔdiàn)* is at 113 Yanjiang West Lu (at the corner of Changdi Lu). Opened in 1937 but fully refurbished, this grand old place overlooks the Pearl River. Given the high standards, prices are reasonable at Y212/308 for singles/doubles. Pricier rooms have a riverfront view. The hotel seems to have restaurants tucked away in every corner, including one on the rooftop that revolves. Three stars.

The *White House Hotel* (☎ 8188-2313; fax 8188-9161) *(bái gōng jiǔdiàn)* at 17 Renmin Lu is a pleasant and friendly place. Doubles are Y422.

Across the street from the White House is the *New Asia Hotel* (☎ 8188-4722) *(xīnyà jiǔdiàn)*, 10 Renmin Lu, where doubles are Y278. The hotel is an old but elegant-looking place popular with Hong Kongers. Two stars.

Just to the south of the New Asia is the *Xinhua Hotel* (☎ 8188-2688; fax 886-8809) *(xīnhuá dà jiǔdiàn)* at 4 Renmin Lu. Another large, Chinese-speaking place geared towards the Hong Kong crowd, rooms are Y422. Two stars.

The *Nanfang Hotel (nánfāng dàshà)* is a huge place, yet it's a little hard to find the entrance because the hotel sits atop the Nanfang Department Store on Yanjiang West Lu. Doubles in this building cost Y278. Two stars.

The *GD Hotel* (☎ 8188-3601; fax 8188-3667) *(guǎngdōng dà jiǔdiàn)* is at 294 Changdi Lu, one block north of the Aiqun Hotel and next to the fancier Furama Hotel. It's a large and attractive hotel with rooms for Y395. Two stars.

The *Furama Hotel* (☎ 8186-3288; fax 8186-3388) *(fùlìhuá dà jiǔdiàn)*, 316 Changdi Lu is a splashy place near the river. Rooms start at Y400. Three stars.

The *Lido Hotel* (☎ 8332-1988; fax 8332-3413) *(lìdū dà jiǔdiàn)*, 182 Beijing Lu, is on Guangzhou's main shopping street. Doubles are Y363 and Y385. Three stars.

North-West Guangzhou Zhanqian Lu has a large collection of hotels in the middle price range. At 90 Zhanqian Lu is the *Overseas Chinese Hotel* (☎ 8666-3488; fax 8666-3230) *(huáqiáo jiǔdiàn)*. Doubles are Y353 and Y417, and you get a good discount by booking through CTS. Three stars.

A popular option is the *Leizhou Hotel* (☎ 8668-1688) *(léizhōu jiǔdiàn)* at 88 Zhanqian Lu. Rooms are priced between Y250 and Y350.

The *Guangdong Building (guǎngdōng dàshà)* is on Dongfeng Centre Lu just west of Xiaobei Lu. Doubles here are from Y363 to Y470. Three stars.

The *New Mainland Hotel* (☎ 8667-8638; fax 8667-6880) *(xīn dàdì bīnguǎn)* is in the same neighbourhood at 108-122 Zhanqian Lu. Doubles in this cavernous place start at Y315. Three stars.

The *Liuhua Hotel* (☎ 8666-8800; fax 8666-7828) *(liúhuā bīnguǎn)*, is the large building directly opposite Guangzhou railway station at 194 Huanshi Lu. At one time this place was the lap of luxury in Guangzhou but it has been superseded. The range of prices for double rooms is Y360 to Y398, suites are Y600 to Y1480. Three stars.

China Merchants Hotel (☎ 8668-1988; fax 8666-2680) *(zhāoshāng bīnguǎn)*, 111-8 Liuhua Lu, has doubles beginning at Y428. Three stars.

The *Hutian Hotel (hútiān bīnguǎn)* is on the south-west corner of Dongfeng Centre Lu and Renmin North Lu. Doubles cost Y300 to Y375. Three stars.

The *Financial Hotel* (☎ 8332-1688; fax 8331-4477) *(jīnróng jiǔdiàn)*, 199 Dongfeng Centre Lu, is affordable at Y395 for a double. Three stars.

North-East Guangzhou This is Guangzhou's exclusive neighbourhood. High-rise hotels and office blocks are being built here like mad. If there's any part of Guangzhou determined to mimic Hong Kong's skyscraper canyons, this is it.

The *Hakkas Hotel* (☎ 8777-1688; fax 8777-0788) *(jiāyìng bīnguǎn)*, 418 Huanshi Lu, is aimed at the business traveller. Standard/de luxe doubles are Y353/417. Three stars.

Zhejiang Building (☎ 8777-2998; fax 8775-3564) *(zhèjiāng dàshà)*, 85 Xianlie Lu, is also known as the *Fuchun Hotel (f'chūn bīnguǎn)*. Prices start at Y250.

Huatai Hotel (☎ 8778-9888; fax 8778-8118) *(huátài jiǔdiàn)*, 23 Xianlie Lu has rooms beginning at Y260.

Shahe Hotel (☎ 8770-5998) *(shāhé dà fàndiàn)*, 318 Xianlie Lu. Low-end rooms here are Y220.

The *Overseas Chinese Friendship Hotel* (☎ 8551-3298; fax 8750-1823) *(huáqiáo yǒuyí dàshà)*, 44 Tianhe East Lu. You can get a good double here for Y270.

Tianhe Guesthouse (☎ 8551-5888; fax 8551-4996) *(tiānhé bīnguǎn)*, 188 Tianhe Lu has rooms from Y240.

The *Unic International Hotel* (☎ 8775-8888; fax 8775-8618) *(huánghuā gǎng guójì jiǔdiàn)*, 96 Xianlie Lu has rooms starting from Y370.

The *Star Hotel (jǐngxīng jiǔdiàn)*, Linhe Xilu, is just south of Guangzhou East railway station. This new place was offering deep discounts at the time of writing. Doubles can be had for Y365. Four stars.

South-East Guangzhou Honourable mention goes to the *Foreign Businessmen's Club* (☎ 8731-1288; fax 8737-9288) *(wàishāng huódòng zhōngxīn)*, 293 Guangzhou Centre Lu. You don't have to be a businessman to stay here, but you do have to pay at least Y430 for a double.

The *Zhujiang Hotel (zhūjiāng bīnguǎn)* is in a small park two blocks west of the Ramada Pearl Hotel. Doubles begin at Y360.

Places to Stay – top end
North-West Guangzhou The *Hotel Equatorial* (☎ 8667-2888; fax 8667-2582) *(guìdū jiǔdiàn)*, 931 Renmin North Lu, is a short walk from Guangzhou railway station and offers plush doubles for Y512. Four stars.

Parkview Square (☎ 8666-5666; fax 8667-1741) *(yuèxiù tiān'ān dàshà)*, 960 Jiefang North Lu, has doubles at Y556. Three stars.

The *Guangdong Guesthouse* (☎ 8333-2950; fax 8333-2911) *(guǎngdōng yíng bīnguǎn)*, 603 Jiefang North Lu, has standard/de luxe doubles for Y430/535. It's an exclusive-looking place with its own grounds and a wall around it. A sign by the lobby reminds you that 'proper attire' is required at all times. This place is about half way between Guangzhou railway station and the Pearl River. Three stars.

The *Dongfang Hotel* (☎ 8666-9900; fax 8668-1618) *(dōng fāng bīnguǎn)* is at 120 Liuhua Lu near Jiefang North Lu and next to the China Hotel. One of the greatest attractions is the beautiful garden in the hotel's central courtyard, where there are a number of restaurants. Singles/doubles begin at Y556/663. It's about a 15-minute walk from Guangzhou railway station and bus No 31 runs right by. Five stars.

Towering over the Dongfang Hotel is the gleaming *China Hotel* (☎ 8666-6888; fax 8667-7014) *(zhōngguó dà jiǔdiàn)*, which boasts wall-to-wall marble, a disco and a bowling alley. Doubles are Y1166, Y1332 and Y1749. Five stars.

The *Central Hotel* (☎ 8657-8331; fax 8659-2316) *(zhōngyāng jiǔdiàn)*, 33 Jichang Lu, is north of Guangzhou railway station on the way to the airport. Doubles begin at Y525. Four stars.

South-West Guangzhou The *White Swan Hotel* (☎ 8188-9891; fax 8186-1188) *(báitiāné bīnguǎn)*, 1 Shamian Nanjie, is one of the few hotels in the world to boast a waterfall in the lobby. Other amenities include a pool, sauna, disco and a great location on Shamian Island. The hotel has played host to some of China's biggest big shots, including Deng Xiaoping. If you're not wearing a necktie or high heels, you'll feel the glaring hostility from the staff – the management is trying to scare off backpackers who wander in to cash travellers' cheques, buy magazines, send faxes and so on. In the process, the hotel is also scaring off their guests. Doubles with discount begin at Y727. Five stars.

The *Guangzhou Hotel* (☎ 8333-8168; fax 8333-0791) *(guǎngzhōu bīnguǎn)* is at Haizhu Square. The square's name means 'sea pearl' though some Westerners have dubbed the place 'McDonald's Square' due to a certain restaurant's prominence here. Doubles cost Y483 and Y504.

Also on Haizhu Square is the *Hotel Landmark Canton* (☎ 8335-5988; fax 8333-6197) *(huáshà dà jiǔdiàn)*. Rates for standard doubles are Y581 and range up to Y2700 for a suite. Four stars.

South-East Guangzhou The *GITIC Riverside Hotel* (☎ 8383-9888; fax 8381-4448) *(guǎngxìn jiāngwān dà jiǔdiàn)*, 298 Yanjiang Lu, is a towering new place overlooking the river. Doubles are Y481 to Y642. Four stars.

The *Ramada Pearl Hotel* (☎ 8737-2988; fax 8737-7481) *(kǎixuán huáměidá jiǔdiàn)*, 9 Mingyue 1 Lu (near the waterfront) is a favourite in this development area of the city. Doubles cost Y605. Four stars.

North-East Guangzhou The *Baiyun Hotel* (☎ 8333-3998; fax 8333-6498) *(báiyún bīnguǎn)*, 367 Huanshi Dong Lu, is one of the oldest (but still excellent) hotels in this part of town. Doubles begin at Y420. Three stars.

Opposite the Baiyun Hotel is the *Garden Hotel* (☎ 8333-8989; fax 8335-0467) *(huāyuán jiǔdiàn)* at 368 Huanshi Lu. This place positively drips with elegance; it's one of the most spectacular hotels in China. The hotel is topped by a revolving restaurant, and there's a snooker hall and a lobby large enough to park a jumbo jet. Doubles start at Y750. Five stars.

Also in the same neighbourhood is the *Ocean Hotel* (☎ 8776-5988; fax 8776-5475) *(yuǎnyáng bīnguǎn)* 412 Huanshi Lu. Doubles begin at Y400. Three stars.

Immediately to the north-west of the Ocean Hotel is the *Holiday Inn* (☎ 8776-6999; fax 8775-3126) *(wénhuà jiàrì*

jiǔdiàn), 28 Guangming Lu (a tiny side street off Huanshi Lu). Doubles are from Y620. Four stars.

Yuehai Hotel (☎ 8777-9688; fax 8778-8364) *(yuèhǎi dàsha')* is far to the north-east at 472 Huanshi Donglu. Standard doubles start at Y230 and fancier rooms are Y550 and Y575.

The *Cathay Hotel* (☎ 8386-2888; fax 8384-2606) *(guótài bīnguǎn)*, 376 Huanshi Donglu, is slightly cheaper than its neighbours at Y385 for a double. Three stars.

At 63 storeys, the *Guangdong International Hotel* (☎ 8331-1888; fax 8331-1666) *(guǎngdōng guójì dà jiǔdiàn)*, 339 Huanshi Lu, was once the tallest building in China. The building is also known as *GITIC Plaza*. Home of Guangzhou's first McDonald's, this edifice probably rates as a tourist attraction in itself. Doubles rooms start at Y684. Five stars.

South of the River The south side of the Pearl River is a rapidly developing area. The best place in this district is the *Plaza Canton Hotel* (☎ 8441-8888; fax 8441-2695) *(jiāngnán dà jiǔdiàn)*, 348 Jiangnan Lu. Doubles begin from Y406. Four stars.

The *Haizhu Hotel* (☎ 8444-9711), 4 Jiangnan Centre Lu is just over the bridge. Doubles begin at Y330.

PLACES TO EAT

The Chinese have a saying: to enjoy the best in life, one has to be 'born in Suzhou, live in Hangzhou, eat in Guangzhou and die in Liuzhou'. Suzhou is renowned for beautiful women, Hangzhou for scenery and Liuzhou for the finest wood for coffin-making. It's too late for me to be born in Suzhou, I don't like the weather in Hangzhou and I have no enthusiasm for dying in Liuzhou, but when it comes to eating, Guangzhou is a pretty good place to stuff your face.

Bakeries Up in Beijing or out in Tibet, you can break your teeth on Chinese bread. One of the great delights of Guangzhou is that the Cantonese bake the best bread and pastries in China – soft, mildly sweet and tasty. It's great for breakfast and snacks, and goes down well with the ubiquitous yoghurt. The *Victory Bakery* next to the Victory Hotel on Shamian Island is just one of many good places to start.

Chinese Food On Shamian Island, most budget travellers head for the *Li Qin Restaurant (lì qún yǐn shídiàn)* on Shamian 4 Jie near the Victory Hotel – distinguished by a large tree growing right inside the restaurant and out through the roof. Some foreigners have dubbed it the *Tree Restaurant*. Prices are relatively low and the food is excellent, but as Shamian Island eateries go, it's rather dingy and the seats (stools) are uncomfortable. Little English is spoken, but the menu is bilingual.

Right next door is the *Kiu Mei Restaurant* (☎ 8188-4168) *(qiáoměi shíjiā)*. Prices are at least 50% higher than at the Lin Qin, but the environment is more cheery and the chairs infinitely more comfortable. The food is superb.

The *New Litchi Bay Restaurant (xīn lìzhī wān jiǔlóu)* is just to your right as you face the Shamian Hotel on Shamian Nanjie. All kinds of seafood squiggles and squirms in fish tanks near the entrance, but the most exotic dish is snake. Before choosing your eel or cobra, ask the price – some of these creatures cost more than the tanks they're kept in.

Also on Shamian Island is the *Victory Restaurant*, attached to the Victory Hotel. Prices are amazingly reasonable for such a high standard of service. An English menu is available. Near the new annex of the Victory Hotel is the *Sea Dragon Restaurant (hǎilóng yúgǎng)*.

The China Hotel is where you'll find *Food St*, an arcade offering what could be considered gourmet food at very reasonable prices.

Food St in the China Hotel was magnificent. Superb food, friendly service, English menu. To cite you: It is something to write home about!
Gerhard Kotschenreuther

The *Aiqun Hotel* has a great restaurant on the 14th floor. Besides the food, it's worth coming up here just for the views overlooking the Pearl River.

One of the city's most famous restaurants is the *Guangzhou* (☎ 8188-8388) *(guǎngzhōu jiǔjiā)*, 2 Wenchang Lu near the intersection with Dishipu Lu. It boasts a 70-year history and in the 1930s came to be known as the 'first house in Guangzhou'. Its kitchens were staffed by the city's best chefs and the restaurant was frequented by the most important people of the day. The four storeys of dining halls and private rooms are built around a central garden courtyard, where potted shrubs, flowers and landscape paintings are intended to give the feeling (at least to the people in the dingy ground-floor rooms) of 'eating in a landscape'. Specialities of the house include shark fin soup with shredded chicken, chopped crabmeat balls and braised dove. It does tend to be expensive and reservations are sometimes necessary.

The *Muslim Restaurant* (☎ 8188-8991) *(huímín fàndiàn)* is at 325 Zhongshan 6 Lu, on the corner with Renmin Lu. Look for the Arabic letters above the front entrance. It's an OK place, but go upstairs since the ground floor is dingy.

In the west of Guangzhou, the *Banxi* (☎ 8181-5718) *(bànxī jiǔjiā)*, 151 Longjin Xi Lu, is the biggest restaurant in the city, and was opened in 1947. It's noted for its dumplings, stewed turtle, roast pork, chicken in tea leaves and a crabmeat-shark fin consommé. Its famed dim sum is served from about 5 to 9.30 am, at noon and again at night. Dim sum includes fried dumplings with shrimp, chicken gizzards, pork and mushrooms – even shark fin dumplings! You can try crispy fried egg rolls stuffed with chicken, shrimp, pork, bamboo shoots and mushrooms. Monkey brains are steamed with ginger, scallions and rice wine, and then steamed again with crab roe, eggs and lotus blossoms.

In the same general direction is the *Taotaoju* (☎ 8188-5769) *(táotáojū)*, 288 Xiuli 2 Lu. Originally built as a private academy in the 17th century, it was turned into a restaurant in the late 19th century. Tao Tao was the name of the proprietor's wife.

Dim sum is the speciality here; you choose sweet and savoury snacks from the selection on trolleys that are wheeled around the restaurant. Tea is the preferred beverage and is said to be made with Guangzhou's best water – brought in from the Nine Dragon Well in the White Cloud Hills.

Beijing Lu has two of Guangzhou's 'famous' restaurants. The *Wild Animals Restaurant (yěwèixiāng fàndiàn)* at No 247 is where you can feast on dog, cat, deer, snake and bear. Spare a thought for the tiger, which was once served up at this restaurant like there was no tomorrow.

Highly recommended is the *Taipingguan* (☎ 8333-2938) *(tàipíngguǎn cāntīng)* at 344 Beijing Lu, which serves both Western and Chinese food. Zhou Enlai fancied their roast pigeon.

The *South Garden Restaurant* (☎ 8444-9211) *(nányuán jiǔjiā)* is at 142 Qianjin Lu and the menu features chicken in honey and oyster sauce or pigeon in plum sauce. Qianjin Lu is on the south side of the Pearl River; to get to it you have to cross Haizhu Bridge and go down Jiangnan Lu. Qianjin Lu branches off to the east.

Just to the west of Renmin Lu at 41 Jianglan Lu is the *Snake Restaurant* (☎ 8188-2317) *(shé cānguǎn)*, with the snakes on display in the window. This place opened at the turn of the century, when it was called the 'Snake King Moon'. To get to the restaurant you have to walk down Heping Lu, which runs west from Renmin Lu. After a few minutes turn right into Jianglan Lu and follow it around to the

Location of Snake Restaurant

0   50   100 m

To Riverfront

restaurant on the left-hand side. Creative snake recipes include fricasseed assorted snake and cat meats, snake breast meat stuffed with shelled shrimp, stir-fried colourful shredded snake, and braised snake slices with chicken liver.

Cheap Eats Small government-owned dumpling *(jiǎozi)* restaurants are cheap and the food is usually good, but the service leaves a lot to be desired. Before you get your food you must pay the cashier and obtain tickets which you take to the cook. Especially when they are busy, customers tend to be ignored, so if you want something to eat you have to be aggressive. Just watch how the Chinese do it. Join the push and shove match, or else come back later in the off-peak hours.

Innumerable *street stalls* are open at night in the vicinity of the Aiqun Hotel. If you walk around the streets, and particularly along Changdi Lu on the north side of the hotel, you'll find sidewalk stalls dishing up frogs, toads and tortoises. At your merest whim these will be summarily executed, thrown in the wok and fried. It's a bit like eating in an abattoir, but at least there's no doubt about the freshness.

Snakes & Bladders

The Chinese believe eating snake gall bladder dispels wind, promotes blood circulation, dissolves phlegm and soothes one's breathing. Snake meat is said to cure all sorts of ailments, including anaemia, rheumatism, arthritis and asthenia (abnormal loss of strength). Way back in the 1320s the Franciscan friar Odoric visited China and commented on the snake-eating habits of the southern Chinese: 'There be monstrous great serpents likewise which are taken by the inhabitants and eaten. A solemn feast among them with serpents is thought nothing of.' ■

Anyone for hot dog? The Chinese believe that dog meat has tonic properties that fight off colds and flu, so it's only served during the winter months. If it's January and you need your flu shot, all sorts of doggie dishes are available from little *back-alley restaurants* along Liu'ersan Lu north of Shamian Island (and elsewhere). By the way, only black dogs are thought to be good medicine, a big break for the St Bernards.

Vegetarian The *Caigenxiang Vegetarian Restaurant* (☎ 8334-4363) *(càigēnxiāng sùshíguǎn)*, 167 Zhongshan 6 Lu, is Guangzhou's most famous venue for vegie meals. It's also one of the few places in the city where you don't have to worry about accidentally ordering dogs, cats or monkey brains.

Less famous but certainly worth tracking down is the *Buddhist World Vegetarian Restaurant (fó shìjiè sùshí shè)*. It's on Tongfu Lu on the south side of the Pearl River.

Fast Food *McDonald's* made its debut in Guangzhou in 1993, and has become all the rage with the face-conscious Chinese. While cheeseburgers on sesame buns rarely turn heads in the West, McDonald's is considered one of Guangzhou's most prestigious restaurants, the venue for cadre birthday parties and other important gatherings. On Sundays, the restaurants pack out as the city's chic social climbers get dressed up in their best and order a banquet of Chicken McNuggets which they enjoy in air-conditioned comfort. Ironically, at Y9.50, China's Big Macs are the cheapest in the world. There are at least four McDonald's in the city – the most accessible branches are in the GITIC Plaza Building, at the intersection of Beijing Lu and Zhongshan 5 Lu, and on Renmin Lu near Changshou Lu.

KFC, the new cryptic name for 'Kentucky Fried Chicken', spreads its wings at 171 Changdi Lu near the Aiqun Hotel.

Fairwood Fast Food (dà kuàihuó) is a branch of the Hong Kong instant food chain of the same name (which means 'big

happy'). You'll know this place by the red plastic clown face by the door. As fast food goes, you could certainly do worse. There is a Fairwood in the basement of the Nam Fong International Plaza next to the Friendship Store on Huanshi Lu, and another on Jiefang

---

Fast Feud

Guangzhou's first McDonald's opened in 1993 on the ground floor of the 63-storey GITIC Plaza. Since then, the golden arches have risen in practically every neighbourhood around the city. However, some old China hands recall the heady days before Chicken McNuggets made their debut in Guangzhou:

It was a hot and steamy summer afternoon. I was sitting in Hasty Tasty, Guangzhou's premier fast-food restaurant, enjoying the air-conditioning and sipping a large Coke with ice. As I sat there contemplating where I would go next in this sizzling weather, a foreign tourist stepped up to the counter. His name was George.

George's wife was sitting at a table by the door. She wore a purple jump suit, gaudy fake jewellery, horn-rimmed sunglasses and enough perfume to be a fire hazard. Her hair – flaming orange and held rigid by hair spray – looked like cotton candy. She was carefully explaining to her two children how she would break their arms if they didn't shut up and stop fighting with each other.

As George approached the counter, the waitress grinned at him. Perhaps she did that to all the customers, or perhaps it had something to do with the way George was dressed – in pink shorts, a flowered shirt and a white sunhat embroidered with a picture of a fish and the words 'Sea World'.

'May I take your order?' the waitress said. George looked relieved, obviously pleased that the waitress could speak English.

'Excuse me,' George said, 'I don't want to order anything right now, but could you tell me where the nearest McDonald's is?'

'Sorry sir' the waitress replied, 'we don't have McDonald's in Guangzhou. I have never eaten there. But they have in Hong Kong – I saw on television.'

You might as well have hit George with a freight train. He turned his back on the waitress without saying another word and trudged fearfully towards the table where his wife and two charming children were sitting.

'Well George', she bellowed, 'where's the McDonald's'?

'They haven't got one here,' he answered coarsely and immediately the kids started yelling 'we want a Big Mac!'

'Shut up!' George said, 'we have to go back to Hong Kong!' ∎

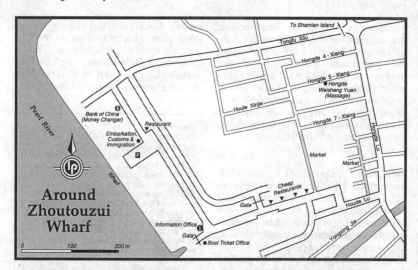

Around Zhoutouzui Wharf

Lu just to the north and east of Guangzhou railway station.

The China Hotel's *Hasty Tasty Fast Food* shop (which opens on to Jiefang Lu) is China's home-grown answer to instant capitalist cuisine. It looks and tastes much like any Hong Kong or American fast-food venue, with banks of neon lights in the ceiling, laminex tables and victuals served in the finest paper and plastic packaging.

Western If you'd like something Western but more avant-garde than an Egg McMuffin, try *Kathleen's Cafe* (☎ 8387-8045). It's next to the Friendship Store and the Baiyun Hotel on Huanshi Lu.

The *Cafe de Paris* (☎ 8441-8888) in the Plaza Canton Hotel at 348 Jiangnan Dadao Zhong is French right down to the white table cloths.

For Italian food you can try *The Pizzeria* (☎ 833-8989) in the Garden Hotel at 368 Huanshi Lu.

Mexican dishes (Californian variety) can be had at the *California Cafe* (☎ 8777-1988) in the Ramada Pearl Hotel.

Holiday Inn's contribution to good Western cooking is *Oscar's* (☎ 8776-6999).

ENTERTAINMENT

Back in the days of Mao, 'nightlife' often meant revolutionary operas featuring evil foreign devils who eventually were defeated by heroic workers and peasants frantically waving copies of Mao's 'Little Red Book'. Even as late as 1990, the only thing in Guangzhou for foreign visitors to do at night was go to bed. Then came cocktail lounges at joint-venture hotels, bowling alleys, STAR TV and now a proliferation of bars and discos catering to a mixed expat and local crowd. You'll still have to choose your discos carefully (unless you're deaf or happen to enjoy Canto-pop), but no longer is the music selection limited to renditions of the national anthem, *The East is Red*.

Shamian Island is a good place to begin. The Guangzhou city government has ambitious plans to transform the island into a Westernised eating and entertainment spot to compete with Hong Kong's Lan Kwai Fong. It's fair to say that it will be many years before Lan Kwai Fong pub owners throw in the towel.

Lucy's Bar & Cafe (lùsī kāfēi shì) occupies a prime piece of real estate on Shamian Island near the river. The cafe is open in the evening and is the most popular spot in the area with expats. Also on the island is the *Chicago Café* and the *Shamian Bar*, though the latter attracts more local Chinese than Westerners.

For late night carousing, one of the most popular places in town is *One Love Disco (húngfēngchē)*. It has a Y10 cover charge, an inky black dance area with a hip DJ, and a large beer garden and live music area upstairs. You can find it on the north-west corner of Dongfeng Lu and Guangzhou Lu. Friday and Saturday nights see the place at its liveliest.

JJ Disco (☎ 8381-3668), Lingyuan Xilu, has to be seen to be believed. Space-pod lights lead you into a warehouse-size dance complex with laser light shows. On a Friday or Saturday night this place is packed with sweaty bodies. Techno beats feature heavily, along with happy-happy Filipino DJs.

Another dance club popular at the time of writing is *Hit Disco* (☎ 8331-3889) at 1 Tongxin Lu (just off Huanshi Lu). Hidden away in an extremely tacky castle structure, it's essentially a small-scale JJ clone.

The *Rock'n Roll Club* at 130 Yanjiang Xilu is just south-east of the huge Nanfang Department Store, east of Shamian Island. This should not be confused with the *Rock Bar*, another good place at 815 Jiefang Lu.

Adler's Pub is a fine place in the Guangdong Trade Centre on the north-west side of Haizhu Square (near the Pearl River).

The *Hill Bar* next to the Baiyun Hotel on Huanshi Lu is good for both pub grub and a mellow drinking session. The excellent food is remarkably inexpensive. Try the fish & chips at Y20 – a bargain. The steaks here are also highly rated.

Besides the expat bars, karaoke has taken over the nightlife scene in China and you won't have any trouble finding it. The Guangzhou Youth Hostel is probably the only hotel in Guangzhou that does *not* have a karaoke lounge, but maybe it will by the time you read this.

Around Guangzhou

WHITE CLOUD HILLS
(báiyún shān)

The White Cloud Hills, in the north-eastern suburbs of Guangzhou, are an offshoot of Dayu Ling, the chief mountain range of Guangdong Province. The hills were once dotted with temples and monasteries, though no buildings of any historical significance remain.

At the southern foot of the hills is **Lu Lake**, also called Golden Liquid Lake, which was built for water storage in 1958 but is now pretty much ornamental.

The White Cloud Hills has long had a **cable car**, the entrance to which has recently been renovated into a massive tourist attraction. It features a large aviary, artificial waterfalls, rock carvings, gardens and much more.

The highest peak in the White Cloud Hills is **Star Touching Hill** *(mōxīng líng)*. At 382m it's considerably smaller than Hong Kong's famed Victoria Peak (554m), but anything higher than a sandcastle is a mountain in the Pearl River Delta area. On a clear day, you can see a panorama of the city, with the Xiqiao Hills to one side, the North River and the Fayuan Hills on the other side, and the sweep of the Pearl River. Unfortunately, clear days are becoming a rarity in Guangzhou.

The hills are popular with the local people, who come here to admire the views and slurp cups of tea. The Cloudy Rock Teahouse, by a small waterfall on the hillside, is recommended if you want to do the same.

The Chinese rate the evening view from **Cheng Precipice** as one of the eight sights of Guangzhou. The precipice takes its name from a Qin dynasty tale. It is said that the first Qin Emperor, Qin Shi Huang, heard of a herb which would confer immortality on whoever ate it. Cheng On Kee, a minister of the emperor, was dispatched to find it. Five years of wandering brought Cheng to the White Cloud Hills, where the herb grew in profusion. On eating the herb, he found that the rest of it disappeared. In dismay and fearful of returning empty-handed, Cheng threw himself off the precipice, but having been assured immortality from eating the herb, he was caught by a stork and taken to heaven. The precipice, named in his memory, was formerly the site of the oldest monastery in the area.

North of the Cheng Precipice, on the way up to Star Touching Hill, you'll pass the **Nine Dragon Spring**, the origins of which are also legendary. During the 18th century, the governor of Guangzhou is said to have visited the temple during a drought. As he prayed he saw nine small boys dancing in front of the temple, but they vanished when he rose from his knees. A spring bubbled forth from where he had knelt. A monk at the temple informed the amazed governor that these boys were in fact nine dragons sent to advise the governor that his prayers for water had been heard in heaven.

1 Donghu Amusement Park
东湖乐园
2 Baiyun Airport
白云机场
3 Sanyuanli Bus Terminal
三元里客运站
4 Central Hotel
中央酒店
5 Cable Car Station
白云索道
6 Xijiao Bus Station
西郊汽车站
7 Panyu Bus Station
番禺汽车站
8 Watson's & Park 'n' Shop
屈臣氏，百佳超市
9 Haizhu Shopping Centre
海珠购物中心
10 Plaza Canton Hotel
江南大酒店
11 Zhongshan University
中山大学
12 Horse Racing Track
跑马场

GUANGZHOU

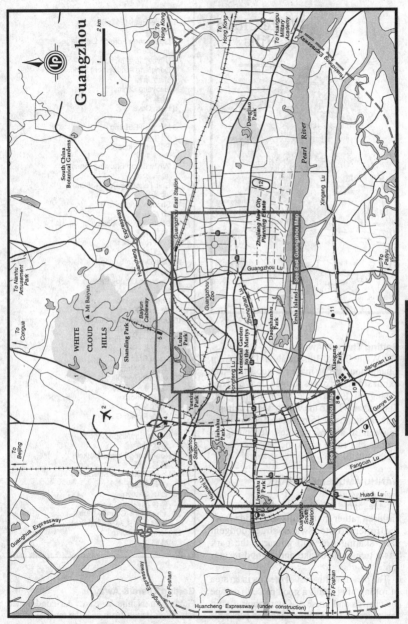

GUANGZHOU

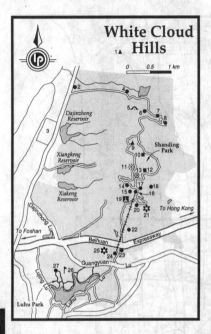

White Cloud Hills

1 Wulei Peak (247m)
　五雷岭
2 Guangzhou Foreign Language
　Institute
　广州外语学院
3 Dongfang Amusement Park
　东方乐园
4 Liaoyang Clinic
　疗养院
5 Hero Cave
　英雄洞
6 Mingzhu Building
　明珠楼
7 Billowing Pines Villa
　松涛别院
8 White Cloud Billowing Pines
　白云松涛
9 Star Touching Peak (382m)
　摩星岭
10 Shanzhuang Inn
　山庄旅舍
11 South Sky Viewpoint
　锦绣南天
12 Twin River Villa
　双溪别墅
13 Nine Dragon Spring
　九龙泉
14 Embrace Clouds Pavilion
　抱云
15 Cheng Precipice
　白云晚望
16 Upper Cable Car Station
　白云索道上部站
17 Southern Sky First Peak
　天南第一峰
18 Cloud Crag
　云岩 (郑仙岩)
19 Nengren Temple
　能仁寺
20 Keqi Teahouse
　可憩茶座
21 White Flower Garden
　白花园
22 Shengjian Village School
　省建村学校
23 Rongchang Flower Market
　荣昌花场
24 Lower Cable Car Station
　白云索道下部站
25 Baitai Garden
　白台花园
26 Luhu Golf & Country Club
　麓湖高尔夫球乡村俱乐部
27 Honghu Building
　鸿鹄楼

Getting There & Away

The White Cloud Hills are about 15 km from Guangzhou and it makes a good half-day excursion. Express buses leave from Guangwei Lu, a little street running off Zhongshan 5 Lu to the west of the Children's Park, about every 15 minutes. The trip takes between 30 and 60 minutes, depending on traffic. The cable car is the best way to get up the hill.

NANHU AMUSEMENT PARK

(nánhú lèyuán)

As the name implies, this is geared for children rather than adults. But aside from the roller coaster, water slide, dodgem cars, skating rink and go-carts, the park has a tree-shaded lake and a good restaurant.

The park is north-east of the city in an area of rolling hills and is a good place to escape the crowds and noise of Guangzhou. Avoid this place on weekends, when it is packed.

Getting There & Away

Getting to Nanhu is easy. Air-conditioned minibuses depart from near the main entrance of Guangzhou train station and go directly there. You can pay in RMB.

DONGFANG AMUSEMENT PARK
(dōngfāng lèyuán)

Yet another venue for roller coasters and fairy floss, this one is even tackier than Nanhu Amusement Park. Expats looking to keep the kids amused might want to pay a visit. Travellers who want to see a bit of China should go elsewhere.

The park is just to the west of the White Cloud Hills, less than 10 km from central Guangzhou and therefore close enough to reach by taxi.

SOUTH CHINA BOTANIC GARDENS
(huánán zhíwùyuán)

Although it has a long way to go to become world class, the botanic gardens are a welcome respite from the concrete and exhaust fumes of Guangzhou. With the city's rising fortunes, it's likely that more money will be spent to improve the site.

The botanic gardens are about 10 km north-east of Guangzhou.

HUANGPU MILITARY ACADEMY
(huángpǔ jūnxiào)

While not highly rated as a tourist attraction, the Huangpu (formerly Whampoa) Military Academy is of some interest to history buffs.

No longer an active school, it is maintained as an historical site. It's on Changzhou Island in the middle of the Pearl River, 20 km downstream (east) from Guangzhou. The academy was opened in 1924. Dr Sun Yatsen, first president of the Republic of China, presided at the opening ceremony, and his statue is on display at the school.

The institute trained people who played major roles in China's turbulent history. The most interesting figure was Chiang Kaishek, who became the school's president. After leaving the academy, Chiang became the head of the Kuomintang (or 'Nationalist Party'). In 1926, in an effort to unify China, the Kuomintang embarked on the Northern Expedition to wrest power from China's warlords. In an uneasy alliance, Chiang

Kaishek was appointed commander in chief by the Kuomintang and the communists. The campaign was successful and Chiang unified China, but he also turned against the communists in a notorious massacre in Shanghai in 1927. Despite this, another alliance between the communists and the Kuomintang had to be arranged in order to fight the Japanese during WWII.

With Japan's defeat, full-scale war broke out between the Kuomintang and the communists. The communists emerged successful and Chiang Kaishek and his troops fled to Taiwan in 1949.

The school's other big celebrity is Zhou Enlai. Zhou barely escaped being killed by Chiang's troops in the 1927 Shanghai massacre. He then endured the brutal Long March of 1933, was a loyal ally of Mao Zedong and became premier of China after the communist victory in 1949. He died in 1976.

PANYU
(pānyú)

Developers are attempting to turn Panyu into a tourist haven, but from all appearances they've still got some work to do. This small city about 20 km south of Guangzhou (46 km by road) is being developed along family-type recreation lines. Clifford Estates is a high-class residential and recreation development for expats.

Tourists can stay at the *Panyu Today's World Recreation Village (jīnrì shìjiè dùjiàcūn)*, which boasts a four-star hotel with rooms for Y350 to Y460. There is also the *Panyu Hotel (pānyú bīnguǎn)* with doubles priced from Y440 to Y650, and the *Miramar Hotel* (☎ 482-6833; fax 483-8335) *(měilìhuá dà jiǔdiàn)*.

Somebody must be visiting, because there are direct boats running between Panyu and Hong Kong. Two jet-powered catamarans do the run – the fastest takes one hour and 25 minutes, the slow-poke takes two hours. Departures from Hong Kong are at 7.55 and 9 am, and at 1.30 pm. From Panyu, boats to Hong Kong depart at 11 am, and 4 and 5 pm.

There are also buses between Panyu and

Guangzhou, but because of heavy traffic the ride takes about an hour.

LOTUS MOUNTAIN
(liánhuā shān)

This interesting and unusual place is only 46 km south-east of Guangzhou and makes an excellent day trip. The name Lotus Mountain might conjure up images of some holy mountain like Emeishan in Sichuan Province, but it's nothing like that.

Lotus Mountain is an old quarry site dating back to the Song dynasty (960-1279). Most people wouldn't think of a quarry as being attractive, but this place is an exception. The stonecutting ceased several hundred years ago and the cliffs have since eroded to a state where it looks almost natural. A little historical interest is added by the fact that Lin Zexu garrisoned his troops here during the Second Opium War.

Attempts to dress up the area by building pagodas, pavilions and steps have made the area into a sort of gigantic rock garden. Dense vegetation and good views of the Pearl River add to the effect. The nine-storey **Lotus Pagoda**, constructed in 1612, is the tallest structure on the site.

Overall, most of the buildings fit in well with the scenery and there are some nice walks. If only someone could persuade Chinese tourists to stop filling up the lotus ponds and gorges with bottles, drink cans and plastic bags.

However, Lotus Mountain is now a popular summer weekend stop-off for tour boats from Hong Kong, which means that it would be best to visit on week days or during the low season (winter).

There are a few restaurants here, and one hotel, the *Lotus Mountain Villa (liánhuā shānzhuāng)*.

Getting There & Away

Get there either by bus or boat – the boat is more interesting. The old lumbering ferry was recently replaced with a speedy jet-boat, so the one-way journey takes only one hour. The boat leaves Guangzhou at 8 am and departs Lotus Mountain at 4.30 pm. That gives you about five hours on the mountain, which I found was about right for a relaxing hike and picnic. Departures are from Tianzi Pier *(tiānzi mǎtóu)* on Yanjiang Lu, one block east of Haizhu Square. It's not a bad idea to buy a ticket one day in advance.

Buses depart from outside Guangzhou train station. In theory the bus should travel at the same speed as the boat, but with Guangzhou's traffic jams it works out to over two hours by bus.

There are fast boats direct from Hong Kong (2.5 hours, HK$250) which run at touristy times like weekends, summer holidays and public holidays. For the latest schedule, enquire at CKS *(zhūjiāng kèyùn)* in Kowloon's China-Hong Kong City ferry terminal. It can be fascinating to see these tour groups, usually led by a young woman in uniform holding up a big flag and talking through a megaphone as her troops march in step, leaving behind a trail of rubbish.

CONGHUA HOT SPRINGS
(cōnghuà wēnquán)

The springs are 85 km north-east of Guangzhou in a pleasant forested valley with a river flowing through it. Twelve springs have been found; the temperature of most varies from 30 – 40°C, with the highest over 70°C.

Many foreigners come here to enjoy a soak during Guangzhou's chilly winter. The Chinese come here because they believe the hot springs can cure everything: arthritis, dermatitis, migraine headaches, high blood pressure, constipation, impotence – the lot. One tourist leaflet even claims relief for 'fatigue of the cerebral cortex' and gynaecological disease.

Unfortunately, there are no longer any outdoor pools. The water is piped into the private bathrooms of nearby hotels, so you'll have to enjoy the water without the benefit of open-air scenery. Nevertheless, Conghua is a pleasant place to visit.

Information

CTS For what it's worth, CTS has an office in the CTS Travel Hotel.

Places to Stay

Hotels are thick on the ground here, though during public holidays accommodation can be a little tight. CTS operates the *CTS Travel Hotel (lǚyóu bīnguǎn)* which is just next to the Happy Forever Restaurant. The three-star *Wenquan Binguan* charges Y290 to Y370 for a double. Other choices include the *Hot Springs Hotel (wēnquán dà jiǔdiàn)* and *Guangdong Hot Springs Guesthouse (guǎngdōng wēnquán bīnguǎn)*. *Wēnquán Shānzhuāng* is a huge resort village.

Getting There & Away

Buses to Conghua depart all day from the Guangzhou City bus station and Baiyun Lu bus station. Some buses go directly to the hot springs, but most terminate in the town of Conghua, an ugly place 16 km from the hot springs. In that case, you have to catch another bus (20 minutes) to the hot springs.

The one-way trip takes three hours or more, depending on traffic. There are two departures directly to the hot springs at 7.35 and 10.35 am; departures to Conghua town are at 8, 9 and 10 am, 1.40, 2.30, 3.30, 4, 4.30, 5 and 5.30 pm.

The place is thick with bodies at the weekend, so try to avoid going then. If you do go on a weekend or holiday, buy a return ticket to Guangzhou on arrival because the buses fill up fast at those times.

FEIXIA GORGE & QINGYUAN

(fēixiá, qīngyuǎn)

This pretty gorge on the North River *(běi jiāng)* is nine km long and makes for an excellent boat trip. There are also numerous footpaths starting from the river's edge, passing several interesting grottos which have been built into mini-temples. The two most important grottos are Feixia *(fēixiágǔ dòng)* and Cangxia *(cángxiá dòng)*.

On the west bank of the river about three km downstream from the gorge is **Feilai Temple**, with a history of more than 1400 years. It's one of the three largest temples in Guangdong Province.

To get to the gorge you first must take a bus from the main bus station to Qingyuan,

Feixia

Not To Scale

To Feilai Temple

North River

1 Lion Mountain
   狮山
2 Songfeng Pavilion
   松峰亭
3 Changtian Pagoda
   长天塔
4 Feixia Grotto
   飞霞古洞
5 Clear Spring Pavilion
   清泉亭
6 Stone Buddha
   石佛
7 Feixia Hotel
   飞霞宾馆
8 Cangxia Grotto
   藏霞古洞
9 Tiger Mountain
   虎山
10 Cangxia Gate
   藏霞牌坊
11 Ligeng Academy
   礼耕书屋
12 Feixiatongjin Gate
   飞霞通津坊
13 Jinxia Temple
   锦霞禅院
14 Meiting Pavilion
   梅亭
15 Yidongtian Rock
   一洞天
16 Cangxiashanjing Gate
   藏霞善径坊
17 Feixiagu Cave Gate
   飞霞古洞坊

GUANGZHOU

about 100 km north-west of Guangzhou. From there, minibuses or taxis do the last 20 km to Feilai Temple plus the additional three km to Feixia. Make local enquiries at Feixia about doing boat trips on the North River. Reasonably priced accommodation is available at the *Feixia Hotel*.

FOSHAN

(fóshān)

Just 22 km south-west of Guangzhou is the town of Foshan ('Buddha Hill'). The story goes that a monk travelling through the area enshrined three statues of Buddha on a hilltop. After the monk left, the shrine collapsed and the statues disappeared. Hundreds of years later, during the Tang Dynasty (618 – 907), the Buddha figurines were suddenly rediscovered, a temple was built on the hill and the town was renamed.

Whether or not the story is true, from about the 10th century onwards the town became a religious centre and, because of its location in the north of the Pearl River Delta and its proximity to Guangzhou, Foshan was ideally placed to thrive as a market town and trade centre.

Since the 10th or 11th century, Foshan has been one of the four main handicraft centres of old China. The other three were Zhuxian in Henan Province, Jingdezhen in Jiangxi and Hankou (Wuhan) in Hubei. The nearby town of Shiwan (which is now just an extension of Foshan) became famous for its pottery, and the village of Nanpu (which is also now a suburb of Foshan) developed the art of metal casting. Silk weaving and paper cutting also became important industries and now Foshan papercuts are a commonly sold tourist souvenir in China.

Foshan has been devoured by urbanisation – complete with heavy traffic, factories and ugly buildings – no respite here from Guangzhou! However, it is smaller, and a bit easier to get around. The city is worth at most about two hours of your time. The chief reason for coming is to visit a couple of temples. It's convenient to stop here on the way to the scenic Xiqiao Hills (which *are* worth visiting).

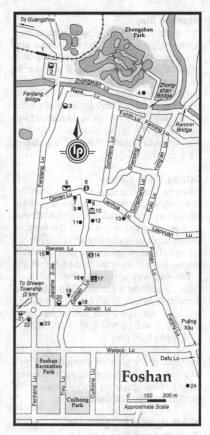

Information

CITS (☎ 335-3338; fax 335-2347) is in the Foshan Hotel at 75 Fenjiang Lu. CTS (☎ 222-3828; fax 222-7625) is in the Overseas Chinese Hotel at 14 Zumiao Lu.

Ancestors' Temple

(zǔ miào)

Foshan's only real tourist attraction, the Ancestors' Temple, draws large tour groups from Hong Kong and elsewhere. Recognising the opportunity, several hotels and restaurants have sprouted in the neighbourhood, but the temple grounds are still quiet and peaceful.

reign of the first Ming emperor, Hong Wu. The Ancestors' Temple was converted into a Taoist temple because the emperor worshipped a Taoist god.

The temple was developed through renovations and additions during the Ming and Qing dynasties. The structure is built entirely of interlocking wooden beams, with no nails or other metal used at all. It is roofed with coloured tiles made in Shiwan.

The main hall contains a 2500-kg bronze statue of a god known as the 'northern emperor' (Beidi). He's also known as the 'black emperor' (Heidi) and rules over water and all its inhabitants, especially fish, turtles and snakes. Since South China is prone to floods, people often tried to appease Beidi by honouring him with temples and carvings of turtles and snakes. In the courtyard is a pool containing a large statue of a turtle with a serpent crawling over it, into which the Chinese throw money, plus the odd drink can.

The temple also has an interesting collection of ornate weapons used on ceremonial occasions during the imperial days. The Foshan Museum is in the temple grounds, as is the Foshan Antique Store and an arts & crafts store. The temple is open daily from 8.30 am to 4.30 pm.

Renshou Pagoda
(*rénshòu sì*)
The architecture is impressive and the name means 'benevolent longevity', but that's about all you can learn about this pagoda. You can admire the structure from the outside, but the doors seem to be permanently locked and there are no resident monks or worshippers. The pagoda is just south of the Rotating Palace Hotel on Zumiao Lu.

Folk Arts Studio
(*mínjiān yìshù yánjiū shè*)
Just to the north of Renshou Pagoda, the Folk Arts Studio has some unusual exhibits, including fossils. Other more predictable exhibits and workshops include lanterns, stencilled pictures, silk paintings and pottery.

At the southern end of Zumiao Lu, the original temple was built during the Song dynasty in the latter part of the 11th century, and was used by workers in the metal-smelting trade for worshipping their ancestors. It was destroyed by fire at the end of the Yuan dynasty in the mid-1300s and rebuilt at the beginning of the Ming dynasty, during the

GUANGZHOU

The studio comes complete with a souvenir shop.

Places to Stay
Around Guangzhou

The cheapest in town is the *Pearl River Hotel* (☎ 228-7512) *(zhū jiāng dà jiǔdiàn)* which has doubles for Y210 to Y250. It's on 1 Qinren Lu in the centre of town, across the street from the post office.

Around the corner and just opposite Renshou Pagoda is the *Overseas Chinese Hotel* (☎ 222-3828; fax 222-7702) *(huáqiáo dàshà)*, 14 Zumiao Lu. Standard doubles cost Y360 to Y450, de luxe class is Y550 and de luxe suites are Y918. Most intriguing are the 'honeymoon rooms' for four persons which are a bargain at Y400.

The *Rotating Palace Hotel* (☎ 285622) *(xuángōng jiǔdiàn)*, is in the centre of town at 1 Zumiao Lu. A double room costs Y360. The hotel doesn't rotate but the rooftop restaurant does, and even if you don't eat there, you can pay a visit to the 16th floor for a sweeping view of Foshan's haze and industrial smokestacks.

Foshan Electronic Hotel (☎ 228-8998; fax 222-5781) *(diànzi bīnguǎn)*, 101 Renmin Lu, has doubles ranging from Y288 to Y420. This 19-storey building is readily identified by a large red 'FEG' (Foshan Electronic Group) sign on the roof. The hotel features receptionists who giggle uncontrollably at every foreigner who approaches the front desk; the FEG's colourful brochure explains '...the solicitous and attentive service by the desk girls makes the guest feeling warmth at home'.

The *Golden City Hotel* (☎ 335-7228; fax 335-3924) *(jīnchéng dà jiǔdiàn)*, 48 Fenjiang Lu, is pleasant enough, though the location at a busy intersection is not especially aesthetic. Doubles are Y663.

The *Foshan Hotel* (☎ 335-3338; fax 335-2347) *(fóshān bīnguǎn)*, 75 Fenjiang Lu, is notable as the home of CITS. Singles are Y238 to Y668, doubles from Y368 to Y668.

Places to Eat

The *Rose Restaurant (méiguì jiǔjiā)* on Zumiao Lu just opposite the entrance to the Ancestors' Temple is one of the better places in town.

Also near the Ancestors' Temple is *McDonald's*. For some reason, this particular branch has no public toilet.

All sorts of mouth-watering aromas emanate from the *Rainbow Bakery (tiānhóng bāobǐng zhuānmén diàn)* just opposite the Renshou Pagoda.

Hotel restaurants serve their usual excellent and pricey food.

Getting There & Away

Air There is a little-used airport seven km north-west of the city. Unless you charter your own flight, you aren't likely to arrive this way.

Bus From Guangzhou, the easiest way to Foshan is to catch one of the numerous minibuses at either the Guangzhou City bus station or the Guangfo bus station. Be sure to ask if the bus takes the expressway *(gāosù gōnglù)*. The fare is Y10.

The bus from Guangzhou will probably drop you off at a small terminal next to Foshan railway station. However, going from Foshan to Guangzhou you should *not* catch the minibus at this place. Instead, go to the Zumiao bus station *(zǔ miào qìchē zhàn)* on Jianxin Lu. This bus station also has minibuses heading for Shenzhen and Zhuhai.

Train International trains No 102 and 104 run between Kowloon (Hong Kong) and Zhaoqing with a stop-off in Foshan. Train No 102 departs Kowloon at 7.50 am, arrives Foshan at 11.07 am, departs Foshan at 11.22 am and arrives Zhaoqing at 12.48 pm. Going the other way, train No 104 departs Zhaoqing at 2.50 pm, arrives Foshan at 4.16 pm, departs Foshan at 4.31 pm, and arrives Kowloon at 7.45 pm. For international trains, you should try to be at the station about one hour before departure time. The gates close 20 minutes before actual departure.

Taking the train from Guangzhou to Foshan (30 minutes) might seem like a good way to beat the maddening traffic, but you'll waste more time and energy organising a ticket at chaotic Guangzhou railway than you will sitting on the bus in a traffic jam. Still, it's worth considering the train, especially if you're heading west, because the line from Guangzhou passes through Foshan, then continues westwards to Sanshui, Dinghushan, Zhaoqing, Maoming and Zhanjiang (the gateway to Hainan Island).

The schedule will doubtless change, but at the time of writing there are six departures in each direction as follows:

Train No	From	To	Depart	Arrive
271/274	Guangzhou	Foshan	2.55pm	3.22pm
281/284	Guangzhou	Foshan	9.30pm	9.57pm
351	Guangzhou	Foshan	7.22am	7.52am
353	Guangzhou	Foshan	5.10pm	5.41pm
355	Guangzhou	Foshan	7.20pm	7.47pm
391	Guangzhou	Foshan	2.02pm	2.29pm
272/273	Foshan	Guangzhou	10.08am	10.35am
282/283	Foshan	Guangzhou	5.57am	6.28am
352	Foshan	Guangzhou	7.53pm	8.20pm
354	Foshan	Guangzhou	12.23pm	12.50pm
356	Foshan	Guangzhou	9.35am	10.02am
392	Foshan	Guangzhou	3.41pm	4.08pm

Getting Around

Motorcycle Taxi You won't have to look too hard for the two-wheeled taxis – they will be looking for you. Motorcycle drivers wearing red helmets greet minibuses arriving from Guangzhou and practically kidnap disembarking passengers. There are no meters and fares are strictly by negotiation. Many drivers assume that every foreigner wants to head immediately for the Ancestors' Temple. If that's not where you want to go, make that clear straight away.

Pedicab There aren't too many of these, but you will see them about town. Foshan's pedicabs are really designed for hauling freight – there are no seats, just a cargo area behind the driver. Fares are negotiable.

XIQIAO HILLS

(xīqiáo shān)

If you're tired of Guangzhou's filthy air and traffic jams, these hills are well worth visiting. Just 68 km south-west of Guangzhou,

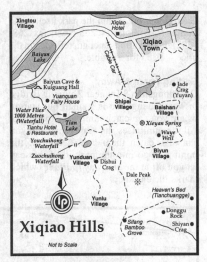

Xiqiao Hills

Not to Scale

Xiqiao Hills can be visited as a long day trip or a pleasant overnighter. Seventy-two peaks (basically hills) make up the area, the highest rising to a mighty 345m. There are 36 caves, 32 springs, 28 waterfalls and 21 crags. A number of tourist facilities have been built, including a luxury hotel, kiosks, kiddie minitrain and paddle boats on **Baiyun Lake**. Despite these intrusions, the area offers pleasant walks and is an excellent retreat provided you avoid weekends and public holidays. It's popular with Chinese tourists – foreigners of any kind are rare.

At the foot of the hills is the bustling **market town** of Xiqiao, where the main attraction is the busy river port area. The hills themselves are protected in a large park and, unusually, there is no admission charge (yet). Around the upper levels of the hills are scattered several centuries-old villages, but don't expect to find ancient China here. Most of the area is made accessible by stone paths. You can cheat your way to the top by taking the **cable car**, but don't count on it since it's often not in operation.

Places to Stay

Most travellers do this as a day trip from

Guangzhou, but within the park itself is the *Xiqiao Hills Hotel* (☎ 268-6799; fax 268-2292). It's luxurious enough, reflected in the price – Y365 for a double.

Getting There & Away

On Zhongshan 8 Lu near Zhujiang Bridge in west Guangzhou is a small bus station where you can catch minibuses to Xiqiao. All the minibuses run via Foshan and you can also catch them there. None of the minibuses go into the park itself, but can let you off at the archway *(páifáng)* which marks the entrance.

ZHAOQING

(zhàoqìng)

For almost 1000 years people have been coming to Zhaoqing to scribble graffiti on its cliffs or in its caves – often the scrawls take the form of poems or essays describing the beauty of the rock formations they are defacing.

If you're going to breathtaking Guilin or Yangshuo, you could give this place a miss, but it's fair to say that Zhaoqing is one of the most beautiful places in the Pearl River Delta region.

Orientation

Zhaoqing, 110 km west of Guangzhou on the

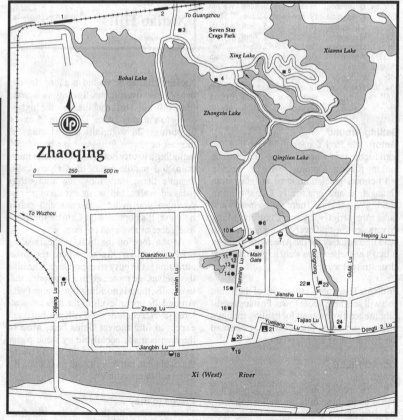

Xi (West) River, is bounded to the south by the river and to the north by the immense Seven Star Crags Park. Zhaoqing is a small place and much of it can be seen on foot.

Seven Star Crag

(qī xīng yán)

Zhaoqing's premier attraction, the Seven Star

1 Zhaoqing Railway Station
　肇庆火车站
2 Seven Star Crags Railway Station
　七星岩火车站
3 Bohailou Hotel
　波海楼
4 Songtao Hotel
　松涛滨馆
5 Xingyan Hotel
　星岩宾馆
6 Star Lake Amusement Park
　星湖游乐园
7 Long-Distance Bus Station
　市汽车站
8 Star Lake Hotel
　星湖大厦
9 Local Bus Station
　公共汽车站
10 Huguang Hotel
　湖光酒店
11 Dynasty Hotel
　新君悦皇朝酒店
12 Huaqiao Hotel
　华侨大厦
13 Duanzhou Hotel
　端州大酒店
14 Bicycle Rentals
　租自行车店
15 Xinhua Bookstore
　新华书店
16 Holiday Hotel
　假日酒店
17 Plum Monastery
　梅庵
18 Passenger Ferry Terminal
　肇庆港客运站
19 Floating Restaurant
　海鲜舫
20 Yuehai Hotel
　粤海大厦
21 Yuejiang Temple
　阅江楼
22 Jinye Hotel
　金叶大厦
23 Flower Tower Hotel
　花塔酒店
24 Chongxi Pagoda
　崇禧塔

Crags is a group of limestone towers – a peculiar geological formation abundant in the paddy fields of Guilin and Yangshuo. Legend has it that the crags were actually seven stars that fell from the sky to form a pattern resembling the Big Dipper constellation. In keeping with their celestial origin each has been given an exotic name like 'Hill Slope' and 'Toad'. The artificial lakes were built in 1955, and the park is adorned with concrete pathways, arched bridges and little pavilions.

The crags are in a large park on the north side of town. Hire a bicycle and head off along the paths away from the lake. Old villages, duck ponds, door gods, buffalo swimming in ponds, strange pavilions and caves can all be found.

Chongxi Pagoda

(chóngxī tǎ)

This nine-storey pagoda on Tajiao Lu in the south-east was in a sad state after the Cultural Revolution, but was restored in the 1980s. On the opposite bank of the river are two similar pagodas. Tajiao Lu, a quiet riverside street, has interesting old houses.

Yuejiang Temple

(yuèjiāng lóu)

This is a restored temple about a 30-minute walk from the Chongxi Pagoda, just back from the waterfront at the eastern end of Zheng Lu.

Plum Monastery

(méi ān)

This small monastery is in the western part of town off Zheng Lu.

Places to Stay

Many budget travellers stay at the *Flower Tower Hotel* (☎ 223-2423) *(huātǎ jiǔdiàn)*, 5 Gongnong Lu. Doubles range from Y100 to Y200.

The *Duanzhou Hotel* (☎ 223-3215) *(duānzhōu dà jiǔdiàn)*, 77 Tianning Lu, is certainly one of the better deals in town. Although it looks frightfully expensive on the outside, standard doubles cost Y170 to Y220.

Another reasonable alternative is the *Holiday Hotel* (☎ 222-1688; fax 222-1898) *(jiàrì jiǔdiàn)* at the southern end of Tianning Lu. Singles/doubles are Y220 to Y350.

The *Xinghuwan Songyuan* (☎ 222-7521) is a collection of three hotels right in Seven Star Crag Park. On the north side is the *Bohailou Hotel (bōhǎilóu)* – attractive and quiet but not as pleasant as the other two. More towards the centre of the park is the *Xingyan Hotel (xīngyán bīnguǎn)* and just to the west of that is the very pleasant *Songtao Hotel* (☎ 222-4412) *(sōngtāo bīnguǎn)*. Double rooms cost Y150 to Y320.

Also on the lake, but not quite as nice, is the *Huguang Hotel* (☎ 222-4904, 222-4905) *(húguāng jiǔdiàn)*. Rooms are Y200 to Y225. The hotel is just inside the main gate off Duanzhou Lu.

The *Yuehai Hotel (yuèhǎi dàshà)* on Jiangbin Lu and Tianning Lu does doubles for Y230.

The *Jinye Hotel* (☎ 222-1338; fax 222-1368) *(jīyè dàshà)* is at the south of Gongnong Lu and has doubles from Y195 to Y280.

The *Huaqiao Hotel* (☎ 223-2952) *(huáqiáo dàshà)*, 90 Tianning Lu, has an excellent location but prices to make you pause. Singles, doubles and triples are Y400, Y600 and Y800 respectively, or check out the presidential suite for Y5000.

The *Star Lake Hotel* (☎ 222-1188) *(xīnghú dàshà)*, 37 Duanzhou 4 Lu, is a multi-storey glass high-rise priced from Y480.

The *Dynasty Hotel* (☎ 223-8238; fax 222-3288) *(xīnjūnyuè huángcháo jiǔdiàn)*, 9 Duanzhou Lu has doubles from Y300.

Getting There & Away

Bus From Guangzhou, there are buses to Zhaoqing from the Guangzhou City bus station on Huanshi Lu. There are half a dozen buses a day and the trip takes about 2.5 hours. Try to avoid returning to Guangzhou on a weekend afternoon; traffic jams are common on this road.

Privately run minibuses operate between Zhaoqing and Guangzhou. In Zhaoqing, the minibus ticket office is inside the main gate

of the Seven Star Crags Park (at the top of Tianning Lu).

Train By rail, Zhaoqing is 110 km from Guangzhou, 256 km from Shenzhen and 291 km from Kowloon (Hong Kong).

There are two railway stations in Zhaoqing. All trains stop at Zhaoqing railway station *(zhàoqìng huǒchē zhàn)* – almost no trains stop at Seven Star Crags railway station *(qīxīngyán huǒchē zhàn)*. If you get into a taxi and say you want to go the railway station, drivers will automatically assume you mean Zhaoqing railway station.

International trains 102 and 104 stop at Foshan en route, but not at Guangzhou.

Train No	From	To	Depart	Arrive
102	Kowloon	Zhaoqing	7.50am	12.48pm
104	Zhaoqing	Kowloon	2.50pm	7.45pm
14	Shenzhen	Zhaoqing	9.40am	2.42pm
13	Zhaoqing	Shenzhen	3.58pm	9.57pm
271/274	Guangzhou	Zhaoqing	2.55pm	9.35pm
281/284	Guangzhou	Zhaoqing	9.30pm	11.48pm
351	Guangzhou	Zhaoqing	7.22am	10am
353	Guangzhou	Zhaoqing	5.10pm	7.42pm
355	Guangzhou	Zhaoqing	7.20pm	9.45pm
272/273	Zhaoqing	Guangzhou	8.08am	10.35am
282/283	Zhaoqing	Guangzhou	4.02am	6.28am
352	Zhaoqing	Guangzhou	5.50pm	8.20pm
354	Zhaoqing	Guangzhou	10.08am	12.50pm
356	Zhaoqing	Guangzhou	7.20am	10.02am

Boat The ferry terminal and ticket office for boats to Wuzhou and Guangzhou is at 3 Jiangbin Lu, just west of the intersection with Renmin Lu. It appears that only lower-class boat tickets can be bought here since Zhaoqing is an intermediate stop. Boats to Wuzhou and Guangzhou depart in the early evening. From Zhaoqing to Wuzhou it takes around 12 hours. From Zhaoqing to Guangzhou is a 10-hour trip. The boat is not popular because it's so slow. In Guangzhou, departures are from Dashatou Wharf.

In the tourist season (basically summer and public holidays), there are direct boats to and from Hong Kong. There are two boats: the *Xijiang*, which is an overnight ferry taking 12 hours; and the *Xinduanzhou*, which is a high-speed catamaran taking four hours. The *Xijiang* departs Hong Kong on odd-numbered dates at 7.30 pm, and departs Zhaoqing on even-numbered dates at 7 pm. The *Xinduanzhou* departs Hong Kong on odd-numbered dates at 7.45 am and departs Zhaoqing on even-numbered dates at 2 pm. Fares are as follows:

Xijiang (overnight ferry)

Class	Fare
Special A	HK$671
Special B	HK$378
1st	HK$338
2nd	HK$303
3rd	HK$248

Xinduanzhou (catamaran)

Class	Fare
Special	HK$353
1st	HK$323
Common	HK$293

Getting Around

The local bus station is on Duanzhou Lu, a few minutes' walk east of the intersection with Tianning Lu. Bus No 1 runs to the ferry terminal on the Xi (West) River. Bus Nos 4 and 5 go to the Plum Monastery.

The railway station is well out of town near the north-west corner of the lake. Taxis and minibuses into town are cheap.

Next to walking, the best way to get around Zhaoqing is by bicycle. There is a hire place diagonally opposite the main entrance to the Seven Star Crags, and another south of the Duanzhou Hotel. They ask exorbitant fees if you have a foreign face, but will accept Y35 per day.

DINGHUSHAN

(dǐnghú shān)

This is one of the best scenic spots in Guangdong. Apart from its streams, brooks, pools, hills and trees, the mountain is noted for the Qingyuan temple, built towards the end of the Ming dynasty.

Dinghushan can be visited as a day trip from Zhaoqing, but there are hotels on the mountain.

Dinghushan is 20 km north-east of Zhaoqing along the Guangzhou-Zhaoqing highway. You might get a minibus directly

from Zhaoqing, but if not, take any highway bus heading towards Guangzhou and get off at the Dinghushan junction. Then walk or flag down a minibus to go the last two km up the mountain.

Two trains serve Dinghushan from Guangzhou:

Train No	From	To	Depart	Arrive
351	Guangzhou	Dinghushan	7.22am	9.42am
351	Dinghushan	Zhaoqing	9.44am	10.00am
352	Zhaoqing	Dinghushan	5.50pm	6.06pm
352	Dinghushan	Guangzhou	6.08pm	8.20pm

LUOFUSHAN

(luófúshān)

Possibly the best sight in Guangdong Province, Luofushan ('Catch Fortune' mountain) is one of China's principal Taoist sites. It's also the place where the third patriarch of Buddhism wrote poems, and the mountainside is appropriately dressed for the occasion with temples. However, you need not have any interest in Buddhism or Taoism to enjoy the fine scenery. Luofushan presents a dramatic face, rising sharply from the plains to an elevation of 1281m. Silver pheasants breed on the mountain and the local herbs have a good reputation. These days there is a thriving tourist kitsch industry – products on sale include stuffed panda dolls, plastic toys and Luofushan Hundred Herbs Oil.

Despite Luofushan's enchanting scenery and religious appeal, surprisingly few Hong Kongers have ever heard of the place. Most residents of Guangzhou have been here at least once, but the mountain has yet to make it on the international tour circuit. Perhaps that alone is a reason to visit it.

Getting There & Away

Luofushan is approximately 100 km east of Guangzhou, and about the same distance north of Hong Kong. The easiest approach is from Guangzhou, where there are early morning buses direct to the mountain from the Guangzhou City bus station.

Coming from the direction of Shenzhen,

GUANGZHOU

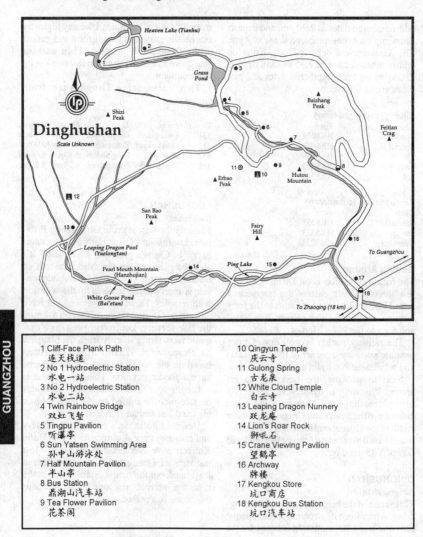

Dinghushan
Scale Unknown

Heaven Lake (Tianhu)

Grass Pond

Baizhang Peak

Feitian Crag

Shizi Peak

Erbao Peak

Hutou Mountain

San Bao Peak

Fairy Hill

Leaping Dragon Pool (Yuelongtan)

Pearl Mouth Mountain (Hanzhujian)

White Goose Pond (Bai'etan)

Ping Lake

To Guangzhou

To Zhaoqing (18 km)

1 Cliff-Face Plank Path 连天栈道	10 Qingyun Temple 庆云寺
2 No 1 Hydroelectric Station 水电一站	11 Gulong Spring 古龙泉
3 No 2 Hydroelectric Station 水电二站	12 White Cloud Temple 白云寺
4 Twin Rainbow Bridge 双虹飞堑	13 Leaping Dragon Nunnery 跃龙庵
5 Tingpu Pavilion 听瀑亭	14 Lion's Roar Rock 狮吼石
6 Sun Yatsen Swimming Area 孙中山游泳处	15 Crane Viewing Pavilion 望鹤亭
7 Half Mountain Pavilion 半山亭	16 Archway 牌楼
8 Bus Station 鼎湖山汽车站	17 Kengkou Store 坑口商店
9 Tea Flower Pavilion 花茶阁	18 Kengkou Bus Station 坑口汽车站

it is possible to reach Luofushan by making a number of transfers, but this is advised only if you can speak some Chinese. First take the train to Shitan. When exiting the railway station at Shitan, turn left and walk nearly one km to reach the main road where you get buses to Zengcheng (22 km north of Shitan). Zengcheng is on a major east-west highway and you can get buses or minibuses to Changning, which is six km from Luofushan. From Changning there are many minibuses going the remaining distance to the mountain.

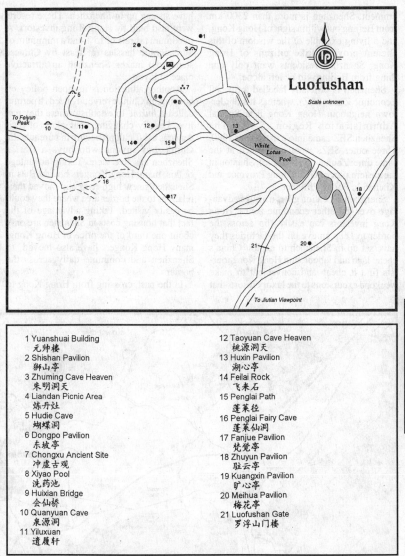

Luofushan

Scale unknown

White Lotus Pool

To Feiyun Peak

To Jiutian Viewpoint

1 Yuanshuai Building
   元帅楼
2 Shishan Pavilion
   狮山亭
3 Zhuming Cave Heaven
   朱明洞天
4 Liandan Picnic Area
   炼丹灶
5 Hudie Cave
   蝴蝶洞
6 Dongpo Pavilion
   东坡亭
7 Chongxu Ancient Site
   冲虚古观
8 Xiyao Pool
   洗药池
9 Huixian Bridge
   会仙桥
10 Quanyuan Cave
   泉源洞
11 Yiluxuan
   遗履轩

12 Taoyuan Cave Heaven
   桃源洞天
13 Huxin Pavilion
   湖心亭
14 Feilai Rock
   飞来石
15 Penglai Path
   蓬莱径
16 Penglai Fairy Cave
   蓬莱仙洞
17 Fanjue Pavilion
   梵觉亭
18 Zhuyun Pavilion
   驻云亭
19 Kuangxin Pavilion
   旷心亭
20 Meihua Pavilion
   梅花亭
21 Luofushan Gate
   罗浮山门楼

SHENZHEN

(shēnzhèn)

'The mountains are high and the emperor is far away' says an ancient Chinese proverb, meaning that life can be relatively free if one keeps far enough away from the central government. Shenzhen is more than 2300 km from Beijing but within sight of Hong Kong, and a living example of the wisdom of this ancient proverb. Like citizens of Hong Kong, Shenzhen residents want only one thing from Beijing – to be left alone.

Shenzhen is officially labelled a Special Economic Zone (SEZ), whereas it's border-town neighbour Hong Kong is a Special Administration Region (SAR). The Shenzhen SEZ came into existence in 1980. Three other SEZs were established at the same time: Zhuhai (near Macau), Shantou in the eastern part of Guangdong Province and Xiamen in Fujian Province.

Shenzhen's location gives it a huge advantage over the other economic zones. Hong Kong investors can easily slip across the border to keep an eye on the factories they have set up in Shenzhen to exploit China's cheap land and labour; and Hong Kong tourists find it cheap and convenient to make weekend excursions to the luxury resorts that

have sprung up in Shenzhen. These resorts were also built by Hong Kong investors. A maximum tax rate of 15% and a minimum of bureaucratic hassles (at least by Chinese standards) makes Shenzhen an attractive place to invest.

Another attraction is its open policy on housing. In China everybody needs a permit, called a *hukou*, to establish where they can live. Legally changing your place of residence is a difficult procedure in bureaucratic China, but anyone who buys a flat in Shenzhen can live there. Taking advantage of this, many Hong Kongers bought flats in Shenzhen's new high-rises and moved their relatives to the border area where they could be easily visited. Taking advantage of the fact that housing costs in Shenzhen are only about one third of the price in Hong Kong, many Hong Kongers have also moved to Shenzhen and commute daily across the border.

In the past, crossing from Hong Kong to

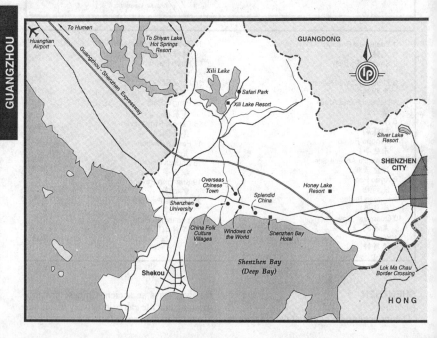

Shenzhen was like entering another world – the two cities couldn't have been more different. But these days, the only major difference is that cars in Shenzhen drive on the right side of the road.

Shenzhen is China's leading boom town (if you don't include Hong Kong). Not only is the economy exploding, so is the population. While hardly anyone wanted to live in Shenzhen when it was first designated a SEZ, today the government has to fight to keep people out. Access to the SEZ is restricted – Chinese citizens need a special permit to visit, though foreigners can drop in by just showing a passport. Indeed, Shenzhen experiences the same problem as Hong Kong with illegal immigrants. To stem the human tide, an electric fence has been installed around the SEZ. Nevertheless, the population of more than 3.5 million continues to expand, and Shenzhen seems destined to become one of China's largest cities.

Shenzhen is a bold experiment. The Chinese government is learning from running Shenzhen just how a modern capitalist economy works (or doesn't work). And if there's one thing the people of Hong Kong sincerely hope, it's that the Chinese government will learn the cardinal rule of capitalism – nonintervention.

Orientation

The name 'Shenzhen' refers to three places: Shenzhen City (opposite the Hong Kong border crossing at Lo Wu); Shenzhen Special Economic Zone (SEZ); and Shenzhen County, which extends several km north of the SEZ. Most of the hotels, restaurants and shopping centres are in Shenzhen City, along Renmin Lu, Jianshe Lu and Shennan Lu.

In the western area of the SEZ is the port of Shekou, where you can get a hoverferry to Hong Kong. Shenzhen University is also in the west, as are the holiday resorts of Shenzhen Bay and Honey Lake. The main

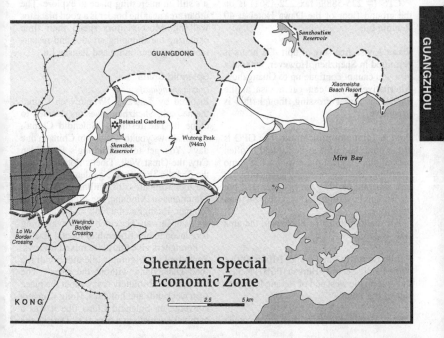

attraction in the eastern part of the zone is the beach at Xiaomeisha.

The northern part of the SEZ is cut off from the rest of China by an electric fence, to prevent smuggling and to keep back the hordes of people trying to emigrate illegally into Shenzhen and Hong Kong. There is a checkpoint where you leave the SEZ. You don't need your passport to get out but you will need it to get back in, so don't leave it in your hotel if you decide to make a day trip outside Shenzhen.

To get from the front (east) side of the railway station to the back (west), you have to find the pedestrian underpass *(dìxià dào)*. It's not at all conspicuous and you may have to ask someone where it is.

Information
Tourist Office CITS (☎ 220-2320; fax 223-0473) has it's office in a wing of the Guangdong Hotel on Shennan Lu (the entrance is from Nanhu Lu).

CTS (☎ 225-5888; fax 222-4561) is on the ground floor of the Dawa Hotel at 40 Renmin Lu.

Visas A visa-free stay of up to 72 hours is permitted in Shenzhen. However, without a visa you cannot continue on to Guangzhou. Alternatively, you can get a visa at the Shenzhen border crossing, though this is expensive.

Post & Telecommunications The GPO is at the north end of Jianshe Lu and is often packed out – a great place to practise sumo wrestling. The telecommunications office is in a separate building on Shennan Lu, but most hotels now offer IDD service right from your room.

For dialling direct to Shenzhen, the area code is 0755.

Public Security The Foreign Affairs Office of the Public Security Bureau (PSB) (☎ 557-2114) is on the west end of Jiefang Lu, north side of the street.

Money Hotels change money or you can do

it right at the Hong Kong border crossing. There is also a large Bank of China at 23 Jianshe Lu.

Black market money changers will often approach you on the street and yell *'gǎngbì'* ('Hong Kong dollars'). Like elsewhere in China, they are skilled rip-off artists.

HongkongBank, on Chunfeng Lu, has an ATM machine which accepts Hong Kong-issued ETC cards, plus foreign cards which use the Cirrus system.

Maps Chinese-character maps of Shenzhen are widely available from stalls near the railway station and elsewhere. There is at least one edition that is partially in English, though you may have to hunt around to find it. Maps of Shenzhen published in Hong Kong are, surprisingly, not too good.

Shenzhen City
(shēnzhèn shì)
There isn't much in Shenzhen City to see, but it's still an interesting place to explore. The urban area near the border is a good place for walking. Most visitors spend their time exploring the shopping arcades and restaurants along Renmin Lu and Jianshe Lu.

Splendid China
(jǐnxiù zhōnghuá)
Inspired by Taiwan's 'Window on China' theme park, Shenzhen investors decided to clone it. The result is 'Splendid China', which allows you to 'visit all of China in one day'. You get to see Beijing's Forbidden City, the Great Wall, Tibet's Potala Palace, the Shaolin Temple, the gardens of Suzhou, the rock formations of Guilin, the Tianshan Mountains of Xinjiang, the Stone Forest in Yunnan, Huangguoshu Falls and even some sights in Taiwan. The catch is that everything is reduced to one fifteenth of its real size.

Foreigners give this place mixed reviews. Some find it intriguing while others call it a 'bad Disneyland without the rides'. The Chinese are absolutely crazy about the place – on weekends and holidays, Hong Kongers converge on Splendid China like it was a carnival – which, in a way, it is. Despite the circus atmosphere, it might at least give you some idea of just what parts of China you'd like to visit.

Splendid China is in the western end of the Special Economic Zone, near Shenzhen Bay. From the railway station there are frequent minibuses. If you're entering Shenzhen by hoverferry, you could take a taxi from Shekou.

Windows of the World
(shìjiè zhīchuāng)
This takes the concept of Splendid China one step further by providing models of sights in foreign countries. Thus you can admire miniaturised versions of the Eiffel Tower and the Golden Gate Bridge.

For most Chinese, this is about as close as they can get to making a trip abroad. Westerners tend to be less impressed, but if you're feeling homesick it could be worth a shot.

Windows of the World is sandwiched between Splendid China and the China Folk Culture Villages (see next section).

China Folk Culture Villages
(zhōngguó mínsú wénhuà cūn)
In this case, rather than admiring miniaturised temples and statues, you get to see real-life ethnic minorities. To add to the effect there are over 20 re-creations of minority villages, including a cave, a Lama temple, drum tower, rattan bridge and a statue of Guanyin (Kuanyin), the Goddess of Mercy. Just to remind you of China's claim to Taiwan, the 'Gaoshan' ('high mountain') minority was invented to represent Taiwan's 10 aboriginal tribes. However, as of yet there are no representatives of Hong Kong's *gwailo* ('foreign devil') minority – could be an employment opportunity there.

China Folk Culture Villages is on the west side of Windows of the World.

Overseas Chinese Town
(huáqiáo chéng)
This is not really meant to be a tourist attraction, but rather a residential area for upper-crust Overseas Chinese investors who operate businesses in Shenzhen. There are

some factories in this district too, but they are not the dirty, smoke-belching type. The official name for this place is the Overseas Chinese Town Economic Development Area and it covers some 5 sq km, of which only half is yet developed.

CTS (Hong Kong branch) has invested heavily in this place, and there is an Overseas Chinese Town CTS branch office (☎ 660-1163). If you're interested in coming here to invest or speculate in real estate (a popular Hong Kong activity) this is the office to contact. The Overseas Chinese Town is just to the north of Splendid China.

Safari Park
(yěshēng dòngwùyuán)
This is essentially a zoo, but the animals get to stay outdoors and the people are inside – inside cars and tour buses, that is. It's a drive-through experience and well-suited to families – Hong Kongers are most enthralled by the place.

The park features a wide range of animals including deer, lions, tigers, baboons, giraffes and zebras. To avoid the tourist stampede, it's best to visit on week days.

The Safari Park is adjacent to Xili Lake to the west of town and about seven km north of Splendid China. The easiest way by far to get there is by taxi.

Botanic Gardens
(zhíwù gōngyuán)
While not necessarily spectacular, the gardens are spacious, green and one of the few places in the area not yet covered by concrete, skyscrapers or factories. The Botanic Gardens are north-east of town on the shores of the Shenzhen Reservoir.

Shekou
(shékǒu)
A rapidly growing port city at the western end of the Shenzhen SEZ, Shekou is of minor interest to tourists. However, over 1000 expat Westerners live here, employed chiefly in oil exploration and high-tech industries. Many of the foreigners are housed in pricey

GUANGZHOU

GUANGZHOU

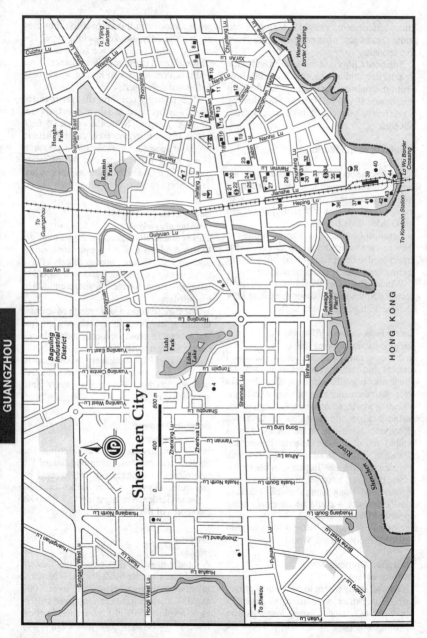

PLACES TO STAY
8 Nam Fong International Hotel
南方国际大酒店
9 Jingpeng Hotel
京鹏宾馆
10 Tung Nam International Hotel
东南国际大酒店
12 Sunshine Hotel
阳光酒店
13 Far East Grand Hotel & Cafe de Coral
远东大酒店
14 Gold Hotel
富丽华大酒店
16 Airlines & Guangdong Hotel
航空酒店
19 Landmark Hotel
富苑酒店
20 Wah Chung & Dawa Hotels & CTS
华中国际酒店，大华酒店
21 Shenzhen Hotel
深圳酒店
24 Petrel Hotel
海燕大酒店
25 Nanyang Hotel
南洋酒店
26 Shentie Hotel &
   Tiecheng Restaurant
深铁大厦，铁城酒家
28 Guanxin Hotel & McDonald's
广信酒店，麦当劳
29 Hong Yan Hotel
鸿厌大酒店
30 Century Plaza Hotel
新都酒店
32 Kingwu Hotel
京湖大酒店
35 Shangri-La Hotel
香格里拉大酒店
37 Forum Hotel
富临大酒店
42 Overseas Chinese Building
华侨大厦
43 Overseas Chinese Hotel
华侨酒店

PLACES TO EAT
7 McDonald's
麦当劳

11 McDonald's
麦当劳
15 Wendy's Hamburgers
云狄斯
27 Banxi Restaurant
泮溪酒家
31 Wendy's Hamburgers
   & HongkongBank
云狄斯，汇丰银行
33 Cafe de Coral
大家乐快餐
36 Fairwood Fast Food
大快活

OTHER
1 CAAC
航空大厦
2 China Eastern Airlines
中国东方航空公司
3 Xinhua Bookstore
新华书店
4 Shenzhen City Hall
深圳市政府
5 PSB
公安局外事科
6 Post Office
邮局
17 Telecommunications Building
电信大楼
18 CITS
中国国际旅行社
22 Bank of China (large)
中国银行
23 International Trade Centre
国贸大厦
34 Bank of China (small)
中国银行
38 Luohu Bus Station
罗湖汽车站
39 Railway Station & Dragon Inn
火车站，港龙大酒店
40 Luohu Commercial Plaza
罗湖商业城
41 Laundry Service
洗衣店
44 Customs & Immigration
联检大楼

GUANGZHOU

villa-style homes, and their tight-knit community is not unlike an upscale suburb in the USA or Australia.

There are many factories here, though really ugly structures are kept out of sight. North of the centre is Shenzhen University, which has acquired a reputation for its computer skills (including the ability to pirate Microsoft's hologram logo).

There are a number of posh and pricey hotels, some shopping centres and a few expat bars which are open only in the evening.

As a tourist attraction, Shekou doesn't offer much beyond an attractive waterfront

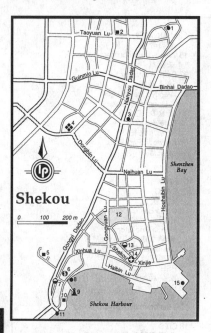

1 Shenzhen University
深圳大学
2 Anhua Xintaoyuan Hotel
安华新桃园大酒店
3 Zhubao Building
珠宝大厦
4 Star Moon Shopping Centre
星月广场
5 Marina Ming Wah Hotel
明华中心
6 Bank of China
中国银行
7 Bus Station
汽车站
8 Sea World
海上世界
9 Goddess Statue
女娲补天
10 Nanhai Hotel
南海酒店
11 Passenger Wharf
蛇口港客运站
12 Sihai Park
四海公园
13 Bus Station
汽车站
14 Shekou People's Hospital
蛇口人民医院
15 Shekou East Port
蛇口东角头港

park called Seaworld. Perhaps the most interesting thing about Shekou is its name, which means 'snake's mouth'.

Places to Stay – bottom end

The bad news is that there are no dormitories in Shenzhen. But the good news is that in Shenzhen you can get a much larger and more luxurious room than you could in Hong Kong for the same amount of money. The definition of 'bottom-end' accommodation in Shenzhen would be any hotel costing less than Y300 a night.

Hotels in Shenzhen typically give discounts during week days, as much as 40% off the regular price. This is also partially offset by an additional 10% tax, plus (in some hotels) an additional 5% surcharge.

The bottom of bottom-end lodgings is the *Overseas Chinese Hotel* (☎ 559-6688; fax 558-3975) *(huáqiáo jiǔdiàn)* at 68 Dayuan, Heping Lu. By way of compensation for its rather bleak surroundings, the staff are

friendly. Singles cost Y208 and doubles are Y272 and Y388.

It's easy to confuse the aforementioned with its near neighbour, the *Overseas Chinese Building* (☎ 557-3811) *(huáqiáo dàshà)*. It's also a bit tattered around the edges, but not bad. Doubles cost Y238. It's on Heping Lu, close to the railway station.

Another cheapie is the two-star *Shentie Hotel* (☎ 558-4248) *(shēntiě dàshà)* at 63 Heping Lu. Standard/de luxe doubles are Y220/260. More spacious flats cost Y320/520.

The *Jingpeng Hotel* (☎ 222-7190; fax 222-7191) *(jīngpéng bīnguǎn)* on Shennan Lu is an attractive place that offers good value for the money. However, it's a rather long walk from the border station. Doubles with twin beds are Y228.

Also towards the east end is the *Tung Nam International Hotel* (☎ 228-8688; fax 229-1103) *(dōngnán guójì dà jiǔdiàn)* at 82 Shennan Lu, with doubles for Y228, Y311 and Y498.

The *Guanxin Hotel* (☎ 223-8945; 225-5849) *(guǎnxìn jiǔdiàn)* at 22 Renmin Lu is quite a bargain. Doubles on week days cost Y280, though on weekends and holidays the tariff rises to Y360.

The *Kingwu Hotel* (☎ 232-6666; fax 232-6983) *(jīnghú dà jiǔdiàn)*, 66 Renmin Lu, is centrally located and easy to find. Singles/doubles are Y130/250.

The *Shenzhen Hotel* (☎ 223-8000; fax 222-2284) *(shēnzhèn jiǔdiàn)* at 156 Shennan Lu has doubles for Y252 and Y270. By Shenzhen standards this is good value for the money.

The *Nanyang Hotel* (☎ 222-4968; fax 223-8927) *(nányáng jiǔdiàn)* has standard/de luxe doubles for Y276/323. The hotel is on Jianshe Lu just north of Jiabin Lu.

The *Petrel Hotel* (☎ 223-2828; fax 222-1398) *(hǎiyàn dà jiǔdiàn)* on Jiabin Lu is a 29-storey luxury tower offering incredibly cheap singles/doubles for Y246/353. As for the name, the hotel's brochure clearly explains: 'Petrel hover at sea of the red sun shine upon.'

The *Dawa Hotel* (☎ 220-2828) *(dàhuá jiǔdiàn)* – home of CTS – is at 40 Renmin Lu. This new place has double rooms priced from Y238 to Y468.

The *Hong Yan Hotel* (☎ 225-4168; fax 225-4268) *(hóngyàn jiǔdiàn)* on Renmin Lu is another new place. Doubles are Y239 to Y269.

Places to Stay – middle

In Shenzhen, 'mid-range' would have to be defined as a hotel costing between Y300 and Y600.

The *Wah Chung Hotel* (☎ 223-8060) *(huázhōng guójì jiǔdiàn)* at 140 Shennan Lu has a very central location. Spacious singles/doubles cost Y300/380; suites are priced at Y440.

For a convenient location, you can hardly beat the *Dragon Inn* (☎ 232-9228; fax 233-4585) *(gǎnglóng dà jiǔdiàn)*, which is on the ground floor of the railway station. Compared to most of the train station hotels in China, this one is relatively luxurious (with prices to match). Standard doubles are Y600 and suites range from Y950 to Y1800.

The *Airlines Hotel* (☎ 223-7999; fax 223-7866) *(hángkōng dà jiǔdiàn)* at 130 Shennan Lu, has doubles for Y300, Y353 and Y567. It's modern, clean and ruthlessly air-conditioned.

The *Guangdong Hotel* (☎ 222-8339; fax 223-4560) *(yuèhǎi jiǔdiàn)* is a sparkling glass and concrete edifice on Shennan Lu. Doubles cost Y567 to Y727; suites are Y941 to Y2782.

In the same neighbourhood as the preceding is the *Far East Grand Hotel* (☎ 220-5369; fax 220-0239) *(yuǎndōng dà jiǔdiàn)*, 104 Shennan Lu. Singles are Y468 and doubles are Y492 and Y524.

Nam Fong International Hotel (☎ 225-6728; fax 225-6936) *(nánfāng guójì dà jiǔdiàn)* is an attractive place at 55 Shennan Lu. Doubles cost Y580 to Y1070.

The *Gold Hotel* (☎ 218-0288; fax 217-7436) *(fùlìhuá dà jiǔdiàn)* at 97 Shennan Lu is quite a bargain for what appears to be a luxury hotel. It even offers 40% discounts during off-peak times. Regular rates for doubles are Y580 to Y850 while suites are Y1180 to Y1380.

Places to Stay – top end

As in Guangzhou, a way to get a good discount at top-end places is to book through CTS in Hong Kong. Week day off-season rates are also discounted. The following are for the regular rates.

The very posh *Century Plaza Hotel* (☎ 232-0888; fax 233-4060) *(xīndū jiǔdiàn)* has a good spot on Chunfeng Lu, between Jianshe Lu and Renmin Lu. Standard/de luxe doubles are Y1100/1210. Four stars.

The *Forum Hotel* (☎ 558-6333; fax 556-1700) *(fùlín dà jiǔdiàn)* is at 67 Heping Lu, just to the west of the railway station. This place positively radiates luxury and gives discounts up to 37% on week days during off-season. Regular prices for doubles are Y1177 to Y1337; standard suites cost Y1979. Four stars.

If you really want to go first class, the *Shangri-La Hotel* (☎ 223-0888; fax 223-9878) *(xiānggé lǐlā dà jiǔdiàn)* has it all. It's on Jianshe Lu facing the railway station and

GUANGZHOU

is topped by a revolving restaurant. Doubles cost Y1260 and Y1365. Five stars.

The newest top-end place is the excellent *Sunshine Hotel* (☎ 223-3888; fax 222-6719) at 1 Jiabin Lu. Doubles start at Y1000 but can be discounted by up to 40%. You can book rooms through the hotel's Hong Kong agent (☎ 2575-5989).

Also new is the *Landmark Hotel* (☎ 217-2288) *(fùyuàn jiǔdiàn)* at 2 Nanhu Lu. Singles/doubles start at Y1124/1263. Five stars.

Shekou Best in town is the *Nanhai Hotel* (☎ 669-2888; fax 669-2440) *(nánhǎi jiǔdiàn)*. Doubles are Y920 but big discounts are possible. Five stars.

Marina Ming Wah (☎ 668-9968; fax 668-6668; HK 2838-3855) *(mínghuá zhōngxīn)* on Guishan Lu, has rooms starting from Y320.

Resort Villages Although the Shenzhen SEZ was originally meant to attract high-technology manufacturing, one of its chief sources of foreign exchange are the luxurious hotel-recreation complexes. These places defy description, but are a bit like Club Med, Disneyland, old European castles and Hong Kong's Ocean Park all rolled into one. They offer discos, saunas, swimming pools, golf courses, horse riding, roller coasters, supermarkets, palaces, castles, moats, Chinese pavilions, statues and monorails – not to mention luxury hotels. The huge dim sum restaurants are transformed into nightclubs in the evening, with Las Vegas-style floor shows.

The resorts are crowded on the weekends, so avoid visiting unless you consider watching the crowd one of the amusements.

Week day prices are about Y400 for a double, which often includes a free breakfast and transportation to and from the Shenzhen border crossing (train station area). On week days, the resorts often throw in free use of their facilities (sauna, disco, swimming pool, etc) or else offer sizeable discounts. You can often get some coupons or a discount at the resort's shopping arcades if you stay in their hotel.

You can book directly through the hotels or the resorts' Hong Kong offices. Hong Kong travel agents, including CTS, can tell you about special package deals that the hotels won't bother to mention. The major resorts include:

Honey Lake Country Club – (☎ 370-5061; fax 370-5045) *(xiāngmì hú dùjià cūn)* west of Shenzhen City. It's known for its amusement park, a miniature version of Disneyland called China Happy City *(zhōngguó yúlè chéng)* which is complete with monorail, roller coaster and castles. Despite the name, Honey Lake itself is little more than a duck pond. Doubles cost HK$250 to HK$400. Hotel guests receive a 20% discount in the restaurant, amusement park, sauna and other facilities. Three stars. The Hong Kong booking office (☎ 2380-8080, 2780-0351) is in the Park-In Commercial Centre at Dundas and Tung Choi Sts in Yau Ma Tei.

Shenzhen Bay Hotel – (☎ 660-0111 ext 8888; fax 660-0139) *(shēnzhèn wān dà jiǔdiàn)* is on the beach and has good views across the bay to the New Territories. On week days doubles cost Y550 to Y700. Hotel guests have free access to the swimming pool, night club shows and other facilities. Guests also receive a discount at the shopping centre. Four stars.

Xili Lake Holiday Resort – (☎ 662-6888; fax 662-6123) *(xīlì hú)* has a nice lakeside view and good facilities. There is boating on the lake and a water-oriented sports park similar to Hong Kong's Water World (though not as good). The nearby Safari Park is an added attraction and there is even a camping ground. Doubles in the hotel range from HK$300 to HK$500 on week days. Three stars.

Shiyan Lake Hot Springs Resort – (☎ 996-0143) *(shíyán hú wēnquán dùjià cūn)* is five km to the north-west of Shenzhen outside the SEZ. There are good country club facilities here. Doubles range from Y320 to Y420 on week days.

Xiaomeisha Beach Resort – (☎ 555-0000) *(xiǎoméishā dà jiǔdiàn)* is the most beautiful of all. It's on the east side of the SEZ on the shore of Mirs Bay and has the best beach in Shenzhen. *Xiaomeisha* means 'little plum sand' and next door an annex is being built at *Dameisha* ('big plum sand'). Doubles cost Y400, which includes breakfast and a 20% discount on other meals. Weekend rates are higher. Three stars.

Silver Lake Resort Camp – (☎ 222-2827; fax 224-2622) *(yín hú lǚyóu zhōngxīn)* is very close to Shenzhen City but is not as nice as the other resorts. Doubles range from Y290 to Y430 on week days.

Places to Eat

Shenzhen railway station has a collection of reasonably priced takeaway *food stalls*, *fast-food eateries* and *cafes*.

Dim sum breakfast and lunch is available in all but the scruffiest *hotels*. Usually the dim sum restaurants are on the second or third floor rather than by the lobby. Prices are slightly lower than in Hong Kong.

You'll find quite an exotic menu at the *Tiecheng Restaurant* at 63 Heping Lu. Choose your meal while it's still hopping around in its cage (rabbits, pheasant, etc) or taking a swim (eel, octopus and so on). Vegetarians had better pass this place up.

One of Shenzhen's most famous eateries is the *Banxi Restaurant* (☎ 223-8081) *(bànxī jiǔjiā)* at 33 Jianshe Lu.

Shenzhen is the site of China's first *McDonald's* (that is, outside of Hong Kong). Whether or not you want to eat here, you might wish to visit for historical reasons. The restaurant can be found on the north side of Jiefang Lu.

Yet another symbol of creeping Westernisation is *Wendy's Hamburgers (yúndísī)*. You'll find one of its branches at the corner of Shennan Lu and Dongmen Lu.

Fairwood Fast Food (dà kuàihuó) offers Hong Kong-style fast food – not bad actually. The easiest branch to find is on the west side of Heping Lu, just north of the flashy Forum Hotel.

Café de Coral is another Hong Kong fast-food chain – it does a mean curry chicken and rice. There's a branch near the southern end of Heping Lu.

On the north-east corner of Jiabin Lu and Renmin Lu is the International Trade Centre *(guómào dàsha')* which has no English sign, but is easily recognised by its mammoth high-rise topped with the *Revolving Restaurant* (☎ 225-1464) *(xuánzhuǎng cāntīng)*. Though not the cheapest restaurant in town, you can't beat the view. The ground floor lobby is often flooded with Chinese tourists taking photos of each other standing in front of the fountains. There is a supermarket and several good

shops on the third and fourth floors by the fountains (not in the high-rise section).

Entertainment

In the central city, the lack of a gwailo community pretty much limits the nightlife to karaoke sessions. There are a couple of discos in the five-star hotels.

It's a somewhat different story out in Shekou, where about 1000 expats live and work. Gwailo pubs seem to pop up (and close just as fast) in the vicinity of the Nanhai Hotel. Some of those that have come (and perhaps gone by the time you read this) include the Red Rooster, Casablanca, Joe Bananas, Hammers and the Hennessy Bar.

Activities

Hong Kongers with a passion for golf often head to Shenzhen because the green fees are lower and the golf courses more spacious. For information, contact the Shenzhen Golf Club (☎ 330888). The club has a contact office in Hong Kong (☎ 2890-6321) in Hang Lung Centre at Paterson and Yee Wo Sts in Causeway Bay.

There is also the Shenzhen Famous Businessmen's Outdoor Sport Club (☎ 336-3698 ext 11906) in room 1906 of the Grand Skylight Hotel *(gélán yúntiān dà jiǔdiàn)* at 68 Shennan Lu.

Getting There & Away

Air Shenzhen's Huangtian airport is rapidly becoming one of China's busiest, offering direct flights to most major Chinese cities. This makes Shenzhen a useful alternative for reaching China's hinterland when all flights from Hong Kong are full.

Airline booking offices are inconveniently located about three km west of central Shenzhen. Therefore, it may be easier to book through a travel agency such as CITS or CTS, or maybe even at Huangtian airport itself. If you don't mind trekking out there, the two airline offices can be found as follows: CAAC (☎ 324-1440), Shennan Lu just west of Huaqiang South Lu; and China Eastern Airlines (☎ 322-2931), corner of Hongli West Lu and Huaqiang North Lu.

Bus From Hong Kong bus services to Shenzhen are run by Citybus (☎ 2736-3888) and the Motor Transport Company of Guangdong & Hong Kong, from the Guangdong bus station on Canton Rd (between Austin and Jordan Rds in Kowloon). Citybus operates direct buses to various places in Shenzhen, including Huangtian airport, Safari Park, Windows of the World, Shenzhen Bay and central Shenzhen. For most foreign travellers, buses are not a likely option unless you are on a tour. For information and tickets, contact CTS or Citybus.

There are long-distance buses to Fuzhou, Xiamen and other coastal cities departing from the Overseas Chinese Travel Service (*huáqiáo lǚyóu bù*), next to the Overseas Chinese Building on Heping Lu.

Minibus There are frequent minibuses running between Guangzhou and Shenzhen. Fares are approximately Y80 and travel time is 2.5 hours (provided the bus takes the new expressway).

In Shenzhen, departures are from the Luohu bus station (*luóhú qìchē zhàn*) just to the east of the railway station next to the Hong Kong border crossing.

In Guangzhou, buses depart from the Guangzhou City bus station near Guangzhou train station. Minibuses also run directly from Guangzhou's Baiyun airport to Shenzhen.

Train The Kowloon-Canton Railway (KCR) offers the fastest and most convenient transport to Shenzhen from Hong Kong. Trains to the border crossing at Lo Wu begin from Kowloon KCR station in Tsim Sha Tsui East. Unless you want to walk to Kowloon KCR station, take the MTR to Kowloon Tong station, then change to the KCR. The trains start running at 6.05 am. The fare from Kowloon to Lo Wu is HK$29. The last train to Lo Wu is at 9.45 pm (there are trains departing until 12.41 am which do *not* go all the way to Lo Wu). The border closes at midnight and reopens at 6 am. From Kowloon to Lo Wu it's 34 km and the trip takes 37 minutes. Avoid taking the train on weekends, when it's packed to overflowing and the stampede at the border crossing is a horror.

There are frequent local trains running between Guangzhou and Shenzhen and the journey takes a little over two hours. There are departures from Shenzhen about every 30 minutes throughout the day from 6.15 am to 8.40 pm.

Car It is possible to drive across the Hong Kong-Shenzhen border, but it makes little sense to do so given the convenience of public transport. There is also a pretty long queue of vehicles at the border checkpoints.

The original border crossing is at Man Kam To on the Hong Kong side and is called Wenjindu on the Chinese side. Another border crossing was opened at Lok Ma Chau in 1991.

Boat Hoverferries run between Hong Kong and Shekou, Shenzhen's port on the west side of town. In Hong Kong, departures are from the China-Hong Kong City ferry terminal on Canton Rd in Tsim Sha Tsui and from the Hong Kong-Macau ferry terminal in Sheung Wan. The fare is HK$104 and HK$135 depending on the class. The journey takes 45 minutes and the schedule is currently as follows:

Kowloon – Shekou

From Kowloon	From Shekou
7.50am	9am
10.15am	11.30am
1.30pm	2.45pm
4pm	5.15pm

Hong Kong Island – Shekou

From Hong Kong	From Shekou
8.20am	8.15am
9.30am	10.45am
2pm	3.15pm
4.30pm	5pm

There is one jetcat (jet-powered catamaran) daily from Macau to Shekou. It departs Macau at 8.30 am and arrives at 10 am. The cost is M$79.

There are many boats between Shekou and Zhuhai (near Macau). Departures are about once every 30 minutes throughout the day from 7.30 am to 5 pm.

Getting Around

The Airport There are shuttle buses between the airport and the CAAC office at Shennan Lu. Minibuses and taxis also add to the choices, but remember that in Shenzhen's traffic, getting to the airport can take a considerable amount of time.

If you want to travel directly between the airport and Hong Kong, there is a rapid boat service (jet-powered catamaran) that takes 60 minutes, at least twice as fast as the bus. The sole ticketing agent in Hong Kong is the branch office of CTS (☎ 2736-1863) in Kowloon's China-Hong Kong City ferry terminal on Canton Rd. In Shenzhen, you can purchase tickets at the airport. Deck class is HK$175; super-deck HK$275; and VIP cabin HK$1650 (at that price why not charter a helicopter?). Currently, there are six sailings daily as follows:

Hong Kong – Huangtian airport (Shenzhen)

From Hong Kong	From Shenzhen
7.30am	9am
9am	10.30am
10.30am	noon
1pm	2.15pm
2.30pm	4pm
3.45pm	5.15pm

Getting to Huangtian airport by direct bus from Hong Kong is also possible. Citybus No 505 costs HK$150 and tickets can be bought from CTS in Hong Kong. Another place in Hong Kong selling these tickets is MTR Travel, which has offices in the following MTR stations: Admiralty, Causeway Bay, Central, Kwun Tong, Mong Kok, Tai Koo, Tsim Sha Tsui and Tsuen Wan. The schedule is limited and subject to change, so ring Citybus (☎ 2736-3888) to enquire about changes. Currently, departures from Hong Kong are in the morning only at 7.45, 8, 9.15, 9.30 and 9.45 am.

Bus & Minibus The government-run city buses are not nearly as crowded as elsewhere in China. However, destinations are written exclusively in Chinese.

The minibuses are faster. These are privately run and cheap, but if you can't read the destination in Chinese characters, you will need help.

Taxi Taxis are abundant but not so cheap because their drivers have been spoilt by free-spending tourists. There are no meters so negotiate the fare before you get in. Make sure you understand which currency is being negotiated – drivers will usually ask for payment in Hong Kong dollars.

Getting There & Away

The easiest way to get to the resorts is to take a minibus from the train station area in Shenzhen. These are operated by the hotels and only accept payment in Hong Kong dollars. The privately run minibuses that run up and down Shennan Lu are cheaper and accept payment in RMB, but you'll have to find out which minibus goes where.

HUMEN

(hǔmén)

The small city of Humen on the Pearl River is only of interest to history buffs with particular curiosity about the Opium Wars that directly led to Hong Kong's creation as a British colony. According to one Chinese leaflet:

Humen was the place where the Chinese people captured and burned the opium dumped into China by the British and American merchants in the 1830s and it was also the outpost of the Chinese people to fight against the aggressive Opium War. In 1839, Lin Zexu, the then imperial envoy of the Qing government, resolutely put a ban on opium smoking and the trade of opium. Supported by the broad masses of the people, Lin Zexu forced the British and American opium mongers to hand over 20,285 cases of opium...and burned all of them at Humen Beach, Dongguang County. This just action showed the strong will of the Chinese people to resist imperialist aggression...

At the end of the First Opium War, after the Treaty of Nanking, there was a British Supplementary Treaty of the Bogue, signed 8

October 1843. The Bogue Forts *(shājiǎo pàotái)* at Humen are now the site of an impressive museum which commemorates the destruction of the surrendered opium which sparked the First Opium War. There are many exhibits – including large artillery pieces and other relics – and the actual ponds in which Commissioner Lin Zexu had the opium destroyed. When the new museum opened, there was a special exhibition commemorating the 150th anniversary of the war.

The only problem with this place is getting there. No buses go directly to Humen, but buses and minibuses travelling from Shenzhen to Guangzhou go right by. You could ask to be let off at the Humen access road, and then get a taxi, hitch or walk the five km into town.

At least on paper, there are daily ferries directly from Hong Kong to Taiping, which is almost walking distance from Humen. These depart Hong Kong at 8.45 am and 2.20 pm, returning to Hong Kong at 11.50 am and 4.50 pm. However, you'd be wise to enquire about the current schedule at the ferry ticket office in the China-Hong Kong City ferry terminal in Tsim Sha Tsui.

In Guangzhou, buses direct to Taiping depart from the Guangzhou City bus station near Guangzhou train station.

ZHUHAI
(zhūhǎi)

From any hilltop in Macau, you can gaze to the north and see a mass of modern buildings just across the border in China. This is the Zhuhai Special Economic Zone (SEZ). Like the Shenzhen SEZ, Zhuhai was built from the soles up on what was farmland less than a decade ago. The areas near the beach have several high-class resort playgrounds catering to Chinese residents of Hong Kong and Macau as well as the occasional foreigner. Cadres also come to Zhuhai for 'meetings', usually returning to Beijing with a good suntan and a suitcase full of electronic goodies which can be sold for a profit up north.

Many travellers conclude that, having seen Shenzhen, they will bypass Zhuhai.

This is a pity since Zhuhai has its own character and in many ways is more attractive than Shenzhen.

However, Zhuhai is changing, and the speed of development is almost frightening. Travellers from the 1980s (even *late* 1980s) remember Zhuhai as a small agricultural town with a few rural industries and a quiet beach. Nowadays, high-rise hotels, factories and workers' flats have crowded out the few remaining farms and half of the beach has been paved to make way for a new waterfront freeway.

Be that as it may, Zhuhai is more laid-back than Shenzhen and definitely cleaner than Guangzhou (for now, at least). If you're looking for an easily accessible getaway from Hong Kong and Macau, but with all the modern conveniences, Zhuhai is worth a visit. Zhuhai is so close to the border that a visit can be arranged as a day trip from Macau, and you can see many of the sights just travelling by foot. Most travellers don't linger for long, but if nothing else, Zhuhai can be used as a stepping stone to Guangzhou and beyond.

Orientation

Zhuhai City is a sprawling municipality and Special Economic Zone (SEZ) larger in land area than all of Hong Kong. The central area is opposite Macau and is divided into three main areas. The area nearest the Macau border is called Gongbei and is the main tourist area with lots of hotels, restaurants and shops. To the north-east is Jida, the eastern part of which has Zhuhai's harbour *(jiǔzhōu gǎng)*. Xiangzhou is the northernmost part of Zhuhai's urban sprawl.

West of the central area it's flat and fertile delta country. Until recently, the west was entirely farmland but land reclamation and factory building should be taken as a sign of the urban horrors to come.

Information

Tourist Office CTS (☎ 888-8056) has its office inside the Overseas Chinese Guesthouse (also called the Huaqiao Hotel) on Yingbin Dadao.

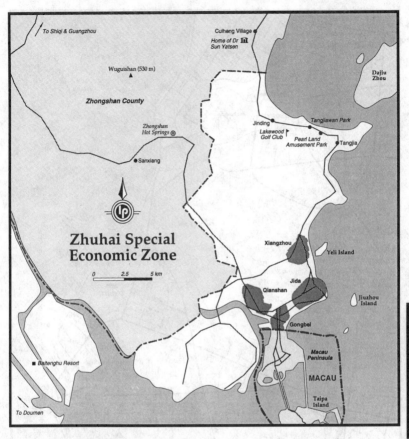

Zhuhai Special Economic Zone

To Shiqi & Guangzhou

Culheng Village
Home of Dr
Sun Yatsen

Dajiu
Zhou

Wuguishan (530 m) ▲

Zhongshan County

Jinding
Tangliawan Park
Lakewood
Golf Club
Pearl Land
Amusement Park
Tangjia

Zhongshan
Hot Springs ◎

Sanxiang ●

Xiangzhou
Yeli Island

Jida
Qianshan
Jiuzhou
Island

0   2.5   5 km

Gongbei

Macau
Peninsula

MACAU

Baitenghu Resort ■

Taipa
Island

To Doumen

GUANGZHOU

Visas Like Shenzhen, Zhuhai permits a visa-free stay for up to 72 hours, but at the moment it's not available to British nationals. No matter what your nationality, this type of visa limits your stay to the Zhuhai SEZ and you cannot continue northwards to Guangzhou unless you have a regular Chinese visa.

Public Security The Public Security Bureau (PSB) (☎ 822-2459) is in the Xiangzhou district on the corner of Anping Lu and Kangning Lu.

Money The Bank of China is a gleaming building next to the towering Yindo Hotel on the corner of Yuehai Lu and Yingbin Dadao. You can also change money in most hotels, but another good place in the Gongbei district is the Nan Tung Bank on the corner of Yuehai Lu and Shuiwan Lu. There is an official money changer at the Macau border entry/exit station.

The black marketeers hanging out by the border crossing are basically thieves.

Post & Telecommunications The most useful post office is on Yuehai Donglu. You

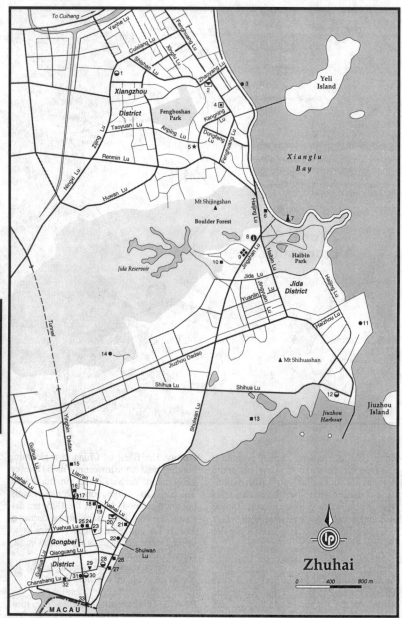

To Cuiheng

Yanhe Lu

Cuixiang Lu

Fengshuang Lu

Xinglu Lu

Shishan Lu

Zhaoyang Lu

Xiangzhou

District

Fengboshan Park

Kangning Lu

Fenghuang Lu

Taoyuan Lu

Anping Lu

Dongfeng Lu

Ziling Lu

Ninpoi Lu

Renmin Lu

Huwan Lu

Haijing Lu

Xianglu Bay

Yeli Island

Mt Shijingshan

Boulder Forest

Jida Reservoir

Jinghai Lu

Haibin Lu

Haibin Park

Jida District

Jida Lu

Yuanlin Lu

Jingxian Lu

Haijing Lu

Haizhou Lu

Tunnel

Jiuzhou Dadao

Shihua Lu

Shihua Lu

Mt Shihuashan

Jiuzhou Island

Shuiwan Lu

Jiuzhou Harbour

Yingbin Dadao

Guihua Lu

Yuehai Lu

Lian'an Lu

Yuehai Lu

Yuehua Lu

Yuehai Lu

Gongbei

Qiaoguang Lu

Shuiwan Lu

District

Guihua Lu

Chansheng Lu

MACAU

Zhuhai

0   400   800 m

GUANGZHOU

PLACES TO STAY
6 Jiari Hotel
假日酒店
10 Zhuhai Hotel
珠海宾馆
13 ZHR Hotel
珠海度假村
15 Huaqiao Hotel
华侨宾馆
16 Yindo Hotel
银都酒店
18 Good World Hotel
好世界酒店
19 Guangdong Hotel
粤海酒店
21 Popoko Hotel
步步高大酒店
24 Overseas Chinese Hotel
华侨大酒店
26 Gongbei Palace Hotel
拱北宾馆
27 Jiuzhou Hotel
九洲酒店
32 Fortune Hotel
福海大酒店

PLACES TO EAT
23 Fairwood Fast Food
大快活
29 Restaurant Row
餐厅

OTHER
1 Xiangzhou Bus Station
香洲汽车站
2 Post Office
邮局

3 Xiangzhou Harbour
香洲码头
4 Martyrs' Mausoleum
烈士陵园
5 PSB
公安局
7 Zhuhai Mermaid Statue
珠海渔女
8 Shijingshan Tourist Centre
石景山旅游中心
9 Jiuzhou Cheng (shopping mall)
九洲城
11 Helicopter Pad
直升机场
12 Jiuzhou Harbour Passenger
Terminal
九洲港客运站
14 Bailian Grotto
往白莲洞公园
17 Bank of China
中国银行
20 Post Office
邮店局
22 Beauty Salons
美容院
25 Gongbei Market
拱北市场
28 Gongbei Bus Station
& Yongtong Hotel
长途汽车站，永通酒店
30 Local Bus Station
拱北公共汽车总站
31 Zhuhai-Gongbei Bus Company
珠海拱北客运站
33 Customs & Immigration
海关

can make IDD calls from your room in most hotels. The area code for Zhuhai is 0756.

Gongbei Market
(gǒngběi shìchǎng)
Most visitors start their exploration of Zhuhai from the area near the Macau border. It's worth taking a look at the Gongbei Market on Yuehua Lu, next to the Overseas Chinese Hotel. It's reasonably clean and not nearly as 'exotic' as the Qingping Market in Guangzhou – they keep the butchered dogs hidden when the tour buses come through here.

Haibin Park
(hǎibīn gōngyuán)
This park in the Jida district just keeps on

developing. At one time it was just trees, but now there's a swimming pool, shooting range, roller-skating rink, barbecue pits and the **Zhuhai Mermaid**. The mermaid, symbol of Zhuhai, is a statue just off the coast. She looked great until the new highway obscured the view.

Bus Nos 2, 4 and 9 can drop you off by the park entrance.

Bailian Grotto
(báilián dòng gōngyuán)
Bailian ('White Lotus') Grotto is in a small park on the slopes of Banzhangshan ('Camphor Mountain'). Features of the park include the Huatuo temple and the adjacent Dashi and

Liujiao pavilions. There is also the **Jidan Gardens** and a few villas.

Bailian Grotto is on the north side of Jiuzhou Dadao, which runs between Gongbei and Jida districts. Bus No 2 passes right by and can drop you off by the park entrance.

Resorts
(dùjià cūn)

The Zhuhai Holiday Resort (ZHR) just west of Jiuzhou harbour has the nicest beach in Zhuhai – or at least, it did have. The beach is largely being wasted by development and there isn't much open sand left. Still, the walk along the coastline from Gongbei to this beach is pleasant if not spectacular. Be sure to wander around the resort itself. You can't say it's not a beautiful place, though the statue of Mickey Mouse waving hello doesn't quite fit in with most Westerners' idea of paradise. The Chinese apparently don't agree. Carloads of them come to this place just to get their picture taken in front of the giant Disney rodent.

West of Haibin Park is an area called Shijingshan Tourist Centre *(shíjǐngshān lüyóu zhōngxīn)*. The tourist centre itself is no big deal, just some gardens, an artificial lake, a supermarket and shops selling tourist junk. However, if you go inside the centre, and head towards the back you'll find some stone steps going uphill. Follow them up and up and you'll quickly find yourself in a forest with big granite boulders all around. Keep climbing to the ridge and be rewarded with outstanding views of Zhuhai City, Zhongshan and Macau.

On the south side of Shijingshan Tourist Centre is Jiuzhou Cheng. From the outside, you'll probably think it's some kind of restored Ming dynasty village. Inside, you'll find that it's a fashionable shopping centre.

Nearby is the Zhuhai Resort *(zhūhǎi bīnguǎn)*, another playground for rich Hong Kongers and cadres attending 'meetings'. It's worth stopping for a brief look.

Pearl Land Amusement Park
(zhēnzhū lèyuán)

At the northern end of Zhuhai is the Pearl Land Amusement Park (☎ 331-1170), a land of Ferris wheels, roller coasters and various other rides capable of allowing you to see your lunch for the second time. Other features include 'Popeye World' and 'Thriller House'.

The park is open from 9 am to 5.30 pm. Minibuses running from Zhuhai north to Cuiheng can drop you off at Pearl Land.

Lakewood Golf Club
(zhūhǎi cuihú gāo'ěrfū qiú huì)

Adjacent to Pearl Land is the Lakewood Golf Club. Facilities include a 36-hole championship golf course, club house, putting green and driving range. If belting a little white ball isn't your style, the other major feature here is the **Zhuhai International Racing Circuit**. This is the first formula-one racing course in China, though so far no schedule of races has been announced.

Two hotels are being built here, along with villas and luxury apartments. Although the country club is basically for members, hotel guests are also permitted to play.

In Zhuhai, the place to contact for information is the Zhuhai Nanhai Oil Silver Bay Resort (☎ 335-2502; fax 335-2504). There is a separate phone number for membership (☎ 338-0591). There is also a Hong Kong office (☎ 2877-1128; fax 2877-8770) and a membership phone number (☎ 2877-1215).

Baitenghu Resort
(báiténghú dùjiàcūn)

To the west of central Zhuhai and near the town of Doumen is the Baitenghu Resort. It was originally set up as a recreation centre for the peasants, but recently the place has sprouted a parish of luxury hotels which look too pricey for the average Chinese rice farmer. The most attractive things here are the **lotus ponds** which cover nearly half the resort. Hong Kongers descend on the place, and the seafood restaurants here do a brisk business.

The resort is about 20 km west of central Zhuhai and minibuses make the trip. There are even direct boats from Hong Kong to

Doumen, which is a short taxi ride from the resort.

Lingding Island
(wài língdīng dǎo)

Rather than see all that revenue from the slot machines and dice going into Macau's pocket, Zhuhai has decided to launch a gambling resort of its own: Lingding Island. To entice customers, Hong Kong residents are permitted to visit the island without immigration and customs formalities, but this privilege is not granted to foreigners.

Not that it matters much. The whole project has been long on rhetoric and short on action. Direct ferries from Hong Kong to Lingding Island are supposed to be in operation and CTS is the ticket agent – unfortunately, no one at CTS knows anything about it. The island is only about 10 km due south of Cheung Chau in Hong Kong, but over 50 km from central Zhuhai. For this reason, Hong Kongers wanting to visit have chartered boats from Cheung Chau.

I confess that I haven't been to Lingding Island, and probably won't bother going until a regular ferry service begins. Right now, the only ferries from Zhuhai go once daily and stop along the way at Guishan Island.

Still, Zhuhai officials confidently predict Lingding Island will be the next Las Vegas. If so, don't forget you read it here first.

Places to Stay – middle

The good news is that hotels in Zhuhai are slightly cheaper than in Shenzhen. The bad news is that there really isn't much of a bottom end – you'd be hard pressed to find anything under Y270. There are no dormitories open to foreigners. As might be expected, hotel prices rise by at least 10% on weekends and public holidays.

The accommodation situation has been made more complicated by the Zhuhai PSB, which has placed many perfectly acceptable hotels off-limits to foreigners. This includes many hotels which allowed foreigners just one year ago. The excuse given for this is to 'improve the standards for our foreign guests', but the reality has to do with covering up Zhuhai's growing reputation as a haven for prostitution. It's not that prostitution has been cracked down on, it's just that foreigners can no longer stay in the hotels which have made a speciality out of this business. While a nightly parade of young women ply their trade along the eastern end of Yuehai Lu, the message from the Zhuhai PSB is that this service is strictly for the domestic market (which now includes Hong Kongers).

Near the border gate and in the same building as the Gongbei bus station is the *Yongtong Hotel* (☎ 888-8887; fax 888-4187) *(yǒngtōng jiǔdiàn)*. Because of its good location and affordable price, it's now the favoured place for backpackers. Doubles are Y278 to Y368.

A little further from the border is the *Overseas Chinese Hotel* (☎ 888-5183) *(huáqiáo dà jiǔdiàn)*, on the north side of Yuehua Lu between Yingbin Dadao and Lianhua Lu, right next to the Gongbei Market. Doubles are Y280 and Y360.

The *Fortune Hotel* (☎ 888-0888; fax 887-3787) *(fúhǎi dà jiǔdiàn)* is on Changsheng Lu, a road which always seems to be hopelessly torn to shreds by construction equipment. If they ever get the road repaired, this could be a good place to stay. Doubles are Y298 to Y520; suites are Y550 to Y8888.

The *Overseas Chinese Guesthouse* (☎ 888-6288) *(huáqiáo bīnguǎn)* on Yingbin Dadao, one block north of Yuehai Lu, has singles/doubles for Y245/260 and suites priced from Y436 to Y746.

The *Popoko Hotel* (☎ 888-6628; fax 888-9992) *(bùbùgāo dà jiǔdiàn)* is at 2 Yuehai Lu, on the corner with Shuiwan Lu near the waterfront. Double rooms cost Y273 to Y676.

Tucked away in the forested grounds of Haibin Park is the quiet (except on weekends) *Jiari Hotel* (☎ 333-3277) *(jiàrì jiǔdiàn)*. Double rooms are Y248 to Y416. Haibin Park is in the Jida district north-east of Gongbei, within walking distance of the Shijingshan Tourist Centre and luxurious Zhuhai Hotel.

Adjacent to the *Gongbei Palace Hotel* is

GUANGZHOU

the *Jiuzhou Hotel* (☎ 888-6851; fax 888-5254) *(jiŭzhōu jiŭdiàn)*. Doubles start at Y278 and skyrocket to Y498 for the cushier rooms, but breakfast is thrown in free. It's at 19 Shuiwan Lu, near Qiaoguang Lu.

The *Good World Hotel* (☎ 888-0222; fax 889-2061) *(hăo shìjiè jiŭdiàn)*, 82 Lianhua Lu, is a fine place for the price. De luxe doubles are Y321. There is a 10% surcharge with another 10% on weekends or 20% on public holidays.

Places to Stay – top end

The *Gongbei Palace Hotel* (☎ 888-6833; fax 888-5686) *(gŏngbĕi bīnguăn)* is the most luxurious place close to the border. It's by the waterfront at 21 Shuiwan Lu near Qiaoguang Lu, about a one-minute walk from the border crossing. Among the facilities are a disco, video game arcade, sauna and swimming pool (including water slide). Unfortunately, the 'beach' is just for looking – it's too rocky for swimming. The hotel runs bus tours of the surrounding area. Doubles are Y661 and Y736, but single/double rooms in a villa only cost Y460/535. There is a 15% service charge.

Guangdong Hotel (☎ 888-8128; fax 888-5063) *(yuèhăi jiŭdiàn)* at 30 Yuehai Lu, is a flashy place where doubles cost Y590 to Y800 and suites range from Y1180 to Y6250. There is a 15% surcharge.

The ultra-modern *Yindo Hotel* (☎ 888-3388; fax 888-3311) *(yíndū jiŭdiàn)* is a gleaming glass and steel high-rise dominating Zhuhai's skyline. It's Zhuhai's only five-star hotel, and easily the best in town. Amenities include a bowling alley and miniature golf course. The budget rooms cost a mere Y690 but the tariff for the presidential suite is a cool Y19,500. If it helps, you can get an extra bed thrown in for Y190. There is a 15% surcharge plus 10% more on weekends and public holidays. The hotel is on the corner of Yuehai Lu and Yingbin Dadao.

The *Zhuhai Hotel* (☎ 333-3718; fax 333-2339) *(zhūhăi bīnguăn)* near the Jida reservoir is meant to be a playground for the upper classes. It doesn't have the benefit of a beach or a casino, and nearby Macau is

more interesting so it's hard to see what the attraction is. Nevertheless, the Hong Kongers keep coming, and the hotel caters to them with a sauna, tennis courts, billiard room, swimming pool, nightclub and even mahjong rooms. For all that, it's not so unreasonable – double rooms cost Y450 to Y700 and villas start at Y900. There is a 15% surcharge.

The *Zhuhai Holiday Resort* (☎ 333-2038; fax 333-2036) *(zhūhăi dùjià cūn)*, or *ZHR* for short, is a four-star complex with spacious grounds. At one time it had the best beach in Zhuhai, but the sand has nearly disappeared under some new construction. Still, there are amenities such as a bowling alley, roller-skating rink, tennis courts, club house, go-kart racing, horse riding, camel riding, disco, karaoke, video game parlour and sauna. On the downside, service seems to have fallen off. The resort is on the shoreline north-east of Gongbei near Jiuzhou Harbour. Single rooms in the main hotel are Y650, but a villa for two people is a better deal at Y490. There is a 15% surcharge.

Places to Eat

The area near the Macau border crossing has the most of everything – restaurants, bakeries, night markets and street vendors. It also has the most pickpockets! Little kids who approach you as beggars will sometimes try to relieve you of your wallet. They work in groups and practically glue themselves to foreigners. Their parents can be equally aggressive. Hang on to your wallet and you'll find plenty to spend your money on.

Right near the border crossing is *Maxim's* (☎ 888-5209) at 4 Lianhua Lu, the Hong Kong fast-food chain famous for its cakes. It's a good place to catch a quick breakfast. You'll see many other restaurants around the border area.

The ubiquitous Hong Kong chain *Fairwood Fast Food (dà kuàihuó)* has made its debut in Zhuhai. You'll find it close to the corner of Lianhua Lu and Yuehua Lu.

The north-east corner of Youyi Lu and Yingbin Dadao is Zhuhai's unofficial food alley. There is a good collection of *streetside restaurants* here plus a few *street vendors*.

If you haven't already made the discovery, *dim sum restaurants* are to be found in most hotels, usually on the 2nd or 3rd floors. Prices are low. There's one on the 2nd floor of the *Huaqiao Hotel* on Yingbin Dadao (north of Yuehai Lu) that I really liked .

From personal experience, the in-house dim sum restaurant in the *Overseas Chinese Guesthouse* can be highly recommended.

Getting There & Away

Air While Zhuhai can claim to have an airport, there are almost no flights – most are made by small aircraft doing short hops to neighbouring towns in the Pearl River Delta. Cancelled flights are the norm, but at least on paper there is a daily shuttle to Guangzhou. This flight departs Zhuhai at 11 am and arrives in Guangzhou at 11.30 am. Going the other way, it departs Guangzhou at 3.40 pm and arrives in Zhuhai at 4.10 pm.

Considering the amount of time you spend getting to and from the airports at each end, plus checking-in and going through airport security (not to mention the possibility of cancelled flights), you might as well take the bus.

To/From Macau Simply walk across the border. In Macau, bus Nos 3 and 5 lead to the Barrier Gate, from where you make the crossing on foot. The Macau-Zhuhai border is open from 7.30 am to 11.30 pm.

To/From Guangzhou Buses to Zhuhai depart from the Guangzhou City bus station near Guangzhou train station. Minibuses from this station are air-conditioned and leave according to a posted schedule. Other minibuses cruise in front of the station, travelling south on Renmin Lu then back on Zhanqian Lu, looking for passengers – some of these buses are notoriously unreliable.

From Zhuhai, you can catch minibuses to Guangzhou from the Gongbei bus station adjacent to the Yongtong Hotel. Departures are about once every 40 minutes throughout the day.

Forging Ahead

Once upon a time in China you got what you paid for – if the sales clerk said it was top-quality jade then it was top-quality jade. Times have changed. Now there are all sorts of cheap forgeries and imitations about, from Tibetan jewellery to Qing coins, phoney Marlboro cigarettes, fake Sony Walkmans (complete with fake Maxell cassette tapes), imitation Rolex watches, even fake Garden biscuits (Garden Bakeries is Hong Kong's biggest seller of bread, cakes and biscuits).

While eating counterfeit name-brand biscuits probably won't kill you, phoney jewellery is disappointing at best and fake electronic goodies have a life expectancy of a few weeks.

Fakes aren't limited to consumer items either. As high technology filters down to the masses, the manufacture of fake railway tickets, fake lottery tickets and fake Y100 notes have become new cottage industries. Some cadres now pad their expense accounts with fake receipts – one reason why state-run companies are losing money.

While counterfeiting name-brand goods is supposedly illegal, enforcement has been slack. China's foreign trading partners are none too happy about the fake Rolexes and CDs, and have threatened retaliation if China doesn't crack down. Meanwhile, the government is having a hard enough time stopping the haemorrhage of state funds caused by the fake tickets and receipts.

What to do? It's not easy to say, but if you want to buy things like genuine antiques, try to get an official certificate of verification – just make sure the ink is dry. ■

To/From Hong Kong Hovercraft and jetcats (jet-powered catamarans) between Zhuhai and Hong Kong do the trip in about 70 minutes. Departure times from Hong Kong are at 7.45, 8.40, 9.30 and 11 am, noon, 2.30, 4 and 5 pm. Boats depart from the ferry terminal at the China-Hong Kong City terminal on Canton Rd in Tsim Sha Tsui. They cost HK$183 to HK$223, depending on the class.

Going the other way, departures are from Jiuzhou harbour passenger terminal (*jiǔzhōu gǎng*) in Zhuhai at 8, 9.30 and 10.30 am, 1, 2, 5 and 5.30 pm. Even when you buy the ticket in Zhuhai, foreigners must pay in Hong Kong dollars! If you don't have Hong Kong dollars and try to argue the point, the staff will tell you to swim.

GUANGZHOU

To/From Shenzhen Ferries operate between the port of Shekou in Shenzhen and Jiuzhou harbour in Zhuhai. There are a variety of craft plying this route – the fastest take only 50 minutes while the old clunkers take about twice that. Departures are about once every 30 minutes throughout the day from 7.30 am to 5 pm. On this boat too, if you belong to the wrong racial group you have to pay in Hong Kong dollars. After all, why should the Chinese have to accept their own currency from foreigners?

Getting Around

Bus & Minibus Zhuhai has a decent public transport system. Buses travel most of the main roads shown on the Zhuhai map. You might have to stand, but the buses aren't nearly as packed as in Guangzhou.

Even better is the minibus system. You'll never have to wait more than 30 seconds for one of these to come along. To flag one down, just wave and they will come screeching to a halt regardless of any traffic behind them. Minibuses will stop in the public bus stops and most other places, but they cannot stop right at major intersections.

On minibuses, the destination is written in Chinese characters and displayed on the windscreen. Even if you can't read Chinese it hardly matters because there are only two basic routes: one runs along Shuiwan Lu by the waterfront; the other route goes up Yingbin Dadao and terminates in Xiangzhou. Actually, there are variations of these routes, but all you have to do is tell the driver where you want to go (before you get in). If he doesn't go there, he'll just wave you off and drive away. If you can't pronounce the Chinese, point to it on a map.

The fare for minibuses is Y2 for any destination within the city limits.

Taxi You are most likely to use taxis to shuttle between your hotel and the boats at Jiuzhou harbour. Zhuhai taxis have no meters and fares are strictly by negotiation. Drivers typically try to charge foreigners double. A fair price from the Macau border to Jiuzhou harbour is around Y40, but given

China's inflation, it's best to first ask a neutral bystander (try the desk clerks at your hotel) what the current proper fare is.

ZHONGSHAN CITY

(zhōngshān shì)

Just to the north of Zhuhai is Zhongshan City. Like Zhuhai itself, Zhongshan City is not so much a city as a sprawling political entity. It's basically a collection of towns, industrial parks and farmland, with a total area actually larger than Hong Kong.

Shiqi

(shíqí)

Shiqi is the administrative and industrial centre of Zhongshan City. Shiqi itself could hardly be called a major tourist attraction, but it's easy enough to pay it a visit. Hong Kong tour groups usually stop here and the city has a couple of worthwhile sights.

The one and only real scenic spot in town is **Zhongshan Park**, which is pleasantly forested and dominated by a large hill *(yāndūn shān)* topped with a pagoda. It's visible from most parts of the city so it's easy to find. It's nice and quiet in the park (except on Sunday) and a climb to the top of the pagoda will reward you with a sweeping view of the city's factories and air pollution. Perhaps this explains why the English translation of the hill's name is 'smoky mound'.

There is a large **Sun Yatsen Memorial Hall** *(sūn zhōngshān jìniàn táng)* on Sunwen Lu to the east of Zhongshan Park. The car park here is often jammed with tour buses from Macau, though there is nothing special about this place. The most worthwhile sight is the old MIG fighter parked on the lawn, a relic of the Korean War.

Apart from the pagoda in Zhongshan Park, the other dominant feature on the skyline of Zhongshan City is the Fu Hua Hotel, a huge golden building topped with a revolving restaurant. The hotel has a disco, sauna, bowling alley, billiard room and swimming pool. You might be curious as to why anybody would build this stunning resort hotel in the middle of an industrial wasteland such as Zhongshan City. I asked numerous Hong Kongers this question and the answer was always the same – 'everyone is here on business'.

Places to Stay Should you be so taken with Zhongshan City, you could stay at the three-star *Tiecheng Hotel* (☎ 873803; fax 871103) *(tiĕchéng jiŭdiàn)*. The hotel's name means 'Iron City', which is a fair description of the landscape of factories and scrap yards. The hotel is on Zhongshan Lu. Doubles are Y360 to Y480.

Perhaps a better deal is the new *Xiangshan Hotel* (☎ 887-4567; fax 887-4929) *(xiāngshān jiŭdiàn)* at 1 Xiangshan Dajie. Agreeable doubles are Y250.

Moving upwards in price is the *Zhongshan Building* (☎ 887-3838; fax 887-1133) *(zhōng-shān dàshà)*, 3 Fuhua Dao. Rooms with twin beds are Y280 to Y384.

Across the street is the *International Hotel* (☎ 887-4788; fax 887-4736) *(guójì jiŭdiàn)*, 1 Zhongshan Lu, where singles/doubles cost Y500/700. Four stars.

Top of the line is the *Fu Hua Hotel* (☎ 886-6888; fax 886-1862) *(fúhuá jiŭdiàn)*, near the river. It has singles/doubles for Y300/700. There are honeymoon suites for HK$1000. On weekends and holidays there is a 10% surcharge. Four stars.

Most likely, you won't want to stay in Zhongshan City or Shiqi unless you decide to open a factory here.

Places to Eat In addition to the usual abundance of *cheap noodle shops*, elegant seafood dining is available at the *Jumbo Floating Restaurant (zhēnbăo hăixiān făng)* which floats on the Qi River.

Fast food has made its debut in Zhongshan City. *Timmy's (tiān mĕi shí)* on Zhongshan Lu (south of Sunwen Lu) can satisfy a sudden attack of uncontrollable lust for French fries, hamburgers and milk shakes.

Getting There & Away All buses running between Guangzhou and Zhuhai pass through Zhongshan. The quickest way out of town is to catch a minibus from the car park of the Tiecheng Hotel.

Because of its importance as a manufacturing centre, frequent high-speed catamarans ply the route directly between Zhongshan and Hong Kong in just one hour and 45 minutes. Tourists seldom make use of this route, but if you're sick of Zhongshan, this is one quick way to make an exit. Fares are Y160.

Sun Yatsen's Residence
(sūn zhōngshān gùjū)
China's most famous revolutionary, Dr Sun Yatsen, was born in a house on this site on 12 November 1866. That house was torn down and a new home was built in 1892. This second house is still standing and open to the public. The site also has a museum, but the Chinese have turned the place into something of a circus.

Sun dedicated his life to the overthrow of the corrupt and brutal Qing (Manchu) dynasty. His goal was to do away with dynasties altogether and establish a Chinese republic based on Western democratic principles. He organised several uprisings, all of which failed. As a result, he spent much of his life in exile because there was a price on his head. There is no doubt that he would have faced a horrible death by torture if the emperor had succeeded in capturing him.

When the actual revolution came in 1911, Dr Sun wasn't in China. Still, there is no denying his role as a major organiser and instigator of the revolution. His Tokyo-based Alliance Society coordinated the uprising which led to the sudden collapse of the Qing dynasty, and the subsequent establishment of the Provisional Republican Government on 10 October 1911. Sun Yatsen is widely regarded as the father of his country and has been deified by both the Communist Party and the Nationalists in Taiwan. He briefly served as the first president of the Republic of China. He died in 1925 from liver cancer at the age of 59. His wife was Soong Ching-ling, the sister of Soong Mayling (Madame Chiang Kaishek).

Dr Sun's house is in the village of Cuiheng, north of the city limits of Zhuhai.

GUANGZHOU

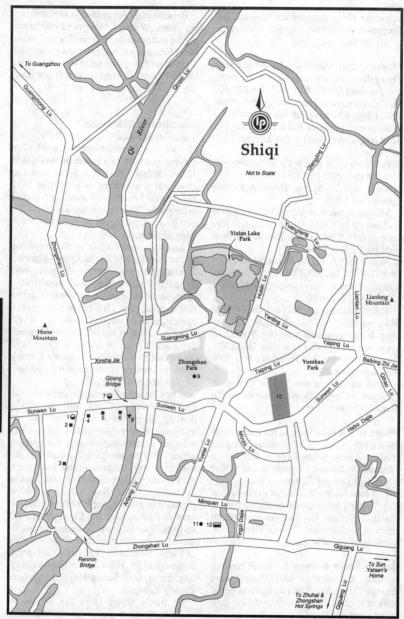

Shiqi

Not to Scale

To Guangzhou

Guangzhong Lu

Qijiang Lu

Qilong Lu

Qi River

Qiangjing Lu

Yuangfeng Lu

Yixian Lake Park

Hubin Lu

Liantan Lu

Lianfeng Mountain ▲

Yanling Lu

Yaiping Lu

Baibing Zhi Jie

Zhongshan Lu

Horse Mountain ▲

Guangming Lu

Zhongshan Park
● 9

Taiping Lu

Yueshan Park

Sunwen Lu

Cehao Lu

Xinsha Jie

Qijiang Bridge

7 ☕

Sunwen Lu

Sunwen Lu

10

Hebo Dajie

1 ●
2 ■   ■   ■   ▼
     4   5   6   8

3 ■

Minzu Lu

Yuelai Lu

Anlang Lu

Minquan Lu

11 ● 12 🏨

Tingzi Dajie

Zhongshan Lu

Qiguang Lu

Renmin Bridge

To Sun Yatsen's Home

To Zhuhai & Zhongshan Hot Springs

Qipeng Lu

GUANGZHOU

1 Minibuses to Zhuhai
开往拱北的小汽车
2 Tiecheng Hotel
铁城酒店
3 Xiangshan Hotel & Timmy's
Fast Food
香山酒店, 添美食
4 International Hotel
国际酒店
5 Zhongshan Building (hotel)
中山大厦
6 Fu Hua Hotel
富华酒店
7 Bus Station
汽车站
8 Jumbo Floating Restaurant
珍宝海鲜舫
9 Pagoda
烟墩山宝塔
10 Sun Yatsen Memorial Hall
孙中山纪念堂
11 Renmin Athletic Field
人民体育场
12 Swimming Pool
游泳池

There are frequent minibuses to Cuiheng departing from Gongbei near the border checkpoint.

In Cuiheng, there are two hotels – the enormous three-star *Cuiheng Hotel* (☎ 550-2668; fax 550-3333) *(cuìhēng bīnguǎn)* and the smaller *Cuiheng Jiudian*. It's doubtful you'll want to spend the night here unless you're a Sun Yatsen-ophile.

Zhongshan Hot Springs

(zhōngshān wēnquán)

Just north of Zhuhai city limits on the way to Guangzhou is the town of Sanxiang. Here you'll find Zhongshan Hot Springs, much touted in the glossy tourist pamphlets produced by CTS. In fact, the hot springs are not such a big attraction – they are piped into the hotel. In the past, the area was known for its pleasant countryside, but this has recently been replaced by factories and worker flats.

Aside from the mineral baths, the resort is famous for its **golf course**. Just how much longer before the golf course also becomes an industrial park is open to speculation. The first professional golf championship ever held in China, the 1988 Dunhill Cup Pacific, took place here. Nowadays you'll have trouble distinguishing the sand traps from the waste dumps.

Thanks to the rapidly deteriorating environment, prices at the hotel have stayed reasonable for such plush amenities. The *Zhongshan Hot Springs Hotel* (☎ 668-3888; fax 668-3333) charges Y220 to Y460.

A minibus drops you by the entrance to the resort, then it's a walk of nearly 500m to the hotel. For Y2 you can hire someone to carry you on the back of a bicycle. You won't have to look for them as they'll be looking for you. To get back to Gongbei, flag down any minibus you see passing the resort entrance.

GUANGZHOU

Health

In general, health conditions in Hong Kong, Macau and southern China are good, but a little awareness of potential hazards could prevent illness from ruining your trip.

Predeparture Preparations

Health Insurance A travel insurance policy to cover theft, loss and medical problems is a wise idea. There are a wide variety of policies and your travel agent will have recommendations. The international student travel policies handled by STA Travel or other student travel organisations are usually good value. Some policies offer lower and higher medical expenses options; the higher one is chiefly for countries which have extremely high medical costs, like the USA. Check the small print:

1. Some policies specifically exclude 'dangerous activities', which can include scuba diving, motorcycling, even trekking. If such activities are on your agenda you don't want that sort of policy. A locally acquired motor cycle licence may not be valid under your policy.
2. You may prefer a policy which pays doctors or hospitals direct rather than you having to pay on the spot and claim later. If you have to claim later make sure you keep all documentation. Some policies ask you to call back (reverse charges) to a centre in your home country, where an immediate assessment of your problem is made.
3. Check if the policy covers ambulances or an emergency flight home. If you have to stretch out you will need two seats and somebody has to pay for them!

Medical Kit If you require an unusual medication take an adequate supply. You can almost certainly buy any drug in Hong Kong, but you might have to get a local prescription and that will take time and money. It's a wise idea to have a legible prescription with you to show you legally use the medication – customs inspectors at border checkpoints can get sticky about unlabelled bottles filled with different coloured pills.

If you wear glasses, bring an extra pair and/or a copy of your lens prescription with you. Sunglasses come in useful, and a hat will help protect you from sunburn.

You can buy almost any medication across the counter in Hong Kong, or get it by prescription. Given this situation, it really isn't necessary to carry a first-aid kit around with you as you would in India or Cambodia, for example. On the other hand, if you're going to spend time hiking in the mountains or exploring remote islands, a basic medical kit would be handy. It could include: headache tablets for pain and fever, a pin and tweezers for removing splinters, plaster for blisters, Band-aids, an antiseptic, rehydration salts (for heat exhaustion), insect repellent, sunscreen and Chapstick.

Vaccinations No special vaccinations are required for Hong Kong or Macau. However, that doesn't mean you shouldn't get any. For Hong Kong, the most useful vaccinations are for hepatitis B, tetanus and influenza (during winter).

Plan ahead for getting your vaccinations: some require an initial shot followed by a booster, and some vaccinations should not be given together. It is recommended you seek medical advice at least six weeks prior to travel.

If you need vaccinations while in Hong Kong, the Port Health office (☎ 2961-8852) can give you a low-cost jab for cholera and typhoid. They occasionally stock other vaccines, depending on which epidemics are ravaging this part of Asia. Port Health has two branch offices: Kowloon (☎ 2368-3361), room 905, Government Offices, Canton Rd, Yau Ma Tei; and Hong Kong Island (☎ 2961-8840), 18th floor, Wu Chung House, 213 Queen's Rd East, Wan Chai.

For Guangzhou and southern China, few people will be required to have vaccinations but there are several that are certainly recommended. If you're arriving within six days after leaving a yellow fever-infected area, then a vaccination is required.

Vaccinations which have been recommended by various health authorities include: cholera, meningitis, rabies, hepatitis A, hepatitis B, BCG (tuberculosis), polio, and TABT (protects against typhoid, paratyphoid A and B, and tetanus) and diphtheria.

You should have your vaccinations recorded in an International Health Certificate. If you are travelling with children, it's especially important to be sure that they've had all necessary vaccinations.

Guangzhou may not look very clean, but health standards are reasonably OK. There is very little chance of picking up some nasty tropical bug like malaria or dysentery. The main thing is to watch what you eat and drink.

Food & Water

The Chinese are pretty conscientious about handling food and there is little to worry about. If you want to be particularly cautious, then avoid seafood during summer – it spoils quickly if not freshly killed or refrigerated.

The government insists that Hong Kong's tap water is perfectly safe to drink and does not need to be boiled. However, most local Chinese boil it anyway, more out of habit than necessity. In urban areas there should be no problem with tap water, though in some agricultural backwaters in the New Territories and Outlying Islands, surface water may be contaminated by fertiliser. If you're going to be hiking in the countryside, be sure to bring a sufficient water supply and avoid drinking unboiled surface water. Bottled water is widely available from shops.

In Macau, the water supply is purified and chlorinated and considered safe to drink. Nevertheless, many locals boil it anyway. Distilled or mineral water is widely available from shops.

In Guangzhou and surrounds, tap water is chlorinated and safe for brushing your teeth, but it's still advisable to boil it before drinking. Virtually all hotels provide flasks with boiled water. Bottled water is widely available from kiosks and stores. Shellfish and seafood of any kind pose the greatest risks of all, from spoilage (due to lack of refrigeration) and water pollution. Some of the rivers

and bays in China are positively toxic, yet you often see people fishing in them. Better restaurants only buy fish which are raised in commercial ponds, and the fish are kept alive in aquariums until just before cooking – unfortunately, not all restaurants are so scrupulous.

Qigong

Kungfu meditation, known as *qigong*, is used as a form of self-defence training and as a healing technique in Chinese medicine. *Qi* represents life's vital energy. Qigong can be thought of as energy management – practitioners try to project their qi to perform nearly magical acts.

Qigong practitioners occasionally give impressive demonstrations, driving nails through boards with their fingers or putting their fists through a brick wall. Less spectacular but potentially more useful is the ability to heal others, and it's interesting to watch them do it. Typically, they place their hands above or next to the patient's body without actually making physical contact. To many foreigners this looks like a circus act, and even many Chinese suspect that it's nothing but quackery. However, there are many who claim they have been cured of serious illness through qigong, even after more conventional doctors have told them that their condition is hopeless.

In China during the Cultural Revolution of the 1960s, qigong practitioners were denounced as a superstitious link to the bourgeois past. Many were arrested and all were forced to stop the practice. It is only recently that qigong has made a comeback, but many of the highly skilled practitioners are no longer alive.

Does qigong work? It isn't easy to say, but there is a theory in medicine that all doctors can cure one-third of their patients regardless of what method is used. So perhaps qigong gets its one-third cure rate too. ■

Hospitals

Although Hong Kong's medical care is of a high standard, there is a real shortage of qualified medical staff. This is because China's takeover has driven many of the best medical staff to emigrate in droves to Western countries. This has led some cynics to suggest that perhaps the best place to get sick in Hong Kong is at the airport.

Hong Kong and Macau's public hospitals

HEALTH

charge much less than private clinics, but you may have to wait a long time to see a doctor. Residents pay less than foreign visitors. Most four- and five-star hotels have resident doctors.

Hong Kong

Public hospitals in Hong Kong include:

Queen Elizabeth Hospital
    Wylie Rd, Yau Ma Tei, Kowloon (☎ 2710-2111)
Princess Margaret Hospital
    Lai Chi Kok, Kowloon (☎ 2310-3111)
Queen Mary Hospital
    Pok Fu Lam Rd, Pok Fu Lam (☎ 2819-2111)
Prince of Wales Hospital
    30-32 Ngan Shing St, Sha Tin, New Territories
    (☎ 2636-2211)

There are some excellent private hospitals in Hong Kong, but their prices reflect the fact that they operate at a profit. Some of the better private hospitals include:

Adventist
    40 Stubbs Rd, Wan Chai, Hong Kong Island
    (☎ 2574-6211)
Baptist
    222 Waterloo Rd, Kowloon Tong (☎ 2337-4141)
Canossa
    1 Old Peak Rd, Mid-Levels, Hong Kong Island
    (☎ 2522-2181)
Grantham
    125 Wong Chuk Hang Rd, Deep Water Bay,
    Hong Kong Island (☎ 2554-6471)
Hong Kong Central
    1B Lower Albert Rd, Central, Hong Kong Island
    (☎ 2522-3141)
Matilda & War Memorial
    41 Mt Kellett Rd, The Peak, Hong Kong Island
    (☎ 2849-6301)
St Paul's
    2 Eastern Hospital Rd, Causeway Bay, Hong
    Kong Island (☎ 2890-6008)

Macau

There are two government-run hospitals in Macau:

Government Hospital
    Estrada de a Sao Francisco (☎ 51449, 313731)
Kiang Vu
    Estrada do Repouso and Rua Coelho do Amaral
    (☎ 371333)

Guangzhou

Hospitals in Guangzhou include:

Guangzhou No 1 People's Hospital
    602 Renmin Lu (☎ 3333090)
Sun Yatsen Memorial Hospital
    107 Yanjiang Lu (☎ 8882012)

Medical Problems & Treatment
Cuts, Bites & Stings

Insects Wasps, which are common in the subtropics, are a more serious hazard than snakes because they are more aggressive and will chase humans when stirred up. If you see a wasps' nest, the best advice is to move away quietly.

It would take perhaps 100 wasp or bee stings to kill a normal adult, but a single sting can be fatal to someone who is allergic. In fact, death from wasp and bee stings is more common than death from snakebite. People who are allergic to wasp and bee stings are also allergic to bites by red ants. Those with this sort of allergy usually know it. If this includes you, throw an antihistamine and epinephrine into your first-aid kit and keep it with you when exploring the countryside. Epinephrine is most effective when injected, but taking it in pill form is better than nothing.

Except during the dead of winter, mosquitos are a year-round annoyance in Hong Kong, even in the urban jungles of Kowloon and Central. They are especially annoying at night when you're trying to sleep. Electric mosquito zappers are useful, but are too heavy for travelling. A portable innovation is 'electric mosquito incense', also known as 'vape mats' or 'mosquito mats'. Mosquito mats and the mosquito mat electric heater are sold in grocery stores and supermarkets all over Hong Kong, Macau and southern China. The mats emit a poison – breathing it over the long-term may have unknown health effects, though all the manufacturers of this stuff insist that it is safe.

Mosquito incense coils accomplish the same thing as the vape mats and require no electricity, but the smoke is nasty. Mosquito repellent is somewhat less effective than incense, but is probably less toxic and gives protection outdoors where incense is impractical. Look for brands that contain DEET (diethyl toluamide). Some effective brands include Autan and Off!. Sleeping under a blowing electric fan all night (not recommended during winter) will also keep mosquitos away.

Snakes The term 'snake' is used by the Cantonese to describe someone who smuggles illegal aliens into Hong Kong. However, I speak here of the non-human kind.

The countryside of Hong Kong in particular is home to some poisonous snakes which you'd be wise to avoid. Most dangerous are the cobras, and some species show very little shyness about living near areas inhabited by people. The king cobra is most dangerous by far, but fortunately it's not common and avoids contact with humans. Two common poisonous snakes include the green bamboo pit viper and coral snake. There are a number of poisonous freshwater snakes and sea snakes. Non-poisonous snakes include rat snakes (which find plenty to eat in Hong Kong), copperhead racers, pythons and boas.

Don't be a fool and attack a snake with a stick – it's the easiest way to get bitten. The only safe option is to get out of its way quickly – back off if possible – because most snakes will retreat from humans. Cornering a snake will very likely make it assume the striking position. Cobras can spit their venom some distance; they aim for the eyes and can cause blindness.

If by some chance you do get bitten, the important thing to remember is to remain calm and not run around (sounds easier than it is). Opinions differ widely on how to treat a snake bite in emergencies without a specific antivenin, but the conventional wisdom is to rest and allow the poison to be absorbed slowly. A constricting band (tourniquet) can be useful for slowing down the poison, but it's also very dangerous – if too tight, a tourniquet can cut off circulation and cause gangrene, a possibly fatal complication. If a tourniquet is applied, be sure you *do not* use

a narrow band like a shoelace. Use something wide and soft, like strips of cloth or a T-shirt. Furthermore, be sure that you can feel the pulse below the tourniquet – if you've cut off the pulse, it's too tight! Keep the affected limb below the heart level.

The old 'boy scout' method of treating snake bite – cutting the skin and sucking out the poison – has also been widely discredited.

Treatment in a hospital with an antivenin would be ideal. The Hong Kong police will dispatch a helicopter to pluck snake-bite victims from remote mountaintops and they don't even charge for the service. However, *this is emergency service*, so don't call for a helicopter because you're tired and would like a lift into town.

Although no one likes to admit it, there isn't a whole lot you can do for a snake-bite victim if you are far from civilisation. Fortunately, the vast majority survive even without medical treatment.

Sharks In addition to the shopkeepers along Nathan Rd, there are several other species of sharks in Hong Kong. The tiger shark seems to be particularly nasty – there is typically about one fatal attack on humans every year. Most of these attacks have occurred at beaches in the Sai Kung area of the New Territories.

Diarrhoea Even though the tap water is safe, some people rapidly develop that well-known ailment, 'travellers' diarrhoea'. Should it happen to you, don't automatically assume that you've caught some dreaded disease. It's more likely that your body needs a few days to adjust to the change of diet and the mineral content of the local water supply. Indeed, chlorinated tap water may be the culprit – you will soon get used to it.

Diarrhoea is caused by irritation or inflammation of the intestine. First try a simple cure by switching to a light, roughage-free diet for a few days. White rice, bananas, pudding and boiled eggs will usually see you through. Further relief can be obtained by chewing tablets of activated charcoal. Tea, coffee, cola and other caffeinated drinks are irritants and may worsen the diarrhoea. Ditto for spices and alcohol.

More serious cases can be treated with drugs such as Lomotil and Imodium. These drugs only treat the symptoms, not the underlying disease. Your intestine will still remain irritated or inflamed. Use anti-diarrhoeal drugs with caution because they can have nasty side effects. Also, you don't want to take so many drugs that you become plugged up, because the diarrhoea serves a function – your body is trying to expel unwanted bacteria or irritants. Only take the minimum dose needed to control yourself.

The diarrhoea should clear up in a few days. However, if you continue to suffer, you may have a serious infection that requires antibiotics or anti-amoebic drugs. If you get to this stage, you should visit a hospital or clinic and get some medical tests to determine just what the problem is.

Eye Problems Amber and grey are said to be the two most effective colours for filtering out harmful ultraviolet rays.

Some people suffer mild inflammation of the eyes (conjunctivitis) caused by irritants such as dust, cigarette smoke or the chlorinated water in a swimming pool. If you wake up in the morning with a headache and stinging in the eyes, this is likely to be the problem. You could just go to any pharmacy and tell them you want eye-drops for *mild* conjunctivitis – a few days of treatment should clear up the problem. Be careful – there are more powerful eye-drops containing steroids and antibiotics. These medications may be sold across the counter in Hong Kong, but their use requires medical supervision. If you suspect that you have a serious eye infection, you should not attempt to treat yourself – see a doctor.

Flu The Chinese call it *ganmao* and it's usually the most common and serious ailment to afflict visitors to China. In most countries it's known as influenza or even the common cold, but it's uncommonly bad in China. Few probably remember the notorious 'Hong Kong flu' of 1968, but you may

have heard of the 'Shanghai flu' which in 1989 killed over 26,000 people in the UK alone. There have been various other influenza strains named after Chinese cities. The fact is that China is the world's prime reservoir of influenza viruses.

What distinguishes Chinese viruses from the Western variety is the ubiquitousness of the infections – practically the entire population of 1.2 billion is stricken during the winter. Many wonder why this is so. Medical experts give several reasons: respiratory infections are aggravated by cold weather, poor nutrition and China's notorious air pollution. Smoking definitely makes it worse, and practically everyone in China smoke. Overcrowded conditions increase the opportunity for infection. But the main reason is that Chinese people spit a lot, thereby spreading the disease. It's a vicious circle: they're sick because they spit and they spit because they're sick.

The law of natural selection guarantees that the average Chinese person has a fairly high level of immunity to influenza. However, foreigners are easy prey for these diseases. Now that so many people visit China, the viruses are easily spread worldwide.

Like any bad case of the flu, it starts with a fever, chills, weakness, sore throat and a feeling of malaise normally lasting a few days. After that, a prolonged case of coughing sets in, characterised by coughing up large quantities of thick green phlegm, occasionally with little red streaks (blood). This condition is known as bronchitis and it makes sleep almost impossible. This exhausting state of affairs can continue for as long as you stay in China, and many foreigners find that they can only get well by leaving the country.

If nothing else, winter visitors to China should bring a few favourite cold remedies. These can easily be purchased from any good chemist in Hong Kong or Macau. Such items can be found in Guangzhou, but with considerably more difficulty.

If you become seriously afflicted with bronchitis, you may have to nuke it with antibiotics. This is not a decision to take lightly – antibiotics can have serious adverse effects. On the other hand, it's better than dying from influenza or pneumonia. If you are that ill, you really should see a doctor. But if worse comes to worst, tetracycline (250 mg) taken orally four times daily for a minimum of five days is usually highly effective. Antibiotics are not readily available in China, and they are a prescription item in Hong Kong. Finally, if you can't get well in China, leave the country and take a nice holiday on a warm beach in Thailand.

Hepatitis A Hepatitis is a disease which affects the liver. There are several varieties, mostly commonly hepatitis A and B. Hepatitis A occurs in countries with poor sanitation – this would have to include the backwards parts of China. It's spread from person to person via infected food or water, or contaminated cooking and eating utensils.

Hepatitis is often spread in China due to the Chinese custom of everybody eating from a single dish rather than using separate plates and a serving spoon. It is a wise decision to use the disposable chopsticks now freely available in most restaurants in China, or else buy your own chopsticks and spoon.

Symptoms appear 15 to 50 days after infection (generally around 25 days) and consist of fever, loss of appetite, nausea, depression, complete lack of energy, and pains around the bottom of your rib cage (the location of the liver). Your skin turns progressively yellow and the whites of your eyes change from white to yellow to orange.

The best way to detect hepatitis is to watch the colour of your urine, which will turn a deep orange no matter how much liquid you drink. If you haven't drunk much liquid and/or you're sweating a lot, don't jump to conclusions since you may just be dehydrated.

The severity of hepatitis A varies; it may last less than two weeks and give you only a few bad days, or it may last for several months and give you a few bad weeks. You could feel depleted of energy for several months afterwards. If you get hepatitis, rest and good food is the only cure; don't use alcohol or tobacco since that only gives your liver more work to do. It's important to keep up your food intake to assist recovery.

A vaccine for hepatitis A came on the market in 1992. It's not widely available yet, but it should be possible to get it. Check with your doctor.

Hepatitis B Hepatitis B is transmitted the same three ways the AIDS virus spreads: by sexual intercourse; contaminated needles; or inherited by an infant from an infected mother. Some Chinese 'health clinics' reuse needles without proper sterilisation – no one knows how many people have been infected this way. Acupuncture can also spread the disease.

There is a vaccine for hepatitis B, but it must be given before you've been exposed. Once you've got the virus, you're a carrier for life and the vaccine is useless. Therefore, you need a blood test before the vaccine is administered to determine if you're a carrier. The vaccine requires three injections each given a month apart, and it's wise to get a booster every few years thereafter. Unfortunately, the vaccine is expensive.

Hepatitis C and Others Recent research has found other varieties of hepatitis of which little is yet known. Hepatitis C and other strains are considered serious. Fortunately, these are usually spread by blood transfusions and therefore are not diseases that you're going to pick up through casual contact.

Sexually Transmitted Diseases China does not issue visas to foreigners known to be HIV positive, and foreigners who wish to work in China must submit to an AIDS test. Those who test HIV positive at Chinese hospitals are routinely deported. Beijing isn't known for respecting an individual's right to confidentiality. For decades, authorities pretended that prostitution, premarital and extra-marital sex simply didn't exist in the People's Republic, and that sexually transmitted diseases (STDs) were a foreign problem. The Cultural Revolution may be over, but the sexual revolution is booming in China and STDs are spreading rapidly.

HEALTH

Under British rule, Hong Kong has been fairly tolerant towards victims of AIDS/HIV. For example, AIDS testing is free at all public hospitals in Hong Kong and medical records are kept strictly confidential. For this reason alone, Hong Kong is a good place to get an AIDS test. Not only are the testing facilities reliable, but the government does *not* deport people who test positive for the disease. Some fear that after 1997, HIV-positive expats could be deported en masse.

If you can't be 'good', be careful. The sexual revolution reached Hong Kong long ago, as did the 'social diseases' that go with it. While abstinence is the only 100% preventative, using condoms helps. Gonorrhoea and syphilis are the most common of these diseases; sores, blisters or rashes around the genitals, and discharges or pain when urinating are common symptoms. Symptoms may be less marked or not observed at all in women. Syphilis symptoms eventually disappear, but the disease continues and can be fatal. Gonorrhoea is not fatal but can lead to sterility and other problems. Both diseases can be cured by antibiotics.

There are numerous other sexually transmitted diseases, for most of which effective treatment is available. However, there is no cure for herpes and there is also currently no cure for AIDS. Using condoms is the most effective preventative.

AIDS can be spread through infected blood transfusions and dirty needles – vaccinations, acupuncture and tattooing can potentially be as dangerous as intravenous drug use if the equipment is not clean.

Tuberculosis The tuberculosis (TB) bacteria is transmitted by inhalation. Coughing spreads infectious droplets into the air. In closed, crowded spaces with poor ventilation (like a train compartment) the air can remain contaminated for some time. In overcrowded China, where the custom is to cough and spit in every direction, it's not hard to see why infection rates remain high.

Many carriers of tuberculosis experience no symptoms, but the disease stays with them for life. The infection is opportunistic – the patient feels fine, but the disease suddenly becomes active when the body is weakened by other factors such as injury, poor nutrition, surgery or old age. People who are in good health are less likely to catch TB. Tuberculosis strikes at the lungs and the fatality rate is about 10%.

There are good drugs to treat tuberculosis, but prevention is the best cure. If you're only going to be in China for a short time there is no need to be overly worried. Tuberculosis is usually contracted after repeated exposures. Budget travellers – those who often spend a long time staying in cramped dormitories and travelling on crowded buses and trains – are at greater risk than tourists who remain relatively isolated in big hotels and tour buses.

The effective vaccine for tuberculosis is called BCG and is most often given to school children (a high-risk group). The disadvantage of the vaccine is that, once given, the recipient will always test positive with the TB skin test.

Skin Problems Sunburn can be more than just uncomfortable. Among the undesirable effects of frying your hide are premature skin ageing and possible skin cancer in later years. Bring sunscreen lotion and wear something to cover your head.

Sunburn is not the only hazard to your skin. Indeed, the most common summertime afflictions that visitors to Hong Kong suffer from are skin diseases. This is because of the hot, humid climate. The most common varieties are 'jock itch' (a fungal infection around the groin), athlete's foot (known to the Chinese as 'Hong Kong feet'), contact dermatitis (caused by a necklace or watch band rubbing the skin) and prickly heat (caused by excessive sweating). Prevention and treatment of these skin ailments is often a matter of good hygiene.

For fungal infections, bathe twice daily and thoroughly dry yourself before getting dressed. Standing in front of an electric fan is a good way to get thoroughly dry. An antifungal ointment or powder should be applied to the affected area. It's more effective to use an ointment and a powder in combination. Some popular fungicides available in Western countries include Desenex, Tinactin and Mycota. Whatever ointment and/or powder you use, it should include the ingredients undecylenic acid and zinc undecylenate. Wear light cotton underwear or very thin nylon that 'breathes'. Wear the lightest outer clothing possible when the weather is really hot and humid. For athlete's foot, wearing open-toed sandals will often solve the problem without further treatment. It also helps to clean between the toes with warm soapy water and an old toothbrush.

Treat contact dermatitis by removing the offending necklace, bracelet or wristwatch. Avoid anything that chafes the skin, such as tight clothing and, especially, elastic. If your skin develops little painful red 'pin pricks', you probably have prickly heat. This is the result of excessive sweating, which blocks the sweat ducts, thus causing inflammation. The treatment is the same as for fungal infections: drying and cooling the skin. Bathe often, soak and scrub with hot soapy water to get the skin pores open and dust yourself with talcum powder after drying off.

Women's Health

Gynaecological Problems Poor diet, lowered resistance from the use of antibiotics for stomach upsets, and even contraceptive pills can lead to vaginal infections when travelling in hot climates. Keeping the genital area clean, and wearing skirts or loose-fitting trousers and cotton underwear will help to prevent infections.

Yeast infections, characterised by a rash, itch and discharge, can be treated with a vinegar or even lemon-juice douche, or with yoghurt. Nystatin suppositories are the usual medical prescription. Trichomonas is a more serious infection; symptoms are a discharge and a burning sensation when urinating. Male sexual partners must also be treated, and if a vinegar-water douche is not effective medical attention should be sought. Flagyl is the prescribed drug.

Pregnancy Most miscarriages occur during the first three months of pregnancy, so this is the riskiest time to travel. The last three months should also be spent within reasonable distance of good medical care, as quite serious problems can develop at this time. Pregnant women should avoid all unnecessary medication, but vaccinations should still be taken where possible. Additional care should be taken to prevent illness and particular attention should be paid to diet and nutrition.

Glossary

amah – domestic servant

cheongsam – formal tight-fitting dress with a revealing slit up the side, often worn at weddings and by restaurant hostesses

chau – a Cantonese word meaning 'land mass' - you'll see it everywhere, like in the Outlying Islands (Cheung Chau, Peng Chau, etc)

congee – watery rice porridge

dai pai dong – street market

dragon boat – a long and narrow boat used in races on Dragon Boat Day

fungshui – geomancy, the art of manipulating the environment to blow away bad spirits

gam bei – 'cheers' or 'bottoms up', literally 'dry glass'

godown – warehouse

gwailo – literally 'ghost person' and interpreted as 'foreign devil', but now a term of both ridicule and endearment

hong – large company

joss – luck, fortune

joss sticks – incense

junk – traditional Chinese fishing boat, but the name now includes most small to mid-sized Chinese boats

kaido – a small to medium sized ferry

mai dan – the bill or check in a restaurant

oolong – high grade Chinese tea, partially fermented

sampan – a motorised launch which can only accommodate a few people and is too small to go on the open sea

shroff – cashier

snake – a smuggler of illegal immigrants

taipan – big boss of a large company

walla walla – a motorised launch used as a water taxi and capable of short runs on the open sea

yum cha – dim sum meal, literally 'drink tea'

wan – the Cantonese word for 'bay' which pops up on all sorts of maps, including the map of the MTR system (Tsuen Wan, Chai Wan, etc).

Index

LONELY PLANET JOURNEYS

FULL CIRCLE: A South American Journey *by Luis Sepúlveda (translated by Chris Andrews)*
Full Circle invites us to accompany Chilean writer Luis Sepúlveda on 'a journey without a fixed itinerary'. Extravagant characters and extraordinary situations are memorably evoked: gauchos organising a tournament of lies, a scheming heiress on the lookout for a husband, a pilot with a corpse on board his plane . . . Part autobiography, part travel memoir, *Full Circle* brings us the distinctive voice of one of South America's most compelling writers.

THE GATES OF DAMASCUS *by Lieve Joris (translated by Sam Garrett)*
This best-selling book is a beautifully drawn portrait of contemporary Syria. Through her intimate contact with local people, Lieve Joris explores women's lives and family relationships – the hidden world that lies behind the gates of Damascus.

IN RAJASTHAN *by Royina Grewal*
Indian travel writer Royina Grewal takes us behind the exotic facade of this fabled destination: here is an insider's perceptive account of India's most colourful state. *In Rajasthan* discusses folk music and architecture, feudal traditions and regional cuisine . . . Most of all, it focuses on people – from maharajahs to itinerant snake charmers – to convey the excitement and challenges of a region in transition.

ISLANDS IN THE CLOUDS: Travels in the Highlands of New Guinea *by Isabella Tree*
This is the fascinating account of a journey to the remote and beautiful Highlands of Papua New Guinea and Irian Jaya. The author travels with a PNG Highlander who introduces her to his intriguing and complex world. *Islands in the Clouds* is a thoughtful, moving book, full of insights into a region that is rarely noticed by the rest of the world.

KINGDOM OF THE FILM STARS: Journey into Jordan *by Annie Caulfield*
With honesty and humour, Annie Caulfield writes of travelling in Jordan and falling in love with a Bedouin. Her book offers fascinating insights into the country and unpicks some of the tight-woven Western myths about the Arab world within the intimate framework of a compelling love story.

LOST JAPAN *by Alex Kerr*
Lost Japan draws on the author's personal experiences of Japan over a period of 30 years. Alex Kerr takes his readers on a backstage tour: friendships with Kabuki actors, buying and selling art, studying calligraphy, exploring rarely visited temples and shrines . . . The Japanese edition of this book was awarded the 1994 Shincho Gakugei Literature Prize for the best work of non-fiction.

SEAN & DAVID'S LONG DRIVE *by Sean Condon*
Sean and David are young townies who have rarely strayed beyond city limits. One day, for no good reason, they set out to discover their homeland, and what follows is a wildly entertaining adventure that covers half of Australia. Sean Condon has written a hilarious, offbeat road book that mixes sharp insights with deadpan humour and outright lies.

SHOPPING FOR BUDDHAS *by Jeff Greenwald*
Shopping for Buddhas is Jeff Greenwald's story of his obsessive search for the perfect Buddha statue. In the backstreets of Kathmandu, he discovers more than he bargained for . . . and his souvenir-hunting turns into an ironic metaphor for the clash between spiritual riches and material greed. Politics, religion and serious shopping collide in this witty account of an enlightening visit to Nepal.

LONELY PLANET PHRASEBOOKS

Nepali phrasebook — Listen for the gems

Ethiopian Amharic phrasebook — Speak your own words

Latin American Spanish phrasebook — Ask your own questions

Ukrainian phrasebook — Master of your own image

Greek phrasebook

Vietnamese phrasebook

Building bridges,
Breaking barriers,
Beyond babble-on

- handy pocket-sized books
- easy to understand Pronunciation chapter
- clear and comprehensive Grammar chapter
- romanisation alongside script to allow ease of pronunciation
- script throughout so users can point to phrases
- extensive vocabulary sections, words and phrases for every situations
- full of cultural information and tips for the traveller

'*...vital for a real DIY spirit and attitude in language learning*' – Backpacker

'*the phrasebooks have good cultural backgrounders and offer solid advice for challenging situations in remote locations*' – San Francisco Examiner

'*...they are unbeatable for their coverage of the world's more obscure languages*' – The Geographical Magazine

---

Arabic (Egyptian)
Arabic (Moroccan)
Australia
  Australian English, Aboriginal and Torres Strait languages
Baltic States
  Estonian, Latvian, Lithuanian
Bengali
Burmese
Brazilian
Cantonese
Central Europe
  Czech, French, German, Hungarian, Italian and Slovak
Eastern Europe
  Bulgarian, Czech, Hungarian, Polish, Romanian and Slovak
Egyptian Arabic
Ethiopian (Amharic)
Fijian
Greek
Hindi/Urdu

Indonesian
Japanese
Korean
Lao
Latin American Spanish
Malay
Mandarin
Mediterranean Europe
  Albanian, Croatian, Greek, Italian, Macedonian, Maltese, Serbian, Slovene
Mongolian
Moroccan Arabic
Nepali
Papua New Guinea
Pilipino (Tagalog)
Quechua
Russian
Scandinavian Europe
  Danish, Finnish, Icelandic, Norwegian and Swedish

South-East Asia
  Burmese, Indonersian, Khmer, Lao, Malay, Tagalog (Pilipino), Thai and Vietnamese
Sri Lanka
Swahili
Thai
Thai Hill Tribes
Tibetan
Turkish
Ukrainian
USA
  US English, Vernacular Talk, Native American languages and Hawaiian
Vietnamese
Western Europe
  Basque, Catalan, Dutch, French, German, Irish, Italian, Portuguese, Scottish Gaelic, Spanish (Castilian) and Welsh

---

LONELY PLANET TRAVEL ATLASES

Lonely Planet has long been famous for the number and quality of its guidebook maps. Now we've gone one step further and in conjunction with Steinhart Katzir Publishers produced a handy companion series: Lonely Planet travel atlases – maps of a country produced in book form.

Unlike other maps, which look good but lead travellers astray, our travel atlases have been researched on the road by Lonely Planet's experienced team of writers. All details are carefully checked to ensure the atlas corresponds with the equivalent Lonely Planet guidebook.

The handy atlas format means no holes, wrinkles, torn sections or constant folding and unfolding. These atlases can survive long periods on the road, unlike cumbersome fold-out maps. The comprehensive index ensures easy reference.

* full-colour throughout
* maps researched and checked by Lonely Planet authors
* place names correspond with Lonely Planet guidebooks
  – no confusing spelling differences
* legend and travelling information in English, French, German, Japanese and Spanish
* size: 230 x 160 mm

Available now:
Chile & Easter Island • Egypt • India & Bangladesh • Israel & the Palestinian Territories • Jordan, Syria & Lebanon • Laos • Thailand • Vietnam • Zimbabwe, Botswana & Namibia

LONELY PLANET TV SERIES & VIDEOS

Lonely Planet travel guides have been brought to life on television screens around the world. Like our guides, the programmes are based on the joy of independent travel, and look honestly at some of the most exciting, picturesque and frustrating places in the world. Each show is presented by one of three travellers from Australia, England or the USA and combines an innovative mixture of video, Super-8 film, atmospheric soundscapes and original music.

Videos of each episode – containing additional footage not shown on television – are available from good book and video shops, but the availability of individual videos varies with regional screening schedules.

Video destinations include: Alaska • American Rockies • Australia – The South-East • Baja California & the Copper Canyon • Brazil • Central Asia • Chile & Easter Island • Corsica, Sicily & Sardinia – The Mediterranean Islands • East Africa (Tanzania & Zanzibar) • Ecuador & the Galapagos Islands • Greenland & Iceland • Indonesia • Israel & the Sinai Desert • Jamaica • Japan • La Ruta Maya • Morocco • New York • North India • Pacific Islands (Fiji, Solomon Islands & Vanuatu) • South India • South West China • Turkey • Vietnam • West Africa • Zimbabwe, Botswana & Namibia

The Lonely Planet TV series is produced by:
Pilot Productions
Duke of Sussex Studios
44 Uxbridge St
London W8 7TG UK

Lonely Planet videos are distributed by:
IVN Communications Inc
2246 Camino Ramon
California 94583, USA

107 Power Road, Chiswick
London W4 5PL UK

Music from the TV series is available on CD & cassette.
For video availability and ordering information contact your nearest Lonely Planet office.

PLANET TALK

Lonely Planet's FREE quarterly newsletter

We love hearing from you and think you'd like to hear from us.

When...is the right time to see reindeer in Finland?
Where...can you hear the best palm-wine music in Ghana?
How...do you get from Asunción to Areguá by steam train?
What...is the best way to see India?

For the answer to these and many other questions read PLANET TALK.

Every issue is packed with up-to-date travel news and advice including:

* a letter from Lonely Planet co-founders Tony and Maureen Wheeler
* go behind the scenes on the road with a Lonely Planet author
* feature article on an important and topical travel issue
* a selection of recent letters from travellers
* details on forthcoming Lonely Planet promotions
* complete list of Lonely Planet products

To join our mailing list contact any Lonely Planet office.

Also available: Lonely Planet T-shirts. 100% heavyweight cotton.

LONELY PLANET ONLINE

Get the latest travel information before you leave or while you're on the road

Whether you've just begun planning your next trip, or you're chasing down specific info on currency regulations or visa requirements, check out the Lonely Planet World Wide Web site for up-to-the-minute travel information.

As well as travel profiles of your favourite destinations (including interactive maps and full-colour photos), you'll find current reports from our army of researchers and other travellers, updates on health and visas, travel advisories, and the ecological and political issues you need to be aware of as you travel.

There's an online travellers' forum (the Thorn Tree) where you can share your experiences of life on the road, meet travel companions and ask other travellers for their recommendations and advice. We also have plenty of links to other Web sites useful to independent travellers.

With tens of thousands of visitors a month, the Lonely Planet Web site is one of the most popular on the Internet and has won a number of awards including GNN's Best of the Net travel award.

http://www.lonelyplanet.com

LONELY PLANET PRODUCTS

Lonely Planet is known worldwide for publishing practical, reliable and no-nonsense travel information in our guides and on our web site. The Lonely Planet list covers just about every accessible part of the world. Currently there are eight series: *travel guides*, *shoestring guides*, *walking guides*, *city guides*, *phrasebooks*, *audio packs*, *travel atlases* and *Journeys* – a unique collection of travellers' tales.

EUROPE

Austria • Baltic States & Kaliningrad • Baltic States phrasebook • Britain • Central Europe on a shoestring • Central Europe phrasebook • Czech & Slovak Republics • Denmark • Dublin city guide • Eastern Europe on a shoestring • Eastern Europe phrasebook • Finland • France • Greece • Greek phrasebook • Hungary • Iceland, Greenland & the Faroe Islands • Ireland • Italy • Mediterranean Europe on a shoestring • Mediterranean Europe phrasebook • Paris city guide • Poland • Prague city guide • Russia, Ukraine & Belarus • Russian phrasebook • Scandinavian & Baltic Europe on a shoestring • Scandinavian Europe phrasebook • Slovenia • St Petersburg city guide • Switzerland • Trekking in Greece • Trekking in Spain • Ukrainian phrasebook • Vienna city guide • Walking in Switzerland • Western Europe on a shoestring • Western Europe phrasebook

NORTH AMERICA

Alaska • Backpacking in Alaska • Baja California • California & Nevada • Canada • Florida • Hawaii • Honolulu city guide • Los Angeles city guide • Mexico • Miami city guide • New England • New Orleans city guide • Pacific Northwest USA • Rocky Mountain States • San Francisco city guide • Southwest USA • USA phrasebook

CENTRAL AMERICA & THE CARIBBEAN

Bermuda • Central America on a shoestring • Costa Rica • Cuba • Eastern Caribbean • Guatemala, Belize & Yucatán: La Ruta Maya • Jamaica

SOUTH AMERICA

Argentina, Uruguay & Paraguay • Bolivia • Brazil • Brazilian phrasebook • Buenos Aires city guide • Chile & Easter Island • Chile & Easter Island travel atlas • Colombia • Ecuador & the Galápagos Islands • Latin American Spanish phrasebook • Peru • Quechua phrasebook • Rio de Janeiro city guide • South America on a shoestring • Trekking in the Patagonian Andes • Venezuela

Travel Literature: Full Circle: A South American Journey

ANTARCTICA

Antarctica

ISLANDS OF THE INDIAN OCEAN

Madagascar & Comoros • Maldives & Islands of the East Indian Ocean • Mauritius, Réunion & Seychelles

AFRICA

Arabic (Moroccan) phrasebook • Africa on a shoestring • Cape Town city guide • Central Africa • East Africa • Egypt • Egypt travel atlas • Ethiopian (Amharic) phrasebook • Kenya • Morocco • North Africa • South Africa, Lesotho & Swaziland • Swahili phrasebook • Trekking in East Africa • West Africa • Zimbabwe, Botswana & Namibia • Zimbabwe, Botswana & Namibia travel atlas

ALSO AVAILABLE:

Travel with Children • Traveller's Tales

MAIL ORDER

Lonely Planet products are distributed worldwide. They are also available by mail order from Lonely Planet, so if you have difficulty finding a title please write to us. North American and South American residents should write to Embarcadero West, 155 Filbert St, Suite 251, Oakland CA 94607, USA; European and African residents should write to 10 Barley Mow Passage, Chiswick, London W4 4PH; and residents of other countries to PO Box 617, Hawthorn, Victoria 3122, Australia.

NORTH-EAST ASIA

Beijing city guide • Cantonese phrasebook • China • Hong Kong, Macau & Guangzhou • Hong Kong city guide • Japan • Japanese phrasebook • Japanese audio pack • Korea • Korean phrasebook • Mandarin phrasebook • Mongolia • Mongolian phrasebook • North-East Asia on a shoestring • Seoul city guide • Taiwan • Tibet • Tibet phrasebook • Tokyo city guide

Travel Literature: Lost Japan

MIDDLE EAST & CENTRAL ASIA

Arab Gulf States • Arabic (Egyptian) phrasebook • Central Asia • Iran • Israel & the Palestinian Territories • Israel & the Palestinian Territories travel atlas • Istanbul city guide • Jerusalem city guide • Jordan & Syria • Jordan, Syria & Lebanon travel atlas • Middle East • Turkey • Turkish phrasebook• Yemen

Travel Literature: The Gates of Damascus • Kingdom of the Film Stars: Journey into Jordan

INDIAN SUBCONTINENT

Bangladesh • Bengali phrasebook • Delhi city guide • Hindi/Urdu phrasebook • India • India & Bangladesh travel atlas • Indian Himalaya • Karakoram Highway • Nepal • Nepali phrasebook • Pakistan • Rajasthan • Sri Lanka • Sri Lanka phrasebook • Trekking in the Indian Himalaya • Trekking in the Karakoram & Hindukush • Trekking in the Nepal Himalaya

Travel Literature: In Rajasthan • Shopping for Buddhas

SOUTH-EAST ASIA

Bali & Lombok • Bangkok city guide • Burmese phrasebook • Cambodia • Ho Chi Minh city guide • Indonesia • Indonesian phrasebook • Indonesian audio pack • Jakarta city guide • Java • Laos • Lao phrasebook • Laos travel atlas • Malay phrasebook • Malaysia, Singapore & Brunei • Myanmar (Burma) • Philippines • Pilipino phrasebook • Singapore city guide • South-East Asia on a shoestring •South-East Asia phrasebook • Thailand • Thailand travel atlas • Thai phrasebook • Thai audio pack • Thai Hill Tribes phrasebook • Vietnam • Vietnamese phrasebook • Vietnam travel atlas

AUSTRALIA & THE PACIFIC

Australia • Australian phrasebook • Bushwalking in Australia • Bushwalking in Papua New Guinea • Fiji • Fijian phrasebook • Islands of Australia's Great Barrier Reef • Melbourne city guide • Micronesia • New Caledonia • New South Wales & the ACT • New Zealand • Northern Territory • Outback Australia • Papua New Guinea • Papua New Guinea phrasebook • Queensland • Rarotonga & the Cook Islands • Samoa • Solomon Islands • South Australia • Sydney city guide • Tahiti & French Polynesia • Tasmania • Tonga • Tramping in New Zealand • Vanuatu • Victoria • Western Australia

Travel Literature: Islands in the Clouds • Sean & David's Long Drive

THE LONELY PLANET STORY

Lonely Planet published its first book in 1973 in response to the numerous 'How did you do it?' questions Maureen and Tony Wheeler were asked after driving, bussing, hitching, sailing and railing their way from England to Australia.

Written at a kitchen table and hand collated, trimmed and stapled, *Across Asia on the Cheap* became an instant local bestseller, inspiring thoughts of another book.

Eighteen months in South-East Asia resulted in their second guide, *South-East Asia on a shoestring*, which they put together in a backstreet Chinese hotel in Singapore in 1975. The 'yellow bible', as it quickly became known to backpackers around the world, soon became *the* guide to the region. It has sold well over half a million copies and is now in its 8th edition, still retaining its familiar yellow cover.

Today there are over 180 titles, including travel guides, walking guides, language kits & phrasebooks, travel atlases and travel literature. The company is one of the largest travel publishers in the world. Although Lonely Planet initially specialised in guides to Asia, we now cover most regions of the world, including the Pacific, North America, South America, Africa, the Middle East and Europe.

The emphasis continues to be on travel for independent travellers. Tony and Maureen still travel for several months of each year and play an active part in the writing, updating and quality control of Lonely Planet's guides.

They have been joined by over 70 authors and 170 staff at our offices in Melbourne (Australia), Oakland (USA), London (UK) and Paris (France). Travellers themselves also make a valuable contribution to the guides through the feedback we receive in thousands of letters each year.

The people at Lonely Planet strongly believe that travellers can make a positive contribution to the countries they visit, both through their appreciation of the countries' culture, wildlife and natural features, and through the money they spend. In addition, the company makes a direct contribution to the countries and regions it covers. Since 1986 a percentage of the income from each book has been donated to ventures such as famine relief in Africa; aid projects in India; agricultural projects in Central America; Greenpeace's efforts to halt French nuclear testing in the Pacific; and Amnesty International.

'I hope we send the people out with the right attitude about travel. You realise when you travel that there are so many different perspectives about the world, so we hope these books will make people more interested in what they see. These are guidebooks, but you can't really guide people. All you can do is point them in the right direction.'
– Tony Wheeler

LONELY PLANET PUBLICATIONS

Australia
PO Box 617, Hawthorn 3122, Victoria
tel: (03) 9819 1877 fax: (03) 9819 6459
e-mail: talk2us@lonelyplanet.com.au

USA
Embarcadero West, 155 Filbert St, Suite 251,
Oakland, CA 94607
tel: (510) 893 8555 TOLL FREE: 800 275-8555
fax: (510) 893 8563
e-mail: info@lonelyplanet.com

UK
10 Barley Mow Passage, Chiswick,
London W4 4PH
tel: (0181) 742 3161 fax: (0181) 742 2772
e-mail: 100413.3551@compuserve.com

France:
71 bis rue du Cardinal Lemoine, 75005 Paris
tel: 1 44 32 06 20 fax: 1 46 34 72 55
e-mail: 100560.415@compuserve.com

World Wide Web: http://www.lonelyplanet.com